READERS AND WRITERS IN PRIMARY GRADES

A Balanced and Integrated Approach

Second Edition

Martha Combs

University of Nevada, Reno

Upper Saddle River, New Jersey
Columbus, Ohio

Library of Congress Cataloging-in-Publication Data

Combs, Martha.
Readers and writers in primary grades: a balanced and integrated approach / by Martha Combs.—2nd ed.
p. cm.
Rev. ed. of: Developing competent readers and writers in the primary grades. © 1996.
Includes bibliographical references and indexes.
ISBN 0-13-093150-0
1. Language arts (Primary) 2. Reading (Primary) 3. English language—Composition and exercises—Study and teaching (Primary) 4. Language experience approach in education. I. Combs, Martha. Developing competent readers and writers in the primary grades. II. Title.

LB1528 .C64 2002
372.6044—dc21

2001030239

Vice President and Publisher: Jeffery W. Johnston
Editor: Linda Ashe Montgomery
Production Editor: Mary M. Irvin
Design Coordinator: Diane C. Lorenzo
Project Coordination and Text Design: Carlisle Publishers Services
Photo Coordinator: Sandy Lenahan
Cover Design: Ceri Fitzgerald
Cover Art: Erin Jesse, Age 7
Production Manager: Pamela D. Bennett
Director of Marketing: Kevin Flanagan
Marketing Manager: Krista Groshong
Marketing Coordinator: Barbara Koontz

This book was set in Cheltenham by Carlisle Communications, Ltd., and was printed and bound by Courier Kendallville, Inc. The cover was printed by Phoenix Color Corp.

Photo Credits: Andy Brunk/Merrill: 3; Anne Vega/Merrill: 8,18, 40, 143, 144, 256; Scott Cunningham/Merrill: 12, 69, 71, 105, 112, 233, 236, 323; Anthony Magnacca/Merrill: 25, 281; Laima Druskis/PH College: 28, 183; Todd Yarrington/Merrill: 196; Barbara Schwartz/Merrill: 365.

Pearson Education Ltd., *London*
Pearson Education Australia Pty. Limited, *Sydney*
Pearson Education Singapore Pte. Ltd.
Pearson Education North Asia Ltd., *Hong Kong*
Pearson Education Canada, Ltd., *Toronto*
Pearson Educación de Mexico, S.A. de C.V.
Pearson Education—Japan, *Tokyo*
Pearson Education Malaysia Pte. Ltd.
Pearson Education, *Upper Saddle River, New Jersey*

10 9 8 7 6 5 4 3 2

ISBN 0-13-093150-0

For the children of Roger Corbett Elementary School,
their teachers, and principal.
Thank you for all that you have shared with me
throughout the years.
You are all a testimony to possibility!

CREDITS

p. 82 Excerpt from *Ten in the Bed* by Mary Rees copyright © 1988 by Mary Rees. Reprinted by permission of Little, Brown & Company.

p. 82 Excerpt from *The Napping House* by Audrey Wood, illustrated by Don Wood. Text copyright © 1984 by Audrey Wood. Published by Harcourt Brace & Co. Reprinted by permission of Harcourt.

pp. 31, 82-83 and 310 Excerpt from *Chicka Chicka Boom Boom* reprinted with the permission of Simon & Schuster Books for Young Readers, an imprint of Simon & Schuster Children's Publishing Division from *Chicka Chicka Boom Boom* by Bill Martin, Jr., and John Archambault, illustrated by Lois Ehlert. Illustrations copyright © 1989 by Lois Ehlert.

p. 83 Excerpt from *A Very Hungry Caterpillar* by Eric Carle, copyright © 1984 by Eric Carle. Used by permission of Penguin Putnam, Inc.

p. 32 *How Is a Crayon Made?* by Charles Oz, copyright © 1988 by Charles Oz. Reprinted by permission of Simon & Schuster Books for Young Readers.

pp. 33-34 From *A Chair for My Mother* by Vera B. Williams, copyright © 1982 by Vera B. Williams. Published by Greenwillow/William Morris. Reprinted by permission of HarperCollins Publishers.

p. 39 From *The Snowy Day* by Ezra Jack Keats, copyright © 1962 by Ezra Jack Keats. Used by permission of Viking Penguin, a division of Penguin Putnam, Inc.

p. 85-86 Excerpt from *The Chick and the Duckling* by Vladimir Suteyev, translated by Mirra Ginsburg, illustrated by Jose and Ariane Aruego. Copyright © 1972. Reprinted by permission of Macmillan Company.

p. 129 Excerpt from *It Looked Like Spilt Milk* by Charles G. Shaw, copyright © 1947 by Charles G. Shaw, renewed 1975 by Ethan Allen. All rights reserved. Reprinted by permission of HarperCollins Publishers.

p. 268 Excerpt from *Stone Fox* by John Reynolds Gardiner. Copyright © 1980 by John Reynolds Gardiner. Published by permission of Ty Crowell Co.

p. 310 From *On Market Street* by Arnold Lobell, illustrated by Anita Lobell. Text copyright © 1981 by Arnold Lobell, illustrations copyright © 1981 by Anita Lobell. Published by Greenwillow Books. Reprinted by permission of HarperCollins Publishers

p. 310 From *A My Name is Alice* by Jane Bayer, illustrated by Steven Kellogg. Copyright © 1984 by Jane Bayer, illustrations copyright © 1984 by Steven Kellogg. Reprinted by permission of Dutton Children's Books, a division of Penguin Putnam, Inc.

p. 310 From *An Edward Lear Alphabet* by Edward Lear, illustrated by Vladimir Radunsky. Text copyright © 1999 by Edward Lear. Reprinted by permission of HarperCollins publisher.

p. 441 From *Brown Bear, Brown Bear, What Do You See?* By Bill Martin Jr. Copyright © 1995 by Bill Martin, Jr., published by Harcourt Brace & Co. Reprinted by permission of Harcourt.

p. 443 From *The Ghost Eye Tree* by Bill Martin, Jr., and John Archambault, illustrated by Ted Rand. Copyright © 1988 by Bill Martin and John Archambault, illustrations copyright © 1988 by Ted Rand. Reprinted by permission of Henry Holt.

Preface

Every child has the right to know firsthand the power and possibility that come from being a literate individual! For over thirty years, I have been a teacher of children and adults, and during that time I have learned that effective teachers have at least two things in common—a commitment that all children can learn and a commitment to providing the assistance necessary for every child to become literate. There is much that we must know about children, language, and literacy if we are to support all children as learners. This book is a beginning!

Imagine that we are helping a young child learn to ride a bike. At first we provide a great deal of support, patiently demonstrating the parts of bike riding that the child needs to know and seems ready to learn. Teaching this child to ride requires repetition, redirection, and careful observation of his or her responses. Slowly, as the child demonstrates new levels of skill, we adjust the amount and types of support we provide, until the child is riding without our support. There may be spills along the way, even regressions, but we intervene only as the child demonstrates need because we want the child to become independent.

The story about riding a bike could just as easily be a story about helping a child learn to read and write. Young children who learn to read and write early usually do so with the support of a responsive adult—an adult who listens to them, talks with them, reads with them, and writes with them. This is what we want for every child, to be that responsive adult who supports their acquisition of literacy skills and strategies, because our goal for children is independence! To this end, this book is organized around teaching strategies that can help each of us be responsive to the literacy needs of young children.

LITERACY FRAMEWORK

This second edition of *Readers and Writers in Primary Grades* focuses on a balanced and integrated approach to literacy, meshing theory and practice in every chapter. The illustration on page vi clearly identifies the components of our literacy framework. Each chapter focuses on one or more components, providing the theory base for the component and illustrations of effective classroom practices with the component.

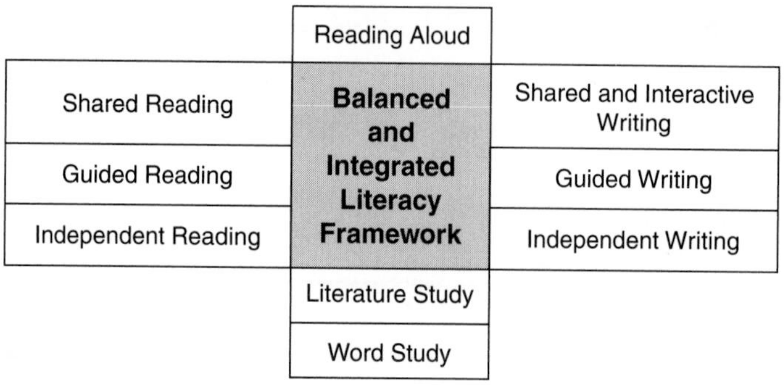

	Reading Aloud	
Shared Reading	**Balanced and Integrated Literacy Framework**	Shared and Interactive Writing
Guided Reading		Guided Writing
Independent Reading		Independent Writing
	Literature Study	
	Word Study	

PART I: LITERACY METHODS FOR K–3 CLASSROOMS

- *Chapter 1* provides an overview of a balanced and integrated approach to literacy, children's growth as readers and writers in the primary grades, and an examination of our role as responsive adults in the literacy process.
- *Chapter 2* introduces the foundation of a balanced literacy framework—reading aloud to children. This component is a powerful tool that is often overlooked for its instructional value. In this chapter we explore ways of engaging children in read-aloud to enhance language development and knowledge of what print has to offer.
- *Chapters 3* and *4* provide an in-depth examination of shared reading and writing experiences. Shared experiences provide excellent opportunities to model reading and writing processes for and with children. When we share the pen, and children write with our support, we provide a truly interactive writing experience in which children model and demonstrate their understandings of print.
- *Chapters 5* and *6* provide an in-depth examination of guided and independent reading and writing. It is through these components that we are able to assess the effectiveness of our instruction. Guided reading and writing provide an intermediate step on the way to independence, with assistance as needed to extend children's learning that began in read-aloud and shared reading and writing.
- *Chapter 7* provides background needed to organize activities that extend children's interactions with quality literature through whole-class, small-group, and independent study of books. Literature study is a complement to other forms of reading experiences provided in a balanced framework.
- *Chapters 8, 9,* and *10* build background for the scope of word knowledge development that takes place during the primary grades. We begin with phonological awareness, which is the basis for success in reading and writing. Then we develop an understanding of both phonics and the structure of words to enable us to read and write multisyllable words.

PART II: MAKING CONNECTIONS: LINKING CHILDREN'S LEARNING EXPERIENCES WITH A BALANCED LITERACY PROGRAM

An Integrated Unit Study: Learning about Amphibians in Two Second Grade Classrooms, serves as a culminating illustration of how a group of second-grade teachers link instruction in literacy through their use of all the components in our framework. Reading this classroom illustration along with Chapter 1 provides a more comprehensive overview of our literacy framework. Rereading this section throughout the text provides continued clarification of the possibilities for components.

TEXT FEATURES

This is an all-new edition of *Readers and Writers in Primary Grades.* A number of features in the text are provided to support learning:

- ***Literacy framework illustration***—Each chapter opens with the illustration showing the focus component(s) for the chapter. Throughout the text, the logo serves as a reminder of our framework for literacy instruction.
- ***In this chapter . . .***—Identifies the major concepts, issues, and ideas on which the chapter will focus. This feature provides an opportunity to think ahead about familiar ideas that might appear in the chapter.
- ***Focus Literature***—Identifies on the opening pages of each chapter what literature will be highlighted. Familiarity with the literature enhances understanding of chapter activities.
- ***Looking into Classrooms . . .***—Each chapter opens with a classroom vignette that provides a practical connection to a real classroom in which the focus component is being practiced. Often, the teacher featured in the vignette will reappear later in the chapter as we focus in more depth on classroom practices.
- ***Building a Theory Base . . .***—Following *Looking into Classrooms . . .*, we turn our attention to the particular background knowledge needed to implement the focus component(s) for each chapter. To be able to expand upon the ideas of others we must understand the theories upon which the ideas are based.
- ***Take a Moment to Reflect . . .***—At the close of *Building a Theory Base . . .*, we take a moment to consider the major ideas presented in the section. This is a good opportunity to check comprehension of main ideas before considering the application of theory to practice. This section also appears at the end of each chapter to help summarize the final portions of the chapter.
- ***Putting Theory into Practice . . .***—The remainder of each chapter provides extensive applications of theory to classroom practices. Classroom dialogues, expanded illustrations, and assessment features appear in each chapter.

- ***Your Turn . . .***—Suggests practice activities that apply to ideas presented in each chapter. To retain new ideas we must re-collect and reconstruct our ideas to make them our own. The activities suggested in the *Your Turn . . .* section are best if completed with someone else. Sharing ideas and teaching each other help us refine and solidify our thinking.
- Issues of ***Assessment*** and ***Respecting Diversity*** are integrated into each chapter, as they apply to the focus component. Discussions are easy to find, as they are the final two sections of each chapter.
- ***A Handbook for Children's Literature,*** Appendix A, provides an overview of genre and literary elements to support planning for the use of children's literature, particularly in read-alouds and literature study.
- Sample pictures and word lists for word study activities are provided in Appendix B and Appendix C.

ACKNOWLEDGMENTS

First, and foremost, to my husband, Randy, who is the most patient, understanding, and loving husband—Thank you for everything. Thanks to the teachers at Roger Corbett Elementary, who are a constant source of inspiration, especially Jeana Milligan, Marcie Humes, Nikki Perkins, and Mary Ballinger, who inspired the Making Connections section, and to Coral Poore, an amazing teacher and colleague. A special thank you to their principal and friend, Pat Casarez, for making me feel like I am one of the faculty. Many thanks to everyone at Merrill/Prentice Hall who work their magic to make books come to life—especially Linda Montgomery, Jeff Johnston, Lori Jones and Mary Irvin. My thanks also to each of the reviewers who provided helpful ideas and constructive criticism for this second edition—Carol J. Fuhler, Iowa State University; Larry Andrews, University of Nebraska—Lincoln; Karen Robinson, Otterbein College; Joan Simmons, University of Wisconsin—Oshkosh; and Helen Abadiano, Central Connecticut University. And finally, thank you to the readers, who breathe life into the ideas on these pages, and hopefully draw upon them to touch the lives of children. Thank you.

Martha Combs

Aa Bb Cc Dd Ee Ff Gg Hh Ii Jj Kk Ll Mm
Nn Oo Pp Qq Rr Ss Tt Uu Vv Ww Xx Yy Zz

Contents

Part I
Literacy Methods for K–3 Classrooms

Aa Bb Cc Dd Ee Ff Gg Hh Ii Jj Kk Ll Mm

CHAPTER

1

Reading and Writing in the Primary Grades: A Balanced and Integrated Approach

An Introduction

	Reading Aloud	
Shared Reading	**Balanced and Integrated Literacy Framework**	Shared and Interactive Writing
Guided Reading		Guided Writing
Independent Reading		Independent Writing
	Literature Study	
	Word Study	

In this chapter, we . . .

- Consider the following elements, which are important to developing an effective literacy program in your primary grade classroom:
  - Components of a balanced and integrated approach to literacy
  - Classroom environments that support children's development and independence as learners

- The teacher's role in creating learning experiences
- The monitoring of children's literacy development
- Respect for the diversity that individual children bring to the classroom

Looking into Classrooms . . .

It is October in Carmen's first-grade classroom, and the children have gathered on the floor near the painting easel that also serves to hold their favorite songs, poems, and big books for shared reading. Jeremy holds the pointer and confidently touches each word on the chart the class has made of "Old MacDonald Had a Farm" as the children sing along. Jeremy's face shows the pleasure that he has in being the "pointer" for that day. Following cries of "Let's do it again!" Jeremy places the pointer at the beginning of the song, and in a loud voice begins to point and sing, "Old MacDonald . . .."

Later that morning the children are allowed to choose activities as part of their morning work. Jasmine sits at the small table in the corner by the mouse cage, which holds a mother mouse and her four new pink babies. The cage bears the label, Minnie Mouse. As Jasmine writes, she looks intently at the cage and also up to the wall that displays words the class uses frequently in reading and writing. Jasmine puts the finishing touches on a birth announcement for the baby mice:

Come see the babez
Minnie Mouse haz 4 babez

As she writes the last word on her announcement, Jasmine says aloud with great pleasure, "There! Now everyone will know about the babies." Carmen encourages Jasmine to tape the birth announcement outside the classroom door so that neighboring classes can read the news.

At the end of the day, Carmen pins a note on Ruben's shirt. "What's this say?" he demands, pulling at the note. "Read it to me. Is my mom gonna be happy or mad?" As Carmen unpins the note and opens it, Ruben sees some letters and the drawing of a happy face and smiles. He has had a note like this before. Carmen reads the note, "Ruben helped a friend on the playground today. I am proud of him."

Building a Theory Base . . .

Like the children in Carmen's classroom, we learn that becoming literate enables us to "read and write the world to meet our needs and interests, taking from and making of the world what we will" (Shannon, 1992, p. 1). As we strive to make meaning in our lives, we are able to:

- experience satisfaction in our work,
- communicate important feelings to others,
- resolve personal problems,
- satisfy our desire to know,
- experience vicariously what we may never know in real life,
- escape, through the narratives of others' lives, the stresses of our own,
- record and save our thinking in written form for a later time, and . . .

What would you add to this list? What does it mean to you to be literate? Being literate is more than just learning how to read and write. Being literate involves the orchestration of cognitive abilities, such as problem solving, that lead to a satisfying and enriched life. Being literate enables each of us to participate effectively as citizens in our community, state, and country.

Although literacy involves complex cognitive challenges, it is also a social activity. We know that through children's interactions with more knowledgeable others they learn to use language to think about their world and organize their thoughts in ways that are useful in their daily lives. However, children's cognitive development is greatly dependent upon whether they live in a world that provides assistance in meeting their personal needs and desires. How adults respond to children during the preschool years has a great deal to do with the level of children's cognitive functioning as they enter school.

Because literacy is so important, we must find ways to organize learning experiences in school that have the possibility of supporting the literacy development of all children, and when needed, accelerating that development to enable children to realize their literacy potential. An integrated and balanced approach to becoming literate should be provided for all of our children.

DEFINING LITERACY

Historically, literacy has been defined in ways that reflect the nature of the times. In the 1700s, literacy might have been defined as the ability to read and write one's own name, or in the early 1900s as simply the ability to read and write. The National Literacy Standards for Language Arts (1996) suggest that "a much more ambitious definition of literacy today includes the capacity to accomplish a wide range of reading, writing, speaking, and other language tasks associated with everyday life" (p. 73). Literacy is also used to describe competence in a technical field, such as computer literacy. Being literate enables us to have greater access to the benefits of citizenship in a technological society. Yet, each year we are reminded by reports in the media and from government agencies that large numbers of children are not functioning at adequate literacy levels.

Trends in literacy development, reported by the National Assessment of Educational Progress (NAEP, 2000), show that for all fourth-grade students tested, 93% have rudimentary skills to carry out simple, discrete reading tasks; 64% have partially developed literacy skills, being able to understand specific or sequentially related information; and only 16% are able to search for specific information and interrelated ideas, and make generalizations. In addition, substantial disparities continue between white students and students of ethnic minorities. Since the first NAEP results were reported in 1971, a disproportionate number of children of minorities and children of low socioeconomic status (SES) demonstrate limited reading ability.

The failure of some children to reach their literacy potential, however, is not a recent phenomenon. Literacy research throughout the twentieth century reveals that children with normal intelligence frequently have difficulty learning to read and write proficiently. Growing out of the struggles that some children endure when learning to read and write, a variety of theories concerning early literacy development and instruction have been widely debated. Just as definitions of literacy change, so do educators' beliefs about effective literacy instruction.

Recent discussion centers on the importance of a balanced approach to literacy, with the possibility of serving the needs of all children. A report of the Commission on Reading, entitled *Becoming a Nation of Readers* (Anderson et al., 1985), called for a balance between explicit instruction in word recognition and comprehension and daily opportunities to read and write meaningful, connected text. More recently, the report of the *Committee on the Prevention of Reading Difficulties in Young Children* (Snow, Burns, & Griffin, 1998) identified the need to balance instruction that emphasizes meaningful reading and writing with specific attention to the features of print, particularly the features of the alphabetic system of English. In addition to issues of balance in instruction, discussions of integrating or linking literacy components may provide multifaceted learning opportunities. If we truly believe that children learn in different ways and at different paces, then we must provide more than one route to acquiring literate knowledge, skills, and strategies.

A FRAMEWORK FOR LITERACY

In this book we take an important approach to literacy instruction that is meaningful, integrated, and balanced. What does this mean for our classroom practices? Our approach to literacy provides four ideals:

1. a strong emphasis on children receiving and producing oral, written, and visual modes of communication in meaningful contexts
2. an appropriate balance of authentic, skills-based learning experiences that provide appropriate support (scaffolding) for children's learning
3. a continual linking of learning experiences to support children's views of literate behavior and also their varied needs and interests as learners
4. an overview of children's progress toward independence and self-regulation in their reading and writing in a variety of contexts, with appropriate interventions as needed

Let us consider what these goals might mean in a primary grade classroom. From the scenario of Carmen's first-grade classroom, it seems apparent that Carmen considers language, both oral and written, to be central to the development of her students. Because language is a central aspect in her curriculum, Carmen consciously organizes learning experiences that encourage and extend children's language abilities.

As we view young children learning to read and write, be reminded of the following:

> The more children read and are read to, the more words, concepts, and language patterns become a part of their listening vocabulary. Soon children are using these words in their everyday oral language and including them in their writing. The more sophisticated their oral language becomes, the more understandings and vocabulary they have to bring to the tasks of reading and writing (Depree & Iversen, 1994, p. 87).

Carmen understands that language involves the negotiation of meaning between two or more persons: between speaker and listener, between writer and reader. These negotiations require the knowledge of multiple skills and strategies that enhance understanding by another, and personal interpretations that are appropriate to a particular context.

Carmen believes that people learn from each other, so consequently she encourages a collaborative environment for learning. Through assistance and cooperative activity, her children perform at developmental levels beyond what they could do by themselves. Many of Carmen's ideas about teaching and learning are drawn from the Russian psychologist Lev Vygotsky. We consider his ideas about learning and development throughout this book.

A balanced and integrated approach to literacy draws upon a combination of learning experiences or components to provide literacy support and development for all types of learners. These learning experiences or components form a framework for our classroom literacy program, as shown on page 2. Throughout this text we explore the theoretical base of each component and apply it to classroom practice.

We can observe the integration of the components of this literacy framework in Carmen's first-grade classroom. Throughout a unit of study about farms and farm animals, for example, Carmen uses the song about Old MacDonald's farm as a foundation for linking, or integrating, literacy experiences. Integration through content increases learning opportunities for all of the children.

> The children learn to sing "Old MacDonald," playing with sounds and developing their **phonological awareness,** or ability to hear sounds in words. Carmen uses **oral language development,** through music and talk, as an anchor for other literacy experiences.
>
> Several times each day Carmen **reads aloud** to the children. She finds several versions of the "Old MacDonald" song that have been published as books and shares them with the children through reading aloud. She also reads aloud both fiction and nonfiction books about farms and farm animals. Her purposes are for children's enjoyment and for building their background knowledge for this theme unit.
>
> When the children know the words to the song, Carmen introduces a large chart with the basic frame of the song, and blanks in the appropriate place for an animal.

Old MacDonald had a farm
E-i-e-i-o
And on this farm he had a ________
E-i-e-i-o

She models the reading/singing of the text, placing a picture of an animal in the appropriate blank spaces for children to "read." Children are encouraged to share the reading/singing as soon as they feel comfortable predicting the print based on their knowledge of the song. During repeated reading/singing, individual children, such as Jeremy, lead the shared experience. Carmen has used the song as a text for **shared reading,** in which she models what readers do and supports children's efforts.

At another time, the class composes a new verse for the song, sharing ideas about the writing. At various times during the writing, Carmen shares the marking pen with individual children. Everyone works together to assist the writer in figuring out the mechanics and spellings for the new verse. Carmen uses **shared/interactive writing** experiences to model how ideas can be written and enables children to demonstrate what they know about producing meaningful print.

When the words of the song are very familiar to children, the song is made into individual books for each child. Carmen guides daily small-group reading, listening carefully to the control that individual readers have over the text. **Guided reading** provides an opportunity for Carmen to observe what knowledge, skills, and strategies children are taking from whole-class literacy experiences. Carmen meets small groups of children each day for guided reading experiences, using books that slightly challenge the children.

On other days, Carmen assists individual children as they write their own versions of animal songs and stories. **Guided writing** enables Carmen to observe the level of control that children are developing over the production of written language. She is available to help children think about their composition and to help them as they wrestle with spelling and the mechanics of written language.

Carmen gathers a variety of books about farms and farm animals and places them in the library corner for children to explore independently. She understands that **independent reading** provides daily opportunities to explore books and practice reading skills and strategies. Frequently she listens in on children's independent reading to better understand the skills and strategies over which they are gaining control.

In the writing center, Carmen places a variety of writing materials such as colored and plain paper, farm-related pictures, little blank books shaped like animals, scissors, tape, a stapler, and writing implements for children to compose stories during the daily "choice time." She understands that **independent writing** provides time to practice writing skills and helps children develop a sense of control over written language.

Carmen collects multiple copies of two versions of the Old MacDonald song that are published as picture books, and multiple copies of several other easy reading books that focus on the subject. Carmen provides an opportunity for children to select the book that they wish to read and discuss during **literature study.** In contrast to guided reading, the children in this small group direct much of the book discussion and have the opportunity to explore quality literature with their peers. Such groups frequently contain children of varying reading levels.

Finally, as part of this farm unit, the children select words from the Old MacDonald text, as well as other texts, to add to the wall of words they use to talk about letter–sound patterns and also for help during their writing. Carmen is

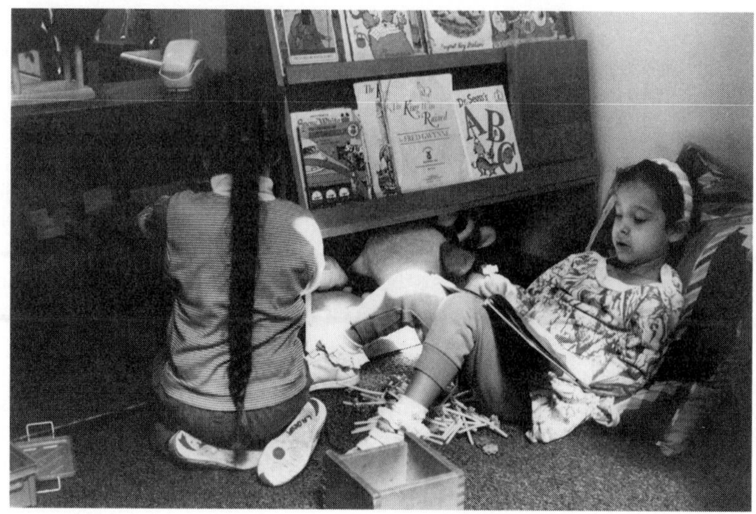

Children become literate individuals by participating in such meaningful activities as daily independent reading.

committed to helping children develop a broad and deep knowledge of words, including knowledge of letter–sound patterns and the structure of words in the English language. She provides daily **word study** opportunities that are geared to children's current developmental levels.

Throughout the week, Carmen is able to engage students in a range of literacy activities that vary in the amount of assistance she provides. Carmen continuously returns to the words of the song as a text that provides multiple learning opportunities. Each day she engages all students in literacy activities that integrate oral and written language and provide opportunities for students to demonstrate their growing knowledge of how to use language effectively. She provides balance between the use of fiction and nonfiction materials. She balances children's experiences between reading and writing, between reading for pleasure and reading for information. Carmen's classroom is one example of the way that teachers draw upon a variety of literacy components to create a balanced and integrated program for learning.

In upcoming chapters we explore the components of a balanced and integrated literacy framework in order to develop an effective early literacy program. As we do so, we consider the theory base of each component and how theory informs our classroom practices. The effectiveness of the literacy components that we select and implement in the classroom is directly influenced by our knowledge of children, by the role we take as teachers, and by the learning environment we construct. To begin, what should we know about children's development in literacy?

CHILDREN'S LITERACY DEVELOPMENT

Becoming literate is a developmental process during which children make gradual, but predictable, changes over time. Qualitative differences are observed in children's literacy behaviors (Adams, 1990; Biemiller, 1970; Bissex, 1980; Chall,

1967, 1983; Clay, 1967; Ehri, 1991, 1998; Juel, 1991; Mason, 1984; Snow, Burns, & Griffin, 1998; Sulzby & Teale, 1991a). Children's concepts about oral and written language are formed from the earliest years by observing and interacting with other readers and writers as well as through their own attempts to read and write (Sulzby & Teale, 1991a). Over time, as children gain knowledge about language and experience in using that knowledge effectively, we can observe changes in their behavior as listeners, speakers, readers, and writers. Such changes are typically referred to as stages of development (Piaget & Inhelder, 1969).

In this text, the stages of children's literacy development are described as either emerging, developing, or transitional.

Emergent Readers and Writers

The term "emergent literacy" was first used by Marie Clay (1966) as she studied the acquisition of literacy by young children in Australia. Emergent literacy is a term used to describe the gradual development of literacy behaviors in children, typically from birth to age five (Sulzby & Teale, 1991a). Children's natural desire to understand leads them to explore and emulate what the significant people in their lives show them about language and print (Teale, 1986). This initial phase of development has also been characterized as "learning about print" (Brown, 1999/2000).

Prior to school entrance, responsive adults support and extend emerging literacy behaviors by encouraging children to:

- reread favorite books with an adult,
- practice reading-like behaviors by "reading" favorite books to stuffed animals or to self,
- "write" a note to a grandparent,
- talk about favorite books during bedtime reading,
- recognize signs that indicate familiar foods, such as cereal, at the grocery store,
- leave a message for a family member using magnetic letters on the refrigerator,
- recognize which building is the favorite place for hamburgers or tacos, or
- play word games, chant rhymes, or sing songs with an adult while riding in the car.

Such activities typically grow out of meaningful interactions between young children and more knowledgeable readers and writers who encourage children's interest in language and print. As children participate in early literacy experiences, speech serves as a mediator for their transition into print. Through their interactions with others, children learn to use speech to develop problem-solving skills. With assistance, language skills can serve as a tool to enable them to unlock the mysteries of written language.

In each literacy situation that children encounter, their understanding of oral and written language is both increased and constrained by their existing beliefs about language and print (Snow, Burns, & Griffin, 1998). Children use their existing understandings to explore language, text, and meaning and, as they do, their previous understandings are modified or reorganized. In this way, the breadth, depth, and nature of children's engagement with text determine a great deal of their literacy learning.

Tremendous growth takes place during this stage of literacy development. Children begin to internalize purposes of print and understand that print is used to communicate and make meaning. They develop knowledge about and appreciation of different types of text through repeated exposures and show increasing interest in reading and writing independently. Their increased exposure to print supports their development of concepts about it, including book-handling skills and an understanding of its permanence. They develop concepts about words including distinguishing letter shapes, letter names, and the sounds represented; and basic levels of phonological awareness (sounds in language), including the concept that words are composed of strings of sounds that can be manipulated to make other words. They are able to make meaning from simple books but rely heavily on memory of familiar wordage, illustrations, story context, and selected letter cues. The knowledge about print developed during this time is important, but not more so than the attitudes and motivations children have toward print and its usefulness in their lives.

Emerging writers need assistance to understand how meaning can be transferred from the head to the page, taking shape through the movement of a pen on paper or fingers on a keyboard. Marie Clay (1975) noted that emerging writers demonstrate a rudimentary understanding of writing. They are beginning to understand that English moves from left to right and top to bottom on a page, that the same shapes reoccur, that there are a variety of letter arrangements, and that certain letters stand for a particular object. They use print to construct simple texts, drawing upon familiar letters and sounds but often inventing word spellings for unfamiliar patterns. Later in this stage, children demonstrate the beginnings of personal narratives as they write single sentences or make lists of ideas such as things they like.

Developing Readers and Writers

Children in this developing stage are learning to sense the patterns of our language as they gain competence with the directional nature of print. They understand the alphabetic principle and that letters map to sounds in words. Combined with their growing phonological awareness, they are able to manipulate letter–sound patterns to recognize and write many new words. They begin to consciously try to match the visual cues of print with what they know. Holdaway (1980) refers to the early part of this stage as "word-to-word matching." It is common for early developing readers to do quite a lot of rerunning or self-correcting as they struggle to make sense of print. Consequently, this stage has also been characterized as the "breaking the code" stage of literacy development (Brown, 1999/2000).

During this stage, it is important for children to spend a great deal of time in text with relatively little challenge so they build the confidence that will help to sustain them in more difficult text. In addition to confidence, easy text enables children to develop a large sight vocabulary—a bank of familiar words that are recognized automatically in text and need not be decoded. Children's practice in easy text during this stage allows them to better organize what they know about print and the thinking processes readers use to coordinate decoding and create meaning from text.

Confidence grows as self-correction becomes more natural. Self-correction shows children's meaning-making abilities. As children move from oral to silent reading, the art of reading becomes a private affair and the children then focus on their own reactions to the text, not merely on the words. Emphasis on comprehension becomes possible at this part of the stage. As Holdaway (1980) states, "Evaluation procedures should now be directed more clearly to appropriate emotional response, identification, creation of sensory imagery, and the whole range of comprehension skills, from word meaning in context to critical and creative reading" (p. 29).

During this period of development, children's close attention to print while reading provides a base for exploring ways to represent those same sounds in their personal writing. They are able to associate sounds and letters to write many one-syllable words with both short and long vowels. Children's compositions show development of ideas that are well beyond simple lists of things they know. We begin to see rudimentary stories, many personal narratives, written retellings of favorite stories, and simple informational pieces that grow out of classroom studies.

Transitional Readers and Writers

Early in the transitional stage, children experience some difficulty moving back and forth between oral and silent reading. As children move into silent reading, they increase the likelihood of becoming really absorbed in a book. When children interact with a book silently, they begin to sense their own style of reading. Style may include the rate at which they are comfortable moving through text, the amount of attention needed by different reading tasks, and the way in which they make meaning with text. Because of such behaviors, this stage has also been characterized as the "going for fluency" stage (Brown, 1999/2000).

Holdaway (1980) suggests that this stage may not be a very active period of reading development. We may not see much progress until the child breaks through into more mature silent reading where ease, and possibly pleasure, increase dramatically. During this stage we should encourage children to read widely in easy text. Such practice enables children to further develop fluency through increased coordination of decoding and comprehension skills. To support children's progress toward fluency, we should provide additional instruction and practice with strategies for chunking longer words, which are becoming more prevalent in the books they read.

During the primary grades, a few children will move into the latter part of the transition stage and become flexible readers. In a third- or fourth-grade classroom, these children might be the ones who meet reading as if it is a challenge. They are highly confident readers who spend hours reading. Because these children read with incredible speed and flexibility, one of the best things teachers can do for them is to get out of their way and let them read!

How can we create a classroom environment that encourages and supports children's literacy development?

Transitional writers, with their growing knowledge of the possibilities of organizing and expressing ideas in print, blossom as writers. They can create a story with a clear beginning, middle, and end; explore ideas through some forms of poetry; organize ideas into an informational piece with a main idea and details; and expand their ability to retell familiar text, borrowing from an author's style and phrasing.

We may notice that, as children acquire new literacy behaviors, their use of new knowledge is clumsy and not yet automated through practice. Behavior in the early part of a stage may look very different from behavior at the end of that same stage. Our instruction should lead or encourage this development. To provide appropriate support for their development we must understand reading and writing processes and the progressions that are possible for developing literacy behaviors. Then through careful observation of children's developing literacy behaviors we are able to select appropriate levels of support during learning experiences to enhance that development.

To support children's literacy development we must carefully consider the nature of the environment in which that development takes place. How can we suppport and extend children's development? What must we do to establish a meaningful learning environment in the classroom for all children?

MEANINGFUL LEARNING ENVIRONMENTS

As each of us strives to meet our personal needs and interests, the environments in which we live take on great importance. The social context of the classroom plays a central role in the development of mental processes in young children (Bedrova & Leong, 1996). The environment we promote in the classroom affects children's views about the nature and importance of reading and writing in their lives and in the lives of significant others. Interaction and exploration through oral and written language provide tools with which young children begin to develop higher mental functions.

Theories of development provide the basis for building learning environments that support readers and writers. From Lev Vygotsky (1978) we learn that:

> From the very first days of the child's development his activities acquire a meaning of their own in a system of social behavior and, being directed towards a definite purpose, are refracted through the prism of the child's environment. The path from object to child and from child to object passes through another person. This complex human structure is the product of a developmental process deeply rooted in the links between individual and social history (p. 30).

Vygotsky states that learning is a social activity, deeply embedded in the interactions between people within a particular cultural context. The nature of that cultural context affects the types of interactions that people have within that context. Children growing up in an aging part of a crowded city live different lives than children growing up in wealthy suburban neighborhoods. Children of parents who were born and raised in the United States experience life differently than children of immigrant parents whose first language is not English.

Let us consider for a moment the social nature of learning. Think of a time when you provided assistance to someone who thought a task was too difficult to do alone. Imagine that with continued interaction and appropriate scaffolding, or support, the person you are helping begins to internalize the new knowledge or skill. This process is what Vygotsky referred to as learning occurring in the social plane, or between people. In these interactions the person is most likely not merely a passive recipient of your guidance and assistance. Rather, talk and action occur between the two of you, which enables the person to internalize new understandings and begin, with some continued support, to use the new knowledge or skill on his or her own. This internalization enables the individual to reconstruct old understandings in new ways. Social psychologists have referred to this process as "guided reinvention" (Fischer & Bulloch, 1984). With the addition of new knowledge, old knowledge is reinvented. The old knowledge is a part of the new, but probably not in the same form.

When we utilize Vygotsky's ideas, a meaningful learning environment for young children will usually contain the following characteristics:

- At least one "more knowledgeable other" who models clearly for students how to use the knowledge, skills, and strategies they are to learn
- Assistance within the learners' zone of proximal development
- Creation of a noncompetitive learning environment
- Opportunities for practice that are motivated and paced by learners
- Opportunities for learners to regulate their own behavior
- Encouragement and support for learners to demonstrate independence

A "More Knowledgeable Other"

Young children learn by emulating the behavior of significant people in their lives. Learning is made easier when the models demonstrate behaviors that are obviously purposeful and successful. Think about how acts of "real" reading and writing might look to young children:

- Following directions to get the new basketball hoop ready for use
- Making a grocery list before going to the store
- Laughing and making comments about an article being read in a favorite magazine
- Writing and mailing invitations to a party

Young children need to observe many successful models of literate behavior over long periods of time to develop a clear understanding of the purposes of written language. This aspect of learning has provided great challenge for teachers because children do not always see school reading and writing tasks, such as completing workbook pages, as useful or purposeful for their lives.

In her first-grade classroom, Carmen serves as a model of purposeful reading and writing. For example, before Jeremy leads the singing of "Old MacDonald," Carmen models how knowing the song can help with reading the words on the song chart. The children frequently see Carmen write notes to herself and others, read to find answers to class questions, and read for personal pleasure during the daily quiet reading time. She realizes the importance of her modeling as a successful reader and writer.

Assistance within the Zone of Proximal Development

According to Vygotsky's theory of human development, a person's ability to learn a new knowledge or skill exists within a zone of proximal development (ZPD). Vygotsky (1978) explained a ZPD as:

> *The distance between the actual developmental level as determined by individual problem solving and the level of potential development as determined through problem solving under adult guidance or in collaboration with more capable peers.* The zone of proximal development defines those functions that have not yet matured but are in the process of maturation, functions that will mature tomorrow but are currently in an embryonic state (p. 86; italics in original).

Vygotsky suggested that the interactions that facilitate children's development are most likely to occur with tasks that are within a child's reach only if assistance is provided. Without adult assistance, there are many forms of thinking that children would not discover, either alone or during interaction with peers. Children learn how to perform tasks appropriately within their ZPD by interacting with more competent and responsive others who provide hints and prompts on an as-needed basis.

We know that learning begins on a social plane, between child and adult, before we see that skill within children's independent functioning. Learning is regulated socially, by a more knowledgeable other, before it is self-regulated by the child. The amount and the kind of other regulation required depend on the age of the child and the nature of the task.

Early in learning a task or skill, children's understanding of what is to be learned and why may be very limited. Consequently, adults offer explicit directions or modeling and children respond in an imitative way. Later, children gradually come to understand the relation between parts of the activity, or come to understand the meaning of the performance. This understanding typically develops through conversation during the task performance. Later direction may come through questions, or further cognitive structuring such as suggesting a strategy for children to try. When adults assist in this fashion they provide a *scaffold* for children (Wood, Bruner, & Ross, 1976). Like the scaffolding of a building under construction, responsive adults provide support to the development of children's concepts that are under construction.

Through doing the task with support, children eventually perform the task without assistance, having internalized the kind of thinking that was previously supported by the adult. To accomplish this move toward self-regulation, adults gradually remove the scaffold as children demonstrate the ability to control the task themselves. Eventually, children come to take over the actual structuring of the task. At this level, the children are capable of redirecting themselves through such strategies as talking themselves through a task, similar to the support previously offered by adults. As children leave their ZPD, performance of the task is smooth and integrated, internalized and automatized. They no longer need adult assistance for the task.

As children move to higher levels of similar tasks their automatized behaviors become de-automatized as they move back through the zone of proximal development for that skill or task. Remember that individuals will have numerous zones depending upon what they are trying to learn. "For every individual, at any point in time, there will be a mix of other-regulation, self-regulation, and automatized processes" (Tharp & Gallimore, 1988, p. 38). Lifelong learning is made up of the same regulated sequences recurring again and again for the development of new capacities.

Learning to talk is an excellent example of how adults scaffold, or assist children within their ZPD. Adults pay close attention to what children are trying to communicate, provide models of how speech sounds are structured, and at appropriate times assist children with the vocabulary and sentence structures they are trying to use to be understood. Over time, children gain control of certain vocabulary and are able to use it accurately and without adult assistance. As children gain inner control over particular speech patterns and structures, the range of that zone moves upward, toward more complex speech patterns for which adults continue to provide assistance as needed by the child.

We can observe such growth of a ZPD at work in Carmen's classroom. Do you recall the birth announcement that Jasmine composed about the baby mice? The announcement contained some unconventional spellings. Jasmine is six years old and lacks extensive experience with written language. Carmen believes that over time, as Jasmine gains meaningful print experience, her spelling will more consistently approximate adult spelling. To assist Jasmine and other students in feeling successful about their early writings, Carmen gives some attention each day to noticing particular letter and sound patterns in high-use words and then adds those words to a place on the classroom wall for all to see. Carmen also models how looking for words in the room can help during writing time. After only one month of school she observes that Jasmine has learned to help herself during writing by looking at various labels around the classroom and on the wall of words to see if the words she wants to use are there. Carmen encourages Jasmine to use writing in meaningful ways, because she knows that overemphasis on correction rather than encouragement may reduce Jasmine's intrinsic desire to learn and may hinder her development as a successful, competent writer.

Noncompetitive Environments

Natural learning environments are typically free of imposed competition. If intrinsic motivation is allowed to drive learners, competition is not needed as a motivator for developmental learning. Once behaviors are learned, friendly competition between learners becomes a part of self-selected practice to maintain and improve competencies. In such cases, though, the competition is the choice of the learners.

Holdaway (1980) wisely speaks to the issue of competition in learning, especially for children, when he states, "The real business of learning is concerned with performing better today than yesterday or last week; it has absolutely nothing to do with performing better than someone else. Children want to learn any developmental task in order to be the *same* as their peers, not better than them" (p. 18). The goal of competition should be to enjoy accomplishing skillful behavior, not simply to be competitive.

In her first-grade classroom, Carmen does not emphasize group competition. Instead, using children's work collected in individual portfolios, she encourages all her students to compare their current work with their own past accomplishments as reflected in the portfolios. Jeremy, Jasmine, Ruben, and the other students share their work with their classmates, and certainly the children compare what they have done, but a personal sense of accomplishment remains the focus.

Opportunity for Self-Paced, Self-Motivated Practice

Learning complex processes such as reading and writing requires much time and practice. As learners, we are more likely to practice when it is our own desire that drives our learning. The amount and intensity of our practice is regulated best by our own motivation (Holdaway, 1979). If an adult takes over the function of regulating practice for a child, the child may become less motivated to learn. In addition, the child's self-confidence to make decisions about learning may be jeopardized.

Every day the children in Carmen's classroom choose writing topics. Almost every day during October, Jeremy wrote stories that had something to do with helicopters. Carmen allows this choice because, as she watches him during the writing time, she can see that he is involved in his work. Jeremy enthusiastically shares his writing with his neighbors and with Carmen. During that four weeks, Jeremy gains control over some specialized helicopter vocabulary and demonstrates a growing depth of knowledge on the topic. Carmen notices that Jeremy's drive to "master" this topic also leads to more conventionally spelled words and more complex sentence structures.

Self-paced, self-motivated practice allows the learner to control the amount of repetition needed to master a particular skill. Who knows better than the individual how comfortable and confident he feels about the task at hand? Repetition is a natural part of children's play as they strive to acquire that sense of control necessary to confidently attempt more mature stages of learning.

Self-Regulation

When children are encouraged to exercise control over their own learning, they are well aware of their level of effort and have a sense of the progress they are making. If someone else controls the learning, children tend to look outside of themselves for evaluation. A primary goal of developmental learning environments is for learners to develop the ability to be self-corrective, and ultimately to be self-evaluative. For children to learn self-regulation as a way of thinking about learning, they must participate in a learning environment in which knowledgeable adults support their attempts to learn and treat them as worthwhile, self-aware individuals. Children must be encouraged to trust their knowledge of themselves, combined with corrective feedback from reliable sources, to move toward independence.

Jasmine and her birth announcement provides a good example of self-regulation. At one point, while writing the announcement, Jasmine stops writing, looks intently at the paper, erases, and writes again. She ends on a note of self-evaluation—"There! Now everyone will know about the babies." Jasmine decides that the task is completed satisfactorily and her goal is met.

Moving toward Independence

Developmental learning environments exist to help children move toward independence as learners. Parents instinctively foster independence when they encourage children to talk, walk, eat, and dress themselves. Often without deliberate planning or conscious knowledge, parents provide a developmental learning environment that fosters children's natural desire to learn and to be independent.

Our goal for learners in school should be independence, because independent learners are confident in their own abilities and skills. If we are to successfully promote independence, we should let the success of developmental learning environments outside of school teach us about the possibilities for learning in school. Within a meaningful learning environment, as described in the preceding section, what is our role as teacher? What function do we serve in the learning environment?

THE TEACHER'S ROLE IN LITERACY DEVELOPMENT

We can all point to learning experiences in which a more knowledgeable person provided the support and guidance that enabled us to advance to the "next level" in our learning. As the teacher, we are a "more knowledgeable other" for our students, assisting them to become independent and competent readers and writers. How will we choose to function in this role?

In this book, the role of teacher is viewed as that of a mediator between children and the learning environment (Dixon-Krauss, 1994), with the goal of moving children toward independence as readers and writers. Remember that as

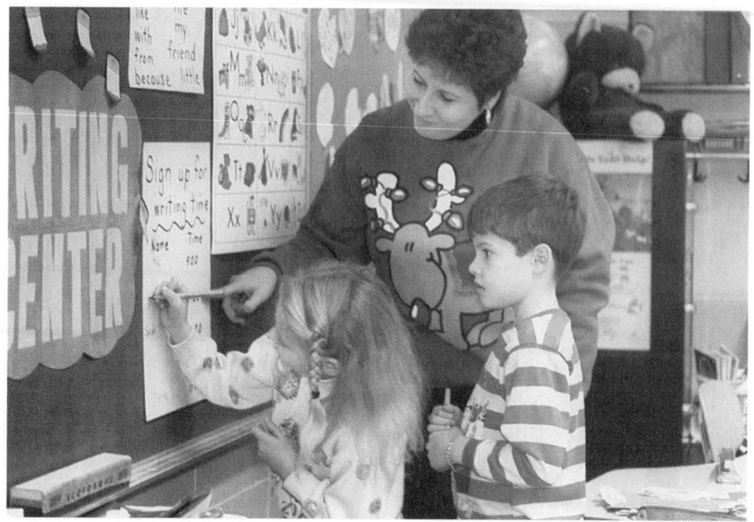

Children need our guidance as they move toward independence as readers and writers.

cognitive functions develop, the ZPD moves forward toward more complex functioning. Such growth led Vygotsky (1962) to conclude that instruction should lead development. He states, "What the child can do in cooperation today he can do alone tomorrow. Therefore the only good kind of instruction is that which marches ahead of development and leads it; it must be aimed not so much at the ripe as at the ripening functions" (p. 104).

As we plan meaningful learning experiences for children, we should use what we know about their development to set purposes for instruction that are just beyond what children can do independently. As we mediate during instruction we should adjust the support and assistance we provide to children based on our observations and on children's feedback to us. Because independence in reading and writing is the goal, we should slowly withdraw our assistance as children demonstrate that they are able to perform independently.

When I began as a classroom teacher, the role I had observed teachers take was primarily a dispenser of knowledge or an assigner of tasks, usually to the class as a whole. Such teachers seemed to focus their efforts on end products such as completed papers or correct answers to questions. Learning to be a mediator was a new role for me, one that required that I be more responsive and flexible than in my past experiences. I found I had to give my full attention to the students and to the feedback they provided during instruction. Does your past experience influence your current understanding of teaching and learning? Try to become more aware of the ways that your past experience informs your current views.

To implement any instructional approach in the classroom, it is important that we understand the theory base—the assumptions about learning—that undergird that approach. Such knowledge allows us to make thorough choices as we organize activities and provide support to children. Knowing the theory base for an approach also allows us to integrate parts of other approaches that are consistent and that share common beliefs about children's literacy development.

ASSESSMENT: MONITORING CHILDREN'S LITERACY DEVELOPMENT

Teaching from a developmental perspective requires that we consider each child's progress in light of what we know about that individual and what we know to be possible based on developmental and literacy learning theories. To build a whole picture of what children know and do as readers and writers, both teacher and child should be active participants in assessing and evaluating growth.

Working from a developmental perspective suggests that we will not hold the same expectations for all children at any one point in the school year. Our assessments of their strengths and needs should:

- be based on continuous observation of children engaging in authentic reading and writing tasks over a substantial period of time, and
- use a variety of measures, by both teacher and child, that reflect appropriate instructional purposes and account for diversity among children as learners.

To consider the rationale for assessing children's progress in this book, we should ask ourselves these two questions:

- What will I need to know about children as readers, writers, and learners to evaluate their growth?
- How can I use what I know about reading, writing, and learning to monitor children's growth in various approaches to instruction?

Today's classrooms challenge us to move beyond our individual recollections of school and be open for today's children to teach us about who they are as individuals and as learners. We should be cautious as we draw on our own memories of school to inform us in this rapidly changing world. Instead, our experiences with children and our knowledge of what research teaches us should exert a strong influence on our views of children and school.

RESPECTING DIVERSITY AMONG CHILDREN

As we think about the children who enter our classrooms, we are reminded that:

> Diversity is the norm in our society, even when homogeneity appears on the surface. . . . When educators do not notice diversity, when they give negative notice, or when they lose the opportunity to give positive notice of the natural diversity that is always there, they create a bogus reality for teaching and learning (Hilliard, 1994, p. x).

Throughout this book, we consider how different aspects of curriculum and instruction may affect the unique individuals in the classroom. Children are diverse in their backgrounds of experience, in their ability to make use of those experiences, in their preferences for learning, and in their motivation to engage in new learning experiences. Historically, we have always found diversity among individuals, diversity of gender, social class, ethnic group membership, learning styles, physical or mental abilities, personal interests, and the like. Issues of multicultural education should address all of these entities (Harris, 1994).

Gender differences have always existed in our classrooms. Boys and girls are not only different physiologically, but are also socialized differently into a culture. To see this process in action one only need look at the portrayal of male and female roles in advertisements, literature, or television and film.

Our capitalistic system traditionally produces an economically stratified society. The opportunities for life that are determined by economics affect the experiences and outlook that children from different social groups bring to the classroom. The conditions associated with poverty help to explain much of the variation in achievement among individuals.

We are a nation of many different racial and ethnic groups, each with a rich cultural heritage of language, values, and traditions. We are what we are because of the unique contributions that each group has made to our way of life (Ramirez & Ramirez, 1994). What we have in common is that we all belong to a democratic society that in turn has its own values and traditions. Somewhere in the mingling of culture and citizenship, we each find our place.

In any group of children, we see diversity in preferred learning style, in physical, intellectual, social, and emotional abilities, and in personal interests. Sometimes this diversity in children has been labeled, for example, in special education or compensatory programs such as Title I; and children have been segregated from others based on their differences. More recently, the trend has been to as far as possible accommodate these differences within a single educational environment.

In this book we examine ways to respect the diversity that each child brings to the classroom. Our challenge is to find ways to enable all children to contribute, with dignity, to the culture of the classroom. Teachers of young children can have far-reaching impact. Our world always needs concerned individuals who are competent to deal with the problems that face us. The curriculum and learning environment that we create for young children will be an important part of their foundation as literate, fully developed individuals.

Take a moment to reflect on issues of reading and writing in the primary grades . . .

Literacy is the ability to competently use language to read, write, and think for personal satisfaction and success.

A balanced and integrated literacy framework provides appropriate support for all children to become literate.

A balanced and integrated literacy framework includes:

- reading aloud;
- shared, guided, and independent reading;
- shared, interactive, guided, and independent writing;
- literature study; and
- word study.

Literacy develops over time and experience, as children progress through identifiable stages of development.

Emergent readers and writers

- use speech to develop problem-solving skills;
- learn that speech can be represented with print; and
- develop a concept about words in print and how words can be made.

Developing readers and writers

- develop knowledge and skills to decode simple words in written language;
- develop fluency in appropriate-level books;
- learn to use visual, meaning, and language cues to understand what they read;
- develop some strategies to monitor their own reading; and
- write many familiar words and some unfamiliar words with predictable letter–sound patterns.

Transitional readers and writers

- sink into silent reading;
- are becoming more flexible in their skills;
- have a large storehouse of known words for fluent reading and writing;
- have a number of strategies to monitor their own reading and writing; and
- incorporate reading experiences into models for writing.

Learning environments that contribute to literacy development in the primary grades typically contain:

- a "more knowledgeable other" who provides assistance within the zone of proximal development (ZPD);
- collaboration rather than competition;
- opportunities for self-paced, self-motivated practice;
- opportunities for self-regulation; and
- direction toward independence.

The teacher:

- works to develop a meaningful learning environment for all children; and
- serves as a "more knowledgeable other," supporting children toward independence as learners.

Assessment

- is a constant and careful monitoring of children's literacy development during authentic reading and writing experiences; and
- uses a variety of measures or sources of information about children.

Diversity is the norm of society. We expect diversity in the classroom and we have respect for all children as learners when we consider issues of gender, social class, ethnicity, language, learning styles, physical or mental abilities, and personal interests as we develop curriculum and plan instruction.

YOUR TURN . . .

1. What are your current beliefs about how children learn to read and write? What experiences have influenced your current view? Take time to record those beliefs. Later in this book you can revisit the beliefs you record now to consider how your study of early literacy is or is not being influenced by your interactions with this book, your conversations with others, and your observations in schools.
2. Imagine that you are teaching in a primary grade classroom. What would you do to create a classroom environment that gets children excited about reading and writing?
3. How do your current beliefs about reading and writing compare with your potential actions? How do the things you identified for the classroom environment in question 2 relate to your beliefs about reading and writing that you listed in question 1?

Aa Bb Cc Dd Ee Ff Gg Hh Ii Jj Kk Ll Mm

CHAPTER

2

Reading Aloud to Children

Beginning to develop our literacy framework . . .

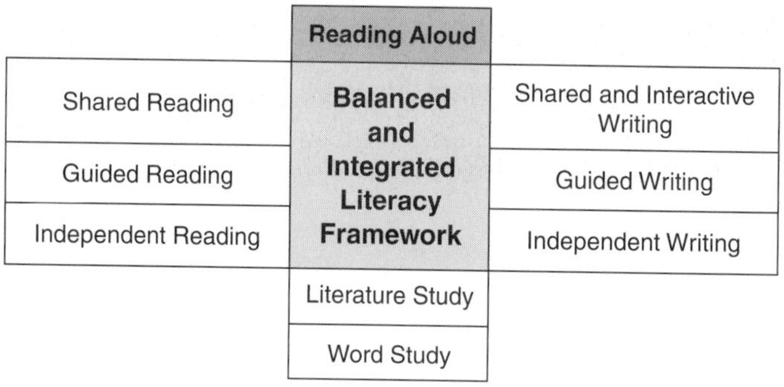

	Reading Aloud	
Shared Reading	**Balanced and Integrated Literacy Framework**	Shared and Interactive Writing
Guided Reading		Guided Writing
Independent Reading		Independent Writing
	Literature Study	
	Word Study	

In this chapter, we . . .

- Focus on the powerful role that reading aloud to children plays in literacy development.
- Explore the instructional possibilities of read-aloud as a central component of a balanced and integrated literacy framework.

Focus Literature:

- *A Chair for My Mother* by Vera B. Williams
- *Trains* by Gail Gibbons

Looking into Classrooms . . .

The kindergarten children in Sheila's classroom are just completing their morning calendar routine. Sheila moves to a chair at the corner of the carpet area and prepares for the daily read-aloud time. Without being directed to do so, the children move away from the calendar and settle themselves in front of Sheila.

Sheila always begins the read-aloud with an old favorite. Today she holds up several books from past readings and asks the children which they prefer. A show of hands indicates that Amazing Grace *by Mary Hoffman and Caroline Binch (1991) is the "old favorite" for today.*

The children know this story well and love the way that the main character, Grace, pretends to be all kinds of different characters and earns the lead in a school play as Peter Pan. The children are quick to say, " Grace can be anything she wants, if she puts her mind to it," just like Grace's Nana says.

As Sheila turns each page, the children respond in chorus with the different characters that Grace pretends to be. The children are completely engrossed in the story. Story time spills over into activity time as several children play dress-up and are overheard to say, "I'm just like Grace. Guess what I am."

Building a Theory Base . . .

"Language is a gateway to new concepts, a means of sorting out confusions, a way to interact with people, or to get help, a way to test out what one knows. It enters into every activity we can envisage" (Clay, 1998, p. 11). Language is a universal cultural tool used in many contexts to solve problems (Bedrova & Leong, 1996), and is central to becoming literate:

> As a cultural tool, language is a distillation of the categories, concepts, and modes of thinking of a culture . . . Language allows the acquisition of new information: context, skills, strategies, and processes. While not all learning involves language, complex ideas and processes can only be appropriated with the help of language. . . . Language delays impact of other areas of development: motor, social, and cognitive (p. 96).

Children's developing brains are marvelous for learning language! Language development begins on the day a child is born and, for a short time, every child becomes a linguistic genius and with great creativity learns to construct his or her first language (Lindfors, 1987). Children receive stimulation and communication from other humans in their environment. Slowly they develop the physical ability to respond and make their needs and desires known. They learn to use language to interpret and negotiate meaning with others in their environment.

When speech and thinking merge, a special kind of speech ensues, which Vygotsky called *private speech.* Although private speech is audible, it is directed to the self rather than to other people and is used to inform and regulate one's own behavior or learning. When faced with a difficult task as adults, we may also use private speech and talk aloud to ourselves as a means of support and self-regulation. As development proceeds, private speech becomes inner speech, then verbal thinking. Over time and experience these internal mental processes become automatic and enable humans to think and function at higher cognitive levels. By the time children enter school they know a great deal about using language to comprehend and interpret their own world (Halliday, 1975).

LANGUAGE AT HOME

What children know about language is quite dependent upon the environment in which they develop. "For the first five years a child's language growth is entirely dependent on what people say to him—on how much they speak to him, about what things, in what dialect or language, and in what manner, whether gentle and explaining or peremptory and imperative" (Clay, 1991, p. 70). Depending upon socioeconomic status (SES) and the educational background of the adult(s) in the home, some children receive more scaffolding, or support, for thinking and learning language than do others. There can be large differences in the quality of language interactions that children experience as a function of social class (Hart & Risley, 1995).

Through interactions with others during the preschool years, most children acquire the sounds and structures of the language spoken around them. Although there are commonalities among speakers of a language such as English, it is also possible that individuals will develop unique ways of using that language in their lives. The same possibilities for language variation exist between members of different neighborhoods in the same city, between people living in different regions of a country, and between people of different cultural groups.

Rules of language are learned through children's interactions with others, particularly parents. Language use is influenced by the dialect used within the home and community. There is no formal curriculum for learning language, only situations when adults enter into conversations with children because they have a desire to help them learn to communicate. Without formal training, many parents seem to know how to adjust the level of language to that which is useful to their children. Adults make language available and easy by listening to children, responding to what they say, repeating words and phrases, altering sentence structures, and encouraging children to produce language at whatever level they are able. As children produce more language, the adults produce less.

Children learn to negotiate meaning with those around them through their interactions. Every sentence construction is based on an intuitive hypothesis about language. Children constantly test out their hypotheses about how they think other speakers structure language. Through their interactions children are able to judge the correctness of their thinking. Because they want to be understood, they ask questions, search for more information, revise their concepts, and work to connect ideas. Responsive parents help to expand the language capabilities of their children. When children's hypotheses about language structure are not correct, responsive parents provide a more complete model, not merely correction. This model may be the correct pronunciation of a particular word or the conventional organization of words within a sentence, but the message to children emphasizes the important role of language in communicating intentions clearly and accurately in order to be understood.

Responsive parents also introduce their children to the world of language in print through bedtime stories. They share the sounds and rhythms of language in print. They engage in rich discussions and animated conversations with children about the images of the world that are presented in books. As they do so, parent and child work out the meaning of a text (Morrow, 2001). During bedtime story reading, a parent models skillful reading and brings the words in books to life. They demonstrate that reading is both pleasurable and worthwhile. Children begin to learn about book language and the type of meaning making associated with books through participation in book-reading experiences with adults or older peers at home (Elster, 1998).

Children's favorite stories are usually reread numerous times by parents. Children can be very persuasive with their requests: "Please, read this again. It's my favorite!" The more familiar the book, the more children participate in the rereading. Familiarity breeds confidence. Children use the illustrations and their recollections of the text to help in the rereading. They join in with the phrases they remember, such as "Run, run, as fast as you can. You can't catch me I'm the Gingerbread Man." They delight in telling what will happen just before it actually does, so that the parent can say, "You're right! You remembered that part." This knowledge of what is in a book brings a feeling of confidence and a sense of power for children.

Engagement with books also presents new language-learning opportunities for young children. Although children negotiate meaning and understanding quite well in daily conversation, the presentation of ideas in print can present a challenge for making meaning. Daily conversation takes place in a familiar context that children understand and make interpretations about. If they lack understanding, they are able to interact with the speaker to clarify or gain other needed information. In addition, voice intonation, facial expressions, and body language of a speaker provide additional support for understanding.

In contrast to speech, books are written in such a way that a reader can reconstruct the author's message, but without the benefit of the author being present to help clarify ideas. While children listen to stories, they can begin to develop an ear for book language. With the assistance of a responsive adult, children come to understand many things:

- A book's contents can be either make-believe or real.
- Pictures can help to tell the story.
- Books can provide information about many details that, in face-to-face conversations, can be observed (for example, when authors tell who is talking by using such words as *said, exclaimed,* and *asked).*
- All books are not the same. "Once upon a time . . ." signals a make-believe rather than a true story, for example.
- Stories can provide us knowledge about the world.

As children listen to stories they begin to discover the symbolic power of language. As Wells (1986) suggests, this power will "create a possible or imaginary world through words—by representing experience in symbols that are independent of the objects, events and relationships symbolized and that can be interpreted in contexts other than those in which the experience originally occurred, if indeed it occurred at all" (p. 203). The long-term effects of this discovery can be seen in children's learning as they read and write in meaningful ways. Strong positive correlations exist between storybook reading during preschool years and subsequent vocabulary and language development, children's interest in reading, and early success in reading (Sulzby & Teale, 1985).

One of our challenges as teachers is to re-create in the classroom the joy and excitement of bedtime story time.

LANGUAGE AT SCHOOL

Remember that language has its beginning within the social setting of the home and within a particular cultural context. Given the diversity within the American society, it is likely that the home language of many children will differ from the language used for instruction in schools. Such differences may be found in the sounds, accent, or intonation of children's language, vocabulary, grammatical forms the children know, and type and range of sentence forms they use (Clay, 1991). Regardless of the range of differences, teachers must remember that children have already learned how to learn language. If children are assisted in expanding their language knowledge, they will be able to do so. Marie Clay (1991) states:

> The child may not know as much about language as some of his peers, or he may find the rules for talking in school are different from those of his culture or ethnic group, or he may see little similarity between talking in his family and the more formal teacher–pupil talk of the classroom, or he may even speak a different language from the teacher's. Yet in all these cases the child has already learned how to learn language (pp. 26–27).

Learning experiences in school must assist children in successfully using what they already know about language and adding to that knowledge as they acquire literate behaviors. Teachers must strive to be like the responsive parent, expanding children's language knowledge and scaffolding as children strive to use their knowledge of oral language as a foundation for experiences with written language. Conversations with and about books become an essential tool for assisting children with language learning as required by school.

During bedtime stories, young children learned much about the world and how language is used in print to help people think about the world. Teachers can re-create some of the power of bedtime stories by the way they read aloud to children. When a more experienced reader reads aloud, children can learn to think like a reader. Part of thinking like a reader is realizing that a reader has intentions for the reading that influence how that reader approaches print, the expectations that reader has for print, and how much that reader is willing to think about the print to make it meaningful.

DEVELOPING AN EAR FOR THE SOUNDS OF LANGUAGE

In school, teachers will also expect children to draw upon their knowledge of sounds in oral language in order to read and write. To a young child, the spoken words "How are you?" are an idea that has meaning, not words or sounds. Concepts about words, what they are, and how they are made develop slowly as children observe and participate in print experiences with more knowledgeable readers and writers. While emergent readers and writers already have some knowledge of phonemes through their oral language ability, they are not consciously aware that spoken language has a structure. Knowledge of oral language is so automated that conscious control is not necessary. To learn to read and write an alphabetic script, such as English, children must learn to pay attention to the very sounds (phonemes) to which they have learned not to attend (Adams, 1990). They must also become keenly aware that sounds can be manipulated in language to form many varied words.

Even with extensive language support and storybook experiences at home, many kindergarten and first-grade children lack the awareness that words are streams of sounds that can be disentangled, and that sounds can be assembled to produce words (for example, Adams, 1990; Pennington, Grossier, & Welsh, 1993; Pressley, 1998; Stanovich, 1986). This ability to hear sounds in language is referred to as phonological awareness. Researchers have been able to identify levels of awareness, with the more complex levels having a strong relationship to the developing understanding of letter–sound relationships and learning to spell (Griffith, 1991; Juel, Griffith, & Gough, 1986), as well as a strong relationship to skilled reading (Adams, 1990; Slocum, O'Connor, & Jenkins, 1993; Stahl & Murray, 1994; Wagner, Torgensen, Laughon, Simmons, & Rashotte, 1993; Yopp, 1988; Yopp & Yopp, 2000).

DEVELOPING EXPECTATIONS FOR WRITTEN LANGUAGE

Through extensive exposure to print, children learn that it appears in many different places and forms in our world. In and out of school, children see and respond to print in the form of books, charts, logo T-shirts, magazines, signs, posters, computer games, restaurant menus, television, and the like. Based on their experiences with print, children develop a schema that leads to expectations about what a particular form of print might mean. A well-formed schema for written language helps children organize personal experiences into abstract representations that are independent of the originals (Shanklin, 1982). Abstraction allows knowledge to be used in different contexts to make sense of new experiences. Within a schema, knowledge is organized into a hierarchical framework of concepts and procedures that allows for access of knowledge and ideas (Adams & Collins, 1985; Schank & Abelson, 1975).

A child's schema for reading books, for example, includes concepts about reading (we read print rather than pictures, we follow the words from left to right and from top to bottom on a page, and so on) and procedures for reading (for example, pages are turned to read a book, and when we come to a word we do not know we can use context and/or letter–sound clues to figure it out). Depending upon the demands of the reading situation, the child arranges these concepts and procedures in order of importance within an organized framework.

As children gain more experience with books, they add new information about reading to their "reading" schema by "filing" the new information with similar concepts and/or procedures within their existing framework. If their schema for reading does not already include an appropriate place to file the new information, they must create one within their framework by inferring how the new information might relate to existing concepts or procedures.

What does participation in read-aloud experiences contribute to children's schema for reading—their knowledge of what reading is and what readers must do to make meaning? As a more knowledgeable adult reads aloud and guides children through books, children gain knowledge of the distinctive discourse structures, meaning-making strategies, and vocabulary that distinguish written language, especially language found in books, from spoken language (Elster, 1998). Such linguistic knowledge underlies children's emergent reading behaviors.

DEVELOPING EXPECTATIONS FOR DIFFERENT GENRE

Experiences with the different genres of literature help children develop schema for the various forms of written language. Children's knowledge and their emergent reading behaviors are influenced by the types of books they hear (Elster, 1998). The different types of books we choose to read aloud can be particularly helpful along the developmental path as emergent readers rely first on pictures, then on story language, and finally on print (Sulzby, 1985). Reading aloud books from a variety of genre provides effective scaffolds for emergent readers, who, like older readers, orchestrate visual information with memorable story language, content, or predictable story structures (Elster, 1994, 1995).

To build background and expectations for print, children in primary-grade classrooms should have extensive experiences with a range of genre:

- Contemporary realistic fiction
- Information books
- Fantasy
- Poetry
- Folk literature
- Biography and autobiography
- Limited amounts of historical fiction

When reading or listening to a book that belongs to a particular genre, we have expectations for it based on our knowledge of other books in the genre. For example, *Mufaro's Beautiful Daughters* (Steptoe, 1987), an African Cinderella tale, begins, "A long time ago . . . . " Our experience with other picture books that begin similarly leads us to expect a fairy-tale-like story, containing characteristics such as a clear problem needing to be solved, a struggle between good and evil, and the use of magic to help solve the problem. In this case, we would be correct. These characteristics are typically found in the genre of traditional literature.

In contrast, we open another picture book, *Chicka Chicka Boom Boom* (Martin & Archambault, 1989), and we hear:

A told B,
And B told C,
I'll meet you at the top
Of the coconut tree.

Realizing that what we hear is poetry, we probably have different expectations for this book than for *Mufaro's Beautiful Daughters.* Our experiences with poetry lead us to expect rhythmic language, rhyming words, or sensory images. As we read or listen, we find that the author is using poetry to tell a story about letters of the alphabet that are trying to race each other up a tree.

In yet another book with a colorful cover, entitled *How is a Crayon Made?*, we hear:

> It's hard to imagine a world without crayons. If all
> the regular size crayons made in the United States last year
> were laid end-to-end around the equator, they would circle
> the globe four and a half times!

From these first two sentences we are aware that this text will probably provide factual information about crayons.

Our previous experiences with various genres help us realize that poetry, fairy tales, and information books may not have the same purposes or characteristics, so we read each type of book with slightly different expectations. As we become more aware of expectations for different forms of written language, we should think about helping children learn how to use their knowledge of these differences to respond and make meaning during read-aloud experiences.

THINKING LIKE A READER

Reading to children allows them to think like readers without having to be the decoders of the text. As children gain experience working with an author's ideas, especially through repeated experiences with a single text, they have many opportunities to learn how it feels to think like a reader. Retelling their version of a familiar text can affirm their own capabilities as readers to make meaningful renditions.

Readers' Intentions

Part of thinking like a reader is realizing that, as a reader, we have intentions when we read. Our intentions influence how we approach print, the expectations we have for print, and how much we are willing to think about the print to make it meaningful to us. If we think that the print has something for us, we probably are motivated to spend more time thinking about the ideas that the author expresses and relating the author's ideas to our own. If we do not want to be involved with the print, we are less likely to work to make sense of it, especially if the text is difficult for us. Our interests, needs, and desires as human beings influence the types of texts we find meaningful. Our past experiences with text, positive and negative, may also influence our intentions when we engage with books.

Authors' Intentions

Another part of thinking like a reader is realizing that authors have intentions when they write, intentions that direct how they communicate with the reader. The more that we are aware of and consider an author's possible intentions, the closer we may come to meaningfully interacting with that author's ideas.

What intentions might a sports journalist have? A journalist, who is committed to the purposes of newspapers, provides the relevant facts about a game that has taken place. If, however, the journalist's favorite team was upset or poor officiating had a decided impact on the game, his or her intentions for the column might go beyond reporting the "facts." Our experience with newspapers, and more specifically with the sports section, leads us to work with the author to learn about the outcome of the game. Our newspaper experience also leads us to realize that journalists sometimes take license with their subject, so we must read with an eye for separating the journalist's opinions from the facts.

An author's intentions will, in large part, determine the choice of form; conversely, a predetermined form and purpose for writing influence the author's intentions. Picture books, newspaper columns, and telephone messages each have certain "rules" by which they are written and can influence an author's intended outcome. Extensive experiences with a variety of texts help children develop expectations for different types of writing.

THINKING ABOUT WRITTEN LANGUAGE

Through interactions with others, children have already learned to think and make meaning from those interactions. As children begin to interact with written language, they must learn to use various ways of thinking about texts to make meaning. The meaning that children are able to construct from a written text depends in whole or part on (1) the child's schema for a topic or particular type of text, (2) the context in which the text is being read, (3) the child's understanding of the purpose, (4) the level of attention or motivation the child has for making the text meaningful, (5) the level of difficulty of the text language, and (6) the child's use of how listeners/readers make meaning from text. Listeners/readers can think about or make meaning from a particular written text in a variety of ways, just as they do during verbal interactions. To make a text meaningful, children may need to think about the author's ideas in any or all of the following ways: explicitly, implicitly, critically, creatively, and personally.

Explicit Thinking—Recalling the Author's Words

Explicit understanding of an author's words depends in part on knowing the words in a text and on knowing about the topic. In *A Chair for My Mother* (Williams, 1982), the young girl begins her story by telling us the following:

> My mother works as a waitress in the Blue Tile Diner.
> After school sometimes I go to meet her there. Then her boss
> Josephine gives me a job too.

If, after hearing the story, children are asked to recall what type of work the mother does, the children should state, "waitress." To prove that fact we can return to the text and find that word in the first sentence. Children should be able to agree on explicitly stated ideas or information. If, however, the topic is unfamiliar, children may have difficulty understanding the author's ideas, even if they know all of the author's words.

Implicit Thinking—Linking the Author's Ideas

Authors do not consistently tell readers explicitly what they need to know. It would be impossible for an author to anticipate everything that every reader might need to know about the topic. The author must assume that the reader knows some things about the topic and will "work" to make sense by filling in or linking ideas during the reading. This act of filling in or linking ideas is called *implicit* thinking.

Anderson and Pearson (1984) identify four types of implicit thinking that readers will draw upon to fill in missing ideas or incomplete understanding:

- *Text cues a sufficient schema.* Based on clues in the reading, a reader decides to draw from an existing schema that is sufficient to allow the accurate filling of the empty "slot" (missing information).
- *Reader links specific ideas in text.* The reader decides that a specific piece of information in the text fills a particular empty "slot" in the ideas that the author has been building in the text.
- *Reader combines schema and clues in text.* The reader decides to fill a particular empty "slot" without specific information from the author but in concert with clues gathered from the text.
- *Logical reasoning occurs without support of text.* The reader lacks sufficient schema and draws a conclusion based on logical reasoning, but without clues or support from the text.

The first three types of implicit thinking can lead to appropriate conclusions through varying combinations of children's schemata (plural for schema) and ideas in a text. The fourth, however, can be problematic if children's lines of reasoning lead to misconceptions about the author's ideas.

On the second page of *A Chair for My Mother,* the young girl who is narrating the story tells us that:

> My mama empties all her *change* from *tips* out of her purse
> for me to count. Then we push all the *coins* into the jar.

From the first page of the story we know that her mother is a waitress. If we know about that type of work, we know that customers give tips, or extra money, for good service. We use our schema for what waitresses do and clue words in the text to link ideas from one page to another to complete the intended idea. As competent readers, we have learned to think our way through text and operate as if text should make sense, so at times we will fill in missing pieces to reach a conclusion.

Critical Thinking—Questioning the Author's Ideas

An author writes from a particular perspective and, depending on intentions, may be trying to persuade us toward a particular point of view. It is the responsibility of each reader to make critical judgments about the value or merit of an author's ideas based on a set of criteria determined by the reader. To be an effective critical reader we must decide (1) what is of value, (2) what is accurate, and (3) what is worthy of retaining for future use. Critical judgments require us to use background knowledge accurately and to approach reading as a thinking process. We must know that we cannot ignore the author. While we use our own ideas to make judgments, we must make these judgments in light of the author's ideas or arguments. The author of *A Chair for My Mother* crafts a story that clearly values disciplining oneself to save money for personal wants, but also the importance of helping others in times of need. Critically considering these issues involves identifying both the author's position and one's personal stance.

Creative Thinking—Beyond the Author's Ideas

To engage in creative thinking about a character, for example, we go beyond the author's ideas and let our own ideas take over. Although initially we may be influenced by the author, we soon realize that our response does not *require* us to consider the author's ideas. Creative thinking is influenced both by our purpose for reading and by the type of text. If our purpose is enjoyment, we may decide that we control the reading and the direction of our thinking. The more comfortable we are with a text, the greater our creativity will be. As children listen to the young girl in *A Chair for My Mother* narrate the story of her family, they may think about other ways the family could save money to buy the special chair. Their own experiences compliment, and may exceed, the author's telling of the story as they consider alternatives that the family did not consider.

The type of text we read and our purposes for reading can influence whether we think creatively about a text. If we read text for specific information, we may feel more of a need to attend to the author's thinking rather than to our own, so we might not engage in as much creative thinking. Children need encouragement to think creatively, drawing upon their own ideas about the text.

Personal Response—Personal Connections with an Author's Ideas

We never know all that another reader thinks, understands, or feels about a text. Don Holdaway (1980), an Australian educator, describes reading as "an individual and intensely personal thing. We cannot speak of reading as thinking without emphasizing the individual nature of the process: groups don't think" (p. 51). Do you agree with Holdaway? Consider yourself for a moment. After finishing a book you enjoyed, are you able to recount in great depth all that you understood and experienced while you were reading? I know that I could not retell everything, and what is more, I would not want to be forced to give a detailed account of my responses. I do not feel the need to share all of my responses; some I would rather keep to myself.

As children engage with the main character in *A Chair for My Mother,* they may think of themselves in her place and consider how they would feel if their apartment had burned and everything the family owned was lost. They might also think of someone they know to whom such things have happened. This type of thinking goes beyond the author's control and involves the personal response of the listener/reader.

How effectively students use different ways of thinking to make meaning with text is a national concern. The National Assessment of Educational Progress (NAEP) is "the nation's only ongoing, comparable, and representative assessment of student achievement" (Mullis, Campbell, & Farstrup, 1993, p. 1). In this assessment, fourth-, eighth-, and twelfth-grade students are asked to read for literary experience, to read to gain information, and to read to perform a task. As students read a variety of texts for different purposes, they are asked to demonstrate an initial understanding, develop an interpretation, articulate a personal reflection and response, and demonstrate a critical stance. In 1999, only 64% of fourth-grade students participating in the NAEP assessment could read at or above a basic level of proficiency. Thus, 36% of students tested could not achieve a basic level of reading proficiency, defined as having at least partial mastery of the knowledge and skills needed to be proficient in fourth-grade-level work.

How are the different ways of making meaning as discussed reflected in the NAEP reading assessment? Students are expected to:

- demonstrate an initial understanding (explicit),
- develop an interpretation (implicit),
- articulate a personal reflection and response (personal/creative), and
- demonstrate a critical stance (critical).

As we think about the ways in which a listener/reader makes text meaningful, we should try to distinguish for ourselves when a particular type of meaning making is appropriate or even demanded by the reading situation. In the classroom, we should help children learn how to make text meaningful in different ways and how to judge what a particular text demands of them. Competent listeners/readers should be able to independently judge the demands of a reading situation.

When children come to school they are already experienced language learners. How do we build on children's existing language knowledge to enhance their expectations of print, motivation to read, and knowledge of book language? Reading aloud quality literature is an essential element of our balanced and integrated literacy program in the primary grades. Reading aloud can begin to develop skills and strategies that lead to the literate thinking required of competent readers and writers. The remaining sections of this chapter focus on applications that help us apply theories about reading processes and reading aloud with children to effective classroom practices.

Take a moment to reflect on your theory base for reading aloud . . .

At home, during the preschool years,

- children acquire intuitive rules for language through interactions with more knowledgeable others,
- responsive adults introduce children to purposes of oral and written language,
- reading bedtime stories is a primary way to help children emerge into literacy, and
- children know how to learn language.

Learning experiences in school must support and extend children's learning about the differences between oral and written language.

In school, children will draw on their ability to hear sounds in oral language to figure out written language.

Experience with written language, especially through read-aloud, provides background knowledge, or schema, for understanding written language.

Read-aloud, from a variety of literary genre,

- provides models for types and purposes of written language, and
- develops expectations for the variety of ideas that can be found in print.

Varied experiences with print help children understand that readers and writers have intentions that are communicated through written language.

Readers must be able to think in a variety of ways to make meaning with and through print.

- Explicit thinking occurs when we recall the author's words.
- Implicit thinking occurs when we link the author's ideas across a text.
- Critical thinking occurs when we question the author's ideas.
- Creative thinking occurs when we think beyond the author's ideas.
- Personal response occurs when we make connections with an author's ideas.

Putting Theory into Practice . . .

We know that responsive adults initiate literacy experiences at home when they engage in meaningful conversations with their children, introduce children to written language through bedtime stories, and help children to find meaning in print found in their surroundings. We also know that children's understandings about language and print develop through interactions with others, interactions involving a lot of dialogue in which adults and children work on problems together. As adults support and scaffold children's understandings, it is possible for children to internalize knowledge about language and print that will support their learning to read and write in school.

When children come to school, we should build upon and extend their understandings of language and print in much the same manner. The literacy program we develop for young children should be rooted in the meaningful conversations that surround exploring the contents of books, attending to the sounds and meaning of oral language and the unique features of print. In the remainder of this chapter, then, we explore ways to engage children with books through reading aloud, we help them attend to sounds of oral language, and we introduce children to the basic features of print.

ENGAGING CHILDREN WITH BOOKS

The single-most important thing we can do to help children build knowledge about reading and the language of books is to read to them (Anderson et al., 1985). Think of that! Read-aloud is our "most direct way of communicating the special qualities of written language to children" (Holdaway, 1980, p. 17). With such potential, reading aloud should be "the centerpiece of the curriculum from which all else flows" (Kristo, 1993, p. 54).

Through reading aloud:

- adults share the sounds and rhythms of language in print,
- adults engage in rich discussions and animated conversations with children about the images of the world as presented in books,
- both adult and child work out the meaning of a text (Morrow, 2001),
- adults model skillful reading as they bring the words in books to life and show children that reading is both pleasurable and worthwhile, and
- the child learns to think like a reader and to navigate through the ideas in books without needing to be the decoder.

READING ALOUD IS AN INVITATION INTO BOOKS

During read-aloud we invite children into books, creating opportunities for them to become more receptive to written language. Inviting children into books should:

- be in a comfortable environment,
- expose children to new books,
- provide time to revisit old favorites,
- encourage children to share their responses,
- enable you to help children interpret and/or appreciate literature,
- encourage children to give direction to read-aloud discussions, and
- happen more than once per day.

Create a Comfortable Environment

When we gather children close around for reading aloud, we re-create the warmth of bedtime story reading. Make an inviting place in the classroom for the reading to happen. This says to children that read-alouds are important and deserve a special place. Think about where to sit in relation to the children. Sit in a comfortable chair and have the children gather on the floor nearby. Sitting near or in the classroom library corner is another good choice because it is usually a comfortable area where children feel welcome.

Expose Children to New Books

We should use read-aloud time to expose children to new books, new ideas, new authors, and new illustrators. When we read a new book, make a special introduction. Tell children where we found the book and what made us select the book to share with them. If the author or illustrator is new, we can share information about that person to help children understand that real people write the books they love. Interesting pieces of information about authors and illustrators can be found on the inside flaps of a book jacket and in *Something about the Author* (Telgen, 1986), *Children's Literature Review* (Senick, 1990), and other similar resources. For example, children delight in knowing that Tomie dePaola really took dancing lessons as a boy just like Oliver in *Oliver Buttons Is A Sissy* (1979) or that Gail Gibbons, author/illustrator of such books as *Weather Words and What They Mean,* puts people and places she knows in the information books that she writes.

Provide Time to Revisit Old Favorites

Children of all ages need opportunities to realize that the worth of a book is not used up after one reading (Beaver, 1982). By dedicating part (at least 25%) of the read-aloud time each week to rereading old favorites, we show children that their enjoyment, understanding, and confidence are increased by relistening to stories. Revisiting an old favorite also enables emerging readers to see that texts remain the same from reading to reading, thus reinforcing the concept of permanence of print.

Encourage Children to Share Responses to Books

Watch children during a read-aloud and notice the variety of responses they have to books. The types and frequency of children's responses will vary depending on the way that we encourage response, the connection between the book and children's background knowledge, and children's familiarity with the book. Children's responses may be nonverbal, responsive, or evaluative among others (Kristo, 1993). We observe children's nonverbal responses as they smile, grimace, lean forward, squirm, and hold their breath in anticipation. This body language tells us that children are involved with the story. We should acknowledge these responses, realizing that children may not yet be ready to make public verbal responses.

Children also show their response when they repeat words or ask about words in a text. Sometimes the words will catch children's attention, such as in *The Snowy Day* (Keats, 1962):

> Down fell the snow—
> plop!
> —on top of Peter's head.

Children might repeat "plop" because it has an interesting sound and creates pleasing sensations in the mouth when it is repeated; or they may ask about "heaping mountain of snow," wondering what that means.

Children also make evaluative statements or ask evaluative questions about books. Children reveal their thinking when they make statements such as:

> "I don't like that mean sister."
>
> "He looks like my grandpa."
>
> "Why did they tease him? That hurts."

The more experience children have with stories, especially in conversational settings, the more likely they are to tell us about their responses to books. Young children form opinions and feelings about books and we should encourage them to share and explore those opinions and feelings to validate their thinking as readers.

Help Children Interpret and Appreciate Literature

When we read aloud, we are doing more than just making the print come alive; we also have the opportunity to help children make connections between themselves and books. We can serve as a guide who will help children begin to focus on what the author has to share. We can model our own response to the author's choice of words, the mood set by the illustrator, and an important theme in the text or a character's motives.

Encourage Children to Direct Read-Aloud Discussions

If we encourage children to respond during read-aloud, we open the possibility that their responses may direct discussions about books. Letting children direct the discussion during and after read-aloud can be the beginning of independent thinking about text. For example, Tony's first-grade children are listening to *Hattie and the Fox* (Fox, 1986), a cumulative predictable story about a fox that is stalking a hen. One child commented that the repetition of the animals' talking reminded him of *The Little Red Hen* (Galdone, 1973). There were comments about the repetitions and how the children delighted in knowing what would come next. Tony values the children's thinking and allows their responses to direct the discussion of books.

Engage Children in Many Ways and More Than Once a Day

If we read aloud more than once each day we may feel the freedom to let children set direction on some occasions, while we set the direction during others. Sometimes reading aloud should be for pure pleasure, whereas at other times we may take more of an instructional focus and teach children more directly about literature and the use of certain skills or strategies. The more often we share books aloud, the more familiar children will become with a wide variety of genre and authors.

What literacy knowledge and skills are we able to model as we read aloud to children?

TIPS FOR QUALITY READ-ALOUD

Reading aloud well requires much thought and practice. The following tips are suggestions from authors (Freeman, 1992; Trelease, 1989) and teachers who bring books to life for children.

- *Pick books that you like or are your old favorites.* When you "love" a book you are more likely to share that book with genuine enthusiasm. Children will know when books are special to you.
- *Preview the book.* Read a new book to yourself to become acquainted with its language and ideas before presenting it to class. Then decide what to emphasize or eliminate during the read-aloud.
- *Allow ample time.* Do not start a read-aloud session unless you have time to do it justice. Filling a ten-minute space in the school day by reading aloud is not always a good idea.
- *Think about the position of the book as you read aloud.* If you are reading a picture book, hold the book to your side, about shoulder high, to let both you and your listeners see the illustrations.
- *Children need to see illustrations.* Be sure that children sit close enough to see details, because much of the plot, characters, and setting is told through the illustrations.
- *Connect with your audience.* To let your listeners know they are involved in the reading with you, make frequent eye contact with the children as you read.
- *Read with expression.* Try to maintain good pitch, volume, and expression while you read. Practice reading aloud by tape recording yourself to hear your expression and pacing. When you actually read aloud, you may be so preoccupied with other details that you are not able to evaluate your reading.
- *Read in your own style.* Your read-aloud style should fit your personality. You do not need to create voices for every character. If you are comfortable with your style, you will be more likely to relax and enjoy the experience with your children.
- *Adjust your pace as you read.* When you reach parts of a story that are complex or require careful mental processing, slow the pace of your reading to give your listeners time to process the ideas. When the writing is primarily descriptive, allow your listeners ample time to build mental pictures.
- *Do not read above a child's emotional level.* Consider children's emotional maturity and background knowledge when selecting books. Children may not always be ready for the emotional demands of specific events or themes such as death.
- *It is okay to abandon a book.* Sometimes, even when we preview and thoughtfully select books, we find the choice of a book may be a poor match for a particular group of children. This can be especially true with chapter books. In such cases, abandoning the book may be the best solution.

- *Make read-aloud books available to children.* As you finish a read-aloud, give the book a place of honor in your library area. Some children will want to revisit the book during independent reading time.
- *Award winners are no guarantee.* Just because a book has won an award does not guarantee it to be a good read-aloud for your children. Be sure to preview the book with an ear for the way that the story sounds when read aloud and an eye to the appropriateness for your children.

TEACHING THROUGH READING ALOUD

Remember that in the classroom each of us as teachers is a more knowledgeable other for our students. When we serve as the decoder of text during a read-aloud, we can help young children learn how to listen to and appreciate good literature, to make meaning with book language, and to think like a reader. Because it is important during reading aloud for us to support and extend children's interactions with text, our techniques must be fluid and responsive to children. We can assist children as they learn to make meaning with text through an instructional technique called mediated read-aloud.

Through reading aloud we can assist children in developing skills and strategies for thinking about and making meaning with written language. Reading aloud can help children focus their thinking about a text before, during, and after the reading and extend their understanding of that text. With the assistance of a more knowledgeable reader, children begin to internalize the strategies for thinking about text. Internalization enables children to begin to independently use skills and strategies in new reading situations.

Helping children focus their attention on salient aspects of a book during read-aloud is not new. Techniques such as a directed listening thinking activity (Stauffer, 1959), in which a teacher directs children to listen or read to obtain certain outcomes, has been shown to improve children's comprehension of a story (Morrow, 1985). Considering current views of how children learn (e.g., Vygotsky's theories of development), viewing the teacher as one who directs and the reader as one who is directed is no longer appropriate. The teacher should act as a mediator, one who adjusts the amount of support or assistance provided to children during instruction, gradually reducing that assistance as children are able to accomplish a task independently. In this text we support children's developing understanding of reading and texts through mediated read-aloud experiences.

PLANNING A MEDIATED READ-ALOUD IN NARRATIVE AND INFORMATION TEXTS

To prepare a read-aloud that assists children in making meaning with text, teachers should:

- think about the *purpose(s)* for engaging children with a particular book,
- plan the *strategies* that are needed to support children and assist as they make meaning before, during, and after the reading of a book, and

- *reflect* on interactions with children before, during, and after the reading to provide indications of where assistance is needed in order to make meaning with a text.

The steps of purpose–strategy–reflection provide a cycle of planning for mediated learning (Dixon-Kraus, 1995) that teachers repeat throughout the reading of a particular text. As we engage children in read-aloud, we adjust the level of teacher assistance as feedback from children indicates their need for support to become independent, self-regulated learners.

A mediated read-aloud involves three time segments: before, during, and after the reading (Powell, 1993). In each segment a teacher considers the purpose for using the selected book, the strategy that will be used to support children, and how reflecting on children's interactions might be used to adjust instruction. An overview of what a teacher and children do during a mediated read-aloud is shown in Figure 2.1. Please review that chart before reading further.

The following sample of mediated read-aloud shows how a teacher assists or supports children's thinking during read-aloud in a narrative, or fictional, text. *A Chair for My Mother,* by Vera B. Williams (1982), is used as an example of how a teacher can mediate between children and a narrative text. An additional sample mediated read-aloud is provided for an information text in order to compare and contrast our use of both fiction and nonfiction in the classroom.

SAMPLE MEDIATED READ-ALOUD IN NARRATIVE TEXT—A CHAIR FOR MY MOTHER BY VERA B. WILLIAMS

A Chair for My Mother is the story of the members of a hardworking family (mother, young daughter, and grandmother) who have lived through a fire in their house and are working to rebuild their lives. The story is told through the voice of the young girl, who often goes to her mother's place of work to help after school. The mother is a waitress at the Blue Tile Diner. The family is saving coins in a large glass jar to buy a special armchair to relax in after a long day. The story features a flashback in the middle that fills in information about the fire and helps the reader understand the strong desire to save for the special chair.

Before the reading of *A Chair for My Mother* we thoughtfully consider our purpose(s) in selecting and reading this text to children. How we engage children is influenced by our perceptions of the text. For *A Chair for My Mother,* we might plan the reading to help children understand the following:

- The references to *I, my,* and *me* in the story mean that the little girl is telling the story (first person is one point of view authors can use to tell stories).
- This story teaches the satisfaction of working hard for something that is important and the value of people helping each other in times of need (theme(s) of a plot can help with understanding life lessons).

Before the reading:

The teacher should plan

- clear purpose(s) for reading a particular text
- identify strategies for meeting that purpose
- consider how support can be adjusted during the reading to help children move toward independent thinking

With children, the teacher should

- encourage children to anticipate reading, using text and background knowledge
- focus children's attention on the reading for identified purposes

In response, the children are assisted as they

- predict what might come in the reading using available information
- connect the prediction to current background knowledge
- prepare for meeting the purpose(s) of the reading

During the reading:

The teacher should

- read aloud in a fluid and lively manner
- stop the reading at appropriate places to assist children in making meaning and meeting reading purposes
- encourage children's use of identified strategies
- encourage children's responses, listening thoughtfully to what they say
- provide assistance and adjust support according to need reflected in children's responses

In response, the children are assisted as they

- use listening–thinking strategies to meet reading purpose(s)
- participate, giving feedback to teacher about thinking during the reading
- receive support, adjusted to level of need, to meet purpose(s) of reading
- receive support with essential vocabulary as needed

After the reading:

The teacher should

- encourage response through open-ended questions such as "Well, what did you think of that story?"
- elicit retelling, first unaided through open-ended questions, then aided by probing for specific points
- based on response, determine which essential words may warrant further discussion
- reaffirm strategies used to meet reading purposes
- depending on purposes and children's responses, determine whether repeated readings are warranted or desirable

In response, children are assisted as they

- share responses to the reading (creative/personal meanings)
- retell most important points (explicit/implicit meaning)
- recall essential vocabulary (explicit/implicit meaning)
- discuss important meanings of text as a whole (implicit/critical meaning)

FIGURE 2.1
Mediated Read-Aloud

As we guide children through this book, keep these two purposes in mind to better engage children in the story and help them make meaning from character's actions and story events.

As we prepare children for the read-aloud, we guide their attention to particular information in preparation for what might come. We ask open-end questions to encourage them to use what they already know and to be curious about what they might find. Each time we ask a question, we pause to give children time to think and we listen carefully to their responses as evidence of their thinking.

To prepare children for the reading of* A Chair for My Mother, *we may do the following:

- Point to the title of the book and say, "The title of this book is *A Chair for My Mother* and it is written by Vera B. Williams."
- Point to the illustration on the front cover and ask, "What do you think this blue shape might be? What do you see as you look through the windows?" Pointing to the back of the girl and the mother in the doorway ask, "Who do you think the people in the picture might be? What do you think this story might be about?"
- Begin the reading of the text by saying, "Let's read and see what we can find out."

Remember, if children are unfamiliar with the story, you are only trying to get them thinking about possibilities, not "right" answers. Responses should be treated as possibilities that can be confirmed or revised throughout the reading. Notice that our questions used the word *might* rather than a more definitive word such as *is*. Remember, also, that our purpose for encouraging children to make predictions at this point in the reading is merely to encourage them to use what they know to anticipate and think ahead.

While reading aloud *A Chair for My Mother,* it is important to keep our purpose(s) for reading clearly in mind, so that our support to children can be adjusted based on what they say in response to the reading and discussion. As we guide children through this book, we focus our assistance around helping them to understand each of the three parts to this story:

Part 1: Introduction to the family and how they are saving money to buy a special armchair for the mother (pages 1–8)

Part 2: A flashback to a fire in their house and how neighbors helped (pages 9–16)

Part 3: A description of getting the new armchair (pages 17–28)

In the first reading of this text, we will not specifically address the flashback in part two. Familiarity with the text, such as in a rereading of the book, would be a more suitable situation for helping young children understand the use of flashback as a literary device. We will return to the use of flashback later in the chapter during our discussion of text rereadings.

Discussion during and after the reading should reveal children's understanding of essential words and their context. Most texts contain words that need explanation or emphasis to assist children's understanding and enjoyment of the story. To decide how to handle essential words, we ask ourselves the following questions:

- Is the word likely to be in the listening vocabulary of the children?
- Is the word used in a context that helps children figure out the meaning?
- Is the word essential to understanding the story during the *first* reading?

If a word is essential to understanding, is in the children's listening vocabulary, and is used in good context, then we give the children the opportunity to figure out the word. We are careful not to overnurture children, reducing their drive for independence as readers (Speigel, 1985). During discussion we can check their understanding. If their background experience or the context is insufficient, then we assist them during the reading to make meaning.

***Sample discussion points during the first reading of* A Chair for My Mother:**

PART 1

Pages 1–2

Point to the illustration on page 1 and say:

- "Here is the same illustration (page 1) that we saw on the front cover of the book, but now instead of the title we can see that this place is called the Blue Tile Diner. What is a diner? Why do you think the girl is going into the diner?"

Read text on page 2, then ask:

- "Who do you think is saying the words 'My mother works as a waitress . . .'?" (Allow children to respond.) Confirm their understanding: "Yes, the little girl is telling this story about her mother."
- "The mother is a waitress. What does a waitress do?"
- "What does the little girl do to help her mother at the diner?"
- "The last sentence says, 'And every time, I put half of my money into the jar.' What do you think that means?" (Pause for children to think.) "Maybe we need to read more of the story to understand these words."

Pages 3–4

Point to the illustration of the jar on page 3, then ask:

- "Do you think this could be the jar the little girl puts money in?"

Read the text on page 4, then ask:

- "What do we know about the jar now? What do you think this jar might be for?"
- "What are the 'tips' that the mother puts into the jar?"
- "Why do you think the little girl says that her mother looks worried?"

Pages 5–6

Read page 6, then ask:

- "Who do you see in the picture?"
- "How does Grandma get money for the jar?" (It may be necessary to reread and explain the sentence, "Whenever she gets a bargain on tomatoes or bananas or something she buys, she puts by the savings and they go into the jar.")
- "Look at the jar here (page 3) and now here (page 5), and what do you notice?"

Pages 7–8 (end of part 1)

Read page 8, then ask:

- "What do we know about the money in the jar now?"
- "What happened to the family's other chairs?"
- "What kind of chair are they dreaming about?"

PART 2

Pages 9–12

Read pages 10 and 12, then ask:

- "What did we find out about their house? Why did the little girl say, 'But everything else in our whole house was spoiled'?"

Pages 13–14

Read page 14, then ask:

- "Now what do you know about how the fire 'spoiled' everything?" (charcoal and ashes)
- "What did the little girl, her mother, and her grandmother do after the fire?"

Pages 15–16

Read pages 15 and 16, then ask:

- "After the fire, what did their friends and family do to help?"
- "How did Grandma feel about that? How do we know?" (Reread her words, "You are all the kindest people," she said, "and we thank you very, very much . . . . ")

PART 3

Pages 17–18

Point to the illustration on page 17 and say:

- "Look at the jar now! How do you think it got so full?"
- "What did the little girl tell us about why they are saving money to buy a chair?"
- "Why did her Mama bring home such a big jar?"

Read page 18, then ask:

- "What did we find out about the jar?"
- "How long has it been since the fire?" (That was last year . . .)
- "What do you think they will buy with the money? What makes you think that?"

Pages 19–20

Point to the illustration, and ask:

- "What is this place? Where do you think the mother and daughter are now?"
- "What do you think they are doing there?"

Read page 20, then ask:

- "What did they do with the money?"
- "What are they going to do now?"
- "What kind of chair do you think they will buy? What kind of chair did they say they wanted in the beginning of the story?" (Recall pages 7 and 8.)

Pages 21–26

Read pages 21 to 26, then ask:

- "What did they do as they shopped for a new chair?"
- "How did the Grandma feel?"
- "Do you think they like the new chair? What makes you think so?"
- "What do you think will happen after they get the chair home?"

Pages 27–28

Read page 28, then ask:

- "Where did they put the chair? Why did they put it there?"
- "Is it a big chair? How do we know?"

After reading *A Chair for My Mother,* help children reflect on the story by asking:

- "What did you think of this story?"
- "Let's see if we can remember all of the important things that happened in the story." (Based on their retelling, determine which essential words/ideas may warrant further discussion.)
- "How do we know that the little girl is telling the story?"
- "What do you think about working hard for something you want? About helping others? Can you think of a time that you helped someone or you worked hard to save for something you wanted? How did you feel?"

Depending on children's responses and what we hope they gain from the first reading of the story, we then determine whether repeated readings of this book are warranted or desirable. How does supporting children in read-aloud with narrative texts compare with the support we provide for hearing and understanding information texts?

SAMPLE MEDIATED READ-ALOUD IN INFORMATION TEXT—TRAINS BY GAIL GIBBONS

When we begin to read a text that is informational we have different expectations than we do for a narrative text. The literary elements we learn to follow in narrative are no longer present: plot, setting, characters, theme. Information, also called nonfiction, text is written in a different style than narrative text. To make meaning we learn to focus on understanding main ideas and important details about a real-world topic. We use our knowledge of the world to make meaning. Understanding essential vocabulary—the technical vocabulary of the topic—is also crucial to developing and extending our understanding of the topic.

As adults, most texts we read are information texts. Throughout school, children find that information texts become increasingly more prominent in the curriculum. To prepare children for reading and being able to learn from information texts, we must help them develop an ear (and an eye) for the differences between narrative and information texts. This requires both extensive and intensive experiences with information texts, the same types of experiences we provide with narrative texts.

Consider that we begin reading narrative texts aloud to children long before we expect them to read such text for themselves. Do we do the same with information texts? Typically not, unless children demand we do because of their personal interests. If we read aloud information texts as frequently as we read narrative texts, can we better prepare children for reading information texts for themselves? How does reading aloud from information texts compare with narrative read-aloud?

Trains, by Gail Gibbons (1987), provides a description of different types of engines and the fuels that are used to power each, information about passenger and freight trains, and types of train cars. Specialized vocabulary to talk about trains is introduced and supported by description and illustrations. In general, each page typically has one detailed sentence, supported by the illustration.

Before the reading of *Trains* we thoughtfully consider our purpose(s) in selecting and reading this text to children. How we engage children is influenced by our perceptions of the text. For *Trains,* we might plan the reading to help children understand the following:

- Information about types and purposes of trains
- Specialized vocabulary pertaining to trains
- Illustrations that accompany specialized train words

As we guide children through this book, keep these three purposes in mind to better engage children in the story and help them make meaning from the information provided about trains.

As we prepare children for the read-aloud, we guide their attention to particular information in preparation for what might come. We ask open-end questions to encourage them to use what they already know and to be curious about what they might find. Each time we ask a question, we pause to give children time to think and we listen carefully to their responses as evidence of their thinking.

To prepare children for the reading of* Trains*, we may do the following:

- Point to the illustration of the train engine on the front cover and ask, "What do you think this book might be about?" We can confirm children's thinking by reading aloud the title, *Trains,* and the author's name (Gibbons is also the illustrator).
- Then we might ask, "What do you already know about trains?" Somewhere in children's background will be ideas about trains. In children's comments, we listen for their ideas about types of engines and trains, and the types of cars found on a train.

We are trying to get the children to think about possibilities, not just "right" answers. Responses should be treated as possibilities that can be confirmed or revised throughout the reading. Notice that our questions use the word *might* rather than a more definitive word such as *is.* Remember, also, that our purpose is to encourage children to make predictions at this point in the reading to anticipate and think ahead.

While reading aloud *Trains,* it is important to keep our purpose(s) for reading clearly in mind, so that our support to children can be adjusted based on what they say in response to the reading and discussion. This text focuses on three aspects of trains. As we guide children through this book, we focus our assistance around helping them to understand each aspect of the text:

Part 1: A little history of trains (pages 1–9)
Part 2: The two main types of trains (pages 10–17)
Part 3: The types of cars found on a train (pages 18–27)

In the first reading of the text we might focus most on parts 1 and 2 which contain main ideas that are attainable without extensive background knowledge. The amount of details in part 3, the types of cars, will be challenging for most children and will require rereadings and closer study.

Before the reading, we try to anticipate the essential vocabulary needed for engagement during the first reading. Some vocabulary will need rereadings and additional background to be understood and retained by children.

Vocabulary that needs attention during the first reading includes *locomotive, steam, diesel, subway, freight, couplers,* and *cargo.*

The types of train cars identified in illustrations in part 3 are flatcars, refrigerator cars, hopper cars, piggyback cars, box cars, tank cars, gondola cars, three-level rack cars, and caboose.

The author uses both illustration and explanation to describe the characteristics and function of each car. This amount of detail, however, should not be expected during the first reading. Rereadings will be needed to provide support for attending to and retaining this specialized vocabulary.

***Sample discussion points during the first reading of* Trains:**

PART 1

Pages 1–3

Point to the illustrations on page 1, then pages 2 and 3 (extension of page 1), and ask:

- "What do you see in the illustrations?" (different kinds of trains)
- "Let's read to see what we can find out about trains."

Read text on pages 1 to 3, then ask:

- "Locomotive. What do you think that might be?"
- "Where is a locomotive in this illustration (pages 2 to 3)?"
- "What do the illustrations here make you think about trains?"
- "What type of trains do you see?"

Pages 4–5

Point to the illustrations on pages 4 and 5, and ask:

- "Do these locomotives look new or old? Listen to what the words say." Read the text on pages 4 and 5. Children find out that trains have been around for a long time, and some used to be powered by wood and coal. Briefly discuss coal and what it is.

Pages 6–9

Look at illustrations on pages 6 to 8, and ask:

- "What types of locomotives do you think these might be? Let's read to find out."

Read pages 6 to 8, and ask:

- "We know that wood and coal were used to make steam to run a train. What other kinds of power did we find out about?"

Read page 9, and ask:

- "Look at the illustration that shows how a train sits on the track. Do you see how the wheels of the train fit on the track?"
- "What do we know so far?" (Retell the most important ideas up to this point, end of part 1. Look back at illustrations to support retelling. It is important to help children begin to connect the details they are hearing about.)

PART 2

Pages 10–13

Look at illustration on pages 10 and 11, and ask:

- "In this part we shift our focus to the two main types of trains, passenger and freight. What type of train do you think this might be?" Call attention to the many people in the illustrations (passenger train). "Let's read to find out."

Read pages 10 to 13, then ask:

- "What did we find out about passenger trains?" Help children notice the labels on parts of the train (e.g., berth, dining car) to support what they know.

Pages 14–17

Look at illustrations on pages 14 and 15, then ask:

- "Does this look like a passenger train? What kind of train could this be? Let's read to find out."

Read pages 14 to 17, then ask:

- "What kind of train is this? What did we find out about freight trains?"
- Review part 2, using illustrations to support. "What are two kinds of trains we learned about? What is a passenger train for? What is a freight train for? How can we tell if a train is a passenger train or a freight train?"
- "We know that a freight train can have many kinds of train cars. Let's see what we can find out about the different kinds."

PART 3

Pages 18–25

- For each two facing pages, read each text, calling attention to the illustrations for clues about the types of cars. After reading, point to illustrations on each page and ask, "What kind of car is this? What does it carry?"

Pages 26–27

- Read the last two pages.

After reading *Trains,* help children reflect on the story by asking:

- "Would you like to be a passenger on a train? What would you do if you were a passenger?"
- "What other type of train is very important today? What are some of the kinds of cars that can be on a freight train? Which cars do you like the best? Why?"
- "How do trains get their power to go?"

Depending on our purposes for selecting this text and children's responses, we then determine the extent to which rereadings of this book are warranted or desired.

Are there differences between reading aloud a narrative and reading aloud an information text? What can we observe as we reflect on each mediated read-aloud? By comparing the texts used as examples in this section—*A Chair for My Mother* and *Trains*—the following comparison might be made:

A Chair for My Mother	***Trains***
• Organized around characters' actions and interactions that tell a life story.	• Organized to explain/teach new ideas about trains, using specialized vocabulary.
• Chronology of actions/reactions among characters creates a sequence that the reader is able to follow.	• Text describes trains. Descriptive writing does not have a particular sequence. The reader must know enough about trains to connect relevant ideas.
• Readers can relate to/link ideas because of life experiences.	• Readers may or may not be able to relate to trains as a result of prior experiences.

Sensitivity to the types of texts we select and how readers relate to, or make sense of, those texts guides us to adjust the assistance we provide before, during, and after the reading. Information texts will typically require increased support before, during, and especially after the reading to help children add new information and understanding to concepts about the world they are forming and refining. Revisiting texts enables all children to continue to build and refine their life and world knowledge.

REREADING AND REVISITING TEXTS

From our knowledge of child development, we are aware that all children do not learn at the same rate or in the same way. We are also aware that children's background knowledge can be an asset to learning. It stands to reason, then, that children with varied backgrounds will need to have varied experiences with books that we read aloud. Supporting children in books for a second, third, or even fourth reading can provide the extended experience that many children need (Beaver, 1982). Texts that are reread become old favorites and are requested again and again, just as children request rereadings of bedtime stories.

Children come to a rereading with a version of that story or text already in their heads. They remember portions of the previous reading of the text, which becomes a schema or background knowledge to use as they revisit the text. During a repeated reading we should help children use their knowledge of the text to derive greater pleasure and understanding.

How might the first reading of a text compare with a rereading of the same text? Figure 2.2 shows a comparison of how a reader might think before, during,

FIGURE 2.2
Thinking about a Text—First Reading versus Rereading

First Reading	Rereading
Before you read, we think: • What is this about? • What do I already know?	**Before you read, we think:** • What do I remember about this from before? • What did I like about this?
While reading, we think: • How does this fit with what came before? • How does this fit with what I already know? • What will happen next? • Do I need to change what I was thinking?	**While reading, we think:** • I think I know what's coming, let's see if I'm right! • That's what I thought it would be! or That's different than I remembered. • Oh, I didn't see that before. That's new.
After you read, we think: • How do I feel about this? • What do I want to remember about this?	**After you read, we think:** • I really know this book! • It feels good to know what is coming.

and after the reading of a text. During a rereading we should support children as they use their knowledge of the text to:

- expand vocabulary and book language,
- achieve a deeper appreciation and understanding of the text, and
- focus on a specific aspect of the text, such as the author's style of writing, use of a literary device, or strategies for understanding the text.

Expanding Vocabulary and Book Language

Rereading text provides additional exposure to new vocabulary and book language. We know that children's familiarity with book language will be important to their future success as readers and writers. Revisiting text enables us to focus on essential words and expand on children's understanding of other interesting language presented by an author.

- We might reread *A Chair for My Mother* to help children add new words to their vocabulary. Words such as *diner, waitress, tips, armchair, pumps, spoiled,* and *delivered* may be unfamiliar or may be presented in a new context.
- Rereadings can also expose children to new phrases or ways of saying things, such as how Grandma "puts by the savings" as a way of talking about the money she adds to the jar.
- Rereading provides repeated exposure to vivid descriptions, such as when the little girl describes the aftermath of the fire as everything "was turned to charcoal and ashes" or that what they are saving for is a "wonderful, beautiful, fat, soft armchair."

Revisiting *Trains* can support children's developing understanding of trains, as well as refining understandings of the specialized vocabulary associated with trains.

- Taking a "book walk" through the text to examine illustrations serves as a way for children to recall what is most familiar.
- Rereading a specific part of the text helps focus children's attention on specific information/descriptions the author/illustrator provides, such as the two main types of trains (part 2) or the variety of freight cars (part 3).

During a rereading, children have a familiarity with a text that enables them to focus on more details in the story. We should encourage them to be more actively involved, recalling and confirming what they already know. Knowing the text and interacting more during the reading brings increased satisfaction for some of our more reluctant readers. Our support helps children feel affirmed for what they already know.

Enhancing Children's Understanding and Appreciation of Literature

In the first reading of a text we support children as they think about new ideas before, during, and after the text is read aloud. We mediate between children and texts so that children will successfully follow the gist of the plot and understand the basic actions and motives of the characters. Supporting children through a repeated reading enables them to become more familiar with the author's expressed ideas or the general language of the book. In addition, rereading provides needed repetition to add new vocabulary introduced by the author. Children find great pleasure in knowing that they already "know" a story and are able to join in the telling.

Rereading also can develop deeper understanding of the themes of a text, such as children's appreciation of how people, sometimes with the help of friends and neighbors, work hard to make a new life after something as devastating as a fire destroys all of their belongings. We might also help children to gain a greater appreciation for how long and hard the characters worked to save money to buy the chair of their dreams.

Another reason for rereading text is to help children learn strategies that they can use to increase their understanding and enjoyment of text. Some texts are challenging and require the reader to notice particular details to gain a fuller understanding; however, noticing such details often requires a familiarity with the text. For this reason a rereading can be useful in guiding children to think about these details. Be sure that children have a general understanding of the text before they attempt to examine specific details.

Children's development as readers should guide us as we select which details of a text seem to be most important to revisit. There are usually more possibilities in a text than we would want to use at any one time. We might choose to revisit *A Chair for My Mother* to help children understand the author's use of flashback to tell about how the fire destroyed all of the characters' belongings. Familiarity with the story will help children develop a better sense of the time during which the story takes place, thus, to place the time of the fire in proper perspective. A flashback is a literary device an author uses to fill in details that are needed to better understand the story. Try reading this book by skipping the flashback (pages 9–16). How is the significance of saving for the chair affected? To make the flashback more concrete for children, we might illustrate the time sequence of this story to understand that the author has flashed back to an important event that occurred before the present event (saving for a chair) began.

Supporting children during the reading and rereading of quality literature is an important beginning to a balanced and integrated literacy program. As we support children, we can extend their language learning and expectations of print through a range of engaging activities. In the section that follows we explore ways of extending children's interactions with literature that is read aloud.

RETELLING: BUILDING CONFIDENCE AND OWNERSHIP OF STORIES

Telling and retelling stories was an oral tradition long before it became a written tradition. Children can use the retelling of favorite stories as a way to solidify their understanding of plot sequence and character traits (Morrow, 1985). Retelling is a way to actively engage children in sharing their understanding of an author's ideas. Retelling requires tellers to identify, clarify, and organize their thinking, thus building a base of literal and implied meaning. We support children's development of sense of story through retelling activities.

Children need to verbalize their retellings to develop their knowledge of language and of using language expressively. There is a "linguistic spillover" as children practice retelling a text. As children retell a plot or main ideas of a text, they borrow particular linguistic forms, structures, concepts, and conventions from that author (Brown & Cambourne, 1987). What children learn about language is useful, not only during the retelling, but also in speech and writing that occurs weeks or months later. The language of authors that we read aloud becomes another model for children. Retelling provides practice with language models that are crucial to children's success in reading and writing.

Retelling through Text Illustrations

Text illustrations can help children who have the language for retelling, but need support in recalling and organizing their thinking. After reading the text aloud, return to the beginning of the text and encourage children to retell important story events as cued by the illustrations. Seeing the illustrations in sequence, as we turn the pages of the text, will help children remember the story events in correct order. We can invite them to participate in shared retellings. The safety of the group may let some children be willing to risk in their retellings. Wordless or nearly wordless books are excellent for this form of retelling, such as *Do You Want To Be My Friend?* (Carle, 1971) or *Rosie's Walk* (Hutchins, 1968). We model the "reading" of a wordless book or story based on the illustrations. Then we would encourage children to help retell the story. Finally, we encourage children to construct their own versions of the "reading" or telling to encourage creative thinking.

Retelling through Story Maps

To help children gain confidence in retelling stories, especially complicated ones, help them develop a visual arrangement of events in the story. A *story map* shows the main parts of a story and should show the relationships among the parts. A story map can be organized either by (1) the beginning, middle, and end of the story (see Figure 2.3) or (2) the problem, events, and resolution of the story (see Figure 2.4). Story maps may be written in words or drawn with pictures. The level of detail and format we choose depends on the children and their experience with complex stories. Picture story maps are most appropriate for emerging and developing readers.

Retelling through Drawings

Drawing is an excellent activity for young children because it slows their thinking and allows them time to recall details and organize ideas about a story. Drawing is appropriate for both retelling and response. Retelling through drawing can be either individual or group. If children do each drawing on a separate piece of paper, they can make a retelling book. As children are drawing, either individually or in groups, they can write or dictate a retelling statement about the story. Folding under the bottom two or three inches of the drawing paper provides am-

FIGURE 2.3
Simple Story Map—Beginning, Middle, End

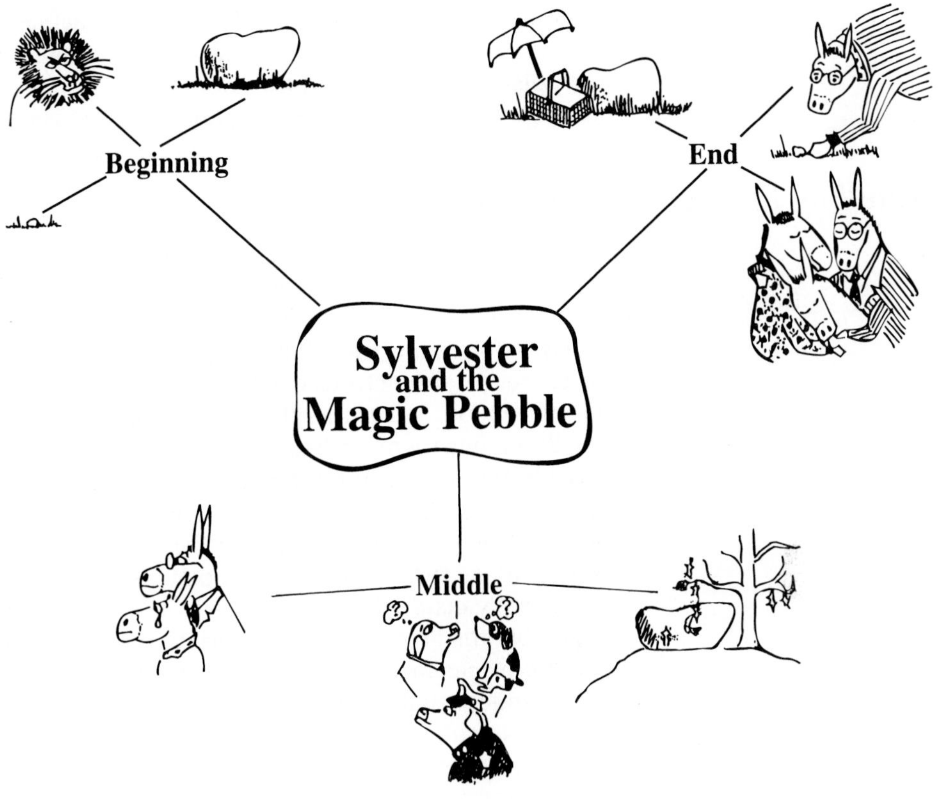

FIGURE 2.4
Simple Story Map—Problem, Events, and Resolution

Sylvester and the Magic Pebble

Problem: Sylvester becomes a rock.

Events:
- Sylvester is scared by a lion.
- He makes a wish.
- He becomes a rock.
- Mother and father look everywhere.
- Time passes.
- Mother and father go for a picnic.
- Father finds a magic pebble.
- He wishes for Sylvester.

Resolution: Sylvester changes back to a donkey.

ple space for written response. When the drawings are complete, children decide the order of the drawings. The children may then hold up the drawings in order, display them around the room or along an inside hallway, or make them into a class or individual retelling book.

Retelling through Felt Boards

A *felt board,* a large display surface covered in felt or flannel, becomes the backdrop for introducing and manipulating pictures of the most important characters and scenes in a story. After we read a text aloud, we encourage the class to retell the story using the felt board props. It is best to begin with uncomplicated stories. Felt board pictures can be made from copies of illustrations of a favorite children's book. Select the illustrations that are essential to the retelling, individually mount them on heavy paper, laminate each picture, then glue felt or flannel to the back so they will adhere to the board. If a commercially made felt board is not available, an old game board, a thin piece of wood, or heavy cardboard can be covered with felt or flannel. An individual student felt board is made by lining the inside top of a box with felt. Pictures for the retelling can be stored neatly inside the box.

Felt boards are also good materials for activity centers. Many teachers like to set up places around the classroom where children can make work choices and continue activities that the class has begun together. With felt board stories, children can independently or in pairs extend their understanding and response to a story by retelling it with picture props. Children can also use felt board props to create their own stories with the characters or change the course of the story by introducing new events. Felt board retellings are especially good for sensory learners. Manipulating the props for a felt board story provides a sensory stimulus for children's recollections of story sequence and details.

Retelling through Writing

Like drawing, writing also slows children's thinking and focuses their attention on the details of a story. The depth of children's written retellings relates to their knowledge of the story, development as writers, and motivation to share their ideas. Individual children do not have to write an entire retelling. A second-grade child shares her response to a class read-aloud of *Mrs. Piggle Wiggle* in Figure 2.5. Groups of children can share the task by each writing one part of the story. Children may also dictate their retellings to a more knowledgeable writer. Children share their written retellings with a peer or class and may also read aloud into a tape recorder.

Retelling through Drama

Bringing physical movement into retellings aids children's sensory learning. Retelling may be easier for some children if they are allowed to pretend to be the character and to play act. The use of props from the story, such as the chairs and bowls of porridge from *Goldilocks and the Three Bears,* supports children's recollections of details and sequence. Early dramatic versions of a story may

FIGURE 2.5
Written Retelling and Response to *Mrs. Piggle Wiggle*

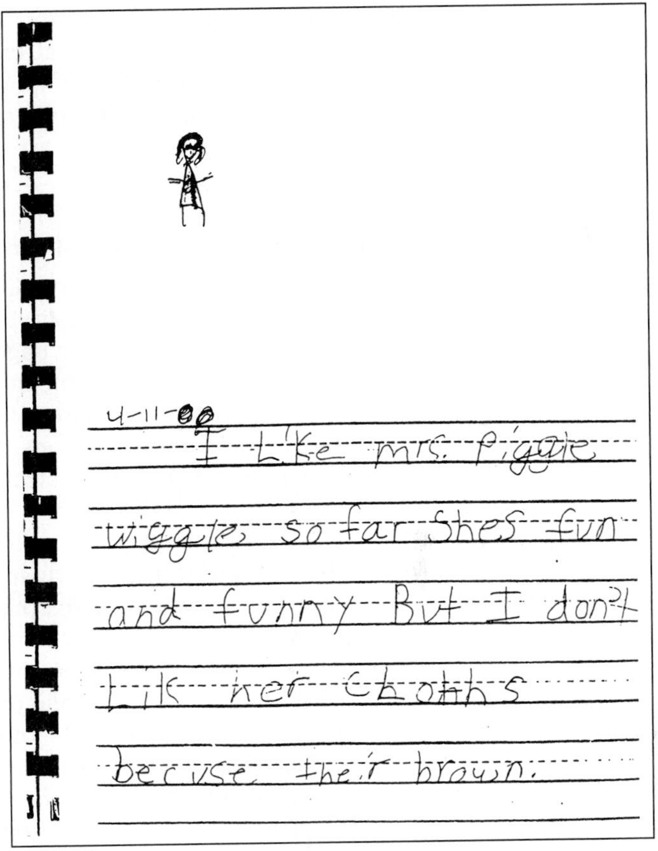

have very little narration or speaking as a part. Some children will need the security of movement to help them remember story events and the language they can use for the retelling. As children gain confidence, encourage more narration or explanation along with the movement.

In this section, we have explored a number of ways to help children gain experience in retelling stories that are read aloud. Retelling helps children notice detail in story events and helps children assign value or importance to story events and order. Retelling activities are helpful in supporting children's development of meaning-making strategies. With quality literature, we also want to encourage children's personal responses for motivation to become lifelong readers.

RESPONDING: DEVELOPING PERSONAL PERSPECTIVES ABOUT LITERATURE

Readers return to books because of the way they feel about the reading, or their response to the text. In helping children develop their responses to literature, we must foster children's belief that their perspectives about stories are valid. We must value their opinions about literature and help them find the words to talk about their interpretations of books. Responding to literature enables children to think in inferential, creative, and critical ways. We know that we support and extend children's responses to literature through discussion. We can also enhance response through the use of response journals, chants and rhythms, creative movement, and art.

Responding through Journals

A *response journal* can contain written and illustrated interpretations to text. For example, from the very first day of kindergarten, Karen provides her children with booklets containing pages of blank paper. As Karen reads aloud to children and engages them in retelling and responding to those tests, she encourages them to write and illustrate their reactions. Karen encourages children to talk about their interpretations. She might also record a child's most important thoughts under their illustrations to serve as a record and to reinforce their understandings about print.

We can direct children toward particular types of responsive journal entries without interfering with their honest responses to literature. Second-grade team teachers, Jena and Marci, provide opportunity for response to read-aloud during independent reading time, as well as during activity centers later in the day. They encourage children to illustrate their favorite part, or explore how they might feel if they were one of the characters. As children gain experience with literature, we can use the journal to explore their understandings of the significance of story events, themes, and character's actions. For nonfiction text we can focus on understanding of key concepts and technical vocabulary.

Illustrations and dictations of emerging readers and writers eventually give way to illustration and child-generated text, especially if we encourage children to be both author and illustrator. Young children can get very caught up in illustration if allowed. We want to gently nudge them toward combining illustration and text. From the very first days of school, we encourage children to explore and share their responses to literature read-aloud, even if that response is scribble, letter strings, or initial attempts at spelling. In her first-grade journal, Madison responds to a rereading of an old favorite, *The Three Little Pigs.* Her teacher encourages her to think about the words she wants to write (see Figure 2.6).

Response journals do not have to be a daily routine. They can be a special activity that follows the readings of favorite texts. The more familiar children are with text, the more potential we have for eliciting meaningful responses. We should keep in mind that children sense whether we value activities by the way we treat the journals and their responses. Responses worth taking the time to write are also worth discussing and sharing.

Response journals can be made from stapled paper, lined or unlined. If children are illustrating and writing, we might alternate lined and unlined paper as needed. Printing companies often dispose of scraps of colored paper that are excellent for making response journals. Children can learn to make their own journals. To spark children's interest, consider varying the size and shape of the journal. For example, children who are exploring *A Chair for My Mother* might have journals shaped like the Blue Tile Diner or a big overstuffed armchair, similar to the one in the story.

FIGURE 2.6
First-Grader's Response to *The Three Little Pigs*

Children's responses in a journal might focus on the story events or go beyond the story to their own lives. Children responding to *A Chair for My Mother* could draw their favorite part of the story and tell why they chose that part, describe their favorite character, take the part of a character and tell how they would have felt, draw pictures and tell about what they might save money to buy, or describe a time when they had to overcome a difficulty like the destruction of the fire in the story. By encouraging response to literature through journals, we offer children a vehicle for exploring the meaning they are making from read-aloud experiences and help them strengthen their understanding of written language.

Responding through Chants and Rhythms

Chants, or rhythmic poems without music, provide an opportunity for a class to create responses to literature. Composing chants is a shared response for the class. We can begin with a simple rhythmic pattern, then fill in with story events. For example, we might develop the following chants after reading *A Chair for My Mother:*

We are saving, saving, saving,
Every nickel,
Every dime,
We are saving, saving, saving,
And soon it will be time—
To buy a special chair.

OR

My mother wants a chair
A soft, soft chair
A velvet chair
A beautiful chair
My mother wants a chair

In *The Snowy Day* (Keats, 1962), Peter explores in the snow. A chant that describes the things that Peter did might be:

Peter went walking in the snow, snow, snow.
Peter went crunching in the snow, snow, snow.
Peter made angels in the snow, snow, snow.
Peter had fun in the snow, snow, snow.

In response to the story problem depicted in *Sylvester and the Magic Pebble* (Steig, 1969), we might compose the following chant:

Sylvester found a pebble,
a magic pebble.
Sylvester saw a lion,
a hungry lion.
Sylvester made a wish,
a foolish wish,
Now Sylvester is a rock,
a donkey rock!

Chants can be combined with creative movement to let children express their response to the rhythms of language. When chants are well known, the words can be written on large charts and used as shared reading text. Shared reading, then, further extends children's literacy experiences. (For more detail about shared reading, see Chapter 3.)

Responding through Creative Movement

Young children have strong feelings, and they find it satisfying to express them through movement. When children have shared an especially exciting story, invite them to "become" a character and show their interpretation of their favorite thing about that character. To support reluctant children, we can involve the whole class in this activity, with everyone becoming a character. Children find a place to stand that is their "own space" and respond to character feelings or story events.

After learning to recite a chant, children can find "their" space, reciting the chant as they move about the room. Encourage children to add movements and use their voice intonation to emphasize the mood of the chant. Props such as scarves, hats, and masks can be used to enhance creative movement. Props can help children lose themselves in the movement and feel less self-conscious. Props also can represent important elements in the literature and usually require much less preparation than most costumes and scenery for plays. Use of props can grow out of children's use of concrete objects to support retelling experiences, as discussed previously.

Where the Wild Things Are (Sendak, 1963) is a favorite for so many children that encouraging creative movement is not difficult. However, keeping the "rumpus" focused might prove to be challenging. To support the creative movement of the "wild things," a chant filled with rhythm can be used:

They roared their terrible roars
They gnashed their terrible teeth
They rolled their terrible eyes
They showed their terrible claws.

The children have their own rumpus as they chant. We focus on feeling like and sounding like a "wild thing." Such response enhances children's enjoyment of the story.

Responding through Art

Art is an excellent vehicle for children to use to respond to literature. Having a wide variety of media available in the classroom helps children explore their feelings about a literary experience. Bold tempera colors suggest very different feelings than do gentle watercolors. Collage combines textures, patterns, and colors to suggest complex feelings, where crayon resist with a black tempera wash might suggest hidden or mysterious feelings.

The quality of art that children produce is directly related to the guidance we give and the value we place on their work. Just as we guide children to "see" particular parts of a story, we also guide their eyes to see ways that artists express feeling. If we are not comfortable with art, we can seek the assistance of another teacher who is. By talking to fellow teachers we learn how they help children develop an eye for art and a willingness to risk sharing personal perspectives.

When we engage children in looking closely at literature that has quality illustrations, we may find that a particular illustrator's style makes a strong impression. The children may enjoy emulating that illustrator's style (Madura, 1995). Attention to style requires spending more time viewing and thinking about a text. Selecting winners of the yearly Caldecott Award, given for best-illustrated children's book, is an excellent starting point.

Children's artistic responses may take the form of individual or group projects. Murals are always a favorite. Children enjoy contributing ideas to a class project. Group projects reinforce interdependence as well as individual accountability, which is essential to developing children's cooperative skills.

We have explored a variety of ways to help children respond to literature read aloud. Helping children develop the ability to express their responses to literature enhances their enjoyment of it and their reading experiences (and ours, too!). We know that children who enjoy literature are more likely to spend time reading.

Retelling, responding, and other discussion activities help reveal which words are unknown or misunderstood during the reading. Literature extension activities provide opportunities for children to revisit words that may need their attention. Literature logs are excellent resources for encouraging children to attend to interesting words, as well as to words that need extra attention.

Be selective in your word study. Children cannot attend to large numbers of words at one time. It is better to study a few words that are within a child's stage of development. As you consider different ways to organize literature-based reading, think about the places where word study would be most natural and would remain in the context of children's interaction with literature.

ASSESSMENT: MONITORING ENGAGEMENT AND UNDERSTANDING DURING READ-ALOUD

Read-aloud provides information about children's attitudes toward reading and their ability to make meaning with text they hear. Careful observation of responses during read-aloud activities gives some indication of children's developing attitudes about reading, as well as foundations of making meaning. Do we observe these behaviors usually, sometimes, or rarely? Making anecdotal records, or notes about informal observations, can document specific behaviors and growth over time. Figure 2.7 provides an example of a sample record-keeping form for observations made during mediated read-aloud experiences.

RESPECTING DIVERSITY DURING READ-ALOUD

Children bring a richness of experience to the classroom that we must acknowledge, support, and enhance through read-aloud. As we use mediated read-aloud and rereadings to engage children with books, we must remain keenly aware of their interests, world knowledge, cultural experiences, and experience with book language. Teachers and children together should select the books to be read aloud in the classroom. Children's selections reflect their interests in books. Our sensitivity to their interests can increase children's motivation to interact with print.

What children know should be our starting point for sharing print in the classroom. Balancing narrative and information texts provides opportunity for children with specialized knowledge to share what they know. In this way, we validate children's lived experience. If uniqueness is to be an asset in the classroom, then we must challenge ourselves to use children's knowledge as one basis of the curriculum. Encouraging interaction especially during read-aloud enables children to share what they know about the world.

Historically, people of different cultures have shared their values, beliefs, and experiences with others through story. Using quality multicultural literature for read-aloud can show children that people with whom they identify are worthy of being central characters in books. Each of us needs cultural models that validate our worth as human beings.

The language of books is a different way of thinking and talking for all children. The difference for individuals is really a matter of degree of experience with books. Our sensitivity to making the transition from oral to written language for all children will be apparent in the books that we select to read aloud. The fewer experiences children have had with the formality of written language, the more conscious we need to be in providing repeated exposure to books. Rereading of stories provides practice for children in this new language—the language of print. We can be a "language bridge" as we guide children in their interactions with print.

Demonstrating Reading Behaviors Name ____________________

Response to Read-Aloud	Usually	Sometimes	Rarely	Comments
Shows positive physical and/or verbal responses during read-aloud.				
Participates in read-aloud discussions.				
Thinking Like a Reader	**Usually**	**Sometimes**	**Rarely**	**Comments**
Uses background knowledge to predict/confirm meaning during read-aloud.				
Is developing a well-formed sense of story, follows sequence, can retell stories.				
Uses knowledge of story elements in response to read-aloud (plot, character traits, setting, theme).				
Uses background knowledge to understand main ideas and details presented in nonfiction.				
Uses oral context to make meaning for unfamiliar words.				
Remembers past stories, relates knowledge to new stories.				
Shows greater depth of understanding through repeated readings.				

FIGURE 2.7
Demonstrating Reading Behaviors

Reading aloud is one part of our literacy framework. We know that reading aloud to children provides wonderful experiences with book language and a world of ideas, but it is not enough to prepare them for independence as competent readers and writers. Even though we share many books with children through read-aloud experiences and we talk extensively with them, we need to do much more to help them develop an understanding of the relationships between oral and written language. We need many other techniques to help them learn how readers decode, or break the code of written language, to make meaning and how writers encode, or create the code of written language, to communicate. In the upcoming chapters of this book we will build on our knowledge base for literacy learning that we have begun in this chapter.

Take a moment to reflect on putting theory about reading aloud into practice . . .

The single-most important thing we do is to engage children in meaningful experiences with books.

We invite children into books when we

- create a comfortable environment,
- introduce new books,
- revisit old favorites,
- encourage children to share their responses, and
- read frequently.

When we read aloud we should:

- pick books we like,
- preview a book before we read, because even award winners are no guarantee of children's response,
- allow ample time to pace the book appropriately for children,
- be conscious of how we position the book so children can clearly see the illustrations,
- connect with the audience through expression and eye contact,
- abandon books that are above children's emotional level or that are otherwise inappropriate, and
- make read-aloud books available for independent reading.

Teach through Mediated Read-Aloud by

- using mediated read-aloud strategies before, during, and after the reading to support children's interactions with a new book,
- using rereadings to enhance understanding and focus on specific features of a book, and
- focusing on children's retelling and responding to texts.

Build children's confidence and ownership of stories by retelling through:

- illustrations,
- story maps,
- drawings,
- felt boards, and
- writing.

Develop children's personal perspectives about literature by encouraging response through:

- journals,
- chants and rhythms,
- creative movement, and
- art.

Monitor children's progress in reading by considering:

- development of positive attitudes toward reading through read-aloud,
- knowledge development about reading through read-aloud, and
- development of independent reading behaviors.

Keep records of observations during read-aloud.

Respect diversity among children by providing for varied reading interests, reading abilities, and reading styles.

YOUR TURN . . .

1. Select a favorite children's book and read the book aloud to a small group of children. Do not rehearse the book. The purpose of this activity is for you to hear your natural style of sharing books with children. Tape record the read-aloud so you can listen to the way you sound. Notice your natural strengths, but especially make note of ways you can improve when you engage children with books.
2. Using your selected text, prepare a mediated read-aloud similar to those shown as examples in this chapter. How would you prepare children for the read-aloud, guide them through the text, and help them reflect on the reading afterwards? When you have completed the mediated read-aloud, take time to compare with your read-aloud in question 1. Notice the elements of your natural style that are also a part of the mediated read-aloud.

Aa Bb Cc Dd Ee Ff Gg Hh Ii Jj Kk Ll Mm

C H A P T E R

3

Shared Reading

Adding to our literacy framework . . .

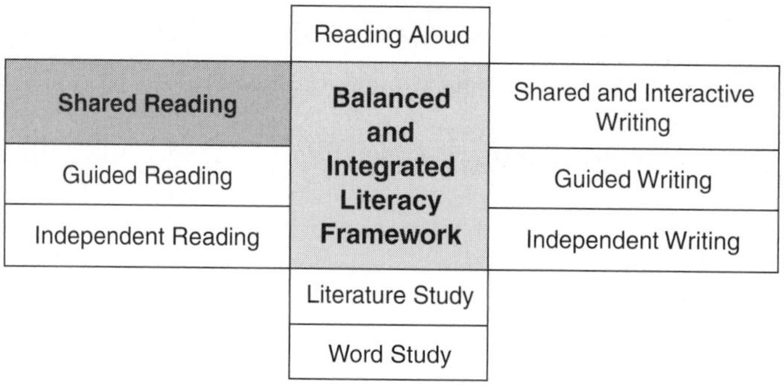

	Reading Aloud	
Shared Reading	**Balanced and Integrated Literacy Framework**	Shared and Interactive Writing
Guided Reading		Guided Writing
Independent Reading		Independent Writing
	Literature Study	
	Word Study	

In this chapter, we . . .

- Explore children's development of concepts about print.
- Support children's transition from speech to print through whole-class reading of enlarged texts.
- Examine shared reading processes, including guiding children through shared texts.

Focus Literature:

- *The Chick and the Duckling* by Mirra Ginsburg

Looking into Classrooms . . .

Antonio gathers the first-grade children on the floor near his chair. On the easel is an oversized book, with print and illustrations large enough for all of the children to see. Antonio uses a pointer to draw children's attention to the front cover, as he says, "Look at this strange creature on the front of the book. What does it make you think this book might be about? The title of this book is Where the Wild Things Are *and it was written by Maurice Sendak (pointing to the words on the cover). What do you think of when you hear the words 'wild things'? I wonder what Maurice Sendak thought about wild things. Let's read and find out."*

Antonio opens the book and, pointing to each word as he reads aloud, leads the children in reading the text, encouraging them to join in the reading whenever they wish. Over the course of the week the class will read, reread, and explore all aspects of this big book together as a whole class, in small groups, with partners, and independently. Antonio is engaging the children in a shared reading experience.

Building a Theory Base . . .

Sharing print experiences with responsive adults is an excellent way for young children to explore what it means to be a reader. Shared reading, which Antonio models in the previous scenario, is a group reading experience that simulates the best aspects of a bedtime reading experience (Holdaway, 1979). Whereas read-aloud, as explored in Chapter 2, enables children to enjoy and think about a text that is read by someone else, shared reading engages children more directly as participants in the reading. To become proficient readers, children must learn to decode and understand print in a fluent and accurate manner.

Shared reading should be a central part of a balanced and integrated literacy program, because it provides appropriate support as children learn to process print. During a shared reading, the more knowledgeable reader points to or tracks print to show what part of the text is being read, models fluent reading, and encourages children's interactions with meaningful texts. Shared reading was originally called "shared book experience" by Don Holdaway (1979), a New Zealand educator. He studied experiences during bedtime story situations to discover how and why this type of interaction between parent and child was related to children who became successful young readers. We know that children who are read to during the preschool years are more likely to succeed in learning to read than children who have not had such experiences.

Emerging readers who are still forming their understandings about how language can be displayed in print need to be shown that the words spoken by the reader are coming from a specific place in the text, and not from the illustrations (Holdaway, 1979). In addition, children who have not participated in the reading of many bedtime stories need the interactions with a more knowledgeable reader to expand their concepts about print and expectations for what a book can contain. Shared reading is an instructional component that exemplifies the importance of the role of a responsive adult in scaffolding children's print experiences.

Shared reading experiences are built upon repeated readings of texts, which has been shown to have great instructional value (Dowhower, 1987; Herman, 1985; Rasinski, 1990; Samuels, 1979). Although extensive reading, such as daily read-alouds, helps children develop expectations for the forms and purposes of print, intensive shared reading helps children begin to focus on the print itself. Intensive reading keeps children involved with one piece of text for an extended time. Details of the text become familiar and may be better understood. Such close inspection of print is absolutely necessary if children are to develop the competencies needed to identify words quickly and accurately. Shared reading, the focus of this chapter, is an excellent way to engage children in intensive reading experiences.

In shared reading, children first become familiar with the text as a whole. Then, through repeated exposure, children begin to see the details that comprise the whole—details they usually do not notice during their initial interactions (Kawakami, 1985). Rereading of texts helps young readers attend to letters and to word formation. As learners we tend to move from whole to part, which means that we do not always see all details in new things. We are more able to distinguish particular parts as we gain familiarity with the whole. As we

Shared reading is an invitation to participate in the development of reading skills and strategies in the safety of a group.

strengthen our schema for the whole, we are able to recognize how new parts may fit within it.

Intensive experiences such as shared reading provide time and opportunity to build the schema needed for making meaning with particular pieces of print. Children teach us about the power of intensive experiences. In their play, children continue at the same game or activity, day after day, until they "get it just right." They ask for the same bedtime story again and again, until they know it so well they confidently join in and even lead the "reading," or telling, of the story. Through such intensive, repeated exposures, children become comfortable with a text or a task and gain confidence in their abilities. Children involved in rereadings of text have been heard to say, "Now it's easy. I know all of the words. I can read it by myself. I can read it to my mom!"

DEVELOPING CONCEPTS ABOUT PRINT

Children's concepts about written language, similar to their concepts about oral language, are formed from the earliest years by observing and interacting with readers and writers as well as through their own attempts to read and write (Sulzby & Teale, 1991a). They already know that speech has meaning for them and others. Slowly they begin to realize that the print around them also has meaning.

From the many meaningful interactions young children have with more knowledgeable readers and writers, their interest in language and print emerges. The environments that support and encourage language and literacy include a variety of literacy materials such as books, writing materials, magnetic letters, and the like, and supportive adults who value literacy and encourage children to explore language and the world through literacy activities (Morrow, 2001).

Children begin to internalize meanings for print, just as they internalized speech. They begin to notice that funny-shaped symbols reoccur—in their name, in their favorite cereal, on billboards that advertise favorite places or foods. Children's interest in print provides wonderful opportunities for knowledgeable adults to help them begin to connect sounds and symbols, to understand that there is a relationship between speech and print.

Basic to all reading and writing is an understanding about the rules of print. To play a game like soccer we must know and understand the rules of the game. Without this knowledge we would have difficulty being a successful player, even if we observe others playing the game. Print also has rules that readers must understand to be successful participants (Clay, 1979). The rules or conventions of print include:

- permanence of print,
- directionality of print,
- concept of word, and
- language to talk about print.

Permanence of Print

Do young children understand that print, when it is on paper, remains fixed and does not change on its own accord? My son, Steve, taught me about permanence of print when he took a favorite book to his babysitter's house. Steve was surprised that Nancy, his babysitter, read the book just as I read it. Before that episode, I had not realized that Steve might think print in books could change from reading to reading. If print could move inside of books as it does on television or on the computer screen, children might come to the conclusion that stories and words could change from reading to reading.

As we work with emergent readers, we use their developing sense of story to help them notice the details of print. Children who do not expect that print in books is permanent may not be able to use their remembrance of past readings to predict words in the text. Expecting stories and words in books to remain the same from reading to reading allows print to become predictable. Children begin to notice details and patterns that aid in distinguishing letters and words from one another.

To emphasize the permanence of print, we help children notice that rereading books, especially big books and charts where print is highly visible, yields the same story or text with each reading. We also emphasize permanence through rereadings of language experience charts that children have watched being written. Such techniques will be examined in this chapter and in Chapter 4 when we explore shared/interactive writing.

Directionality of Print

Understanding directionality of print is essential to the development of word knowledge. When children observe us tracking print, when we slide our finger or a pointer along under words as we read, the left-to-right direction of reading English can be observed. The same directional movement can also be observed when children watch us write.

In her research with young children, Marie Clay (1979) found that concepts about directionality of print are essential to success in reading and that they develop slowly, through many experiences with print. Concepts about directionality of print include the following:

- Books have fronts and backs; we read a book from front to back.
- We read print, not pictures.
- There is a right-side-up to print.
- We read the left page before the right page when text is on both pages.
- We read left to right, top to bottom on a page.
- When we finish one line of print we make a return sweep, returning to the left side of the page and dropping down one line to continue reading.
- Words in a sentence must be arranged in a certain left-to-right order to make sense in our language (e.g., *here is a cat* and *cat is here a* do not communicate the same ideas).

Through many demonstrations of page turning, tracking of print, and watching spoken language be written, children begin to understand that our written language does have rules. Through children's desire to be understood, they have already internalized many rules for meaningful use of oral language. Interactions with print, especially in school, need to provide similar meaningful experiences to focus children's attention on learning the rules of written language.

Concept of Word

As young children gain experience with speech sounds represented by symbols or letters, they begin to develop concepts about words. In speech, words are difficult to detect unless we have experience with written language. To a young child, "How are you?" may be understood as one unit, "Howareyou," and not thought of as being three separate words. The idea itself has meaning to the child, not the separate words. Concepts about words (what they are and how they are made) develop slowly as children observe and participate in print activities with more knowledgeable readers and writers (Read, 1975). Concepts about words include knowing that:

- words in print are set off by white spaces,
- letters make up words and are written in a left-to-right sequence,
- letters within words must be written in a particular order to make specific words (e.g., the letters *a, c,* and *t* can make different words by changing the left-to-right order of the letters: *act, cat,* and *tac*),
- the order of letters in words is not arbitrary as certain patterns are characteristic of English words,
- letters in words represent speech sounds and can be blended to make recognizable words,
- words can be made up of more than one sound part or syllable, and
- the same word is always spelled the same way.

Language to Talk about Print

Print has a language that we use to talk about reading and writing with children. To think about the importance of this language we must think back to our discussion of developmental learning in Chapter 1. As more knowledgeable readers or writers help us learn by demonstrating reading or writing, they use language to clarify their demonstration and call attention to certain behaviors that might not have been noticed. For example, when my daughter, Heather (age 3), and I would read bedtime stories I would say, "Let's start at the *front* of the book so we can read the whole story," as I would turn the book to the front and point to the front cover. I did this because she had a tendency to begin at the back of a new book, working right to left instead of left to right through the book. In addition to *front,* what other words or phrases might be used when we talk about print? When reading with a young child we might use words such as *front, back, title, author, page, beginning, end, top, bottom, left, right, line, sentence, word(s), letter(s), capital letter, period, question mark, quotation marks,* or *exclamation point.*

Children's knowledge will be limited by their experiences with print. The print language that children know will have developed through experiences in which a reader or writer talked about print and demonstrated the meaning of the "print" language. Vygotsky (1962) suggests that competence in oral language enables us to control our thinking. If we apply his ideas to print we might say that knowing the language to talk about print can help children gain control over their thinking about print.

To understand the language of print, children require more knowledgeable readers and writers to demonstrate to them the use of print language in the context of meaningful reading and writing activities. Children, in turn, need to be encouraged to demonstrate their understandings of print language.

THE POTENTIAL OF SHARED READING EXPERIENCES

Shared reading, as a part of our balanced and integrated literacy framework, enables us to engage children with enlarged versions of text to:

- induce a desire to read through participation,
- model literate reading behavior,
- provide access to print,
- develop concepts about print,
- provide guided participation,
- help children gain control over text through repetition,
- help children develop skill in decoding words, and
- help children learn to balance use of meaning, language, and visual cues.

Let us revisit Antonio's first-grade classroom, where we can glimpse some of the potential of the intensive reading experience that shared reading provides.

Inducing a Desire to Be a Reader

Antonio selects texts for shared reading that quickly become known to children because of predictable patterns or familiar content. He uses a style of reading aloud that invites children to interact with him, with other children, and with the text during the reading. Antonio understands that literacy is a social event in which children need to experience reading as pleasurable and purposeful (Bus, van Ijzendoorn, & Pellegrini, 1995; Taylor, 1983).

Modeling Literate Behavior

Antonio begins to read aloud from the big book on the easel. As he reads, he comments on things he notices in the illustrations and story. He shares the memory of a past experience that is evoked by the story. He laughs at a part that strikes him as humorous. Antonio is modeling literate behavior. Children observe his reading behavior and build expectations for their own behavior as literate individuals. Shared reading in Antonio's class will enable children to practice literate behavior (Holdaway, 1979).

Providing Access to Print

When Antonio uses reading materials with enlarged print, all of the children have access to the print. In traditional group read-aloud situations, children are able to hear the content of a written text, but the print in a standard-size children's book is not large enough to be observed by the listeners. Using enlarged print for read-aloud experiences provides opportunity for Antonio's children to gain the familiarity necessary to learn from print. Becoming a reader requires many opportunities for children to become familiar with the features of print.

Developing Print Concepts

Each time Antonio and his children interact with enlarged print, he points to the words he is reading and talks about things he knows about print. Antonio's first-graders develop an understanding that when the English language is printed on paper, it must be printed in a particular way if a reader is going to be able to figure out what the author wrote. Because print is accessible to all, shared reading is an excellent way to support children's growing knowledge of the rules of print (Holdaway, 1979).

Guiding Children's Participation

After Antonio introduces a text to the children, he knows that he needs to allow them opportunity to use their own skills and strategies as they participate in the shared reading. He also knows that the amount and type of support he provides should be determined by his observations of children's response to text and his purpose(s) for instruction. Antonio adjusts his guidance throughout lessons, reducing his support as the children become more responsible for the reading (Vygotsky, 1962). Antonio wants each child to become an independent reader.

Repetition—Gaining Control over Text

Repetition enables Antonio's children to feel a sense of control (Rhodes, 1981), which encourages confidence in their shared reading of familiar text and their sense of self as reader. Confidence is supported by repeated readings in which children will not be asked to do something with text that is beyond their capability without the support of a more knowledgeable other. Antonio knows that repetition over time will deepen the children's understanding (Yaden, 1988).

Develop Skill in Decoding Words

Antonio realizes that children's ability to learn words is closely tied to their proficiency as readers (Adams, 1990; Chall, 1983; Ehri, 1998). As his children gain control over text through a variety of repeated experiences, Antonio plans activities that call attention to patterns of letter–sound relationships. He also encourages his children to become aware of the strategies they use successfully to figure out words.

Balancing Use of Language Cues

Antonio understands that good readers draw upon meaning (semantic), grammar (syntactic), and visual (grapho-phonics) cues to process text. During shared reading experiences, Antonio models how he uses some clues more than others at particular times during reading. He encourages children to anticipate words in text by drawing upon what makes sense as we think about text (meaning), what sounds right in English (grammar), and what looks right in print (visual). He is laying the foundation for the use of strategies during guided and independent reading, when readers monitor their understanding of text as they read.

TYPES OF TEXT FOR SHARED READING EXPERIENCES

Enlarged print can be made available to children through a variety of sources:

- Big books
- Overhead projector
- Using a pocket chart
- Songs, poems, and chants
- Shared writings or experience charts
- Sheltered text

Shared reading often begins with teachers and children reading big books together, then moving to other forms of enlarged print to extend children's interaction with a particular text.

Big Books

Enlarged versions of children's books enable us to turn a read-aloud experience into a shared reading experience, making print accessible for children to join in the reading. Quality big books are readily available from publishers such as Wright Group, Scholastic, and Rigby. In addition to commercial big books, we can also make big books with our children. Gail Heald-Taylor (1987) suggests that class-made big books can:

- be replicas of original books,
- have new illustrations decided by the children, or
- be a new version written jointly by teacher and children during shared writing.

Overhead Projector

The overhead projector can be used to enlarge the text of a book that is not available as a big book. Overhead transparencies of desired pages can project text onto a screen, enlarging the print and making it accessible to a group of children. As the text is shared together, transparency by transparency, we guide the reading by pointing to the text on the transparency. Children are able to participate just as they do with a big book.

Using a Pocket Chart

A pocket chart is a large chart with rows of pockets that display sentence strips, word cards, or picture cards. Text can be arranged in a pocket chart before or during a lesson. The text can also be rearranged in the midst of a lesson to demonstrate a new idea. Engaging children in manipulating text provides opportunity to assess children's understanding of language and/or print. Pocket charts are available through school supply companies or can be made by the teacher from material such as poster board. See Figure 3.1 for suggested teacher-made pocket charts. Charts can vary in size from individual (12" × 18") to large group size (4" × 6").

Songs, Poems, and Chants

Favorite songs, poems, and chants written in large print make excellent shared reading experiences. Songs, poems, and chants are usually rhythmical, rhyming, and repetitious. Children's prior knowledge becomes "text in the head" and can be drawn upon to match against the text printed on a chart. For example, it is not uncommon for children to sing the song as they read the chart, drawing upon the form in which they know the text best. Class songbooks and anthologies can be made to preserve favorite pieces in a class big book that grows over time. In the vignettes of Carmen's first-grade classroom from Chapter 1 we have seen how a song such as "Old MacDonald" can be used for shared reading.

FIGURE 3.1
Pocket Chart

Shared Writing or Experience Charts

Teachers and children can share in compositions that grow out of shared classroom experiences. Children who participate in the composition of a shared writing know its content. Predictability is enhanced through the repeated reading of charts and through extension activities that prolong children's interaction with the text. Primary-grade teachers often compose morning messages on the chalkboard with the help of the children. One example of a morning message might be:

Today is Monday, March 19.
Today is Raul's birthday.
We will make tortillas after lunch.
Raul's grandmother will help us.

Sheltered Texts

The language of charts can be sheltered to support emerging readers and children who are learning English. The essence of a familiar book is represented through carefully selected language. The most meaningful words are placed in simple sentence patterns. The teacher constructs the language of a sheltered text with attention to how ideas are presented and linked together, rather than developed spontaneously with children. Sheltered text works well with content area books that are too difficult for beginning readers.

Imagine that in our second-grade classroom we have a range of reading levels, including a number of emerging readers. We have been studying about weather. We find an excellent resource book about weather called *Weather Words and What They Mean* by Gail Gibbons (1990), but the structure of some sentences and some of the vocabulary is too difficult as written. We might simplify the text by writing a sheltered text. As we do we strive to accurately present concepts and use essential vocabulary, but in sentence structures that are familiar to the children and support their thinking.

Moisture in the air makes clouds.
Moisture comes from water that evaporates.
Water evaporates from rivers, lakes, and oceans.
Vapor is water that evaporates into the air.
The vapor makes drops of water.
The vapor makes ice crystals.
The water and the ice crystals make a cloud.

Notice how, from sentence to sentence, the ideas are related and key vocabulary is explained and repeated. Text that is sheltered helps children make meaning through the use of more familiar sentence structures.

There is a wide range of experiences and texts that can become shared readings. If we lack commercially prepared big books, there are many other ways to have enlarged texts that a group of children can share in reading.

SELECTING TEXTS FOR SHARED READING EXPERIENCES

When we read bedtime stories with children, we quickly learn which books only appeal to them and which are their favorites. Shared reading experiences, drawn from bedtime story reading, must involve texts that will engage children. In the classroom, however, we have a range of interests of many more children than in typical bedtime story situations.

Andrea Butler (1987) suggests that when we use commercially produced materials with large print, such as big books, we consider the following traits as we select materials for shared reading:

- A strong story line in which something actually happens
- Characters and situations with which children identify strongly
- Attractive illustrations that support and enhance the text
- Humor and warmth

- Rich and memorable language features that ensure predictability such as rhythm, rhyme, and repetition (p. 5)

The previous attributes describe quality fiction that might be shared with children. In addition, we might also add attributes related to quality nonfiction:

- Clear photographs that build vicarious background and are supported by text
- Accurate information presented in a clear and concise manner
- Background information provided to enhance reader understanding

Finally, regardless of whether a text is fiction, nonfiction, poetry, or the like, we must consider the size and amount of text on each page so that we can adequately engage all children in the shared experience.

Quality of Illustrations

Young children are influenced by the illustrations on the pages of text (Sulzby, 1985). Illustrations are a representation of the world and are often better understood by emerging readers than the abstractness of print. We should select books for emerging readers, especially, in which the illustrations are simple and clear and have a strong link to the content of the text on that page. In shared reading experiences, we should guide children's eyes to carefully examine illustrations or photographs before the text is shared so their knowledge of the illustration or photograph allows them to anticipate the content of the text.

Size and Amount of Print

It is important that the print of a shared text be clearly visible. If size prohibits all children in a group from being able to distinguish details in the print, then shared reading will be no different than a typical read-aloud. The amount of print should fit our instructional purpose and children's level of functioning. If our purpose is to help children think about written language and directionality, then the amount of print is not as important as children's familiarity with its content. If, however, our purpose is for children to learn to independently read the text, children's reading levels should guide the amount of print.

Structure or Predictability of Text

Text that allows the reader to use patterns or background knowledge to anticipate upcoming text is considered predictable (Barrett, 1982; Holdaway, 1979; Rhodes, 1981). Texts become predictable for readers when there is:

- repetition of vocabulary or story structure,
- cumulative sequence,
- rhythmic, rhyming language patterns,
- familiar sequences, or
- repeated readings of a text.

Figure 3.2 provides a suggested list of predictable books.

FIGURE 3.2
Suggested Predictable Books

Repetitive Pattern

Carle, E. (1987). *Have You Seen My Cat?* New York: Scholastic.
Eastman, P. D. (1960). *Are You My Mother?* New York: Random House.
Flack, M. (1932). *Ask Mr. Bear.* New York: Simon & Schuster.
Fox, M. (1987). *Hattie and the Fox.* New York: Simon & Schuster.
Galdone, P. (1974). *The Little Red Hen.* New York: Scholastic.
Ginsburg, M. (1972). *The Chick and the Duckling.* New York: Simon & Schuster.
Keats, E. J. (1971). *Over in the Meadow.* New York: Scholastic.
Langstaff, J. (1974). *Oh A-Hunting We Will Go.* New York: Atheneum.
Martin, B. (1967). *Brown Bear, Brown Bear, What Do You See?* New York: Holt, Rinehart & Winston.
Raffi. (1988). *The Wheels on the Bus.* New York: Crown.
Rees, M. (1988). *Ten in a Bed.* Boston: Little, Brown.
Shaw, C. G. (1947). *It Looked Like Spilt Milk.* New York: Harper & Row.

Cumulative Pattern

Fox, M. (1987). *Hattie and the Fox.* New York: Simon & Schuster.
Kalan, R. (1981). *Jump, Frog, Jump.* New York: Scholastic.
Mayer, M. (1975). *What Do You Do With a Kangaroo?* New York: Scholastic.
McGovern, A. (1967). *Too Much Noise.* Boston: Houghton Mifflin.
Scott, Foresman Reading Systems, level 2, book A. (1971). *The Bus Ride.*
Shulevitz, U. (1967). *One Monday Morning.* New York: Scribner's.
Tolstoy, A. (1968). *The Great Big Enormous Turnip.* New York: Franklin Watts.
Wood, A. (1984). *The Napping House.* New York: Harcourt Brace Jovanovich.

Rhythm & Rhyme

Ahlberg, J. A. (1978). *Each Peach Pear Plum.* New York: Viking.
Hoberman, M. A. (1978). *A House is a House for Me.* New York: Viking.
Kraus, R. (1948). *Bears.* New York: Scholastic.
Kraus, R. (1970). *Whose Mouse Are You?* New York: Simon & Schuster.
Martin, B. (1970). *Fire! Fire! Said Mrs. McGuire.* New York: Holt, Rinehart & Winston.
Martin, B., & Archambault, J. (1989). *Chicka Chicka Boom Boom.* New York: Holt, Rinehart & Winston.

Familiar Sequences

Carle, E. (1969). *The Very Hungry Caterpillar.* New York: Putnam.
Hutchins, P. (1968). *Rosie's Walk.* New York: Simon & Schuster.
Martin, B. (1970). *Monday, Monday, I Like Monday.* New York: Holt, Rinehart & Winston.
Martin, B., & Archambault, J. (1989). *Chicka Chicka Boom Boom.* New York: Holt, Rinehart & Winston.
Raffi. (1988). *Five Little Ducks.* New York: Crown.
Rees, M. (1988). *Ten in a Bed.* Boston: Little, Brown.
Shulevitz, U. (1967). *One Monday Morning.* New York: Scribner's.

Repeated Readings of Familiar Stories—Predictable Plot

Adams, P. (1974). *This Old Man.* New York: Grossett & Dunlap.
Brown, M. (1957). *The Three Billy Goats Gruff.* New York: Harcourt Brace Jovanovich.
Galdone, P. (1970). *The Three Little Pigs.* New York: Seabury.
Galdone, P. (1972). *The Three Bears.* New York: Scholastic.
Nodset, J. (1963). *Who Took the Farmer's Hat?* New York: Scholastic.
Sendak, M. (1963). *Where the Wild Things Are.* New York: Scholastic.

Repetitive Pattern.
A repetitive pattern uses repetition of words, phrases, or sentences throughout a text. The fewer words that are changed in the pattern, the more predictable the text. Illustrations that clearly support word changes further increase predictability. Consider the pattern in *Ten in the Bed:*

> There were ten in the bed
> and the little one said,
> "Roll over, roll over."
> So they all rolled over
> and one fell out.
>
> There were nine in the bed
> and the little one said, . . .

Once readers know the pattern in *Ten in the Bed,* they can expect it to be repeated and can anticipate the words that are coming. The illustrations show the actual number of children in the bed. The only word that changes in the pattern is the number of children in the bed. Children who know how to count backwards from ten are able to anticipate the appropriate word for the pattern.

Cumulative Pattern.
A cumulative pattern adds one new element, then repeats all previous elements. A cumulative sequence builds to a climax, then either ends or reverses the cumulative order.

> There is a house,
> a napping house,
> where everyone is sleeping.
>
> And in that house
> there is a bed,
> a cozy bed,
> in a napping house,
> where everyone is sleeping. . . .

The pattern in *The Napping House* (Wood, 1984) continues to add and repeat, accumulating a snoring granny, a dreaming child, a dozing dog, a snoozing cat, a slumbering mouse, and a wakeful flea that awakens everyone and reverses the order of the sequence. Children who recognize the pattern are able to join in the repetition of the cumulative sequence. Illustrations cue the reader about each new element.

Rhythm and Rhyme.
Rhythmic patterns can help readers anticipate the rhythm of specific language that could possibly fill the pattern. Rhyming patterns help readers narrow the choice of possible words that could fit a particular pattern, considering sound and meaning.

> A told B, and B told C,
> "I'll meet you at the top of the coconut tree."
> "Whee!" said D to EFG,
> "I'll beat you to the top of the coconut tree."

The rhythm of the language in *Chicka Chicka Boom Boom* (Martin & Archambault, 1989), combined with repetition and rhyme, makes this text predictable. The authors also draw on children's knowledge of sequence of the letters of the alphabet to add to predictability (see familiar sequences).

Familiar Sequences.

Familiar sequences such as the days of the week, months of the year, numbers, and letters of the alphabet increase the predictability of text.

> On Monday he ate through one apple.
> But he was still hungry.
> On Tuesday, he ate through two pears,
> But he was still hungry.
> On Wednesday he ate through three . . .

In *The Very Hungry Caterpillar* (Carle, 1969), children's knowledge of days of the week and counting increase the predictability of a portion of this text.

Repeated Readings.

Another way that text becomes familiar and, consequently, predictable is through repeated readings. Once children have heard a text read aloud, they have a version of the text in their heads, which they can draw upon in subsequent interactions with that text. While the "text in the head" may not be complete or totally accurate, it serves as background knowledge that enables children to anticipate content and thus, gain control over text (Rhodes, 1981). Children's ability to anticipate parts of classic stories such as *The Three Pigs, Jack and the Bean Stalk,* and *The Three Billy Goats Gruff* often comes through repeated exposure.

We have considered the purpose and potential of shared reading experiences through features of various texts. Now we turn our attention to developing shared reading experiences for the classroom. As we do, you may wish to reconsider aspects of our theory base to clarify your own understanding of shared reading experiences.

Take a moment to reflect on your theory base for shared reading . . .

Shared reading is a group participatory reading experience, using enlarged print, that simulates the bedtime reading experiences many children have at home.

Children's experiences with print provide opportunities to develop understandings that:

- on paper, print is permanent, it does not move,
- in English, print moves from left to right, top to bottom on a page,
- the letters within a word must always be in the same left-to-right arrangement to make that word (changing one letter changes a word and in print, spaces define words), and
- there is a language to talk about print, such as *letter, word,* and *sentences.*

Shared reading experiences, led by a more knowledgeable other,

- model reading behaviors,
- support children in print that is often too difficult for them to read independently,
- help children refine their understandings about print, and
- model the use of meaning, language, and visual cues for reading.

Text can be enlarged in many ways to make shared reading possible, such as

- big books,
- overhead projector,
- pocket chart,
- charts with songs, poems, or other experiences, and
- charts with text that has been sheltered to make difficult concepts and vocabulary more accessible.

The texts we select for shared reading should have

- quality illustrations that children are able to use as clues to contextual meaning,
- print that is easily seen by all and with appropriate amounts on a single page, and
- a language structure that is familiar and predictable.

Putting Theory into Practice . . .

In the remainder of this chapter we use our knowledge of intensive reading experiences to consider how enlarged texts can be used to develop children's knowledge of language, print, and reading processes. We will develop plans for a range of instructional experiences that build upon shared reading texts and will help us better understand how shared reading provides important scaffolding for emerging and developing readers.

To begin, we return to Antonio's first-grade classroom to listen to the way that he engages children in the first reading of a big book, entitled *The Chick and the Duckling* (Ginsburg, 1972). He has chosen this big book because it has a highly repetitive pattern and clear illustrations that help to cue key words in the text. He knows that after the children are familiar with text patterns, he will need to support them as they use the text illustrations to make predictions and confirm the key words on the page.

SAMPLE SHARED READING OF A BIG BOOK

Before the reading:
Antonio uses a pointer to point to the cover of the big book and says,

"When you look at the front cover of this book, what do you see?"

He takes responses.

"What ideas does that give you about this book?"

Again, Antonio takes responses, then points to the words as he says,

"The title of this book is *The Chick and the Duckling.*
It was written by Mirra Ginsburg.
Jose Aruego and Ariane Dewey drew the pictures.
Does the title give you any other ideas about this story?"

He takes responses, then opens the big book to the inside title page and asks,

"Do you see the words of the title again? Let's read the title together, *The Chick and the Duckling,*" pointing to the words as he reads.

"Let's take a picture walk and see what we can learn about this story before we begin to read it."

Antonio begins turning the pages of the text and guides children to examine key elements in each illustration that will be useful in predicting new words in the repetitive text.

"Look at what is happening to the egg.
A duckling is hatching.
It breaks out of the shell."

Turning to the next page, he points and says,

"Look, another animal is hatching.
What is this? Yes, it's a chick.
Do you remember the title of this book?
Yes, *The Chick and the Duckling.*"

Antonio turns the page and asks,

"What is the duckling doing? Yes, it's walking.
What is the chick doing? Yes, it's walking too."

Antonio continues in this same manner, moving briskly through the text to help the children see that as the duckling was digging a hole, found a worm, caught a butterfly, and went for a swim, the chick did the same thing. In the end, the duckling must save the chick from drowning and the chick realizes it cannot swim like the duckling.

During the reading:
After the picture walk, Antonio returns to the front of the book and begins the reading, pointing to each word as he reads aloud. He moves fluidly through the text during this first reading to help children develop a sense of the whole text. In this first reading, Antonio's main focus is to help children use the illustration showing the chick to anticipate and join in the reading of the repetitive sentence, " 'Me too!' said the Chick."

The words on the first two pages of text are:

A Duckling came out
of the shell.
"I am out!" he said.

Antonio turns to the next two pages of text and reads aloud to reveal the repetitive pattern:

"Me too," said the Chick.

On each page with the duckling, Antonio calls attention to the illustration and reads the text aloud. Then he turns the page, calls attention to the chick, and reads, " 'Me too,' said the Chick," encouraging children to join him. After several sets of actions, the children begin to join in the reading, showing that they recognize a pattern and can predict the words on the pages where the chick appears.

After the reading:
Antonio invites children to respond to the text. He asks,

"What do you think about that story?"

He takes most all the personal responses that children offer. Then he asks,

"What is your favorite part?"

The children agree that the best part is when the duckling saves the chick from drowning.

Rereading Adds Emphasis to the Language of the Text

Antonio capitalizes on the children's interest in the story by turning back to the front cover in preparation for another quick reading. During this first rereading he continues to emphasize the repetitive "Me too" pattern of the chick, but he also calls attention to key words used to describe the duckling's actions.

He uses a technique called aural cloze procedure, hesitating before he reads aloud a key word so that children can complete the part of a sentence cued by an illustration or predictable language structure. For example, on the first page of *The Chick and the Duckling,* Antonio reads, "A Duckling came out of a sh—." He hesitates at the beginning of *shell,* giving only the beginning sound, to help children distinguish it from *egg* as they complete the sentence.

During this first rereading Antonio wants to know which children are able to use illustrations and language structure to make meaning with this simple text. As he reads aloud and points to the appropriate text, several children join in by finishing the word.

For example, on the next duckling page, Antonio hesitates before the word *walk.* He thinks that children will be able to use their knowledge of language and the illustration to fill in "I am taking a w____." He continues in this manner, using aural cloze procedure, focusing on the most obvious words that are cued by illustration and language structure.

After the rereading, Antonio asks, "How did the illustrations help us read this story?" Children offer their ideas about how the illustrations help them remember that part of the story.

He continues with, "What did you notice about the words that the chick said?" The children clearly understand that repetition helps anticipate the words on the page.

Then Antonio asks, "How did you know what words would fit in the places where I stopped reading? How did you know that the word *walk* would fit in the sentence, 'I am taking a ________' ?" A few children suggest that they just remember the text, but others say, "That's how we talk."

Children intuitively sense the structure of English that is used in oral communication. In subsequent rereadings of this text, Antonio can build on this strategy for checking meaning.

PLANNING SHARED READING EXPERIENCES

How does Antonio make decisions about engaging the children with texts such as *The Chick and the Duckling?* When Antonio plans for shared reading experiences, he considers:

- which literacy skills and/or strategies that the children are ready to learn,
- the variety of ways that he can organize shared reading experiences, and
- how to introduce and develop skill with text that supports the children as readers.

SELECTING SKILLS AND STRATEGIES

To plan effectively Antonio must be responsive to the strengths and needs of the children. He bases his decisions about which skills and strategies children are ready to learn on careful observations of the children's reading behaviors, and his knowledge of the curriculum and instructional possibilities. Antonio knows that responsive instruction:

- has clear instructional purposes,
- uses appropriate texts,
- is based on an analysis of the demands of that text, and
- is accompanied by careful observation of what children know in relation to the selected text and our instructional purposes (Powell, 1993).

CLEAR PURPOSE(S) FOR INSTRUCTION

In Antonio's school district, academic standards have been adopted for language arts. The standards for reading in his school district focus on developing word knowledge, including phonics; strategies for monitoring one's reading; and skills and strategies related to comprehending both fiction and nonfiction texts. Antonio consults the standards document for his grade level, but he knows that not all of the children are at a similar stage of development. He knows that the children have different understandings of any text that is shared as a whole class. Antonio selects skills and strategies currently needed by a majority of children, as well as skills and strategies that introduce some children to new ideas for future development.

Analyzing the Demands of Text

The next part of Antonio's planning involves analyzing the demands of the text he chose for instruction. In *The Chick and the Duckling,* he sees two obvious patterns:

- One pattern is an exact repetition, " 'Me too,' said the Chick," cued by the illustration.
- One pattern is cued by the illustration and related to what the duckling is doing.

In shared readings, Antonio prepares and supports the children through rereadings as the text becomes very familiar. If he helps children effectively use illustration and familiar language patterns, they should be able to read *The Chick and the Duckling* independently after several shared rereadings. Antonio knows that readers make meaning with text by thinking about whether the words in the text make sense—if the language sounds "right" for English and if the words look "right" for English words.

Observing What Children Know

Before beginning instruction with *The Chick and the Duckling,* Antonio observes the children's interaction with other predictable texts, paying special attention to their ability to:

- detect and use pattern in text to support their reading, and
- utilize their natural inclination to use illustration to support their reading.

Based on his observations, Antonio decides how much guidance and support to give during his teacher-led activities. Observations help him decide which extension activities will be most helpful to engage the children in using illustration and pattern in their reading. He listens carefully to what they say before, during, and after the reading of a text. Antonio considers what children might understand about reading based on those interactions.

ORGANIZING SHARED READING EXPERIENCES

To provide maximum support to emerging readers, Antonio combines shared reading experiences with other literacy activities to extend children's interaction with a particular text. In the next section we focus on a variety of choices we have for extending children's engagement with shared texts.

The whole-class shared reading is intended to introduce and practice enlarged text within the safety and support of a large group. This whole-class activity can combine:

- a warm-up activity involving familiar songs, poems, or chants,
- rereading an "old favorite,"
- introducing and reading a new text, and
- highlighting specific skills or strategies related to the new text.

The new text is read, reread, and explored over several days to give all children time for the "new" to become "familiar." Depending upon the text, a shared reading cycle may last up to five days or more. Children's knowledge of print and the demands of the text determine this length.

First Shared Reading

The purpose of the first reading is to make public the storyline and patterns of the text which will allow children to join in the reading. During the first reading we:

- introduce text, encouraging children's anticipation,
- take a "picture walk" through the text with children to help them become familiar with text features they can use to make meaning while reading,
- read the text in a fluent manner, stopping briefly to help children focus their attention on the salient features needed to comprehend text,
- ask for responses after the reading to check for general understanding, and
- reread the text at least one time during that sitting, encouraging children to join in.

These are the same steps that Antonio demonstrated in the first reading of *The Chick and the Duckling* in the opening vignette.

Further rereadings enable children to clarify their understanding of the story line or information presented in the text. Rereadings also provide support as children begin to focus on the salient features of print that are needed for guided and independent reading.

Shared Rereadings

Repeated readings of a shared text over several days enable children to become increasingly more familiar with the language and structure of the text. With background knowledge of a text, we are able to guide and support children as they focus on the salient features of the text. Shared rereadings assist children as they use:

- language knowledge and meaning-making skills and strategies to comprehend text, and
- visual and phonological skills to notice letter–sound patterns and decode unfamiliar words.

Shared rereadings enable us to focus children's attention on the skills and/or strategies we select for instruction. The first reading of *The Chick and the Duckling* allows Antonio to focus children's attention of using text illustrations and knowledge of the predictable text patterns to make meaning. Rereadings of this text provide additional opportunities to model how readers use knowledge of text illustrations and language patterns to predict and confirm the actual words on the page.

Following further shared readings of *The Chick and the Duckling,* Antonio invites children to "Show what you know." While he focuses on the skills and/or strategies identified in his plans (e.g., using text illustrations to anticipate and confirm predictable patterns, and learning how to use a self-checking strategy to confirm meaning in the reading), the children are likely to show him other text features they noticed. For example, during rereadings of *The Chick and the Duckling,* Antonio's children noticed:

- familiar letters that appear throughout the text,
- the use of capital versus lowercase letters, as in the names Chick and Duckling,
- particular words that appear on every page, such as the high-frequency words *I, said,* and *the,*
- expressions on a character's face that are clues to what is happening, and
- "talking marks" (quotation marks) that signal the words of chick and duckling.

Antonio invites children to come up to the text and point our what they notice. As children "show what they know" he pays careful attention to learn more about their understandings of print and reading processes.

The types and number of activities we use in shared rereadings should be adjusted to children's abilities to attend to the print. When children are actually attending to the print, their reading will become less smooth and fluent. To give attention to the print, children must devote their energy to processing the details of words to get meaning (Lynch, 1986). It is a sign of progress when emergent reading becomes halting and hesitant (Holdaway, 1979). To help emergent readers internalize particular skills and strategies we should select text that can become independent and "easy" through repeated readings.

During rereadings we can use the following techniques to focus children's attention on the text:

- Aural cloze procedure: While reading aloud, hesitate before a word that children are likely to know, allowing them to fill in and discussing how they figured out what to fill in (meaning cues, language cue).
- Visual cloze procedure: Focusing on a selected part of the enlarged text, reread the text with a few key predictable words covered, show beginning sound only (if children are ready to use as decoding strategies), and discuss how children figured out what to fill in (visual + meaning, visual + language + meaning).
- Enlist the help of the children to write words/phrases they remember out of the context of the story (see Chapter 4 for interactive writing), discuss the letter–sound patterns needed to write words accurately, and point and read together.

- Practice identifying letter names/shapes or letter–sound relationships that are prominent in text and appropriate for children.
- Reinforce the "reread, read on" checking strategy to confirm meaning. Encourage children to reread any part of a text that does not make sense to them. If rereading does not bring greater understanding, children might need to read on to see if the information they need has yet to be presented in the text.

EXTENDING SHARED READING EXPERIENCES

The longer children are engaged with one particular text, the greater the likelihood they will learn from that text (Beaver, 1982; Yaden, 1988). Extending experiences for children can take place both in small groups with an adult and independently in activity centers. To follow up or extend what begins in the whole group, additional opportunities should be planned for children to practice reading in easy familiar text. Follow-up may be in the form of teacher-led small groups that focus on specific skills and strategies introduced in the whole class; for example, written cloze activities would work well with small groups of four to six children. Children should also have opportunities to practice independently and extend upon their initial responses to familiar texts.

Figure 3.3 shows a week of related activities in which shared reading and rereading are prominent. Each day opens with whole-class activities, which include singing or shared poems, shared reading and rereading of the focus text, and response. Following the opening activities, children break into small groups for shared rereadings, as well as activity choices that support the shared reading. Small-group shared readings can also serve as guided readings, even though the text is already familiar. The level of text will present challenge to several children. Choices for extension activities are related to the content of the text, the knowledge of language patterns needed to successfully read it, and the level of independence of the children. To have access to print, many children will need extended exposure to that print. Shared reading and rereading, combined with extension activities, maintain children's interest in reading and writing.

Retelling and Responding to a Shared Reading

As we discussed in Chapter 2 with reading aloud, retelling and responding activities offer many choices for extending children's shared reading experiences. We can engage children in a variety of retelling and responding modes: discussion; support of text illustrations, story map, or flannel board; drama, chants, and creative movement; and children's art and writing. Retelling focuses children's attention on recalling the author's text in an appropriate order. Responding provides opportunity for children to focus on their personal response to a text. Retelling and responding require readers to think in different ways about a text. Both ways of thinking are needed for effective literacy development.

Explanation of Activities	Monday	Tuesday
Whole-Class Opening: • warm up with song, poem, chant, rereading of "old favorite" • introduce and guide reading/rereading of new text • plan/organize for work time, explain activity choices	**Whole-Class Opening:** • sing "Five Little Ducks," use hand motions • reread "old favorite" (children's choice) • introduce/read new book, *The Chick and the Duckling* • encourage response after reading • explain activity choices	**Whole-Class Opening:** • read "old favorite" • recall first reading of *The Chick and the Duckling* • reread, discuss each page, illustrations • make activity choice
Work Time: Teacher-led Small Group • shared rereading • retelling of text • responding to text • word knowledge skills • reading strategies	**Work Time: Small Group** • reread in small group • encourage response	**Work Time: Small Group** • reread big book, notice patterns (1) use illustrations to support duckling's actions, (2) notice how chick repeats what duckling says • attend to individual responses
Text Extensions • taped books • art • retelling • responding • word knowledge • reading corner • writing center	**Text Extensions** • tape recording of *The Chick and the Duckling* • art center, response to text • reading corner, old favorites • writing center, shape book of chick or duckling, topic open	**Text Extensions** • tape recording of *The Chick and the Duckling* • painting: something chick and duckling could do together • writing center, books shaped like chick or duckling • reading corner
Whole-Class Closure: • share small group/independent activities • plan for upcoming activities	**Whole-Class Closure:** • share art or writing • discuss new activity choices for tomorrow	**Whole-Class Closure:** • share paintings or shape books • plan for puppets tomorrow

FIGURE 3.3
Sample Plan—Extending Shared Reading

In the sample weekly plan that focuses on extending shared reading, shown in Figure 3.3, we use the following retelling and responding activities:

- Puppets in a dramatic retelling
- Felt board retelling
- An artistic response through painting
- Drawn and written response: "Things I Can Do!"

The weekly plan emphasizes retelling and response because we want children to notice the characters' actions, which would lead to noticing patterns in the text. Other extensions we might consider to extend children's responses to a shared text are wall stories and floor puzzles.

Wednesday	Thursday	Friday
Whole-Group Opening: • sing "Old McDonald" • reread text, children join in • record memorable words, phrases • read together • discuss paintings of things chick and duck can do together • encourage others to go to painting • introduce stick puppet activity	**Whole-Group Opening:** • sing/read *Five Little Ducks,* use Raffi book • recall what duckling did to prepare for reread • reread, use oral cloze to anticipate key words, encourage "reread, read on" strategy • reread using puppets to take parts of chick and duckling • introduce new activities	**Whole-Group Opening:** • read "old favorite," children's choice • reread big book, use oral cloze, predictable actions and character names
Work Time: Small Group • reread big book, encourage use of illustrations to cue words about duckling • introduce flannel board retelling of big book	**Work Time: Small Group** • reread big book, take parts, use puppets • return to words/phrases children remember, place in pocket chart	**Work Time: Small Group** • select sentences for written cloze, place in pocket chart • reread, with few key words covered, predict, uncover, discuss
Text Extensions • tape-recorded book • art, painting • make stick puppets of chick and duckling • reading corner • writing center, shape books	**Text Extensions** • tape recording of book, add response sheet • flannel board retelling • reading corner • writing center: (1) shape books (2) draw/write "Things I Can Do" (put on bulletin board)	**Text Extensions** • tape recording, encourage children to take part, use puppets • flannel board retelling • reading center • writing center (continue from Thursday)
Whole-Group Closure: • share puppets, writing, painting • plan for using puppets during whole-group opening tomorrow	**Whole-Group Closure:** • pairs of children use puppets and role-play chick and duckling • help children plan for a center they have not worked at yet	**Whole-Group Closure:** • share pictures for bulletin board, reread others

Using Enlarged Text to Create Wall Stories

Book illustration and text are cut apart, illustrations are placed on a wall or in a hallway in proper order, and text is available for matching. Text must be mounted on paper to be only one-sided. Two copies of a book are necessary to have both sides of a page. Children can retell the story by using illustrations, then matching text. Matching text to illustration reinforces interpretation of illustrations and provides practice in reading sentences without the support of illustrations. Wall stories can also be made from children's illustrations and teacher-written text. Children can also be innovative on a text by composing their own version through shared/interactive writing. Wall stories enable children to "read the room" during activity periods.

Creating Floor Puzzles

Mount text illustrations and text on paper so only one side of page can be seen, then separate by making distinct cuts between picture and text to match like puzzle pieces. Two copies of a book are needed to represent all pages. Pieces are spread out on the floor. Children help each other match pieces and place in proper order to tell the story. Place pieces in a large self-closing plastic bag or box for storage.

DEVELOPING WORD KNOWLEDGE THROUGH SHARED READING

In the primary grades, children must develop many concepts about the generalizations that govern words in the English language. Shared reading of enlarged texts provides many opportunities for adults to scaffold children's understandings about words in print. In this section we focus on how shared reading can support children's developing knowledge of words in print.

Print Concepts

Early reading success relies on children's understandings about print and the "rules" that govern how words are displayed in print (Clay, 1991). Bedtime stories and noticing print in the environment provide an excellent introduction into how written language can be displayed. What do children need to know about print? The list below provides a starting point for literacy development:

- *Purpose of print.* Print is meaningful and carries messages. We read print, not pictures; however, children's early retellings/rereading of a text are guided by illustrations and recollections of the text, before they understand that it is the print that carries the message.
- *Permanence of print.* When we make print on paper, the letters remain where we put them. When a book is closed, letters and words do not move around. With rereadings, children begin to notice that the text is the same from reading to reading. We guide them to notice that words are in the same place on a page as they were during the previous reading.
- *Directional concepts.* We read left to right, and top to bottom on a page. To move through a text we use "return sweep," returning to the left side of a page and dropping down one line of text, to move through text.
- *Concepts about words.* Empty space defines the beginning and end of a word. We match speech to print to help us read words. We need to know letter names, shapes, and sounds that letters represent to read many words. Letters are sequenced from left to right to form a word.
- *The language of print.* We use words in particular ways to talk about print and books, such as *front, back, left, right, top, bottom, letter, word, line,* and *sentence.*

Shared reading with enlarged text, in either whole-class or small-group settings, can be used to reinforce print concepts for children. During shared reading experiences, especially rereadings of text, we model how proficient readers use an understanding of print to read. Then we ask children to demonstrate their understandings of print concepts. Children "show what they know" when they point to the text to guide the class through a rereading, or when they find the word *said* on each page and notice that it is always spelled with the same sequence of letters.

High-Frequency Words

Many words that young readers encounter appear frequently in texts. Readers become fluent when they remember these frequently occurring words. Fluent readers notice certain distinguishing features of these words and commit them to memory after a few meaningful exposures. When they encounter the words in future readings they are able to instantly recall them. Children should be encouraged to notice the features of words that appear with great frequency and think about how to remember those words for future use. Amazingly, young readers often remember longer, distinctive words such as *dinosaur* and *elephant.* Such words are typically nouns that have high meaning for children and are remembered as whole words.

Other high-frequency words must be remembered as whole words because they have unpredictable sounds for the letter patterns within the word. For example, words such as *said* and *have* do not follow typical letter–sound generalizations. Our knowledge of vowel patterns would lead us to expect:

- *said* to decode as *s-ay-d,* rather than *s-e-d.*
- *have* to decode as *h-ay-v,* rather than *h-a-v.*

We call such high-frequency words "sight words." They are words that are unpredictable to decode and best recalled as whole words when seen in text.

Shared reading of texts provides many opportunities to help children develop a large number of words that are recognized quickly:

- Predictable text is an excellent way to help children develop a large sight vocabulary. Bridge, Winograd, and Haley (1983) report that children who participated in repeated reading of predictable books learned more sight words than comparable children who were placed in a basal reading series.
- The use of words from a word bank encourages development of sight vocabulary. Children can build a word bank by selecting their favorite words from a familiar text. The selected words are placed on word cards for the child to keep. These words can be kept in a small box or other container and used for small-group and individual word-build and word-sorting activities. As the word bank grows, dividers can be used so that words are easier for children to find and use. Many teachers divide words by alphabetical order, but Trachtenburg and Ferruggia (1989) suggest the following categories: words that describe (adjectives), people and animal words (nouns), action words (verbs), and words that tell how, when, where (adverbs).

Developing Use of Context

As children gain skill and confidence in using initial consonants, we encourage them to use their "context +" strategy. During shared reading we:

- cover all but the beginning letter(s) of a predictable word,
- ask children to orally predict what would make sense in the context and begin like the letter(s) shown,
- help children check their thinking by discussing appropriateness for meaning and sound and eliminating unreasonable choices that do not have the same beginning sounds, and
- reveal the word and check for meaning by considering beginning and ending sounds of the word.

Written cloze is one way to prepare children for decoding unfamiliar words.

Masking text is very effective for pacing children's reading and focusing their attention on particular words or word parts (Holdaway, 1979). Masking also enables us to encourage children to use their knowledge of context and beginning sounds, with their "reread, read on" strategy, to anticipate words in text. The type and amount of text that we mask depends on children's level of development as readers. Masking text can also be used with older students who are still in emergent or developing reader stages. Figure 3.4 shows examples of masking devices.

- *Big books.* Mask words or portions of words with a "magic window"—a sturdy cardboard rectangle with a small rectangle cut out of the center allows words in the enlarged text to be singled out for sight word development (Trachtenburg & Ferruggia, 1989). A masking device with a sliding opening can direct children to attend to detail within words (Cooper, 1993). We can also mask individual words with small pieces of paper that can be removed after their prediction.
- *Pocket chart.* Mask words or parts of words by placing blank cards in front of text, covering all or portions of words for attention. After predictions, the blank card is removed to enable children to confirm their thinking.
- *Overhead projector.* Text is reproduced on a transparency, then desired portions can be masked. Strips of heavy paper are laid over each line of text. The strips can be moved, one at a time, to reveal text. Individual words, or portions of words, are masked with small pieces of paper to focus attention on particular decoding elements or strategies.
- *Charts.* On a chart, containing a poem or song for shared reading or a text jointly composed through shared writing, portions of words are masked. As children participate in the shared reading or rereading of the text, they are encouraged to use beginning letters plus context to predict the masked words. Words are then unmasked to confirm the accuracy of children's predictions.

FIGURE 3.4
Masking Text

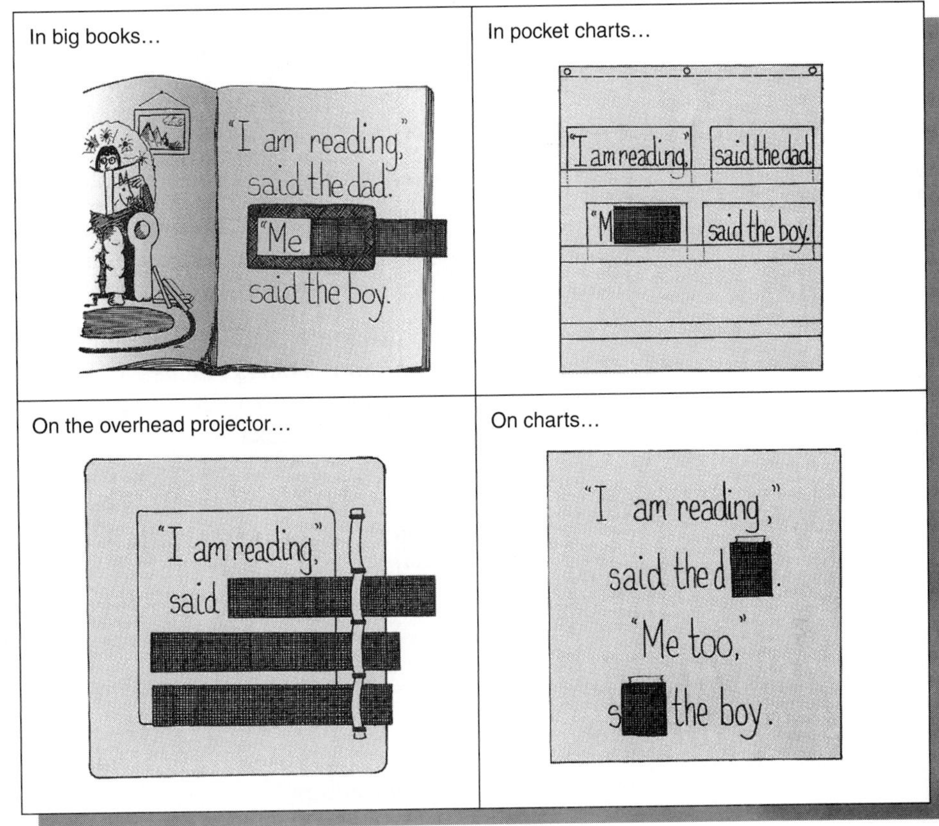

INTEGRATING WRITING WITH SHARED READING

Emerging readers and writers are working to develop their concepts about print, learning letters and associated sounds, and just beginning to consider who they are as authors. Writing should be integrated with shared reading experiences to help children retain, recollect, and represent their ideas about a text.

In the sample weekly plan (Figure 3.3) for *The Chick and the Duckling,* we included a variety of writing opportunities:

- *Annotated drawings.* Throughout the book, the duckling is telling the chick the things he can do. The children draw a picture of something they can do, then they write a statement about what they are doing in their pictures. These drawings are arranged as a bulletin board entitled, "Things We Can Do!" The bulletin board also becomes shared reading during group times.
- *Shape books.* Construction paper that can be cut into meaningful shapes, filled with blank paper, and stapled as a book is placed in the writing center. Poster board templates can also be placed in the writing center for children to make their own blank books. Even first-grade

children are able to trace around a template for the cover of the book, staple a few sheets of blank paper between the covers, and cut out the book along the template lines. (Good scissors are needed.) For *The Chick and the Duckling,* we use the shapes of both a chick and a duck. Children write their own "stories" or respond to the text. This open-ended task enables all children to be successful.

Functional writing can be used to support and extend the shared reading, depending upon our purposes for instruction and the children's background as writers:

- *Idea clusters.* Children could draw a cluster of ideas or list "Things ducks can do" and "Things chicks can do." They can then use intersecting circles, as in a Venn diagram, to identify what is common between chicks and ducks.
- *Journals.* In a journal or learning log, children can record a variety of responses or ideas about the text. They can respond to their favorite part of the story, write their favorite words, or describe what they would have done if they were the duckling or the chick.
- *Innovation on a text.* Use the pattern from the story to create a predictable text. In *The Chick and the Duckling,* the pattern to innovate on might be:

  "I am (action)," said the ________.

  "Me too," said the ______________.

If we are reading this story in October, we might innovate on the pattern by using two Halloween characters.

"I am flying," said the ghost.

"Me too," said the witch.

If we are involved in a unit on families we might use a parent and child for the two characters.

"I am reading a book," said the dad.

"Me too," said the boy.

By innovating on a pattern, the children extend their practice with patterns and also sight words. When appropriate, the pattern can be copied for children to fill in with a personal innovation. Multiple pages can allow children to make a small book.

The innovation can also be made into a class big book. Individuals or pairs can contribute pages. The innovated book is then enjoyed as a shared reading experience by the whole class or a small group. The completed big book is placed in the library corner for independent rereading.

ASSESSMENT: MONITORING DEVELOPMENT IN SHARED READING

In shared reading, children refine their concepts about print, how print is organized on paper, and how words appear in print. To monitor children's early progress in reading we must understand how they are making sense out of print and the rules for print in English. We can evaluate children's concepts about print by carefully observing their behavior as they handle books and respond to print.

Concepts about Books and Print

Concepts about books and print are assessed most effectively in the context of real print sources, such as books. Both commercial and teacher-made instruments can effectively measure concepts about print. Marie Clay (1979, 1993) has developed an assessment that enables us to observe children's print knowledge as we read and the child participates in applying print knowledge. Her assessment uses two specially constructed texts, *Sand* and *Stone.* Clay's books have been altered so that on some pages print and illustrations have been turned upside down. In addition, line order, word order, and letter order within some high-frequency words have been altered.

The examiner reads the text aloud and asks the child what he or she notices about the text. Children can demonstrate their knowledge that print carries the message by noticing a discrepancy between what is read aloud and what is on the page. The items on the assessment have been validated for children, ages five to seven years. Directions for administration and scoring are available in *Early Detection of Reading Difficulties* (Clay, 1985) and *The Observation Survey* (Clay, 1993).

A teacher-made assessment can simulate Clay's Concepts about Print as shown in Figure 3.5. Although a published children's book does not have altered pages, children's concepts about book handling and print can still be observed. As in Clay's assessment, the text is read aloud to the child. During the assessment, the child is asked to demonstrate concepts about book orientation and handling, directionality, and print language.

To assess a child's concepts about books and print, we select a book that is not familiar to the child. We want to be sure there is a title on the front cover and the first page of print also has an illustration. Be sure that text appears on two facing pages somewhere in the book. To document growth, this assessment should be completed with all emergent readers and selectively with developing readers early in the school year and intermittently throughout the year. For comparison, also conduct this assessment with a book that is very familiar to the child. A child who scores better with a familiar text may be showing us the potential for instruction in print concepts with familiar texts. A record-keeping form (see Figure 3.6) is provided.

Over time, emergent and early developing readers show increasing understanding of print and how readers respond to print. We begin administering Clay's assessment early in kindergarten and continue until children demonstrate knowledge of all items. Knowledge of print is essential for children to make accurate predictions about what print can be expected to do in their reading.

As we administer this assessment, we use observations across the class to make decisions about the skills and strategies to emphasize in shared reading experiences. For example, early in kindergarten children may not demonstrate knowledge of return sweep (i.e., when we get to the end of a line of text we return to the left side of a page and drop down one line). If that knowledge is absent in a number of children, as it probably will be, we model that skill in shared reading and ask children to demonstrate that skill by reading sentences that are longer than one line of text.

FIGURE 3.5
Concepts about Books and Print Assessment

Do:	*Say:*	*See:*
Hand child a book, spine first, ask #1, 2, 3.	1. Show me the front of the book. 2. Show me the title of the book. 3. Show me where I should start to read the story?	1. Child points to front cover. 2. Child points to any words in title. 3. Child turns to first page of text.
On first pages of story, ask #4.	4. Where should I start to read?	4. Child points to print, not illustration.
Read first facing pages of text, then ask #5. After child turns page, ask. #6, 7, 8. Then, read facing pages of text. Turn page. Read several more pages.	5. I finished reading this page, now what do I do? 6. Where should I start to read on this page? 7. Which way should I go when I read? 8. Which way should I go after that?	5. Child turns to next page of text. 6. Child points to first word, top left side. 7. Child moves finger to right end of line. 8. Child does return sweep, moves left to right on another line of text.
On two facing pages with print on both sides, ask #9. Turn page, ask #10, 11.	9. Where should I start to read? 10. Show me the first word on this page. 11. Show me the last word on this page.	9. Child points to left-hand page, first word on top left. 10. Child points to first word on top left. 11. Child points to last word on bottom right.
Read last facing pages of text. Then give child two small cards (1" × 2"). Show how to move cards, to close and open like a window. Use for #12, 13, 14.	12. Show me one letter. Show me two letters. 13. Show me one word. Show me two words. 14. Show me a capital letter.	12. Child slides cards apart to show any single letter, any two letters together. 13. Child slides cards apart to show one word, two words together. 14. Child points to any capital letter.
Close the book. Ask #15, 16	15. Show me the beginning of the story. 16. Show me the end of the story.	15. Child shows title page or first page of text in book. 16. Child shows last page of text in book.

FIGURE 3.6
Assessment Record Form

Concepts about Books and Print Assessment

Name ______________________

Date __________ Age _____ yrs. _____mo.

Item/Concept	Score	Comments
1. Front of book		
2. Title of book		
3. Begin to read book on first page of text		
4. Read print, not picture		
5. Turn page when finished reading		
6. Begin to read page on top left, first word		
7. Read line of text left to right		
8. Return sweep		
9. Read left page before right page		
10. First word on page		
11. Last word on page		
12. One letter, two letters		
13. One word, two words		
14. Capital letter		
15. Beginning of story		
16. End of story		
Total	**/16**	

Overall Observations:

RESPECTING DIVERSITY THROUGH SHARED READING

Using enlarged print for reading makes text more accessible to children. However, their background experience as readers and with the English language may not allow them full access to meaning. Your thoughtful use of shared reading experiences can provide:

- support and safety within a group,
- support through modeling and guided participation,
- language support through predictability, and
- extended reading experiences through sheltered text.

Safety and Support of a Group

Within the group during a shared reading experience, children are able to participate at different levels without calling attention to their individual performance. Everyone is absorbed in the activity, whether they are reading every word with the teacher or observing the illustrations and listening. Shared reading allows children, at all levels of development, to take from the reading what they desire. Shared reading also allows all children to participate at a level in which they are comfortable and confident.

Support through Modeling and Guided Participation

As a shared reading begins, you assume the responsibility of showing children what they need to do as readers by modeling. Through extended experiences with the same text, the level of your support for children is adjusted depending on what the children show you they need. Your role as model and guide provides opportunity for children to feel successful at their level of performance within the group.

Language Support through Predictability

Having a sense of pattern and anticipating what will come enables children at all levels of experience to find success in shared reading. Predictable text supports children's efforts to figure out the rules of written language. Combined with your modeling and guidance, predictability will enable children who are learning English to find success in early reading experiences.

Extending Learning through Sheltered Text

Children who are learning English and/or have limited experience with print will find success when text is made more accessible. You can enhance children's feelings of success when you are sensitive to the demands that texts make on less experienced readers. When your analysis of text suggests that it lacks the support of predictability, you should provide sheltered text experiences. Bringing sheltered text to shared reading experiences can be beneficial for all children.

Take a moment to reflect on putting theory into practice with shared reading . . .

Knowing our children, we

- select skills or teaching points to emphasize in the texts,
- set clear purposes for instruction,
- analyze the demands of the text to confirm that our purpose(s) are appropriate for the text, and
- carefully observe children's interactions with other texts as indication of their ability to interact with the chosen text.

In much the same fashion as a mediated read-aloud, we guide children's thinking before, during, and after the reading of a text.

We reread shared texts to emphasize language patterns, especially predictable patterns in language structure, rhythm, and rhyming.

To ensure that more students will be able to access the chosen text, we provide extended experiences with shared texts through integration with other literacy components.

Children's concepts about print are strengthened through intensive experiences with a piece of shared text.

Repeated exposure to a single text heightens the possibility that children will add words they recognize automatically to their sight vocabulary.

Experiences in predicting print characteristics from text that is masked, or covered, enables children to develop and refine their decoding knowledge.

Shared writing can be extended through various forms of functional writing, such as annotated drawings.

We should monitor children's developing concepts about print through daily observation and a one-on-one Concepts about Books and Print (Clay's) assessment.

Shared reading experiences show respect for diversity by:

- providing safety and support within the group,
- modeling reading and guiding children's participation,
- supporting language knowledge through predictability, and
- sheltering text to make it more accessible.

YOUR TURN . . .

1. Develop a list of your favorite books that are simple, repetitive, and/or predictable and will lend themselves to shared reading. Find out if they are available as big books. If not, consider an appropriate way to enlarge the text for possible shared readings.
2. Start a collection of songs, chants, and poems that will make for lively shared readings.
3. Prepare a plan for a shared reading of a big book. Select a predictable text that is available as a big book or can be enlarged with an overhead projector or as a class big book.
   - Analyze the text for predictable pattern and illustrations.
   - Make decisions about possible skill/strategy instruction.
   - Outline a five-day plan that includes the following:

     Whole-group reading and rereading
     Introduction of the text
     Attention to print concepts and word knowledge
     Small-group study of the text with individual copies for the children
     Possible text extensions that encourage children to revisit and respond to the text
     Independent reading of the text
     Independent writing/drawing as response or retelling

Aa Bb Cc Dd Ee Ff Gg Hh Ii Jj Kk Ll Mm

CHAPTER

4

Shared and Interactive Writing

Adding to our literacy framework . . .

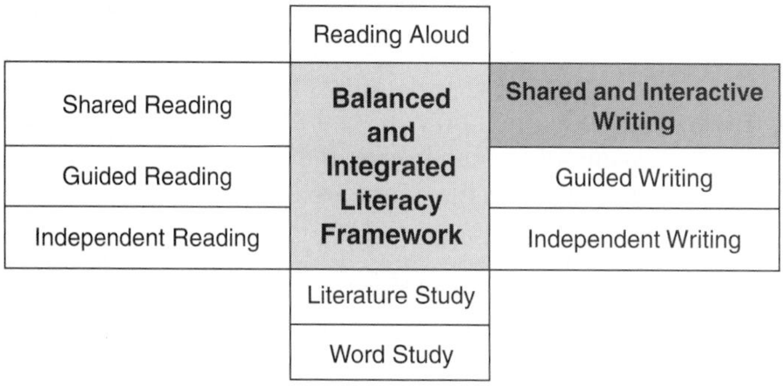

	Reading Aloud	
Shared Reading	**Balanced and Integrated Literacy Framework**	**Shared and Interactive Writing**
Guided Reading		Guided Writing
Independent Reading		Independent Writing
	Literature Study	
	Word Study	

In this chapter, we . . .

- Explore engaging children in the act of shared compositions that model writing processes.
- Examine the process of developing a shared composition, as well as extending children's interactions with the text.

Looking into Classrooms . . .

One morning Renee brings a frog into her first-grade classroom. The class is studying about different ways that animals move and Renee thinks this is a wonderful opportunity for the children to explore the movement of frogs. She places the frog in an aquarium with a screen cover and asks the children to spend time observing the frog during their morning activities. All during the morning children gather around the aquarium in small groups watching the frog and talking with each other.

After lunch Renee gathers the children together and asks them what they notice about the frog. At first, the children talk about the frog's smooth skin, bulging eyes, the long back legs, the markings on the frog's back, and its wide mouth. Then the talk begins to center on how the frog jumps.

Renee asks the children to sit in a large circle on the floor. She removes the frog from the aquarium and places it in the center of the circle. At first the frog sits very still. Then with some prodding, it jumps across the circle, changes directions, and jumps several more times. Each time it jumps, Renee asks the children to notice what the frog does when it jumps. Talk continues as the children explore words that help to describe what they observe in the frog's movement.

Renee puts the frog away and asks the children to pretend they are frogs. The children crouch down, with legs bent and arms out front to steady themselves. Renee asks them to jump once like a frog and notice what they have to do to get off the floor. She asks the children to sit again, where they are, and talk about what they notice about their own jumping. Renee encourages the talking until she feels that the children are comfortable with the language they need to describe the experience.

To begin the shared writing, Renee asks the children, "How do frogs jump?" Several children volunteer ideas. Renee then asks for the children's thoughts on the best way to start the writing, and the class begins to compose. Renee serves as the scribe for the children as she guides the composition. Each time the class reads what is written, Renee asks what should come next. She raises questions about which ideas are most important to include, and she helps children clarify their thinking as they dictate what they are thinking about frogs:

Frogs can jump a long way.
Frogs jump with their back legs.
The back legs get all stretched out.
The front legs are not for jumping.
We jumped like frogs.
We pushed with our legs.

Renee uses shared writing experiences, such as the one above, to model the purposes and process of writing. At appropriate times the writing becomes interactive as Renee shares the pen so the children can do the writing. She invites children to write familiar words or familiar sounds at the beginning or end of words. Renee provides daily shared and interactive writing experiences because she knows that children become writers over a long period of time. It is through their extensive and intensive experiences with making print that children form concepts about what purposes print serves and how people use print.

Building a Theory Base . . .

From previous chapters, we know that shared activity provides a meaningful social context for learning. Children are motivated to interact with others socially. Learning experiences that are grounded in shared activity provide appropriate social contexts for the acquisition of literacy skills. Shared and interactive writing, as demonstrated by Renee in the opening vignette, are powerful instructional tools for us as teachers.

Lucy Calkins (1994), who has great experience in writing with young children, tells us: "The powerful thing about writing with words is that we are really working with thoughts. Writing allows us to put our thoughts on the page and in our pockets; writing allows us to pull back and ask questions of our thoughts. It is this dynamic of creation and criticism, of pulling in to put thoughts on the page and pulling back to question, wonder, remember more, organize and rethink that makes writing such a powerful tool for learning" (p. 222).

Writing with children provides us the opportunity to work collaboratively with children to explore writing's full potential. Shared and interactive writing also provide excellent opportunities to explore this potential with children.

WHAT IS SHARED WRITING?

Shared writing is the use of children's language and thinking as a foundation for developing a written text. Moira McKenzie (1985) is one of the first to use this term to describe the assistance that teachers can provide to model writing processes and support young writers. Children's knowledge, personal experience, and language are used to create written texts that show children the relationship between written language and their already familiar oral language (McCarrier, Pinnell, & Fountas, 2000).

Using children's language to create written texts is a method used by many primary-grade teachers to teach beginning reading. Formerly known as language experience approach, or LEA (Nessel & Jones, 1981; Stauffer & Hammond, 1967), the joint creation of text by teacher and children has been viewed as an effective way to engage children in early print experiences. LEA, however, was primarily used as a personalized approach to reading instruction, during which children read texts created with their own words. Shared writings begin as compositions, but become reading materials, drawn from children's experiences.

In the language experience approach, the teacher does not attempt to shape the content of the text. The children's grammar is recorded just as it is spoken. In contrast, shared writing is a joint composition between children and teacher, guided by the teacher. In a shared writing, we use children's language and our knowledge of writing to construct a joint text. We serve as the scribe, but we use our knowledge of writing to nudge children's thinking in certain directions. In doing so, we raise questions, as if thinking aloud, about the writing. Shared writing allows us to model how writers think while they are writing. Talking about the writing, its content and organization, serves as a verbal composition in preparation for the written composition.

Shared writing is assisted writing. We must work thoughtfully with children's responses, however, so they retain ownership of the writing. Our interactions with children should not impose our ideas on their composition, but rather bring to a level of consciousness children's understanding of possibilities in the writing. For the writing to be shared, we must work from what children know.

Various writing activities are adapted to different groups of children or learners for a variety of purposes, such as to:

- assist children and adults who are learning to read and write,
- model writing processes through shared experience,
- assist children whose first language is not English,
- support handwriting instruction,
- supplement other methods of teaching reading and writing such as basal reading series and literature-based reading,
- supplement language arts and content area instruction at all grade levels, and
- provide a tutorial device for special needs students.

Shared and interactive writing are powerful learning experiences that occur within a social context and enable us to apply our understanding of writing purposes and its process.

Shared writing engages children in different types of thinking. Writing, in general, enables us to retain and recollect what we know. In addition, group writing experiences that deal with vicarious experiences and secondhand information can support children as they learn to reconstruct new ideas. Many of the types of writing that children will be asked to do in school will require them to reconstruct their thinking, or combine ideas from several different sources in a new way. Through our assistance, children become aware of the forms or structures of different types of writing, such as the differences between narrative and information texts. Through our assistance, we are able to model how writers compose various types of texts.

WHEN DOES SHARED WRITING BECOME INTERACTIVE?

As Renee and her children develop a composition, she often shares the pen. At appropriate times, Renee invites children to share in the actual writing of letters and words. When the writing becomes interactive, the act of composing gives way to the appropriate use of symbols, letter–sound relationships, and language conventions. During interactive writing, children are able to demonstrate to themselves and others what they understand about the formation of letters, the order of letters to form words, the function of punctuation and capital letters, and the like.

Interactive writing, a term first used in 1991 by faculty members at The Ohio State University (McCarrier, Pinnell, & Fountas, 2000), continues to focus children's attention on the message of the text, but provides more attention to the principles of written language (Clay, 1975), as discussed on pages 114–116. As Renee invites children to share the pen by writing parts of the frog composition, she considers their literacy development. What children are invited to write depends on their developing knowledge about print. As one child writes, Renee invites the other children to activate their knowledge about letters, sounds, and other language conventions as a way of learning through the experience of others. She often uses a small dry-erase board or a device called a Magna-Doodle to write in response to children's thinking about what is being written on the class chart.

Figure 4.1 shows one of Roseanne's journal entries. This entry was written interactively with her kindergarten teacher. After drawing a picture of herself, Roseanne told the teacher that she was thinking about her first day at school (two months earlier). Roseanne and the teacher shared the writing of the sen-

FIGURE 4.1
Personal Interactive Writing—Kindergarten

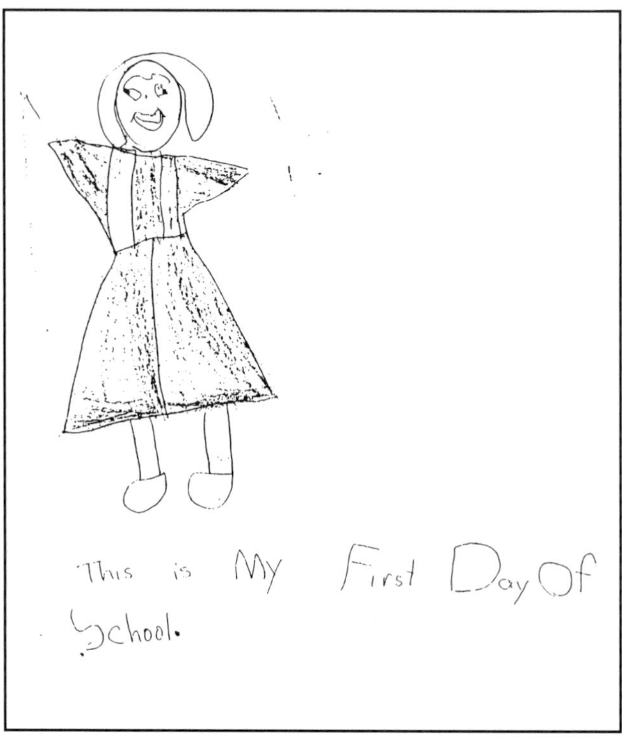

tence, "This is **M**y **F**irst **D**ay **O**f **S**chool." The letters in bold are those that Roseanne was able to hear and write. Notice that even early in the kindergarten year, interactive writing enabled Roseanne to write the first letter of five words.

WHY DO SHARED/INTERACTIVE WRITING?

When a more knowledgeable other assists a child in communicating through writing, the probability is high that the child will realize the communicative value of writing. "As children see their spoken thoughts put into written form, they can grasp the concept that communication is the purpose" (Hall, 1981, p. 2). Children are already aware that oral language serves communication purposes. Shared and interactive writing extend that understanding to include the communication purposes of written language as a part of learning to read and write. Engaging in verbal composition prior to written compositions helps children develop understanding of essential vocabulary and practice appropriate sentence structures.

In shared and interactive writing, instruction in listening, speaking, and writing are integrated with reading. Children think, talk, look, and listen. Teachers write children's spoken thoughts, then read the written thoughts aloud. Children read their thoughts that are recorded by either the teacher or the children and talk about the meanings that the words create. Stauffer (1975) supports the interrelatedness when he states, "The processes that children have developed for oral communication must be used to full advantage in a similar way by having written words trigger the same concepts" (p. 170).

Just as in LEA, shared writings become excellent texts for shared and guided reading instruction. Children are highly motivated to read jointly composed texts. Learning to read is easiest and most enjoyable when the language of instructional materials matches the language of the reader (McCarrier, Pinnell, & Fountas, 2000; Nessel & Jones, 1981). As a main approach to beginning reading instruction, research suggests that jointly constructed texts can be as effective in helping children learn the skills of reading as using a basal reading series (Bond & Dykstra, 1967; Dykstra, 1968; Stahl & Miller, 1989; Stauffer & Hammond, 1967), and may even have some advantages over basal approaches (Hall, 1978; Stahl & Miller, 1989).

As children actively participate in constructing meaningful texts they are able to see a relationship between school learning activities and learning to read and write. Children see writing as functional when it involves such activities as documenting the birth and growth of the class's baby mice or a letter of appreciation to a grandmother who taught the class about making tortillas. Shared and interactive writing is purposeful for children because learning to read and write is integrally linked to personal interests and learning experiences in general.

THINKING WITH WRITTEN LANGUAGE

The environment in our classroom supports children as they think and shape meaning with written language. D'Arcy (1989), working from Frank Smith's ideas about how the "learning brain" functions, identifies several ways that writing supports and enhances our thinking. Engaging in writing enables us to:

- retain memories of experiences with the world,
- "re-collect" memories/experiences,
- "re-create" memories from firsthand knowledge,
- "re-construct" ideas by arriving at new perceptions of experiences with secondhand knowledge, and
- "re-present" in some way what is known now that was not known before.

D'Arcy deliberately hyphenates the terms to call attention to the fact that as we arrive at new knowledge and new understandings, we draw upon what has already been collected, constructed, or created by our brains.

We ask children to write by drawing upon their experiences and their knowledge of language. To do this, children need our support and encouragement as they learn to value their own thinking. A writing program that encourages and supports thinking focuses on what children have already retained from their life experiences, then enables them to "re-collect, re-construct, re-create, and represent" their thinking.

Retaining Experiences

Through our senses we constantly take in new experiences, or "memories" as D'Arcy refers to them. For young children, processing through their senses is a natural way of learning (Piaget & Inhelder, 1969). Our senses influence how we interpret the experiences in which we find ourselves. D'Arcy's use of "retaining" is similar to our previous discussions about schema. We could say that as children retain new experiences they are building schema about their world.

One marvelous aspect of thinking, and perhaps the most problematic, is that the retaining that children do is virtually effortless. Children are often unaware that they are retaining memories or experiences and do not realize all that they know. When we ask children to write about what they know, they may respond in dismay because they do not think they know much about the world. Experiences that are retained, especially without conscious effort, may not be so readily available to children. To draw upon their experiences in school writing activities, children will need help in organizing their thinking and learning to recognize and use what they know.

Re-Collecting Experience

"None of us are in a position to 'know what we know' until we are given opportunity to re-collect what we have retained" (D'Arcy, 1989, p. 4). Re-collecting provides opportunities with each new encounter we have to connect back to past experiences that have begun to take shape. In connecting back, we are able to revisit and also reshape what has been retained. The ease of using what we know is related to the frequency of re-collecting those retained experiences.

When children write, we should encourage them to write from what they know. Planning activities that enable children to re-collect retained experiences is an essential step for successful and satisfying writing. Demonstrating how to re-collect experiences can be done through the recording of children's shared and personal experiences, as Renee did with her first-grade children in the opening scenario. Children can also re-collect their ideas in many forms of functional writing such as notes, idea clusters, diagrams, and short descriptions, which we explore in Chapter 6.

Re-Creating Experience

Our firsthand experiences with the world are usually easier for us to recall than vicarious, or secondhand, experiences. When we sift through the incredible amount of detail we have retained from personal experiences, certain memories stand out as significant to us. We re-create those experiences in our mind, perhaps highlighting some part of the experience differently than we had on previous occasions.

It is also possible that our responses to literature are re-creative. When we identify with the triumphs and struggles of characters, we use literature as a mirror reflecting back on ourselves. In that reflection, we use our own life experience, combined with our literary experience, to look closely at some particularly relevant life event.

Writing should enable children to re-create their lived experience and write about what they know best. Children who struggle with what to write about may be the ones who do not value their lived experience. Carefully selecting literature for the reading program that connects with children's lives can extend their opportunities for re-creating experiences through writing.

Re-Constructing Experience

Clarifying our thinking is valuable to better understand what we know. With each new experience, we gather re-collections of past experiences to understand the proper connections to make with the new. Re-constructing previously held ideas, we adjust our ideas in light of what we know. In other words, we build or revise a particular schema. Much of the knowledge we gain is through secondhand experience, which can be more difficult to manipulate or reshape than knowledge gained through firsthand experience.

Almost daily we ask children to re-construct their previous knowledge in light of new information. We introduce new concepts for which children often lack firsthand experience. To enable children to use this new knowledge effectively we should help them first re-collect what they already know. Writing is instrumental in helping children see what they know in preparation for re-constructing their knowledge.

Re-Presenting Experience

To reinforce children's sense of what they know, they need many opportunities to move thinking and learning outside of themselves. Re-presenting their thinking in writing, using words to stand for what they know, enables children to see their thinking. It is especially important for children to realize when they have learned, when they know something new.

Shared writing becomes interactive writing when we share the pen with children. What can they learn about writing by participating in such an activity?

If in our classrooms we treat writing as an active process, children will have numerous opportunities to re-present their thinking. During the process of developing a piece of writing to completion, children may see a change in their ability to clearly re-present their thinking. By re-presenting their thinking in writing at different points in their learning, children can focus on what they know that was not known before. Seeing their own growth can lead to self-satisfaction with themselves as writers and learners.

HOW IS WRITING USED IN CLASSROOMS?

How do the thousands of hours we spend as students shape our views about writing and of ourselves as writers? Children learn about writing by the ways that writing is used in the classroom and by the things that we emphasize about writing. Children may learn that writing is:

- a symbolic code that must be mastered,
- a medium through which they may communicate,
- an end product to be achieved,
- an active process or activity, or
- a combination.

D'Arcy (1989) suggests that the writing we require from our pupils and the ways in which we respond to that writing will, in their turn, influence the pupils' expectations and consequently their approach to and performance in writing, possibly for life. Lucy Calkins (1994) also comments, "What our students do as writers will largely depend on what we expect them to do and on what they've done in the past" (p. 113).

Writing as a Code

If we view writing as a code, then we give attention to the correct use of language symbols. In our experience as writers, many of us have experienced teachers who view writing as a code. We spent endless hours completing exercises that focused on grammar, sentence structures, spelling, and so forth. We received feedback on our writing in the form of red marks on compositions. We were given specific formats in which to fit our ideas about a topic. Although these practices were intended to focus our attention on the details of written language, we also learned that there was a "right" way to write.

Research in writing (Calkins, 1986, 1994; Clay, 1975; Graves, 1983, 1994) helps us realize that overemphasis on code, at the expense of meaning, can lead children to see writing as a tedious task and themselves as inadequate writers. As young children make the transition from oral to written language, they must learn a new symbol system. Such attention to detail requires an extensive background with print that will be acquired over many years. We know that concepts about written language are best acquired in the context of meaningful activity.

Writing as a Medium

If we consider writing as a medium, we view words as "verbal play dough" (D'Arcy, 1989), out of which something useful can be made. Just as an artist uses a medium as a vehicle of expression, writers use words. Just as an artist experiments with a medium to see what it can do, a writer experiments with language without being quite sure where it will lead. An artist knows that while the medium is visible, its meaning lies within its creator and the individuals who observe it. So, too, the meaning of writing lies within its creator and observers.

By the ways we engage children with written language we help them see language as a flexible and responsive medium, able to be manipulated or reshaped to meet different intentions. Children's experiences with written language impact their views about the possibilities of language.

Writing as a Product

The completion of projects or tasks is important to our sense of self-satisfaction in our work and our lives. It is often a way that we measure our personal success. However, when completion becomes more important than the tasks themselves, work can become personally meaningless and unsatisfactory. In writing, we want children to experience the self-satisfaction of finished products. We can encourage children's writing to move in certain directions, but what will ultimately be most important is the direction that children think their work should take. Producing a written product should never become more important than the meaning it holds for the writer.

Writing as an Active Process

Research in writing has lead us to realize that writing is an active, not a passive, process. Writing is full of activity, mental and physical, that enables us to move our thinking out of our heads, down our arms, and out our fingers by way of a pen or keyboard. In the process of doing writing, we make our thinking and feelings visible. Mental images can also become visible.

Thinking of writing as an active process is tied to viewing writing as a medium that is responsive and flexible. For children to recognize the existence of this process, we must help them become aware of their thinking through talk, drawing, and physical actions, then show them how that thinking can be captured with words to represent the talk, drawing, and actions. Many varied writing experiences help children see that writing serves different purposes, takes different forms, and can be directed to different audiences.

Calkins (1994) pushes our thoughts of writing as a process even further. Her experiences with writing have taught her that "[w]riting does not begin with deskwork but with lifework" (p. 3). Calkins shares comments by Cynthia Rylant, a children's book author, who described her writing process: "We are talking about . . . being an artist every single day of one's life." Calkins believes the process of writing "begins in living with a sense of awareness" (p. 3).

PRINCIPLES OF WRITTEN LANGUAGE

"There are uniform rules governing the relationship between sounds and symbols, between different kinds of words, and between ideas in a paragraph. While children may form some rudimentary ideas about the structure of language as they acquire meta-linguistic awareness, these ideas become crystallized as the child learns to read and write" (Bedrova & Leong, 1996, p. 103). By "metalinguistic awareness," we mean the ability to reflect on and think about the language being used. For example, a child may have a vague understanding that words make up sentences, but when that child participates in creating sentences that are written, the idea of "word" becomes clearer.

Through extensive experiences with written language, emerging writers demonstrate a developing understanding of principles that govern print (Clay, 1975). Over time, their writing shows a growing awareness of the details of print, as shown in Figure 4.2, through the following principles:

- Recurring principle
- Generative principle
- Sign concept
- Flexibility principle
- Directionality

Recurring Principle

Children begin to notice that the same shapes occur repeatedly in English words. They demonstrate their awareness of these recurring shapes by using one or two shapes (perhaps a hump, loop, or cross) over and over again to fill pages of paper.

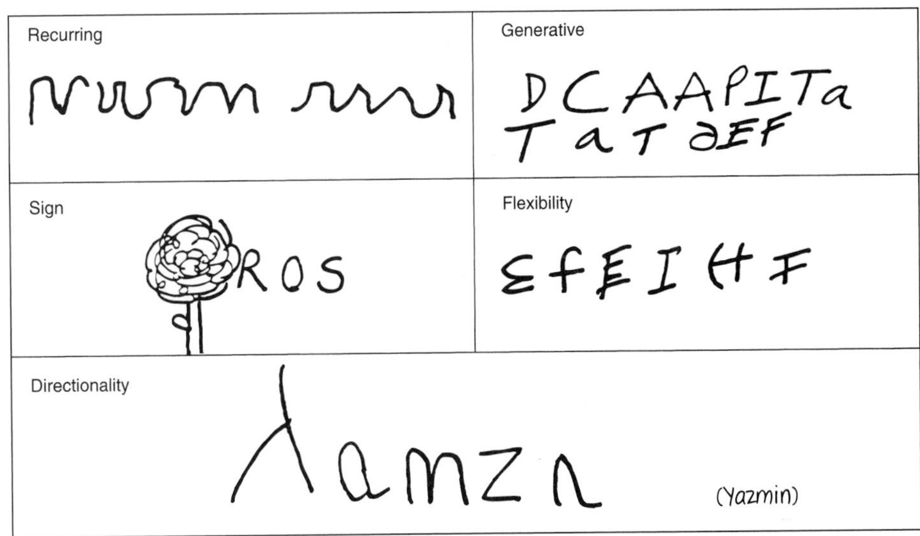

FIGURE 4.2
Examples of Principles of Written Language

Generative Principle

As children notice more of the detail of writing, they use several letters repeatedly (often letters in their name), but vary the patterns or combinations. This suggests their observation of the variety of arrangements of letters in words.

Sign Concept

Children must come to understand the arbitrary nature of signs in written language, in contrast to graphic representations, which are not arbitrary. To facilitate communication, people who use a particular language agree to use the same word to label a particular object or idea. For example, we agree that in English, "cat" will stand for a four-legged animal with fur that purrs and meows. The choice of the letters *c-a-t* is arbitrary. The choice is not necessarily related to the object itself (cat), but speakers of English agree to let the letters *c-a-t* represent the real animal, just as a picture of a cat represents the animal.

Flexibility Principle

In the natural world an object can change its orientation and still be that object. A cup can be turned upside down, but it is still a cup. However, if the letter *b* is turned upside down it becomes a *p.* In English, we name letters by their position in relation to other letters. In addition, the same letter *b* can be written in different fonts or styles of print, which adds to the potential letter forms that children must come to acknowledge as *b.* As children begin to discover this flexibility in print, they will experiment with various symbols to see which are allowable in English. For example, upon discovering that some letters can be made by adding horizontal lines (*I* can be made by adding a horizontal line to *T*, *E* can be made from *F*) , children experiment with horizontal lines on other letters (can lines be added to *H* or *L* to make other letters?).

Directionality

English writing is linear—left to right and top to bottom on a page. The orientation of letters to one another is important. Letters must face in a particular direction on a page. Letters must be in a particular order to make words. Children will draw on the knowledge they gain from reading print as they discover principles of directionality when they write.

As we begin to engage children in writing, we model a variety of purposes for writing, ways that writers think as they compose, how writing can be organized, and the need for convention in writing that it is intended to communicate. Shared and interactive writing are excellent ways to begin to develop children's acquisition of knowledge about written language and to support their progress toward independence as writers.

Take a moment to reflect on your theory base for shared and interactive writing . . .

Shared writing

- is a joint composition between children and teacher,
- is assisted writing, with the teacher recording the jointly drafted composition,
- engages children in different types of thinking, depending upon the nature of the composition,
- supports children as they explore the use of new vocabulary in meaningful contexts, and
- adapts easily to the needs and interests of the children.

Shared writing becomes interactive when we share the pen and have children write all or portions of a text. It engages children in refining concepts about words in print and letter–sound knowledge.

Shared/interactive writing is valuable because it:

- emphasizes communication,
- links communication skills,
- is purposeful and functional, and
- can become personalized text for shared and/or guided reading.

Shared/interactive writing supports and extends children's thinking by helping them

- retain memories of experiences with the world,
- re-collect memories/experiences,

- re-create memories from firsthand knowledge,
- re-construct ideas by arriving at new understandings of past experience, and
- re-present new knowledge or understandings.

Classroom experiences with writing can show children that writing is

- a symbolic code that must be mastered,
- a medium through which they may communicate,
- an end product to be achieved,
- an active process of constructing meaning, or
- a combination.

To be successful readers and writers, children must understand several principles that govern print in English:

- The same shapes appear over and over in words (recurring principle).
- Letters can be arranged in a variety of ways (generative principle).
- Specified letters, in a particular order, have been arbitrarily chosen to stand for a particular object (sign concept).
- Although letters can be written in different font styles and still be the same letter, we cannot change the orientation of a letter in relation to other letters (such as turn it upside down, *b–p*, or add additional lines to a letter, *C–G, T–I*) without making it a different letter (flexibility principle).
- Print must always be written left to right, top to bottom on a page; left page is written before right page; letters in a word are always written left to right (directionality principle).

Putting Theory into Practice . . .

Anything that teachers and children think and talk about in the classroom provides possibilities for shared/interactive writing. It is a matter of what we want to show children about how and why we put ideas on paper.

POSSIBILITIES FOR SHARED/INTERACTIVE WRITING

In the opening vignette, Renee uses shared writing to help children express their observations of a frog in the classroom. She shows how a teacher can guide and extend children's thinking. The resulting writing is a good example of descriptive thinking that is written down. What other options might we have for using shared/interactive writing? Can children express what is being learned or explore their ideas through shared/interactive writing? Can we use shared/interactive writing to help children organize their thinking about what they are learning?

Composing as Expressions of Learning

Shared and interactive writing can serve as an expression of learning. Consider the following examples provided for each grade level.

Kindergarten

- Kindergarten children express what they have learned about farm animals as they create a farm mural with animal names and the sounds each animal makes (see Figure 4.3).
- Kindergarten children explain facts they have gathered about wolves and bears, as they look and listen during read-aloud.

First Grade

- First-grade children chronicle the events of a pumpkin activity that involved categorizing, weighing, and measuring in math (see Figure 4.4).
- First-grade students compose a thank-you letter to a local business after a field trip.

FIGURE 4.3
Kindergarten Interactive Writing—A Portion of a Farm Animal Mural

FIGURE 4.4
First-Grade Interactive Writing—Retelling Sequence of a Math Lesson

Pumpkin Math

Yesterday we worked with pumpkins.
First, we sorted them by size.
Second, we sorted them by long and short stems.
Third, we counted them by twos.
Then we made sets of 15 pennies to buy a pumpkin.

FIGURE 4.5
Second-Grade Shared/Interactive Writing—What We Know about Lightning

Lightning

Lightning is electric. It can be very dangerous. Lightning goes zig zag. It hits tall things first. Sometimes lightning strikes trees and starts a fire.

Second Grade

- Second-grade students state names and definitions of solid geometric shapes being studied to create a classroom display.
- Second-grade students record details about lightning (see Figure 4.5).

Third Grade

- Third-grade students create their own legend about why the owl is awake at night, as a model for personal legends that each child will write as culmination of a unit about nocturnal animals.
- Third-grade students begin a class list of ideas they already know (K) and what they want to learn (W) (the beginning of a K-W-L) as they begin a study about their community. Later they will state what they learned (L) (Ogle, 1986).

Composing as Organization of Thinking

The process of creating a shared or interactive experience can serve as an excellent model for ways to organize thinking. Consider the following examples for each grade level.

Kindergarten

- Kindergarten children make a list of farm animals and the sound that each can make, adding to the list with each book that is read aloud during a farm unit.

- Kindergarten children retell the tale of *The Three Little Pigs* as practice for a class play.

First Grade

- First-grade students collect important details from a read-aloud spanning several days, organizing details into a story summary.
- First-grade students develop accurate retellings of the scientific method followed in a class experiment.

Second Grade

- Second-grade students use a Venn diagram to compare and contrast the attributes of frogs and toads during a unit about amphibians.
- Second-grade students develop a chart to compare the use of literary elements (plot, characters, setting) in several versions of a favorite fairy tale.
- Second-grade students participate in the labeling of a frog drawing prepared by their teacher to "see" what they know, and still need to learn, about frogs.

Third Grade

- Third-grade students develop a chart to organize such questions as "Where Does Our Garbage Go?" in preparation for beginning personal research.
- Third-grade students develop a chart to connect ideas about a text, *The King of the Beasts,* in preparation for writing an essay stating and supporting a personal opinion in response to the text (see Figure 4.6).

In each case, the teacher makes a decision about the importance of the thinking to be done by the children and the need to share in the actual writing. When one goal of the writing is for children to write independently, teachers tend to engage children to "share the pen." From the previous lists, it is apparent that anything that we can think about and talk about with children can become a shared writing experience. Each of the resulting products is then displayed somewhere in the classroom. The text is revisited by the class and by individual children as they "read the room."

If we want to engage children in such assisted writing experiences, how do we develop meaningful experiences from which children can learn about print?

GROUPING FOR THE COMPOSING PROCESS

Shared/interactive writing can be used with a whole class, small groups, or individuals. The grouping we select depends on our purposes for instruction, the needs of our children, and the demands of the shared texts we are using. In Renee's classroom, the composition about the frog comes from the whole class, because Renee believes that the experience is best suited to whole-group interaction. At times, Renee provides a whole-group experience and discussion, but

FIGURE 4.6 Third-Grade Shared/Interactive Writing—Organizing Ideas for Literature Response

Text:	King of the Beast
Introductory Statement	Our favorite character is the elephant.
Appearance & Characteristics	His nose looks like a trumpet. He is fast and strong. He is fat and huge.
Opinion	We like the elephant because he is rough and tough.
Evidence	In the story, he stomped on the ground and picked up the lion and spun him around and threw him away.
Concluding Statement	We think the real king of the beasts is the elephant.

saves the composition and follow-up for small groups in which she can better observe the children.

Early in the school year, emerging and developing readers benefit from the safety and security of whole-group situations. They also benefit from the attention they are able to receive in smaller groups. Whole-group and small-group compositions provide a variety of benefits.

Whole-group composition

- is excellent for introducing children to shared writing and reading,
- makes efficient use of time,
- can be followed up in small groups as needed,
- is excellent when writing is being used as a supplement to other reading/writing activities, and
- gives children equal opportunity to learn.

Whole-group composition also allows children to hear many other ideas and compare their ideas with those of others, but it does not allow for all children to contribute to the dictation.

Small-group composition

- provides more personalized attention,
- can be of mixed ability or similar ability,

- can be compared between groups that compose about the same topic,
- allows teachers to observe student interactions more closely, and
- allows more children to contribute to a dictation.

Individual compositions may also be undertaken, but are extremely time consuming and do not provide the benefit of joint thinking between children. Once we have a composition, we begin thinking about ways to extend children's interactions with the text. In the following sections we explore extending shared/interactive writing experiences.

Word-processing programs can also support group composing (Grabe & Grabe, 1985). Small-group and individual compositions are possible at individual workstations. Children can gather around the workstation as the teacher types their words. Large-group compositions are displayed by linking the computer to a television monitor, which makes text large enough for all to see. Children are still able to observe the left-to-right, top-to-bottom progression of text on the screen as it is typed; however, the formation of letters cannot be observed, which may be a drawback for emerging readers. One advantage of working with word processing is the ease of making changes in a composition and duplicating text for children to work with on subsequent days.

ORGANIZING SHARED/INTERACTIVE WRITING EXPERIENCES

Shared/interactive writing weaves life experience and oral language together with modeled writing to provide reading materials that are personal and meaningful for children. To use shared/interactive writing effectively, some basic steps are important to include in instruction. For example, think back to the vignette of Renee's first-grade classroom at the opening of this chapter. During the shared/interactive writing experience, Renee provides opportunity for:

- a meaningful shared experience,
- talk about the experience to organize thinking and prepare for writing,
- shared composition between teacher and children,
- writing modeled by a more knowledgeable other,
- writing by children, assisted by the teacher to focus on language principles,
- shared reading, discussion, and rereading of a text, and
- follow-up activity to extend the learner's interaction with text.

Meaningful Shared Experiences

Rich experiences such as observation of the frog are easily retained and motivate children to develop understanding. Units of study—drawn from the school curriculum, academic standards, and children's experiences—serve as a base for developing children's understanding about the world. Renee plans connected learning experiences, such as integrated or thematic units, to provide multiple experiences for exploration. In-depth learning experiences enable all her children to build or broaden background knowledge.

Talking about Experiences and Ideas

Renee believes that talking through experiences supports children's developing language for a particular concept or topic. If children can easily talk about a concept, Renee finds that the children are more likely to be able to read and write about that concept also. Renee encourages much talk prior to writing because she believes that this talk serves as a verbal composing process. Through verbal composition, children rehearse the ideas they will write. Rehearsal, with Renee's assistance, provides children with practice in regulating their thinking about the ideas that will be written.

Shared Composition and Modeled/Interactive Writing

By the end of first grade, Renee hopes that children are able to compose simple descriptive or expository texts about familiar topics, personal narratives, or a friendly note. To encourage such compositions, she must model how to think about and organize ideas. While the class talks about and Renee begins to record ideas, she talks aloud about ways that writers think and what writers might need to know about various forms of writing. Renee must also support children's developing concepts about language principles such as how we write words, how letters are formed, sounds that letters represent, and predictable patterns that we can expect in English.

When the writing begins for the frog composition, Renee models how to use print to express ideas. As Renee records the children's ideas, typically she:

- solicits ideas from the children about what to write,
- repeats the sentence that was suggested and confirms its accuracy with the children,
- thinks aloud to nudge children's thinking about the composition,
- says each word aloud before she writes it,
- names letters as she writes each word, thinks aloud about sound patterns that are heard, or invites children to offer information about known letter–sound patterns,
- reads the complete sentence and asks children to check the accuracy of its content, then
- rereads the complete sentence encouraging children to join the reading, then
- begins the process again for the next idea.

When appropriate, Renee moves beyond shared writing to an interactive experience. She invites children to provide the letters that represent known sounds, leaving space for sounds that were unfamiliar (*th__r*), and fills in letters for sounds that are unfamiliar to the children (*th ei r*).

Shared Reading, Discussion, and Rereading of Text

Shared/interactive writings become shared readings. After the initial composition is completed, Renee rereads the entire text. She asks children to listen carefully and watch as she points to the words that are read aloud to be sure that the ideas expressed are what the class intended. Asking children to give such attention to accuracy of recording acknowledges the importance of the text's meaning to the learner. Once a text is read in its entirety, several rereadings follow with children joining the reading as Renee points at each word in the text. Composing the text and participating in several rereadings makes the text familiar and predictable to the children.

Over the next several days, Renee invites children to participate in shared rereadings of the text that was created the first day. As individual children read, Renee adjusts the level of her support to the needs of each child

- Some children still need Renee to lead the reading by pointing to each word and softly reading aloud with the child close behind.
- Other children were ready to take the lead and the pointer, pointing to words and reading aloud with the rest of the group joining in.
- Still other children read aloud as Renee points to the text, needing her support only on occasional words.

To support comprehension development, Renee guides children to predict, read, and prove (Stauffer, 1975) their thinking just as they do with other pieces of literature.

Extending Interaction with Text

Over the remainder of a week Renee brings children back to a text they have written to provide repetition that is needed to increase children's knowledge of fundamental reading processes. Renee chooses follow-up activities that fit her purpose(s) of instruction, are appropriate for the shared composition, and support the level of children's development as readers.

Renee provides several duplicate copies of the shared writing. The copies are used at various times to:

- read and illustrate the main idea or favorite parts,
- cut apart sentences to reconstruct the text (see Figure 4.7),
- underline known words in the text, then place particular known words on small cards that become part of a child's personal bank of words, and
- add a copy to individual folders of past shared/interactive writings.

In addition, Renee also provides extension activities that utilize art, handwriting, and game activities. At the art center, children paint pictures of frogs. The bottom of the painting paper is folded under. After the painting is completed, Renee unfolds the paper and records children's ideas about their painting. The paintings are displayed around the room. Children are encouraged to read each other's dictations and to find words they know in the dictations. To help the children who need practice with their handwriting, Renee duplicates sentences

FIGURE 4.7
Sentences for Reconstructing Text

Frogs can jump a long way.
Frogs jump with their back legs.
The back legs get all stretched out.
The front legs are not for jumping.
We jumped like frogs.
We pushed with our legs.

from the shared writing and provides space for children to practice writing the words, leaving spaces between words.

We jumped like frogs.

Renee also uses several familiar game formats such as concentration, go fish, and basic board games to develop practice activities for sight vocabulary, letter–sound knowledge, and patterns within words. Shared writing is a versatile approach to teaching writing and to reinforcing reading. In the next section we explore a variety of ways to set up the classroom for shared/interactive writing and to develop specific skills and strategies.

EXPLORING COMPOSITION PROCESSES

In Renee's first-grade classroom we observe how she provides children with the opportunity to explore their ideas about the frog experience. We also know that shared/interactive writing can be used to create a composition that helps children consider how writers organize and express ideas, particularly in specific narrative genre or information structures.

We can expand our understanding of the possibilities of assisting children's developing knowledge of composing processes by visiting Brad's second-grade classroom. The children have just finished reading and rereading *The Ugly Duckling* by Hans Christian Andersen, retold by Karen-Amanda Toulon (Silver Burdett Ginn,

1993) in their basal reader. The class has been discussing characteristics of fairy tales and how the authors of retold versions sometimes make changes in the story.

The children are interested in writing their own retold version of a fairy tale. Brad wants to nudge the children to consider the characteristics of fairy tales so that their retold versions will have appropriate characteristics of the genre. He decides to use shared writing to model thinking about fairy-tale characteristics and support children's attempts to retell the story of *The Ugly Duckling.* The dialogue from the children is a composite of many children's ideas.

Brad: Before you write your own a fairy tale; maybe we should write one together. Hmmm. We're going to write a fairy tale, but what makes a good fairy tale? When I'm reading a fairy tale, I feel like I know the characters.

Children: You can tell real easy who is good and who is bad.

Children: Yeah, and people act just like you think they will.

Brad: That's good thinking. I'll write your ideas here so we can use them later on. (Brad writes both statements off to the side of the chart.) I think when people act just like I think they will, I'm not really surprised by the ending of the story.

Children: Yeah. The good characters usually win. (Brad records off to side of chart.)

Brad: Yes, that's what I think too. Is that what happened in *The Ugly Duckling?* Were we surprised by the ending?

Children: No. (Brad records to side of chart that ending is not a surprise.)

Brad: If we are making our own version of *The Ugly Duckling,* what are the things we want to remember to put in our story so we are sure it is a fairy tale? Think about the ideas that have been suggested. (He points to notes on side of board.)

Children: Our ugly duckling has to be really good and the other ducks need to be bad!

Brad: Yes, usually in a fairy tale we care about the good character. We don't want anything bad to happen to that character. Do you feel that way about a character in *The Ugly Duckling?*

Children: Yes, the ugly duckling. (Brad records to side of chart that children care about character.)

Brad: So, at the beginning, do we want to let everyone know who the good and bad characters are? How can we do that? How should we write that part?

Children: We could write, "Once there was a mother duck who was waiting for her eggs to hatch."

Brad: (repeats child's statement) Is that what you want me to write? Does that sound like the beginning of a fairy tale?

Children: Yeah, or we could say "once upon a time"—fairy tales can start like that too.

Brad: (Class settles on the second suggestion and Brad records, then reads back to group to confirm.) What else do we need in our beginning to make it sound like a fairy tale?

Children: "Out came five yellow ducks and a big ugly gray duck."

Brad: How does that fit with our first sentence?

Children: Good. . . . Write that next. (Brad writes and reads aloud.)

Brad: Remember what we are trying to show (points to side notes), that we need good and bad characters.

Children: We could write, "The other ducks picked on the gray duck. He felt ugly so he ran away."

Brad: (repeats children's statements) Does that help our fairy tale? (Based on responses, Brad records both statements, then reads back all that has been written so far.) Okay. Do we have good and bad characters yet?

Children: The ducks are bad.

Brad: (to the class) Do you agree? And do we have a good character?

Children: The ugly duckling.

Brad: How will other people know that the ugly duckling is our good character?

Children: Because the one who gets picked on isn't bad. The ugly duckling didn't do anything to the other ducks.

Brad: Hmmm. When I read fairy tales, there is usually a character that I am rooting for, one that I want to win. For me, it is the ugly duckling. I feel bad that he is picked on and I want things to be better for him. What do you think?

Children: (responses generally concur)

Brad: Then we will need to be sure that we help our good character be the winner in the end. What are some other things we want to have happen in our fairy tale?

The conversation and writing continue as the teacher and children complete the introduction of the characters, develop the events in the middle of the plot, and bring the fairy tale to a close with the triumph of the ugly duckling becoming the most beautiful swan on the lake.

The class continues to work out their ideas and Brad records what the class decides to write. When the fairy tale is complete, the class reads and rereads it. The composition serves as a model experience for writing fairy tales. Later Brad uses the shared composition to compare it with the version in the basal reader. He models strategies for saving ideas by writing notes to the side of the chart.

POSSIBLE FORMS OF SHARED/INTERACTIVE WRITING

Brad used shared writing to model the organization of a literary genre, fairy tales. Renee engaged her children in writing a description of frog movements. The variety of writing that can be modeled through shared or interactive writing is endless. We can model composing processes for literary genre, information text structures, and the functional types of writing we encounter daily. We can also use shared writing to model how authors develop particular literary elements within a composition.

We expose children to a great deal of literature, predominantly narrative forms. We know, however, that information text is structured differently than narrative and is filled with details and concepts that are often new to children. Using a shared writing to explore information text structures, and functional writing which also tends to be informational, can help children retain, re-collect, and reconstruct what they know in disciplines such as science (Daniel, Fehrenbach, & Greer, 1986; Laminack, 1978) and mathematics (Ferguson & Fairburn, 1985).

The possibilities for shared/interactive writing include, but are not limited to:

Literary genre—writing in other genre, such as:

fairy tales	realistic animal stories
folk tales	humorous stories
fables	autobiography and biography
mysteries	realistic adventures
animal fantasies	people fantasies
everyday realism	poetry

See the Handbook of Children's Literature (Appendix A) for a discussion of the characteristics of various genres.

Literary elements—exploring specific literary elements, such as:

- creating a plot with a beginning, middle, and end,
- introducing the problem of the plot,
- building progressively to a climax,
- resolving the problem of a plot, and
- introducing a main character.

See Appendix A for a discussion of the characteristics of various literary elements.

Information texts structures—exploring different informational text structures, such as (Kinney, 1985):

description	compare/contrast
order/sequence	cause/effect
problem/solution	question/answer
explanations	

See Appendix A for discussion of information text structures.

Functional writing—exploring various forms of functional writing that we encounter daily:

lists	notes
clusters	annotated drawings
charts	graphs
labels	explanations
descriptions	record of events

See Chapter 6 for a more detailed discussion of functional writing.

Innovations—Innovating on patterned texts with which children are familiar:

Shared writing enables teachers to make children's versions of predictable books by using children's language to complete the author's pattern. For example, in *It Looked Like Spilt Milk* (Shaw, 1947) the pattern is:

Sometimes it looked like a _____,
But it wasn't a _____.

Through shared composition children create a new text using their language and the author's pattern. The teacher serves as scribe. Shared innovation provides a model for individual innovations during guided and independent writing.

ADDITIONAL IDEAS FOR SHARED COMPOSITIONS

Shared/interactive writing can also be used to prepare and support children's learning in other literacy activities:

- *Building background before reading.* Experiences to build background knowledge and, particularly specialized vocabulary required for fluent reading, can be recorded through shared writing as children re-collect and re-construct their knowledge in preparation for reading. Reading the shared text, which is familiar, rehearses vocabulary and concepts needed in the basal text.
- *Making predictions before reading.* Prediction is encouraged to help children mentally prepare themselves for reading. After previewing the text, record and read back children's predictions. Return to the shared writing to confirm or prove predictions during and after the reading.
- *Responding to the reading.* While children are acquiring fluency as writers, you can encourage response to text by using shared writing to record children's general and specific responses to reading. Typically responses are discussed. Recording responses preserves children's thinking for use on subsequent days.
- *Retelling the story.* Retelling enhances children's comprehension of stories (Morrow, 2001). Verbal retellings are excellent for helping children rethink a story and decide about the most important elements. Shared/interactive writing is an excellent way to preserve the retelling which can reinforce concepts of plot, provide a copy for comparison to the plots of other stories, and provide a model for independent written retellings.
- *Group literature log.* A big book that simulates an individual literature log can be kept in the early stages of literature study to model the possibilities of literature logs, such as responses to literature and collecting words that are of interest to the group.

- *Literature mini-lessons.* Children's literature provides excellent examples of the variety of options open to writers. We can provide short, focused lessons for children, often called mini-lessons, to teach children about specific aspects of literature, reading, and writing. Samples of mini-lessons can be found in Chapter 7, which focus on using children's literature for reading instruction. Shared/interactive writing, on charts and on overhead projectors, becomes an essential tool for helping children process their thinking about the content of the literature mini-lesson.
- *Making strategy use explicit.* When we want to support children's developing understanding of the strategies that they use to read more effectively, we can do more than discuss these strategies with children. After discussion of how children used a particular strategy, we record children's definition of the strategy, when it should be used, and how it helps a reader to use the strategy. These charts are displayed in a visible area and can help to reinforce children's use of reading strategies.
- *Group K-W-L charts.* K-W-L (Ogle, 1986) is a strategy to help children prepare for and focus their attention for learning. Space is provided on a chart to record:

  K = What We Know,
  W = What We Want to Know, and
  L = What We Learned or Still Need to Learn.

  K-W-L charts can also be individual charts depending upon children's experience as writers. The teacher makes a large class chart and records children's dictations in the appropriate area. Reading and rereading occur as children use the chart throughout the unit of study.

- *Adapting difficult information texts.* Information books are often too difficult for children to read independently. Shared/interactive writing can be used to create information texts that are within reach for primary-grade children. We read and discuss information books that provide information that children are interested in knowing. We can begin to record their ideas about the relevant content and add new information to the shared/interactive chart over a number of days as reading and discussions continue. Read and reread charts as new information is added. We then make individual shared/interactive charts or individual books that can be read by the children. Books, made from shared/interactive compositions by small groups and individuals, can be sources of new information with a familiar vocabulary. When a unit of study is completed, content shared/interactive books can be placed in the class library for checkout and at-home reading. This approach has been used successfully in first grade (Siera & Combs, 1990).
- *Developing labeled drawings.* The day before the discussion of information about a topic is to begin, we lightly sketch an outline of our subject, such as a salamander, on a large piece of chart paper and have made notes around the edge of the chart or on "sticky notes," to remind

> us about the facts we wish to discuss with the children. As we engage children in talking about the subject, such as salamanders, we begin to "fill in" the sketch with a marker. We encourage the children to talk about what they know and, as they do, we add the information to the drawing. Children help decide where and what information should be recorded. The completion of the drawing involves the re-collecting and re-presenting what we know about a topic.

With the completion of a composition, we must then consider how to best use that composition to extend children's interactions with print, as well as reading and writing processes. We know that extending interactions provides opportunities for all children to add to their knowledge about reading and writing. Renee extends interactions through rereading, and guided and independent activities with both the original and duplicated copies of the text. How might we make decisions about the ways that we extend interactions with texts? We can draw many ideas from our discussion of shared reading in Chapter 3. Shared compositions can become shared readings, and include all of the types of text extensions we are able to do with text.

EXTENDING INTERACTIONS WITH THE ORIGINAL TEXT

Once the composition is complete, the following activities are appropriate to use with the rereading of the text in a teacher-guided group:

- *Editing text.* To promote comprehension of text, children have the opportunity to edit the text with the teacher. As children carefully reread, they are asked—sentence by sentence—if there is anything about the text they want to change. Edit emphasizes both meaning and correctness. Reasoning for a change or no change is discussed.
- *Concept of word in print.* Child points to text while other children read aloud, matching spoken words with text. Teacher notes accuracy of match. When asked to find a word that should be familiar, child is able to pick out the word. Teacher notes whether the child is developing sight recognition of the word and could find the word without rereading from the beginning of the text.
- *Guided rereading.* Teacher guides reading by asking children to predict, read, and prove their predictions. Even though the text is known, attention to thinking and making meaning should be stressed.
- *Use context, oral cloze.* Teacher hesitates before a key word and children can verbally supply the word. Teacher asks what clues are used to identify the word.
- *Use context, written cloze.* Teacher blocks or masks a word, exposing only the beginning sound(s), children supply the word and tell how they know. A sentence can also be taken out of context and written on the chalkboard.

  We pushed with our l_____.

- *Sight words.* Children use a "magic window" (heavy paper rectangle with a word-size window in the middle) to read words in isolation as sight words (see Figure 4.8).
- *Recognize letters.* Children find multiple examples of a letter in a chart to reinforce letter recognition (see Figure 4.9). Write words on the chalkboard, children circle the target letter(s) in each word and also identify capital and lowercase forms of letters that appear in the text.
- *Letter–Sound patterns.* Depending upon children's word knowledge, use the text to identify particular letter–sound patterns (such as *fr* or short *a*). Write the words on the chalkboard, read in isolation, listen for sound pattern, look for visual pattern, reread in context.

FIGURE 4.8
Magic Window for Sight Word Practice

FIGURE 4.9
Finding Letters in Text

Find "f"

Frogs

Frogs can jump a long way.
Frogs jump with their back
legs. The back legs get all
stretched out. The front legs
are not for jumping. We
jumped like frogs. We pushed
with our legs.

- *Structural patterns.* Depending upon children's word knowledge, use the text to identify appropriate structural patterns. For example, in the frog story, the base word *jump* appears with different inflected suffixes (*jumped, jumping*). Group activities would be selected based on children's background experiences with print and their familiarity with the text.

EXTENDING INTERACTIONS WITH DUPLICATED TEXT

After the text is composed and read on the first day, we can make individual copies of text for the children. For future reference, we want to be sure to date each text. These copies may be typed or handwritten in manuscript. The text should be written in the same format as the original text. Duplicate copies can be used for the following:

- *Rereading.* Practice reading as a group, with a partner, or individually. Cut up and match sentences, phrases, or words to an intact copy (see Figure 4.2). Cut up and reconstruct the original text or revise in a form that makes sense (see Figure 4.2). Make a personal collection of cumulative shared texts for each child. Make a class booklet of shared texts to place in the library corner for independent reading.
- *Class-made big book.* After a text has been composed, read, and discussed, it can be written on separate pages for children to illustrate the next day. The big book can be read by small groups or the whole group, then placed in the library corner for all to enjoy. At-home reading of shared texts, alongside commercially published texts, validates children as authors.
- *Responding to text.* Illustrate the text by leaving space at the top of the copy or make a personal booklet from the shared text by cutting apart text and gluing it on separate pages to create a book which may also be illustrated.
- *Sentence building.* With words from the text, children build meaningful phrases and sentences to practice with sight words and reinforce their knowledge of the syntax of our language. Stauffer (1975) suggests giving children a word-card holder made of flannel-covered cardboard, on which to arrange word cards. Desktop size or 9" × 12" is sufficient. The felt will help to keep the cards in place as children construct phrases and sentences. An individual pocket chart could also be used as children construct text (see Figure 4.10).
- *Word building.* Use letter cards to build words from the text. Focus on letter–sound or structural patterns when possible. Build a rime (*-og*), then add the onset (*fr-*) to complete the word. Build a base word (*frog*), then add a suffix (*-s*) to make a related word (*frogs*) (see Figure 4.11).
- *Word sorts.* Both open and closed words sorts (see Chapters 8 through 10 for more detail) may be done with words that have been accumulated from shared texts. Children determine categories in open sorts, but we determine categories in a closed sort. Word sorts may be

FIGURE 4.10
Sentence Building—Build Sentences from the Text or Create New Ones

Frogs	jump	can	a	long
way	with	their	back	legs
We	jumped	our	like	pushed

FIGURE 4.11
Word Building—Frog, Frogs, Jump, Jumps, Jumped, Jumping

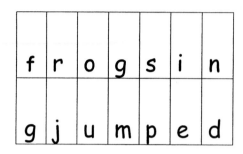

f	r	o	g	s	i	n
g	j	u	m	p	e	d

by meaning or characteristics of words, phonic, or structural patterns. Hall (1981) suggests a variety of meaning sorts as:

descriptive words	food	compound words
naming words	colors	feelings
action words	people	sports
interesting words	animals	science words

- *Word bank books.* Small books can be made out of blank paper, folded, and stapled, with a child-decorated cover. Children write one word bank word, or a meaningful phrase or sentence on each page. The phrases/sentences could have been constructed during the sentence-maker activity. Each page can then be illustrated and taken home to read to parents. Books with a theme can also be made following sorting activities.
- *Magic window words.* Use an index card, with a word-size window cut out of the center, to isolate and read words in the duplicate shared text. Children can test themselves or a partner on sight words.
- *Word searches.* Children enjoy finding their words in other published materials such as newspapers, magazines, and children's literature. These words can be recorded in a list or cut out for sharing.
- *Word posters.* Words can be cut out of newspapers and magazines and used to make word posters. Stauffer (1975) suggests that word posters have a focus or theme, such as words for colors, words for people, *-ing* words, or words that begin like *frog* (*fr*). Word posters can be individual or group. Individual posters can be kept in children's shared writing folders until they are filled. Group posters can be prominently displayed in the classroom so that children can add to the posters as words are found.

- *Picture dictionary.* To stimulate an interest in words, children can keep personal dictionaries where they collect words they want to learn to read and/or spell. A folder of twenty-six pages of blank or lined paper, one for each letter of the alphabet, can become a picture dictionary. When a word is added, children may make a small illustration to remind them of the word.
- *Word wall.* A word wall can be thought of as a group word bank. Words that are common to most individual word banks or commonly needed for writing activities can be drawn from shared texts, placed on large cards, and added to a word wall. It is helpful for the words to be related in some way such as theme (frogs), type of word (verbs), or spelling pattern (__*og* words).
- *Games.* Many common and commercial game formats can be used to extend children's work with words. Lotto (like Bingo), Go Fish, Concentration, and jigsaw puzzles can be made into extension activities.

Once students have been introduced to cutting/reconstructing text and checking self-knowledge of known words in a shared text, these activities can be completed independently with follow-up by the teacher. These are but a few of the possibilities for extending shared texts and children's interest in words. Children will be successful in extension activities if they have adequate practice in appropriate-level activities.

From the ideas and activities discussed in this chapter it is clear that shared/interactive writing is an engaging way to model writing processes and develop accessible reading materials for all students. Composition may be made with the whole class, in small groups, or with individual children. Any topic in our knowledge is a topic about which we can write. The important consideration is that the topic is meaningful to the children and one that is worth preserving for future rereading and rethinking.

ASSESSMENT: MONITORING CHILDREN'S DEVELOPMENT IN SHARED/INTERACTIVE WRITING

Shared/interactive writing provides opportunities for use to observe children's development of:

- knowledge of ways to organize writing,
- how to include appropriate ideas and content in writing,
- use of conventions in writing,
- showing voice in writing,
- ability to reread for meaning, and
- ability to attend to details and patterns in words.

We know that shared/interactive compositions serve as a model for writing. As we compose with children, we should carefully observe the level of their engagement, their thinking that is evidenced by personal contributions, and their interactions with text during rereading and extension activities. Shared/interactive writing is integrally linked to shared, and possibly guided and independent, reading. Children demonstrate their learning from shared writings through subsequent shared readings.

Shared writing will model composing processes for children. Interactive writing will directly engage children in the composing. To observe the full effect of such modeling and engagement, we must observe children during guided and independent writing, as discussed in Chapter 6. We look for evidence of their developing knowledge of the composing process, of the traits embodied in good writing (e.g., organization, ideas/content, voice, conventional use of language). A discussion of writing traits can be found in Chapter 6.

Writing development occurs slowly, over time. Consequently, our observations must also be over time, keeping in mind the changes we observe and making records to accurately recall those changes. A sample form for recording such observations is provided in Figure 4.12. Such record-keeping forms should be developed to fit the particular behaviors that a teacher desires to help children develop and the curriculum standards adopted at a particular grade level.

RESPECTING DIVERSITY WITH SHARED/INTERACTIVE WRITING

In shared/interactive writing, the text comes from the children. The content of the text relates to children's interest and knowledge of a topic. These factors make shared compositions an excellent approach for reading and writing instruction in a diverse classroom. The flexibility of grouping, the nature of the content, and the length and complexity of the text are easily adjusted to the needs of the learners.

Respecting the Language of the Learner

Seeing one's own words in print is affirming. ESL learners understand material that is culturally and/or experientially familiar to them better than they understand unfamiliar content (Barnitz, 1986; Rigg, 1986). The personalized nature of shared/interactive writing provides the opportunity to develop reading materials that are familiar to children for whom English is a second language (ESL). Sharing stories from children's culture provides excellent content for shared writings (Rigg, 1989). The oral language used during shared compositions represents the language patterns and content over which ESL children have control. Compositions should affirm children's ability to communicate their thinking.

Shared writing is appropriate for use with ESL children, with a few modifications. For example, children can illustrate words that are being added to their word bank. We should encourage children to draw a small picture on the back of each word bank card to provide an association with the word. Content words, words that can be pictured, will be most useful in early reading instruction.

We should encourage retellings of well-known stories and information. After reading a text that children enjoy, we encourage children to retell the most im-

Name ______________________________ **Shared/Interactive Writing**

Shared Compositions	**Usually**	**Sometimes**	**Rarely**	**Comments:**
Contributes ideas/content to composition.				
Contributes ideas for organization to composition.				
Demonstrates knowledge of composing processes.				
Demonstrates knowledge of voice by expressing ideas in personally unique ways.				
Attends to the recording of ideas.				

Interactive Compositions	**Usually**	**Sometimes**	**Rarely**	**Comments:**
Contributes ideas/content to composition.				
Contributes ideas for organization to composition.				
Demonstrates knowledge of conventions—letter–sound knowledge to write words.				
Demonstrates knowledge of conventions—capital letters and punctuation.				
Attends to the recording of ideas.				

Read/Reread Text	**Usually**	**Sometimes**	**Rarely**	**Comments:**
Rereads composition, using knowledge of composing process.				
Tracks text while rereading.				
Demonstrates concept of word in rereading.				
Uses familiar context to predict words in text.				
Finds details in text.				
Reconstructs text from sentences, words.				

Developing Word Knowledge	**Usually**	**Sometimes**	**Rarely**	**Comments:**
Adds sight words to writing vocabulary.				
Adds sight words to reading vocabulary.				
Demonstrates knowledge of letter–sound patterns in words.				
Demonstrates knowledge of structure units in words.				

FIGURE 4.12
Record Keeping for Shared/Interactive Writing

portant parts. The language of the retelling will be simplified when compared with the text. We record the retelling and use it for instruction, especially if the original text was not a repetitive patterned text. Sheltering the English of a text and using a simplified version for instruction can be successful with ESL children (Treadway, 1993).

Respecting Special Learning Needs

The personalized nature of shared/interactive writing is an excellent approach for working with children who have special learning needs (Bowyer, 1988; Ewoldt & Hammermeister, 1986). For learners who have special needs, emphasis might be placed on individual compositions. Shared writing results in personalized reading materials. Individual compositions can provide reading material that is appropriate to the needs and interests of the learner. Careful observation during rereading helps us identify strategies that individual readers use successfully and those strategies that are absent or misused. Comprehension is supported by the child's firsthand knowledge of the text. Learners who experience difficulty with decoding text are also supported by familiar content as decoding skills are practiced.

Respecting the Thinking of the Learner

Recording children's language also shows them that their ideas are important and valid. Small-group and individual dictations are especially important in this respect. The smaller the group, the greater the likelihood that individual children will find their ideas reflected in print. They will hear their ideas read aloud by others.

Respecting Experiential Background

Shared texts grow out of classroom experiences and the interests of the children. The flexibility of shared compositions enables the teacher to engage children in writing and reading about experiences that are shared by the class, as well as those that are known and valued by individuals.

Take a moment to reflect on putting theory into practice with shared and interactive writing . . .

Shared/interactive writing experiences can help children:

- capture expressions about what they are learning, and
- use writing to organize their thinking.

We can group children for the composing process in a number of ways:

- Whole-class groupings use time efficiently, enable all children to participate and learn from one another, and enable the teacher to make observations across the class.

- Small-group compositions provide more personal interactions and possibilities for cross-group comparisons of the compositions.
- Individual compositions are personal and can be adapted to individual interests and learning styles, but can also be time-consuming.

We organize shared/interactive writing experiences by:

- providing meaningful shared experiences,
- talking about the experience to organize thinking and prepare for writing,
- sharing the composition between teacher and children,
- modeling writing by a more knowledgeable other,
- children, assisted by the teacher, focusing on language principles,
- shared reading, discussion, and rereading the text, and
- providing appropriate follow-up activities that extend the learner's interaction with the text.

Shared/interactive writing can be used to explore a variety of forms of writing, such as:

- literary genre,
- information text structures,
- literary elements,
- functional writing, and
- innovations on text.

Extending interactions with the original text can provide the following:

- A myriad of activities with both the original text and duplicated copies of the text
- Activities that address most all aspects of reading and writing processes

Careful observation of children provides assessment information concerning their developing understanding about:

- composing processes,
- their ability to use knowledge of print to interactively compose a text, and
- their ability to use knowledge of a text for fluent rereading.

Respecting diversity involves the following key concepts:

- Using children's language in shared compositions respects and validates children.
- Shared compositions can reflect the diverse interests and backgrounds reflected in the classroom.
- Sheltered texts can be composed and used for shared and guided reading.
- The size of the composing group can be adjusted to meet children's needs.

YOUR TURN . . .

1. Imagine that you are in a primary-grade classroom where children are learning about insects. What types of shared and interactive writing might you create with the children? Brainstorm ideas with a peer. Which topics would be best as shared writing? as interactive writing? as a combination?
2. Return to the second-grade composition about lightning presented earlier in the chapter. After the composition is complete, how might you extend children's interactions with this text? What activities might you do with the original chart? What activities might you do with duplicated copies of the text? Provide support for your choices.
3. Return to the first-grade composition about pumpkins. Imagine that it is late October of first grade. If you invite children to write portions of this text interactively, to share the pen and write words on the chart paper, which words might be most appropriate for first-grade children to attempt to spell? Which words might be sight words by this time of the school year? Which words might have beginnings and endings that children will know? Which words have letter patterns that some children might know? Provide support for your thinking.

Aa Bb Cc Dd Ee Ff Gg Hh Ii Jj Kk Ll Mm

CHAPTER

5

Guided and Independent Reading

Adding to our literacy framework . . .

	Reading Aloud	
Shared Reading	**Balanced and Integrated Literacy Framework**	Shared and Interactive Writing
Guided Reading		Guided Writing
Independent Reading		Independent Writing
	Literature Study	
	Word Study	

In this chapter, we . . .

- Explore the difference between guided and independent reading.
- Consider how to set up for guided reading experiences with small groups of children with similar needs as readers.
- Consider how to set up a reading environment that supports and encourages independent reading.

Oo Pp Qq Rr Ss Tt Uu Vv Ww Xx Yy Zz

Focus Literature:

- *Three Little Ducklings*
- *Sylvester & the Magic Pebble by William Steig*

Looking into Classrooms . . .

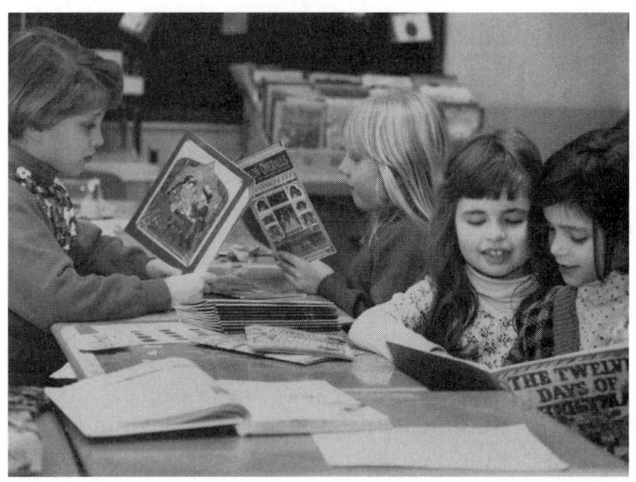

Katarina and four of her first-grade children are sitting at a small table along the side of the classroom. The other children in the class are engaged in independent rereading of familiar books and in activity centers which contain tasks the children can complete independently.

Katarina selects a text she thinks is appropriate for the skills and strategies of these four children. For about twenty minutes, she introduces the book in an engaging manner and assists the children in previewing the book in preparation for guided reading. The children then begin to read the book for themselves while Katarina listens in on each child's reading. These first-grade children still read orally as they read to themselves.

Katarina notices that several words are a struggle for the children. She carefully observes which strategies the children are able to use by themselves. She assists only after a child seems unable to use his or her own skills and strategies successfully. After the reading is a short response time, followed by a focus on a teaching point, which today is ways to decode the contraction I'm, *and the suffixed word* yelled. *Katarina will emphasize how children can monitor their own decoding of such words.*

Building a Theory Base . . .

The more we practice something, such as a sport or a musical instrument, the better our chances of improving our performance. It stands to reason, then, that children who spend a great deal of time practicing reading in the early phases of reading development have an increased chance of becoming fluent and skilled readers. To encourage this development we provide daily opportunities for children to spend significant amounts of time in guided and independent reading.

In the previous chapters we explored ways to provide assistance to all children in a classroom as they learn about print. Although reading aloud, shared reading, and shared writing are important parts of a balanced and integrated literacy program, it is through guided reading that we truly come to know children as readers, giving us a window into their thinking as readers. It is through independent reading that children have the opportunity to come to know themselves as readers.

WHAT IS GUIDED READING?

In contrast to whole-class shared reading, we can see that guided reading occurs in small groups with the support of the teacher:

> Guided reading is a context in which a teacher supports each reader's development of effective strategies for processing novel texts at increasingly challenging levels of difficulty. The teacher works with a small group of children who use similar reading processes and are able to read similar levels of text with support (Fountas & Pinnell, 1996, p. 2).

During guided reading a more knowledgeable other becomes a bridge between the child and a particular text. The adult mediates, assisting the child in linking from what is known to what is new. Guided reading is a key component in any balanced literacy program. It is through guided reading that we come to truly understand children as individuals and how to mediate, or support them, as they move toward independence. Fountas and Pinnell (1996) remind us, "It is through

We should provide careful guidance for children's reading every day. What can we learn as we listen to them read texts that are appropriate to their level of development?

guided reading, however, that teachers can show children how to read and can support children as they read. Guided reading leads to the independent reading that builds the process; it is the heart of a balanced literacy program" (p. 1).

WHAT IS INDEPENDENT READING?

Independent reading is our best opportunity to evaluate the effectiveness of instruction. What children demonstrate during independent reading, without our mediation, are the skills and strategies that are truly their own. It is through independent reading that we can evaluate our effectiveness as teachers. Consider the following classroom example.

> All of the children in Lon's third-grade classroom read independently for twenty to thirty minutes every day. He takes great care to help children learn how to select books that are "just right" for them, books that present a little challenge but not too much. Lon continually builds the classroom library and guided reading group book tubs (plastic tubs filled with familiar books and unfamiliar books of similar levels) to have ample materials from which children select independent reading material.
>
> Over the course of the school year, Lon teaches short lessons about selecting books that fit independent reading—books that allow children to read fluently and enjoy the chosen text. Most children read silently, while a few others whisper read (moving their lips and/or whispering the words). During the reading each day, Lon moves around the room, sitting briefly by a number of children and listening in on what is being read. He uses this time to assess the match between child and text, and measure each child's independent fluency.

Don Holdaway (1984) states: "Traditional practice assumes that independence is a step to be reached after learning to read rather than an integral process within early learning" (p. 5). Isn't independence our goal for all children? To get started in guided and independent reading, we must consider several issues: selecting appropriate texts, matching children with appropriate texts, preparing for small-group instruction, and preparing children for sustained independent reading.

SELECTING APPROPRIATE TEXTS

It is important that we carefully select texts for guided and independent reading through which children can be successful. Fountas and Pinnell (1996) suggest the following factors be considered in selecting appropriate reading materials: length of text, size and layout of print, illustration support, vocabulary and concepts, text structure and genre, language structure, and predictability and pattern of language. When taken together, these factors should guide us as we select and sequence texts in a balanced and integrated literacy program.

- *Length of the text.* Emerging readers should begin with short, simple texts. Developing and transitional readers slowly progress to more challenging books that provide added challenge. Varying the length of texts that are of similar difficulty can help children learn to sustain their own reading. Length of text is also dependent upon the amount of text on a page.

- *Size of the print and layout on the page.* The size of print and amount on a page should match children's visual acuity and ability to process print. For emerging readers, the placement of print on the page should be predictable, such as print appearing on each page below the illustration. As children gain experience with print, it is possible to select books in which print appears in various placements from page to page. Children who understand the rules about the placement of English print on pages of text can handle greater variation in print placement, particularly novel formats such as cartoon style.
- *Illustration support.* Illustrations, including photographs, not only add interest to a text, but can also provide clues to the meaning of the print on the page. Illustrations that cue the key words in a predictable pattern provide excellent support to emerging readers. It is important to select texts for novice readers that are clear and enhance the contents. Illustrations may also support children's development of new understandings, especially in information texts. As the complexity of text increases, illustrations begin to be replaced by descriptive language. Transitional readers begin to understand and use description in place of illustration.
- *Genre and text structure.* Children learn to appreciate the various types of writing that expand their knowledge of what is possible in books. Exposure to a variety of genre also meets the range of children's interests. Some genre, such as information text, may be more challenging for children because their knowledge of a topic or organization of the ideas is unfamiliar. Regardless of genre, texts should be "information-rich texts" (Clay, 1991, p. 262), enhancing children's ability to make meaning.
- *Language structures and concepts.* The closer the match between a child's knowledge of language and the language structures of a particular text, the easier it is for the child to understand the ideas and concepts presented by the author. Sentence structures that are uncommon in a child's language background will present challenge, which at times may be too much to overcome. For example, texts that are written for children in New Zealand typically contain vocabulary and phrases that are not widely used in the United States. We must be sensitive to children's language knowledge and select texts for which they have sufficient background to connect to new ideas they will encounter. Texts that are "information-rich" provide illustrations and explanations that are clear and easy to understand.
- *Predictability and pattern of language.* Repeated patterns of language, along with rhythm and rhyme, provide predictability and support to young readers. Easy text has strong patterns from page to page that emerging readers use to make predictions about the text. As text loses strong patterns, children must rely more and more on their own ability to decode text and make connections with an author's ideas.

- *Linking learning experience through text selection.* The more that we link learning experiences about a particular topic, genre, or author, the more that children are able to bring to the reading. Texts that are related in some way provide natural links for children's thinking. Related vocabulary appears in more than one text. Children have background knowledge and experience to connect to the ideas in a text. Providing opportunities to hear about ideas in read-aloud, write about those ideas in shared writing, and read about similar ideas in guided and independent reading can dramatically increase a child's opportunity to learn.

Many publishers provide readability ratings for texts to indicate a level of difficulty. A readability rating, such as 2.0 or beginning second-grade level, is an attempt at an objective prediction of level of difficulty. A readability formula may simply compare length of sentences with number of complex words in the text. Other methods of calculating readability may consider some of the factors as discussed. Considering the previous factors, our overall assessment of a text may result in a different rating of difficulty than we find for texts in a published reading program. After careful consideration, we should trust our judgments of text difficulty because we take the needs of specific children into consideration. Publishers do not know our children.

Using these factors should allow us to select and sequence texts for guided and independent reading. Of course, the best way for us to judge the appropriate selection of texts is to observe children as they read those texts. By what criteria can we judge our selections? Let us consider variations in matches between children and text.

MATCHING CHILDREN AND TEXTS

In the classroom, we select texts for children to read and we help children learn to select their own texts. We want children to be successful in their reading. Therefore, it is important that we consider the varying levels of text difficulty that are possible when finding suitable materials for children to read. Levels of challenge of reading texts are described as follows:

- Listening level—the highest level at which a listener can hear and make adequate meaning from a text read aloud by another
- Frustration level—high challenge and without high motivation from the reader; may be too difficult for making meaning
- Instructional level—some help needed from a more knowledgeable other to make adequate meaning
- Independent level—low challenge level and can be understood without additional support

These levels describe the challenges that an individual child may have with a text, not the level of the text itself. As we match children with texts, a particular text may be independent for one child but frustration for another. It all depends on a child's knowledge of print, reading processes, and the ability to effectively self-monitor meaning making.

Listening Level

Listening level is typically described as the level at which children can hear and understand the majority of a text, especially with our support. During read-aloud we serve as the decoder, the one who translates the symbols into the language we understand. Children are not asked to decode text. Instead, children use their background knowledge of the content and language to make their own personal meaning. Interaction with a more knowledgeable other during read-aloud—a teacher, for example—provides opportunities for discussion and clarification. This interaction assists children with filling in gaps in their understanding of a text.

It is possible, however, that we may select a text that is so challenging that no amount of interaction and support can help children find meaning. In general, children should be able to listen and comprehend approximately 75% of a text, without our assistance. Children's listening levels can indicate a level at which they can make meaning with the ideas in a text. Having a sense of each child's potential as a reader helps us set appropriate expectations as we plan for reading experiences.

Frustration Level

In contrast to listening to text read aloud, frustration level text is too difficult for children to read themselves or with our support. Frustration may come from an inability to decode a sufficient amount of the text and/or difficulty linking the essential ideas for making meaning. It requires great effort to sustain one's self in a text in which many ideas are only partially understood. If we select frustration level text for children to read, their motivation to deal with the text may not be high enough to avoid harmful effects such as loss of confidence. The development of self-monitoring strategies will not develop in this level of text; in fact, they may actually be thwarted.

In general, text is considered frustration level if, unassisted, children accurately recognize less than 90% of the words and understand less than 75% of the ideas presented. Even with our support, children may not be able to achieve enough understanding of such text to make reading worthwhile without repeated exposures. Text that we use for shared reading may begin as frustration level, but through repeated exposures children's interactions with those texts take on the characteristics of instructional, and even independent, level texts. Considering a child's zone of proximal development (ZPD), frustration text is often beyond this zone. With our support and repeated experiences with a text, children's knowledge of a text grows and they are able to begin to interact with words and ideas in the text with greater accuracy.

Instructional Level

When children have support as they work with a text, they can tolerate a margin of error or inaccuracy and still learn from the text. With support of a more able reader, children will be able to use what they know to fill in missing ideas from the text. Developmentally, we typically think of this level as having sufficient challenge to motivate learning, without being either too easy or too difficult. Instructional text typically falls in the middle to upper end of a child's ZPD.

Children working with instructional level material know enough of the text to be able, with our help, to fill in from their own background to make sufficient meaning. The assistance of a more able reader, usually the teacher, provides support at key points to help students use their knowledge appropriately. Working at the instructional level, with appropriate guidance, allows readers to learn from errors, which they may then practice at an independent or recreational level.

In general, text is considered instructional if children are able to read 90% to 95% of a text and comprehend 75% to 90% of the ideas without our assistance. Through interaction with a more knowledgeable other, children are able to approach independence in text. We use this level of text in guided reading, when we teach children something new about reading processes and strategies and provide supported practice.

Independent Level

Independent text requires very little effort for children to be successful. Extensive reading at this level builds confidence in readers, habituates decoding, and moves many competencies to an automatic level. Extensive experience with independent level text encourages fluency and the control of reading strategies. Independent text represents the lower end of a child's ZPD, the area in which no assistance is needed by a more knowledgeable other. Text at this level enables children to use strategies that move them toward unconscious control and become automatic.

When children read text that is at their independent level, their comprehension and word knowledge is almost completely accurate. They know enough to fill in missing understandings without the aid of a more knowledgeable reader. Developmentally, children need opportunities to spend time in reading tasks that present relatively few challenges. If reading is always a struggle for new readers, they may never build the stamina to persevere with difficult text.

Reading in this level should take place during independent reading times in the classroom when the purpose is successful practice and enjoyment. Teachers often refer to these independent reading periods as uninterrupted sustained silent reading (USSR), sustained silent reading (SSR), or drop everything and read (DEAR).

Comparing Levels of Text

Different levels of text serve different purposes for readers and require different levels of motivation for successful use. We might summarize the match between readers and texts as follows:

Text Level	Purpose	Motivation Required
Listening	Feel potential as a reader	Medium challenge
Frustration	Stretch, test self	High challenge
Instructional	Learn with help	Medium challenge
Independent	Practice, teach self	Low challenge

Emerging readers are making the transition from oral to written language and read with support from a more knowledgeable other. Children in this stage should read highly predictable texts, which may begin as frustration level in shared reading but become instructional and then independent through supported repeated readings. Shared and interactive writings, which are children's own compositions, are quite familiar and offer ease for practice. Texts for guided reading should fall within the instructional range, offering some challenge that is supported by assistance from the teacher. Assisted rereading of these texts quickly allows them to become independent for children. During some quiet reading times, emerging readers may challenge themselves by selecting frustration level library books, which they may have heard read aloud.

Developing readers, children who are becoming more independent as readers, need some instructional level challenge, with the remainder of the day spent in independent level materials. Remember, they are working to gain control over print and need the confidence with text to be willing to persevere. We might describe developing readers as children who are read instructional level texts that are between middle first-grade to late second-grade level. Frustration level text may be self-selected during quiet reading times, but will not be very helpful in gaining control. Shared writing and reading, with supported rereadings of text, provide access to texts that become independent.

Transitional readers, those who know quite a lot about print, are ready to sustain more challenge with guidance or with highly motivating self-selected materials. To help them solidify silent reading, we should be sure they spend much of their day with instructional and independent materials that offer "controlled challenge." We might describe transitional readers as children who read instructional texts that are late second-grade level and beyond. Transitional level children have established effective strategies for making meaning. They are able to learn new skills and refine old ones when the amount of challenge is monitored.

Read-aloud and shared reading are typically whole-class contexts for learning. Guided reading, however, requires a small-group setting for careful observation of children. What factors should we consider as we form small groups for guided reading instruction? Does it matter how we group children?

THE NEED FOR FLEXIBLE GROUPING

As we come to know our children as readers, we are able to form smaller groups for guided reading. These groups consist of children who, at that point in time, are at a similar level of reading development and will benefit from a guided reading experience in the same text. These small groups serve a particular purpose and complement the mixed ability groupings of read-aloud, shared reading, shared or interactive writing, and other learning experiences such as literature circles and theme units that we will discuss in other chapters.

If we intend our smaller groupings to enhance children's development, we must carefully monitor those groupings. Ample evidence suggests that low-ability groupings that are static can impact children's opportunities to learn (e.g., Allington, 1977; Allington & McGill-Franzen, 1989) and damage self-confidence and self-esteem (e.g., Filby, Barnett, & Bossart, 1982). We serve the needs of children best through flexible groupings, including a combination of whole-group instruction and needs-based smaller groups.

How do we achieve flexible, dynamic groupings? Continuous assessment is the key. Our observations of children's behaviors during a variety of reading contexts help us determine the span of a child's zone of performance in a variety of reading situations—the range from independent to instructional to frustration. We conduct running records, making visual records of a child's reading (see the Assessment section later in this chapter). As children demonstrate new skills and strategies, we adjust our groupings. Our groups should always, to the best of our ability, reflect children's current level of functioning.

We want children to become independent readers who find pleasure and satisfaction in reading and are able to monitor their own performance as readers. Children who are motivated to read stand a good chance of becoming lifelong readers. To support children's reading of text we must consider the strategies readers use to make meaning with text and how the level of difficulty of a text may affect the reader.

DEVELOPING STRATEGIC READERS

Strategic readers use knowledge of language and reading processes deliberately, yet flexibly, at appropriate times and under a variety of conditions (Paris, Wasik, & Turner, 1991). Experienced readers integrate use of language cues to make meaning and check understanding of text. As readers, we process language with the help of three cueing systems: meaning, structure, and visual (Clay, 1991).

Meaning cues, or semantics, enable us to use the general sense or meaning of written or spoken language to determine either the meaning of an unknown word or the overall meaning of a piece of text.

Example: Sherlock Holmes, a famous detective, could *crack* criminal cases better than anyone else.

We use our knowledge of what detectives do to determine that *crack,* in this context, probably means "to solve".

Example: *Cinders,* like pieces of red-hot sand, began pouring out of the volcano.

We use information provided by the author (between the two commas) to determine a meaning for the word *cinders.*

Structure cues, or syntax, draw upon our knowledge of the rules and patterns of language to aid in identifying an unknown word or word part by the way it is used in a text.

Example: The noisy carts ______ the street woke ______ the people in ______ houses.

Our knowledge of familiar English phrases and how words can be arranged in sentences enables us to fill in the missing words.

Example: John ran so hard that when he reach__ the store, he stop__ at the door to catch his breath.

Our knowledge of verb forms helps us supply the missing word parts.

Visual cues, or grapheme–phoneme correspondences, draw upon our knowledge of letters and letter patterns and the possible sounds they may represent.

Example: The police *officer* stopped to help.

If we read *man,* instead of *officer,* we may look back at the text because we realize that the word on the page was much longer than the word we thought of and it also began with the letter *o,* not *m.*

Competent readers use meaning, structure, and visual language cues in an integrated manner to make meaning. Which cue(s) a reader uses at any one time depends upon the type of text being read and the reader's purpose for reading that text. Selecting the most appropriate cues to make meaning at the appropriate time is called *strategic reading.*

Marie Clay is a respected educator who researches reading processes among young children. As the title of one of her books suggests, Clay (1979) believes that learning to read involves the "patterning of complex behavior." Through her research, she has identified strategies that children must learn to use effectively if they are to become competent readers. Clay describes these strategies as "in-the-head" operations that "allow a learner to use, apply, transform, relate, interpret, reproduce, and re-form information for communication" (Fountas & Pinnell, 1996, p. 149). Clay believes that, over time, readers establish inner control over reading processes.

Experienced readers draw upon knowledge of language and processes involved in reading, as needed, to make meaning and to monitor understanding of what is being read. The language cues that are used during reading are drawn from semantics (meaning cues), syntax (the structure or grammar of English), and grapho-phonics (the visual cues of print connected to the sounds that those letters can represent). As experienced readers, we use our knowledge of the topic about which we are reading and our knowledge of what we must do as readers to make sense. We use our knowledge of language to decide if what we are reading sounds like the way we say things in English; and, of course, we look for details in print to decide if the words we see in the text look like the words that we are thinking about.

Some strategies we use help us maintain fluency, some enable us to detect and correct errors as we read, and others enable us to problem-solve new words (Fountas & Pinnell, 1996). These strategies may involve *monitoring* ourselves as we read, adjusting our rate to the type of text we are reading and to our purposes for the reading. To make meaning we may draw upon what we know from various sources of information. When we realize that meaning has broken down, we *search* for sources of information that may have been overlooked and may help to repair meaning. We may use our knowledge of the topic, the meaning and structure of language, and/or visual cues from the text itself. When we use several of these sources of information together, we *cross-check.* As we discover what our error in thinking is, we try to *self-correct* to restore meaning.

Because strategy use involves "in-the-head" processes, we are not able to know exactly how a child is thinking while he or she reads. We are able, however, to model, encourage, and support the use of strategies for meaningful reading. Then we observe children's reading behaviors and the miscues they make during reading as a window into children's thinking about reading (Goodman & Burke, 1970).

MOVING TOWARD INDEPENDENCE

We support children's strategy development in order for them to become independent readers.

We know that next to being read to, independent reading is the most important way that children can spend their time if they are to become fluent, competent readers (Center for the Study of Reading, 1990). Regardless of the organization of our literacy program, independent reading should be a daily occurrence in the classroom.

There are worthwhile benefits from independent reading:

- The more words that pass in front of a reader's eyes the greater the opportunity for a child to become a better reader (Allington, 1977).
- One-third or more of vocabulary growth can be accounted for by independent reading (Center for the Study of Reading, 1990).
- Reading skills can improve significantly if children read independently for at least ten minutes per day or one hour per week (Anderson et al., 1985).
- A child's attitude toward reading also improves through self-selected independent reading (Tunnell & Jacobs, 1989).

It is fluent independent reading that typically becomes the motivator for the development of personal reading. Holdaway (1980) tells us that in the acquisition of independent skills, children become their own monitors and critics. They practice repeatedly to gain control over the task and find pleasure and satisfaction in being able to perform it. Their practice is usually at a level that provides little challenge so skills can become automatic. Children must have some control over reading tasks to let their natural desire to monitor and critique their own performance be developed.

Our best opportunities for observing children's reading behaviors and their developing control of strategies are during guided and independent reading. We select texts carefully during guided and independent reading. We select texts that offer some challenge, but not too much. We want children to successfully practice using reading strategies as they develop the inner control that is needed for competent reading. How can we structure learning experiences in small groups and independently so that we support children's developing knowledge about reading processes and the strategies they can use to successfully monitor their own reading?

Take a moment to reflect on your theory base for guided and independent reading . . .

Guided reading is

- small-group reading instruction,
- assisted by a more knowledgeable other,

- using text that is accessible, with some support, to the child, and
- an opportunity to carefully observe children's oral fluency and use of strategies.

Independent reading is

- individual practice in reading,
- unassisted by the more knowledgeable other in the classroom,
- using text that is accessible, without additional support, to the child, and
- an opportunity to carefully observe an individual child's oral fluency and use of strategies.

We select appropriate texts for guided and independent reading by considering:

- length of the text,
- size of the print and layout of the print on the page,
- how well the illustrations support making meaning with the print,
- organization of ideas in the text and their accessibility to children,
- structure of the language and the way in which concepts are presented to children,
- predictability of ideas in the text based on patterns in the language of the text, and how well the text supports and extends concepts being taught in the classroom.

The match between a child and the text they read is an important consideration:

- Independent text is easily accessible for a child, without additional support.
- Instructional text is accessible for a child, with some support.
- Frustration level text is not accessible to a child without intense support by the teacher or high motivation to succeed by the child.
- Listening level is that level at which a child can hear text read aloud and can understand a majority of the ideas in the text.

The manner in which we group children for guided reading must be flexible, constantly adjusted as assessment data indicate a need for change.

Strategic readers use meaning, language structure, and visual cues to continuously monitor the meaning they find in a text.

We support children's progress toward independence in reading when we provide ample time and appropriate materials for reading in independent level text.

Putting Theory into Practice . . .

It is appropriate to consider how the ideas discussed thus far in the chapter can be applied in a classroom setting. In the remainder of the chapter we focus on planning and implementing guided and independent reading experiences in the classroom. We turn our attention first to issues of guided reading. What factors must we consider to plan successfully for children? How do we organize instruction? How might guided reading change as children acquire knowledge as readers?

ENGAGING CHILDREN IN GUIDED READING EXPERIENCES

To understand some of the dynamics of guided reading instruction, we return to Katarina's first-grade classroom while she is working with a small group of children who are preparing to read a short text, *Three Little Ducklings* (created by the author for demonstration, see Figure 5.1). This small book has eleven pages of text, with two to three sentences per page. Three little ducklings get tired from swimming all day and have a funny thing happen while they are sleeping. There is a pattern throughout the book of the first, second, and third duckling responding to a situation, such as being sleepy or needing help.

Observing a Guided Reading Lesson

The guided reading experience that Katarina prepares includes the following steps:

- Teacher and children preview the text to notice unique features.
- Children individually read the text while the teacher listens.
- Teacher engages children in a follow-up discussion and selected teaching points.

Previewing the text:
Katarina engages the four children in considering what they think little duck might do. She shows the front cover of a small book and says, "The title of this book is *Three Little Ducklings.* What is a duckling? Do you see a duckling on the front cover?" The children all point to the picture of the ducklings and let Katarina know that there are three present.

Katarina opens the book and begins to turn the pages, inviting children to observe the illustrations and comment on ideas they have about the story. The story line of this book is quite predictable, with repetition of the actions of the first, second, and third duckling. The class has worked with ordinal numbers (first, second, third, . . .) in math, but Katarina wonders if the children will pick up on those words in this text. For one illustration, she points to the first duckling and asks, "What is the first duckling doing? And the second? And the third?" (Katarina will listen during the reading to see if this is helpful to the children's decoding.)

Katarina is also wondering if the children will be able to decode a new word, *tickle,* that is critical to the humor of the story and also the resolution of the story's problem. When she turns to the page where the word *tickle* is first introduced, Katarina calls attention to the fact that one character, the mother duck,

FIGURE 5.1
Sample Text for Guided Reading
Three Little Ducklings

Three Little Ducklings	Once upon a time, there were three little ducklings. They liked to swim, and swim, and swim all day.
"Time to eat," said Mother Duck. So the three little ducklings went home to eat supper. They were very hungry.	The first little duckling said, "I'm sleepy." The second little duckling said, "I'm sleepy." The third little duckling said, "Me, too!" So they all went to sleep.
In the morning Mother Duck said, "Time to get up." The three little ducklings could not get out of bed. All of their feet were stuck together.	"Where are **my** feet?" asked the first little duckling. "Where are **my** feet?" asked the second little duckling. "And where are **my** feet?" asked the third little duckling.
"I need help," said the first little duckling. "I need help, too," said the second little duckling. "Help!" yelled the third little duckling.	"I can help you," said Mother Duck. She took a big feather from her tail. "I will tickle your feet with the feather," said Mother Duck.
Tickle, tickle! The first little duckling laughed. "Here are **your** feet," said Mother Duck.	Tickle, tickle. The second little duckling laughed. "Here are **your** feet," said Mother Duck.
Tickle, tickle. "He, he, he," laughed the third little duckling. "And here are **your** feet," said Mother Duck.	"Thank you, mother," said the first little duckling. "Thank you, mother," said the second little duckling. "Oh, thank you, mother," said the third little duckling.
	"You are welcome," said Mother Duck. Then they all went for a swim.

has a large feather. She says, "This is Mother Duck. What do you think she might do with this feather?" The children are unsure, so she turns the page to reveal an illustration that causes the children, in chorus, to say, "Tickle their (the ducklings) feet." Katarina holds her copy of the book closer to the children and asks them to identify a word they think might be the word *tickle*. The children identify the first two words on the page that both say "tickle," but one begins with a capital *T*. Katarina wants to be sure that the children are aware that whether written with capital or lowercase letters, the letters *t-i-c-k-l-e*, spell the word *tickle*.

Reading the text:
Katarina now provides individual copies of the book for each child, encourages them to reread the title, then to proceed at their own pace through the first reading of the text. As the children begin to orally read, Katarina listens in for a while to each child's fluency and use of strategies to produce an accurate and meaningful rendition of the story. Today Katarina asks Christiana to sit at the end of the reading table so that Katarina can make a record of her reading in this text. Ben finishes the story before the others, so Katarina encourages him to enjoy rereading the story while the others finish.

During the reading, Katarina notices that several of the children have difficulty with the contraction *I'm* (e.g., I'm sleepy), so she decides to make that a teaching point for the day. She believes that the children know contractions in oral language, but perhaps are not as sure about them in print.

Follow-up discussion and teaching points:
After the reading, the children share their enjoyment of the story—how silly it is that the three little ducklings got their feet stuck together. The children also think it is funny that Mother Duck pulls a feather from her tail to tickle the little ducklings. Katarina encourages a retelling of the text to get a sense of how well the children followed the sequence of the story. Frequently she engages children as a group in retelling, then encourages individual children to retell the story on their own. Retelling builds a framework for telling stories. Katarina finds that verbal retellings provide support for written retellings of stories and the composing of children's personal stories. Then Katarina turns the children's attention to using their knowledge of print to figure out unfamiliar words in a story.

***The contraction* I'm:**
Based on her observations of children's reading that day, Katarina decides to focus attention on a contraction that appeared in the text and seemed unfamiliar to the children. Returning to page 3 in the text, Katarina calls attention to the first sentence on the page,

> "I'm sleepy," said the little duckling.

Once again the children struggle with *I'm* or read it as "I am." Katarina uses magnetic letters on a metal baking sheet to spell the words *I am.* She asks if children can read the two words. Then she replaces the letter *a* with an apostrophe and pushes the letters together into one word. Again she asks the children to read the word, moving her finger from left to right under the word. Then, Katarina gives each child the letter cards:

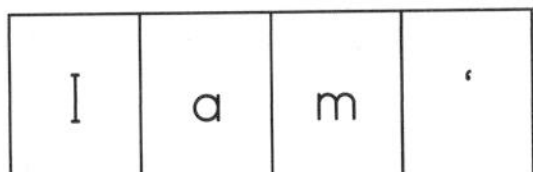

I am = With Katarina's support, each child builds the words *I am.*

I 'm = Then the children remove the letter *a,* and replace it with an apostrophe.

I'm = The children push the letters together to spell the word *I'm.*

Katarina asks each child to read the contraction, moving a finger under the word from left to right. The children mix up the letters and repeat the exercise. Katarina explains to the children that they know many other contractions in talking, but do not always recognize the same contractions in writing. She helps the group think about other common contractions. Katarina writes those contractions on a small white board that she keeps at the reading table. In upcoming texts, Katarina will watch for other contracted forms of words to gradually introduce children to this base + base configuration. After word building, Katarina asks the children to begin on page 1 and scan the text for the contraction *I'm*. The children find two examples on page 3.

***Base + inflected suffix,* yelled:**
Katarina had already decided on another teaching point in this text. She did not think the children would be confident about the word *yelled* on page 5 of the text and she was right. The sentence in the text says:

"Help!" yelled the third little duckling.

ell	With magnetic letters Katarina builds the word chunk *ell.* She reminds the children that they have seen this chunk in other words and encourages them to decode the chunk.
bell	Then she places the consonant letter *b* in front of the chunk to make the word *bell.* Katarina asks, "What word do we have now?" The children respond with "bell." They have encountered this word before.
well	Katarina exchanges the *b* for a *w* and asks, "Now what word is this?" The children respond with "well."
yell	Next, Katarina exchanges the *w* for *y* to make *yell.* The children know the consonant sound that *y* can represent, and respond with "yell."
yelled	Finally, Katarina asks, "What if I put the suffix *-ed* on the end of *yell.* What word do we have now?" Two of the children are quite confident that the new word is pronounced as "yeld," while one child thinks it might be pronounced "yell-ed," making a second syllable, *-ed.*

If this teaching point occurred later in the school year, when the children had acquired several other *-ed* words in their reading vocabulary, Katarina would discuss the three possible pronunciations for the *-ed* suffix (*raked* /t/, *yelled* /d/, *wanted* /ed/), but she thinks it is not yet time for that discussion. Instead, Katarina does the following:

- She asks the children to return to page 5 in the text and encourages the children to consider how they can use their knowledge of language to decide the right pronunciation for *yelled.*
- She asks, "Which word sounds right in the sentence?"—" 'Help!' yelled (d) the third little duck." or "Help! yell-ed the third little duck."
- The children decide that "yelled," not "yell-ed," sounds right. The children think that pronunciation sounds like the way we talk in English. Most of the children say that *yelled* is a word they have heard before.
- She reminds the children that sometimes they can figure out which way to pronounce a word they are unsure about by asking themselves if the word "looks right" and "sounds right" when compared with the text.

For two days Katarina engages the children in reading and rereading *Three Little Ducklings.* The children have the chance to explore other aspects of the text, then the book is placed in the group's book box or book tub for independent reading practice. In addition to guided reading each day, the children also spend twenty to thirty minutes each day rereading familiar books in their group's book tub to build their fluency and confidence as emerging and developing readers.

How did Katarina decide her procedures for this guided reading lesson? What steps did she take to prepare this lesson for the children?

Planning for Guided Reading

In any classroom, children's knowledge and skills as readers vary widely, and should cause us to carefully consider how we form small groups so that we can observe their progress. We need a range of texts for daily, guided reading—texts that meet the range of needs and interests of all the children. We must then question how the texts we select fit with or enhance other literacy experiences that are taking place in the classroom. Linking learning experiences increases children's opportunities to make connections, clarify their understanding, and gain confidence through practice of familiar tasks.

Setting up flexible groups:
At the beginning of the school year Katarina assesses the literacy development of her eighteen children. She evaluates what they know about letters of the alphabet and what sounds letters can represent. She assesses children's concepts about words in print and book-handling skills. She engages children individually with various levels of text to observe their concepts about handling books during reading (e.g., page turning, left page before right page) and what they know about print. For example, she introduces each child to an easy text that has a simple repetitive pattern. She watches to see whether children use the language pattern or the clues in illustrations to "read" the text. Depending upon what she observes, Katarina may use other text with slightly more complex patterns to see what children do with increased challenge. Based upon the concepts that children are able to demonstrate, she forms tentative groups of four to five children who demonstrate similar levels of development. Katarina will adjust these groups as warranted by her frequent assessments (see the Assessment section later in this chapter).

Each week or two Katarina makes a record of reading for each child to monitor development of reading skills and strategies. The reading record shows how accurately the child reads a particular text and what strategies the child employs while trying to make sense of the text. Results of reading records, and observations during guided reading and other literacy activities, provide assessment information that supports moving children between groups to better meet their needs.

Selecting texts for guided reading:
When Katarina selects texts for guided reading, she knows that the text should require children to use skills and strategies that are, for the most part, familiar and with only a few challenges. The type of challenge presented by the text should, with Katarina's support, be within reach for the children in the group. This level of text is referred to as instructional level text. To select a text that is instructional level, Katarina asks several questions:

TEXT CONTENT AND ILLUSTRATIONS

- Do children have adequate background knowledge to understand the main concepts and ideas in the text?
- Is there essential vocabulary the children may not know, but will need to make meaning?
- Are illustrations clear and reflective of the ideas expressed on the page?
- Do illustrations provide additional information and support for understanding the text?

ORGANIZATIONAL FEATURES

- Are children familiar with the manner in which text is laid out on the pages?
- Are sentence structures familiar? Will children be able to use their existing knowledge of language to understand the language of the text?

RELATION TO THE CURRICULUM

- How does the text fit in with, or relate to, the many stories, poems, and picture books we are using with the class?
- Does this text provide an opportunity to link children's learning to other literacy experiences?

Based on answers to these questions, Katarina decides whether she is able to provide appropriate support to help children use their current knowledge, skills, and strategies to successfully read the text. Her observations of the first reading confirms whether her selection is appropriate and the amount of rereading that may be necessary for children to achieve an independent reading of the text.

Guiding the Reading of Texts

Books selected for guided reading are at the instructional level of the children in the small group. While children are able to figure out much of what is in the text, we must guide children to anticipate and make sense of what is new. Before and perhaps during the reading, we provide clues for children to draw upon as they apply existing knowledge, skills, and/or strategies to make meaning from new vocabulary, sentence structure, text format, or literary device used by the author of a text. As teachers, we must anticipate children's need for guidance and support and provide assistance in anticipation of what children will do with a text.

Guiding less complex texts:
Our goal for reading should be to introduce a new book in a way that leads to a successful first reading. In the previous sections we have considered the ways that Katarina guides the reading of a fairly simple text, *Three Little Ducklings.* She provides needed scaffolding to help children have access to the text and feel

successful during the first reading. We know that most of Katarina's first-grade children are in the emerging and early developing read stage. In guided reading with emergent and early developing readers, all children read individually at their own pace, while other group members read simultaneously. We notice in guided reading that Katarina observes, prompts, and provides only the essential support that children need to read independently. In these early stages especially, we must remember that one of our main functions in guided reading is to listen to portions of the reading by each child. As we listen, we assess children's strengths and needs, we provide guidance as needed, and evaluate each child's ability to use the information we provide.

Following the reading of texts that have simple plots and little or no character development, Katarina engages children in personal response and retellings of plot. Simple stories are primarily plot, with little attention to the development of other literary elements. As stories begin to include more complex use of literary elements to tell the story, the nature of the guided reading time begins to change.

Guiding more complex texts:
In guided reading with later developing and transitional readers, we structure the reading and discussion of a text according to the way that ideas are organized in the text. Each child reads the entire text, but the teacher guides the pace of the reading, depending upon the text. Some texts are read in their entirety during the first reading, while other texts are broken into chunks to help children develop strategies for linking ideas. As children are able, reading moves from oral to silent, except when the text needs to be heard to support discussion.

Interactions between adult and child should support and extend children's thinking. Our questions and comments should "agitate" children's thinking by asking them to explain their thoughts and supply supporting evidence, which may include citing, locating, and rereading particular portions of a text. At significant points in the text, we help children connect new ideas to what they already know in order to construct a fuller understanding. Children become active readers by using their background knowledge and what they read in a text to think ahead, anticipating where the text might be going. As children read, we encourage them to pause to reflect on what they think they know, and on where they got their ideas.

As we prepare to support children's reading of more challenging text, we should:

- think about the *purpose(s)* we have for engaging children in reading a particular book,
- plan specific *strategy(ies)* to assist children as they make meaning before, during, and after the reading, and
- *reflect* on how we will adjust our support to children as indicated by their feedback during discussion.

These steps form a purpose–strategy–reflection cycle for mediated learning (Dixon-Krauss and Powell, 1995) that we repeat throughout the reading. We must be prepared to adjust the level of our assistance as children teach us about what they know and understand. We must keep in mind that our goal is to help children learn strategies that will enable them to become self-regulated readers and thinkers.

As we support children's reading and thinking through a text, mediated reading becomes a cycle of *predict–read–explain–connect.* The cycles occur because we pose open-end questions and statements that continue to nudge children's reading and thinking. In response to our questions and comments, children read text, explain and provide support for their thinking, make connections to what they already know, and think ahead about where the text seems to be going. As children mature in their reading, we promote more independent reading and thinking during mediated reading by broadening our questions and offering children more opportunity to set directions during the reading.

Guided readings of more challenging texts are planned in three segments: before, during, and after a reading. In planning each segment, we consider the purpose for using the selected book, the strategy that we will use to support children, and how we will use children's feedback to adjust instruction. As an example, a mediated reading using *Sylvester and the Magic Pebble* (Steig, 1969) follows. We ask open-end questions about the text that encourage children to use a predict–read–explain–connect cycle. Decisions about which events and story elements to emphasize result from an analysis of the selected text.

This text consists of three episodes:

- Episode 1 (pp. 1–9). Sylvester finds the magic pebble, then becomes a rock on Strawberry Hill. Introduction of character and problem.
- Episode 2 (pp. 11–17). Series of events in which Mr. and Mrs. Duncan try to find Sylvester.
- Episode 3 (pp. 18–30). Time passes. Mr. and Mrs. Duncan picnic on Strawberry Hill, discover Sylvester, and bring him back to life. Resolution of problem.

Note that the predict–read–explain–connect cycles are used throughout the mediated reading to focus children's attention on the text and to promote discussion.

Sample Mediated Reading—Sylvester and the Magic Pebble

Purpose: 1. Appreciate use of magic to develop the fantasy
2. Notice author's use of problem–events–resolution plot structure

Strategy: Use illustration and language clues to signal reader.

Essential words: *CEASED,* stone-dumb

Before reading—cover and title

Read: Look at the cover of this book and think about the title.

Explain: What ideas do you have about this book? What leads you to think that?

During reading

Predict: What do you think might happen? Let's read and find out.

Read: (begin Episode 1) Begin mediated reading by reading aloud pages 1–2 to introduce characters and Sylvester's interest in pebbles. Children follow along in their copies.

Explain:	What do you know about Sylvester so far? What makes you think that?
Connect:	What do we know about the "magic pebble," the one that we thought about in the title of the book? (nothing yet from the text)
Predict:	What do you think might happen with the shiny red pebble?
Read:	Read pages 3–5 (silently) and see what you find out.
Explain:	What does Sylvester know about the pebble? What makes you think so? (notice the use of language to describe pebble and its power)
	What do you think *CEASED* means (p. 3)? Why do you think the author printed the word in capital letters?
Predict:	What do you think Sylvester will do now?
Read:	Read pages 6–9 (silently, to the end of Episode 1, and introduction of problem) to find out.
Explain:	What do you think about Sylvester now? What parts of the story give you those ideas?
Connect:	What do we know so far? (problem is established, preparation for beginning of Episode 2)
Predict:	(begin Episode 2) Turn to page 10, notice change of setting shown in illustration, read aloud "Meanwhile back at home, . . ." (pause) Ask, What do you think might happen "back at home"?
Read:	Read pages 10–15 silently and see what you find.
Explain:	What do you think about Mr. and Mrs. Duncan's efforts to find Sylvester? What makes you think that?
Predict:	How do you think Mr. and Mrs. Duncan might be feeling after all of their searching?
Read:	Read pages 16–17. (silently)
Explain:	What did you find out about Mr. and Mrs. Duncan? What makes you think that?
Connect:	Turn to page 18 (beginning of Episode 3—resolution). Ask, What does the illustration suggest to you? What do you think has been happening on Strawberry Hill?
Predict:	(begin Episode 3) What do you think might happen now?
Read:	Read pages 18–23 (silently) to find out.
Explain:	What do you think about Sylvester's problem now? What makes you think that?
Predict:	Now that Spring has come to Strawberry Hill, what do you think might happen?
Read:	Read pages 24–27 to find out what happens next.
Explain:	What do you think about the picnic? What makes you think that? What does it mean to be *stone-dumb?*
Connect:	What do we know about the pebble's magic?
Predict:	What do you think might happen, now that the red pebble is resting on the big rock?
Read:	Read pages 28–29 to see what happens.
Explain:	What do you think about the picnic now?
Predict:	What do you think happened in the "scene that followed" (p. 29)? How do you think the story will end?
Read:	Read page 30 aloud.
Explain:	What do you think about the way the story ended? What makes you think that?

After reading

Connect:	(personal responses) What do you think about this story that William Steig told us?
Explain:	(If responses do not lead to a retelling of major events, we might ask) What did we find out about that magic pebble in the title of the book? What made us think that?
Reread:	Encourage children to support retelling by returning to the text and rereading aloud parts of text that help to explain their thinking and responses.
Connect:	Has there ever been a time that you felt like Sylvester?

Using a mediated reading experience helps us understand the meanings that children are finding in the texts they read. Making meaning is the essence of reading, and most children need daily guided experiences to help them develop their ability to understand more complex texts. We may need to guide some children through a text more than once before they will make meaningful connections with the important ideas in a text.

Now we turn our attention to the other major issues of this chapter—independent reading. How do we establish independent reading as an effective component of our balanced literacy program? How can we know that children are making appropriate selections of the texts they read independently? How can we be assured that they are really making progress as readers?

Selecting Teaching Points to Extend Skills and Strategies

A teaching point is knowledge about reading process or print that is appropriate to a particular text or children's interactions with that text. The teaching point(s) that we select to emphasize with a particular book depends on the needs of the children in the guided reading group and the demands of the text to be read. Teachers use knowledge of children's strengths and needs as readers to predict and confirm the areas in which children need the support of a more knowledgeable reader. A teaching point may also be decided after observation of children's interactions with a text.

Katarina's evaluation of *Three Little Ducklings* text led her to select several possible teaching points. Final selection of those points depended upon children's actual interactions with the text.

Sample teaching points for the text, *Three Little Ducklings,* could include the following:

- Understanding of contraction *I'm* for *I am*
- Sight recognition of ordinal number words *first, second, third*
- Noticing how dialog is presented, especially the use of quotation marks and the words that tell how someone is speaking (e.g., *said, yelled, asked, laughed*)
- Following the sequence of a plot to understand and appreciate a story
- Words with inflected suffix that signal past tense (*yelled, asked, laughed*)

We know from the lesson that Katarina chose to focus only on the contraction *I'm* and the suffix added to *yell.* We must be selective about our teaching points. We can develop other teaching points during the rereading of a text. Which teaching point(s) might Katarina select for the first rereading of *Three Little Ducklings?* At this point in first grade, Katarina's children are encountering many stories with an actual plot line and with stories told partly through dialogue. Either of these teaching points would be valuable to emphasize during a rereading when children are familiar with the story line.

We also select teaching points by considering the development of the children with whom we work. Thinking about stage of development in reading, we might consider the following teaching points:

General teaching points for emerging readers:

- Tracking words left to right on the page
- Reading left page before right page
- One-to-one matching of words being read aloud
- Using illustrations to confirm meaning
- Using illustrations to confirm key words on the page
- Predicting a key word using context and beginning letters
- Reading for sense of ideas

General teaching points for developing readers:

- Seeing familiar chunks in unfamiliar words
- Adding more to a base word (inflected suffix) to make new words
- Predicting a word using context and beginning letters, checked by meaning and/or language
- Connecting events in the sequence of a plot, either beginning–middle–end or problem–events–resolution sequence
- Identifying important details in a text
- Self-monitoring for meaning
- Cross-checking visual cues with meaning and language

General teaching points for transitional readers:

- Connecting important sequences in plots
- Understanding relationships between plot sequences and character actions
- Identifying and inferring character traits
- Identifying and inferring theme
- Identifying main ideas and supporting details
- Finding familiar chunks in unfamiliar words
- Self-monitoring for meaning
- Cross-checking visual cues with meaning and language

Many of these teaching points are introduced during whole-class shared reading, then reinforced during guided reading in instructional level texts.

Our *Three Little Ducklings* text is a simple repetitive text, suitable for first-grade-level readers. Do guided reading procedures change as we move into more challenging texts that we find at second- and third-grade reading levels?

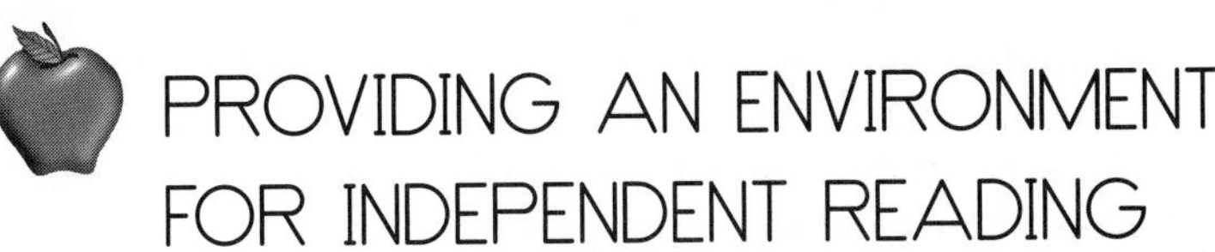

PROVIDING AN ENVIRONMENT FOR INDEPENDENT READING

Earlier in this chapter, we met Lon, a third-grade teacher who provides for daily independent reading in his classroom. What can we learn from Lon about providing a supportive atmosphere for independent reading? What does he consider as he plans for daily independent reading?

- The range of children's reading levels and interests
- A predictable time for independent reading each day
- A sufficient number and variety of quality texts that fit the range of reading levels in his classroom
- An independent reading time so to carefully observe children's progress

Lon knows that the independent reading levels of his third-grade students span from late first grade to fifth grade. How did Lon identify the level at which each child could function independently in text? During the first few weeks of school Lon listened to each child read a variety of texts at various levels. He made careful records of each child's reading, which was a difficult task. Lon had to use precious minutes when the majority of children were at recess or structured work times, when children were occupied and he could evaluate a student or two. Slowly over several weeks, Lon came to have a general idea of where his children were functioning.

Although most children cluster between late second-grade to early fourth-grade reading levels, Lon must be concerned with having appropriate materials for all his children. Thus, he must have an extensive range of books. Children in his classroom who read at third-grade level and above are typically engaged over a period of several days in a chapter book or information books. Many of their books are selected from the school's library. Children at these levels typically are engaged in a single book over a number of days. Lon is most concerned that children who read below third-grade level have books that are truly independent for them. He urges these children to reread familiar books to build fluency and confidence, especially books introduced in guided reading. In addition, he helps children identify unfamiliar books that are at approximately the same level as the familiar texts. These texts will provide some new challenges for children, but still allow them to draw upon familiar strategies to make meaning and check their understanding and ability to decode less familiar words.

While children have short periods of time throughout a day to read independently, Lon chooses to have an independent reading block each day when all children are reading for an extended amount of time. During this time he is free from other instructional activities so that he can move about the room, observing children and listening in on the reading of several "focus" children. Each day Lon focuses on the literacy development of several of his children, make notes about their progress in reading and writing.

Because independent reading time is predictable in Lon's classroom (it occurs every day), children anticipate having time to read books of their choosing and they settle into the routine fairly quickly. Today, Lon particularly watches Darren and Inez, his focus children for the day, noting how they settle into this independent time. While he hears several children read aloud from self-selected books, Lon spends a little added time with Darren and Inez, making a record of their independent reading. As Lon listens to a child read aloud he makes notes about miscues—reading that does not match the text. He notes the correct words from the text and the child's mistaken responses. He estimates the number of correct words to then compare the number of correct words with the number of miscues to determine an approximate difficulty level of the text. Lon wants independent reading to be in texts in which children accurately read 95 to 100 of the words correctly and understand most all of the ideas they read.

During independent reading Lon continues to move about the room. When he sits beside a particular child, that child knows to begin reading orally wherever he or she may be in the text. After listening to a child read a portion of text, Lon asks open-end questions to elicit the child's general response to the text, what the child is learning from the story, what the child predicts might happen next, and the like. Listening to children read aloud in their chosen texts helps Lon know whether children are selecting texts that are truly independent for them.

If independence is to thrive in the classroom, we must plan for independent reading just as we plan other instruction in our literacy program. Children know, by the way that we treat independent reading, whether it is really important. They know of its importance by the time that we allocate for independent reading. We can provide time for independent reading in a variety of ways during the school day:

- Sustained independent reading, SSR or DEAR, when the entire class is reading self-selected books
- a choice during independent or small-group work time that is considered equivalent to paper and pencil tasks
- individualized reading that involves self-selected reading as the center of instruction

Children also know about the importance of independent reading by the range of print materials that we make available. They know by the way that books are treated in the classroom. Children in Lon's third-grade classroom know that Lon values what they do during independent reading time.

Building a Classroom Library

If we want children to value their independent reading time, then we must build a wide and varied collection of books. Children bring a variety of interests into the classroom. Will they find books to feed those interests there and/or in the school library? Children come with varied reading abilities. Will they find appropriate materials to fit their independent reading level?

Ten books per child is a good start for a classroom library. More books are preferable. To develop the classroom library, we can check out books from both the school and public libraries. These books can usually be kept in the classroom for about a month. For children who are reading picture books primarily, we may need to circulate books more frequently. When it is time for new books, we should involve the children in deciding which books should be renewed and which should be changed for new texts.

Reasonably priced paperback books are also available from mail-order book clubs such as Scholastic and Trumpet. One suggestion is, at the beginning of the school year, ask parents if they are willing to buy and donate a few books to the classroom library from book club orders during the year. Most parents are very willing, especially because the books are relatively inexpensive when compared with bookstore prices.

Promoting a Reading Atmosphere

A "reading atmosphere" should permeate everything that is done in the classroom, from the area devoted to a classroom library to the way that we treat independent reading time. The classroom library should invite children to want to read. It does not have to be a large area, but it must be inviting. Throughout the school year, children can help to decide how to make the library area an attractive place where they want to spend time. Involving children in the planning increases their sense of ownership in the classroom.

Consider locating the library near a wall area or bulletin board so that a display of books can be set up about a featured author, a special day such as Earth Day, or other topic of study. After we introduce the display, we can highlight something about the display each day and invite children to share what they are discovering about the books. Reading aloud from the selected books also increases children's interest in exploring the books independently or with a partner. Books can also be featured in other areas of the classroom, such as next to the science inquiry center or near the theme study area.

We must be good at selling some of our children on reading. Just because we find great books and display them in the classroom does not mean that children will automatically become independent readers. We can encourage children's interest in books by giving book talks, or special introductions for new books. As a part of each read-aloud time, we can plan to give a short book talk about a new book. We can tell a few highlights from a book, give a brief summary, or pose an interesting situation that could be explored by reading the book. For chapter books, we can read part of an exciting event aloud as an enticement. We can acquaint children with books, then make then available. Children also enjoy giving book talks about their favorite books.

A reading atmosphere includes physical conditions for reading. Most adults prefer a comfortable, relaxed atmosphere for reading. Children are no different. When they are reading independently, consider allowing children to go anywhere in the room that is comfortable for them, within reason. It may take a while for them to become committed to independent reading, but it will come—with much patience and support.

Book Boxes or Tubs

To facilitate independent reading with emergent and developing readers, we can create book boxes or tubs for each group of children who we see for guided reading. As a group completes the reading of a book in Katarina's first-grade classroom, she places copies of that book in the group's designated book box or tub. Everyone in that guided reading group is familiar with all of the books in the box. Children know they can independently read any of the books. Following daily guided reading, Katarina asks children to independently reread books from the box for fifteen to twenty minutes. Rereading these familiar books builds fluency and confidence.

As new books are added to the book boxes, the oldest books may be removed. It is important to keep enough variety of titles to accommodate the range of interests of children in each group. Book boxes or tubs can be stored near the classroom library for easy access during free choice reading or daily independent reading blocks.

Learning How to Select a Book

Many children will need help to learn how to self-select books for independent reading at an appropriate reading level. One day after returning from a trip to the school library to check out individual books I encouraged my first-grade children to talk about how and why they selected a particular book. What a surprise I had when Tracy said, "I always pick blue books, because blue is my favorite color." Then I realized that I had not done enough to help Tracy know how to select a book that was "right" for her.

Two primary issues involved with selecting books are interest and difficulty. For interest, we can work with the librarian and plan with children before a library visit. If we know about children's interests, we can steer children to areas of the library where particular books are housed. It may be helpful to make a list of children's interests for the librarian, asking that a variety of books be highlighted during the library visit. Before we leave the classroom, we can get the children in the habit of planning for that library visit. We can discuss the type of books they might like to look for that week. Beginning to plan before the visit to the library can make the short library period more productive for selecting books of interest.

Difficulty level of books is another issue in selection. When children select a book they think they would like to read, encourage them to try it out first to see how it suits them. Teach children to use a five-finger test. While they read the first page or two (approximately 100 words) ask them to tuck away a finger every time they come to a word they are not sure about. If they use up all five fingers, they may want to abandon the book because of its level of difficulty. If children are highly motivated to read a particular book, even if the book might be difficult, they should be allowed to try. How will children become independent if we always select their books or try to control their choices?

It can be worthwhile to have discussions with the children about reading easy, medium, and hard level books. Perhaps the term "just right" might have more meaning for children. As in *Goldilocks and the Three Bears,* we want children to feel that their books are "just right." We can talk with them about how we select books for guided reading and for their book boxes and why we want them to have a lot of practice in easy books. We can encourage children to share their book choices and how they made the choice. It is helpful for the children to hear their classmates' views about the pleasure derived from selecting books that are "just right."

Ensuring Adequate Reading Time

Acquiring skill involves practice over time. How much practice time do children need to develop independence in reading? The amount will vary. Some children will practice more reading outside of school. Some children will not require as much reading practice as others. Some children may slow their own progress because they continue to select books that are actually too challenging, such as when they want to read books at the same level as a friend.

How can we respond to children's varying needs for reading time?

- Set a time each day for everyone to read independently.
- Provide flexible time for choosing independent reading during work periods.

As early as kindergarten, time should be set aside each day for children to be engaged independently with books and other forms of print.

- Emergent readers will probably begin with five minutes and slowly progress to ten to fifteen minutes of independent reading.
- Developing readers may also begin with five minutes, but should work toward fifteen to twenty minutes of sustained reading.
- Transitional readers may begin with ten minutes of sustained reading and work up to as much as thirty minutes per day.

Sustained independent reading requires children to build stamina for reading. Children who have not had the opportunity for sustained reading will need patient guidance to learn how readers sustain their own reading.

We can also build independent reading time into the school day by making it a regular activity choice during instructional blocks such as reading/language arts or theme activities. Devoting instructional time to independent reading allows children who either want or need more practice time to have it. Children can read at their desks, in the library area, or at other designated places in the classroom. Remember that in the hustle and bustle of the school day it is easy to let independent reading time slip away. If we want to begin to equalize differences between children's background experiences with books, we must provide time for children to read.

ASSESSMENT: MONITORING GROWTH IN GUIDED AND INDEPENDENT READING

How do we know that children are making progress in their reading? We know it when we listen to them read aloud. We know it when we hear them talk about what they read. It makes sense then to use samples of children's reading as documentation of their growth as readers. Each day we observe children read. On a continuous basis we should make records of those observations, recording what they actually say while reading, then analyze any miscues, or words that differ from those in the actual text. Our analysis should then help us make more appropriate decisions to support their growth as readers.

The study of children's oral reading has a long history as an indicator of performance (Betts, 1946; Durrell, 1937; Gates, 1935; Gilmore & Gilmore, 1951; Gray, 1915; Spache, 1963). Over the past several decades this procedure of making records of children's oral reading behaviors has been referred to by different terms: running records (Clay, 1979), miscues analysis (Goodman & Burke, 1970), and informal reading tests (Beldin, 1970). Because there is a lack of agreement about terms, in this text we simply refer to such records as *reading records,* which is what they are. A record of children's oral reading reflects the strategies they use to monitor for meaning while they read.

Reading records may be made with both familiar and unfamiliar text. When text is familiar we should expect fewer miscues and, consequently, more fluent reading. When text is unfamiliar, we have our best opportunity to see and hear the self-monitoring strategies over which students have control and use almost automatically.

Reading records can either be scripted or unscripted. A scripted reading record uses a duplicate copy of the same text the child reads aloud. We are able to mark directly on the copy to show how a child actually reads. An unscripted reading record is made on a blank sheet of paper or recording form. We make check marks to indicate each correct word in a line of text and also note children's miscues.

When we make a reading record we sit side by side with the child, but slightly behind so that our recording is less distracting. As the child reads, we make a record of the reading. As we are first learning to make reading records, it is a good idea to tape record the reading. The recording enables us to listen again to a child's reading to be sure that we made an accurate record. The tape recording may also be used during conferences to help parents hear a child's strengths and/or need for support as a reader.

Scripted Reading Record

We can use scripted reading records early in the school year as a way of learning about children's self-monitoring strategies. It is best to examine children's reading level in a variety of texts—independent, instructional, and frustration. Making a scripted reading record is an excellent way to check our own instructional decisions, to know we have placed children in appropriate levels of text for guided reading.

On the day before she makes a scripted reading record, Katarina selects and copies an appropriate passage. The next day, Katarina listens carefully for the accuracy of Christiana's reading. Katarina records Christiana's reading by marking her copy of the text with the codes shown in Figure 5.2. Katarina records all miscues, but does not count all miscues when she determines oral reading accuracy. Only miscues that may interfere with meaning and are not self-corrected by the child are counted.

Imagine that Katarina listens to Christiana read *Three Little Ducklings* during guided reading. Using a copy of the text, Katarina makes the scripted reading record shown in Figure 5.3. There are 100 words in this passage. Which errors should we count? Look at Figure 5.2 for help in deciding.

How accurately does Christiana read? Is this text appropriate for her? Why or why not? (Remember that instructional level text is 90% to 95% accuracy of word recognition.)

Miscues that are counted: 6

Miscues that are <u>not</u> counted: 6

FIGURE 5.2
Marking a Scripted Reading Record

Miscues that are counted:

Substitution—Child reads a word differently than the printed text.	three Once upon a time, there were three little ducklings.
Omission—Child leaves out a word printed in the text.	Once upon a time, there were three (little) ducklings.
Insertion—Child adds a word or words that are not in the printed text.	the Once upon a time there were ^ three little ducklings.
Teacher Tells—Child appeals to the teacher for help, teacher first responds, "Try it," child is unable to respond, then teacher tells.	T Once upon a time there were three little ducklings.
Try That Again—Child becomes completely lost in a section of text, teacher brackets passage that has caused the problem and says, "Try that again." The whole passage is coded as TTA and counted as one miscue. Any additional miscues that are made in the rereading are marked with the usual codes. Miscues from the first reading are ignored.	TTA sc tree the tree was the [Once (up)on (a) time there were three little ducks ducklings.]

Miscues that are NOT counted:

Repetition—Child repeats a word or phrase. This usually indicates that they have lost the meaning or they are using rereading as a strategy to figure out an unknown word. One underline is used for each repetition.	R Once upon a time there were three little ducklings.
Self-Correction—Child corrects own miscue *without* assistance. The original miscue is recorded but does not count.	sc three Once upon a time there were three little ducklings.
Teacher Encourages—Child stops reading at point of unknown word, may or may not appeal for help, teacher encourages but does not tell, saying "try it," E (encourage) is recorded, child response is recorded.	E Once upon a time there were three little ducklings.

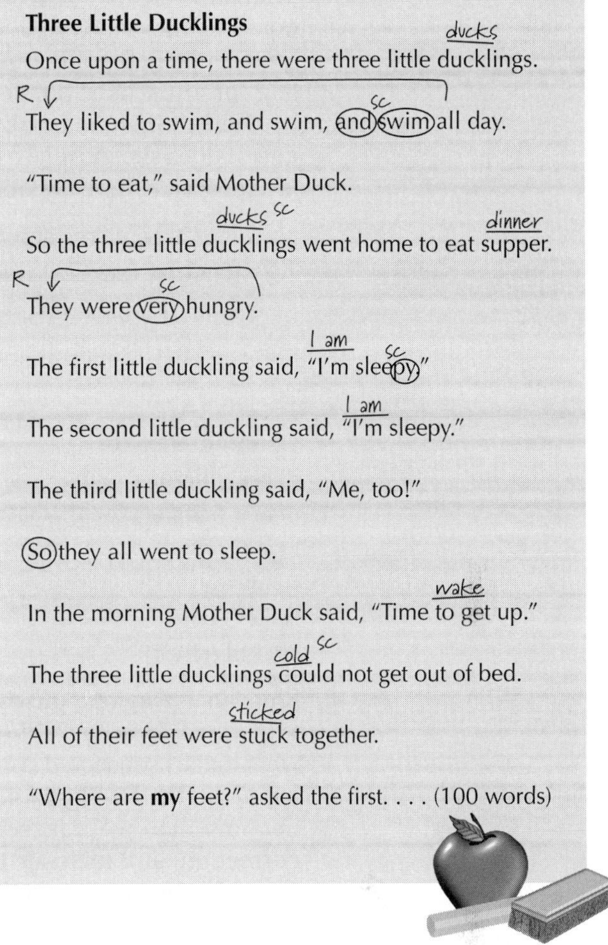

Three Little Ducklings

Once upon a time, there were three little ducklings.

They liked to swim, and swim, and swim all day.

"Time to eat," said Mother Duck.

So the three little ducklings went home to eat supper.

They were very hungry.

The first little duckling said, "I'm sleepy."

The second little duckling said, "I'm sleepy."

The third little duckling said, "Me, too!"

So they all went to sleep.

In the morning Mother Duck said, "Time to get up."

The three little ducklings could not get out of bed.

All of their feet were stuck together.

"Where are **my** feet?" asked the first. . . . (100 words)

FIGURE 5.3
Sample Scripted Reading Record

Calculate Christiana's accuracy rate:

Total words − counted errors = words correct
100 − 6 = 94
Words correct / total = accuracy rate
94 / 100 = 94%

How well does Christiana monitor her own reading? How might you calculate that? Self-corrections and repetitions are signs of self-monitoring. Christiana frequently uses repetition to check her thinking. If she did not self-correct her miscues, there would have been six additional miscues, for a total of twelve miscues. To calculate her rate of self-correction, we must consider all possible miscues compared with the number of miscues that were corrected.

$$\text{Self-correction ratio} = \frac{\text{miscues} + \text{self-corrections}}{\text{self-corrections}}$$

$$\text{Christiana's self-correction ratio} = \frac{6 + 6}{6} = \frac{2}{1}$$

The ratio means that for approximately every two miscues, Christiana self-corrects one—a very good rate of self-correction. She monitors her own reading quite well. If she did not self-correct, her accuracy rate would have dropped to 88%, or into frustration level.

When Christiana makes a miscue that is not self-corrected, what type of miscue(s) does she make? To what information in the text does she seem to attend? It is appropriate here to consider the three types of cues that influence our reading:

meaning (makes sense)
structure (sounds right)
visual (looks similar)

Look at Christiana's miscues. Which cues seem to be influencing her miscues?

	Error Type		
Counted Miscue:	**Meaning**	**Structure**	**Visual**
ducks (duckling)	___×___	___×___	______
dinner (supper)	___×___	___×___	______
I am (I'm)	___×___	___×___	______
(omit so)	___×___	___×___	______
wake (get)	___×___	___×___	______
sticked (stuck)	___×___	___×___	______

From analyzing responses on the reading record, what might we conclude about Christiana's reading? When she makes a miscue, she seems to be thinking about what makes sense and sounds right in the sentence. She does not seem to be asking herself if the word she says looks right when compared with the text. From her miscues, we can see that she makes meaning through repetition, self-correction, and miscues that preserve structure and meaning. Katarina uses a form like the one shown in Figure 5.4 to analyze cues used for each miscue and self-correction.

Unscripted Reading Record

When Katarina wants to assess a child's oral reading without prior planning, she takes an unscripted reading record. She uses a blank form that does not have a copy of the text. While looking at the text the child is reading, she uses check marks to show the child's accuracy (see Figure 5.5). The advantage of an unscripted reading record is the ability to make a record at any time, without advance notice.

If Katarina is listening to a focus child read during independent reading, she does not need to make a copy of the text ahead of time. An unscripted record of Christiana's reading might resemble that shown in Figure 5.6. The reading record is scored and analyzed in the same manner as a scripted reading record.

Keeping accurate records of children's progress in reading is important for planning appropriate instruction and for communicating with parents. Reading records should be made routinely for all children, but especially for emerging and early developing readers. Two reading records per month are the absolute minimum for children at these levels. Frequent records help us to adjust the

Reading Record

Name ______________________________ Date ______________

Text Title ____________________ Level __________ # Words: ______________

Counted Errors = ____ Oral Accuracy: ____ Independent (95–100%) Retelling: ____ Complete/Unaided

Self-Corrections = ____ ____ Instructional (90–95%) ____ Partially Complete

Self-Correction Rate: 1: ____ ____ Frustration (50–89%) ____ Incomplete

Cues used: M = meaning, S = structure, V = Visual

Text Page	Total Miscues	Information Used			Total Self-Corrections	Information Used		
		M	S	V		M	S	V

FIGURE 5.4
Form for Recording Reading Record Showing Cueing Strategies

FIGURE 5.5
Marking an Unscripted Running Record

Miscues that are counted:

Substitution—Child reads a word differently than the printed text.

✓ ✓ ✓ ✓ three ✓ ✓ ✓ ✓
[Once upon a time, there were three little ducklings.]

Omission—Child leaves out a word printed in the text.

✓ ✓ ✓ ✓ ✓ ✓ ✓ (little) ✓

Insertion—Child adds a word or words that are not in the printed text.

✓ ✓ ✓ ✓ ✓ ✓ the ^ ✓ ✓ ✓

Teacher Tells—Child appeals to the teacher for help, teacher first responds, "Try it," child is unable to respond, then teacher tells.

✓ T/upon ✓ ✓ ✓ ✓ ✓ ✓ ✓

Try That Again—Child becomes completely lost in a section of text, teacher brackets passage that has caused the problem and says, "Try that again." The whole passage is coded as TTA and counted as one miscue. Any additional miscues that are made in the rereading are marked with the usual codes. Miscues from the first reading are ignored.

TTA [✓ (upon) (a) the/time tree sc/tree/there was/were the/three ✓ ducks/ducklings]

Miscues that are NOT counted:

Repetition—Child repeats a word or phrase. This usually indicates that they have lost the meaning or they are using rereading as a strategy to figure out an unknown word. One underline is used for each repetition.

R ✓ ✓ ✓ ✓ ✓ ✓ ✓ ✓ ✓

Self-Correction—Child corrects own miscue *without* assistance. The original miscue is recorded but does not count.

✓ ✓ ✓ ✓ three sc/there ✓ ✓ ✓ ✓

Teacher Encourages—Child stops reading at point of unknown word, may or may not appeal for help, teacher encourages but does not tell, saying "try it," E (encourage) is recorded, child response is recorded.

✓ E/upon ✓ ✓ ✓ ✓ ✓ ✓ ✓

FIGURE 5.6
Sample Unscripted Reading Record

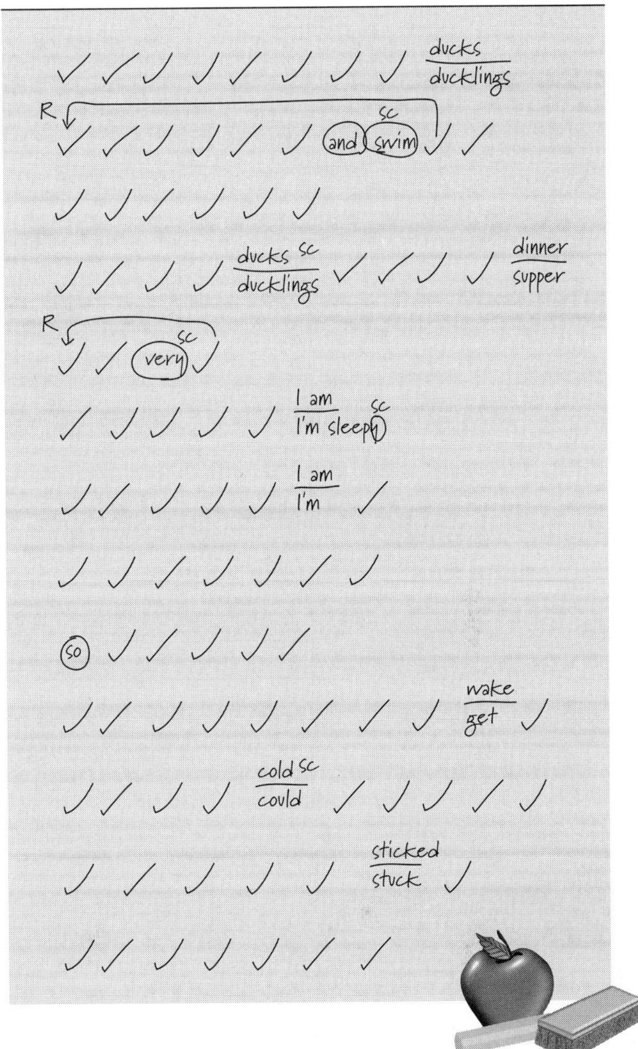

composition of guided reading groups, as well as the level of texts we select for guided reading, and ultimately independent reading.

Charting changes in children's reading levels helps us see the ways in which children are and are not making progress. The chart should show the date of the reading record, the level of the text, and the oral accuracy rate of the child's reading. A sample for a child in first grade is shown in Figure 5.7. The reading levels are adjusted to reflect the appropriate levels for the individual child.

Records of observations of children's performance in reading also help us focus our attention on areas of support that we should provide to individual children. The quality of our notes can remind us of specific behaviors on which we want to focus. Our notes are also helpful when we conference with parents about a child's progress. Figure 5.8 provides a sample record for noting growth in reading behaviors during guided and independent reading.

FIGURE 5.7
A Year-at-a-Glance Reading Record

Oral Accuracy	95	98	98	96	98	98	96	98	99	90	90	90	90
Book Title / Level	Up in a Tree	Sally & the Daisy	Bread	Nick's Glasses	Candle Light	The Little Red Bus	My Sloppy Tiger Goes to School	The Poor Sore Paw	Catch the Cookie	Sean's Red Bike	Dragon w/a Cold	The New Car	Paloma's Party
Late First													
Mid-First													
Emergent													
Date	10/14	10/24	10/28	11/4	11/24	1/22	2/5	2/13	2/20	2/26	3/13	4/3	4/10

RESPECTING DIVERSITY THROUGH GUIDED AND INDEPENDENT READING

Children Will Vary in Reading Interests

When we provide reading time with child-selected materials, we are telling children we realize their reading interests may differ from the classroom instructional materials. Providing a well-stocked classroom library and encouraging frequent browsing trips to the school library further reinforces our understanding that what motivates individual children to read is personal and may require time to discover.

Children Will Vary in Reading Ability

Regardless of socioeconomic levels and background experiences, children vary in their ability to deal with print. The diversity that exists in children's ability to decode and process print in guided groups, as well as independently, should motivate us to build a collection of instructional texts and classroom library

FIGURE 5.8
Record of Reading Behaviors

Name ____________________

Observations of Growth in Reading Behaviors   Date________   Grade__________

Attitudes — **Notes:**

- demonstrates interest/response
- participates in discussions
- chooses to read

Thinks at different levels: — **Notes:**

- recalls explicit information
- makes inferences
- thinks critically, makes judgments
- thinks creatively/responds personally

Uses Literary Knowledge: — **Notes:**

- follows the plot
- understands characters
- describes setting
- identifies point of view
- infers theme
- uses knowledge of genre

Uses Knowledge of Information Text: — **Notes:**

- identifies relevant details
- identifies main idea
- follows sequence
- understands compare/contrast
- understands cause/effect

Use Strategies To Make Meaning: — **Notes:**

- anticipates/predicts before reading
- uses illustrations to make meaning
- anticipates/predicts during reading
- reads with a purpose in mind
- monitors/changes thinking while reading
- can locate important ideas in text

Repairs Breakdown in Meaning: — **Notes:**

- notices when reading does not make sense
- makes an attempt to repair meaning
    - searches illustration
    - rereads/reads on text
    - uses visual to check meaning

Shows Signs of Independence: — **Notes:**

- selects appropriate texts
- reads fluently
- sustains own reading
- reads silently

materials that allow all children to have meaningful reading experiences in materials of a suitable reading level. Sufficient low-challenge materials should be available for guided groups and independent practice.

Children Will Vary in Reading Styles

Guided and independent reading are best within a relaxed reading environment. Allowing children to select the most comfortable situation for reading can facilitate personal learning styles that may vary from sitting to laying, from solo to partners, from quiet to conversational. Allowing choices during independent reading situations can help children come to know their preferences for different learning situations.

Take a moment to reflect on putting theory into practice in guided and independent reading . . .

When we engage children in guided reading, we do the following:

- Prepare children for the reading by previewing the text, including a book walk to notice patterns and key words.
- Provide support as needed for children's independence in the reading of the text.
- Discuss text to focus on retelling and response.
- Base teaching points for that day on children's observed interactions with the text.

Planning for guided reading focuses on:

- setting up flexible groups that are adjusted as needed,
- selecting accessible texts for each group, and
- selecting teaching points, initially based on the demands of the text and our predictions about what children will do, but adjusted by observations during groups.

When we guide reading in more challenging text, we:

- plan based on a purpose–strategy–reflection cycle,
- analyze the demands of the text,
- mediate between children and texts before, during, and after the reading, and
- guide the reading of chunks of the text by helping students predict, read, explain, and connect events and actions.

To provide an environment for independent reading, we

- know the range of children's reading levels and interests,
- provide a predictable time for independent reading each day,

- gather sufficient number and variety of quality texts that fit the range of reading levels in our classroom, and
- use independent reading time to carefully observe children's progress.

Book boxes or tubs contain familiar instructional level texts that are accessible to all children within a guided reading group and are read and reread during daily independent reading.

If independent reading is to provide appropriate practice time and support children's developing fluency, they must learn to successfully select texts that are within their independent, instructional range.

From kindergarten through third grade, children should spend increasing amounts of time in daily silent sustained independent reading.

We assess children's growth in guided and independent reading by means of routine scripted or unscripted reading records of children's oral reading and retelling of either the important sequences of the story or the main ideas and supporting details of an information text.

YOUR TURN . . .

1. To prepare for selecting appropriate texts for guided and independent reading, become familiar with the various levels of text that children might read during the primary-grade years. Pay special attention to changes in the amount and positioning of text on each page and the complexity of the language from level to level.
2. Observe several teachers working with a variety of levels of guided reading groups. Notice how the teacher prepares children for the reading, how children interact with the text, and how the teacher provides support to enable children to read the text fluently and with meaning.
3. Make a point of visiting several primary-grade classrooms to see how teachers arrange for independent reading. Are library corners inviting and organized? Are books given prominent places? Do children have opportunities to talk about selecting new books? What is the teacher's view of the place of independent reading in the curriculum?
4. Gather information about school book clubs and other ways to acquire books in your community. Find out what types of budgets teachers and schools have for building classroom and school libraries.

Aa Bb Cc Dd Ee Ff Gg Hh Ii Jj Kk Ll Mm

CHAPTER

6

Guided and Independent Writing

Adding to our literacy framework . . .

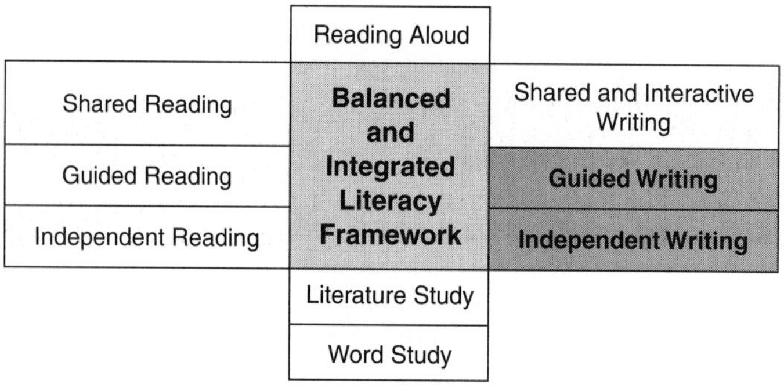

	Reading Aloud	
Shared Reading	**Balanced and Integrated Literacy Framework**	Shared and Interactive Writing
Guided Reading		**Guided Writing**
Independent Reading		**Independent Writing**
	Literature Study	
	Word Study	

In this chapter, we . . .

- Examine writing both as a process and as a functional task.
- Explore how to extend composing processes that began in shared writing, to support children toward independence as writers.
- Consider a variety of types of writing which occur in primary-grade classrooms.

Looking into Classrooms . . .

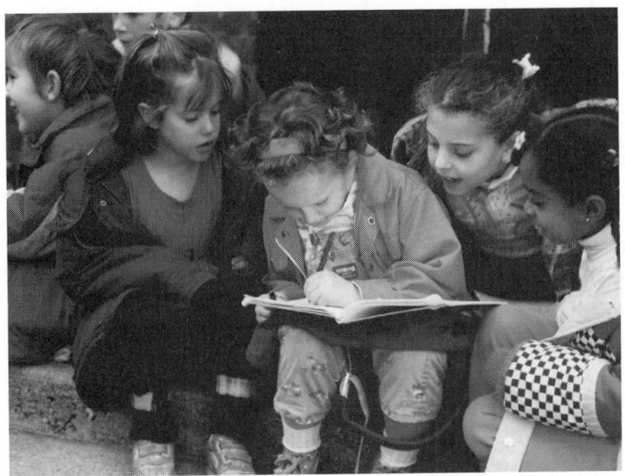

One day in January, Renee begins guided writing, also known as writer's workshop, with her first-grade children gathered on the floor for a read-aloud. The book is about a boy who uses his imagination, pretending he is an astronaut that discovers a new planet. As she finishes the story, Renee begins a mini-lesson about using imagination in writing: "I have noticed that several of you are using your imagination in your writing just like the author of this book." Renee encourages children to share about their imaginative writing and she comments on the writing of two other children. The workshop does not always begin with a read-aloud, but there is usually some "tip" for authors that comes from Renee, the children, or another author such as Tomie dePaola or Ezra Jack Keats.

As the writing folders are passed out, Renee asks the children to turn to their neighbor and tell what they will be doing today during the writing time. Doug asks if Renee will help him brainstorm ideas, because he's "stuck." When everyone has their writing folder, the children are free to find a comfortable place to go and begin a period of sustained writing and talking about their writing.

Four girls settle together on the floor near a bookshelf that has a display of alphabet books. Each of them is making an alphabet book and occasionally they refer to alphabet books by other authors for ideas. William settles at a table and begins to reread aloud what he wrote the day before about a tornado that came near his house. Sarah, who just returned from a three-week absence, has some difficulty settling. She approaches Renee, who is sitting with Doug, helping him brainstorm topics for his writing. Renee encourages Sarah to "ask someone else, because there are lots of other teachers in the room" who can help her. Sarah leaves and finds Bonita at a table in the corner. The girls begin to talk and write, side by side.

When Renee leaves Doug to write on his own, she sees that Sarah has begun to write so she stops and glances around the room. Justin approaches her to tell "facts" he knows about tornadoes. Renee suggests that he share his ideas with William who might find the facts helpful for his story on tornadoes.

From across the room Marty motions to Renee. She kneels down beside him at the reading table as Marty reads aloud his piece about the cold night when his lambs were born. He has signed up for the author's chair today and he appears a little nervous about the questions the other children might ask about his piece.

Forty-five minutes have passed and Renee calls the children back to the carpet for the author's chair. Three children have signed up to share their writing. Marty is first. After he reads his piece aloud, William compliments him saying, "I really liked your story," then asks, "Did the baby sheep really die?" Quickly, Justin echoes, "The cutest one died? The one I saw?" Questions arise about the red light that Marty mentioned but didn't explain in his piece. When the questions and comments cease, the children clap and Marty leaves the author's chair for the next author to share. And so goes a day of guided writing during writer's workshop in this first-grade classroom.

Building a Theory Base . . .

We assist children toward independence as we slowly, deliberately adjust the level of our support to children's needs. In supporting children's development as writers, we move from shared writing to guided and independent writing, as children's actions demonstrate their ability to monitor and guide themselves as writers. In Chapter 4 we explored the potential of shared writing to model writing processes and scaffold children's thinking about producing written communication. Now we turn our attention to guided and independent writing opportunities, in which children learn more about their own strengths as writers.

All journeys take time, and when the going is tough some will take longer than others. It is possible on a journey to have a rest along the way—several rests, if the journey is an extended trek over unfamiliar ground. It is possible to look back over ground already covered and to look forward at least as far as the next bend. It is useful to be able to call on help if you get stuck, and it can be reassuring to have company at least from time to time, as the journey progresses (D'Arcy, 1989, pp. 27–28).

WRITING—GUIDING CHILDREN'S JOURNEY IN THINKING

Writing is like a journey, developed over time through a recursive, or flexible, process (D'Arcy, 1989; Calkins, 1986, 1994; Graves, 1983, 1994). The process of exploring, developing, or examining one's ideas through written language is considered to be a recursive process because writers move between phases of writing as it suits the writer's need. Once children have developed a good sense of letter–sound relationships, are combining words into sentences, and have a beginning understanding of the use of punctuation and capitalization, we should provide scaffolding that moves them toward developing and evaluating their own pieces of writing. "This is a fragile process and very dependent on carefully observing children's readiness" (Soderman, Gregory, & O'Neill, 1999).

When we encourage children to approach their writing as a process, we teach them that writing is indeed a process, a medium, a code, and a product, as we discussed in Chapter 4. Writing as process is a perspective that undergirds the writing from start to finish. Writing as a medium comes into play as students consider their options for shaping ideas. During both composing and editing, knowledge of writing as a code is vital for meaning and clarity. Writing as a product is realized during the publishing/re-presenting phase.

To develop an idea fully, writers go through different phases with their thinking and writing. The phases of writing serve different purposes. In this text we use labels that are descriptive of each phase:

- Getting started
- Finding a focus
- Composing
- Editing for meaning and correctness
- Re-presentation

Getting Started

Getting started with writing is also referred to as prewriting or rehearsal. The term *prewriting* may be misleading for young children, whereas *rehearsal* may be too abstract. Children often describe themselves as "getting started," hence, the choice of the term. During this phase children will do such things as:

- consider their purpose for writing,
- consider what they know about topics,
- use a variety of strategies to explore their thinking, and
- consider who the writing might be for, or the audience.

Children may start their writing in a variety of ways. Some children need to read and think, some need to draw, some need to brainstorm or make a cluster of their ideas, some appear to daydream but are really "writing in their heads" (Murray, 1985). Since writers use different strategies as they get started, we should not dictate one strategy, such as clustering, for all children. If we do, we may limit some children who plan through means other than clustering. Experiences with informal types of writing—such as making lists, writing notes, or writing an explanation of an idea—help children know many different forms that their thinking can take as they prepare to develop a piece of writing.

We should not hurry children through this phase. If we do, we may find they will struggle with a piece that never really takes shape and, consequently, is not self-satisfying. Exploring ideas during this phase is essential if children are to find a focus.

Finding a Focus

At some point during the "getting started" phase, children are ready to clarify their topic and direction. This is when response from someone else may be very helpful. Having another listen to our ideas can affirm or help clarify our thinking. Children can learn to become responsive listeners. We must model what responsive listening looks and sounds like. Then we coach partners as they practice responsive listening. We become responsive listeners as we conference with children about the focus of their writing. This is the point when, as D'Arcy (1989) suggests, we must look through children's writing, rather than at the writing itself. Once children find their focus, sustained writing will usually follow.

Composing

Sustained writing is the goal of this stage. When children have a clear sense of where they are trying to go with a piece of writing, sustaining their effort is not so difficult. Children who continue to struggle with their writing during this phase usually have not really found their focus. Our role during the composing phase is to "get out of children's way." As long as they are sustaining the writing, we let them go. Children can use this phase to build stamina as writers. The composing phase may be the first time for many children that writing continues beyond short bursts.

Composing is the phase when we begin to see something of the recursive nature of writing. Some children will move back to strategies from the getting started phase, especially when they find the need to question or clarify what they know about their topic. Some children will, on occasion, move ahead into the editing phase. For some writers, moving back and forth between composing and editing is a natural activity for checking their thinking. One reason to step back when children are composing is to let them begin to discover their own style as writers. Children cannot learn about their own style if we intrude when they are in a sustained effort with their writing.

In Figure 6.1 we see an example of a composition by a second-grade student, Ramon, in response to a folktale read aloud by his teacher. During the composing process his teacher and classmates were available for guidance and response, but Ramon had a great deal of freedom to organize and develop his composition in ways that pleased him.

Editing for Meaning and Correctness

The phase of the writing process called editing for meaning and correctness is frequently referred to as two separate phases, revising and editing. Revising typically refers to making changes for meaning, while editing usually refers to making changes for language conventions or correctness. In this text we simply use the term *editing.* Children understand that editing means "making changes," changes for meaning and changes for correctness.

Editing for meaning requires a writer to become a reader, and read for meaning. Making meaning may involve more than just changing words. Children may need to restructure sentences or rearrange words to be understood. Minor changes also may be made, such as adding punctuation to clarify the meaning. The more that we are able to help children view language as a medium of communication, the easier it is to get them to mold their words, just as they mold clay. A pinch here, and extra piece there, improves the form of our clay sculpture. We can help children see their words as clay that can be molded into more meaningful and satisfying text.

Editing for correctness requires a writer to become a reader and read for surface details, so that the writing looks the way other readers expect English to look. We want other readers to understand our message, so it must follow the "rules" of English. This phase usually focuses on conventions of writing such as capitalization and spelling. How well children are able to edit for conventions in their writing depends on their stage of word knowledge and spelling development.

We must use what we know about children during this phase, so that we do not have unrealistic expectations for their ability to use correct spelling in the finished piece. For example, if we know that a child is just beginning to spell short-vowel words such as *cap* and *hot,* we should not expect to see most other complex words spelled correctly.

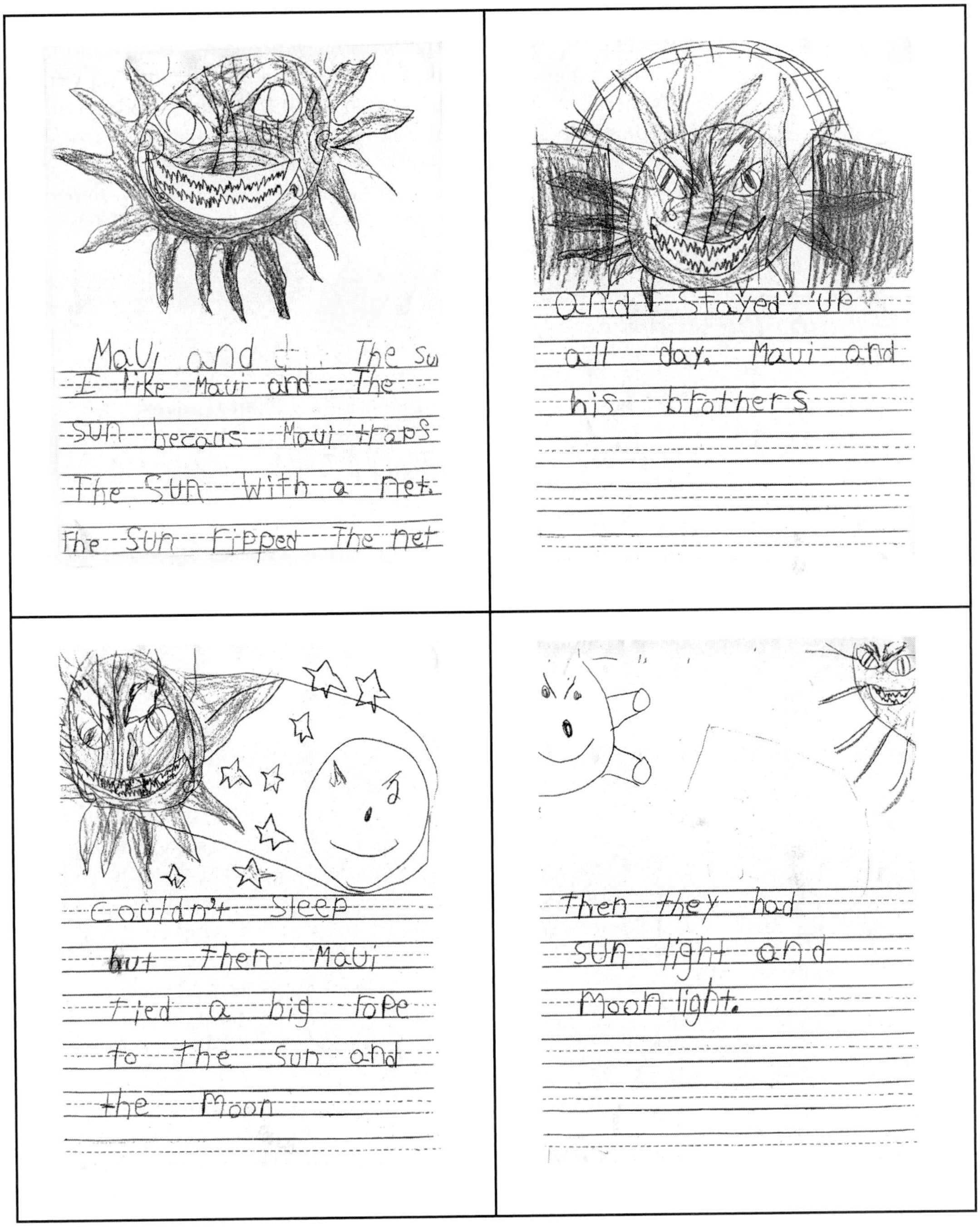

Maui and the Sun

I like Maui and The Sun becaus Maui traps The Sun with a net. The Sun Flipped The net

and stayed up all day. Maui and his brothers

couldn't sleep but Then Maui tied a big rope to The Sun and the Moon

Then they had sun light and Moon light.

FIGURE 6.1
Ramon's Retelling of Maui and the Sun

Forming editing groups can assist children with achieving a satisfactory level of correctness in their writing. Here again, we must model for children how to read someone's writing and help them find details that might need attention. During our modeling, we emphasize that attention to the code is done in order to communicate with others. For example, we spell words in certain ways because we have agreed, as English speakers, that we will all use the same spellings in order to understand one another. If each of us chose our own spellings for a word, or our own grammatical structures, we would probably need for others to interpret their writing for us.

Re-Presenting the Writing

During the re-presenting phase, children should have opportunities for public sharing of their writing. In an author's chair (Graves, 1983, 1994), a child reads aloud a piece of writing to which other children respond and question. Writing should also be prominently displayed in the classroom or published in books that are available for all to read. Children learn about writing through sharing in the writing of their classmates. As children journey as writers, we must provide appropriate assistance, guiding their writing as needed, to help them achieve satisfaction with their ability to communicate with others through print.

MOVING TOWARD INDEPENDENCE AS WRITERS

As we participate with children in many varied writing experiences, such as shared writing and writer's workshop, we scaffold their understanding of ways in which individuals can use written language to communicate with others. We serve as models of fluent writing, we support their developing understanding of concepts about print, we collaborate in the act of composition, we think aloud as authors, and we share some things we have learned about writing.

Children who are fortunate to live with other responsive adults have seen similar models during their preschool years. Slowly, as children become more aware of print and its possibilities, they attempt to produce their own print, making their own messages to self and others. Hand-in-hand with scaffolded writing experiences, we also encourage children to venture out on their own. During independent writing, children have the opportunity to work alone and use their current knowledge of the writing process to compose and construct their own texts (McCarrier, Pinnell, & Fountas, 2000). Their independent writings enable children to orchestrate on their own all that they have observed and participated in as writers. Independent writings enable us to observe and value children's personal development as writers. For example, in Figure 6.2 we can see that an independent writing opportunity allowed Alex to express his sense of satisfaction with himself as he writes, "I like me." In this kindergarten classroom children have daily opportunities to demonstrate their ability to use written language to express ideas and communicate with others.

To encourage independence we can provide daily opportunities for writing in a writer's workshop and throughout the school day. We can provide personal journals in which topic, focus, length, and format are controlled by the children

FIGURE 6.2
Alex's Kindergarten Composition

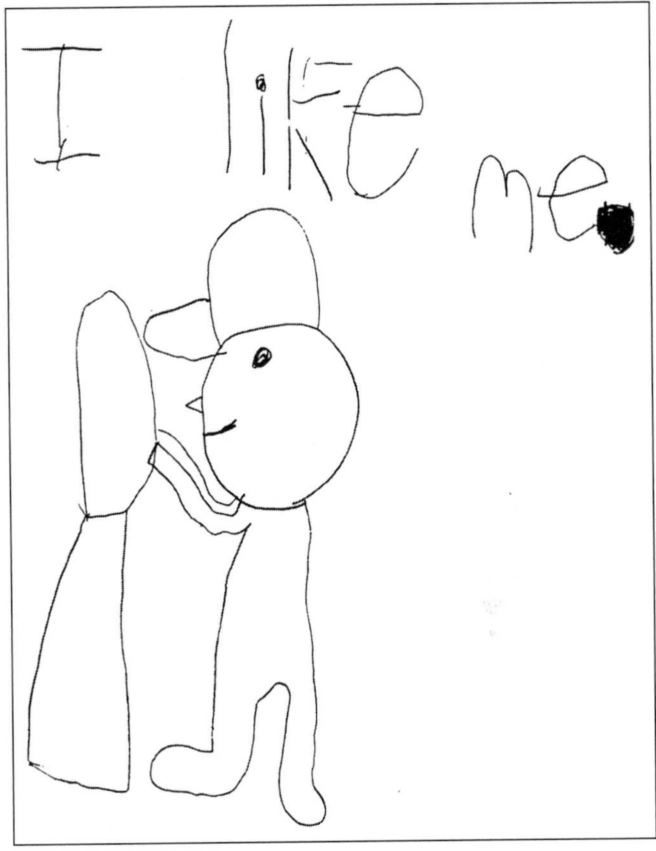

(Soderman, Gregory, & O'Neill, 1999). We can also integrate many shorter writing opportunities into the day, informal writings which will not receive the extended focus of a writer's workshop. Informal writings allow children to experiment with many varied formats for a range of purposes. Informal writings may take the form of annotated drawings, lists, responses, and explanations. The key is daily time to write in meaningful ways.

Take a moment to reflect on your theory base for guided and independent writing . . .

The writing process is like a journey that includes:

- getting started with an idea for a piece of writing,
- exploring the idea to find a focus,
- drafting ideas in sustained writing,
- editing for meaning and conventions, and
- re-presenting the new thinking that has emerged as a result of the writing process.

Functional writing is bursts of writing that are not taken through the writing process, and may not be edited for meaning or conventions, and includes:

- lists and clusters,
- annotated drawings,
- charts and graphs,
- descriptions,
- notes, and
- records of events and explanations.

Functional writing is often recorded in varying types of journals or logs, including:

- personal journal,
- dialogue journal,
- response journal,
- double-entry journal, and
- learning logs.

Learning logs typically include many different types of informal writing that is related by subject area or theme.

Putting Theory into Practice . . .

An excellent way to put the writing process to work in the classroom is through a writer's workshop. A workshop is a very flexible format for organizing learning experiences that can meet the diversity of children's learning styles and preferences (Five, 1988; Hansen, 1987). A workshop format moves from whole-group activity, to a work time for individuals and/or small groups, then back to whole group during a specified time period that can vary from thirty to ninety minutes depending on the activities planned. To maximize children's development as writers, a writer's workshop should occur daily for forty to sixty minutes (Calkins, 1994; Graves, 1994).

GUIDING WRITING IN A WRITER'S WORKSHOP?

A writer's workshop maintains a predictable structure that everyone in the classroom knows. Children have blocks of time for writing, have a choice of certain topics, receive response to their writing, have opportunity to see writing demonstrated, and participate in the evaluation of their writing. The phases of a writer's workshop and the components in each phase are shown in Figure 6.3. Each phase and component is discussed in this chapter.

FIGURE 6.3
Writer's Workshop (40–60 minutes)

Whole Group: (10–20 minutes)	• demonstrations of writing (mini-lessons or shared writing lessons) • plans for the day
Work Time: (20–40 minutes)	• individual writing • conferring • response partners/groups • editing partners/groups
Whole Group: (10–15 minutes)	• author's chair • plans for next day

Whole-Class Preparation

Predictable Time for Writing:
If children are to become writers, they must have a predictable time for writing every day (Calkins, 1994). When the time is predictable and children know when it will happen, they anticipate what they will do with their writing time that day. Calkins tells the story of a child who gets her ideas for writing just as she is about to fall asleep, so she keeps tissues and a pencil near her bed to write down ideas as they come to her, to keep the ideas for her next opportunity to write. For this young girl writing has become an expectation, something she plans for. This type of response to writing is not likely to happen unless your classroom makes a real commitment to time for daily writing.

Time for writing must also be a sustained block. The work of a writer requires time to settle in—to get in one's stride. Graves (1994) suggests a minimum of thirty-five to forty minutes, four days per week, beginning in first grade. Calkins (1994) suggests at least one hour a day. She makes no apologies about the time commitment that is required for quality writing when she states:

> If students are going to become deeply invested in their writing, and if they are going to live toward a piece of writing and let their ideas grow and gather momentum, if they are going to draft and revise, sharing their texts with one another as they write, they need the luxury of time. If our students are going to have the chance to do their best and then to make their best better, they need long blocks of time. Sustained effort and craftsmanship are essential in writing well, yet they run contrary to the modern American way (p. 186).

To find such blocks of writing time, teachers use writer's workshop to:

- complete writing tasks from other subject areas, such as report writing from science or social studies,
- teach and practice handwriting, grammar, punctuation, and spelling as a part of editing for meaning and correctness, instead of teaching each separately at some other time of the day, or

- join reading instruction or literature studies with writing into a reading/writing workshop.

Demonstrations of Writing:
Just like reading, writing involves certain aspects that cannot be observed. Children need to see writing modeled and hear various writers think aloud about the content and process of their writing. Mini-lessons and shared writing experiences provide explicit demonstrations of workshop procedures, writing processes, forms of writing, and conventional uses of language.

Mini-lessons:
As the name suggests, mini-lessons are short and to the point, lasting no more than five to ten minutes. They are intended to address knowledge, skills, and strategies that are helpful for children to know at a particular time or that children are "using but confusing." Mini-lessons serve as a "forum for planning a day's work, a time to call writers together . . . for raising a concern, exploring an issue, modeling a technique, reinforcing a strategy" (Calkins, 1994, p. 193).

Mini-lessons are intended to "put the idea in the room" as Calkins (1986) suggests, so that children can explore the idea if it is helpful to them or share the idea with each other. Mini-lessons plant seeds of ideas or extend upon what children already have demonstrated as awareness. Mini-lessons should extend on what children have begun to learn through informal writing. In the beginning stages of writing workshop, various mini-lessons offer help for learning workshop procedures and routines, such as:

- How to Sustain My Writing
- It's Okay to Abandon a Piece of Writing
- Rereading as I Check for Meaning
- Making Changes in My Writing
- How to Conference with Another Writer
- How to Conference with Myself
- When Am I Ready for Author's Chair?

Topics for procedural mini-lessons must come from the way that we set up a writer's workshop and from our observations of the children's response to the workshop.

An important mini-lesson for emerging writers is to demonstrate that children write in a variety of ways, including:

- using pictures to stand for words,
- scribble writing,
- letter strings,
- using one or two letters to stand for a word, and
- other invented spellings mixed with conventional spelling.

Children need to know that these are all valid ways to write during a writer's workshop.

Acknowledging the range of possibilities for writing that might be seen lets children know that their attempts during writer's workshop are valued.

To develop mini-lessons that draw upon elements of literature, we must consider what we know about various genre, literary elements, and text structures. Primary-grade children can benefit from mini-lessons about the following:

- sequence of a plot,
- using character dialogue to tell the story,
- getting a story started, or
- who's telling the story.

As children's writing develops, mini-lessons might become specific to writing in particular genre, for example, mysteries. For such mini-lessons, examples from literature and children's writing can be used to illustrate:

- How to Get a Mystery Started
- How Authors Use Clues to Build Suspense
- How Authors Resolve Their Mysteries

We can observe an example of a mini-lesson at the beginning of writer's workshop in Kelli's first-grade classroom. She has noticed that a number of her children always write in one particular form—personal narratives using "I" or informative pieces about a familiar topic. Kelli wants children to realize that, as authors, they have many choices about how to tell their "story."

In her mini-lesson, Kelli uses several familiar books as illustrations to call children's attention to the way authors use point of view or "who is telling the story."

> Kelli returns to *The Pain and the Great One,* by Judy Blume, to show children the impact of a first-person point of view.
>
> In *Where the Wild Things Are,* by Maurice Sendak, Kelli helps children notice that this fantasy is told by a narrator who is not a part of story, but knows all that Max, the main character, says and does.
>
> In contrast, Kelli also asks children to think about how Donald Crews, the author of *Freight Train,* told his story.

Comparing these three books, and the difference that point of view can make for the telling of the story, serves as an example of choices that authors have in the way they develop their writing. Kelli encourages children to think about all the literature they read as a potential source of ideas about how other people write.

After this mini-lesson, Kelli notices that several children use the ideas and explore writing "I" stories. These children announce such things to Kelli as, "I am writing like Judy Blume did in *The Pain and the Great One.*" Kelli also observes that some children do not find the mini-lesson helpful until almost two months later when they begin to experiment with point of view. As Calkins (1986) says, the "idea is in the room" and individual children are able to use it when their understanding of writing develops to the place that point of view is useful to them. Examples of other mini-lessons that can be drawn from discussions of literature-based reading in Chapter 7.

Shared Writing:
We know that through shared writing, teachers and children collaborate in the development of a piece of writing, recording the shared thinking on a large chart

or overhead transparency (see Chapter 4). The focus of what we write depends on the particular writing strategies that children need to see us model. Shared writing lessons are typically more in-depth than mini-lessons and allow for both demonstration and discussion. On the days when shared writing occurs, the initial whole-group time is extended and individual writing time or author's chair is shortened.

Like mini-lessons, shared writing helps children explore writing in different genre or using literary elements in new ways. Writing strategies, especially editing for meaning and correctness, are also modeled through shared writing. As an example, instead of using a mini-lesson about imaginative writing in our opening first-grade scenario, Renee could have engaged the children in a shared writing to demonstrate how writers think while writing imaginative pieces. Renee had observed several children who were already using an imaginative style, so she chose to use their sharing during a mini-lesson as her first step, then wait and see what other children chose to do with the idea.

In Coral's second-grade classroom, she has noticed in children's writings that "and" is often used in place of punctuation. She wants to remind children that listening to how language sounds can help us decide where punctuation, such as a period, belongs. At the beginning of a writer's workshop Coral invites children to think about what the class has been learning in the weather unit about the ways that weather affects people. Coral uses this discussion as both a warm-up for writing ideas and a demonstration about rereading to check punctuation. Children talk about a variety of ideas they might use that day for writing about this topic. For the composition, Coral focuses on one of the most frequent suggestions, how we dress, as she writes children's ideas on the easel:

> We wear jackets when it is cold
> and tank tops when it is hot *and*
> we wear raincoats when it rains
> and boots when it snows.

During this shared writing, Coral does not question the children's use of *and.* Coral says, "This is a very long sentence. Is this really only one sentence? Maybe we have more than one sentence and just forgot to put in a period. Let's reread this story and check to see if we need a period to show the end of a sentence." Coral leads the children in rereading the text, encouraging them to listen for places where their voices suggest the end of a sentence. The children decide that a period is really needed after "hot." Coral asks if they still need the word "and" (shown in italics) and the children decide to take it out. They discuss how the word *and* is good for connecting ideas, but to be careful about how many ideas to put together. As children prepare to return to their desks to begin writing, Coral encourages them to reread their own writing, listening for places where they might be using the word *and* instead of punctuation.

Plans for the Day:

As the whole-group meeting comes to an end and children are moving out to their writing time, some teachers use this time to ask children about their writing plans for that day. Asking children about their writing plans each day sends the message that it is the children who are taking charge of their writing and are expected to be thinking about their writing and themselves as writers.

In the opening vignette of Renee's first-grade classroom, she encourages planning by asking children to tell their partners what they will be doing that day during writing. When planning is a regular part of the way we begin a workshop, it moves very quickly because children know what is expected. After the discussion of weather and clothing in Coral's second-grade classroom, she asks children to share with the class an idea for their writing that day. One by one as children share an idea, Coral allows them to return to their desks to begin writing.

Atwell (1998) encourages teachers of older students to conduct a "status check" each day. She quickly checks each child, asking what they are planning to do that day. Will they be getting started with a new piece, getting with a partner to find a focus, composing, conferencing, getting response to their draft writing, working with an editing group, or practicing for author's chair? Beginning in second or third grade, children who are consistently involved in writer's workshops can report their status during group meetings. Status checks encourage children to be aware of, and perhaps more accountable for, their own writing process.

To keep a record, we might use a sheet of paper marked off into boxes with student's names down the left-hand side and days of the week across the top. We can develop a simple code to indicate what students report they are doing. Then we record their response each day as we do our status check. Students come to expect the status check and are prepared to report. Expecting the status check encourages children to plan their work time. Our records show us patterns in ways that children progress through the writing process.

Individual Writing Time

Choice:

Professional writers select their own topics for writing. In an effective writer's workshop, children should have some freedom to choose their topics. Research suggests that children, even as young as first grade, are quite capable of selecting their own topics for writing (Douglas, 1988; Graves, 1973). For young writers whose handwriting is still a slow, laborious process,

> it is all the more important that they choose subjects for which they have an experiential, chronological base, since slow speed hampers access to information as well as the sense of where the word or sentence under construction fits in with the overall idea of the paper (Graves, 1994, p. 252).

At times we might provide a broad focus for the writing, such as exploring how to write a fairy tale or writing in response to part of our unit on moths and butterflies. Within these broad areas children still have many choices for the specific content and form they prefer.

As children move from the whole group to individual writing time, we want to observe how they settle themselves and make the transition to this sustained time. When Renee's children leave the whole group, she sits with Doug to brainstorm ideas, but looks around the room to see what the other children are doing. If children have difficulty getting settled, Renee would leave Doug for a few moments to oversee the transition and troubleshoot if needed. It is Renee's belief, however, that children learn to direct themselves if given the opportunity.

Notice how Renee acts on her belief by the way she responds to Sarah, saying that there are many other teachers in the room who can help Sarah. Renee reminds Sarah about how their classroom works and gives Sarah the opportunity to be more independent.

Sustaining Writing:
Calkins (1994) suggests that we should not underestimate children's ability to sustain their writing by stopping the writing time as soon as children become restless and say they are "done." From the beginning of the school year, forty to sixty minutes should be planned for the workshop. When children indicate they are having difficulty sustaining their writing, our attention should shift to nudging their independence by suggesting they reread their writing to themselves or a partner, and begin to ask the self-conferencing questions suggested in the next section. Observations of children's writing behavior should also suggest minilessons that can help children learn self-sustaining behaviors.

Response to Writing:
Providing opportunity for children to select their own topics requires that we take their choices seriously and respond based upon what each child is trying to accomplish in the writing. Children need the response of others to their writing, "to discover what they do and do not understand" (Graves, 1994, p. 108) about their topic, the writing process, and their desire to be understood by others.

Writing Conference:
Meeting one to one with children enables us to become more personally involved with them as writers and to become more sensitive to their individual needs for instruction. Children can conference with us at different points in their writing— getting a focus, refocusing a piece, questioning a choice of form, thinking about getting started on a new piece, and so forth. We do not need to save conferencing until pieces are near completion. Conferences can be formal or informal. Informal conferences happen as we circulate among children and a con-

As often as we can, we should meet with children to talk about their writing. What can we learn as we listen to them talk about their writing and themselves as writers?

versation begins, initiated by either the child or us. In the opening vignette, Renee and Doug have an informal conference about finding topics for writing. After the conference with Doug, Renee moves about the room responding to children who need assistance.

We can have children sign up for formal conferences ahead of time, by posting a sign-up sheet somewhere in the room. By allowing five minutes per conference, we can set aside time to see several children each day during the independent writing time. When children sign up for the conference we might ask them to indicate their purpose or need for the conference. When a child comes to a conference to talk about his or her writing, our support is most helpful if we direct it toward the child's concerns or what the child is trying to do with the writing. Conferencing is not a time to teach everything that the child needs to know. Supporting the child's concern first, we provide instruction that will help the child take the next step as a writer.

Although it can be very helpful to confer with children about their writing, it may be more important for them to learn to confer with themselves as writers. Smith (1982) tells us: "Writing separates our ideas from ourselves in a way that it is easiest for us to examine, explore, and develop them" (p. 15). Early on in their writing, we must help children learn why and how to step back from their writing to see themselves in their words. In children's writing we must promote self-monitoring, just as we do in their reading.

What questions do writers ask of themselves? Calkins (1994) suggests the following:

- What have I said so far? What am I trying to say?
- How do I like it? How does it sound? How does it look?
- What will my readers think who read/hear this? What questions will they ask?
- What will they notice? Feel? Think?
- What is good here that I can build on? What is not so good that I can fix?
- What am I going to do next? (p. 222–223)

Children can learn to ask these questions by participating in conferences with teachers who ask the same questions. Mini-lessons can also teach self-conferring behavior.

Calkins (1994) suggests that it is important for conferences to focus on children's writing processes, not just the content of the writing. She learned this from Donald Murray, a writing teacher in her graduate program, who focused on her processes as a writer. The art of focusing on process lives on beyond a piece of writing and becomes instructive for future pieces.

Response Partners/Groups:
Response from others can help us as writers. Children also need response to their writing that goes beyond conferencing with us. Helping children learn how to respond to one another's writing strengthens writing in the classroom, allowing everyone to become a teacher. We can plan mini-lessons about how to:

- respond to the writing of another, and
- ask for the type of response that will help your writing.

In the vignette of Renee's first-grade classroom, Sarah has difficulty getting settled, but once she does, she writes about her recent trip to Arizona. Then Sarah talks with Bonita, who listens to Sarah's draft and asks questions just as Renee models as she conferences both formally and informally with children. As the workshop draws to a close Sarah tells Renee that Bonita helped her think about her story.

In the early stages of implementing a writer's workshop, we can use mini-lessons to teach response. Children also learn responding from the models we provide in conferences, during shared writing, and in our other interactions that involve writing. We must remember that it will take time for children to learn to respond in ways that will help them as writers. We must be patient and supportive of their efforts, and compliment the instances when we observe that their responses are sensitive and of help to another. The success of response in the classroom is related to overall climate of support and respect that is fostered.

Finding a response partner can be either formal or informal. We can provide a sign-up sheet on which children can indicate their need for response or encourage children to select their own response partners. The procedure we use to enable children to get response to their writing depends on how our classroom functions. In some classrooms, small groups can work effectively to respond to a child's writing. This typically happens at the upper end of the primary grades. Careful observation of children indicates whether partners or groups are most effective.

Editing Partners/Groups:
At times, children need assistance from a more able writer to notice details in their writing that need attention. Children can be very helpful to each other, teaching strategies such as spell checking and punctuation. As we match children to assist each other, we must consider their respective stages of readers and spellers. Editing is an excellent topic for mini-lessons. Pieces of writing, both our own or our children's, can be used to illustrate editing strategies for meaning and correctness. If we use children's writing, we must be sure that it is with their permission. We should model both editing for meaning and editing for correctness.

Editing for meaning should take precedence over correctness. If we routinely engage in shared writing with our children, we will have modeled our thinking strategies for making meaning. We can help children practice checking for meaning by thinking aloud so that children can understand how different strategies work and consider when certain strategies should be used. Children should be able to edit for meaning at their level of independent reading, where they have enough control over the words to think about the meaning of what is written.

The most common form of editing for meaning that we see in kindergarten and first grade is adding on to a piece. In second and third grade, children may be focused on doing the "right" thing and will revise to please their audience or the adults who respond to the writing. Adding on becomes an editing strategy when children see that adding more paper keeps us from running out of room, which usually ends the writing. Cutting apart a draft and taping or stapling more paper in key places can encourage the process of making changes. Some children will cut apart their writing so that its order can be more easily changed. We must take care with the strategies we suggest to young children because they often take us literally and may think that the same strategy must be used each time they write.

Editing for correctness is encouraged after editing for meaning. Children will not be able to successfully edit the spelling of words that are beyond their level of word knowledge. We may need to coach editing partners or groups to be sensitive to the varying levels of children's knowledge in the classroom. Teaching children to read their work aloud helps them to discover places where punctuation belongs. Punctuation is needed by readers to interpret an author's ideas, so the reader will read the pieces as the author intended. Working with punctuation is another excellent mini-lesson, as well as knowledge that should be modeled in shared writing.

Whether editing for meaning or correctness, we are asking children to let the knowledge they have gained as readers also help them as writers. We should stress this point as we model editing skills for children throughout daily writing activities.

Whole-Class Closure/Sharing

Author's Chair:

In an author's chair, a group of children become the audience for a child to read a piece aloud and receive response. The purpose of an author's chair is to celebrate and receive response to a piece of completed writing. The author usually sits on a chair in front of the group, introduces the piece, then reads the piece aloud.

After the reading, the audience offers remembers, reminders, and questions (Graves, 1994):

- "Remembers" encourages active listening as children are encouraged to tell the author what they heard in the piece.
- "Reminders" occur as children make connections between the piece and their own lives, sharing something they are reminded about by the piece.
- "Questions" also indicate the listeners' connections with a piece, as questions are asked to clarify meaning in what was heard. "Questions" also provide impetus for further editing on some pieces in which authors are heavily invested and wish to publish.

When children learn to listen to and appreciate another's writing, they are also learning more about how to listen to their own writing.

In the opening vignette of Renee's classroom, Marty shared his writing in the author's chair. He rehearsed for the sharing by reading his piece aloud to himself, then to Renee. He anticipated the questions that children would ask, because he had participated in author's chairs since the beginning of first grade, which had been five months ago. The children in Renee's classroom remembered many details from Marty's story and asked many sincere questions. They really wanted to know more about Marty's sheep and what had caused one of them to die.

Author's chair in Renee's classroom evolved over time. Early in the school year, Renee coaxed retellings, connections, and questions from the children and modeled telling the author what she heard in the piece. She also modeled asking questions about the writing, but questions seemed to come more naturally to the children. They wanted to know more about their classmates' experiences. Learning to respond to the writing of another carries over to the group experience of author's chair.

FUNCTIONAL WRITING EXPERIENCES

After viewing a video about whales, the second graders in Ms. Sanger's class discuss and compare the different types of whales they observed. Jason doesn't seem very involved in the discussion. Later we find that during the discussion Jason draws and labels a variety of whales, giving special attention to his favorite, the killer whale. He also writes, "Just because a whale is big don't mean he's dangerous," seemingly comparing size and temperament. Jason uses this piece of informal writing and drawing to explore his ideas (Combs, 1993).

What Is Functional Writing?

We as adults use functional writing every day. We leave notes for others, make notes for ourselves, take phone messages, make shopping or to-do lists, sketch and label directions to someone's house, and complete a variety of forms. These are all examples of functional writing, that which serves a specific function. In our daily lives, functional writing is the dominant type of writing that we do.

Functional writing in school gives children the same opportunities to record their thinking in a variety of forms. Functional writing should be an integral part of a classroom literacy program in which children routinely make written records to capture their thinking and preserve it for future use. We process so much information in today's world that we need mechanisms to retain and sort that information. It is an excellent way to encourage children to retain and recollect an experience, as Jason did with the topic of whales.

Formal writing, pieces of thinking that get fully developed, are not always feasible or the most desirable types of writing to accomplish a goal (Calkins, 1994). In today's busy classrooms, functional writings are very useful. They allow us to easily integrate writing into instruction in any subject area. Through frequent opportunities to write, children come to see writing as a medium that is flexible and useful for thinking.

Functional writing is not typically taken through all phases of the writing process, only those that are appropriate to the purpose of the writing. A cluster or list of what children know about birds, developed in small groups before class discussion, serves as a means of getting started with thinking about the topic of the lesson. It is primarily for children's thinking and will go no further at that time. A chart that children prepare to compare and contrast three versions of *The Three Little Pigs* will be displayed in the classroom, so it is edited for meaning and correctness.

In Carmen's first-grade classroom that we have visited on other occasions, we observe Jasmine who is busy preparing a sign to announce the birth of the baby mice. Above the cage is a sign that states, "This is Minnie Mouse." To the side of the cage are other signs and labeled drawings indicating things the children know about mice. The names of the children who are taking care of Minnie during that week are shown on another sign. Carmen uses many forms of functional writing as a natural part of the classroom environment.

In a classroom, functional writing can take on many other forms:

- lists
- annotated drawings
- graphs
- descriptions
- records of events
- clusters
- charts
- labels
- notes
- explanations

Lists:
Children can use lists to retain information for later use or to re-collect ideas (e.g., Books I Have Read, the lunch menu, special words we are using in our rocks and minerals unit, names of people who will bring items for a party, or the sequence of steps used to make a paper mache project). Class-made lists, such as words-on-the-wall (Cunningham, 1995), demonstrate the making of lists and their potential use for retaining ideas.

At a more elaborate level, children will write "All About . . . " a topic, which is actually a list of what is known about the topic. Figure 6.4 shows an example of a list of characteristics that becomes a descriptive paragraph about birds.

Clusters:
Visual arrangements of ideas are a way to show ideas and perhaps how the ideas are related. Clusters can be thought of as lists that are organized into a visual display that is a helpful tool for retaining and re-collecting specific ideas. Initially, a brainstormed cluster may not be organized to show relationships. Re-collecting the ideas to show relationships can make the ideas more usable. Figure 6.5 shows examples of a cluster that is merely a collection of ideas, as well as a cluster in which the ideas have been organized to support further writing in a second-grade unit about community helpers. Figure 6.6 shows a spider cluster used to re-collect information about spiders during a third-grade unit of study.

FIGURE 6.4
Sample List that Becomes Description—Third Grade

Lists and Descriptions

Birds	All About Birds
- have feathers - fly with wings - beaks crack seeds - claws hold on	Birds have feathers on their body. They have wings that help them fly. Birds have a beak for cracking seeds. They hold on to tree branches with long skinny claws on their feet.

FIGURE 6.5
Sample Clusters

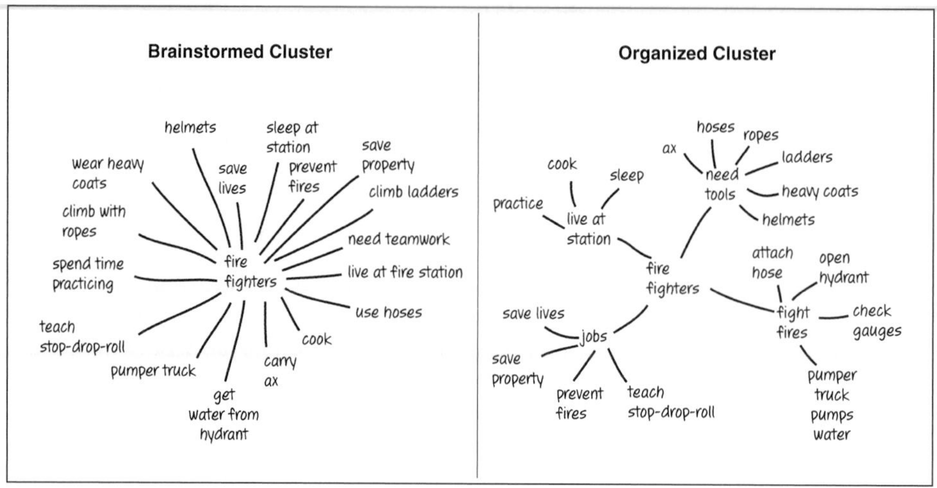

FIGURE 6.6
Organized Cluster for Spiders

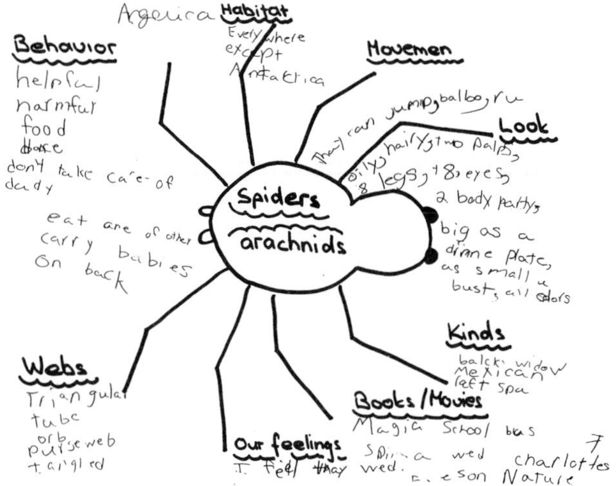

Annotated Drawings:
Writing can elaborate on ideas that are drawn or vice versa. In the opening of this section, Jason used annotated drawings to show his ideas about killer whales. The annotation may be labels, descriptions, or explanations that comment on or clarify the illustration. Annotations may be a way that children reflect of their thinking. For emergent writers, illustration can fill in for ideas that are difficult to put into words. Figure 6.7 shows an example of a plant with parts identified.

Charts:
Sometimes ideas are more helpful if they are arranged in an orderly manner. Charts show ideas arranged so that the relationship of the ideas is clear. Charts can cause children to re-construct ideas, sometimes into new relationships. Figure 6.8 shows an example of a simple chart that supports what a child knows about a topic such as living and nonliving things in second grade.

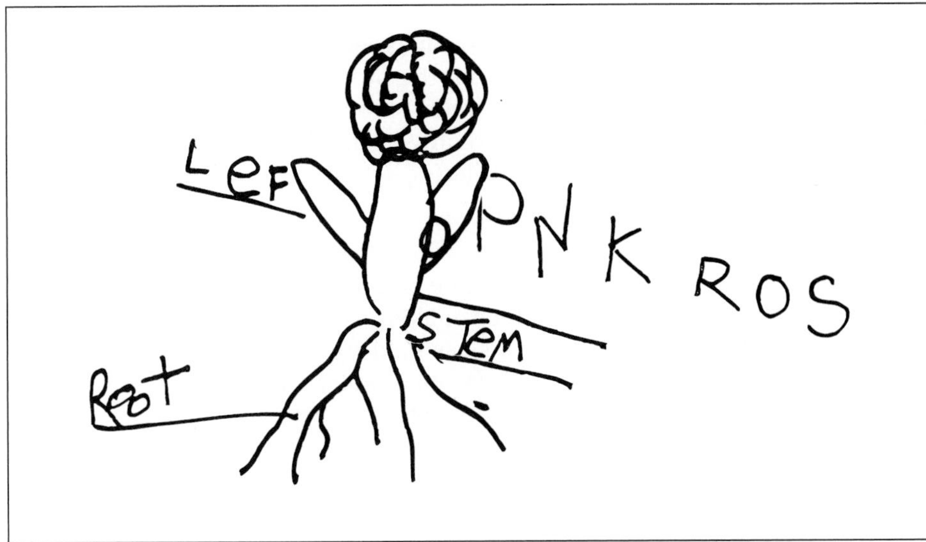

FIGURE 6.7
Annotated Drawing of a Plant

FIGURE 6.8
Sample Chart and Graph

Chart

Living	Not Living
people	rocks
snail	cup
bird	pencil
flower	car
grass	watch

Graph

When Do We Go to Bed?

	X		
	X		
X	X		
X	X		
X	X	X	
X	X	X	
X	X	X	X
8:00	8:30	9:00	10:00

Bedtime

Graphs:
Ideas can be represented in a symbolic form. Graphs use lines, bars, portions of circles, and symbols to represent relationships. Words help to define categories and the type of relationship. Figure 6.8 shows an example of a class-made graph about bedtimes in kindergarten.

Descriptions:
Relationships among ideas can also be shown with words. Descriptions can use words to build images of objects, people, places, and events we know, just as we do with illustrations. In descriptions, we re-collect ideas we have retained or re-create a portion of an experience we have had. Figure 6.4 shows an example of description that began as a list of characteristics about birds in third grade.

Notes:
In the midst of an experience, words, phrases, or sentences can be used to capture and retain the ordeal. Notes are made during experiences or immediately following to retain the happening for future use. Notes should be for personal use and need only be useful to the writer. Note making can be demonstrated by the teacher during activities in which retaining ideas is important.

Record of Events:
Notes can be expanded to become a record of events, or an orderly list that shows sequence and important details. When it is important to recall in an orderly fashion, making a record of events would be a helpful form of informal writing (e.g., a class field trip, a science experiment, life events in preparation for writing an autobiography, or re-collecting the events of a playground disturbance to prepare for problem solving).

Explanations:
When events require elaboration, an explanation is useful. An explanation asks the writer to tell more than the mere ideas or events by providing a rationale or support for one's thinking (e.g., steps in solving a math problem, response to a book or character, hypothesizing in a science experiment, or selecting a particular form for a piece of process writing). Figure 6.9 shows an example of a first-grader's explanation of states of matter in a science lesson.

Informal writing is often collected in a journal or learning log. Journals and learning logs can be thought of as tools for helping children retain, re-collect, re-create, and re-construct their thinking as functional writing.

Journals and Learning Logs

Many people make written records of the everyday events in their lives in some form of journal. While the form of the records may differ, the intention is similar—to capture feelings and experiences for personal, not public, purposes. In school, however, teachers often use journals to provide an outlet for

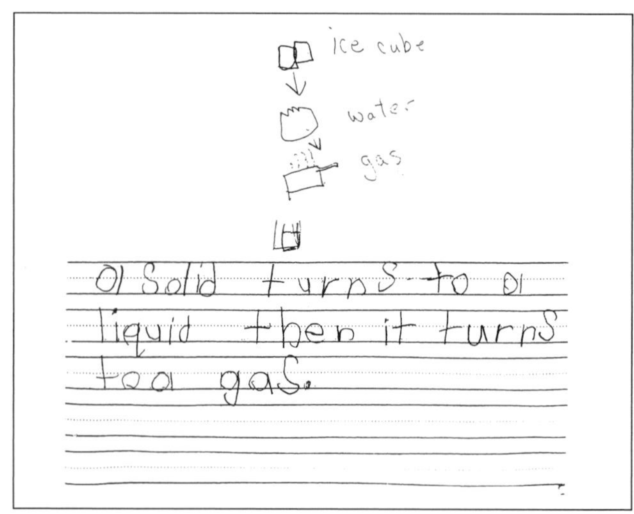

FIGURE 6.9
Explanation of States of Matter—First Grade

children's personal thoughts and as a daily independent writing opportunity. Journals may also become a dialogue between teacher and child.

Some journals are called "working journals," because writers record observations and other information that will be used for another purpose (Tompkins, 1993). Many professions require the observation, collection, and use of data. These professionals keep a working journal, of sorts, as they observe and record progress or outcomes, consider or make predictions about next steps, chart data to consider its meaning or patterns, and consider what data should be shared and in what manner. In this text, working journals are referred to as *learning logs,* to differentiate their intended use from journals. Learning logs are intended to be a vehicle for helping children use writing as a functional tool for learning, particularly in content areas such as science, social studies, and mathematics.

Personal Journals:
Topics for personal journals are usually the choice of the writer. The contents of a personal journal typically focus on events in the writer's life and personal concerns. The personal journal serves as an outlet and is made public only by the choice of the writer. For emerging writers, personal journals may also be annotated drawings. Teachers often write responses to children's entries to stimulate children's writing and model elements of language. Figure 6.10 shows one of Jose's first-grade journal entries about his dog. He usually writes about his personal experiences, especially about his dog.

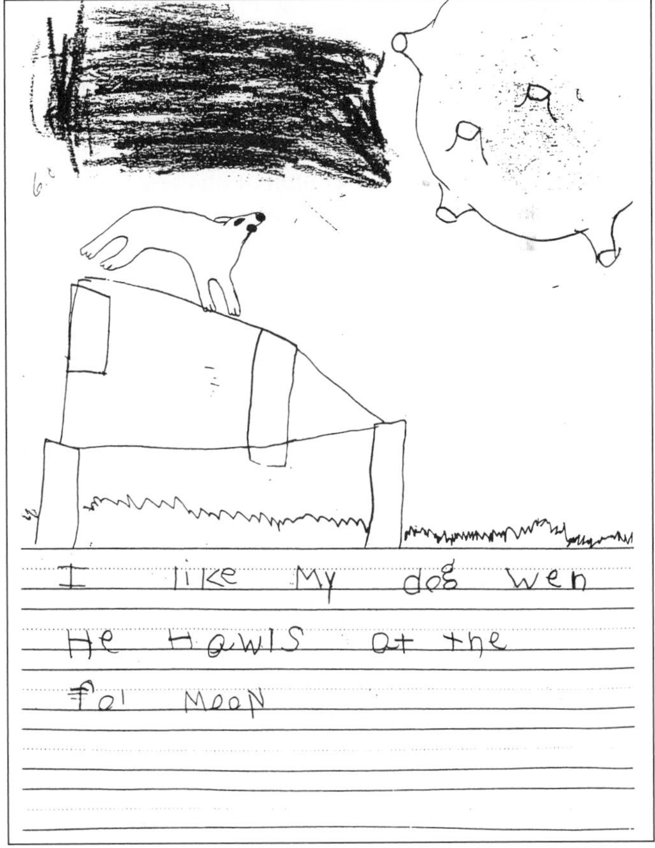

FIGURE 6.10
Personal Journal Entry—First Grade

Dialogue Journals:
Personal journals become dialogue journals when the writer addresses the writing to another who is expected to respond. This exchange is a private conversation through writing (Bode, 1989; Gambrell, 1985; Staton, 1987). The children set the direction for the conversation. Our role is to encourage, support, and nudge or stretch children's thinking. Our goal should be for children to become the question askers (Tompkins, 1993). Dialogue journals can be of great value in bridging the gap between talking and writing (Kreeft, 1984), helping children work out nonacademic school problems (Staton, 1980), and supporting children as they learn to talk about books (Barone, 1990).

Response Journals:
As part of a literacy program, children may be asked to write their responses to books they are reading or to experiences of the class. Tompkins's (1993) review of research reveals that children's responses may include the following:

- Retellings and summaries
- Questions related to understanding the text
- Interaction or empathy with characters
- Predictions of what will happen and validation after reading
- Personal experiences, feelings, and opinions related to the reading
- Simple and elaborated evaluations
- Philosophical reflections (pp. 90–91)

Response journals also serve as an excellent assessment of children's responses to and understanding of class learning experiences. When we include substantial amounts of information text in the curriculum, we want to know how children are forming concepts about those ideas and concepts. Inviting children to comment on their learning provides insight for us. Enrique's second-grade class has been reading about and experimenting with magnets. He uses his journal writing time to comment on his ideas about magnets (see Figure 6.11).

Double-Entry Journals:
Children respond to the authors they read. A double-entry journal (Barone, 1990) combines a quote from a text with the child's response. The journal page is divided into two columns with a quote from the text (noting chapter/page for future reference) on the left and the child's response on the right. Because the quote is provided, double-entry responses are focused and interpretable. Other variations of the double-entry journal can be to place (1) "Reading Notes" on the left, response or "Discussion Notes" on the right, or (2) "Predictions" on the left, validation or "What Happened" on the right (Tompkins, 1993, p. 92). Figure 6.12 shows sample double-entry journals from third-grade children. The first example uses a quote from the narrative text, *Amazing Grace,* as the focus of the response. The second double-entry journal begins with notes from an information text about making crayons, then the child adds a response to the information. From the examples, we can see that double-entry journals are useful for focusing children's responses to a variety of texts.

Learning Logs:
While learning logs can be used to help children record and react to their learning in mathematics, science, and social studies (Fulwiler, 1985), this benefit can

FIGURE 6.11
Enrique's Response to Magnets—Second Grade

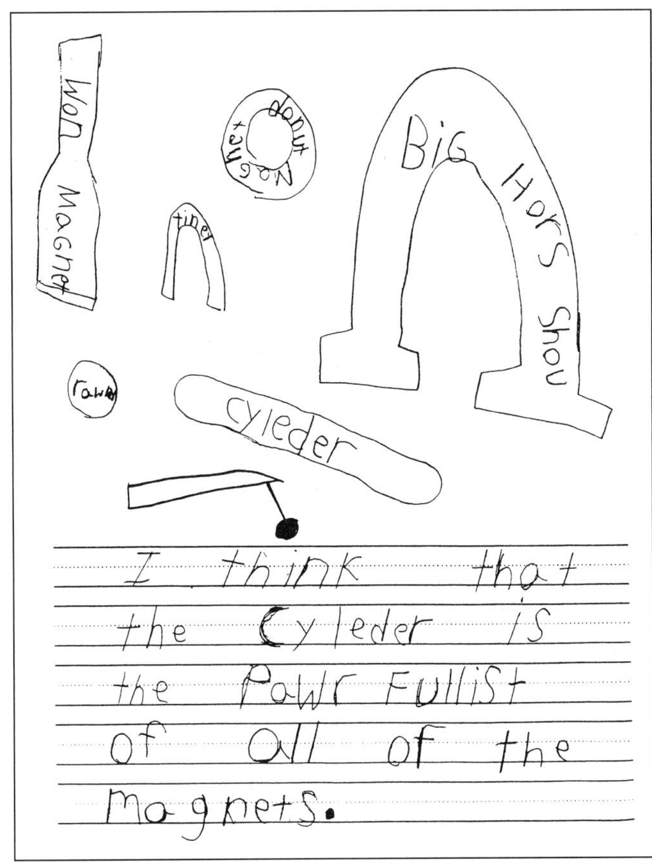
Won Magnet
donut Magnet
tiner
Big Hors Shou
cyleder
I think that the Cyleder is the Powr Fullist of All of the Magnets.

FIGURE 6.12
Sample Double—Entry Journals

Double-Entry Journal	***Amazing Grace,* by Mary Hoffman and Caroline Binch**
Text Quote- "And she always gave herself the most exciting part."	Response- I like to pretend too. I pretend I am in Beauty and the Beast. I think the Beast is the most exciting part.
Double-Entry Journal	***How is a Crayon Made?* by Oz Charles**
Reading Notes from the Text- Crayons are made from clear wax and a colored powder. The hot wax is put in a special mold like a muffin tin.	Discussion Notes- I wondered how crayons got shaped like a pencil. A muffin pan to make crayons is a funny idea.

also be expanded to include literature study. A learning log can be thought of as a collection of journal responses and informal writings that, when taken together, can help children see growth in their thinking.

While participating in a whole-class literature study of *Owl Moon,* by Jane Yolen, children might:

- write a response to the text using a particular journal style,
- draw and label different kinds of owls,
- cluster what they know about owls and add to the cluster as they gain new knowledge,
- make a list of interesting words in the text and add other related words that could be used to describe the setting or the owling experience,
- write a description of a familiar setting, and
- describe a time when they had to be very quiet and still.

While participating in a unit study about the seasons and seasonal change, children might use a variety of informal writings to demonstrate what they are learning, such as the following:

- Draw pictures of changes that occur during each season and identify those changes with labels.
- Write brief descriptions of what they do during each season.
- Add to a chart that compares the four seasons according to average temperatures, amount of daily sunlight, weather, what happens to plants, what happens to animals.
- Cluster or brainstorm ideas on what children know about each season.
- Answer questions posed by the teacher.
- Respond to literature read during the unit.
- Add to shared writings developed by the class.
- Make a list of season words, adding to the list as they find new and interesting words.

Learning logs provide great versatility. In practice, learning logs can combine the formats and intentions of the journals described earlier, as well as a variety of informal and formal writing formats. Learning logs can stimulate writing through the use of a variety of formats, meeting the needs and preferences of individual children. Our experiences with writing help us decide what thoughts need to be re-collected and what form would be best to re-present our thinking. Informal writing may help children see that writing is beneficial and within reach.

TRYING ON DIFFERENT FORMS OF WRITING

When we emphasize writing as a way of exploring and organizing thinking, children have opportunities to "try on" different types of writing. These writing experiences grow out of learning experiences that might be a part of our literacy program using basal readers, authentic literature, or content area materials. Studies of the topics children write about in self-selected writing programs reveal that boys and girls have different interests (Douglas, 1988; Graves, 1973). Boys often write about the world outside of themselves with a focus on informational writing. Girls often write with a focus toward "I" and personal narratives. Knowing this, we can encourage different forms of writing to enhance the writing opportunities for all children.

Extending Personal Narratives

Children's writing often begins with pieces that grow out of their own experience. Early on, the narrative lies mostly in children's drawings with writing to comment on the drawing. To push children's written narratives, whole-class shared writing can demonstrate how to use words to elaborate on what is shown in the drawing with the intention of replacing illustration with written description and to break an experience into "episodes" to encourage more elaboration.

Going Beyond the Illustration:
Young children put a great deal of energy and detail into their drawings, often because writing is slow and tedious compared with drawing. The "story" they have to tell takes shape as the drawing takes shape and is frequently unplanned. To extend children's use of such drawings, we can do the following activities:

- Make an overhead transparency with an illustration similar to what children are doing in their writing.
- With the children, discuss what the drawing shows and read the writing comments on the drawing.
- Brainstorm ideas that are related to the experience but may not be shown in the illustration.
- Taking one idea at a time from the brainstorming, have children compose other things the author could have written, then use interactive writing to record.

Be sure to discuss how the combination of illustration and "new" writing enhances the total composition. Then encourage children to try extending their own illustrated narratives. In the weeks that follow, observe the impact of the interactive writing lesson.

Extend Writing by Making Episodes:
Children's illustrations often describe an experience that actually has several parts. To encourage more elaboration for each part or episode of the experience, demonstrate how writers can break their stories into parts. The illustrations in favorite picture books may be used as examples. Show children how an author elaborates on the illustration that appears on two facing pages to tell a story.

Using an experience that is familiar to children (with a sample one-page illustration), brainstorm the parts or episodes that are part of the experience. Use one piece of paper for each episode. Use shared or interactive writing as children consider what might be written about each part and what the illustration might show. Show children how the parts can be assembled to make a book. Compare the expanded narrative to the one-page illustration telling of the experience. Encourage children to try breaking their experiences into parts, telling about each piece so the reader will know more.

Words in Place of Illustration:
As children acquire more proficiency with handwriting and word knowledge, extended writing becomes more possible (usually by second grade). At this point, demonstrating the use of writing to stand in place of drawings can be helpful.

- With the children's help, brainstorm descriptions that can stand in place of the drawing.
- Using the brainstormed ideas, have children verbally compose sentences that when taken together will "show" what is illustrated.
- Take away the illustration and read the description. Encourage children to build a mental image in place of the illustration.

At the same time, for classroom writing experiences, substitute paper that has all lines instead of the paper that provides a blank space for illustration. Ask children to "show" their narrative with words before drawing.

In these examples, as we brainstorm and record children's ideas, we are also modeling for children the use of functional writing. Many types of writing can begin with clusters of ideas or lists that are moved into phrases, sentences, and descriptive paragraphs. Help children see that functional writing can be very useful to them as they write independently.

Experimenting with Fiction

To try on different forms of fictional writing, children must first have opportunities to listen to literature for the writer's style—to listen like a writer. Instead of listening just for the story line, children listen more for what the author did to create the story. As we read aloud, we encourage children to listen for such things as:

- words that create mental pictures,
- how characters are introduced,
- places in the story where the tension builds, where we say to ourselves, "Something's going to happen,"
- how we come to know about a character, or
- how the author helps us see the setting in our minds.

When we finish the reading we ask, "What did I notice?" and the discussion begins. Learning to listen like a writer can change what children notice about other people's writing. This knowledge begins to inform their understanding of different types of writing. Some forms of writing children will discover, but some forms may be best developed with our guidance. As a reminder about literary elements and genre, see the information provided in Appendix A.

Developing a Plot:
For primary-grade children, plot is an important literary element. The picture books they read are dominated by plot development. To help children enhance their fiction writing, conduct shared writing activities that guide children to think of plot as:

- beginning–middle–end (inexperienced writers), or
- problem–events–resolution (more experienced writers).

A story map is an excellent planning tool for narrative writing. We are familiar with story maps from our discussion of retelling as a response to read-aloud in Chapter 2. A story map is a word or picture diagram that shows the main events in a story and the relationship of those events. Mapping a story can help children identify the detail and sequence they want to use in their plot. A story map can be used to check a child's understanding as a reader or to plan a story as a writer.

To help children plan their own writing, we can study how other authors organize their plots. Originating from the literature that is studied in the classroom, the first step is to develop a story map to examine how a plot can be structured (also see the illustrated story map for *Sylvester and the Magic Pebble* in Figure 2.3).

Beginning–Middle–End Story Map:
Sylvester and the Magic Pebble (Steig, 1969)

Beginning: Sylvester finds a magic pebble and makes the rain stop and start.
Sylvester is scared by a lion and wishes to be a rock.

Middle: Mr. and Mrs. Duncan look for Sylvester.
They ask neighbors, children, police, and dogs.
Fall and spring pass and Sylvester is still a rock.

End: In spring, Mr. and Mrs. Duncan go to Strawberry Hill for a picnic.
Mr. Duncan finds a pebble and puts it on a rock that is really Sylvester.
Sylvester wishes he is himself again.
They all go home together.

Problem–Events–Resolution Story Map:
Sylvester and the Magic Pebble

Problem: Sylvester becomes a rock on Strawberry Hill and he cannot move.

Events: Sylvester finds a magic pebble and makes the rain stop and start.
He is scared by a lion and wishes to be a rock.
Mr. and Mrs. Duncan look everywhere for Sylvester.
They ask neighbors, children, police, dogs.
Fall and winter pass.
In spring, Mr. and Mrs. Duncan go to Strawberry Hill for a picnic.
Mr. Duncan finds a magic pebble and places it on a large rock (Sylvester).

Resolution: Sylvester wishes he is himself again and the wish comes true.
They all go home together.

After we have developed a story map for a familiar book with the children, we help them see how the story map retells the plot of the book. From the story map we can make a class book using one sheet of paper for each major event, which will help children elaborate their ideas. Using shared or interactive writing, we spread out the events on separate pages to emphasize the structure of the plot, as shown in Figure 6.13. We guide the children to reread and check for the flow of the story as we record their ideas. For children with little experience in writing narratives, we leave space for their illustrations on each page, because when they begin to write their own stories both text and illustrations will be used to tell the story.

FIGURE 6.13
From Story Map to Story Writing . . .

Beginning . . . Sylvester found a magic pebble. He made the rain stop and start.	On his way home he got scared by a lion and wished to be a rock. Then he couldn't go home.	Middle . . . Mr. and Mrs. Duncan looked everywhere for Sylvester. They asked the neighbors, children, and police. They were very sad.
Fall and winter passed. Sylvester was still a rock on Strawberry Hill.	End . . . Spring came. Mr. and Mrs. Duncan went to Strawberry Hill. They had a picnic on a big rock. Mr. Duncan found a red pebble and put it on the big rock.	Sylvester wished he was a donkey again and he was! Then they all went home.

After the class has worked together making story maps of familiar books and turning the maps back into stories, children will be ready to write an original group story. As a group, select an idea to develop, brainstorm the plot, and make a map. From the map, work together to tell the story, then write the story in a process similar to the one used for *Sylvester and the Magic Pebble.*

After group writing, children should be ready to try applying their experiences in plot development to their personal writing. As a strategy for getting started, encourage children to develop a map for the story they are thinking about, then have a classmate respond to their ideas. In the writing center provide small sheets of paper that children can use to write their story, spreading out the events as modeled for them. By spreading out the events, making changes in the story is much easier. Ideas can be added or ordered differently by simply changing the pages.

Helping children write well-developed plots is only one element of telling a story that can be modeled in shared writing. Using a process similar to the one just described, children can explore:

- introducing a character in a story,
- letting characters talk to tell part of the story,
- making a story out of one main event, and
- telling stories from different points of view.

Exploring Informational Writing

Informational writing is organized differently than narratives. Whereas narrative seeks to tell a story, information writing:

- describes,
- makes order or sequence clear,
- shows comparison,
- explains cause and effect,
- describes problems and solutions,
- poses questions with answers, or
- attempts to persuade.

Additional discussion of each text form can be found in Appendix A, which provides explanations of literary genre and elements. As we begin to explore information writing, it is helpful to use visual representations, when possible, to help children think about arranging their ideas.

We can use writer's workshop to model specific types of information writing that relate to unit concepts and provide opportunities for children to explore with our support. Taking one type of structure at a time, we develop shared or interactive writings with the children that model possible ways to organize ideas in that structure. Then we encourage children to develop their own ideas during independent writing time.

Description:
Ideas in description can be illustrated like the spokes of a wheel, relating to a central topic but not necessarily to each other in any particular order. To demonstrate description, we work with children to build a cluster of ideas/details about a single topic. We should select a topic that is familiar to children, then help them examine the cluster for relationships among the ideas. Through shared or interactive writing we develop sentences with the related ideas. If we write these ideas on sentence strips and place them in a pocket chart, we can rearrange the ideas until the organization provides a satisfactory description. Figure 6.14 shows an example of descriptive writing about dogs with third-grade children. Notice how ideas from the cluster become sentences in the paragraph.

Order or Sequence:
Describing a sequence of steps involves order, such as giving directions or retelling the steps in a science experiment. Children can retell the steps used to plant seeds and chart the plants' growth during science. An autobiography

FIGURE 6.14
Brainstorm Cluster Becomes a Descriptive Paragraph—Third Grade

FIGURE 6.15
Ordered or Sequential Writing—First Grade

An Alphabet of Favorite Books

A is for...	B is for...	C is for...	D is for...
Amazing Grace by Mary Hoffman and Caroline Binch	Blueberries for Sal by Robert McCloskey	Chicken Sunday by Patricia Polacco	Doctor DeSoto by William Steig

is also a form of ordered writing that children can try. For time sequences, a time line makes a good "getting started" tool. Alphabet and counting books are also good examples of ordered writing for the primary grades. If we examine various types of ABC or number books, we can show children possibilities for presenting their ideas. The topic of the ABC or counting book can be tied to literature the class is reading or a unit of study. Figure 6.15 shows an example of a class or individual book that is sequenced in ABC order.

Making Comparisons:
We can introduce comparison by intertwining a description of one topic with a related topic. Cluster the first topic and identify main ideas. Then introduce and cluster the second topic according to the main points established for the first topic. Identify details that are similar and those that are different. For similarities we can develop "and" statements, and for differences we develop "but" statements.

For example, to compare/contrast the topics of winter and summer, we might identify the following as our main ideas:

- Weather
- Clothing
- Things We Do

We record details for one topic, then compare/contrast those ideas to the second topic. From the details, we write "and" (comparisons) and "but" (contrasts) statements. Figure 6.16 shows an example of the development of compare/contrast writing with second-grade children.

As a group, we must decide how to:

- introduce the piece so that our purpose is clear,
- introduce each part,
- make a transition between parts, and
- conclude the piece.

FIGURE 6.16
Steps in Compare/Contrast Writing—Second Grade

Step 1: Details for Winter–Summer Compare/Contrast

Weather		Clothing		Things We Do	
winter	summer	winter	summer	winter	summer
cold	hot	coats	shorts	snow ski	water ski
snow	dry	hats	hats	play inside	play outside
sunny	sunny	gloves	swimsuit	ride stationary bike	ride bike
		boots	sandals		
			no shoes		

Step 2: Develop Compare/Contrast Statements

Weather	Clothing	Things We Do
Winter is cold but the summer is hot. or Winter is cold and snowy, but summer is hot and dry.	In the summer we wear shorts and swimsuits but in the winter we have to wear coats, gloves, and boots.	We can ski in the summer and winter. In summer we ski on water but in winter we ski on snow.
Days are sunny in summer and winter.	We wear hats in winter and summer.	In the summer we can play outside, but in the winter we play inside a lot. We ride our bikes in the summer and winter.

Thinking about Causes and Effects:
Thinking through cause/effect relationships requires the use of background experience with the topic to recognize how a particular cause and effect are related. Cause/effect relationships also rely on language to give clues about the existence of the relationship with words such as *because, as a result, makes,* or *leads to.*

Cause and effect writing is often seen in social studies and science texts. For example, in a unit that focuses on understanding weather and its impact on land and people, the concept of rainfall may lead to discussion of cause/effect relationships:

Cause—too much rainfall [causes, makes, leads to] floods
Effect—floods happen [because of] too much rainfall

Cause—too little rainfall [causes, makes, leads to] droughts
Effect—droughts happen [because of] too little rainfall

Cause/effect can be illustrated to emphasize the relationship, filling in with the essential language.

too much rainfall → →→→ flood

After the class develops cause/effect statements, we help children brainstorm ideas that elaborate on and explain the relationship. We complete the piece by using brainstorm ideas to explain the relationship. As children gain experience and confidence as writers, we begin to explore cause/effect relationships that have multiple causes and/or multiple effects.

Problem/Solution or Question/Answer:
Another structure that can be found in information writing is the identification of a problem and its solution(s). This relationship can also appear as a question with an answer(s). In information writing, the author may introduce the piece using the problem or a question, then develop the piece by presenting and discussing solutions or answering the question. This type of writing may be most useful as a way to structure the study of a topic, especially using question/answer. Question/answer relationships can be a beginning format for independent research in a unit of study.

The first step may be to generate one problem or question as a group, then brainstorm and write about possible solutions or answers. The second step becomes exploring the use of this structure to organize a number of problems or questions as a way of studying a topic. After a brainstorm session to generate problems or questions about a topic, place each problem or question on a separate chart so that everyone can see it. As children search for information, the charts serve as a means of organizing ideas. Children write important words or phrases on the relevant charts—problem or question. After enough ideas are gathered, hold another shared writing session to discuss how to organize each solution or answer. Then, as a group, decide how to place the problems or questions in a coherent order. On the overhead or another large chart, lead a shared writing activity that shows children how to organize the problem/solutions or questions/answers into a "report." Follow up this exercise by providing an opportunity for children to develop their own "report," using cards for each problem or question rather than large charts. Small groups can also successfully write in this format, assuming you have already been working with small-group writing tasks.

Persuasion:
Children are already well aware of persuasion. They attempt it daily with parents, teachers, and friends! When appropriate, we should provide support for children to begin to use persuasion in their writing. Persuasive writing depends on presentation of facts in a carefully crafted order. Persuasion also requires careful attention to the selection of words that will persuade. The voice of the writer also becomes important. The reader is more likely to be persuaded if the tone is sincere and the argument seems well supported.

Persuasive writing begins with reading aloud particular examples, then modeling how to think about persuading someone else through the shared writing of persuasive pieces. Finally, we should provide opportunities for children to

FIGURE 6.17
Persuasive Letter from Raymond—Third Grade

August 25, 1999

Dear mom

would you Let me bring my mealworm home? I'll keep it locked in a jar. I'll feed it I'll keep it clean. I'll keep it in my room. I'll wash my hands after playing with it. Please let me have It.

Love Raymond

Yes Raymond may bring his mealworm home. Raymond's mom

attempt their own persuasive pieces. Letters are an excellent form to begin persuasive writing in the primary grades. See the example of a persuasive letter from Raymond in Figure 6.17. After his third-grade science project with the mealworm is completed, he wants permission from his mother to bring it home.

Other forms of writing that can be introduced and developed through shared writing include letter writing, biographies and autobiographies, and various types of poetry. For other examples of forms of writing, see Gail Tompkins's (1993) *Teaching Writing: Balancing Process and Product.*

To extend children's interest in writing, provide opportunities for exploration with writing through activity centers in the classroom. Time provided for making choices in activity centers can be highly motivating.

INDEPENDENT WRITING IN ACTIVITY CENTERS

Many teachers in the primary grades use activity centers as extensions of work time or enrichment. The possibilities for centers seem endless, but may include the following:

- Quiet reading or library corner
- Language arts center
- Writing center
- Math center
- Theme/unit center

- Listening center
- Home center (includes dress-up/pretend materials)
- Construction/block centers
- Sand/water/exploration areas

As we set up centers to extend children's work time or for enrichment, we should consider examples of the natural uses of writing that might fit.

- A home center might become a restaurant with menus, order tablets, and so forth.
- The language center might provide materials for children to respond to books they have completed on their own or as extensions of class lessons.
- The writing center might include all types of writing implements and interesting colors and shapes of paper for writing. Materials and ideas for making books are also a must. Additional ideas for making books are provided in an upcoming section. In addition, personal mailboxes can be provided to encourage communication.
- In a math center children might indicate their preference for breakfast cereals on a class graph and record the reason for their selection on a group response sheet.
- Theme or units centers offer extensive possibilities for writing, including:
    - blank booklets in different shapes related to the theme,
    - group response sheets for different theme-related issues such as "My favorite type of weather . . . ,"
    - records of experiments that are tried, or
    - displays of children's drawings, clusters, records, and so on, related to the theme.

Additional ideas for using reading and writing in integrated units can be found in the Unit Study.

EXTENDING WRITING THROUGH BOOKMAKING

Throughout this text we have discussed a variety of ways that we engage children in class-made books. Making individual books is also highly motivating for children, especially when the topic is their choice. A variety of formats are possible. Materials can be provided in a writing center for independent bookmaking or during writer's workshop as children complete drafts, edit for meaning and convention, then prepare to re-present their ideas. Figure 6.18 provides a variety of sample book formats that can be adapted to any topic of study or a child's personal interests.

- Accordion books are made from folded paper, and lend themselves to a variety of shapes. These books work well for both narrative and information writing.

FIGURE 6.18 Sample Designs for Book Making

Accordion Books:

1. Fold paper lengthwise and crease. Folded edge will be top of book.
2. Fold strip in half and crease center.
3. Fold each edge back toward the center fold and crease. The strip should be in the shape of a W.
4. On one side (front) number each panel, 1–4. If more pages are desired, number back panel, 5–8. Panel 8 will be the title page.
5. Write text on separate paper cut slightly smaller than book panels.
6. Glue text on appropriate panels.

Option:

1. Shapes—holding closed book, cut shape leaving some part of fold on sides uncut to keep the book together.
2. Make tag board books by placing tape along edges of pages like a hinge.

Fan Page Books:

1. Decide on the number of pages for the book.
2. Largest page will be the back cover of the book.
3. Cut 1" off right-hand side for next to last page.
4. For each preceding page cut off an additional 1" strip so that each page is 1" smaller than the next.
5. Assemble pages in order of size and staple.

Hint:

1. Using 8½" × 11" paper = max. of 7–8 pages
   Using 11" × 14" paper = max. of 10–11 pages

Pocket Books:

1. Make books with paper pages, stapled on the spine. Pages should be large enough to accommodate a small envelope.
2. Glue an envelope to the lower half of each right-hand page with the flap side accessible.
3. On left-hand page, children place a question or riddle.
4. A small card with the answer is placed in the envelope.

Variation: Flap Books

1. Instead of an envelope, place a paper flap on the lower part of the right-hand page. Glue only the top ½" of the flap to the page.
2. Write the answer under the flap.

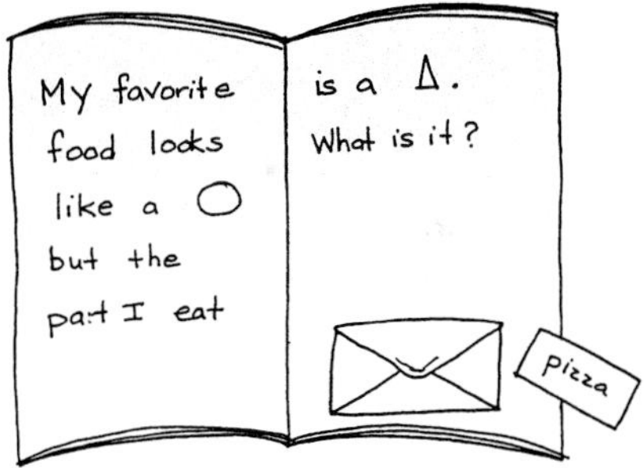

Shape Books:

1. Provide tagboard templates in different shapes to trace for books.
2. Trace shape on paper that will be front cover and cut out.
3. Stack front cover, several sheets of writing paper, and paper for a back cover.
4. Staple on left-hand side for spine.
5. Holding carefully, cut around edge of front cover, being sure to cut through all pages at the same time.

Hint:
Simple shapes work best. Consider the actual writing surface that will be left after cutting the paper.

FIGURE 6.18 (continued)
Sample Designs for Book Making

Pop-up Books:

1. Each page of a pop-up book is made separately.
2. Fold paper in half crosswise.
3. Make two 1" cuts equidistant from the center of the fold to make the pop-up tab.
4. Open the paper, gently pull the tab forward so that it is inside the paper. Crease the fold that is already in the pop-up tab.
5. Close the paper again and press down on the center to crease the top of the pop-up tab.
6. Open the page again. The tab should "pop up."
7. Glue pop-up figures to the front of the tab, leaving 1/8" at bottom of tab to allow for closing.
8. To make a book, the bottom of one pop-up page will be glued to the top of the next page.

Hint:

1. Write text on pages before attaching pop-up figures or gluing pages together.

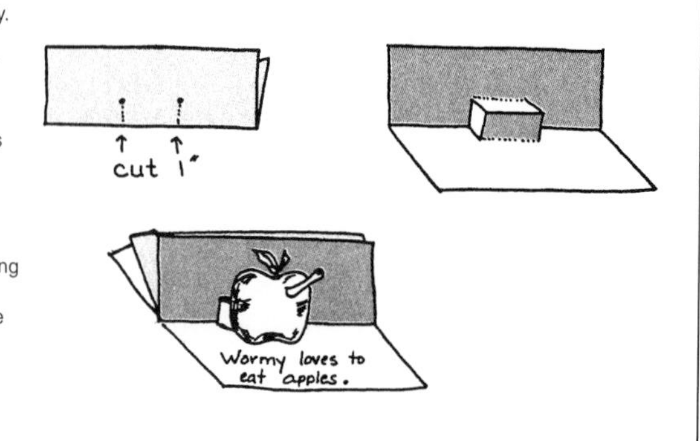

- Fan-page books are made from layers of paper, each page slightly larger than the one before, allowing labels or headings for each page to show. Topics that have distinct sections, such as informative reports, work well.
- Pocket books have envelopes glued to pages in a book, with small cards placed in the envelopes that are just right for the answers to questions (such as riddles), solutions to problems, or cause/effect situations.
- Pop-up books let children represent ideas in three dimensions. Any topic that can be illustrated makes a good pop-up book.
- Sequence books have panels that show sequence of an activity or process.
- Shape books have paper covers cut in various shapes with writing paper inside. Any person, place, or thing can become a fun shape book.

These are but a few ideas for making books. We are only limited by our imagination!

HELPING CHILDREN DEVELOP LEGIBLE HANDWRITING

"The goal of handwriting instruction is to develop fluent and legible handwriting" (Tompkins, 1993). As emerging readers and writers are developing knowledge about print and learning the letters of the alphabet (phonemic stage), it can also be useful to help them develop enough control over the muscles in the hand and arm to form legible letters and become fluent writers.

One caution: We never want to let handwriting become more important than the expression of ideas. Graves (1994) reminds us to keep handwriting in perspective:

> Handwriting is the vehicle carrying information on its way to a destination. If it is illegible the journey may not be completed. Handwriting, like skin, shows the

> outside of a person. But beneath the skin beats the living organism, the life's blood, the ideas, the information" (p. 241).

Young children often interpret our instructional suggestions literally, so we must take care to keep their attention to legible handwriting in balance with the effort they give to composing. If we overemphasize the surface aspects of their writing, how their writing looks on the paper, we may inadvertently be telling them that handwriting is more important than thinking.

Our purposes in handwriting instruction should be twofold:

- To provide instruction in patterns of formation that will allow handwriting to become fluid and eventually unconscious, and
- To help children see the purpose of legibility as a vehicle to clear communication.

The elements of fluent handwriting are letter formation, size and proportion, spacing, slant, alignment, and line quality (Barbe, Wasylyk, Hackney, & Braun, 1984). If the formation of letters is tedious for children, they will soon tire in their attempts to communicate. Handwriting instruction should help children see that some methods of letter formation are less tiring for their hands. Learning to be consistent in letter formation, moving top to bottom and left to right, will generally lead children toward fluid hand motions. To this end, some directed handwriting instruction and practice is warranted, especially when a pattern is first introduced (Farris, 1991). Instruction and practice should be supervised so that children can receive feedback from a more knowledgeable other about the progressions they follow to make letters.

Fluency in the formation of letters becomes a factor when young children are composing. Observation of young writers suggests that, as they are composing, words are produced at a rate of 1.5 letters per minute, or nine minutes for a six-word sentence (Graves, 1994). Graves states:

> If the familiar motor pathways are not built up through regular writing about topics the writer knows, then slowness can hamper the expression of content. The writing goes down on the page so slowly that the writer pokes along word-by-word on the page. That is, each word takes so long to write down that the next word, or even the rest of the sentence, cannot be contemplated at the same time as the one under construction (p. 251).

The manner in which children hold a pencil, marker, or crayon can also be a positive or negative factor in the physical exertion of writing. Some children have taught themselves to hold a pen or pencil in what appears to be an awkward position. Before we attempt to change a child's grip, we should observe the child during writing to see if the grip is functional and that the child's hand does not tire easily.

Legibility for Communication

The real purpose of writing is for communication. Therefore, handwriting's true purpose is a vehicle for communication. Handwriting instruction, then, must reflect this purpose or the message communication will be lost. The most appropriate place to reinforce this idea is in the midst of writing experiences that are shared with others. When children gather together in response pairs or editing groups, it becomes apparent when someone cannot respond because the writing is illegible. The more we engage children in sharing their writing, the more functional opportunities we have to reinforce real reasons for legibility. When children care about communicating, they will care about legibility.

ASSESSMENT: MONITORING CHILDREN'S DEVELOPMENT AS WRITERS

Children develop as writers through both functional and writing process experiences. Understanding the quality of thinking and the processes each child uses to produce meaningful print requires the collection of data that demonstrates:

- what a child understands about writing as a code, a medium, a product, and a process;
- how a child uses writing as a form of thinking to re-collect, re-create, or re-construct ideas;
- how a child uses various forms of functional writing to communicate; and
- how a child uses the phases of the writing process to explore and develop understandings of a topic and/or to communicate that topic to others.

In many respects, monitoring growth in writing is somewhat easier than in reading, because the results of writing are more visible. However, it is still important to go beyond the product to understand children's thinking processes and response to writing as a means of communication.

Observing Writers at Work

When we watch someone writing, what can we observe? In a room full of writers, will we see different styles, different levels of understanding about how and why one writes, or different levels of confidence and experience as writers? As we observe, we should ask, "What do I know about each child as a writer and how did I gain that knowledge?" To answer this question, we return to our instructional purposes of writing, the writing activities that have grown out of those purposes, and our observations of the child. Did we watch children based on our knowledge of their development and our goals for instruction? We make anecdotal records of our observations so that, over time, our notes serve as more detailed reminders of children's writing behaviors.

In a writing process classroom there is a great deal of activity. Conscious effort must be made to watch children in a systematic manner. As we do with independent reading, each day we make careful notes about the writing behavior of one or two children so that over the course of a month every child is observed. Systematic observation provides opportunity for all children to be seen.

Informal observation notes should also be made as needed. What behaviors might we look for? We want to observe how children respond to mini-lessons and shared writing activities, how they settle into their writing each day, how they give and receive help during response and editing activities, how their attitudes reflect their own writing and the writing of others, how they sustain themselves during independent writing, and how they choose writing strategies. Observation notes should be reviewed routinely, reflecting on each child's progress. A scarcity of information for some children should be a signal that more frequent and focused observations are needed.

Evaluating Writing Traits

Samples of children's writing serve as a starting point for assessment and evaluation. We must pay careful attention to our thinking as we look at a piece of a child's writing. What can samples of writing show us? Over time, samples can be compared for growth with the following:

- Overall organization
- Quality and appropriateness of ideas and content
- Development of personal voice
- Use of language
- Use of writing conventions

These elements listed are called writing traits. Although evaluating traits of a child's writing may allow us to talk about the writing in more detail, traits may not reveal aspects of the "child as writer" that ought to be known. The traits view writing as a code, a medium, and a product. Writing traits are usually analyzed in writing that has been taken through the writing process.

Our instruction in writing should provide children with experiences in selecting ideas and content for writing, ways to organize their writing, how to bring themselves to their writing, and how they use language. The use of conventions is always an issue, and one that usually is emphasized in school. Through reading aloud from quality literature we show children how other authors use writing traits to tell their stories or share their ideas. Then through shared writing we model the use of particular writing traits, as they are appropriate to various forms of writing. Through writer's workshop, we guide children to evaluate the traits of their own writing. Figure 6.19 provides a sample form for the ways that we might begin to help children think about the traits of their own writing. It is best to focus on one trait at a time, typically beginning with ideas and content. Organization is one of the most difficult traits for children and develops slowly over many writing experiences.

Conferencing with Writers

Providing a forum for children to talk about their writing is essential to understanding their motivations and intentions as writers. The writing process has response built into it through child–teacher conferences, response partners and groups, and editing partners and groups. Conferring with children while they are

FIGURE 6.19
Rubric to Help Children Evaluate Writing Traits

Evaluating My Writing

Writing Trait	1	3	5
Ideas & Content	When someone else reads my paper, it is hard for that person to understand what I mean or what it is all about.	The reader usually knows what I mean. Some parts will be better when I tell just a little more about what is important.	I know a lot about my topic, my ideas are interesting, the main point of my paper is clear, and my topic is not too big.
Organization	The ideas and details in my paper are sort of jumbled and confused. I don't really have a good beginning, middle, and end.	The details and order of my paper make sense most of the time. I have a beginning but it may not really grab the reader. I have a conclusion but it seems to sum up my paper in just an OK way.	My beginning gets the reader's attention and makes the reader want to find out what's coming next. Every detail adds a little more to the main ideas. I ended at a good place and at just the right time.
Voice	I can't really hear my voice in this paper. It was hard for me to write this paper. I really need to know much more about my topic.	Although readers will understand what I mean, they may not "feel" what I mean. My personality comes through sometimes. I probably need to know a little more about my topic to show, rather than tell, the reader about it.	My paper has lots of personality. It really sounds like me. People who know me will know it is my paper.
Use of Language	Even when I read this paper, I have to go back, stop, and read over, just to figure out the sentences. A lot of my sentences seem to be the same. The words I chose don't seem to be very interesting.	Some of my sentences are choppy and awkward, but most are clear. Some words are very general, but most readers will figure out what I mean.	The sentences in my paper are clear and sound good when read aloud. Words fit just right.
Use of Conventions	There are a lot of spelling and grammar errors in my paper. Punctuation and capital letters seem to be missing. My paragraphs are not indented.	My spelling is correct on simple words. Most of my sentences begin with capital letters and end with the right punctuation.	There are very few errors in my paper; it wouldn't take long to get this ready to publish.

FIGURE 6.20
Making Notes about Writing Conferences

Writing Conference Notes Name Roberto

1/25	2/14	3/3
1/25 Illustrations only. When asked to tell about his "story" he points to and identifies objects, partly in Spanish. I asked if I could write his words. Roberto agreed so I labeled objects in his drawing.	2/14 Roberto has been drawing pictures about blue houses for a week—family has moved out of apartment to house. I encouraged him to label his own picture. He wrote, "Mi Hs bl Hs" (my house blue house).	3/3 Roberto wrote "We wnt to se rs crz." When he reads his story he reads an elaborated version, with many details. He has a story in his head. His illustrations tell only a part. Roberto tells episodes (then, then).

engaged in functional writing also provides a window into their thinking. Talk can focus on how thinking is organized, why a particular format is chosen, other forms that are considered, and explaining the ideas/content of the writing. Assessment and evaluation must begin with and build on what children see in their writing.

Teachers, who use the writing process extensively in their classrooms, confer with children in a number of different ways (see conferring section in writer's workshop). From conferences during writer's workshop we have notes about each child. Conference notes may be kept in a separate folder or notebook or combined with the anecdotal records we make from observations. These records must be considered as we evaluate pieces of children's writing that are to be placed in our assessment portfolio, a folder of selected pieces that best illustrate a child's growth as a writer.

Notes from our conferences help us understand how children think as writers. We may not be able to adequately evaluate samples of children's writing unless we are able to go beyond the surface of their writing and into the processes they use as writers. For example, we review our notes in Figure 6.20 about Roberto, a first-grade child. The conference notes remind us that Roberto has a concept of story that is limited both physically and linguistically for the time being. Our discussions with him let us know that his oral language is well ahead of his knowledge of written language at present. By conferring with Roberto, we have a context for evaluating his drawings and spelling. When we really listen to children, they teach us about themselves and their writing.

Samples of Writing

A set of writing portfolios should be used to develop a comprehensive picture of each child as a writer, including:

- a work folder containing most all of a child's work completed during a particular grading period,
- the child's portfolio for self-evaluation of selected pieces, and
- the teacher's portfolio for assessment and evaluation of growth.

Work Folder:
During a grading period, all writing that children have begun and/or completed should be kept. From the work folder, the child and teacher can select writing to be placed in the child's portfolio and/or the teacher's assessment portfolio. Some teachers choose to divide this writing into two folders for ease of handling—work in progress and past work. The work-in-progress folder often holds three-hole paper and has pockets for loose papers. Only the most recent pieces are kept in this folder so that it is not cluttered. A running list of ideas and self-assessment checklists can also be kept in the inside pocket of the folder. The past-work folder holds all other writing that is not needed on a daily basis. This folder should be accessible to the child, as needed. The writing in this folder might be divided between "completed pieces" and "drafts and ideas." Even if a piece is initially abandoned, the first attempts should be kept in case the child might decide to return to the piece.

Child's Portfolio:
During each marking period children should have the opportunity to select pieces of writing to go into their portfolio. Graves (1994) suggests that along with selecting what children think is their "best" work, they should also be asked to select work that represents specific writing strategies or behaviors. For example, if developing detail or description has been a focus of that marking period, children are asked to select the piece that is their best example of using detail or description. In addition to focused selections, children should also have the option of selecting an additional piece they want to place in their portfolio.

To help children make selections, Graves (1994) suggests that children frequently spend time during writer's workshop reviewing past writing and reflecting on the merit of that writing. We may want to focus mini-lessons on how to reflect on one's own writing by modeling this activity. Mini-lessons may also encourage children to share their thinking as they reflect on their past writings.

For each piece selected, children should provide an explanation for their selection. Self-evaluation is not a natural process and needs to be taught. We may devote mini-lesson time to self-evaluation, hold self-evaluation conferences with children to encourage particular self-evaluation strategies, or provide self-evaluation checklists for children. A child's self-evaluation should be attached to the finished piece of writing when it is placed in the portfolio. With very young children, the self-evaluation may be dictated to the teacher. For other children, a self-evaluation form may be provided on which children record their explanation. Sample evaluation forms for children are shown in Figures 6.21 and 6.22.

The self-evaluation that we encourage in children should be linked to our observations of their writing behavior and the writing strategies that have been encouraged during that grading period. Children will learn more about themselves as writers if we help them focus on evaluating particular traits of their writing, instead of giving them the impression that "whatever they want to say about

FIGURE 6.21
Forms To Help Children Monitor Their Own Writing

Checking my story . . .

My story has ____ a problem in the beginning

____ a middle with 2 or 3 events

____ an end that solves the problem

FIGURE 6.22
Form for Child's Self-Evaluation for Portfolio Selection

I chose this piece for my writing portfolio because it shows...

____

____

____

____

Signed ____________________

their writing is fine." Writing is a complex process and involves the use of many skills and strategies. We can help children evaluate by focusing their attention on particular strategies for some pieces, yet leaving the evaluation of at least one piece open for them to decide the focus.

Teacher's Portfolio:
During the marking period, we should select samples of a child's work that document areas of growth as a writer, as well as areas of need. Selecting a piece of writing for the teacher portfolio constitutes an assessment. How we judge the piece becomes our evaluation. The pieces we select should be photocopied so that originals can remain in the work folder or the child's portfolio. Our evaluation of what each piece represents for the child should be clearly identified and should relate to instructional goals during that marking period. A sample evaluation form we might attach to a child's writing is shown in Figure 6.23.

As we consider evaluating a child's writing, we should evaluate according to our instructional goals that are reflected in:

- the topics of our mini-lessons,
- shared writing topics,
- writing strategies suggested in conferences, and
- behaviors we noted in anecdotal records of observations and conferences.

FIGURE 6.23
Form for Teacher's Evaluation of a Portfolio Selection

This piece was selected for ____________________'s assessment portfolio because it shows. . .

____

____

____

____

____

____

FIGURE 6.24
Record Form for Children's Progress in Writing Processes

Growth in Using Writing Processes Name ________________

Date				
Getting Started . . . • uses informal writing strategies • explores new topics • uses background experience				
Finding a Focus . . . • focuses after exploring ideas • abandons unproductive topics				
Drafting . . . • shows sustained effort • shows meaning is more important than conventions				
Editing for meaning . . . • rereads to check meaning • receives input from others • uses input from others • changes words/sentences • changes order • adds on				
Editing for conventions . . . • receives input from others • checks for capital letters • checks for punctuation • checks for spelling (in word knowledge stage)				

Our goals can be turned into a checklist format that will enable us to quickly and clearly indicate children's overall progress in areas such as using the writing process, types of writing, and organization of ideas/content or using conventions. The best checklists are self-made, because they accurately reflect the goals of our literacy program. A sample checklist is provided in Figure 6.24.

Monitoring children's progress in writing is a continuous process and will require your focused attention. You cannot develop an appropriate writing program for children if you do not know them as writers. You cannot know a child as a writer without carefully observing and talking with that child over a long period of time. Careful monitoring is a commitment you must make if you are to have an effective writer's workshop.

RESPECTING DIVERSITY IN WRITING DEVELOPMENT

If children come to school with different experiences, then we can assume that their knowledge of writing and interest in communicating through writing will also be different. Like reading, writing is very personal. Writers develop through a personal desire to communicate with themselves and others. In your classroom, you can support diversity by honoring children's thinking, and supporting their independent development as writers.

Honoring Children's Thinking

When we ask children to put their thoughts on paper to make their ideas visible, we are asking them to trust us with their thoughts and feelings. How we treat their ideas will tell children a great deal about how we see them as human beings, how we value them as individuals. If we view writing as an extension of oneself, we will treat children's writing with respect. It will be very easy for us, as adults, to see things that are missing from children's writing, things that we wish children had included, things that we think they know and should use. When we see such missing pieces, we might be inclined to impose our ideas on their writing.

When children write, they have intentions. Our response to children's writing should be to help them accomplish their intentions. As we do this, we can nudge their writing, offering suggestions that might be helpful but not imposing our ideas on their writing.

Supporting Independence

Developmental learning environments promote independence, which can then strengthen one's view of self. During their preschool years, children have learned to be quite independent in their activity, including dressing and feeding themselves and finding their way around the neighborhood. Developing as writers should encourage a similar independence.

Young children believe they know much about writing (Calkins, 1994). Unlike reading, the products of writing have been quite visible to them. They most likely have experimented with their own writing in a variety of forms. Writing activities in primary-grade classrooms must encourage children to explore and experiment rather than merely copy and imitate. When children spend the majority of their writing time copying or imitating the writing of another, they learn that someone else's ideas are more valuable than their own.

Observing developmental learning environments has taught us that children want to be independent. By supporting their independence as writers, we will value their ideas as individuals and provide many opportunities for them to show us who they are.

Take a moment to reflect on putting theory into practice with guided and independent writing . . .

We guide writing in writer's workshop by providing:

- whole-class instruction through mini-lessons and shared writing,
- blocks of individual writing time that occur daily, and
- response to writing through response partners/groups, individual teacher conferences, and whole-class author's chair.

Daily writing should include functional writing to help children retain, re-collect, and re-construct ideas and concepts.

Functional writing includes such forms as lists, charts, annotated drawings, explanations,clusters, and journals.

Learning logs go beyond journals to include a wide range of functional writings, usually relating to a central idea or topic.

Guided writing should be used to help children develop skills in writing personal narratives, fiction, and information texts.

Writing, as a part of activity centers or bookmaking, is an excellent way to provide extended exploration and practice with various forms of writing.

Legible handwriting is important when communicating with others. Children should receive handwriting instruction that helps them develop fluency and legibility.

To monitor children's growth as writers, we must carefully observe them as they write and collect many samples of writing to become familiar with their individual preferences and knowledge about writing processes.

We must collect samples of children's writing over time to observe their growth and development as writers.

We should provide instruction in and evaluation of traits in children's writing, including:

- depth and breadth of ideas and content,
- ways to organize writing, especially differences between genre,
- how to bring out personal voice in a piece,

- ways to use language effectively, and
- the purpose and use of conventions of English.

Individual writing conferences between teacher and child are essential to help both parties better understand the child's development of writing skills and strategies. Writing development should:

- respect diversity in children's thinking, and
- support independence in development.

YOUR TURN . . .

1. Plan to interview several primary-grade teachers to learn about the components of the writing program in their classrooms. Develop a form to record notes from the interviews so that you can compare and contrast responses of different teachers. Be sure to ask about essential components for writing: predictable time to write, demonstrations of writing, blocks of guided/individual writing time, choice, opportunities to have response to writing, and opportunities to self-evaluate. Also be sure to ask the teachers to explain their rationale for the decisions they have made about writing. Consider other important ideas you might like to know about each writing program. What conclusions did you reach as a result of your interviews?
2. Practice developing the dialogue for several mini-lessons that you might present at the beginning of a writer's workshop to support children's development in guided and independent writing. Work with a peer to help each other think about how to state your ideas and the most appropriate examples to use. Suggestions include:
   - Focus one mini-lesson on teaching a writer's workshop procedure, such as how to be a helpful response partner.
   - Focus one mini-lesson on a writing strategy, such as how to reread your own writing as a first step in editing for meaning or conventions.
   - Focus one mini-lesson on a literary strategy, such as using character dialogue to tell a story.
3. Ask a child who you know to share a piece of writing with you and talk with you about it. Remember to focus more on finding out about the processes the child used to develop the piece rather than on the content of the piece. After the conference, reflect on your response to talking with this child about his or her writing. What do you think you did well? If you could repeat the conference, what might you do differently?
4. Collect ideas for functional writing. Consider academic standards and the topics that are typical in the curriculum at each grade level, K–3. Also consider writing that you have observed in primary classrooms. What types of functional writing tasks might support and encourage development of children's understanding of the purposes and possibilities for writing?

C H A P T E R

7

Literature Study

Adding to our literacy framework . . .

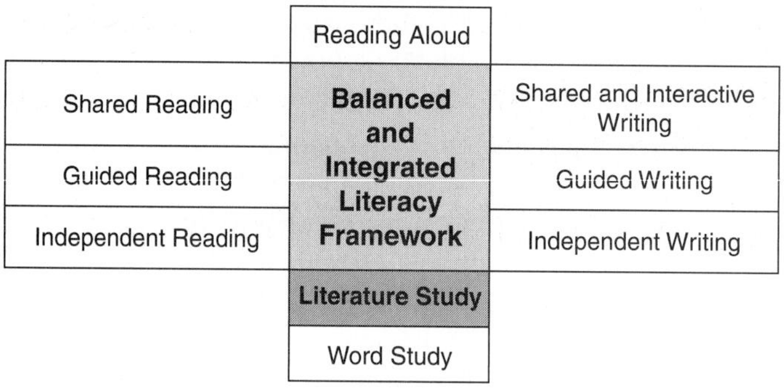

	Reading Aloud	
Shared Reading	**Balanced and Integrated Literacy Framework**	Shared and Interactive Writing
Guided Reading		Guided Writing
Independent Reading		Independent Writing
	Literature Study	
	Word Study	

In this chapter, we . . .

- Consider the value of including literature study in the classroom, in addition to shared and guided reading.
- Examine a variety of ways to organize literature study to complement other classroom literacy activities, including focused units of study.
- Consider how to extend children's interactions with books, including use of a literature response log.

Focus Literature:

- *The Snowy Day* and other books by Ezra Jack Keats
- *Chocolate Fever* by Robert Kimmel Smith
- *A Chair for My Mother* by Vera B. Williams
- *Stone Fox* by John Reynolds Gardiner

Looking into Classrooms . . .

Gabrielle settles her third-graders on the carpet area and begins to read aloud from Chocolate Fever. *Pairs of children follow along in copies of the text as Gabrielle reads aloud. There is occasional laughter and commentary that pauses the reading. At the completion of that chapter the children break up into small groups to talk in more depth about their responses to the new chapter. After about fifteen to twenty minutes, the class gathers again on the carpet area to share ideas generated in the small groups. Each day the children gather to read and talk about a chapter or two of* Chocolate Fever. *Gabrielle is using this whole-class study of a chapter book as a way to introduce literature study to the children.*

Building a Theory Base . . .

In addition to what we already know about supporting children's development as readers and writers, we take the opportunity in this chapter to consider how quality children's literature can be an enhancement to our balanced and integrated literacy framework. Children's literature is already a part of read-aloud and we are quite familiar with its potential as we watch children's reactions to the books that we share. For developing and transitional readers, especially the latter, we want to consider the possibilities of adding literature study as a valued component in our literacy framework.

WHY STUDY LITERATURE?

Why should we engage children in reading quality children's literature as a part of a balanced and integrated literacy framework?

- Meaningful experiences with literature develop knowledge and strategies typically taught in reading programs, and teach children strategies for processing literary texts (Walmsley, 1992).
- Quality literature allows us to mentally rehearse experiences we might some day have, it enables us to draw analogies between stories we read and our own lives, and it causes us to reflect on life and to experience lives that we might not otherwise know (Cullinan, 1989).
- Quality literature has been shown to have a powerful impact on children's language development (Britton, 1970; Rosen & Rosen, 1973) and the way children talk about books (Eeds & Wells, 1989; Raphael & McMahon, 1994).
- Quality literature is engaging, encourages children to become fluent readers (Durkin, 1966; Wells, 1986), and provides a stimulus for critical reading and writing (Blackburn, 1985; DeFord, 1981; Graves, 1983, 1994; Hansen, 1987).

Teaching reading with "real" books is not new. In a review of research from 1936 to 1988 using authentic children's literature for reading, Tunnell and Jacobs (1989) conclude that all types of students in many different types of programs have been successful in reading instruction that is based on quality literature. Teachers who are committed to teaching reading with quality children's literature share the belief that children are makers of meaning and deserve quality literature, with rich language, that is likely to evoke a strong response from readers.

Reader-response theory, which arises out of literary criticism, attempts to explain how readers interpret literature (Rosenblatt, 1978). Reader-response theory holds that meaning resides in the transaction that occurs between readers and texts and not in the texts alone (McGee, 1992). Reading is viewed as a literary experience, one that often involves literary analysis. It is not, however, a series of literature "skills" taught in isolation. Although shared and guided reading provide important scaffolding for children's learning, the quality of the text may not provide the same richness of language and complexity of literary elements as quality literary experiences.

COMPONENTS OF LITERATURE STUDY

Drawing upon the ideas of those who advocate for study of quality children's literature (Atwell, 1998; Five, 1988; Hagerty, 1992; Hansen, 1987; Raphael & McMahon, 1994), literature study within our classrooms should include the following:

- Time
- Choice
- Response
- Community
- Structure

Time

Successful literature study must commit blocks of time for reading, particularly silent reading, because of the belief that children learn to read by reading (Holdaway, 1980). Independent reading in preparation for literature discussions is a central element of literature study. When time for daily independent reading is predictable, children realize that they will not be hurried and can read in more natural ways, just like adults who enjoy pleasure reading (Hagerty, 1992). Ample time for browsing and selecting books is provided. Time for personal reflection is also an important part of the time devoted to literature study.

Choice

Advocates of literature study recognize the role of personal motivation to read in the process of making meaning (Holdaway, 1980). Learning to make good personal choices for reading requires practice and knowledge of the possibilities in literature. In literature study, choice is a joint responsibility between child and teacher. Children must come to know themselves as readers and their personal preferences for topic and style. We must come to know children's interests and provide quality literature and opportunities for children to discover the wide range of possibilities. Unlike guided reading selections at student's instructional reading level, literature study selections may be a bit more challenging.

Response

Literature study encourages readers to explore and extend their personal responses to literature as a part of becoming independent readers. Through reader-response theory (Rosenblatt, 1978) we realize that it is a reader's personal response to literature that encourages that reader to return to literature

In literature study children read the same books and share their responses with classmates. When children guide their own discussions, what can we learn about them as readers?

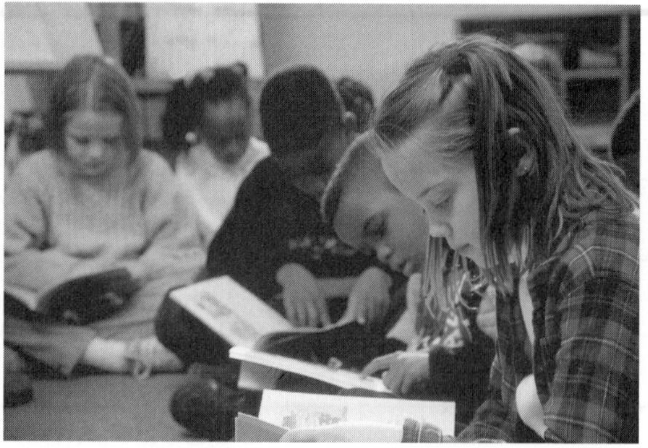

experiences. Response comes from the reader; personal response can be encouraged, but not controlled, by an outside force.

Community

We are well aware of the power of interaction and collaboration in learning (Johnson, 1981; Slavin et al., 1991; Vygotsky, 1962). Sharing sessions and encouraging cooperation during work time provide opportunities for children to learn to depend on each other and to learn from each other. The teacher is a model for how to listen to and respect the ideas of others. A sense of community in a classroom creates the feeling that everyone in the room is a teacher and a learner, with knowledge to share (Hagerty, 1992). Much of what we know we taught ourselves or learned by observing and interacting informally with more knowledgeable others. In literature study, children teach each other what they know if we give them the opportunity and an environment that supports risk-taking.

Structure

Literature study requires a well-planned organization and consistent management that children can count on (Hagerty, 1992). Our role is one of guide and facilitator, anticipating the types and degree of support children will need to become independent readers. We provide some directed instruction in whole-class and small groups. Individual conferences with children can be added to monitor and evaluate their progress.

ORGANIZING LITERATURE STUDY

We can organize literature study in a variety of ways (Daniels, 1994; Heibert & Colt, 1989; Hill, Johnson, & Noe, 1995; McMahon, 1991; Raphael & McMahon, 1994; Zarrillo, 1989):

- *Whole-class* study of one book read aloud by the teacher or read jointly by teacher and students
- *Small-group* study of different books, sometimes in units, led by teacher or students
- *Independent study* of student-selected literature, paced by the student

We can organize literature study around picture books or chapter books, depending upon the range of reading levels in the classroom.

Whole-Class Literature Study

In whole-class literature study, an entire class reads and studies one book together. We know that whole-class instruction can be effective in read-aloud and shared reading experiences. Using read-aloud or read-along (when children have access to the book being studied) enables us to lead the whole class in the study of one text.

The text may be a picture book or a chapter book. It is important that the piece be authentic—a text that has not been altered. In whole-class study:

- each child may have a personal copy of the text,
- children may be sharing copies, or
- we may have a copy of a text that is read aloud, with enough copies for small groups of children to study.

Whole-class study can be followed by small-group study to enhance discussion. Heibert and Colt (1989) refer to this whole-group pattern as teacher-selected literature in teacher-led groups. Zarrillo (1989) refers to this pattern as the study of a core book. Both patterns have the same intention: for the teacher to lead children in studying and responding to the same piece of quality literature.

Small-Group Literature Study

We know from guided reading that organizing children in small groups enables us to monitor their growth more closely than in large groups. In literature study, the teacher typically selects several different books, with multiple copies of each title, from which children select the book they most want to read. Each child's choice of text creates heterogeneous groups, which stand in contrast to homogeneous groups created for reading instructional level texts in guided reading groups. Also in contrast to guided reading groups, the intention for literature study groups is to move from teacher-led to child-led discussions.

Independent Literature Study

Individualized reading programs, such as reader's workshop, use independent reading of literature as the primary focus with group work as the supplement. Because children are on their own much of the time, individualized reading is more appropriate for children who are moving into the transitional reader stage. Independent study requires that children learn to make appropriate selections of text for reading and that teachers are able to routinely conference with individual children to monitor their progress.

These forms of literature study are one piece of a balanced literacy framework. Literature study occurs alongside other components, such as read-aloud and shared and guided reading.

FOCUSING LITERATURE STUDY

Literature study may simply be the study of one text, but it can also include a focused study across multiple texts that provide time and opportunity for deeper examination of an author, topic, genre, or literary element.

The books selected for focused literature study may:

- cluster around a topic,
- be written by the same author and/or illustrator,
- represent the same genre, or
- provide opportunity to study a particular literary element, such as character.

Selecting books that are related can make planning and instruction more coherent and effective. Related texts can also provide opportunities for children to focus their attention and develop deeper understanding.

Focusing on Topics or Themes

Integrated units drawn from science or social studies standards provide an excellent opportunity to include literature study. Both narrative and information literature are appropriate. Topics in the language arts also provide areas of interest for your children. Some example topics include the following:

- animals
- insects
- families
- human body
- community
- friendship
- problem solving
- service
- various types of animals
- motion
- weather
- famous Americans
- holidays
- other cultures
- environments/habitats

Focusing on Author/Illustrator Studies

One way for children to become committed readers is to help them be personally involved with the writers and illustrators of their books. In-depth study of an author enables children to become interpreters of an author's style. Beginning with a favorite children's author is a good way to begin author studies. Another way to find good candidates for an author study is to watch children's responses during read-aloud activities. Authors of books that get a favorable response from children are worth investigating. In the library, we find easy fiction classified by the author's last name. We can see whether other books are available by that author.

Focusing on Genre Studies

Reading several pieces of literature from a particular genre, such as fairy tales, helps children understand how ideas in that genre are organized and presented. Understanding a genre helps us become a more critical reader of that genre. Examining the characteristics of a particular genre provides opportunities to encourage critical thinking, such as comparing and contrasting texts and ideas. Being familiar with various genres can widen children's reading horizons, making them more aware of the variety of literature that is available. Appendix A provides a discussion of the various genres that are appropriate to study in the primary grades.

Focusing on Literary Elements

As children discuss books, their talk naturally moves to issues of characters, plot, setting, and other literary elements. To help them deepen their understanding of how authors use elements to develop narratives, it is appropriate to focus attention on books in which authors use literary elements skillfully. Appendix A provides an overview of the development of literary elements in children's books.

LEARNING TO DISCUSS BOOKS

A major goal of literature study is to help young children learn how to talk about, or discuss, books with their peers—without the guidance of a teacher. We know that children in the middle grades enjoy discussing books with their peers and can gain new perspectives through discussion (Peterson & Eeds, 1990). Primary-grade children deserve similar opportunities to experience the enjoyment of participating in discussions about books. Discussion takes on greater importance in literature study as children transition from picture books to chapter books. Whole-class literature study provides focused experiences with discussion. Small-group discussions can be an effective follow-up to the whole-class reading, to learn and practice discussion skills. The teacher is not a member of the small groups so that children have the opportunity to independently think and talk about books.

To begin a focus on discussion skills, the class talks about what makes a good discussion and the skills needed for discussion before they move to the small groups. Initially, children need our assistance to think about what discussion is and how it compares with past experiences in reading groups. Most children may have participated in groups that are actually question–answer sessions, but not in discussions in which they initiate the talk. Learning how to listen attentively and to take turns talking are two important parts of discussion that must be practiced.

Children learn to be independent if given enough time and proper support. During preschool years, children learn to be quite independent because an adult is not always around to take care of things. Successful literature study also must promote independence as a part of growing as a reader and thinker. We must learn various ways to structure literature study in order to promote children's engagement with quality literature.

Before we consider how to put theory into practice in literature study, take a moment to reflect . . .

Why study literature?

- The study of literature allows us to live through the lives of others, across time and place.
- Interactions between readers and texts motivate readers to return over and over to texts to experience the richness of language and ideas exemplified by good literature.

Components of literature study:

- provide predictable blocks of time for reading and personal reflection,
- provide for personal motivation to read,
- allow personal response to literature that motivates continued reading,
- provide a sense of community in a classroom and create the feeling that everyone in the room is both a teacher and a learner, with knowledge to share, and
- provide a well-planned structure which is necessary to support children's continued growth as readers and thinkers.

Literature study can be organized by:

- whole-class study of the same text,
- small-group study of different texts, and
- independent study of personally selected texts.

Literature study can focus on one item in particular, such as

- topic,
- author/illustrator,
- genre, or
- literary element.

A major goal of literature study is help children feel comfortable and confident when discussing their responses to books with other readers.

Putting Theory into Practice . . .

In this section of the chapter we consider various groupings for literature study, selecting texts, extending children's engagement with texts, providing appropriate skill and strategy development, and issues in monitoring children's progress.

WHOLE-CLASS LITERATURE STUDY

In whole-class literature study, developing skill in thinking about and responding to literature takes on greater importance. An essential element is the opportunity for interactions with other readers. Learning to talk about books with others is a major goal, so whole-class study is an appropriate place to start. A whole-class study of literature may be used as the beginning of a unit study or to introduce the use of a particular literary element. Following the whole-class study, children have the opportunity to participate in small-group or independent literature experiences.

Whole-Class Picture Book Study

We can begin with a mediated read-aloud, then move to guided reading and extension activities that encourage response and exploration.

- The text is read aloud with the whole class, tapping into children's background knowledge of snow. The rich descriptive language used by the author is emphasized during the read-aloud. This read-aloud is a highly interactive time.
- Analysis of books determines teaching points, often delivered through whole-class mini-lessons and reinforced in small groups.
- Guided reading groups can meet to reread and extend children's engagement with language, moving toward independence in reading.
- Time is provided for independent writing in a literature response log, and for other activities to extend children's engagement with the text (see section focused on extending literature experiences in this chapter).
- Community sharing sessions at the end of a literature study period bring children together for another sharing of their responses, emphasizing what they have thought about and gained during the work time.

Figure 7.1 provides an overview of whole-class literature study. The outcomes that we intend for a particular text determine the way we use the literature study time. If independent reading of the picture book is our goal, we need to provide time for children to work with the text under our guidance, with partners and/or independently, depending upon the level of the text. If response to the literature is our goal, we provide opportunities for children to talk with each other about the text and numerous extension activities that allow them to explore their response to the text.

Studying The Snowy Day *by Ezra Jack Keats*

Keats's language is simple, yet descriptive, and supported by the illustrations. Focus on children's responses to Peter, using illustrations to retell the story.

FIGURE 7.1
Organizing Time for Whole-Class Literature Study

Whole Class: 60% of time	• Teaching points—mini-lessons Procedures Literary knowledge Reading skills & strategies • Mediated read-aloud & whole-class and/or small-group discussions • Planning for the day
Work Time: 30% of time	• Small-group discussions (optional) • Response activities Literature log Art Related reading Drama
Whole Class: 10% of time	• Sharing/closure discussion • Planning for next day

DAY 1: WHOLE-CLASS MEDIATED READ-ALOUD AND DISCUSSION:

Prereading strategies:

Discuss favorite things to do in snow.
Make a cluster of children's ideas (shared/interactive writing).
Preview illustrations in *The Snowy Day* and make predictions.

Mediated read-aloud and response:

How did our favorite things about snow compare with Peter's?
Focus on Keats's use of language:

crunch, crunch, crunch
dragged his feet s-l-o-w-l-y
smacking a snow-covered tree
a great big tall heaping mountain of snow—

DAYS 2–5: WHOLE-CLASS REREADING AND DISCUSSION:

Teaching points:

Descriptive language
Plot structure—beginning, middle, and end
Using illustrations as context to predict words in text
Using aural context clues to predict words in text

Guided rereading in small groups:

Reread in small groups, teacher support as needed to move toward independence.

Respond/discuss text as driven by children's interests.

Literature response log possibilities:

Illustrate and describe what you would do if you were Peter.

Try to use interesting words like Keats.

Draw a story map (retelling).

Illustrate/describe favorite part.

Create own "Snowy Day" story.

Word study possibilities:

Make personal cluster of snow words/experiences.

Locate favorite words in story.

Hunt for descriptive words.

From these possibilities, activities would be selected that provide the support needed for children to learn from the text and be able to read the text either independently or with support. A literature log can become a record of each child's participation in whole-class literature study. Retelling, response, and word study activities can be placed in the literature log and referred to during whole-group and small-group activities. Entries for several picture books can be combined, especially related books.

Whole-Class Chapter Book Study

Whole-class study of chapter books provides support to children who are making the transition into more challenging literature. Initially, chapter book study should focus on a unique feature of chapter books—the need to mentally link chapters from reading to reading. We must provide support to children as they learn to think about connecting the ideas into a whole that they gain over the course of reading a text. With transition to chapter books, increased time for independent reading and writing is needed. Whole-class shared reading is suggested for transitional readers in chapter books.

A class set of books allows literature study to move from read-aloud to a shared read-along. A book may still be presented through read-aloud, but children are able to read orally or silently while the teacher reads. Chapter books are most effective when children have access to the text while it is read aloud. If children can read along, the teacher can call attention to specific passages that children can both hear and see. The text is already familiar when children move into small groups or partner situations to give the text closer study.

For children at the transitional stage, discussion skills should be emphasized, with the ultimate goal of literature study being student-led small groups. To work toward greater student participation in literature study, students should have the opportunity to meet in small groups to discuss text that has been read aloud. To overcome the effect that teacher control of small-group instruction may have had in the past, we want to structure small-group discussions so that children can learn to lead their own discussions. Consequently, plans are suggested to teach discussion skills during whole-class literature study.

Studying Chocolate Fever *by Robert Kimmel Smith.*

Chocolate Fever by Robert Kimmel Smith (1972) serves as an example of a whole-class study of a chapter book. *Chocolate Fever* is humorous, presents little challenge, and is an easy transition into chapter books. The story is a fantasy about Henry Green, who loved chocolate so much that he made medical history with the only cure for Chocolate Fever. The book has twelve short chapters, which can be easily read over one week by reading two to three chapters per day.

Small-group and independent extension activities provide additional engagement with the text. The sample chapter book study provides time for partners to reread and study part of the text each day. Selection of small group versus partner or independent reading is the teacher's option. The literature response log becomes an integral part of a child's response to that chapter book. Extensions emphasize independent reading and writing over elaborate teacher-made or commercial materials.

DAY 1: WHOLE-CLASS MEDIATED READ-ALOUD OR SHARED READ-ALONG:

Prereading strategies:

Introduce the story *Chocolate Fever* and the author Robert Kimmel Smith.

Preview text cover, table of contents, and limited illustrations and make predictions.

Read-aloud, read-along, chapters 1 and 2 (pages 13–23)

Encourage continued predictions, including revising predictions based on new information.

Discussion centers on: What do we know about Henry? How did we find out?

Reality versus fantasy: How do we know this is a fantasy? What are the clues?

DAYS 2–5:

Day 2 Chapters 3–5, pages 24–40

Day 3 Chapters 6–7, pages 41–55

Day 4 Chapters 8–9, pages 57–71

Day 5 Chapters 10–12, pages 72–93

Retell previous chapters.

Link chapters to have a sense of the whole.

Make inferences about motivations for characters' actions.

Follow the plot and clearly identify problem and events that lead to resolution of the problem.

Support use of meaning, visual, and language cues to determine unfamiliar words.

Daily small-group discussions:

Provide a discussion guide to help children learn to guide their own discussions (see discussion and samples in next section).

Literature response log possibilities:

Make a chart of all the chocolate things Henry ate.

Henry discovered brown freckles on his skin. What are freckles?

Could freckles just appear on Henry's skin? Why or why not?

Make a prediction—Henry said he was "feeling funny," then he discovered brown freckles. What do you think might happen next?

The length and complexity of chapter books offer more possibilities for study than picture books. Care must be taken to select a few essential elements that allow children to focus their attention while reading. The study of other chapter books during the school year provides additional opportunities for skill and strategy development. How we select skills and strategies for the focus of instruction depends upon other daily reading and writing activities that are occurring.

With chapter books, the literature response log becomes the collection place for a variety of written retellings, responses, and word study activities. Extended study in chapter books provides many opportunities for a literature response log to become an integral part of the classroom literature study. Literature response logs and extension activities can be shared in a community session that ends the literature study period each day.

Developing Discussion Skills

To focus on developing discussion skills, we prepare a daily discussion guide that children use in small groups to develop their student-led discussion skills. To encourage use of discussion skills at all levels of thinking we design questions for the discussion guides that encourage children to think in different ways. A copy of the questions is given to each child so they can think about their response to the text. We might want everyone in the group to record their ideas or have one child serve as the recorder each day. Discussion guides can also become a part of each child's literature response log.

During the small-group discussions, we circulate among the small groups, listening to the tone and direction of the talk. Our job is to listen, to notice what children are thinking and talking about. Children need time to learn to make decisions for themselves. They will seek our affirmation that they are doing the "right things." Our response to their requests for help might be, "What do you think about . . . ?" When they see that we really want to know what they think, they will stop asking and begin to trust themselves. We must be patient.

As we begin to focus on discussion skills, children's responses may be primarily focused on only answering the questions on the discussion guide and not much more. We should not be disappointed. This is what they know how to do! Slowly we begin to make the questions more general and open-ended to facilitate children's willingness to direct the discussion. They took several years to learn to answer our questions. Now they need time to learn to answer their own questions.

At the end of the small-group discussion, fifteen minutes or so, we gather children back together for a sharing session. We provide opportunity for each group to contribute ideas from their discussion. During this time we also help groups focus on what helped the discussion in the small groups work well. Slowly, children begin to have confidence in their abilities to guide book discussions, with our patience and support.

To make a discussion guide, we consider the reading that will take place during one day and create three to five questions to help children focus their attention on the major issues being revealed in the text. We know the entire text, so we select questions that will help children focus on the main themes of the text.

SAMPLE DISCUSSION GUIDE QUESTIONS—CHOCOLATE FEVER:

Day 1 discussion guide:

Chapter 1 Daddy Green said that Henry liked his chocolate, "bitter, sweet, light, dark, and daily" (page 18).
What do you think he meant by that?
How can you tell that Henry REALLY loves chocolate?

Chapter 2 What was the first clue you noticed that something was happening to Henry?
At the end of chapter 2, what do you think is happening to Henry?

Day 2 discussion guide:

Chapter 3 On page 25, what do you think the word *phenomenon* means?
What are freckles? Do you think Henry's spots are really freckles?
How do you think Henry feels at the end of chapter 3?

Chapter 4 On page 30, Nurse Farthing looked at Henry through her spectacles.
What are spectacles? What clues helped you figure it out?
What is happening to Henry at the end of chapter 4?

Chapter 5 What did you think when the doctors discovered that Henry's spots were pure chocolate?
How would you feel if you were Henry right now? What would you do?

Over the course of the twelve chapters in *Chocolate Fever,* the questions become more general and more open-ended. Notice the change in questions from chapter 1 to chapter 5. By chapter 5, we are asking more general questions as a reflection of that chapter. About two-thirds of the way through the text, we begin inviting children to pose personal questions. To model the forming of questions, we invite children to brainstorm questions during the read-aloud that can be answered in the small groups.

During the next book that the children study, the questions on the discussion guide can be half teacher made and half child made. We must remind ourselves that we have the opportunity to guide discussion during the whole-class time. We should think of the small group as children's opportunity to learn independence in discussion.

SMALL-GROUP LITERATURE STUDY

Small-group literature study of picture books and chapter books provides more personalized interaction than a whole-class study allows. In contrast to whole groups that study the same book, each small group in a classroom can study a different book (Zarrillo, 1989). Children select texts that are typically chosen by the teacher. Literature groups can be either teacher led or student led (Heibert & Colt, 1989). In classrooms that already have guided reading groups in instructional text, it is preferable to have literature study focus on student-led groups. The development of discussion skills is an important aspect for the success of student-led literature groups (Pierce, 1990). An overview of small-group literature study is provided in Figure 7.2.

FIGURE 7.2
Organizing Time for Small-Group Literature Study

Whole Class: 10–15% of time	• Teaching Points—Mini-lessons Procedures for groups, discussions Literary knowledge Reading skills & strategies • Planning for the day
Work Time: 80% of time Silent reading (40%) Small groups (20%) Other activities (20%)	• Reading & writing period to prepare for small groups • Small-group discussions • Response activities Literature log Art Related reading Drama • Flexible skill groups
Whole Class: 20% of time	• Sharing/closure discussion Relating books Application of teaching points • Planning for next day

Sample Four-Week Literature Study for Picture Books

To explore small-group study with picture books, imagine that we have multiple copies of four picture books about families to complement a unit study about families and individual roles within families:

Book A: *A Chair for My Mother* by Vera Williams
Book B: *Dad Told Me Not To* by Susan Talanda
Book C: *Now One Foot, Now the Other* by Tomie dePaola
Book D: *The Terrible Thing That Happened at Our House* by M. Blaine

Imagine that we want children to have the opportunity to read each of the four picture books, spending one week with each book, over the course of the month-long unit on family. The time period can be adjusted as needed. For example, children might read three of the four books if a three-week time period works.

In the weeks before the small-group literature study begins, we carefully analyze the demands of each text and possible ways each text could be extended during a week of study. Depending upon the other literacy activities that are taking place in the classroom at that time, we plan a sufficient number of activities for one week of study with each book. When planning is complete, we may have as much as one month of literature study prepared—one week for each book.

Our plans focus on ways to encourage interactions among children in the groups. In addition, we focus on ways to extend children's engagement that complement other classroom literacy activities. During these weeks of study, small-group literature discussions may take the place of some guided reading activities. The literature response log may take the place of some independent writing activities. Independent and partner reading may take the place of some time otherwise devoted to independent reading.

During the week before we intend for the small groups to begin we introduce and read aloud each picture book during daily read-aloud time. On the Friday before the groups begin, we ask each child to select their first and second choice of books. Children's choices create four interest groups and allow them first choice when possible.

Over the next four weeks (if we choose to have children read each book), the children spend a week studying each book. On the Friday before a new rotation begins, children choose their next book to read. New choices typically create different group compositions.

Analyzing texts:

To support children's reading of quality literature, we must know well the possibilities of a text. A careful analysis of a text helps us know what directions we might take with it. In our analysis we think about the development of literary elements in the text and how such elements potentially affect children's engagement with a particular text.

As we begin our analysis we must remember that the focus of this sample four-week study is on families and the roles of individuals within families. Consequently, two aspects of the texts selected for this unit will be very important to enhance children's potential engagement with a text: namely, plot and character.

Plot—The ability to identify the problem presented in the text is at the heart of understanding the family and the importance of family roles that are presented; and

Character—The understanding of characters' actions is essential to understanding the importance of individual's roles within a family, how individuals contribute to a family.

The focus of the unit thus guides the way we think about small-group discussions of texts, select possible teaching points for mini-lessons and flexible skill groups, and use the literature response log and other possible extension activities. Literature response logs could be used to help children focus their attention on retelling, responding, and word study. Extensions will enable children to extend retelling and responding to a particular text.

An example of a text analysis of *A Chair for My Mother* (also discussed in Chapter 2) might contain:

Plot	Flashback to a fire that destroyed characters' house (problem) sets up for the desire of the characters to save for a new chair.
Setting	Location is integral to the telling of the story; interpreting illustrations will help to clarify character actions.
Characters	Understanding of characters is developed through child's (teller of story) point of view. Consider how child's telling influences reader's understanding of characters.
Point of view	First person—child is teller. Check for children's response to child's point of view.
Theme	Important, strong values are communicated; saving for what you want, family and neighbors help each other; may take rereading for children to understand content implied by the flashback.
Style	Child's language is simple and clear.
Vocabulary	Check for children's understanding of tips (money), "she puts by the savings," bargains, pumps (shoes), spoiled (ruined).

Complete an analysis such as this for each book to determine what might be emphasized during its one-week study.

Literature log possibilities:

Illustrate favorite part of story and tell why.

Make a list of ways that people in this family help each other.

Tell something you did to help your family during a time of trouble.

Draw and tell about something that your family would like to save for.

Word study:

Children select new words/phrases from the text to illustrate such as *tips, waitress, pumps, spoiled, delivered.*

From these possibilities we select the activities that we believe will be best suited to our children, engage them in meaningful study, and thus extend their enjoyment of literature.

Managing small groups—picture book study:

Each of the four picture book groups might meet with the teacher on Monday, then group meetings could alternate between teacher-mediated and independent/partner study of the literature for the remaining four days of that week.

Four-Group Rotation Plan—Picture Book Study

Group	Monday	Tuesday	Wednesday	Thursday	Friday
A	Teacher reads aloud	Small-group discussion	Independent/Partner reading	Small-group discussion	Independent/Partner reading
	Log: Extensions	Log- Extensions	Log- Extensions	Log- Extensions	Log- Extensions
B	Teacher reads aloud	Small-group discussion	Independent/Partner reading	Small-group discussion	Independent/Partner reading
	Log- Extensions	Log- Extensions	Log- Extensions	Log- Extensions	Log- Extensions
C	Teacher reads aloud	Independent/Partner reading	Small-group discussion	Independent/Partner reading	Small-group discussion
	Log- Extensions	Log- Extensions	Log- Extensions	Log- Extensions	Log- Extensions
D	Teacher reads aloud	Independent/Partner reading	Small-group discussion	Independent/Partner reading	Small-group discussion
	Log-Extensions	Log- Extensions	Log- Extensions	Log- Extensions	Log- Extensions

FIGURE 7.3
Possible Group Rotation in Literature Study

Depending upon other literacy activities taking place in the classroom, we must decide how much time to devote to this literature study.

During a week of study, groups would be alternated as shown in Figure 7.3. Our decisions about ways to extend interactions with texts would enable us to complete the chart with specific activities for small-group discussions, literature response logs, and appropriate extension choices for each group.

Sample Four-Week Literature Study for Chapter Books

To explore the use of chapter books for small-group literature study, imagine that we have multiple copies of four chapter books for a study of characters (literary element study). The books selected vary in their complexity and level of difficulty, from early second-grade reading level to fourth grade.

Book A: *Stone Fox* by John Gardiner (most challenging)
Book B: *Beans on the Roof* by Betsy Byars
Book C: *Staying Nine* by Pam Conrad
Book D: *The Poppy Seeds* by Clyde Robert Bulla (least challenging)

Children should have the opportunity to read two of the four books so that they are able to compare and develop characters. We estimate that each book may need up to two weeks for completion.

Analyzing texts:
To begin planning, we read each of the books, considering children's background knowledge and experience as readers of chapter books. (Imagine that

our class has already completed several chapter books in whole-class studies.) We analyze the development of literary elements in each book, particularly as the other elements influence the development of character. We also consider how children will respond to vocabulary and writing styles of each text.

An example of a book analysis for* Stone Fox *might be:

Plot — Provides a quick-paced, progressive, exciting climax. Open-ended resolution allows reader to know Little Willy (main character) wins the race but not what happens afterward to Willy and Grandfather. Leaves reader to speculate on resolution, provides a good focus for discussion and follow-up activity.

Setting — Jackson, Wyoming, a highly integral setting, serves as an antagonist to show us Willy's courage and highlights his relationship with Searchlight, his dog. Children may need help understanding that authors sometimes use setting like it is a character in the story.

Characters — Pay special attention not only to understanding the main character, but also to understanding how the other characters and the setting contribute to the reader's response to Little Willy.

- Little Willy is round and dynamic; in our comparison with the other flat characters we are able to learn about him.
- Searchlight is flat and static, reflecting Willy's growth.
- Stone Fox is flat but dynamic, changing at the end to accentuate the climax.
- Grandfather and Doc Smith act as foils, pushing Willy in certain directions that the reader needs to see.

Point of view — A limited-omniscient narrator outside of the characters tells the story. The narrator lets readers know what Willy is thinking about and helps them understand Willy's drive to win the race.

Theme — This book is about perseverance, personal strength, and finding courage in the face of defeat. The theme can be seen through the characters.

Style — There is a good balance between description and dialogue: Descriptions are clear, language is simple and straightforward.

As we know from whole-class studies, a book analysis similar to the one presented is necessary to determine what to emphasize in each chapter book.

Literature log possibilities:

Open response to group discussions that can provide a glimpse of how children are dealing with the text

Double-entry journal responses for independent reading days:

A double-entry journal consists of a quote from the text on the left side of the page in the literature log and the reader's personal response to the quote on the right side of the page. Other ways to use the double- entry journal are suggested in Chapter 4. A sample entry is shown in Figure 7.4.

Focus on words:

Identify interesting words that need attention or study in the log and use during group discussions. Attend to decoding of words in the group. Encourage children to determine meanings; record how words are used in text.

FIGURE 7.4
Sample Double-Entry Journal for *Stone Fox*

Stone Fox

Quote from text: p. 12	Response:
"A ten-year-old boy cannot run a farm. But you can't tell a ten-year-old boy that. Especially a boy like little Willy."	I'd be scared to try to do what Willy did. He was brave. His grandfather taught him to work hard. I don't have to work so hard at my house. Maybe if I did I'd be more like Willy.

Character sketches:

Keep notes on different characters, what we are learning about them, how we learned it. Add to sketches with each reading; use in group for character discussions.

Discussion guides:

If children are new to literature study, we might want to develop a discussion guide for each chapter to help in their thinking. Over the two-week period of study, the questions could become more open-ended. If students study more than one book in the selected group, questions could be used for the first book, but more child-initiated direction in log responses could be permitted with the second book.

These are but a few of the possibilities that can be used. A later section of this chapter explores other types of extensions for literature study.

Managing Small Groups—Chapter Book Study

How we manage the four groups that are studying these texts depends on our intentions for the literature study. Are we just beginning small-group study and wish to continue to have teacher-led groups? Are we trying to provide opportunities for children to begin to move toward child-led groups? Our intentions should cause us to structure differently the way that groups will meet and use their time together.

Example of teacher-led groups:* Stone Fox *(Group A)

Day 1 — Teacher reads aloud chapter 1 (9 pages) to begin the book study. Discuss plans for reading and how children will get independent/partner reading completed; begin a group character chart of major characters.

Day 2 — Independent/partner reading, chapters 2 and 3 (18 pages); no group meeting but children work on log and extension activities.

Day 3 — Group meets, reads chapter 4 in group (8 pages) and discusses, shares literature log entries from day 2; add to group character chart; make new log entry as response to group discussion of character.

Day 4	Independent/partner reading, chapters 5 and 6 (18 pages); no group meeting, log entry, extension work.
Day 5	Group meets, reads chapter 7 (8 pages) and discusses, adds to character sketches, shares log entries, makes new entries after group.
Day 6	Independent/partner reading chapters 8 and 9 (15 pages); no group meeting, literature log, extension work.
Day 7	Group meets, reads chapter 10 (6 pages) and discusses open resolution and personal impact, makes log entry after group.
Day 8	Children are involved in independent follow-up activities, extensions.
Days 9/10	Groups meet and share work, revisit character sketches, engage in overall responses to book.

When the focus is on teacher-led groups, it is best to stagger the reading plans for the four chapter books, just as we did for the four picture books (Figure 7.3). We can meet with all four groups on the first day of each new book to introduce the books and get the children started. Then we stagger the group meetings, seeing two groups each day while the other two groups read independently. For example, *Stone Fox* readers will meet on days 1, 3, and 5 of the first week. One other book group will follow a similar schedule. To stagger the group meetings, two groups will meet on days 1, 2, and 4 of the first week.

When deciding how to stagger the groups, we consider having the readers of the least challenging books begin with independent reading after the introductory meeting. Readers of the most challenging books could follow the day 1, 2, and 4 schedule to give two days of guided reading before children read independently.

***Example of child-led groups:* Stone Fox**

There are at least two important distinctions between the procedures we use for teacher-led and child-led groups: how we use time during literature study and the roles of teacher and child.

In child-led literature study, all reading and writing that is done to prepare for group meetings can take place at the beginning of the literature study period. Children are then reading and writing ideas or questions for that day's discussion at the same time, so we can provide support to the children who are most in need of it. Following such preparation, all groups can meet for discussions at the same time because their group meetings do not require our attendance. We attend one group meeting each day, listening, observing, and participating as needed to support children's growing discussion skills. Following group meetings, all children can participate in extension activities, which we are then able to oversee.

Observation of group interactions and individual participation in literature activities provide us with information about instruction that may be needed for either the class as a whole or for groups of children within the class. For example, after the groups meet for discussion on day 1, we provide instruction in how to develop a character chart for each text. We provide a blank chart for each child. After instruction, each group identifies the characters that were introduced in chapter 1 and places names in the appropriate place on the chart. The group brainstorms characteristics and places them on the chart. Additional instruction might come in the form of mini-lessons that focus children's attention on how they might infer character traits from dialogue and descriptions in text, using examples from the four different texts. Ideas for literature study mini-lessons can be found in a later section of this chapter.

Based on our analysis of each book, we make daily suggestions to the class and/or groups for literature response log entries that children complete following small-group discussions. On appropriate days after the groups meet, we bring the class together to discuss ideas that have been entered into the literature response logs. Children bring their logs to this discussion and may even read aloud from their entries as a way of sharing their ideas about the literature.

Day 1	Teacher meets with each group to help children develop a reading plan for the two-week period; children then independent/partner read chapter 1 (9 pages).
Days 2–8	Independent/partner read, one chapter each day (7–9 pages); make log entries in preparation for discussion, group meets for discussion, continue log and extension activities as time permits.
Day 9	Independent/partner read, chapters 9 and 10 (13 pages); make log entries in preparation for discussion; group meets for discussion; continue log and extension activities as time permits.
Day 10	Group meeting/sharing of work; revisit character sketches; engage in overall response to book.

Small-group literature study provides a variety of opportunities to engage children in quality literature for the purpose of enhancing their understanding of the potential that literature has for telling stories about life, and also enhancing motivation to read those stories. We turn our attention now to the possibilities that independent study of literature provides for primary classrooms.

INDEPENDENT LITERATURE STUDY

Independent literature study, with texts chosen by the child, is also known as reader's workshop (Atwell, 1998; Hagerty, 1992; Hansen, 1987). Children spend extensive amounts of time reading independently, keeping records and responses for literature in a response log, and conferencing individually with a teacher. Figure 7.5 provides an overview of independent literature study. Teachers who use independent reading or a reader's workshop for a major portion of their literacy program face a number of issues: helping children select literature at an independent reading level, providing ample time for silent reading, carefully monitoring children's growth through teacher–child conferences, encouraging exploration of literature through response activities, and providing whole-class and small-group skill/strategy instruction.

Helping Children Select Literature

Children in independent literature study must learn to select books that are appropriate for their interests and reading level. We help children learn to effectively select books in a variety of ways:

- Reading aloud from a wide assortment of books provides children with knowledge of the topics and styles of writing in different genre.

FIGURE 7.5
Organizing Time for Independent Literature Study

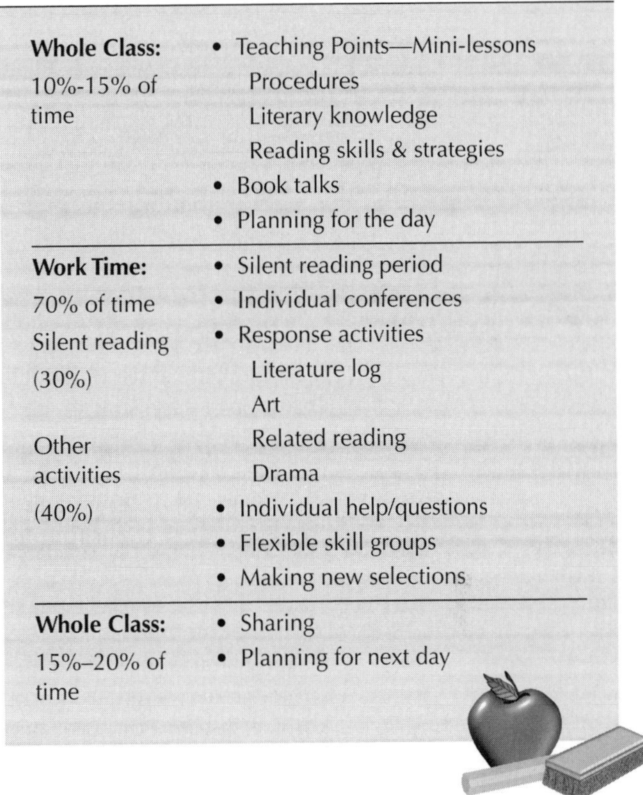

Whole Class: 10%-15% of time	• Teaching Points—Mini-lessons Procedures Literary knowledge Reading skills & strategies • Book talks • Planning for the day
Work Time: 70% of time Silent reading (30%) Other activities (40%)	• Silent reading period • Individual conferences • Response activities Literature log Art Related reading Drama • Individual help/questions • Flexible skill groups • Making new selections
Whole Class: 15%–20% of time	• Sharing • Planning for next day

Children also become acquainted with the work of various authors and the possibilities that books offer.

- Book talks, given by teachers or other children, can provide just enough information about a book to motivate a child to read. Librarians can also give book talks during routine library visits to inform children about new books that have recently been acquired. Book talks should give an overview of a book without giving the plot away.
- Author studies provide opportunity to focus on the work of one author and can link a child to a series of books for extended reading. A few of an author's books can be read aloud, with others displayed in a prominent place in the room. Sharing information about the author's life, especially how that life was reflected in the author's work, can be of particular interest to children. Becoming aware of an author's work also helps children learn where to look for books in a library.

Sharing personal responses to books, along with personal projects completed during independent work time, can interest other children in reading a particular book. When a sense of community has been developed in a classroom, children will place importance on the views of their peers and will allow those views to influence selection of new books for reading. Children who happen to read the same book can also form small sharing groups during the work time to talk about their responses.

Making a commitment to a book is also a part of the selection process. In the reading log, children should make a dated record of the title of each selection they make. This list serves as a chronicle of a child's progress through books. If a child abandons a book, he or she should explain why in the log. Making such a record encourages children to view selection as an important part of reading.

Silent Reading

To become independent, a reader must develop "the ability to persevere at a personal pace that makes efficient use of current skills" (Holdaway, 1980, p. 34). Perseverance requires sustained practice. In this way, independent reading becomes a reflection of reading proficiency (Fielding, Wilson, & Anderson, 1984).

A block of time each day, in which only silent reading is permitted, enables children to settle into their reading. Independent reading can extend beyond the "quiet time" if children so choose, because independent reading is also self-paced reading. The time that had been devoted to sustained silent reading (SSR) can become a part of the literature study. Combining SSR time with literature study helps to extend the amount of time available for sustained reading. We must make silent reading a comfortable time, allowing children to move to a place in the room that is conducive to their reading.

Conferences

Conferences are short meetings, about five to ten minutes, between teacher and child that provide time for open dialogue about a book the child is reading or has just completed. Conferences are intended to give children an opportunity to share their personal responses to their reading. In addition, con-

Conferencing with children is an excellent way to learn about them as readers. What can we do to encourage children to share themselves as readers?

ferences are intended to give us an opportunity to personally monitor a child's progress, provide guidance where needed, diagnose difficulties, and encourage the use of particular skills or strategies (Hagerty, 1992; Holdaway, 1980). Conferences are not the time for instruction. Mini-lessons and skill groups are better suited to that purpose (see later section for discussion of mini-lessons). The conference should be used to learn about how children are handling the books they have chosen.

Conferences may begin during the quiet reading period and extend into the activity period when some children will be adding to their literature response logs or continuing their work on other extension activities. Schedule conferences on a regular basis and when children request a conference after completing a book. For example, we might plan to see three or four scheduled children per day with one or two open slots each day for other children. It is appropriate to spend thirty to forty-five minutes each day in conferences, because they are central to independent literature study.

Conferences should contain:

Child sharing personal responses
Teacher probing those responses
Oral reading by child of selected passage
Review and discussion of a child's reading log
Teacher encouraging and guiding child's efforts as reader based on conference dialogue
Teacher making records to monitor child's progress

Child shares personal response:
We open a conference by asking children about their response to the book they are reading or have just finished. We should be accepting of their responses. We must remember that children's responses are an indication of their level of involvement with the book. We listen carefully not only to what the child says, but also to how the child talks about the book.

Possible response questions might be:

How is your book going?
What is your book about?
What do you think about your book so far?

Teacher probes responses:
Based on children's responses to a book, we ask thought-provoking questions. We must be sensitive to the direction children set in the conference because our goal is reader independence. Our only role is to help children take the next step in thinking about the book. Possible probing questions include:

What makes you think that?
Based on what you have told me, what do you think might happen next?
Why did you choose this book?

Child oral reads:
Once children know how conferences work, they will come prepared to share a part of their book. (How to pick a part to read can be the topic of a procedural

mini-lesson.) As children share their text, we want them to share a sufficient amount of text that allows them to get in their stride as readers and to show word recognition and fluency abilities. At least once per grading period (four to six times per year), we should tape-record this oral reading as a record of children's growth. We listen carefully during the reading for miscues, intonation, fluency, and strategies children use successfully.

We compliment children on the productive use of strategies during oral reading, saying such things as:

> I noticed the way that you went back and corrected that word, once you realized it didn't make sense. That's what good readers do.
>
> When you read the dialogue, it sounded just like people talking to each other. That is the way that good readers make their reading interesting to others.
>
> I noticed the way you emphasized some words. I could tell that you thought they were important and wanted to be sure I heard them.
>
> Then, we probe one aspect that is relevant to the child's selection of a favorite part:
>
> Tell me a little about your favorite part.
> Tell me what you think about . . .
> that character,
> what the character did,
> the conflicts the character is having,
> the impact of who is telling the story.

Review child's literature log:
Children should bring their literature response log to each conference sharing. We look at the entries that have been made since the last conference. We want children to feel accountable for their entries. We may also consider asking children who are scheduled for a conference to turn in their log the day before so that we are able to read their entries and use the content of the entries during the conference.

Possible questions about the response log entries include:

> How is your response log going?
> What kinds of things do you like to put in your response log?
> How do you choose what to write in your response log?
> Tell me a little more about this entry.

Teacher encourages and guides:
As we end the conference, we make a suggestion for children based on our observations and impressions of their progress. We focus on one thing. Remember, the conference is not our only opportunity to make suggestions. We will have other opportunities to direct children's attention. This is not an instructional time; it is a relaxed time to let children teach us about who they are as readers.

Possible comments to encourage and guide further growth include:

> As you continue on in this book,
> you might think about . . .
> you might try to . . .

As you make entries in your log,
you might think about . . .
you might try to . . .
When you come to words that you are not sure about,
you might think about . . .
you might try to . . .
As you choose another book,
you might think about . . .
you might try to . . .

Teacher provides help:
When we are not conferencing with children, we circulate among the children, providing support and encouragement for their individual endeavors. We may be able to build upon suggestions made in the conferences. Think of this also as a time to continue learning about children as individuals and as readers. We may want to make notes about our observations, and add them to our conference records (see Figure 7.6). We may find it helpful to carry a clipboard for note making. Some teachers prefer to transfer their notes to the conference record, while others prefer to use sheets of computer labels, with twenty to thirty labels on a sheet. We write a child's name on each label. When we fill a label, we peel it off and place it in a child's reading folder. Empty labels can also be a signal to us of children who we are not watching closely.

Teacher makes a record of conference:
We should keep careful records of our conferences with children. In our conference notebook should be a space set aside for each child (see Figures 7.7 and 7.8). Immediately following each conference we make notes about children's behaviors, including:

Fluency
Word recognition and self-monitoring
Level of response and understanding
Ability to select appropriately
Self-pacing
Self-evaluation

Terra:	Jango:	William:	Ivy:	Chi Chi:
11/12–read all of work time 11/15–helped Ivy with project	11/12–spent 30 minutes selecting book	11/13–book may be too difficult, asking about many words	11/15–sought help, big step!	11/14–sustained reading for 15 minutes, that's good progress

FIGURE 7.6
Example of Recording Observations during Work Time

FIGURE 7.7
Example of an Open Conference Entry

Date	Book Title	Comments
November 17	Stone Fox	fluency increasing, good intonation, improving on multi-syllable words, challenging level but more appropriate than last selection

FIGURE 7.8
A Focused Conference Entry with Prearranged Categories for Comment

Date Book Title	Comments
November 17 *Stone Fox*	Response/understanding: ____________
	Fluency/intonation: ____________
	Word recognition/self-monitoring: ____________
	Pacing: ____________
	Other: ____________

Independent literature study provides a number of challenges for us in meeting the needs of each child. At least some portion of the school year, however, should be devoted to having children select their own reading materials. Children can thrive when their personal interests in reading are being met.

SUPPORTING SKILL AND STRATEGY DEVELOPMENT IN LITERATURE STUDY

Whether we engage children in whole-class, small-group, or independent literature study, we will probably have some concerns about their interactions with texts. Through whole-group mini-lessons and follow-up small-group lessons come the necessary skills and strategies related to literature and reading. Extension activities are planned to encourage children to use skills and strategies with a particular text.

Teaching Points—Instruction through Whole-Class Mini-Lessons

Analysis of the books to be used in literature study and observation of children's interactions with those books provide information that we use to select teaching points each day. Mini-lessons provide excellent instructional opportunities in literature study. Mini-lessons (Five, 1988; Hagerty, 1992) are short, whole-class lessons, lasting only five to ten minutes, in which children focus on an essential aspect of the reading and on how to implement a particular skill or strategy in their reading. Mini-lessons help to plant seeds for further development.

In a mini-lesson, we think aloud about using a skill or strategy as we demonstrate for, rather than tell, children what they should know or do. Illustrations are usually drawn from the book being studied or books that are familiar to all of the children. Thinking aloud helps children learn how readers make the decisions that they do, what information gets considered, and why some possibilities get discarded (Davey, 1983). Remember, reading is a thinking process as well as an emotional response. Because thinking cannot be observed, it must be shared verbally.

The possibilities for mini-lesson topics are limitless. The literature selected for study and the needs of the children as readers determine our selections. We might focus on helping children develop their understanding of how authors use literary elements in various genre to develop engaging stories, how to better use skills and strategies as readers to make meaning or help the literature study run more smoothly.

Possible mini-lesson topics: genre and literary elements

Plot	Stories have beginnings, middles, and ends
	Plots that go forward
	Plots that sometimes go backward
	When conflict is a good thing
	Does there have to be a problem
	Different ways that authors end stories
Character	Learning about a character
	Different types of characters
	What purpose an antagonist serves
	Why does an author use a foil character
Setting	Roles that settings can play
	What happens when the setting acts like a character
Point of View	Who is telling the story
	What difference does point of view make
Genre	Characteristics of a particular genre
	How genres make different kinds of stories
	Recognizing the difference between narrative and information writing

Possible mini-lesson topics: reading skills and/or strategies

- Word Knowledge
  - How to tell when a book is easy, just right, or too hard
  - How to figure out unfamiliar words
    - when to use context (words and/or illustrations)
    - when to use structural patterns
    - when to use particular phonics patterns
  - Can I skip words I don't know?
  - How to use my "checking system"
  - Asking myself, "Is this making sense to me?"
  - Tips for fluent expressive audience reading
- Making Meaning
  - How to use prediction on my own
  - How to use a *predict–read–prove* cycle on my own
  - Retelling stories
    - making a story map
    - preparing a felt board retelling
    - storytelling the story
    - sequencing important events
  - Summarizing what I read
  - Finding main ideas
  - Recognizing important details
  - Drawing conclusions
  - Making inferences
  - Distinguishing fact and fiction/opinion
  - Distinguishing reality and fantasy

Possible mini-lesson topics: procedures for literature study

- What to do during independent work time
- Recording and responding in a literature log
- Deciding what type of response to make
- Choosing words to put in the response log
- Learning how to participate in discussions
- What to do when I have finished my reading
- How to get ready for a teacher conference
- What to do during a community sharing session
- Responding to other reader's ideas

Sample mini-lesson dialogues:

Following are sample mini-lessons that teachers can present to children. We can listen to the ways that teachers talk with children during mini-lessons and notice how mini-lessons are very focused and serve as "seeds" of ideas about reading and writing development.

Learning about a character:

We might say, "Each time I read a new book, I'm introduced to a new character. I've noticed there are different ways that an author helps me get to know the character. In *A Chair for My Mother* (a picture book the class read), the main character is a girl and she tells the story. To get to know her, I have to listen to how she tells the story and what she says about herself and others. I know that I'll have to look at the story through her eyes. There's not much dialogue for me to listen to, mostly description of people, places, and events."

"In *Stone Fox* (a chapter book we are in the process of reading), the story is told by a narrator who is not part of the story. The narrator tells me everything that's happening and what everyone says. Then I can decide for myself about the characters. In this type of story, I have to listen to what people say about a character, what the character says, and how the narrator describes what goes on. I think about characters talking just like I think about my friends and me talking. I learn about what my friends are like by listening and watching them. That's how I learn about characters in *Stone Fox.*"

"When you are reading today, try to notice how your author lets you learn about what your characters are like. Perhaps some of you might like to share what you find in our closing group time."

Notice how we end this mini-lesson with a suggestion of what children might do. Then we observe to see how useful this particular suggestion was for children.

Word knowledge—using context clues for a word with multiple meanings:

We might say, "When I'm reading, sometimes I come to a word that I think I know, but the way it's used in the story doesn't seem to fit what I am thinking. Then I remember that in English some words can have more than one meaning. So I have to look carefully at how the author used the word."

"Yesterday we started reading *Chocolate Fever* by Robert Kimmel Smith. When we got to page 16, we came across the word *stunt* and several of you asked me if it meant something about doing tricks. Let's look at that part of the text again."

"Remember, we were reading about how much Henry loved chocolate and how chocolate even seemed to love him." (We place a copy of that page of text on the overhead with this sentence highlighted:

> *It didn't* stunt *his growth. (He was just about average height, perhaps even a little taller for his age.)*

"In this sentence, *tricks* doesn't make sense. Then I look past that sentence, because I know that clues can come after a word, as well as before a word. I see that the author put something in parentheses. Maybe he wanted me to pay attention to those words, like he was giving me a hint. So I think if Henry is average height or taller he must be growing; he didn't stop growing. Maybe *stop* fits, so let's try it in the sentence:

> *It didn't* stop *his growth.*

That makes sense to me and fits with the other sentences. Stunt is one of those words that can have more than one meaning. Sometimes I can find out what meaning the author is using if I look at the other words around it for clues."

"In our reading today, if we come to a word where the meaning you are thinking of doesn't fit with the way the author is using it, let's stop and see if we can figure it out by looking at the other words around it."

After the mini-lesson, the class continues the reading of *Chocolate Fever*. We follow up the reading with questions such as, "How did you figure out what a 'light *dusting* of cocoa' meant in the story?"

Procedures for literature study—how to get ready for a reading conference:

> We might say, "We've been having reading conferences for several weeks now and I've noticed that you've been remembering to bring your book and literature log to the conference. That's part of getting ready for a conference.
>
> Another part of getting ready takes place in your head. When I'm going to conference with you, I think back to our last conference. I think about the things you told me about your book; I look at the notes I made about our conference; and I think about the book you were reading. I also think about what I've seen you doing in reading since that last conference and the mini-lessons we've had that might help you enjoy reading your books more. Then I anticipate what you might say to me when we meet. That's what I do in my head.
>
> When you get ready for a conference with me, you should also spend some time thinking about what will happen in the conference. You'll think about what you want to tell me about your book. Since you know that our conference is also to help you be a better reader, you might think about something I can do to help you enjoy your book the most.
>
> Tomorrow I will be conferencing with Chi Chi, William, Terra, and Rhonda. Each of you might spend some of your work time today getting your head ready for our conference tomorrow."

As children gain background experience in reading literature, mini-lessons can become more interactive. We invite children to share their thinking about how to use a skill or strategy. We encourage children to provide support for their thinking. One caution: When we open the mini-lesson for interactions, we must plan for a slightly longer mini-lesson time.

Making decisions about mini-lessons:
Whole-group mini-lessons should focus on the commonality of the books children are studying. To decide on appropriate mini-lessons we might ask ourselves, "What will all of the books in the selected study require of the reader?" For example, the group of picture books described earlier on families and responsibilities would provide opportunities for whole-group mini-lessons about the following:

- How to use your background knowledge about families to help you better understand a text
- What to do when your knowledge about families differs from the book
- Comparing/contrasting yourself with a character

Small-group instruction should grow out of the analysis of individual books and observations of children's responses to the books. The sample analyses for *A Chair for My Mother* and *Stone Fox* provide the starting point for selecting one or two skills to emphasize; however, skill/strategy instruction must be adapted if your observations of children's interactions with a particular book suggest that either they are already successfully using the skills/strategies we selected for instruction or there are other skills/strategies needed before the selected skills can be understood.

For independent literature study, mini-lessons grow out of our observations during conferences and during children's work time. We look for trends across children by reviewing the notes from our observations. Based on our observations we may design either whole-class or small-group instruction. We select whole-class instruction when the majority of children demonstrate a need for specific support.

Using Skill/Strategy Groups for Personalized Instruction

Flexible small groups can extend the ideas that are emphasized in whole-class mini-lessons and provide practice that may be needed by some, but not all, children. Skills groups serve a limited purpose—to develop a particular skill or knowledge—and then are disbanded. Ideas should first be presented to the whole class in mini-lessons. When we notice that a number of children are still not using specific literary knowledge or particular reading skills and/or strategies, more extensive small-group work is warranted. Skills groups can fill this need.

Topics for skills groups may be drawn from the lists of suggested mini-lesson in this text, from our knowledge of reading process and children's literature, from our school district's curriculum standards, or from a basal reading series if you are using one. Skills group instruction is teacher-led and may resemble small groups used in other patterns of reading instruction. Holdaway (1980) suggests that skills groups should be by invitation, letting children attend if they want help in that particular area.

> Example: Imagine that we notice a number of children who are experiencing some difficulty with multisyllable words now that they have moved almost exclusively into chapter books. Over a period of several weeks we offer small-group work in strategies for decoding multisyllable words, cross-checking for sources of information to help with decoding, and self-monitoring for meaning. We offer these groups only for the children who demonstrate need. Examples for instruction are drawn from what we notice during observations, and from books that children are currently reading. Following instruction we observe children to see whether their decoding of multisyllable words shows improvement. As necessary, additional instruction is provided for children who continue to demonstrate a need.

Skill/strategy groups are an effective tool for reaching children within their zone of proximal development. We can focus our teaching points and observe how children use the instruction we provide.

During literature study we want to provide activities to increase children's engagement with a particular text and enhance the intensity of their response to the literature. Retelling, responding, and word knowledge are three areas in which we might provide activities.

RETELLING

Learning to summarize chapters, verbal and written

Creating group and individual story maps; adding new information to the map each day

Distinguishing relevant from irrelevant details

Distinguishing reality from fantasy

RESPONDING

Responding to humor; exploring how the author uses humor

Identifying with a character

Determining how it feels to get inside the head of a character (omniscient and limited omniscient points of view)

WORD KNOWLEDGE

Using context effectively to confirm word meanings

Using multiple-meaning words

Decoding multisyllable words

Extending Literature Study—Using Literature Response Logs

Each day of literature study, we ask children to make some type of entry in their literature response log. In the early stages of literature study, we focus children's entries. Later, we allow for more child-centered choices.

A literature response log may be:

- a daily reading record that includes date, book title, and pages read,
- a page(s) devoted to words that are of interest or are unfamiliar, and
- responses to reading (open, focused, double-entry journals, story frames, dialogue letters, story map, and so on).

Keep a daily log of reading:
This record can be useful in helping children evaluate the pace of their reading and their ability to persevere with a book (see Figure 7.9).

FIGURE 7.9
Sample Daily Record Log

Date	Book Title	Pages Read
Nov. 12	Stone Fox	Ch 1, 3-11 in group
Nov. 13		Ch 2 & 3, 12-21 Home- 22-29
Nov. 14		

Make a list of words from reading:
Independence in word recognition means helping children become aware of their ability to work with new words. Word lists can be reviewed in whole-class discussions, in small groups of children who are at similar stages of development of word knowledge, and in individual conferences. Recording page numbers makes it possible to refer to the use of a word in the text (see Figure 7.10).

Responses to reading:
The types of entries children make and the time when entries will be made are things we need to decide. For the most part, we will focus on retellings, responses, and word study.

Possible response topics include:

- Illustrated retelling
- Written retelling
- Story maps

Types of responses include:

Open response	personal responses to content, theme, characters, and so on, as child chooses
Focused response	grows out of group discussions or analysis of book; for example, with *A Chair for My Mother,* children might be asked to respond to what they learned about people from this book
Illustrated response	illustrate and comment on favorite part

Focus on words includes:

- Favorite words
- Words I want to learn
- Words I am not sure about
- Phrases I like

The literature response log is an excellent place to collect words and demonstrate knowledge of individual words. A page in the log can be devoted to words that children want to discuss with others. Entries in the response log can also illustrate children's comfort with using the vocabulary of a specific text:

FIGURE 7.10
Sample Personal Word Lists

Interesting Words	Words I Need to Study
Stone Fox	p. 4 explanation
p. 7 harmonica	p. 9 examination
p. 16 hand-and -finger code	p. 16 inspected

Example: On page 28 of *Stone Fox,* as Willy and Searchlight practiced for the sled race, Searchlight "forged ahead with such speed . . ."

By the time children are ready to read this book, they should know enough about letter–sound relationships to decode *forged,* but they may not know its meaning. Children can be asked to note this word as they are reading and, perhaps, record their understanding of its meaning. The literature log is then brought to the group or the teacher conference for discussion.

Group discussion is a vehicle for word knowledge development. Focused rereading of text can lead children back to words in context to check for their decoding of the word, as well as their understanding of meaning as used in the text. In preparation for such discussions, words in a text can be underlined or highlighted in the teacher's copy as a reminder.

Extending Literature Study—Independent Book Extensions

Over the period of time that a book is being studied, children should engage in meaningful activities that help them continue to think about a book, for example, characters in the chapter book unit described in this chapter. We try to keep the activities simple. As children become more comfortable with chapter book study, invite them to make suggestions for extensions. This list is only a beginning.

Tape recorded books for repeated reading and fluency—We can make tapes as we read books in preparation for the literature study. Perhaps we can tape the books that we think will be most inviting to our less experienced readers.

Art—We provide opportunities for children to share and/or create displays of artistic responses using painting, drawing, collage, crayon resist, or dioramas as a medium for responding to the book or extending into personal experience.

Drama—When appropriate, encourage children to re-create and respond to books through role playing, playlets (scenes), puppets, or reader's theatre. For chapter books, the dialogue is a natural for making plays. We can make copies of text for children to highlight their spoken parts, then decide if a narrator is needed.

Writing—Children can create personal and/or creative stories or poems as spin-offs from the books they had read. Shape books are always available for independent writing.

Extending Literature Study—Integrating Content Areas

A Chair for My Mother:

Math—Children can use different-size jars to estimate the amounts needed to fill the jars using rice, cereals, or other small items. Relate back to the book to compare. This work can be placed in the literature log or made into a display of what children find out.

Math—Search newspapers and catalogues for prices of chairs similar to what the mother wanted. Consider how long it might have taken the mother to save up for the chair if she got $3.00 in tips each day she worked. Children can estimate with other amounts and chairs of different prices. Place in literature log or make posters to display.

Stone Fox:

Geography—Where is Jackson, Wyoming? What is the geography like? Did the author portray it accurately? Is there anything else about the geography that Gardiner might have used in his story, but did not? Use pictures and/or illustrations to prove your ideas.

Science—What do you know about dog sleds and sled racing? Did the author portray sled racing accurately? What factors might affect how fast a sled can go? Prove your answers.

Social Studies—Do we know who invented sleds? What types of sleds have been used in times past? Do people use sleds on something other than snow?

Chocolate Fever:

Science—Research the making of chocolate. Start a K-W-L-H chart about chocolate

What do I know (K) about chocolate? What do I want to know (W)?

What did I learn (L) about chocolate? How did I learn this information (H)?

Use encyclopedias, CD-ROM, and other print materials for research

Children should have opportunities to share their responses to books with others both formally and informally. Sharing becomes more formal when children are able to give book talks or share projects during community sharing. Children who have read the same books may elect to form small sharing groups during work time to comparing their ideas.

INTEGRATING LITERATURE STUDY: ONE-WEEK LITERATURE UNITS

Sample Author Study

The study of books written by Ezra Jack Keats, including *The Snowy Day*, provides an example of integrated literature study. This plan includes whole-class study and small-group study. Shared reading, using enlarged versions on an overhead projector, could reduce the need for multiple copies of picture books.

An example of a whole-group author/illustrator study of Ezra Jack Keats is shown in Figure 7.11. A number of Keats's books are read aloud and discussion of Keats as an author and illustrator takes place over five days. Small groups meet with the teacher to study one book in depth. Keats's other books are displayed in a center. Shared writing is integrated as a text for a class big book about Ezra Jack Keats. A literature log, which is an independent writing activity, is used for vocabulary and response. The remainder of the time is devoted to independent reading, listening, and art.

Explanation of Activities	Monday	Tuesday
Whole class • Shared reading • Mediate read-aloud • Rereadings • Shared writing	Shared writing—snow cluster What do we know about snow? Mediated Read-Aloud—*The Snowy Day* Introduce—Keats as author/illustrator Second mediated read-aloud—*Peter's Chair*	Shared reading of snow cluster—review and add new ideas Compare with *The Snowy Day* Rereading of *The Snowy Day* Mediated read-aloud—*Whistle for Willie* Begin shared writing—We Like Ezra Jack Keats!
Small groups • Guided reading & rereadings Independent writing in literature response log Extension activities	Guided reading—*The Snowy Day* (multiple copies) Literature log • Copy & expand snow cluster • Response to *The Snowy Day* • Vocabulary—choose three favorite words from *The Snowy Day* Extensions • Tape recorder—Keats's stories taped, choice of texts • Art—collage in Keats's style • Independent reading—Keats's books	Guided reading—choral reading of *The Snowy Day* Literature log • Add to personal snow cluster • What I Know about Snow • Vocabulary—illustrate and describe three favorite words Extensions • Tape recorder—Keats's stories • Art—continue making collage • Independent reading—Keats's books
Community Closure	Share favorite words written in literature response log Plan for tomorrow	Share collages, make comparisons with Keats' artistic style as shown in his books Plan for tomorrow

FIGURE 7.11
One-Week Literature Unit—Author Study

INTEGRATING LITERATURE STUDY: EXTENDED UNITS

It is possible to create a flexible integration of language arts instruction by using a combination of whole-class, small-group, and independent reading. The literature selected for a six- to nine-week unit is typically related by topic/theme, author/illustrator, genre, or a particular literary element. The intention of the whole-class study is to introduce the focus of the unit and provide teacher-led instruction. The books selected for the small-group literature study enable children to further explore the concepts introduced in the whole group and deepen understanding with moderate teacher guidance. Independent reading serves as the culmination of the unit, allowing children to explore the unit focus on their own, applying what has been developed in the previous whole and small groups.

Wednesday	Thursday	Friday
Shared reading—weather poem Listen for "noisy" words Mediated read-aloud—*Goggles* Reread—a Keats favorite Shared writing—Reread and add to We Like Ezra Jack Keats!	Shared rereading—weather poem Mediated read-aloud—*Louie* Reread—a Keats favorite Shared writing—reread, add, revise, prepare to make a big book	Mediated read-aloud—*Maggie and the Pirates* Reread—a Keats favorite Shared writing—make final revisions for class big book
Guided reading—choral reading of *The Snowy Day*, compare with language in weather poem Literature log • Write "noisy" words you like • Respond to favorite Keats character Extensions • Tape recorder—Keats's stories • Art—continue collage • Independent reading—Keats's books	Guided reading—partner reading of *The Snowy Day*, share favorite part with group members Literature log • Sentence building using favorite Keats words, "noisy" words • Begin What I Like about Ezra Jack Keats (continue on Friday) Extensions • Tape recorder—Keats's stories • Art—decide how to use collages in big book and Keats bulletin board. • Library corner—Keats's books	Guided reading—class big book, divide shared writing into pages for a big book Guided reading of What I Like about Ezra Jack Keats Literature log— • Continue What I Like about Ezra Jack Keats Extensions • Tape recorder—Keats stories • Art—add collages to complete big book • Library corner—Keats's books
Share logs of favorite Keats characters Plan for tomorrow	Share logs of What I Like about Ezra Jack Keats Plan for completion of class big book	Share class big book

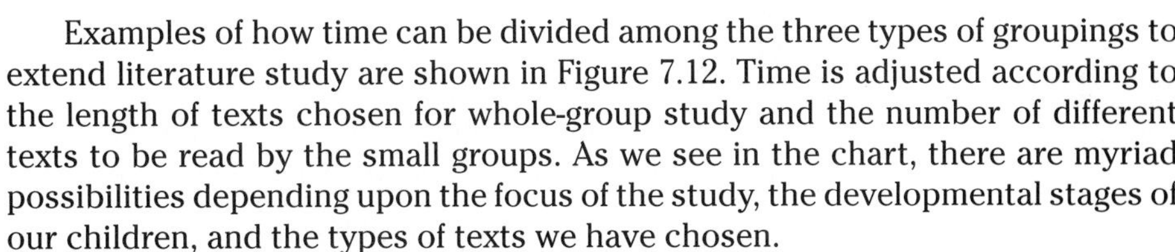

Examples of how time can be divided among the three types of groupings to extend literature study are shown in Figure 7.12. Time is adjusted according to the length of texts chosen for whole-group study and the number of different texts to be read by the small groups. As we see in the chart, there are myriad possibilities depending upon the focus of the study, the developmental stages of our children, and the types of texts we have chosen.

Sample Six-Week Unit: Making Friends

Imagine that it is the beginning of the school year, we are teaching second grade and we want to introduce children to literature study. Friendship is often an issue early in the school year when children are coming together from other classrooms and schools and may not know each other well. In the first unit of

FIGURE 7.12
Integrated Literature Unit Possibilities

	4 Weeks		6 Weeks		9 Weeks	
Types of Grouping	Some Types	All Types	Some Types	All Types	Some Types	All Types
Whole-Class Literature Study	1	1	2	1–2	2–3	2
Small-Group Literature Study	3	2	4	3–4	6–7	4–5
Independent Literature Study	———	1	———	1	———	2–3

our second-grade basal reader are three stories about best friends. The basal stories are well written and provide multiple copies of texts that can be used in small groups or for independent reading. We also have multiple copies of a picture book about friends, *We Are Best Friends*, by Aliki. We decide to use this literature as part of a six-week unit on "Making Friends."

To help us get to know our children as readers and writers, the unit will contain read-aloud, independent reading, and group work over a period of six weeks. This extended time frame will allow us to conduct our beginning-of-the-year assessments. Figure 7.13 shows an overview of a possible unit on making friends, including the literature to be read.

Beginning with whole-class literature study:
To get the unit started with a clear focus on friendship, we decide to read an old favorite, *Charlotte's Web* by E. B. White. This tale shows the development of a strong friendship between Wilbur the pig and Charlotte the spider. The story is familiar to many children, but they will not have studied the book as a piece of literature. We decide to read the text aloud over a two-week period and prepare discussion guides each day so that children will get to know other children and gain confidence in their ability to talk about books (see discussion guides in an earlier section of this chapter).

For the first two weeks of school, reading instruction focuses on making meaning through mediated read-aloud and learning about literature discussions. The reading aloud of *Charlotte's Web* would be used to guide children to:

- use their background knowledge of language and literature to make meaning without needing to be the decoder of words,
- learn how to think through a chapter book by linking previously read chapters to a new chapter, and
- learn how to talk about books in child-led discussion groups guided by printed questions to focus each day's discussion.

This two-week period near the beginning of the school year gives us an opportunity to begin to know the children through a familiar activity, read-aloud. The small-group discussions provide support to children who may not yet feel com-

FIGURE 7.13
Six-Week Making Friends Unit

Whole-Class Study (2 weeks)	Mediated Read-Aloud: *Charlotte's Web* by E. B. White	**Skills/Strategies:** • linking chapters • learning to discuss • using context to make meaning
Small-Group Study Select 3 of 4 books (3 weeks)	*We Are Best Friends* by Aliki Basal Selection: *Lizzie and Harold* by Elizabeth Winthrop Basal Selection: *Ira Says Goodbye* by Bernard Waber Basal Selection: *Gloria Who Might Be My Best Friend* by Ann Cameron	**Skills/Strategies:** • Identifying story problem to understand character motivation • Identify character traits related to friendship • Recognize conflict between self & others to interpret character motivations & actions
Independent Study (1 week)	• Offer wide assortment of books about: — friends, — unit authors (Aliki, Waber, Cameron, White)	**Skills/Strategies:** • Applying skills from unit independently • Focus on sustaining reading • Conference with each child for assessment

fortable sharing with a new adult. In preparation for the small-group discussions, the whole group talks about how to have discussions. A small group, with our support, should model a discussion on the first day of the literature study.

We provide simple discussion guides to help children formulate questions for discussion. The content of the discussion guides is carefully chosen to accommodate children who may still be early-developing readers. For example, on day 1, after reading chapters 1 and 2 of *Charlotte's Web*, the discussion guide questions might focus only on personal responses:

> What do you think of the story so far?
> Which character do you like best? Why?
> Would you sell Wilbur? Why or why not?
> What do you think will happen in the next chapter?

For each response, children are encouraged to give reasons for their thinking. For the first week, the discussions could be structured so that each group member has an opportunity to talk.

The questions are addressed one at a time, with each group member giving a response. Our job is to help keep the discussions going. We encourage group members to listen to the ideas of others. One recorder is selected to write ideas that are shared when the whole group comes back together.

In this first phase of the unit, each child begins a literature response log by recording their personal responses each day to the reading and discussion. Shared writing activities (see Chapter 4) and other forms of functional writing (see Chapter 6) can encourage early writing attempts. In addition, interesting words and words that are not familiar can be collected. The written response, either open-ended or focused, provides additional assessment information.

During this period of mediated read-aloud, group discussions, and literature log responses, extension activities can also be offered. Tape-recorded stories about friends, an attractive reading area, a well-stocked writing center and an art center provide constructive choices for children and additional assessment opportunities for you. A separate SSR or DEAR time would be offered daily, in addition to the literature study.

Small-group literature study:
In the middle of the unit, small-group literature study provides the opportunity to have more focused interactions with children and provide opportunities for some directed teaching. In the six- week time frame, three weeks are allotted for small-group study. With one week per story, each child participates in small groups with three of the four stories. The actual number of small groups we use will depend on the number of children in the class.

The planning process for small groups, described earlier in this chapter, is used. The skills identified in the right-hand column of Figure 7.13 relate to the overall purposes of the unit and the four stories chosen for the small groups. Interpreting character is an important element for understanding friendships. Identifying story problems situates a character's actions. Understanding the nature of the conflicts that characters experience as a result of the story problem makes it possible to interpret character actions and motivations. Consequently, during the three weeks that are spent in the small groups, we focus on interpreting characters.

Independent reading:
The culmination of the unit is a week of child-selected independent reading. For this first unit, one week of independent reading is sufficient as children are becoming accustomed to classroom routine and monitoring their own progress as readers. During the other five weeks of the unit, children will still have SSR or DEAR time for self-selected reading. The time that had previously been devoted to group work will now be entirely for independent reading and responding.

ASSESSMENT: MONITORING CHILDREN'S PROGRESS DURING LITERATURE STUDY

In whole-class, small-group, and independent literature study, children are involved in a combination of literacy components with which we are familiar. We are aware of assessment in:

read-aloud discussions (see Chapter 2),
shared reading and writing (Chapters 3 and 4)
guided and independent reading experiences (see Chapter 5), and
independent writing in response logs (Chapter 6).

We draw upon this knowledge depending upon our choice of literacy component. For example, during the study of *Charlotte's Web* or *The Snowy Day*, accomplished through whole-class mediated read-aloud, we draw upon observations of behaviors discussed in Chapter 2. During small-group literature study, we make records of oral reading and comprehension discussed in Chapter 5.

To effectively monitor children's progress during literature study, we draw upon careful observation of children's interactions with texts, skills that we develop as we make reading records during guided reading, and our ability to evaluate children writing for use of writing traits. We can refer to previous chapters for reminders about assessment strategies that are appropriate to use during literature study.

RESPECTING DIVERSITY DURING LITERATURE STUDY

Whole-Class Instruction

When we organize whole-class instruction, we should become particularly sensitive to our selection of literature and interactions with children. It is easy in a whole group to lose contact with some children.

Literature selection:
In children's eyes, studying a book as a whole class places great emphasis on what the book stands for. Characters and character actions are validated. Consequently, we need to be sure to select literature over time in which all of the children can see themselves portrayed. Multicultural literature should figure prominently in our selections. In addition, the main characters with whom children interact should be both male and female, and reflect different types of personalities and ways of solving problems. A variety of lifestyles and family structures should also be represented.

Group interaction:
Whole-group instruction also increases the possibility that we will not be keenly aware of what each child is doing or thinking. Developing skill as a "kid-watcher" (Pappas, Kiefer, & Levstik, 1999) becomes vitally necessary. We should challenge ourselves to make anecdotal records of our interactions with children. We should be especially sensitive to children we may be watching too much because of behavior and others we may not be noticing at all.

Provide for varying needs:
During whole-class literature study, we should reflect on the choices we make for extending children's interactions with texts. Small-group and independent activities should provide many opportunities for children to share their knowledge and skills, as well as their needs. A balance between directed activities and choice allows children the flexibility that is needed to meet the wide range of interests and needs in one classroom.

Small-Group Instruction

As we move toward more independent work with children, their individual backgrounds as readers and thinkers should be considered. Selecting a variety of literature should also be a consideration.

Providing support to children:
As children work in small, self-selected groups, we must be prepared to vary the support we provide within each group. Reading picture books aloud and providing a tape-recorded version makes the text available to all children for repeated readings. Arranging for reading partners supports children during independent reading time. When we set the pacing of group reading, we must also consider children's ability to successfully meet that pace. Sufficient reading time for individuals must be the top priority even if it means reducing time spent on other supporting activities. Some children will need extended reading time that may be achieved through SSR or at-home reading. In addition, providing extra copies of books for at-home reading relieves children of the burden of remembering to bring the book each day.

Selecting a variety of literature:
As we select books for small-group study we need to be aware of children's interests and reading levels. Within a selected grouping of books, there should be something of interest for everyone. While personal reading interests are also provided for during SSR, instructional materials should also have appeal for children to sustain their reading. This is particularly true for chapter books. The manner in which we prepare children for selecting a book for small-group study is also important. Book talks and making books available beforehand for examination can help children select a book that will meet their needs and interests.

Independent Instruction

Independent literature study provides opportunity for children to pursue personal reading interests in the literature of their choice. Of the different organizational patterns we have explored, independent literature study is the most responsive to children's needs and desires as readers. Providing for independent choices tells children that you trust their judgment. Just as adults come to know their own taste in literature, so can children. Sometimes poor choices will be made, but it is difficult to learn about poor choices if you never have the opportunity to make them yourself. Independent literature study allows children to learn to pace their own reading.

We provide large blocks of time for reading so that, through self-pacing, children can find their rhythms as readers. Selecting one's own books helps individual readers learn to effectively monitor their own reading, to recognize levels of comfort with different types of reading material. Strategic readers develop through many opportunities to monitor their own reading. It is not enough to know what a skill is and how to do it. The real test comes when we must tell ourselves that now is the time to use a particular skill and to know how to activate and use that skill in real reading. Self-selection can support the development of self-monitoring. Self-monitoring one's own reading provides opportunity to evaluate personal performance. Independent reading can provide opportunities for children to develop trust in their own judgment and ability to evaluate reading performance.

In this chapter we have explored a range of ways to engage children in the study of literature that augments the other literacy components we have at work in the classroom. Literature study has as its goal the appreciation of quality literature. It goes beyond the teaching of reading and writing, to engage children in the thoughtful examination of other people's lives. Literature study is a complement to other components of a balanced and integrated literacy program.

Take a moment to reflect on the application of theory to practices in literature study . . .

Whole-class literature study:

- allows a class of children to study the same book together,
- can be combined with small-group and/or independent instruction, and
- focuses skill and strategy instruction on the broad needs of the class.

Whole-class picture book study includes:

- mediated read-aloud with a whole group,
- closer study in small groups,
- use of literature response logs, and
- independent extension activities.

Whole-class chapter book study includes:

- mediated read-aloud or read-along,
- small-group discussions, with discussion guides,
- use of literature response logs, and
- independent extension activities.

Small-group literature study:

- emphasizes small-group over whole-class activities,
- can be extended through multiple-week units, and
- focuses skill and strategy instruction on the broad needs of the class, with opportunities to reinforce in small-group setting.

Organizing for small-group literature study involves:

- an emphasis on small-group work,
- careful analysis of each book selected for study,
- developing a reading plan for each small group, and
- the possibility for either same- or mixed-ability groups.

Independent literature study includes:

- helping children learn how to select books,
- providing ample blocks of silent reading time,
- conferencing with individual children to monitor progress,
- teachers and children keeping accurate records of reading progress,
- response activities that enable children to know themselves as readers and share themselves with others, and
- skill/strategy instruction that is responsive to individual student need.

YOUR TURN . . . .

1. Plan a whole-group literature study for a picture book that would be appropriate for developing and/or transitional readers in the primary grades. To receive feedback about your thinking, (1) plan collaboratively with another or (2) select the same book as another, then compare your plans. Prepare a three- to five-day plan that includes:
   - whole-class mediated read-aloud,
   - small-group discussions,
   - literature log, and
   - extension activities.

   Your activities should address retelling, response, and word knowledge development.
2. Prepare an annotated list of picture books and/or chapter books that would be appropriate for literature study with developing readers. Provide justification for each choice.
3. Practice preparing discussion guides:
   (a) Select a picture book that would evoke good discussion in a whole-group literature study. Prepare a discussion guide to use with developing or transitional readers. Be sure to vary the level of thinking that is asked for by the questions.
   (b) Select a chapter book that would evoke good discussion. Decide how you would divide the book for literature study. Prepare a discussion guide for each chapter or group of chapters that would be read and discussed each day of the study. Be sure to vary the level of thinking that is asked for the questions.
4. Practice developing mini-lessons to support literature study:
   (a) Develop a mini-lesson that would help primary-grade children learn the procedures of whole-class or small-group literature study as might be applied in your classroom.
   (b) Develop a mini-lesson that would support your selected text and address a skill/strategy most likely needed by the majority of the whole group.

5. Select four picture and/or chapter books that are related in some way and would be appropriate for primary-grade children during a four-week literature study. Work collaboratively with at least one other person to develop this plan. Be sure you are very familiar with each book so that you understand why particular decisions are made for group work, logs, or extensions.
   - Read and analyze each book for one to two things you would try to emphasize during a week of study. Especially highlight the relationships among the books (topic/theme, author, genre, element).
   - Develop literature log activities that will help children focus on essential elements and explore their response and study words in the book.
   - Develop enough extensions that, over the course of the text, children can explore and share their response.

Aa Bb Cc Dd Ee Ff Gg Hh Ii Jj Kk Ll Mm

CHAPTER

8

Word Study I: Developing Phonological Awareness

Adding to our literacy framework . . .

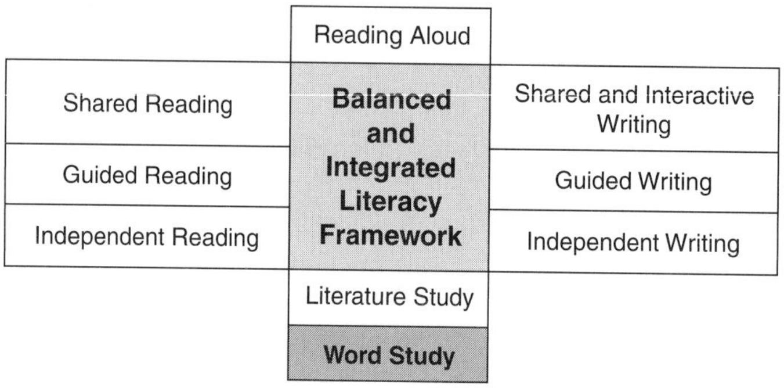

	Reading Aloud	
Shared Reading	**Balanced and Integrated Literacy Framework**	Shared and Interactive Writing
Guided Reading		Guided Writing
Independent Reading		Independent Writing
	Literature Study	
	Word Study	

In this chapter, we . . .

- Consider the purposes and scope of word study in the primary grades.
- Examine the importance of phonological development in emergent reading and writing.
- Explore a myriad of ways to support phonological development in the literacy program.
- Explore how to assess concepts about words in young children.

Looking into Classrooms . . .

The children in Marion's kindergarten class gather on the alphabet carpet for their morning opening. While everything that the children do during the half-day kindergarten relates to literacy and language in some way, Marion plans the morning opening to emphasize awareness of sounds in language, encouraging children to be playful with language. Marion leads the children in word-play songs such as a version of Old MacDonald in which the children separate sounds in the names of animals such as sh-eep, shared reading of songs and poems with rhyming words, and noticing the sounds of words in books read aloud. She knows that during the emergent stage of literacy development it is very important that children notice sounds in language and develop the ability to manipulate sounds in words in a variety of ways.

Building a Theory Base . . .

Knowledge of words is an important aspect of making meaning with oral and written language. Children who experience difficulties in learning to read and write often lack the critical awareness that words are composed of separable sounds, or phonemes, that are blended to produce words. They may know little about how spoken words are represented through print. Early literacy experiences must guide children to be curious about language, how sounds in language are meaningfully represented in print.

WHAT IS WORD STUDY?

In classrooms that focus on developing children's knowledge of language and print, the study of words occurs throughout the school day. We "do" word study with children when we:

- read aloud from fiction, information, or poetry and encourage children to listen for sounds in the language author's use or appreciate interesting words and phrases,
- engage children in shared reading and notice features of words in the text that have similar sounds at the beginning or end of the word,
- encourage children to participate in literature discussions with peers and help each other use familiar contexts to figure out unfamiliar words or phrases,
- interactively write a thank-you letter to the principal and use letter patterns in familiar words to figure out the spellings of some unfamiliar words,
- focus children's attention on patterns in words through activities that include word sorting and word building to see relationships between words that share similar meaningful parts,
- provide opportunities for children to independently explore words in familiar texts as they "read the room" and to extend word-building and word-sorting activities through activity centers,
- provide opportunities for children to write on topics they care about in writer's workshop and participate with peers in editing their work for conventions so that their ideas are clearly heard, or
- engage children in the intensive study of concepts in science, social studies, or mathematics to develop their knowledge of the specialized vocabulary of the topic, applying that knowledge through personal reading and writing.

As we encourage children to focus on new or interesting words, we give attention to making meaning through the effective use of meaning, structure, and visual language cues. It is essential, however, that we focus children's attention daily on the features of words that are appropriate for their current stage of development.

GUIDING PRINCIPLES FOR WORD STUDY

Regardless of children's stage of development, the following principles should guide us as we plan meaningful learning experiences for them. Word study should:

- be developmentally appropriate, focused on individual children's needs and not on a predetermined sequence of phonics concepts such as those found in commercial reading or phonics programs,
- build on a child's rich concepts about how print functions and a foundation of phonemic awareness,
- be learned in the context of meaningful reading and writing, not as isolated rules,
- draw upon multiple sources of information, including teacher demonstration, showing children how to think about letter–sound and structural relationships within the context of daily classroom activities,
- develop independent and automatic word recognition strategies in reading, including knowledge of onsets and rimes, to enable children to devote their full attention to making meaning, and
- encourage the use of invented or temporary spellings in writing to increase the time children spend thinking about and using letter–sound and structural relationships in a meaning-making process (Freppon & Dahl, 1991; Stahl, 1992).

As we plan learning experiences for young readers and writers, we will reflect on these guiding principles. We draw on these principles as we focus on emergent readers and writers. In addition, we will return to these guiding principles as we explore word study in the developing and transitional stages in Chapters 9 and 10.

OVERVIEW OF WORD KNOWLEDGE AND LANGUAGE CUES

We know that readers and writers use meaning, structure, and visual cues to make meaning. Through the use of these cueing systems we are able to develop a bank of words that we know on sight and effectively use the context of words and text to make meaning.

Sight Words

A large storehouse of sight words is necessary for the development of fluent reading (Holdaway, 1980). As a word takes on meaning for a reader and the reader notices enough detail in the word to distinguish it from other words, the reader is able to store the word in memory for later use. Reviews of research suggest that sight words are stored in memory by linking distinctive spelling features to the phonological (speech sound) structure of words in memory (Ehri, 1991).

Meaningful words are easier for readers to remember. Familiar words from children's home environment are often the first words they are able to read at sight, such as their own name, *mom, love,* and the like. Reading environmental print is possible because children have connected the distinguishing contexts of such words with personal experience. Such print becomes familiar through repeated exposure and the efforts of children to make meaning from their experience.

Context

How do readers use context? Imagine that we come to an unfamiliar word in a text we are reading. Up to that point, we have most likely processed the meaning of the text. Using that meaning, we may look at the unfamiliar word for clues to sound and/or meaning and ask, "What word do I know that could look like this and fit in this phrase, sentence, or paragraph?" When we think in this way, we are using context both as an aid to begin to decode the unfamiliar word and as a means of checking if our word choice(s) makes sense.

Young children already know how to use the context of oral language as a check for meaning. We must help them learn that written language also uses context as a means of figuring out words and checking for meaning. Young readers find the use of context especially helpful when they have only partial knowledge of the phonics or structural patterns within an unfamiliar word. They are able to use that partial knowledge to predict a word that fits the current context and confirm it through meaning and structure cues.

Phonics

The term *phonics* actually refers to instruction that emphasizes connecting an individual sound in speech (phoneme) to the letter(s) combinations (graphemes) that represent those sounds. When we encounter an unfamiliar word, we need an efficient way to determine a possible pronunciation of the word to match against words we know. Knowledge of the possibilities of letter–sound patterns in English is an aid to decoding, or determining how to pronounce a given word.

Young readers who have a strong sense of sounds within spoken words also have a strong foundation for phonics. Understanding that words are composed of a stream of sounds, or phonemes, serves as an anchor for connecting sounds with letters of the alphabet. Children must come to understand that it is a single phoneme that determines whether a word is *hat* or *bat, mom* or *mop, like* or *lake.* Changing one phoneme changes the word and, consequently, the meaning. Extensive and intensive exposures to language, both oral and written, provide opportunities for children to refine their phonological awareness and make connections to recurring visual patterns in the English language.

The difficulty with phonics is that many letters or letter combinations can represent more than one sound. At best, teaching children to use visual cues, such as phonics, to decode unfamiliar words provides a means for making a prediction that can only be confirmed by meaning and structure cues. Consider the word *bow.* We cannot know the pronunciation of this word without its context, because the letters *ow* can be decoded in two ways—as "ow" and "oh." While knowledge of the possibilities of letter–sound patterns is very important, especially to early reading and writing, we must always remember that phonics knowledge is only part of the knowledge children need to be competent readers and writers.

Structural Analysis

Analysis of the structural units of a word—roots, base words, compounds, contractions, prefixes, hyphenated forms, and inflected and derived endings or suffixes—can be helpful in determining the overall meaning of an unfamiliar word.

Many words in the English language are composed of two or more language, or morphological, units that have meaning. For example, *doghouse* is a compound word, composed of two base words (*dog* + *house*), when combined each unit contributes to the overall meaning of the new word—a house for a dog. *Overdrawn* is also a compound word, composed of two base words (*over* + *drawn*), but when the units are combined a new meaning emerges. Determining the meaning of *overdrawn* requires knowledge beyond merely decoding the two individual units.

Effective use of structural analysis relies on a reader's ability to see meaning units within the larger word, to draw upon phonics knowledge to determine the pronunciation of each unit and possibly blend the units into a pronounceable word, then relate that pronunciation to meaning and language cues to confirm its meaning within the context of the reading. Structural analysis requires the orchestration of all aspects of word knowledge to achieve understanding.

KNOWLEDGE OF WORDS IN THE EMERGENT STAGE

Our knowledge about words in print grows more complex as we read, write, and think about language. We progress through broad stages of development in our knowledge about words in print (Henderson, 1985; Henderson & Beers, 1980; Morris, 1981; Temple et al., 1993).

Children in this stage of development are just making a start with print. Their interactions with print are guided predominately by illustrations and their recollections of books read aloud to them, rather than by the print. Learning in this stage is dominated by a growing awareness of sounds in language and the representation of those sounds by letters.

Writing in this stage begins with scribbles and forms that begin to resemble letters and numbers. With added print experience, writing becomes strings of letters that have no relationship to sound and frequently no spaces to acknowledge the beginning and end of words. Finally, letters are used to represent sounds in words. One letter, typically the first sound in the word, may stand for an entire word, as in *b* for *bed.* By the time that children make the transition to the developing stage, beginning and ending consonant sounds in words are being consistently represented. Middle vowel sounds are beginning to be represented, though often not accurately.

Children's literacy development becomes more and more dependent on their experiences as learners (Wells, 1986). Early in the emergent stage, children:

- "read" by illustration and recollection of text that was read aloud to them,
- recognize familiar words in their environmental context, such as McDonald's, but typically not recognize it out of that context,
- are realizing that writing is meaningful,
- use strings of familiar letters to stand for words,
- begin to show words in writing by making spaces between groupings of letters, and
- begin to use some letters that accurately represent sounds in words, especially single consonants at the beginning of words, such as using *b* to spell *bed.*

With developmentally appropriate learning experiences, by the later part of the emergent stage, children may:

- read familiar, predictable texts with a limited number of words and repetitive patterns, from a combination of memory and text, guided by visual distinctions at beginnings of words and clues from illustrations,
- be more aware of the streams of sounds that make up words,
- know the names of most letters of the alphabet,
- realize that names of some letters contain clues to sounds they represent; for example, saying the name of this letter, *b,* makes the consonant sound, /b/, for which it typically stands,
- distinguish many single consonant sounds at the beginning of one-syllable words they read, and
- be consistent in the representation of familiar single consonants at the beginnings of words they write.

As children progress through this stage, we must be concerned about how they are learning to use various language cues to become competent readers and writers. How do they begin to develop use of meaning, structure, and visual cues in order to recognize words on sight, to use context in meaningful ways, and to decode print using their knowledge of phonics?

The Beginnings of Sight Vocabulary

Until children have a firm concept of word and knowledge of letter–sound patterns, they will have few sight words. The words that are known at sight are usually supported by strong emotional context. In addition to words in the context of familiar environmental print, emergent readers may also know some important names as sight words. A child's own name is certainly an important word and is usually a sight word in the emergent stage. In addition, children are likely to recognize the words *mom* or *dad*, sisters' or brothers' names, and eventually names of other children in the classroom who are important to them.

children to discriminate when it is heard at the beginning of a rime, as in *-ag.* Learning to listen for chunks of words—chunks that contain a manageable number of sounds—provides an essential piece of becoming a good speller.

After children are successful in splitting a syllable into an onset and a rime, sorting or categorizing activities are appropriate. To sort or categorize by beginning sound is a two-step process requiring syllable splitting, then sound matching. A child must separate the onset from the rime within a syllable, then decide which phoneme is similar to the onset.

Example: Looking at three pictures, bird, girl, and ball.
Child thinks, b-b-b-bird, g-g-g-girl, b-b-b-ball, then compares the beginning consonant to find the two that sound the same and feel the same way in the mouth, bird and ball.

This thinking strategy is essential for making generalizations about the sounds that letters represent.

Changing beginning and ending sounds to make new words is a natural extension of children's play with language. For example, children often play with each other's names by changing phonemes, such as Heather Feather or Silly Billy. Changing phonemes begins as an oral word play activity, then later becomes a decoding or spelling activity as children make associations with letters of the alphabet. Changing the beginning sound or onset in the word *can* makes *man, ran, fan, tan,* and *van.* The skill of changing phonemes gives children flexibility to decode or encode many words that have related letter–sound patterns.

Phonemes

Ultimately, children should be able to show the sounds they hear in words by clapping or tapping an appropriate number of times. Discriminating the vowel in the middle of a syllable present the greatest challenge.

Example: Teacher says /m/-/a/-/n/.
Children clap three times, once for each phoneme.

Hearing the number of sounds in a word helps children stretch words for themselves, hear phonemes, and begin to match sound to symbols in order to write words.

Example: Teacher stretches "man" to let children hear each phoneme.
Children say, "/m/—/a/—/n/."

Example: Teacher says "/m/—/a/—/n/", emphasizing each phoneme.
Children blend the phonemes and say "man."

Changing phonemes in a word helps children see how words can be related to each other by sharing particular letter patterns or sounds.

Example: Teacher asks, "What do you hear at the beginning of *bell?*"
Children say, "b."
Teacher asks, "What word can we make if we change the *b* to *sm?*"
Children say, "smell."

Changing the ending sound of the rime in the word *can* makes *cat, cab, cap, calf,* and *cast.*

Example: Teacher asks, "What do you hear at the end of *cat?*"
Children say, "t."
Teacher asks, "What word can we make if we change the *t* to *p?*"
Children say, "cap."

When children progress to the stage where they are "glued to print," they may decode words as individual phonemes, saying each phoneme aloud just as the teacher did above. Children who are able to decode and blend sounds are then able to hear the recognizable word.

To read and write competently, children must be able to blend, split, or change syllables in print. Consequently, as children are developing phonological awareness they also should be learning about the printed symbols that represent sounds.

LEARNING ABOUT LETTERS OF THE ALPHABET

As children become aware of sounds in words they also begin to notice print in the world around them. Children who are learning to speak English must come to understand that:

> "all twenty-six of these strange little symbols that comprise the alphabet are worth learning and discriminating one from the other because [they stand] for . . . the sounds that occur in spoken words" (Adams, 1990, p. 245).

With exposure to print, children typically begin to show an interest in what the print represents. When that occurs, it is appropriate to help them focus on the symbols used to create words—the letters of the alphabet. Reviews of research suggest that instruction in letters of the alphabet be sequenced in the following manner:

- Learn to say letter names, such as the ABC song, and recognize those sounds as names of letters of the alphabet.
- Match letter names to their corresponding shapes.
- Match letter names and shapes with corresponding sounds (Adams, 1990).

Letter Names

Knowing letter names is a good predictor of reading achievement and seems to transfer to an interest in learning letter–sound relationships. Prior to coming to school, most English-speaking children are introduced to the names of letters by learning to sing "The Alphabet Song." It is often sung to the tune of "Twinkle, Twinkle Little Star." A popular version goes like this:

Example: A, B, C, D, E, F, G
H, I, J, K, L, M, N, O, P
Q, R, S, and T, U, V
W, X, Y, and Z
Now I said my ABCs
Next time won't you sing with me?

Similar alphabet songs, chants, and rhymes help children develop an ear for the sound of letter names when spoken. The sound of letter names becomes an anchor in children's concepts about words and print to which letter shapes, and eventually letter sounds, can be attached. Having a name for letter shapes hastens children's ability to generalize similarities about letters across various print experiences.

Letter Shapes

Matching names of letters with shapes can be challenging for children. The shapes of letters are not graphically memorable; that is, the shape of a letter has very little to do with the name it was arbitrarily given. Instruction must help children learn to attend to distinctive features of print as they make associations between names and shapes.

There are actually four sets of letter shapes that children must learn over time:

- Manuscript lowercase
- Manuscript uppercase or capitals
- Cursive lowercase
- Cursive uppercase

Before entering school, children typically know the most about uppercase manuscript letters. Knowledge of lowercase manuscript letters, however, is most important for learning to read.

For children with limited print experience, it is best to avoid introducing both upper- and lowercase letters at the same time. Being faced with two distinctly different shapes that bear the same name may be confusing. If a choice must be made, Adams (1990) suggests that instruction in kindergarten should emphasize uppercase letters, while instruction in first grade should emphasize lowercase letters.

Instruction in the formation of letters that focuses on the contrasts between letters hastens children's ability to recognize and distinguish letter shapes. Discriminating letter shapes requires children to attend to the visual features of letters. Many children do not naturally notice the subtle differences in the lines and curves used to form letters.

Example: The difference between making a C and a G is a short horizontal line at the opening of the G.

Becoming sensitive to the differences among letter shapes develops over time, through many varied print experiences. It is best to separate instruction about confusable forms of letters, such as *b* and *d,* until at least one of the forms is known well.

Children must also understand that it is the position of a letter in relation to other letters that enables us to know how to name a letter shape.

Example: *b* turned upside-down becomes *p*
b reversed becomes *d*
p reversed becomes *q*
n reversed and turned upside-down becomes *u*

In the real world, a pencil remains a pencil regardless of its position or orientation to other objects. In contrast, children must learn that the position or orientation of a particular letter shape can change the name we give it.

Varied experiences with print should lead children to realize that letters can be found in many different types and sizes of fonts. Children's experiences with print in their neighborhood environment have already shown them some possibilities that they may not yet understand.

Example: The letter *g* may appear in many forms, such as

G g G g G g G g

To become independent readers, children must be able to generalize their knowledge about letters to new forms. When letter shapes are highly familiar and able to be discriminated, introducing letter sounds to children will be more successful.

Connecting Letters to Sounds

To unlock the sounds of unfamiliar words, children must be able to connect letter names and shapes to the sounds they represent. For instruction in letter sounds to make sense to children, they must have developed some phonemic awareness and the concept that letters make up words in print. Without an awareness of sound within words, children will find little purpose in letter–sound activities.

Children who know the names of letters find it easier to make connections to their associated sounds. Eighteen letters of the alphabet have sounds that consistently resemble the letter's name. Knowing the names of the letters, then, becomes an anchor for letter sounds.

Example: A, E, I, O, and U name the long vowel sounds.
B, D, F, J, K, L, M, N, P, R, S, T, V, and Z name consonant sounds.

To aid associations between letter names and shapes with their corresponding sounds, letter shapes can be introduced through pictures that integrate the shape of a familiar object with the shape of the letter (Ehri, Duffner, & Wilce, 1984). The name of the object should begin with the corresponding letter sound, and the pictorial representation should include the letter shape.

Example: Lower case *b* is presented as a baseball bat and ball.
Lower case *h* is presented as a house with a chimney.
Upper case *M* is presented as a mountain.
Upper case *V* is presented as a vase of flowers.

Pictorial mnemonics, such as those shown in Figure 8.1, are remembered by very young children (Pressley, 1997) and can increase the rate at which they learn letter–sound associations (Ehri et al., 1984).

Early consonant instruction that focuses on letter names and sounds that are similar is most effective.

Example: When we say the name of the letter "b", we also make the sound, /b/, that represents the sound of the consonant in words, such as *b*ell and ri*b*.

FIGURE 8.1
Pictorial Mnemonics for Alphabet Letters

FIGURE 8.2
Letter Names that Correspond to Consonant Sounds

Sound at Beginning of Name			Sound at End of Name		
Shape	**Name**	**Sound**	**Shape**	**Name**	**Sound**
b	"bee"	"bbb"	f	"eff"	"fff"
d	"dee"	"ddd"	l	"ell"	"lll"
j	"jay"	"jjj"	m	"emm"	"mmm"
k	"kay"	"kkk"	n	"enn"	"nnn"
p	"pee"	"ppp"	r	"arr"	"rrr"
t	"tee"	"ttt"	s	"ess"	"sss"
v	"vee"	"vvv"			
z	"zee"	"zzz"			

We refer to letters, such as *b,* as letter-name consonants because the letter name is a clue to the consonant sound. There are thirteen single consonants that have letter names that consistently represent the consonant sound when they appear in the initial position. Because of utility and ease of learning, these consonants should be taught before other, less consistent consonants. The letter-name consonants are listed in Figure 8.2. Notice that while all of the consonants name their sound, some do it at the beginning of the name and others at the end.

The letters *h* and *q* are consistent in the sound they represent, but do not name their consonant sound. These consonants challenge children's early understanding about the sounds that consonants represent. Emergent readers and writers may overgeneralize the use of letter-name clues, trying to make all consonants fit the letter-name strategy.

Example: The letter name *h,* pronounced "aaa-ch," represents the sound "huh." It is frequently confused with the sound for /ch/. The single consonant *h* appears at the beginning of a syllable.

Example: The letter name *q,* pronounced "ku," represents the sound "kwuh." *Q* is always followed by the vowel *u* and found only at the beginning of syllables. An awareness of vowels is helpful in decoding *qu.*

Finally, the letters *c, g, s, w, x,* and *y* represent variable sounds. As we help children associate a letter name with a symbol and a particular sound, we must remain keenly aware that the application of this knowledge to the decoding of words will become dependent upon the arrangement of letters within words.

WRITING ALPHABET LETTERS

In the early stages of writing letters of the alphabet, children will not necessarily have accurate mental images of letters. They should be taught to write a letter and check its formation against a model. As they write, they should be encouraged to talk aloud about:

- the name of the letter,
- the directions they move the pencil while forming the letter, and
- the sound it can represent.

Talking aloud as they write helps to bind the visual, motor, and phonological images of the letter together (Adams, 1990). Helping children make connections between letter names, shapes, and sounds is accomplished best in the context of real reading and writing activities. Children need many hours of watching more knowledgeable readers and writers performing tasks that they will one day perform. To be motivated to attend to print, children must believe that reading and writing have value for them.

Take a moment to reflect on your theory base for word study, especially at the emergent stage . . .

Word study is the focused study of words, including concepts about print, that is integrated throughout the components of a balanced literacy framework.

In general, the guiding principles for setting up a word study program in a primary classroom are as follows:

- Be developmentally appropriate and presented in the context of meaningful reading and writing
- Be sequenced in a way that is focused and responsive to children's needs
- Build on children's concepts about how print functions and about phonological awareness
- Draw on multiple strategies for reading and writing words
- Develop independent and automatic word recognition strategies in reading
- Encourage the use of invented or temporary spellings in writing to keep children thinking about print

In the emergent stage, word knowledge involves these steps:

- Beginning to develop a vocabulary of words that are recognized automatically, starting with familiar words in familiar contexts
- Using familiar contexts to recall whole words
- Beginning to understand the relationship between letters and sounds in print

Instruction in the emergent stage should focus on developing phonological awareness in spoken language, including:

- sensitivity to rhyming words,
- ability to discriminate syllable units in spoken words,
- ability to segment onsets and rimes within spoken words, and
- ability to discriminate phonemes in one-syllable words.

As children focus on sounds in language, they should receive instruction in making associations between sounds and the letters of the alphabet that can represent those sounds.

During the emergent stage of word knowledge development, children:

- begin to understand that print can have permanence,
- develop more refined concepts about print and concept of word through experiences with printed language,
- can use oral context to identify words for text,
- know some favorite words by sight,
- learn to listen to detail in spoken language, especially in words,
- develop phonics patterns through phonemic blending, segmenting, sorting, and exchanging single initial and final consonants,
- learn alphabet names, shapes, and sounds in the context of real reading and writing,
- learn most single, consistent consonant sounds at beginnings and ends of words, and
- are encouraged to try the "context +" strategy as the first step in self-monitoring behavior as a reader.

Putting Theory into Practice . . .

Word study for emergent readers and writers is best organized around word play through music, chants, and rhymes; reading aloud and storytelling (Adams & Bruck, 1995; Beck and Juel, 1995; Yopp & Yopp, 2000); and shared/interactive writing and reading. In this portion of the chapter, we explore socially stimulating ways to engage young children in language-rich environments. While we consider playful and engaging experiences as best for young children, we must always remember that our instruction should be deliberate and purposeful. Word study, especially the development of phonological awareness, is only one part of a balanced and integrated literacy program and must be placed in the context of real reading and writing experiences (Griffith & Olson, 1992).

INSTRUCTIONAL FOCUS DURING THE EMERGENT STAGE

Figure 8.3 summarizes the focus of instruction in the emergent stage. Notice how our instructional focus is centered on helping children understand the fundamentals of print and its relationship to spoken language. We will explore ways to

FIGURE 8.3
Overview of Instruction in the Emergent Stage

Emergent Readers and Writers . . .	In this stage children learn . . .
Function from preschool to early first-grade reading level. **They read —** words in meaningful contexts and some high-frequency sight words **They write —** words that range from letter strings, to initial & final consonants, to short-vowel words, to long-vowel words without long-vowel markers	• print has meaning, such as environmental print • print has rules • letters have names • words are made up of sounds • letters represent sounds in words • all sounds in a word can be represented by letters • letter names can be a clue to letter sounds • begin to discriminate initial and final single consonants • begin to acknowledge vowels in words

organize learning experiences to best serve the needs of children in this stage of development. Uses of music, oral word play, sound boxes, and sorting activities are among the activities suggested for developing awareness of sound, and relationships between sounds, letter names, and letter shapes. These activities are frequently integrated with other components of balanced literacy instruction to provide extended practice for children.

USING MUSIC TO FOCUS ON SOUNDS

Rhyming

To encourage attention to sound, children must first be able to detect rhyming patterns. Songs such as "The Ants Go Marching," provide excellent opportunities for children to play with language and attend to rhyme. The main portion of the verse is illustrated below:

> . . . .The ants go marching one by one,
> The little one stops to have some fun,
> And they all go down in the ground,
> To get out of the sun. . . .

With each verse, the number of ants changes and, consequently, the rhyming words change (e.g., two—tie her shoe, three—scratch her knee).

Blending Syllables

The song "Clap, Clap, Clap Your Hands" provides a pattern that is useful to play with joining the syllables of two-syllable words. The pattern of the verse is:

Clap, clap, clap your hands,
Clap your hands together,
Clap, clap, clap your hands,
Clap your hands together.

Yopp & Yopp (2000) suggest the following verse to encourage the blending of syllables:

Say, say, these parts,
Say these parts together,
Say, say, say these parts,
Say these parts together.

The teacher, then, says the two syllables, and children blend the syllables together.

Example: Teacher says, "rab" (pause) "bit."
Children say, "rabbit"
Teacher says, "farm" (pause) "er."
Children say, "farmer."

We want to select a variety of types of words, for example:

compound words—dog + house
words with inflected suffixes—jump + ing, horse + es
words with independent prefixes—un + tie
two-syllable base words—rab + bit, riv + er, mar + ket

Blending Phonemes

To provide practice in blending phonemes in words, use the tune of "If You're Happy and You Know It" (Yopp, 1992):

If you think you know this word shout it out—/m/-/oo/-/n/
If you think you know this word shout it out—/m/-/oo/-/n/
If you think you know this word,
Then tell me what you've heard,
If you think you know this word, shout it out.

This activity is used with one-syllable words. Children can also be encouraged to provide segmented words for others to blend.

Splitting Syllables

To encourage identifying the onset, or beginning, consonant sound for a syllable, use a familiar tune, "Old MacDonald Had a Farm" (Yopp, 1992). The song frame would be:

What's the sound that starts these words
moon, man, mask?
/m/ is the sound that starts these words:
moon, man, mask.
With a /m/, /m/ here, and a /m/, /m/ there,
Here a /m/, there a /m/, Everywhere a /m/, /m/.
/m/ is the sound that starts these words:
moon, man, mask.

Onset and Rime

"Old MacDonald" provides an opportunity to segment onsets and rimes, depending upon the words chosen.

Segment the onset only:

Example: Old MacDonald had a farm
E-I-E-I-O
And on his farm he had some *sheep*
E-I-E-I-O
With a sh- sh- (onset) here
And a sh- sh- there
Here a sh-, there a sh-
Everywhere a sh- sh- . . . .

Segment onset from the rime:

Example: Old MacDonald had a farm
E-I-E-I-O
And on his farm he had some *sheep*
E-I-E-I-O
With a sh- (onset) -eep (rime) here
And a sh- eep there
Here a sh-, there an -eep
Everywhere a sh- eep . . . .

Matching Phonemes

Practice in phoneme matching helps children select a phoneme that is the same as another. Using the tune of "Jimmy Cracked Corn and I Don't Care" you might sing (Yopp, 1992):

Who has an /m/(phoneme) word to share with us?
Who has an /m/ word to share with us?
Who has an /m/ word to share with us?
It must start with the /m/ sound!

In reply, a word is suggested and the class sings together:

Moon is a word that starts with /m/.
Moon is a word that starts with /m/.

Moon is a word that starts with /m/.
Moon starts with the /m/ sound.

Both initial and final sounds may be used in this song.

Changing Phonemes

Practice adding or substituting sounds in words encourages flexibility in making new words. Yopp (1992) suggests using a part of "I've Been Working on the Railroad," which begins with "Someone's in the kitchen with Dinah."

I have a song that we can sing
I have a song that we can sing
I have a song that we can sing
It goes something like this:

Fe-Fi-Fiddly-I-O
Fe-Fi-Fiddly-I-OOOO
Fe-Fi-Fiddly-I-O

Now try it with the /m/ sound

Me-Mi-Middly-I-O
Me-Mi-Middly-I-OOOO. . . .

Initial consonants, blends/clusters, and consonant digraphs can be used to make new words. For example:

ch digraph—Che-Chi-Chiddly-I-O
gr blend/cluster—Gre-Gri-Griddly-I-O

When children demonstrate ease of blending phonemes, splitting syllables to segment the initial phoneme, and matching phonemes, consider connecting oral activities to print. For some children, visual cues are a necessary anchor for sounds.

GAMES

Many game formats lend themselves to attention to words and sound units. Yopp & Yopp (2000) suggest "Mother, May I?" In this game children line up and ask the "mother" for permission to move a specified number of steps. Children can be asked to attend to the number of syllables (beats or chunks) in a word to determine the number of steps they may move.

Example: Teacher says, "Hop the number of syllables in the word *happy.*"
Children say, "Mother, May I? Hap-py!" (children hop twice)

The words used should vary in number of syllables, depending on children's ability to pronounce words correctly and count syllables. After learning to play the game, children can serve as the "mother." Children who play can check each other for correct syllable count. See Yopp & Yopp (2000) for numerous suggestions.

SORTING ACTIVITIES

Sorting Phonemes

In the emergent stage, children are developing their ability to discriminate initial and final consonant sounds. They do not yet recognize many words out of familiar contexts, such as shared readings. They can, however, demonstrate their ability to focus on particular phonemes and match phonemes at the beginning and end of words by sorting small picture cards. Sorting pictures, and eventually words, provides individual and guided group opportunities to refine phonemic awareness.

When we ask children to distinguish between sounds we want to be sure that we begin with phonemes of high contrast, phonemes that sound dramatically different and are formed in different places in the mouth (b/f, m/d). We do not want to begin with phonemes that are low contrast, especially those formed in a similar place in the mouth (f/v, b/p, d/t). These sounds are more difficult for a young sensory learner to discriminate.

Children can sort pictures in at least two ways:

- They can form their own groupings of picture cards, clustering cards they believe share the same beginning (and eventually ending) sounds (open sort).
- Teachers can also guide the sorting, by asking children to cluster pictures that share a particular sound (closed sort).

Sample picture cards for sorting can be found in Appendix B.

When children choose how to group the items for sorting, we refer to this as an open sort. The groupings or categories of pictures are open, or decided by each child. Their groupings show relationships they see among the pictures. Using an open sort is a good way to assess the general level of students' understanding about a particular grouping of cards.

When we guide children to focus on particular groupings of items, we refer to this as a closed sort. The categories, such as making a group of all pictures that begin like *ball* and another category of pictures that do not, focuses children's attention on particular phonemes and enables us to assess students' understanding of specific phonetic elements.

Early sorting activities should use pictures of objects that begin with a single consonant, such as *ball.* Words that begin with more than one consonant, such as *bread* or *ship,* should not be used at this time. At this stage of development, discriminating a single consonant may be challenging enough. Two consonants, such as *br,* are difficult to separate from each other. Two consonants that represent one new sound, such as *sh,* do not represent any one consonant letter. Single consonants should be the initial focus.

An open picture sort (see Figure 8.4) can be set up in the following manner:

1. We provide a group of ten to fifteen pictures that represent particular consonants for each child or pair of children.
2. Children spread out their pictures and orally name each one (a child cannot sort a picture accurately that is named incorrectly).

FIGURE 8.4
Sample Open Picture Sort

Jason said, "Things that are in a house."

"Things that are not in a house."

3. Children listen for the phoneme at the beginning of the word.
4. They isolate and say the phoneme, such as "b-b-b."
5. Children place the pictures together that they think begin (or end) with the same sound.

A closed sort (see Figure 8.5) can be set up in the following manner:

1. We provide a group of ten to fifteen pictures that represent particular consonants for each child or pair of children.
2. Children spread out their pictures and orally name each one.
3. We direct children to select one or more example pictures to guide the forming of categories.
4. One picture at a time, children name the picture and listen for the phoneme at the beginning of the name.

Sorting by Letters

Children need varied experiences to associate letter names with their corresponding shapes and sounds:

- Sorting words according to length—With familiar words on individual cards children sort all words with one letter into the same group, two letters in the same group, and so forth (Cunningham, 1995).

Example:

1	2	3	4	5	6
I	*go*	*and*	*make*	*funny*	*little*
A	*me*	*big*	*come*	*three*	*yellow*
	no	*can*	*down*		
		for	*jump*		

- Sorting words according to letters—Each child has a word on a card. Focusing on one letter at a time, children search their word for that letter. When the letter is found, children show that letter to a partner or the class, then the class makes a tally of the number of times each letter was found (Cunningham, 1995).

Example: The letter t *is found in words such as* it, little, the, three, to, two, at, *and* eat.

- Sorting words according to placement of a letter—Using familiar one-syllable words, the class sorts words according to the position of a particular letter (beginning, middle, or end of the word). We sort in this manner to help children begin to generalize where particular letters are most likely to occur.

Example: Sorting for the letter b

beginning	middle	end
big		*cab*
blue		*tub*
be		
brown		

Example: Sorting for the letter a

beginning	middle	end
a	*ball*	
and	*can*	
are	*make*	
at	*what*	

As children acquire words that are known in isolation, typically as developing readers, sorting activities begin to include the sorting of words to study visual patterns needed for decoding unfamiliar words in text.

USING SOUND BOXES

Say-It-and-Move-It

Blachman (1991) suggests an activity called, "Say-It-and-Move-It." Each child is given three flat buttons or chips and a sheet of paper with several connected

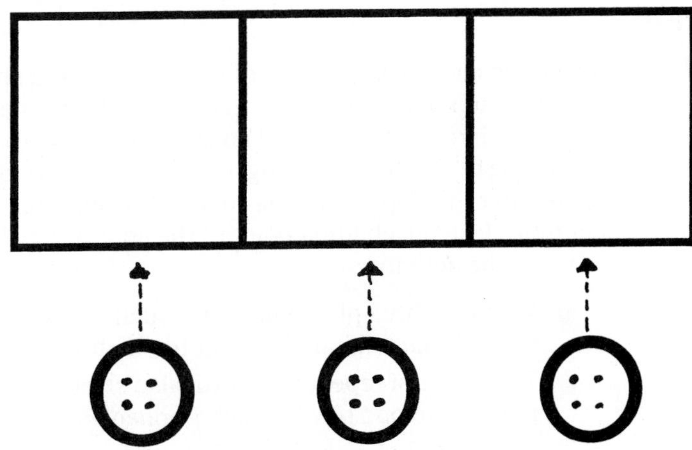

FIGURE 8.6
Sound Boxes for Say-It-and-Move-It

boxes drawn side by side, as shown in Figure 8.6. The number of boxes corresponds to the number of phonemes in the selected words. We usually begin with words that have three phonemes, such as *h-a-t.*

One button or chip is moved into a box to show each phoneme that is heard in a one-syllable word. Before the lesson we prepare a set of boxes with buttons for each child, as well as a set for modeling on an overhead projector. In addition, we prepare a list of words with three phonemes, such as:

bag, ball, bed, bug, cup, dig, dog, duck, fan, fish,
gum, hen, hop, jet, jug, leg, man, mud, net, pig, pop,
red, run, sun, ten, top, van, web, yes, or zip.

We select words that contain phonemes that are familiar to the children. For emergent readers and writers, we select only words that have single consonants.

Begin the activity:

- Let children practice with the manipulative before the activity begins by pushing each button up into a box as the teacher counts, "1 - 2 - 3."
- We say a word aloud, stretching the word enough to segment the phonemes, such as b-a-t.
- We ask the children to repeat the word, stretching the word and listening for each phoneme. They know by the boxes that there are three phonemes.
- We repeat the word and model on the overhead projector how to move a button as we say each phoneme. At the end of saying a word each of the three buttons have been pushed up into a box.
- The children repeat the word and push one button into a box for each phoneme.
- Then, together, we touch each button and isolate that phoneme and the corresponding letter name for that sound.
- Then we try another word.

Say-It-and-Write-It

As children acquire knowledge of letter names and shapes, letter shapes can be written in each box to represent each sound that is heard. In this activity, a sheet of paper with rows of connected boxes is prepared (see Figure 8.7). At first we continue to use the buttons, pushing a button into a box for each phoneme, then writing the letter that represents the sound we hear. Later, we can discontinue the use of buttons. Instead, children point to the appropriate box, then write the letter.

Begin the activity:

- We say a three-phoneme word, such as b-a-t, stretching the phonemes for children to hear. We point to one box for each phoneme.
- The children repeat the word, also stretching it to hear the phonemes, pointing to one box for each phoneme they hear.
- We ask, "What sounds do you hear?" or "What sound did you hear first?"
- Children reply with the phonemes they hear.

  Note: Some children will remember the last sound best. As children supply sounds, we repeat the word, emphasizing that phoneme and encourage children to point to the appropriate box. We confirm by pointing to the appropriate box on the overhead projector.
- We ask, "What letter makes that sound?" Children reply.
- We say, "Write that letter in the box (to which children are pointing)." We confirm by writing in the box on the overhead projector.
- In the same manner, we elicit other sounds that are heard.

Until children are aware of short-vowel sounds, the teacher may choose to supply the vowel. As children gain confidence with segmenting sounds within a syllable, the pace of the activity picks up, working toward more fluent writing of the sounds within a word.

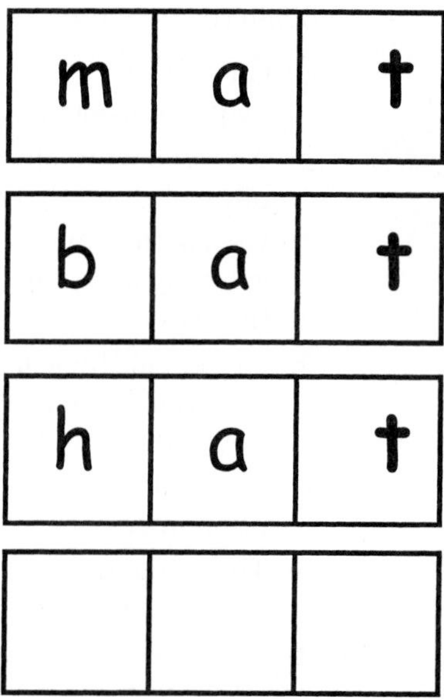

FIGURE 8.7
Sound Boxes for Say-It-and-Write-It

USING ENVIRONMENTAL PRINT TO FOCUS ON LETTERS AND SOUNDS

Environmental print has a context of its own that children "read." Through instruction we help children consider how they use the context of environmental print to read words. While children watch:

- we separate environmental print from its familiar packaging,
- compare the separated print with the print on an uncut package, then
- discuss how the context of the packaging helped us know the words.

Environmental Print Books

Collect multiple copies of logos and labels of environmental print that focus around a particular category, such as favorite foods.

- Children use one label to cut out the key word(s), such as cutting just the word "McDonald's" from a container that holds fried potatoes.
- On each page for the book, children glue a full logo and, underneath, the isolated word.
- Children can write the word in the label under the image. A handwritten sentence can also be written about the label or logo.
- A highly predictable sentence structure, such as "This is ________," should be chosen. The pages are stapled into a book for individual, partner, and group reading.

Environmental Word Wall

Words on the wall (Cunningham et al., 1989) made of environmental print, in and out of context, can be read by the class and referred to often. Children can also look for print around the school to add to the wall, such as the school name on the front of the building, labels on restrooms and offices, or labels on food in the cafeteria that can be read because it is in context.

USING CHILDREN'S LITERATURE TO FOCUS ON SOUNDS AND LETTERS

Alphabet Books

Alphabet books provide a rich source of exposure to the names of letters, both upper- and lowercase, and letter sounds. As books are read aloud, we take time to call attention to letter shapes, encourage children to provide letter names, and talk about the words that represent the sound of the letter. Rereading of alphabet books provides practice in hearing letter names and sounds, and seeing letter shapes in a meaningful context.

Chicka Chicka Boom Boom (Martin & Archambault, 1989) uses a rhyming pattern to name the letters of the alphabet. Letters in the illustrations are shown in lowercase, while letters in the text are shown in uppercase.

Example: A told B,
and B told C,
"I'll meet you at the top
Of the coconut tree."

On Market Street (Lobel, 1981) identifies objects that begin with each letter, one letter per page.

Example: *A apples,* (shows a person dressed in apples)
B books, . . .

A My Name is Alice (Bayer, 1984) uses words that begin with a specific letter to make rhythmical patterns with names of people, places, and objects.

Example: A—my name is Alice and my husband's name is Alex.
We come from Alaska and we sell ants.

An Edward Lear Alphabet (Newsom, 1983) provides opportunities for word play with each letter, changing to onset to make rhyming words.

Example: A a
A was once an apple-pie,
Pidy,
Widy,
Tidy,
Pidy,
Nice insidy,
Apple-pie!

Alphabet books can be enlarged to provide shared reading experiences. Children can participate in making a class version of a favorite alphabet book, supplying the illustrations for the text. Transparencies of pages from a favorite alphabet shown on the overhead projector also become a "big book" for shared reading.

Feed the Hungry Thing

The children's books *The Hungry Thing* (Slepian & Seidler, 1967) and *The Hungry Thing Returns* (Slepian & Seidler, 1990) provide excellent opportunities to encourage language play and changing onsets to create new, rhyming words. In the texts, the Hungry Thing points to a sign around his neck that says, "Feed me." The townspeople try to figure out what it means when he says that he wants some "hookies" (cookies) or "shmancakes" (pancakes).

Children experiment with changing the initial phoneme, or onset, as they feed the Hungry Thing:

- Read *The Hungry Thing* aloud so that children hear the nonsense words introduced in the text.

- Reread, hesitating after nonsense words for children to fill in the real words.

  Example: *"I think," said the little boy, "it's all very clear. Tickles . . . sound like Sickles . . . sound like . . . P_____ to me." (hesitate for children to complete)*

- Encourage children to say the nonsense words and real words aloud to hear the sounds. Discuss how the beginning sound was changed to make a new word.
- From a large paper bag create a "Hungry Thing," such as the example shown in Figure 8.8.

The first time, the game is played as follows:

- Teacher provides ten to fifteen pictures of familiar foods, displayed so that children can see them.
- Teacher says, "The Hungry Thing wants some 'schmandy.' What does he want?"
- Children look at the pictures and identify "candy."

Discuss how beginning sounds were changed. Make up other words that can also be candy, such as "dandy" or "jandy."

Try another version of the game:

- Provide plain paper for children to draw their favorite foods or magazines from which they may cut pictures of foods and paste the pictures on pieces of paper.

FIGURE 8.8
Feed the Hungry Thing

- Children take turns feeding the Hungry Thing by changing the phoneme at the beginning of their food, making it a nonsense word as in the text.
- The class tries to guess the real name of the food.

Following the whole-class activities, place the Hungry Thing in an activity center, along with food cards drawn by the class or pictures cut from magazines. Encourage children to continue their practice of changing beginning sounds. *Note:* As children build background knowledge of letter names and sounds, encourage children to state the letter name for the sound that was changed and write the letter that represents the sound. This should be done first in whole group, then in activity centers or independently. It is best to begin with single consonant changes, such as dandy for candy, stating that dandy begins with the letter *d,* d-d-d.

WORD STUDY IN SHARED AND GUIDED READING

Emergent readers should participate daily in shared and guided readings of texts. Shared readings will be reread to build background for the text. Guided reading engages children in texts that are instructional level. During shared and guided reading we select teaching points depending upon children's knowledge of words and their reading of the text.

Shared and guided readings of text provide opportunities to reinforce concepts about letter names, shapes, and sounds:

LETTER SEARCH

- Children point to or cup their hands around words that begin with a particular letter.
- The teacher places an acetate sheet over the text so that children can circle particular letters with an erasable crayon or marker.
- The teacher writes words from the text on a chalkboard and children circle the target letter(s) in each word.
- The teacher helps children notice the position(s) within words that letters seem to appear in most frequently, as well as never at all.
- Children identify capital and lowercase forms of letters that appear in the text.

SOUND SEARCH

- Children point to or cup their hands around words that begin with a particular sound.
- The teacher writes words from the text on a chalkboard that begin or end with the same sound and circles the target letters.
- The teacher helps children notice the position(s) within words that letters seem to appear in most frequently, as well as never at all.
- Oral cloze—The teacher hesitates before a key word in familiar text, providing only the beginning sound and children supply the word using the context plus the beginning sound.

WORD SEARCH

- Children point to or cup their hands around familiar words, such as the high-frequency sight words *I, can,* and *make.*
- Children search for words in a text and match a word card of a familiar word in isolation, such as *like,* with the same word in context.
- Teacher places familiar words on word cards to add to the word wall for class study. Words with the same beginning letter are grouped together.

WORD STUDY IN SHARED/INTERACTIVE WRITING

Shared writing uses children's language and thinking to create texts for reading. A more knowledgeable writer records children's dictations and provides opportunities to reinforce their concepts about letter names, shapes, and sounds. The recording is usually done on a large chart so that it may be kept for future rereadings.

With assistance from the teacher, children might compose and dictate the following story during the class opening one Monday morning.

Example: Today is Monday.
We go to music today.
Our favorite song is B-I-N-G-O.
Scott lost a tooth on Saturday.
Our class has lost 21 teeth.

As the teacher records the children's dictations, she supports the various levels of knowledge about print in the classroom by:

- repeating the sentence that was suggested and confirming its accuracy,
- saying each word aloud before she writes it, and
- inviting children to provide the letters that represent phonemes in the word, leaving space for sounds that are unfamiliar or that were not suggested by the children. Then the teacher provides information about unfamiliar sounds.

Example: The teacher elicits what children know about the word *teeth.*
Many children suggest the beginning *t, t*______.
Several children hear an *e,* so the teacher writes *te*____.
A few children suggest the ending *th, te*__*th.*
The teacher fills in the additional *e*, and explains that the *e* sound in teeth is made by two *e*s.

The teacher may choose to "share the pen" with children during the writing of certain words, making the composition more interactive. During interactive writing, children not only offer verbal suggestions for letters within words, but also write those letters as other children watch.

One advantage of shared writing, over the use of shared reading charts, is that children see a more knowledgeable writer record their words. In this process they have the opportunity to participate in the writing by using their letter–sound knowledge to suggest spellings for words.

During the rereading of a dictated text, the teacher encourages children to apply their knowledge about letters and sounds to the writing of words. As with big books, teachers should guide children to search for letters and sounds that are familiar.

ENCOURAGING SELF-MONITORING STRATEGIES

Competent readers and writers monitor the effectiveness of the skills they use. Children must learn to think strategically, knowing when to use specific knowledge and ways to monitor its effectiveness. When we discussed developmental learning in Chapter 1, we noted that in children's drive to learn, they monitor when and how much they use a particular skill, such as in learning to bounce a large ball. To continue to support developmental learning in school, we must encourage self-monitoring behaviors in the literacy activities that we plan.

We must help children in the emergent stage learn how to use word-getting strategies that are built on:

- expecting reading to make sense,
- knowing that print carries the author's message, and
- knowing that English has letter patterns that readers use to figure out words that are not immediately known.

A "central method of attack," described by Holdaway (1980), should be encouraged by the end of the emergent stage. Holdaway's central method is:

context + beginning letters,
checked by sense (and other letters).

This strategy is an example of cross-checking visual cues in a text with meaning and language cues. In this text we refer to this strategy as the "context +" strategy because its sophistication grows as children acquire greater word knowledge.

During the initial stages of word knowledge development, children are encouraged to use aural context as a way of making meaning during reading aloud activities. As soon they begin to link letters and sounds, we support the use of familiar visual cues to this "context +" strategy.

We encourage the "context +" strategy use when we talk out loud about how to figure out new, or unfamiliar, words:

> The way I figure out a "new word" is to look at the beginning letter(s). Then I think about what the author has been saying and what words might make sense that start with the letter(s) in the "new word."

When children are ready, we add the next step in the use of this strategy:

> When I think I know what the "new word" might be, I check my idea by looking at the letter(s) at end of the word to see if that word ends like the word I'm thinking about.

This "context +" strategy changes over time as children progress through stages of word knowledge. The strategy becomes more complex as children gain additional letter–sound knowledge and a solid concept of word. If children are to become competent in their ability to figure out words, this "context +" strategy must become an unconscious behavior, one that children use every time a word is not immediately known.

Although children in the emergent stage certainly are not fluent readers, they are learning to think about themselves as readers. Part of the process of becoming a competent reader is thinking that we are competent. Success in reading can build the self-confidence that will lead to further competence. Strategies, especially strategies over which readers have control, are essential behaviors to foster from the very beginning.

ASSESSMENT: MONITORING DEVELOPMENT IN THE EMERGENT STAGE

Viewing growth in children's knowledge of words from developmental stages provides a frame of reference for assessment and evaluation. What we intend to evaluate should guide the data we collect for assessment. Careful observation of reading and writing behavior, along with samples of reading and writing, enables us to ask important questions about children's growth in word knowledge.

The questions that we ask about children's growth in word knowledge change across stages of development. The answers to these questions come as we consider word knowledge instruction. In the emergent stage, we seek answers to the following questions:

- What reading and writing behaviors suggest that children understand there is a relationship between speech and print?
- What concepts about print have developed? How does the child demonstrate knowledge of such concepts, including letters of the alphabet?
- How firm is the child's concept of word in print? What behaviors during reading and writing activities suggest an understanding of "word"?
- How well does the child use oral context to predict and confirm words in print that is read aloud?
- Does the child know some words by sight? What type of words? How were those words learned?

To collect evidence of children's growing knowledge about print, we make observations of daily literacy experiences. In addition, we focus children's attention on particular aspects of literacy to learn more about what children know, are beginning to attend to, and have not yet begun to notice about print.

Concept of Words in Print

Concept of words in print is the ability to match speech to print, integrating knowledge about what words are and how they are formed. Concept of word is essential to the development of word knowledge and to success in early reading. Emergent and developing readers are formulating and consolidating their concept of word in print.

For children who seem confused by reading or are having difficulty learning words, the concept of word assessment may provide new insights into the child's understandings about print. To assess concept of word, a short piece of patterned text is needed that the child can verbally repeat, but cannot read. For example, the song "Twinkle, Twinkle, Little Star" might be used. Children should know how to sing this song, but not how to read the song when it is printed. Other familiar rhymes such as "Mary Had a Little Lamb," songs, or chants can be used.

In the selected text, be sure that there are several words with more than one syllable, and repeated words, so that children can find more than one instance of a word. Print or type the text clearly on a page, leaving some space between lines, with five to six words per line. Be sure to have one copy of the text for the child to read and one copy on which to record the child's responses.

As the child reads and points, mark each syllable (not word) above the place in the text where it was said. For example, a child, with a strong concept of word, matches word to word during reading and would be marked as:

| | | | | | |
Twinkle Twinkle Little Star

A child, who is still formulating a concept of word, will not match the oral and written text word to word. Instead, the child may match syllables, rather than words, so we mark the text as:

|(Twink) |(le) |(Twink)|(le)
Twinkle Twinkle little star

|(lit) |(tle) |(star)
How I wonder what you are

A child who is just beginning to formulate a concept of word may also treat each letter as equivalent to a speech unit or syllable, touching one letter for each syllable. This child may only be at the end of the first line of text by the time the oral rendition of the song is finished.

Procedure for concept of words in print:

- We rehearse the rhyme orally with the child several times to be sure it is in memory. The rhyme may also be taught to the entire class in anticipation of assessing each child's concept of word. This will save time with individual assessments.
- Then, we present the written text and tell the child this is the same song, poem, or chant that was just said together.
- We tell the child that we will read the text first and the child should carefully watch as we read and point. Then the child will read and point.
- We read at a normal pace, clearly pointing to each word as we read the text.
- We ask the child to read the text and point to the words he/she is reading.
- We use a copy of the text to show how the child read and pointed at the text.
- After the reading, we ask the child to locate several words in the text. We select words of different lengths. We ask the child to find a word

that is repeated. In the sample text above, we could ask a child to find Twinkle, twinkle (repeated), world (there are other w words), or sky (or other short words that appear once). We watch to see how the child locates the word—do they go right to the word, hesitate at first and then locate the word, or go back to the beginning to the text and reread/point again to find the word in the text?

Concept of words assessment shows some of the same knowledge as the concepts about print assessment, such as print language or letter/word concepts, but in greater detail. This assessment should be used early in the school year and periodically throughout, while a child is in the emergent or early developing reader stage.

Keeping Records of Word Knowledge Development

Each time that we evaluate children's reading or a piece of focused or unfocused writing for evidence of word knowledge it will be helpful to record our observations. Record-keeping forms, such as Figures 8.9 and 8.10, can be made to reflect the knowledge and strategies for which we provide instruction and expect to see develop at this stage. Such forms are combined with other assessments to serve as a more complete picture of development.

In this chapter we have explored issues of word knowledge development that are specific to emergent readers. In Chapters 9 and 10 we do the same with developing and transitional readers and writers. Before you move to those chapters, take a moment to reflect on what you know about emergent readers and writers.

RESPECTING DIVERSITY IN DEVELOPMENT OF WORD KNOWLEDGE

Learning words is very important in the processes of reading and writing. Confidence in one's own ability to read and write words can greatly influence daily reading and writing performance. If children are to be successful in learning words, we must consider their experiences with print, their knowledge of how to monitor their own reading and writing, and their knowledge of the language you use for instruction. In addition, we should provide a variety of opportunities for children to make sense of reading and writing words.

Experience Sets Children Apart

As we engage children in word study activities, we should keep in mind that it is often experience that sets children apart from one another (Allington, 1994). As we plan a word study program, expect children's differences in experience to enrich daily talk about words. Expect that children will make sense of their word study experiences in different ways and will, if given the opportunity, teach each other what they understand about reading and writing words.

FIGURE 8.9
Development of Word Knowledge: Emergent Stage

Context:	**Usually**	**Sometimes**	**Rarely**
Uses aural context to figure out unfamiliar words during read-aloud			
Recognizes print in familiar environmental contexts			
Sight Vocabulary:			
Recognizes some familiar words in isolation			
Phonics:			
Is developing phonemic awareness			
-remembers rhymes & rhyming words			
-can split words into syllables			
-blends syllables to make a word			
-can split syllable into onset & rime			
-can segment one-syllable word into phonemes			
-can categorize phonemes			
Self-Monitoring Strategy:			
Searches for information in illustrations to make meaning			
Is beginning to use context + first sound to identify words in familiar text			

Observations/Comments:

FIGURE 8.10
Print Knowledge—Alphabet

Reads letters of the alphabet:

A	a	B	b	C	c	D	d
E	e	F	f	G	g	H	h
I	i	J	j	K	k	L	l
M	m	N	n	O	o	P	p
Q	q	R	r	S	s	T	t
U	u	V	v	W	w	X	x
Y	y	Z	z				

Writes letters of the alphabet:

A	a	B	b	C	c	D	d
E	e	F	f	G	g	H	h
I	i	J	j	K	k	L	l
M	m	N	n	O	o	P	p
Q	q	R	r	S	s	T	t
U	u	V	v	W	w	X	x
Y	y	Z	z				

Phonics Knowledge—Initial and Final Consonants

Distinguishes initial consonants in reading: consistent consonants

b-	d-	f-	h-	j-	k-	l-	m-
n-	p-	r-	t-	v-	x-	y-	z-

variant consonants:

c-(hard)	c-(soft)	g-(hard)	g-(soft)	s-(s)	s-(sh)	x-(ks)	x-(z)

Distinguishes initial consonants in writing: consistent consonants

b-	d-	f-	h-	j-	k-	l-	m-
n-	p-	r-	t-	v-	x-	y-	z-

variant consonants:

c-(k)	c-(j)	g-(g)	g-(j)	s-(s)	s-(sh)	x-(ks)	x-(z)

Distinguishes final consonants in reading:

-b	-d	-f	-g	-k	-l	-m	-n
-p	-r	-t	-v	-w	-z	-s (z)	

Distinguishes final consonants in writing:

-b	-d	-f	-g	-k	-l	-m	-n
-p	-r	-t	-v	-w	-z	-s (z)	

Teaching according to developmental levels also acknowledges difference in experience with words. Adopting one level of a spelling or phonics program for all children in a classroom does not acknowledge or respect the diversity that experience brings.

Encouraging Self-Monitoring

While we encourage children to adopt the "context +" strategy in their work with words, we also expect that children will adapt the strategy to their way of thinking as readers and writers. We can provide support to the diverse ways that children work as learners by encouraging them to think aloud about the knowledge and strategies they use as they read and write words.

Language of Instruction

For children whose first language is not English, the language we use for instruction can be a mystery. Who else will they hear talk about long and short vowels or base words? Teachers have a special language they use in school with children. Consider how well children will know that special language. It is our responsibility to teach the meaning of that language of instruction to all children, so that everyone has a more equal opportunity to benefit from word study instruction.

Variety of Opportunities

In this text, building and sorting words is encouraged as a major instructional approach for word study. However, while word building and sorting may look similar when they are completed, the thought processes used by different children may vary widely. Encourage variety in thinking by providing opportunity for children to share with others during word study. Encourage variety in the ways that you accept children's recordings in their word study notebooks.

We must be open in our thinking about how children learn words. Some children will learn words easily by reading many books or writing for a long period of time. Some children will learn words by saying words and spelling them aloud. Some children will find that cards with words, seen over and over, help them to remember. Some children will have to think they are playing to learn words, such as in word games. Some children will be motivated to learn most when working on a computer. The instructional strategies suggested in this chapter are only a start—a foundation for your word study program. Be prepared to add to these ideas, especially as children teach you what works best for them. Be open!

Take a moment to reflect on putting theory into practice with word study at the emergent stage . . .

Phonological awareness is an essential element for successful reading and writing development. Children develop phonological awareness through attention to language in activities such as:

- manipulating sounds through music,
- playing games with words,
- sorting picture cards by segmenting the onset from the rime,
- using sound boxes to count the number of sounds in words and to segment the phonemes, and
- playing with sounds in words found in children's literature.

Concepts about print, which are essential to word knowledge, develop as children explore:

- environmental print, in and out of context,
- children's literature, especially alphabet books,
- print through other literacy components such as shared/interactive writing and reading, as well as guided reading.

Interactions with print should encourage the beginning of mental strategies in which children expect reading and writing to make sense, and begin to search for information to repair meaning.

Children's concepts about print can be assessed through matching speech to print with written text that is already in the child's memory.

Children's varying experiences with language and print will lead to differences in their knowledge of words. We must provide support for oral language development and increased exposure to print to enable all children to experience optimum growth in word knowledge.

YOUR TURN . . .

1. Begin a collection of teaching ideas for developing phonological awareness, including:
   - songs that can be adapted to rhyme, segment, and blend words,
   - games and sorting activities that can be adapted to focus on sounds within words, and
   - literature that emphasizes sounds, such as ABC books.
2. Observe classroom activities that emphasize phonological awareness. Notice ways that teachers engage children to help them focus on sounds in language. Particularly notice their responses to oral and written activities. If possible, interview the teachers to better understand how they make decisions about selecting phonological activities for instruction.
3. Use the words to "Twinkle, Twinkle Little Star" or another familiar song to assess children's concepts about words. Make two copies of the song, one for the children to read and one on which you can record the child's responses. Be sure that the print is clear and of appropriate size for the children to read and point. Consider placing extra space between words and between lines of print so that you will be able to follow the child's pointing. Consider administering this assessment with a partner so that you both can observe the child and compare your observations with each other.

Aa Bb Cc Dd Ee Ff Gg Hh Ii Jj Kk Ll Mm

CHAPTER

9

Word Study II: Developing A Strong Phonics Base

Adding to our literacy framework . . .

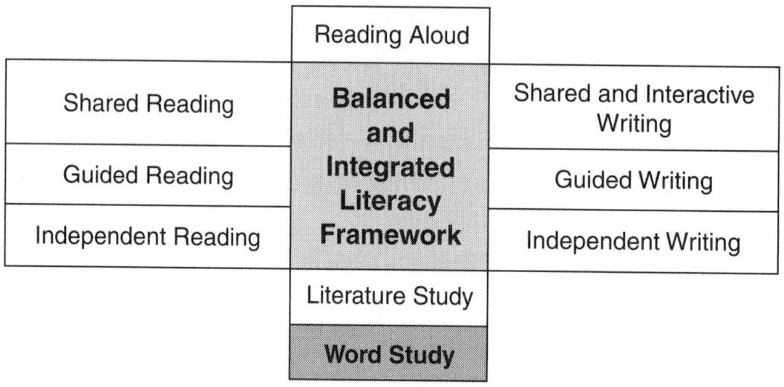

	Reading Aloud	
Shared Reading	**Balanced and Integrated Literacy Framework**	Shared and Interactive Writing
Guided Reading		Guided Writing
Independent Reading		Independent Writing
	Literature Study	
	Word Study	

In this chapter, we . . .

- Consider issues in phonics instruction for developing readers and writers.
- Explore whole-class word study through building new words with varying patterns.
- Explore small-group word study that includes sorting, building, and hunting for words of particular patterns.

- Consider a possible sequence for developing phonics knowledge for developing readers and writers.
- Examine ways to assess the word knowledge using focused and unfocused samples of writing.

Looking into Classrooms . . .

"Look at all of the words we can build from the word prince,*" exclaim the children in Nikki and Mary's second-grade, team-teaching classroom. The class has been studying different versions of* The Frog Prince, *so Nikki and Mary decide to use the word* prince *for a whole-class word building activity. Using all of the letters in the word* prince, *the children are able to build the words* in, pin, rip, pen, ice, rice, nice, ripe, pine, cried, price, *and* prince. *The children each have the letter cards—* p, r, i, n, c, e. *Nikki and Mary begin with two-letter words and work up to using all of the letters to spell* prince. *Together the class talks about sounds in words and how parts of words are similar. The variety of the words that can be spelled from the letters in* prince *provides opportunities for every child to find some familiar words and some challenging words. These developing readers and writers find word building to be very engaging.*

Building a Theory Base . . .

With some foundation in phonological development, children are ready to explore visual cues of print in more depth. It is not possible, nor advisable, that we teach children to recognize each word they will meet in print. Our goal is to work toward an understanding of useful patterns in words and encourage the application of patterns to words that are unfamiliar or occur infrequently.

We focus on word knowledge with young children because literacy research suggests that knowledge of words is a major predictor of future success in reading and writing:

- Differences in word knowledge consistently account for variations in performance among readers and writers (e.g., Biemiller, 1977/78; Gough & Tummer, 1986; Perfetti, 1985; Rack, Snowling, & Olson, 1992; Stanovich, 1982; Stanovich, Cunningham, & West, 1981).
- Children who do not develop effective code-breaking strategies early in their reading histories are likely to experience reading difficulties as they progress through the school grades (Byrne, Freebody, & Gates, 1992; Clay, 1991).
- Developing power with words depends on children's ability to automatically recognize or produce words, combined with their ability to think with those words (Holdaway, 1980).
- For knowledge of words, both speed and effortlessness are integral to competent reading (Adams & Osborn, 1990).

Developing readers and writers need opportunities to focus their attention on the distinctive features of words in order to develop both a rich meaning vocabulary and an extensive sight vocabulary (Ehri, 1991). They need our guidance to understand phonetic and structural patterns in the words they read and write. They must also be able to use meaning and structure cues to cross-check for understanding while reading and writing text.

CHILDREN'S KNOWLEDGE OF WORDS IN THE DEVELOPING STAGE

Developing readers typically function between a mid-first-grade and an early-third-grade reading level. Early in this stage, readers are described as being "glued to print" (Chall, 1979, 1983), because they are intent upon generalizing their concepts about words in print and letter–sound patterns to the words that dominate their reading texts. Unfamiliar words with more than one syllable present much challenge early in this stage, but by the end of the stage students are becoming quite proficient at reading two- and some three-syllable words. Through extensive reading in independent text, they develop a large sight vocabulary during this stage.

As writers, these students are gaining control over one-syllable words, particularly predictable vowel patterns, and are attempting to represent two-syllable words. The vowel in the second syllable, however, is frequently absent. The word *beaches* might be written as *bechs, beechs,* or *beachs,* instead of *beaches.* Word study instruction during this stage focuses primarily on phonics, or learning about words through letter–sound relationships and patterns. Through extensive writing with attention to communication, they develop more conventional spelling.

From the description above it is obvious that as children progress from the emergent to the developing stage, knowledge of print takes on great importance. The texts that children read and write during first, second, and third grades require an understanding of a wide range of words. Are there basic generalizations about the formation of words that children must come to understand?

By third-grade reading level, when children typically transition into silent, and much more fluent, reading, they must be able to effectively and efficiently "break the code" of written language. Knowledge of visual language cues, by way of letter–sound patterns, is one means to achieving fluency.

Developing Sight Vocabulary

Children in this stage are developing a substantial sight vocabulary. Meaning and repetition are key elements in learning sight words for children who are not yet rapid decoders. Sight words become the basis for word study during this stage, which enables children to further develop knowledge about patterns in words. Rereadings in predictable texts and shared writings are excellent ways to help children develop sight words.

Repetition in familiar contexts:
Early in this stage children are not yet independent readers. They are still heavily dependent on familiar contexts for reading connected text. The most appropriate texts for reading instruction are predictable, with a limited amount of text. Shared compositions also make excellent texts for developing sight vocabulary. To help children progress from using familiar words in context to knowing words at sight, we plan activities that call attention to details in words. Rereadings in groups, with partners, or alone are always helpful. In addition, word walls, word books, word rings, and word card activities can focus attention on detail in words and provide additional exposure.

Sample sight word activities may include:

- a portion of a word wall devoted to pairs of rhyming words which are taken from a predictable text,
- word books, made of favorite words or words to learn, with one word on a page and a supporting illustration,
- favorite words put on cards or on a metal or plastic ring to be carried around, shared, and compared, and
- words on cards to be spilled on the floor for group word sorts, building meaningful phrases, or constructing sentences from the familiar text.

Frequency of reading also influences the development of sight vocabulary. Children in this stage need to spend increased time each day in independent reading experiences. Their confidence in easy text reinforces pleasure with their growing independence. The classroom library must be restocked frequently with low-challenge books on a wide variety of subjects, crossing different genre.

Children should be able to sustain their reading in several picture books with easy text for at least fifteen to thirty minutes during independent reading and longer for reading with a partner or in a group.

Repetition is still a factor for developing a memory for words. Continue to provide predictable, repetitive books, along with topics of high interest to the children. Their motivation to read material of interest can take the place of repetitive text when they choose to read and reread favorite books. Success leads to needed repetition! Success breeds confidence, and confidence brings developing readers back to the same books over and over, the books in which they feel successful.

Refining Concepts about Words in Print

For children to become competent readers and writers, they must understand the "rules" that govern the arrangement of letters within English words.

- Each sound in a word can be represented by a letter or letters.

  Example: /ch/-/i/-/n/ is written as *chin.*
  /f/-/o/-/ks/ is written as *fox.*
- Just as letters represent sounds in words, some letters represent silence.

  Example: In *bike* the *e* is silent, in *light* the *gh* is silent, and in *write* the *w* is silent.
- Letters must be written in a particular left-to-right order to make specific words; therefore, a particular word is always spelled the same way.

  Example: The letters *a, s,* and *w* can be arranged to spell both *was* and *saw.* To make the word *saw,* the letters must always be arranged left-to-right as *s-a-w.*
- The position of letters within a word can influence the sound represented.

  Example: The letter *s* typically has the /s/ sound at the beginning of a syllable, as in *sun,* but can also have a /z/ sound at the end of a syllable, as in *his.*
- The sound of a phoneme can be changed by a letter or letters that immediately follow.

  Example: In *mad, a* is pronounced as short *a.*
  In *maid,* with *i* added, *a* is pronounced as long *a.*

  Example: In *sin, i* is pronounced as short *i.*
  In *sign,* with *g* added, *i* is pronounced as long *i.*
- The sound of a phoneme can be changed by one or more nonadjacent letters.

  Example: In *kit, i* is pronounced as short *i.*
  In kite, with silent *e, i* is pronounced as long *i.*
- The sound of a phoneme can be changed by the division of syllables.

  Example: In *mu-sic, c* is pronounced as /k/.
  In *mu-si-cian, ci* is pronounced as /sh/.

- Some spelling patterns that appear in more than one word can represent the same sounds.

  Example: The pattern *-eal* can be found in *meal, steal, conceal,* and *appealing.*
- Some spelling patterns can have more than one pronunciation.

  Example: The vowel pattern *ou* can be pronounced as:
  long *o* (*soul*),
  short *u* (*young*),
  oo (*through*),
  aw (*ought*), and
  ow (*cloud*).
- Some letter patterns are never found in certain positions within a syllable.

  Example: The blend *nt* never begins a syllable. It is always found at the end of a syllable, as in *went.*
- Certain letter patterns are characteristic of English words, but other patterns are not.

  Example: *Boat* would never be spelled *b-a-o-t* because *ao* is not a common English vowel pattern.

Throughout the developing stage, we help children refine their understandings about how words are formed. We provide extensive experiences with print in order for children to make generalizations about patterns that are likely to occur in English. Knowledge of phonics generalizations enables readers to make predictions about the pronunciation of unfamiliar words. The accuracy of predictions must then be checked against readers' knowledge of English words (structure cues) and the appropriateness of the context in which the words appear (meaning cues). Knowledge of letter–sound possibilities by themselves does not lead to meaning. Thus, refining our knowledge about words continually requires that we integrate phonics knowledge with our knowledge of language to make meaning with print.

Knowledge of letter–sound patterns within syllables will also be an aid to decoding longer, multisyllable words that are the focus of the transitional stage (see Chapter 10). Complex words are often composed of patterns that are already known in one-syllable words. The challenge is to recognize those familiar syllable patterns within longer words.

GUIDING PRINCIPLES FOR PHONICS INSTRUCTION

We support students' learning when we plan phonics instruction that, in general, focuses on:

- single-letter patterns before double-letter patterns,
- consistent patterns before variant patterns,
- initial position before final position,

- sounded patterns before silent patterns, and
- development in reading usually before writing.

An overview of phonics, organized by broad patterns, is shown in Figure 9.1

Phonics makes more sense to children when pattern and predictability are emphasized. Seeing patterns means looking for the related "chunks" of knowledge and considering the types of thinking processes used with phonics patterns. The brain is a pattern detector, not a rule applier. When a reader attempts to decode a word, his or her brain either recognizes a familiar spelling pattern or searches through its store of words for similar patterns (Adams, 1990).

Utility is important to learning. The patterns that we study with children should always be applicable to the vocabulary appearing in their reading materials. Spelling, or encoding, instruction should focus on words that are currently appearing in children's writing. If children are not able to use new phonics knowledge, their progress toward fluency may be hindered.

Children come into the developing stage knowing that sounds heard in words can be represented by one or more letters. A new concept to be developed in this stage is that both vowels and consonants can be silent and that when vowels are silent they often influence a preceding vowel.

As we plan for word study, we want to remember that children are likely to demonstrate knowledge of letter–sound patterns in reading before they gain enough control over the same patterns in writing (Temple et al., 1993). In reading words, familiarity with the whole word (sight word) often comes before familiar-

Phonics Patterns

Consonants		Vowels	
Single	Teams	Single	Teams
Consistent • letter name represents sound (d = /d/) • letter name does not represent sound (w = /w/, not /d/)	**2 Consonants—2 Sounds** • blends/clusters initial position (stop) final position (fast)	**Short** • CVC pattern (bed)	**Long—Consistent** • vowel digraphs (rain)
Variant • vary by position, (sun, his) • vary by vowel that follows (go, age)	**2 Consonants—1 Sound** • double consonants (bell, dress) • Consonant Digraph h digraphs (shop) silent letter (write, duck)	**Long** • CV pattern (me) • CVCe pattern (make)	**Long & Short—Vary** • vowel digraphs (meat)
		Neither Long Nor Short • r-controlled (car)	**Neither Long Nor Short** • diphthongs (oil, boy) • r-controlled (fair)

FIGURE 9.1
Overview of Phonics Patterns

ity with word parts or chunks. Keeping in mind that there is much to be learned in the developing stage, how do we begin to consider instructional issues? What should guide us as we plan word study experiences for developing readers?

Take a moment to reflect on your theory base for phonics . . .

Knowledge of words is a key factor in children's development as readers and writers.

Developing readers are "glued to print," refining their knowledge of letter–sound patterns to recognize familiar sound parts in unfamiliar words.

Developing writers gain control over many consonant and vowel patterns in one-syllable words, while they continue to invent spellings for portions of multisyllable words.

An important part of the developing stage is providing support for children's concepts about the rules that govern the arrangement of letters in English words.

As we consider instruction in phonics, several basic principles should guide the ways that we plan learning experiences for developing readers:

- single-letter-before double-letter patterns,
- consistent before variant patterns,
- initial before final position, and
- sounded before silent patterns.

As we observe children, we must remember that they are likely to use their knowledge about print to respond in reading before they are about to use the same knowledge to compose through writing.

Putting Theory into Practice . . .

Developing readers and writers have much to learn about letter–sound and meaning patterns in the words they will encounter as they progress toward the transitional stage. By the time children are able to make meaning with texts at approximately third-grade reading level, they must know a great deal about words.

INSTRUCTION IN THE DEVELOPING STAGE

A major focus of word study during the developing stage is learning to "break the code" of the English language. As children develop concepts about words in print, they must learn to attend to details within words, discriminate letter–sound patterns, and make generalizations about the patterns that are likely to occur in English. Figure 9.2 provides an overview of the patterns that children explore during the developing stage. Instruction in these patterns is the focus of the remainder of this chapter.

Developing Readers and Writers	In this stage, students learn . . .
Function at early-first-grade to early-third-grade reading level.	**Phonics—Consonants**
read— one-, two-, and three-syllable words "glued to print"	• initial and final single consonants (b-, -b) • initial & final digraphs (sh, th, ch) • initial blends (br, gl, st) • variant (c, g, s) • final blends (nt, lk)
oral reading, moving toward silent	• digraphs with silent letters (wr, kn, wh)
write— One-syllable words with long and short vowels, varying vowels are not yet consistent.	**Phonics—Vowels** • short (a, e, i, o, u) • long vowel, no vowel marker (me, go) • silent e (a_e, i_e, o_e, u_e, e_e)
Familiar two-syllable phonetic words, such as rabbit	• consistent long double vowels (ai, ay, ee, igh, oa) • long & short double vowels (ea, ei, ey, ie, ou)
Familiar base words + inflected suffix when the base does not change, such as jumping	• double vowels, nor long nor short (au, aw, oi, oy, oo, ow, ou, ui, eu, ew)
	• r-controlled, single vowel (ar, er, ie, or, ur) • r-controlled, long vowel (are, ere, ire, ore, ure) • r-controlled, double (air, ear, eer, oar)
	Introduce Structural Patterns • recognize base + base (compounds, contractions) • recognize affixes added to base (no change) • base + inflected suffix, no change to base (s, es, ed, ing)

FIGURE 9.2
Overview of Instruction in the Developing Stage

To develop an effective word study program for children at any stage of development, we must consider:

- how words are selected for study,
- how to organize whole-class and small-group study,
- possible sequences for studying words, and
- assessment of children's development of word knowledge.

SELECTING WORDS FOR STUDY

We select words for study based upon children's stage of development and our knowledge of phonics and structural analysis. The focus of study in the developing stage is primarily on understanding consonants and vowel patterns within words, as shown in Figure 9.1. We begin with patterns that are prevalent in one-syllable words.

As we gather words for study, we sort words into categories that coincide with the skills to be taught in phonics and structural patterns at a particular stage of development. We must remember that any single word contains elements of several patterns. For example, the word *map* may be used in lists of words that:

- begin with /m/,
- end with /p/,
- contain short *a,* or
- contain the rime (or phonogram), *–ap.*

In the lists of words that we collect for a particular phonetic element, such as short *a,* are varying levels of complexity. For example, a list of short *a* words can fit the varying needs of children in a classroom:

Short *a*, with single consonants		**Short *a*, with blends and digraphs**	
can	*map*	*black*	*bath*
sad	*fat*	*stamp*	*match*
bag	*ham*	*flat*	*crash*

The vowel, short *a,* is typically studied by developing readers and writers. Within a particular classroom, however, some children will be ready to focus on single consonants, whereas other children are ready for the challenge of spelling words with consonant blends and digraphs. Still other children will use some of these words to compare with long *a* patterns and demonstrate their understanding of how letter patterns can be clues to pronunciation. Children's current reading materials are an important source for words that will have high utility. Sample lists of words are also available in Appendix B.

WHOLE-CLASS WORD STUDY: BUILDING WORDS

With the diversity of knowledge about words that is likely to exist among any group of children, building words is an excellent way to approach whole-class word study. Building words, letter by letter, requires that children use their skills in phonemic awareness to segment sounds in words, connect those sounds to the appropriate letters, and place letters in sequence from left to right on the desk or table in front of them. Word building provides children the opportunity to experience firsthand that changing just one letter or the sequence of the letters within a word changes that word (Cunningham & Cunningham, 1992). This concept is essential to children's developing concepts about words, especially words in the English language.

Selecting Words

We have at least two options for the words we will use for building words.

1. Work with a particular pattern, such as a group of short *a* words that vary in difficulty.

Example: *can, map, sad, fat, bag, ham, flat, bath, match, black, stamp, crash*

2. Select a longer word that contains letters from which two-, three-, four-, and more letter words can be constructed (Cunningham & Hall, 1994).

   Example: Select the letters for the word *scratch,* to make the words—*at, art, tar, car, cart, cars, scar, star, cash, rash, trash, crash, chart,* and *scratch* (p. 9).

The advantage of selecting a particular pattern, such as short *a,* is repetition of pattern within one lesson and some control of the amount of challenge. The advantage of selecting a longer word from which smaller words can be made, as suggested by Cunningham and Hall (1994), is the ability to challenge the various levels of development in a classroom. Care must be taken when selecting a longer word to consider the appropriateness of the patterns that the word will make.

Preparing Materials

To build words, children need a set of letter cards that can be manipulated to make words. Bags of individual letters must be duplicated and cut apart. Cunningham and Hall (1994) suggest that the vowel cards be written in a contrasting color (red) to consonant cards (black), to call attention to the position of vowels within words. Cards have the uppercase letter on one side and the lowercase letter on the other.

At the beginning of a word building session, children assist with passing out the particular letters that are needed that day.

Example: To build the short *a* patterns above, children will need one letter each of *a, b, c, f, g, h, k, l, m, n, p, r, s,* and *t.*

Example: To build words from the word *scratch,* children will need *a*-1, *c*-2, *h*-1, *r*-1, *s*-1, and *t*-1.

After the session, the same children collect the particular letters they distributed and place them back in the appropriate bags.

In addition to individual letters for each child, teachers need a set of large letter cards to display the correct spelling of each word in a pocket chart, and make a large card for each word. After the word building, we will engage children in sorting words in the pocket chart to discover patterns in the word for that day.

Basic Procedures

During a word building session, each child has letter cards for each letter needed that day. From the letters in front of the children, the teacher identifies the word that everyone will build and the number of letters it will take. Cunningham & Hall (1994) suggest the following procedure for making words.

- Teacher holds up each letter, one at a time, and names the letter. Children do the same.
- The teacher states the number of letters and the word to be made, such as "Let's make the two-letter word *at.*" The teacher then observes to see that children understand the direction.
- One child, who made the word correctly, then comes to the board and places large letters for the word in the pocket chart for all to see.

- The teacher helps children check their spelling of the word, letter by letter, against the model in the pocket chart.
- The children continue building words.

  Build a pattern—build each possible word in the pattern.

  Build a long word—build longer and longer words, until a word is made that uses all of the letters for that day.
- After children build the words for the day, the teacher uses large word cards to help them sort words in the pocket chart that have similar spelling patterns and to consider the meaning of particular words.
- To end the lesson, the teacher asks children to speculate on how a word might be spelled that contains a chunk of a word made that day (p. 8).

To provide ample opportunity for all children to participate, ask questions, spell, sort, and write words, it may take several days to complete the activities for word building with a particular set of words.

Sample Lesson—The Frog Prince

In the opening vignette, we visited a second-grade classroom where children were building words from the letters used to spell *prince.* After playing with the letters in this word, Nikki and Mary discover that the following words can be made.

Example: *in, rip, pin, ice, pen, rice, nice, ripe, pine, cried, price, prince*

By selecting the word *prince,* which spelling patterns can the children build? We want to be sure that the children are ready for the patterns that this word will produce.

short *e*	**short *i***	**long *i***	**soft *c***	**blend**	**suffix**
pen	in	ice	ice	price	cried
	rip	rice	rice	prince	ripen
	pin	nice	nice	cried	
	prince	ripe	price		
		pine	prince		
		price			
		cried			
		ripen			

Building many words from one word provides a variety of opportunities to revisit letter–sound patterns that have been introduced before. The word *prince* provides opportunities to focus on several rimes (*-in, -ip, -ice, -ine, -ipe*) that form sound chunks within words. We can notice the effect of silent *e* (*pin, pine; rip, ripe*). We can also be reminded of the difference between single consonants and consonant blends (*rice, price*).

From all possible words to build, which words would we select for a word building lesson for second-grade children? We would consider the range of children in the classroom and select words that the majority can spell, with a few challenging words for the more advanced students. We can provide some support for children by working together as a class.

Developing readers and writers are refining their consonant knowledge and learning a great deal about vowels. The letters in the word *prince* automatically set up for attention for long and short *i*. In addition, it is possible to review initial blends *pr-* and *cr-*. The letters *c* and *e* provide an opportunity to focus on how *c* represents the *s* sound when followed by *e*.

If we have transitional readers and writers in the classroom, children who function between third- and sixth-grade reading levels, we might decide that the words *cried* (*cry* + *ed*) and *ripen* (*ripe* + *en*) are appropriate because of the change to the base word when the suffix is added.

To encourage children to apply their new knowledge, we also consider several new words that they can figure out by using patterns from this lesson.

Example: If we want to write the word *strip*,
which words in our list will help us spell *strip?* (*rip*)
What letters will we need to add? (*st-*, at the beginning)

If we want to write the word *princes?* (*prince*)
What letters will we need to add and where? (*-s*, at the end)

Children who use their knowledge of one word to spell another related word are spelling by analogy. Children focus on known chunks to spell new words.

As we build words, we should also encourage children to write the words they make. Writing is an excellent reinforcement for letter–sound correspondences. A word study notebook, described in an upcoming section, can be quite useful in word building lessons.

To increase students' engagement in sorting words, they might be given blank cards on which they write the selected words. Individual sorting provides the opportunity for each child to participate in discovering patterns in the words they spelled. Increasing the amount of writing that children do in a word building lesson may lead to two- or three-day lessons. Lengthening the amount of time that children attend to one set of words can increase learning for many children in the class.

Word building experiences such as the one above can occur daily in primary-grade classrooms. Word building provides opportunities for children to hear spoken words, then use letters to construct words. Children also have opportunities to participate in sorting words by patterns and spelling by analogy. Children can extend their vocabulary knowledge through discussion of the relationship among words.

In addition to whole-class word building, word study can also occur in small groups. In word study groups, children focus on sorting, building, and hunting for words with patterns that are at their developmental level.

SMALL-GROUP WORD STUDY: SORTING, BUILDING, AND HUNTING WORDS

Children who are at approximately the same level of word knowledge are grouped together for word study. Within one class there will probably be at least three to four different levels of word study. In addition to sorting words, small group study can also include word building and word hunting for patterns in instructional and independent reading materials.

Organizing small-group word study requires:

- a chart of ten to fifteen words that follow a pattern(s) and are developmentally appropriate for the children who will work with the words,
- blank word cards on which children write words that can be sorted and categorized,
- a word study notebook in which children record their thinking about words,
- discussion with a partner/group and teacher about sorting and patterns to confirm or redirect children's thinking about words, and
- guidance by the teacher to enhance children's understanding of spelling patterns.

Children participate in a weeklong study of particular patterns. This study takes the place of traditional spelling instruction. Approximately twenty minutes per day is given to small-group word study activities. This time is in addition to whole-class word building and/or word study that is integrated into other daily literacy components. It is recommended that all children meet in their small groups at the same time so that the teacher is able to interact with children and closely observe their progress. Children can move to a particular place in the room to meet their "word study group."

A week of small-group word study may include the following:

Monday

- Get new list of appropriate words.
- Children check to be sure they can read each word.
- Write list of words in word study notebook.
- Make word cards (about 1" × 3") for sorting activities.
- Take a spelling pretest with a partner.

Tuesday

- Review word cards, individually or with partner.
- Complete a closed word sort for sound, visual, or meaning pattern.
- Write the results in the word study notebook.
- Discuss patterns observed with a partner.
- Discuss patterns observed in sorts in a word study group.

Wednesday

- Individually review word cards.
- Participate in word building or word hunting activities.
- Write results in the word study notebook.
- Discuss results with partner.
- Discuss patterns in a word study group.

Thursday

- Individually review word cards.
- Participate in word build or word hunting activities.
- Write new words in word study notebook.
- Compare new words and word list, note similarities and differences in notebook.
- Discuss with partner.
- Discuss in word study group.

Friday

- Take posttest including two to three new words that fit the pattern, to test ability to generalize pattern.
- Discuss comfort/confidence with patterns following test.
- Plan for next week of word study.

Teacher's Role in Small-Group Word Study

For small-group word study to be effective, we must do the following:

- Become knowledgeable about the stages of word knowledge development and the content of phonics and structural analysis.
- Develop lists of words that fit patterns in each stage of word knowledge. Suggested sequences, such as the ones in this text, should be helpful in selecting words for study. Word lists are also drawn from words that are appearing in instructional and independent reading materials.
- Determine each child's stage of word knowledge and make functional word study groups that will allow children to study words that are sight words and within reach for learning to write conventionally.
- Create manageable word study groups of children with similar word knowledge and instructional need.
- Prepare weekly charts listing the words for each group and provide sheets of blank word cards for the children to prepare words for sorting.
- Take time to teach the routines for weekly word study. This may take several weeks at the beginning of the school year.
- Circulate while children are working on sorting activities and plan for group meetings to discuss what children have noticed. Mediate between what children already know and what they might need to clarify to make sense of the patterns being studied (Vygotsky, 1962).
- Use assessment information to continually monitor groups for appropriate placement of all children.

To implement a word study program, we help children to do the following:

- Understand the purpose for each part of the weekly study.
- Learn to be good partners, assisting and supporting the efforts of another to learn words.
- Learn to record in their word study notebook the results of their picture and/or word sorts, as well as their thinking about their sorts.

Forming Groups for Word Study

Children can be effectively grouped for word study by their stage of word knowledge development. For word study to be most beneficial, children must be able to focus on patterns that they are beginning to notice, but may not fully understand. If children are asked to attend to patterns in words that are above their own reading level, they will not be able to make full use of the instruction you offer. This same principle determines the level of reading text we select for guided reading. We select text from which children can learn, text that is neither too hard nor too easy.

To have a sense of what children are noticing about language, we look at the developmental, or inventive, spellings that appear in their writing. As children are learning about letter–sound relationships, they will invent spellings to stand for patterns they have not yet internalized (Temple et al., 1993). Children represent words as best they can with what they know at their independent level of performance.

Children's writing is one of our best ways to see what they know about written language. From children's writing we can see what they:

- have gained control over and consistently use,
- are just beginning to figure out and use inconsistently or incorrectly, and
- have yet to notice or understand because it is absent from their writing.

For example, Figure 9.3 shows a sample writing from Beatrice's journal in December of second grade. Beatrice's first language is Spanish. Looking at what Beatrice wrote in her journal suggests that she might benefit from a closer look at digraphs that contain a silent letter, such as *-ck* in *chicken* and *stick*. It is helpful to recall that in Spanish, the /k/ sound is represented by only one letter. She might also benefit from examination of the inflected suffix, *-es,* and the sounds that are possible when *-es* forms its own syllable. To determine the types of patterns that will be most helpful to Beatrice at this time, we evaluate this and other samples of her writing.

To identify children's stage of word knowledge development, we can also analyze a sample of words of varying difficulty that children attempt to spell on their own. This inventory is constructed of words that represent a particular level of knowledge, or are of increasing difficulty to determine a level of knowledge. Some example words are provided in the assessment section of this chapter. Children write the example words as we dictate them. It is important to observe children during the writing for signs of their level of confidence in spelling each word. Assessing and evaluating children's stage of word knowledge is discussed again in the assessment section of this chapter.

Sorting Activities

Sorting activities may be done with pictures or words and may be either an open or a closed sort.

- *Open sorts* allow children to determine categories for the cards (either pictures or words) by showing the patterns they notice independently. Some focus can be given to the sort without stipulating categories, by asking children to sort for either sound or meaning patterns.

FIGURE 9.3
Beatrice's Journal Entry from Second Grade

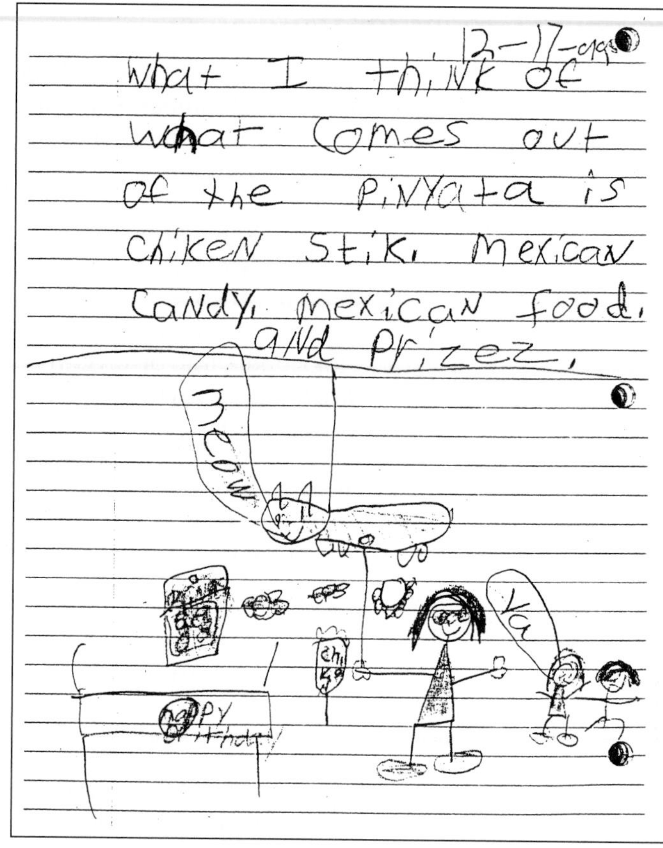

- *Closed sorts* direct children to attend to specific, predetermined characteristics, showing their depth of understanding about particular letter–sound patterns or word structures.

Until children have acquired a sight vocabulary of words that can be studied, pictures are used to focus on sound units, or phonemes, in words. Picture sorts are conducted with small clear pictures, about 2" × 2", which can be moved and grouped according to a particular attribute. Children demonstrate their ability to segment and match phonemes at the beginning, then at the end, of words. Children must be able to verbally name pictures in a picture sort.

Picture sorts are also helpful to use with more proficient readers when you introduce a new pattern, such as vowel digraphs or r-controlled vowels, and want to be sure that children can identify the particular sound they will use in printed words. If children can sort pictures successfully, they are ready to sort known words for the new pattern.

When children have a sight vocabulary of at least 100 words, they are usually ready to begin sorting words. As with picture sorts, word sorts can either be open (focused or unfocused) or closed. At the beginning of a week of word study, we may want to see what children already recognize about pattern(s) in the words. In that case, we have children first complete an open sort, during which they determine the categories by either sound or meaning patterns. When we want to know about the depth of children's understanding of a particular pattern(s) we focus their attention by selecting categories for a closed sort. In a closed sort we give children the exemplars for categories.

Imagine that children will sort the following words:

ship	*chop*	*shot*	*chin*	*and*	*was*
chip	*shop*	*she*	*chat*	*said*	

They have exemplar pictures of a shell and a chick as a representation of the sounds to be sorted. The teacher asks children to place those pictures at the top of their sorting area. The other exemplar is a "crazy pile" card, for all of the pictures that children think do not belong in either of the other piles. Notice that we have included three familiar words to serve as distracters. To sort, the child:

- says the name of each word aloud,
- listens for the onset at the beginning of the word,
- segments the onset (*sh-* or *ch-*) and says it aloud,
- compares the onset with that of *shell* and *chick,*
- places the words that begin like *shell* under the shell picture, and places the words that begin like *chick* under that picture, and
- places all other pictures in the crazy pile.

A sample closed word sort is provided in Figure 9.4a & b.

FIGURE 9.4a
Sample Closed Word Sort—Digraphs *ch-* and *sh-*

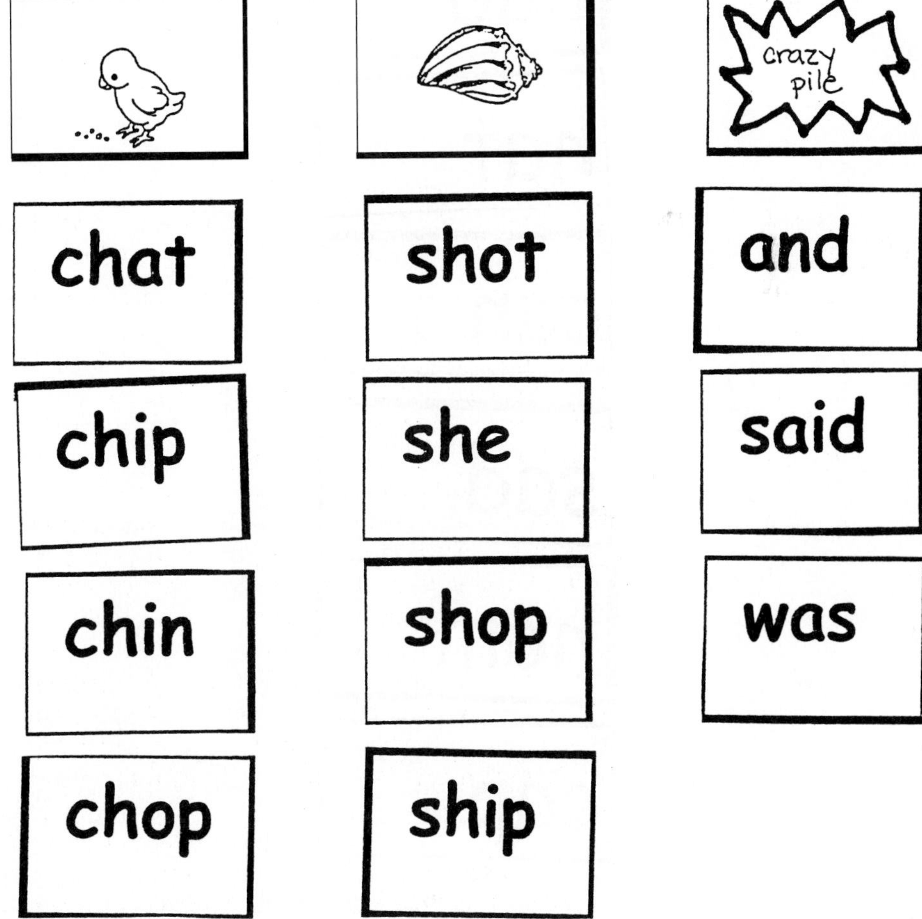

FIGURE 9.4b
Two-Level Word Sort

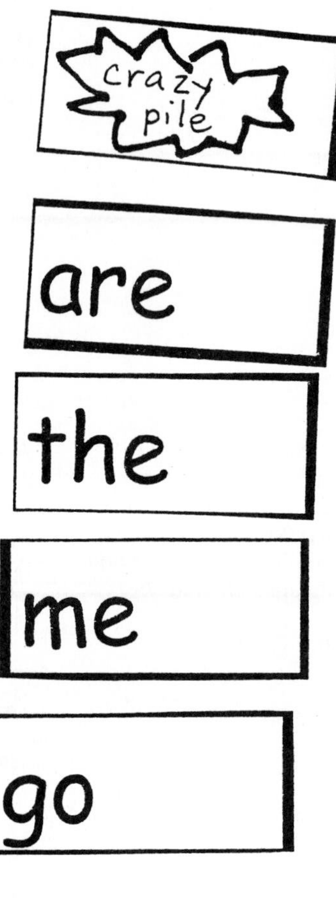

When children work with words that have a particular phoneme, a two-level sort should be used so children focus on the new sound. This sort creates two categories:

- Identified phoneme
- Discard pile for all other phonemes

The complexity of word sorts is increased when we add additional categories with exemplars (for closed sorts) for each category, as children gain experience with identifying phonemes (sound units) and morphemes (meaning units) in words. The sort shown in Figure 9.3 is a three-level sort—/sh-/,/ch-/, and neither (crazy pile). We compared two different sound patterns, plus the discard pile. In Figure 9.4 and 9.5 we compare other sound patterns, plus a discard pile.

Examples of multilevel word sorts:

Two-Level Sort	short *a* (*bat*)	not short *a* (crazy pile)	
	br- (*brown*)	not *br-*	
Three-Level Sort	short *a* (*bat*)	short *i* (*ship*)	crazy pile
	sh- (*ship*)	*-sh* (*fish*)	crazy pile
	short *a* (*bat*)	long *a* (*cake*)	crazy pile
Four-Level Sort			
long *a* (*cake*)	long *a* (*rain*)	short *a* (*bat*)	crazy pile
/b-/ (*bat*)	/br-/ (*brown*)	/bl-/ (*blue*)	crazy pile

In most sorting activities, it is helpful to include a discard or crazy pile. Use of such a pile indicates children's uncertainty or confusion about words or patterns. Without a discard pile, children may feel forced to place words in a category even if they are not certain about the characteristics of the word or picture. Talking with children about the placement of the words reveals the clarity of their thinking.

FIGURE 9.5
Four-Level Word Sort

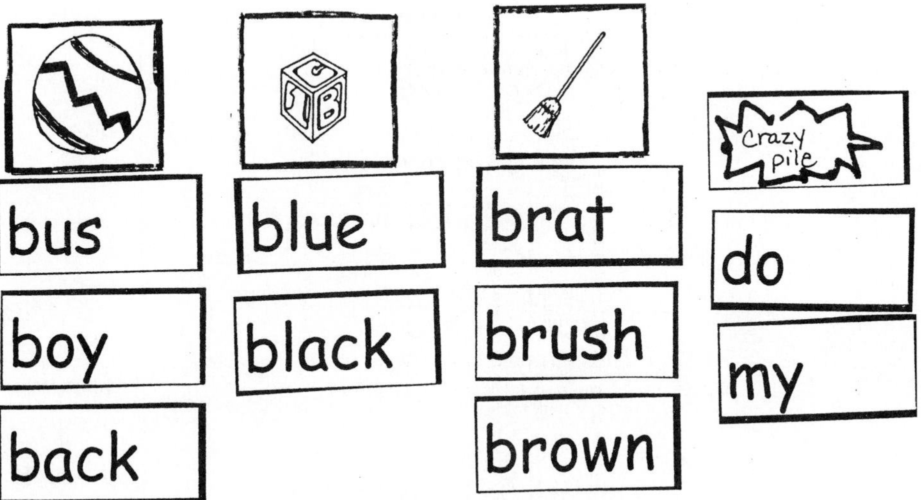

WORD STUDY NOTEBOOKS

Whether we organize word study for the whole class or a small group, we should utilize word study notebooks as a record-keeping device. Each child should have a notebook or folder for recording words that are studied each week. Pages may be duplicated with a particular format that aids children's recording of various activities. The pages should be secured in the notebook. There should be enough pages to record several months of study. Children should be able to refer to past lists and sorts to remind themselves about patterns they have studied. The notebook also enables children to see growth in their knowledge of words.

Referring back to the suggested schedule for daily word study activities, we see that the word study notebook is used for recording:

Monday	List of words for the week Pretest (not shown)
Tuesday	Closed sort and the patterns observed
Wednesday	Words from word building or hunting Explanation of patterns
Thursday	Words from word building or hunting Explanation of patterns
Friday	Posttest (not shown)

The word study notebook is a functional writing experience for children. Even children who are completing picture sorts can record the results of sorting by drawing pictures and recording sounds they hear. Children should be asked to

FIGURE 9.6
A Week of Word Study

My Word Study Notebook

1/16 new words

fish	she	dish
shake	wish	flash
ship	his	stop
sad	shop	

1/17 word sort

begins with sh	ends with sh	crazy pile
she	dish	his
shake	fish	sad
ship	wish	stop
shop	flash	

dish, wish, and fish have -ish.

1/18 building words

sh, i, a, o, f, l, k, e, w, d,

fish	ship	she	flash
dish	shop	shake	
wish			

new words—dash
wishes

1/19 word hunt

fishing	wishes
milkshake	shopping
sheep	

sh can be in bigger words too.

use what is recorded in the notebook on a daily basis. If not, they may feel that the recording is a worthless exercise. Children should refer to their notebooks during word study discussions. Figure 9.6 shows a sample of notebook entries for one week. This notebook shows words being studied by a developing reader early in second grade. At this stage, children are able to tell more about patterns verbally than they can in writing. The word study notebook can also be used to record whole-class word building lessons as described in the previous section.

POSSIBLE SEQUENCES FOR STUDYING PHONICS PATTERNS

We begin with an overview of basic consonant and vowel patterns that are found in the words selected from first-grade-level reading texts. The sequences suggested assume that the words chosen for study are reflected in children's reading and writing and will have multiple opportunities to be applied.

Phonics for Early Developing Readers

Single consistent consonants:
Children come to this stage with knowledge of most single consistent consonants (see Figure 9.7). They typically learn to read and write single, consistent consonants before other letter patterns. To continue refining knowledge of single consonants, we combine the study of consonants with the study of single vowels. As we select words for the study of vowels, we carefully consider the consonant patterns that are reinforced.

Short vowels:
An overview of vowel patterns is provided in Figure 9.8.

- We begin short vowels by returning to phonemic awareness activities to develop ability to blend, segment, and classify pictures containing short vowels.
- Next we focus on the letter patterns of one vowel at a time. Each time a new vowel is introduced, check children's phonemic awareness with picture sorts to be sure they can segment the sound, then move to using known words to examine letter patterns through word sorts and word building.
- Begin word sorts for a particular vowel with an open sort to let children show what they already notice as they compare words. Then move to the closed sorts suggested in the sequences below.
- Begin word building with familiar rimes, such as *-at* or *-an,* then add the onset to complete the word.
- When children are becoming proficient in a particular vowel pattern, check their understanding by introducing a few new words into the word sorting or building activity. Be sure that the new items are the same pattern(s). The purpose of the new words is to see if children can apply their knowledge to unfamiliar words.

Single Consonants				Consonant Teams					
Consistent Sound		**Variant Sound**		**2 Consonants—2 Sounds**				**2 Consonants—1 Sound**	
letter names sound		**varies by vowel that follows**		**initial blends**				**H digraphs**	
b	bat, cab	c	(hard c=/k/)	**r family**				ch	chip, each
d	dot, mad		cage	br	break	cr	crown		chef, —
f	fan, leaf		cone	dr	drop	fr	frog		school, —
j	jam, —		cut	gr	grapes	pr	prize	gh	—, laugh
k	kid, peek	c	(soft c=/s/)	tr	tree			ph	phone, graph
l	lid, pail		cent, face					sh	ship, dish
m	man, ham		city	**l family**				th	this, breathe
n	nut, bun		cycle	bl	blue	cl	clown		thin, breath
p	pin, map			fl	flag	gl	glass		
r	rug, car	g	(hard g = /g/)	pl	play			**double-letter digraph**	
t	tag, cat		gate, bag	**s family**				bb	rabbit
v	van, —		girl	sc	scarf	sk	skip	dd	add
z	zoo, quiz		gone	sl	slide	sm	smile	ff	cuff
			gum	sn	snap	sp	spoon	gg	egg
letter does NOT name sound				st	stop	sw	swim	ll	ball
h	hat, —	g	(soft g = /j/)	scr	scrap			nn	inn
qu	queen, —		gem, cage					ss	dress
			giant	spl	split	spr	spray	zz	fuzz
			gym	squ	squirt			**silent letter digraph**	
		varies by position		str	street			gh	ghost, —
		s	sand, bus					gn	gnat, sign
			sure, —	**w family**				kn	knock, —
			—, his	dw	dwell	sw	swim	wh	what, —
				tw	twin				who, —
		w	win, saw	**final blends**				wr	write, —
				lb	bulb	ld	hold		
		x	x-ray, fox	lf	golf	lk	milk	ck	—, duck
			xylophone	lt	belt			dge	—, fudge
								mb	—, lamb
		y	yes my	mp	lamp			tch	—, match
			baby						
			say	nd	hand	ng	bang		
				nk	pink	nt	went		
				sk	mask	sp	crisp		
				st	fast				

FIGURE 9.7
Overview of Consonant Patterns

Single Vowels						Vowel Teams					
Short		**Long**		**Neither Long nor Short**		**Long—Consistent**		**Long—Short Variable**		**Neither Long nor Short**	
vc	**cvc**	**cv**	**vce**	**r-control**		**vowel digraph**		**vowel digraph**		**diphthong**	
a - at	bag	a- —	cake	ar	car	ai	rain	ea	meat	au	haul
e - egg	bed	e- me	——	er	her	ay	may		bread	aw	saw
i - in	hit	i- —	hide	ir	bird	ee	feet		great		
o - on	log	o- go	rope	or	for	igh	night			oi	oil
u - up	sun	u- —	cute	ur	fur	oa	boat	ei	seize	oy	boy
			rude						vein		
				are	care					oo	boot
		y- fly	——	ere	here			ey	key		foot
		—	baby		there				they		
				ire	fire					ou	through
				ore	more			ie	pie		round
				ure	sure				chief		
										ow	grow
								ou	soul		cow
									young		
										ui	fruit
										ue	blue
										ew	flew
										r-control	
										air	fair
										ear	hear
											bear
											learn
										eer	peer
										ier	pier
										oar	roar

FIGURE 9.8
Overview of Vowel Patterns

- Suggested sequence of short vowels: *a, i, o, u,* then *e.*
  Note: Short *e* and short *i* are not easily distinguished.
- Beginning to sort short vowels
  Example: two-level picture sort — short *a* not short *a*
  two-level word sort — short *a* not short *a*
  When children are comfortable with short *a* and short *i,* you may compare the two vowels in a three-level sort.
  Example: three-level sort — short *a* short *i* neither
- After children are familiar with short *a* and short *i,* remaining short vowels can be interspersed with consonant blends and digraphs to provide a wider assortment of words for sorting.

Consonant digraphs:

- Teach "h" digraphs in the initial position (phonemes and letter patterns). Remember most "h" digraphs represent a consonant sound that does not have a letter-name match; thus, children must learn to let a new sound represent two letters in place of the one-to-one letter-sound matches of single consonants. Focus on "h" digraphs with short-vowel patterns.
- Sort "h" digraphs (sh, ch, th)

  These words contain variations of short *a* and short *i* words from previous study (for example, *sip* becomes *ship*).

Two-level sort	/sh-/	not /sh-/	
	/ch-/	not /ch-/	
Three-level sort	/sh-/	/ch-/	neither
	/th-/ (voiced)	/th-/ (voiceless)	neither

  Note: The digraph /th/ has two possible sounds that children must learn to distinguish. In the initial position, there is no visual clue to the voiced or voiceless sound. Teach children to try one, and listen for a word that is familiar and makes sense.

  Note: /ch-/ has three possible sounds. In this stage, select words with /ch-/ such as *chip.*

- After initial position is comfortable, introduce words with the digraph in the final position and compare with initial.

Three-level sort	/sh-/	/-sh/	neither

- Silent letter digraphs (e.g., wr-, -ck) should be postponed until after children have an understanding that some letters can be silent.

Consonant blends or clusters:

- When children are functioning well with several short vowels (perhaps *a* and *i*), and one or more "h" digraphs, return to consonants and teach/reinforce one blend family (*r, l, or s*). Remember the concept here is to take sounds that are known and blend or link them to see them working together in the word and hear them when spoken.
- Intersperse blend families with remaining short-vowel work and with "h" digraphs. Include blends and digraphs in word choices for sorting.
- Sort consonant blends/clusters:

Two-level sort in one family (r, l, s)	/br-/	not /br/
	/cr-/	not /cr/

- Contrast the initial blend with the single consonant:

Three-level sort in one family (r, l, s)	/b-/	/br-/	neither
	/p-/	/pr-/	neither

Single long vowels:

As with short vowels, begin at the auditory level with picture sorts, then move to word sorts with sight vocabulary. Remember, the purpose of the picture sort is to segment and compare long-vowel sounds. The words represented by pictures do not have to be spelled by single long vowels, because the letter pattern is not represented with the picture. Sorting or classifying pictures with long-vowel sounds should be relatively easy because the letters of the alphabet name long-vowel sounds. Try an open sort first to see what knowledge children demonstrate about vowel sounds.

- Basic sorting pattern for each vowel:

Two-level sort	long *a*	not long *a*	
Three-level sort	long *a*	short *a*	neither

  In the three-level sort, we are interested in children's understandings about silent *e*.

- After long *a,* we develop long *i.* Then we compare the two different long vowels, and add the short vowels for each letter for comparison (and to maintain the short vowels).

Five-level sort	long *a*	short *a*	long *i*	short *i*	none

- Complete the remaining single long-vowel patterns (CVCe and CV) with the other vowel letters (*e, o,* and *u*). The CV pattern (*go, me*) is a single long-vowel pattern without a vowel marker and is not represented in all vowels. When this pattern is introduced, help children compare it with silent *e.* Follow the same sequence with each letter as shown, then compare vowels.
- Remember that *u,* as a single long vowel can represent two sounds, "u" (*cute*) and "oo" (*rude*). Help children learn to try both sounds if needed and select the appropriate sound, checked by context. If one sound does not make sense, try the other—just like the two sounds of /th/.
- Recall that such patterns as *-igh* and *-ight* consistently represent long *i.* These words can be added to the long *i* sort after the single-vowel long *i* pattern (CVCe) is known.

Phonics for Later Developing Readers

Single variant consonants:

Some time during this stage we return to consonants to teach or reinforce single variant consonants (*c, g, s*) as they become useful for children's current reading material.

- In this stage children will have enough vowel knowledge to work with the patterns of *c* and *g.* When these letters are followed by an *a, o,* or *u,* the vowel sound is usually hard, as in *can* or *gate.* When these letter are followed by an *e, i,* or *y,* the vowel sound is usually soft, as in *cent* and *gem.*

- The variation in *s* is determined by placement in a syllable—initial /s/ (*sun*), final /s/ (*bus*), or /z/ *his,* or /sh/ (*sugar*) when followed by the letter *u.*
- Sorting variant consonants:

Three-level sort	hard *c*	soft *c*	neither
	hard *g*	soft *g*	neither
Four-level sort	*s* = /s/ /z/ /sh/ none		

Vowel digraphs:
Once children's knowledge of single long-vowel patterns is solid, then it is time to tackle vowel digraphs. Typically this occurs as children progress to second-grade-level texts in reading. Like consonant digraphs, vowel digraphs have two letters (usually vowels, except in the case of *-igh*) that represent one phoneme, usually either the long- or short-vowel sound represented by one of the letters in the digraph.

Some of us were taught, "When two vowels go walking, the first one does the talking (long sound)." However, the first letter of a vowel digraph has a long-vowel sound only about 45% of the time, more frequently with certain patterns than others. The second letter in the digraph is often the vowel marker, or silent letter, but not always.

Some double-vowel patterns are digraphs of varying sounds. Spend time on these only when needed for reading and writing. Frequency of use is always our guide as we decide which patterns to emphasize.

There are two ways we can consider approaching the double-vowel (and later the varying vowel) combinations to help children see patterns. As we think about double vowels, consider which vowels:

- look the same, but sound different, and
- look different, but sound the same.

Thinking of double vowels in this way supports the development of a strategy for figuring out the sound of a particular vowel combination.

- Begin with the most consistent vowel digraphs (*ai, ay, ee, igh, oa*). Since children have already demonstrated they are able to discriminate long and short vowels, picture sorting is not necessary.
- Teach or reinforce varying vowel digraphs (*ea, ie, ei, ey*) as children's reading materials warrant.
- With visual patterns, which look the same but sound different, children need to realize that the visual pattern of these words will not help them with accurate decoding; rather, only context and knowledge of the possible sounds will help. If children are aware of the possible sounds the letters may represent, they can try each possibility until context helps them confirm an appropriate word.

/ea/ = long *e* (*meat*)	short *e* (*bread*)	long *a* (*great*)
/ei/ = long *e* (*receive*)	long *a* (*vein*)	
/ey/ = long *e* (*key*)	long *a* (*prey*)	
/ie/ = long *e* (*believe*)	long *i* (*tie*)	
/ou/ = long *o* (*soul*)	short *u* (*rough*)	ow (*out*), oo (*soup*)

For sorting activities, sort the sounds of one letter pattern (for example, *ea*) against itself so that children see its possibilities. For example,

long *e*	**short *e***	**long *a***
meat	*bread*	*great*
cheap	*deaf*	*steak*
read	*read*	
please		

- With sound patterns, which look different but sound the same, children should know that a single sound can be spelled in different ways. This understanding is particularly important in writing. Word sorts for this pattern can begin as a two-level sort—long *a*, and not long *a*. Then have children examine the words in the long *a* column to identify characteristics. What generalizations can be made?

Two-level sort	long *a*	not long *a*
	ea, ei, ey	
	long *e*	not long *e*
	ee, ea, ie, ei, ey	

Final consonant blends:

- As children are refining their ability to discriminate sound, notice in their inventive spelling whether the consonants that are difficult to hear in final blends are beginning to be distinguished. At that point it would be appropriate to teach/reinforce final consonant blends (*ld, lt, lk*) (*nd, nk, nt*).
- Sorting activities should be modeled after the sorts for initial blends/clusters in the letter-name stage.

Two-level sort	*-ld*	not *-ld*		
Three-level sort	*-ld*	*-d*	neither	
Four-level sort	*-ld*	*-lt*	*-lk*	none

Double consonants (double letter, one is silent):

- Teach double-consonant letters in the same syllable (*ll, ss*) that represent one single consonant sound that children already know. Picture sorting is not needed because the phoneme is usually the same as the single consonant.
- Two-level sort, final single and double consonants are combined because they represent the same phoneme.

  Two-level sort /-l/ and /-ll/ not /-l/

  Children need to generalize that, within the same syllable, double consonants represent one phoneme, just as single consonants represent one phoneme.

Variant vowels (neither long nor short):

- R-controlled patterns (from short vowels). When single long vowels are well understood, children are usually able to work with the single-vowel r-controlled patterns (*ar, or, ir, er, ur*). Notice that in a single syllable the letter patterns *er, ir,* and *ur* are usually decoded as /er/.

- Begin with *-ar*. Sort to distinguish its unique sound, then compare with long *a* and short *a*. Complete the same sequence with *-or*, then sort *-ar* against *-or*.

Two-level sort	*-ar*	not *-ar*		
Four-level sort	*-ar*	long *a*	short *a*	none
Two-level sort	*-or*	not *-or*		
Four-level sort	*-or*	long *o*	short *o*	none
Three-level sort	*-ar*	*-or*	neither	

- Move to *-er, -ir, -ur*. Help children notice the similarity in sound even though the spelling patterns are different.

Two-level sort	/er/ (*-er, -ir, -ur*)	not /er/		
Four-level sort	/er/	long *e*	short *e*	none
Four-level sort	*-ar*	*-or*	/er/	none

- R-controlled patterns (from long vowels). These r-controlled patterns can also be developed during this stage, when children are working easily with double vowels. The two patterns are:

  Vre (*are, ere, ire, ore,* and *ure*) from single long vowels
  VVr (*air, ear, eer*) from vowel digraphs

  As always, frequency of use is our guideline for the appropriate time to study these patterns. Be sure that children are confident of regular long-vowel patterns before introducing this pattern.
- Long-vowel r-controlled patterns. Sorting should focus on the sound that is heard and then be compared with the *-ar* pattern made from short vowels. Help children generalize that the e-marker and double-vowel patterns can produce similar sounds.

Two-level word sort	long *-ar* (*are, air*)	not long *-ar*		
Three-level word sort	long *-ar*	short *-ar*	neither	
	long *-ar*	long *a*	neither	
Five-level word sort	long *-ar*	short *-ar*	long *a*	short *a* none

  Repeat this sequence for other long-vowel r-controlled patterns.

Consonant digraphs with silent letters:

- During this stage, children become very aware of letters that are silent and how they influence other phonemes. When children are comfortable with silent e-markers and silent vowels in double-vowel combinations, we can introduce the concept of silent consonants in consonant digraphs.
- Children will already have words in their sight vocabulary that include silent consonant digraphs, but they may not have drawn generalizations about these consonant patterns. Identify appropriate words that are known to children.
- Create a closed sort that focuses on the use of silent consonant digraphs in the initial and final positions in words, preferably single syllable. Include other words in the sort that begin with the same

phoneme but are represented by a single consonant. For example, to help children recognize the silent letter *w* in *wr,* include words that begin with /r/ (r, wr).

- After children sort by sound, have them examine the words in the /r/ pile and make generalizations about words that begin with *wr.* To reinforce the silent *w*, ask children to sort words that begin with *w, wr,* and *r.* Children must come to understand that when they see words that begin with *wr,* they must think /r/.
- Sorting activities should include:

Two-level sort for sound	/r/ (wr)	not /r/	
Three-level sort for visual pattern	/r/ (r, wr)	/w/	neither

- Continue to examine other silent digraph patterns (ck, kn, gn, pn, ng, dge, tch) as appropriate words are identified.

Diphthongs (typically neither long nor short):
Remember that diphthongs are two vowels or a vowel and a semi-vowel that, when blended together, represent a vowel sound that is neither long nor short. The letters *w* and *y* can function as semivowels, or consonants that can function as both a consonant and a vowel.

Many of these patterns are in children's sight vocabulary, but need to be studied to generalize patterns for use with unknown words. Sorting diphthongs should be modeled after other double-vowel sorts that discriminate between visual and sound patterns.

VISUAL PATTERN

- Vowels look the same but sound different.

  Several diphthong patterns are visually similar but produce different sounds.

  oo = *boot, foot*

  ow = *cow, tow*

  Children can successfully use an either–or strategy with these vowels. For example, with *ow* children can think, "If it's not *ow,* then it's probably *o.*" Thinking in this way adds to children's ability to use prediction + checking for sense strategy to identify unfamiliar words.
- Sorting activities should compare letter patterns with each other, then with other vowel patterns of similar letters.

Three-level sort	*boot*	*foot*	neither		
Five-level sort	*boot*	*foot*	long *o*	short *o*	none

SOUND PATTERN

- Vowels look different but sound the same.

  Several diphthong patterns are visually different but produce the same sounds.

  au (*haul*), *aw* (*saw*)

  oi (*oil*), *oy* (*boy*)

  ui (*fruit*), *ue* (*blue*), *ew* (*flew*)

Children can be confident in their attempts with these patterns that become highly predictable in sound, then checked by context.

- Sorting activities will compare letter patterns to show they produce the same sound, compared with other "a" patterns to show the difference.

Two-level sort	*au/aw*	not *au/aw*		
Four-level sort	*au/aw*	long *a*	short *a*	none

SELF-MONITORING STRATEGIES IN THE DEVELOPING STAGE

As developing readers and writers are gaining confidence with letter–sound relationships, we must encourage them to use a "context + familiar parts of words" strategy when they read books or other connected text. We encourage them to apply their phonics knowledge with other contextual clues (illustrations, story line, predictable language) to make more accurate predictions about words in text. We also want to nudge children to invent only those spellings that are beyond their current level of knowledge.

By the time that children are in the latter part of the developing stage, mid to late second-grade reading level, they have acquired many skills as readers. They are becoming quite proficient at decoding one- and two-syllable words, and even words with variant vowels. They have also begun to chunk words into meaningful units (base + inflected suffix) to read unfamiliar words.

If self-monitoring has been taught and encouraged throughout this stage, self-monitoring of individual words and overall meaning should be rather natural. Children who expect reading to make sense will naturally monitor their reading, especially in low-challenge materials. Our response to children's reading during this stage is crucial. As Spiegel (1985) suggests, "Don't over nurture children" (p. 78). Developing readers and writers know much about written language. What they need from us is our responsive support, giving them ample opportunity to self-monitor so they can see what they know and need to know. We must resist "rescuing" children.

Sometime during this stage children become independent readers. Developing readers work hard to learn new words. Their attention to individual words causes their reading to be rather halting, with a number of stops, starts, and rerunning of text to make sure the text makes sense. These children will probably point to words as they read and their preference for reading will be oral. Oral reading allows children in this stage to hear their own voice as a check for whether the words they read make sense. Reading materials should be easy, to encourage children's fluid reading behavior and confidence to develop.

SINKING INTO SILENT READING

Up to now children's reading has been dominated by the need to read orally as they work to gain control over print to the point when ideas in written language flow together and make sense. By the time children are late in this stage they have acquired a great deal of knowledge about written language. They have worked hard during this stage to figure out complicated letter–sound patterns and to understand the meaningful use of structural units in our language.

To support children's acquisition of phonics and structural analysis skills and to promote the use of self-monitoring strategies, texts for instruction and independent reading should be carefully chosen. Easy, low-challenge text should dominate children's independent reading to allow newly acquired word knowledge to move to an automatic level, needing less conscious control by the child. Text for instruction should be at an instructional level, offering some challenge with assistance only as needed.

In easy text, children should be moving from oral to silent reading as their preferred mode. However, oral reading will reappear when children are in difficult text, because this too requires much attention to words with phonic or structural patterns that are not yet internalized. In this stage, such difficult text should be kept to a minimum to help children build fluency and confidence.

ASSESSMENT: MONITORING GROWTH IN WORD KNOWLEDGE

To begin to determine how well children are developing as readers and writers, we might ask ourselves the following questions:

Early in the developing stage:

- What strategies does the child appear to use in developing sight vocabulary? How much extensive and intensive reading seems to be necessary to learn new words?
- How consistently does the child use context + consonant knowledge to decode words?
- Is the child actively searching to represent most phonemes when writing one- or two-syllable words?
- Is the child becoming more accurate in representing short-vowel phonemes in one-syllable words?
- Is the child beginning to notice that some words have parts (base + inflected suffix)?

Later in the developing stage:

- Does the child's sight vocabulary show a marked increase over the early part of this stage?
- Does the child's reading and writing reflect a growing knowledge of single- and double-vowel patterns? What behaviors suggest that the child understands that some letters in English will be silent and may serve as markers for a vowel in the same syllable?
- How consistently is the child able to use the context + strategy with consonant knowledge? with vowel knowledge? with structural knowledge?

- How consistently is the child able to find base words within structural patterns in which the base does not change?

To assess and evaluate word knowledge development, we collect data concerning:

- children's use of decoding knowledge and strategies during reading, in and out of context,
- children's use of word knowledge in spelling development, and
- evaluated writing samples.

Decoding in Context

Children show what they know. Children's oral reading, independent writing, and talk about words can reveal both independent and emerging phonics and structural knowledge. As we learned in Chapter 5, when children read orally, they often miscue, or give an oral response to print that is different from what might have been expected. Miscues provide a "window" into a reader's thinking in response to print. As we listen to children read orally, we should listen for patterns in miscues. For example, consider the following miscues:

Text:	The white and brown horse trotted along.
Child 1 reads:	The white and brown house trotted along.
Child 2 reads:	The white and black horse totted along.
Child 3 reads:	The white and brown horse galloped along.

The first and second child attend to visual patterns (horse–house, brown–black, trotted–totted) but are either missing some phonics knowledge or do not apply strategies to the entire word, and they do not cross-check for meaning. The third child does not attend to letter–sound patterns (trotted–ran), but instead appears to use known language patterns and context to make sense. We should continually make reading records, recording samples of reading that show children's miscues in the context of real reading. As children progress through this stage, we should notice marked differences in their ability to accurately decode words, moving from one-syllable to multisyllable words.

We can also make records of focused decoding of particular patterns in isolation as a contrast to decoding in context. Words in isolation demonstrate children's ability to use visual cues, checked by knowledge of word meanings. A focused assessment of decoding is provided in this section of the chapter.

Independent writing can show letter–sound knowledge over which children have control and can write confidently, as well as knowledge about spelling–sound correspondences that a child may be "using but confusing." For example, four different children spell float as *ft, flot, flote,* and *float.* These spellings show different levels of knowledge about phonetic patterns.

During reading and writing opportunities, children make comments or ask questions about words that provide a glimpse into what children notice or may find confusing. While showing the illustrations in *The Snowy Day,* a child sees the word *slowly,* written in the text as "*s-l-o-w-l-y,*" and comments, "That word has *slow* in it." Later, while the child is writing about the same story, she asks about the word *plop;* "It sounds like *pop.* How do I make it say *plop?*"

Word Knowledge in Writing

To identify and monitor children's growth in word knowledge we formally analyze their writing at the beginning of the school year and at least two or three other times during the year. Collect and analyze writing samples for evidence of word knowledge, both focused and unfocused.

Unfocused writing sample:
Examine Enrique's writing about magnets as shown in Figure 9.9. This sample came from his independent journal and was written near the end of the second-grade year. The word *magnet* probably came from the word wall that grew out of the class study about magnets. Also be aware that Enrique's first language is Spanish, which may account for the omission of the letter *s* on the word *magnet* as a plural marker.

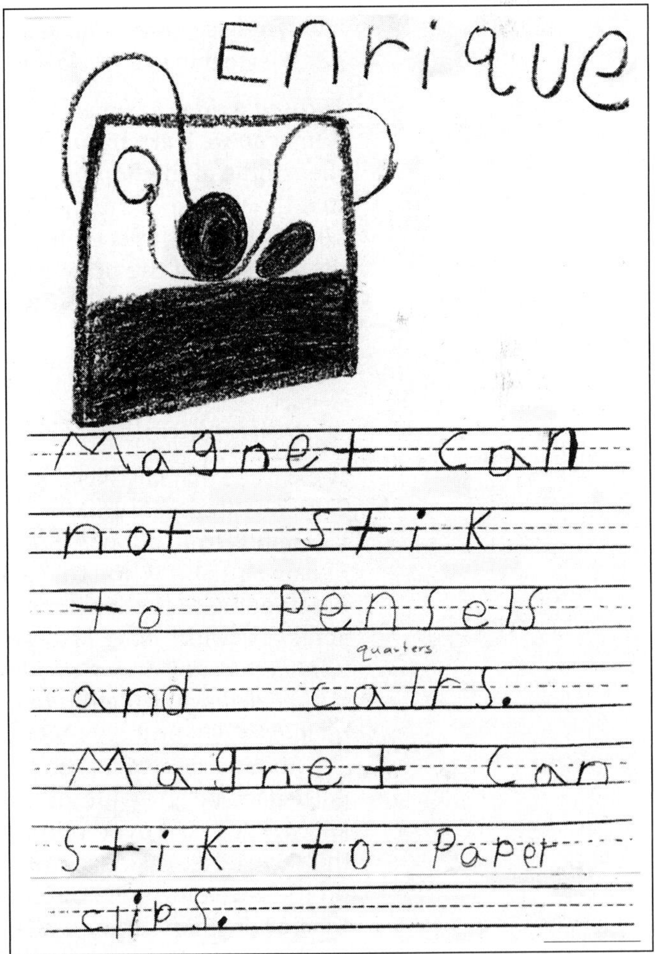

FIGURE 9.9
Enrique's Journal Entry—Second Grade

What does Enrique know about words that appear frequently in reading materials? As a developing reader/writer, Enrique is expected to be nearing mastery of most single-syllable short- and long-vowel words.

- Notice the words *can, and, not,* and *clips.*
- Notice also the correct spelling of a two-syllable word, *paper.*
- How might we explain Enrique's spelling of *stik?* In his acquisition of a new language, Enrique may not understand that English words that have a short-vowel sound and end with *-k* will usually spell that sound with the letters *-ck.* In English, *-ck* has a silent letter and represents one sound, /-k/.
- How might we explain Enrique's spelling of *pensels* (pencils)? We wonder if he knows that the sound of *c* (and *g*) can be softened when a vowel (*e, i, y*) follows immediately behind? He hears *s,* so he writes *s.* Perhaps that is the regularity he would expect in Spanish.
- The knowledge needed to spell the word *quarters* is beyond Enrique's current level of development and we would not expect a correct spelling. We might expect *kw* as a beginning sound or *t* in the middle, but that really depends on how he is pronouncing this word.

If we study several samples of Enrique's independent writing, we can begin to see patterns that help us make decisions about appropriate words for Enrique to study.

Focused writing sample:
What can we learn from children's writing when we focus on what they write? In the middle of the first-grade year, Leslie's teacher asked her to write a sentence that the teacher dictated. The sentence contained many high-frequency words. Leslie's teacher asks children to write the same sentence in the beginning, middle, and end of the first-grade year. Her teacher can then evaluate growth over the year. What do you notice about the sentence that Leslie wrote? What does she know about words?

Teacher dictates: **I can see the red boat that we are going to have a ride in.**

Leslie writes: I kan see the red bot that we are going to hav a ride in.

We can see that she has control over most high-frequency words (*I, see, the,* . . .). The substitution of *kan* for *can* is logical, given that the letter *c* actually borrows its sounds from *k* and *s.* From the word *ride,* we think that Leslie may be aware of using a silent vowel to mark a long-vowel sound. Does she generalize that understanding to the long vowel needed to spell *boat* (*bot*)? Not yet. Leslie represents the word *have* as a short vowel (*hav*), which is the way that it is pronounced. Based on her spellings of *kan* and *hav* we might suggest that attention to the spellings of high-frequency words might be worthwhile. The double vowel *oa* in *boat* will probably be a while in coming.

Another type of focused assessment is to select a list of words that represent particular spelling patterns. In Figure 9.10, we can see five samples of Leslie's word knowledge taken over a three-year period, beginning in first grade. The words in this focused assessment are drawn from a sample of words used for assessing children's stage of word knowledge (Bear & Barone, 1989). By using the same words, we are able to observe growth in Leslie's knowledge. What do you notice?

Looking across the spelling of each word, we are able to see how Leslie's knowledge of words changes over the period of three years. She continues to

FIGURE 9.10
Focused Spelling Assessment for Leslie, Grades 1–3

Focused Spelling Assessment **Name – Leslie**

Focus Words	Beginning 1st Grade	Beginning 2nd Grade	End 2nd Grade	Beginning 3rd Grade	End 3rd Grade
bed	be	bed	bed	bed	bed
ship	hep	ship	ship	ship	ship
drive	r	driv	drive	drive	drive
bump	bup	bup	bump	bump	bump
when	wen	when	when	when	when
train		trene	train	train	train
closet		closet	closit	closet	closet
chase		chaes	chas	chas	chase
float		flowt	flowt	flot	flote
beaches		beches	beaches	beaches	beaches
preparing			preparing	preparing	preparing
popping			poping	poping	poping
cattle			catol	cattle	catel
caught			cote	cote	cot
inspection					inspection
puncture					punksher
cellar					seller
pleasure					plesher
squirrel					squirle
fortunate					forchynet

struggle with how long-vowel sounds are shown in English. In this list we have long vowels spelled with silent e-markers, as well as double vowels such as *ai, oa,* and *ea.* Leslie is not yet consistent with long vowels. By third grade, Leslie is ready to focus on hearing sounds within multisyllable words. She represents each syllable, but does not yet relate the chunks in longer words to what she already knows, except for familiar inflected suffixes. Multisyllable words present their own challenges, as we explore in Chapter 10.

We can design our own focused assessments by having children write several words that represent particular knowledge within the continuum of word knowledge.

Example: To assess a child early in the developing stage, we would select single-syllable words with a variety of short vowels and single consonants.

rag	*jet*	*kid*	*log*	*tub*
fan	*men*	*win*	*hop*	*sun*

These ten words provide two opportunities to spell each short vowel, as well as a variety of single consonants.

Focused assessments are most useful when administered individually. We watch as a child writes each word. We decide what the writing is showing and how much farther we should go with the child in gathering useful information. For example,

Leslie's assessment in third grade could have stopped after the fifteenth word, *inspection.* We should have been able to see that these multisyllable words were not appropriate and the spellings of the last group of words did not add to our knowledge of Leslie's development.

Samples of focused and unfocused writing, and records of miscues during reading (see reading records in the assessment section of Chapter 5), should be primary sources of information about phonics and structural knowledge which children can use independently. Emerging knowledge can also become the focus of instruction for reading and writing.

Keeping Records of Word Knowledge Development

Each time that we evaluate children's reading or a piece of focused or unfocused writing for evidence of word knowledge, it will be helpful to record our observations. Record-keeping forms, such as those provided in Figures 9.11 through 9.13, can be made to reflect the knowledge and strategies for which we provide instruction and expect to see develop at each stage. Such forms are combined with other assessment data to form a more complete picture of children's development.

Take a moment to reflect on putting theory into practice for phonics instruction . . .

Early in the developing stage, children . . .

- become independent readers,
- continue to develop sight vocabulary through repeated reading of text and meaningful contexts,
- know most single, consistent consonant sounds,
- use the names of letters to find sounds that match phonemes in words they are trying to write,
- spell short-vowel sounds,
- spell initial blends and some h digraphs,
- begin to recognize and use words with inflected suffixes,
- are encouraged to use "context +" strategy with initial consonants, and
- are primarily oral word-by-word readers.

Later in the developing stage, children:

- broaden their sight vocabulary through repetition of words in wide reading,
- refine their phonics knowledge for use in decoding new words,
- generalize vowel patterns and vowel markers,
- spell single-syllable words using vowel and consonant knowledge,
- begin to use structural units to identify words,

Context:	Usually	Sometimes	Rarely
Uses written context to determine unfamiliar words and word meanings.			
Sight Vocabulary:			
Adds meaningful words to sight vocabulary.			
Frequently reads low-challenge text.			
Increases amount of independent reading time.			
Reads widely.			
Returns to familiar texts for rereadings.			
Phonics Patterns:			
Uses familiar sound chunks to read unfamiliar words.			
Uses familiar sound chunks to write unfamiliar words.			
Structural Patterns:			
Recognizes familiar words with added inflectional suffix (jump + ing).			
Recognizes compound words as familiar base + base.			
Recognizes/uses contractions -are family ('re) -not family (n't) -will family ('ll) -is/am family ('s, 'm)			
Recognizes/uses independent suffix + base.			
Recognizes/uses base + derivational suffix.			
Self-Monitoring Strategy:			
Uses context + beginning letters strategy, checked by sense and remaining letters to decode 1-syllable words.			
Uses context + beginning letters strategy, checked by sense and remaining letters to decode 2- or 3-syllable words.			
Self-monitors for meaning, searching for clues and cross checking sources of information when meaning breaks down.			
Is moving toward silent reading in easy text. Oral reading reappears in difficult text.			
Oral reading is very fluent in familiar text, and somewhat fluent in unfamiliar text.			

FIGURE 9.11
Development of Word Knowledge: Developing Stage

FIGURE 9.12
Phonics Knowledge—Consonants

Consonants:
blends/clusters—initial

Reads	br-	cr-	dr-	fr-	gr-	pr-	tr-			
Writes	br-	cr-	dr-	fr-	gr-	pr-	tr-			
Reads	bl-	cl-	fl-	gl-	pl-					
Writes	bl-	cl-	fl-	gl-	pl-					
Reads	sc-	sk-	sl-	sm-	sn-	sp-	st-	scr-	spr-	str-
Writes	sc-	sk-	sl-	sm-	sn-	sp-	st-	scr-	spr-	str-

h digraphs—initial

Reads	sh-	th-	ch-
Writes	sh-	th-	ch-

h digraphs—final

Reads	_sh	_th	_ch	Writes	_sh	_th	_ch

single variant consonants

Reads	c-	g-	s-	x-	Writes	c-	g-	s-	x-

double consonants (2 letters, 1 sound)

Reads	_bb	_dd	_ff	_gg	_ll	_ss	_tt	_zz
Writes	_bb	_dd	_ff	_gg	_ll	_ss	_tt	_zz

silent letter consonant digraphs—initial

Reads	gh_	gn_	kn_	wh_	wr_
Writes	gh_	gn_	kn_	wh_	wr_

silent letter consonant digraphs—final

Reads	_ck	_gn	_ng	_dge	_tch
Writes	_ck	_gn	_ng	_dge	_tch

FIGURE 9.13
Phonics Knowledge—Vowels

Vowels:
short vowels:

Hears phoneme	a	e	i	o	u
Reads words	a	e	i	o	u
Writes words	a	e	i	o	u

single long vowels (CVCe, CV)

Reads	a_e	_e	i_e	_o, o_e	u_e
Writes	a_e	_e	i_e	_o, o_e	u_e

vowel digraphs (long, consistent)

Reads	ai_	_ay	ee_	_igh	oa_
Writes	ai_	_ay	ee_	_igh	oa_

vowel digraphs (short & long)

Reads	ea_	ei_	_ey	ie_	ou_
Writes	ea_	ei_	_ey	ie_	ou_

diphthongs—look same, sound different

Reads	oo	ou	ow
Writes	oo	ou	ow

look different, sound same

Reads	au	aw	oi	oy	eu	ew	ui
Writes	au	aw	oi	oy	eu	ew	ui

r-controlled—single vowel + r

Reads	_ar	_or	_er	_ir	_ur
Writes	_ar	_or	_er	_ir	_ur

long-vowel marker + r

Reads	_are	_ere	_ire	_ore	_ure
Writes	_are	_ere	_ire	_ore	_ure

vowel digraphs + r

Reads	_air	_ear	_eer	_oar
Writes	_air	_ear	_eer	_oar

- recognize contractions as the combination of two base words,
- become more proficient at using inflected suffixes that do not change base words,
- become aware of the meaning of derivational suffixes attached to base words,
- become aware of the meaning of independent prefixes attached to base words,
- become self-monitoring and use the "context +" strategy more automatically, and
- move from oral to silent reading.

Words for study should be developmentally appropriate and have utility because they are appearing in children's texts for reading and writing.

Building words is an excellent whole-class word study activity that focuses on a variety of letter–sound patterns in words that range from two to eight letters.

Small groups can also be formed for word study by:

- using lists of ten to fifteen words in patterns,
- using developmentally appropriate words from stages of word knowledge, and
- using word sorting and building to focus children's attention on distinctive features.

Word study notebooks are an excellent way to use writing to help children retain and recollect their thinking about words and patterns within words.

We can assess children's knowledge of patterns in words by analyzing focused and unfocused samples of writing.

Word study in the early developing stage:

- extends use of context, introduces written cloze,
- emphasizes sight vocabulary through meaningful words and repetition,
- develops phonics patterns such as
  - initial and final consonants
  - short vowels
  - h digraphs
  - consonant blends/clusters
  - e-marker
- helps with self-monitoring, context + initial consonants, and
- helps children become oral readers and attend to words.

Word study in the later developing stage:

- broadens sight vocabulary through repetition and wide reading
- refines phonics knowledge (silent letters) of both

-vowels
- single—long
- double—digraphs, diphthongs
- variant—r-controlled, l-controlled

-consonants
- single variants
- double consonants (ll)
- final blends
- digraphs with silent letters

- helps self-monitoring to become covert
  -context + initial sounds, checked by sense and remaining letters one- and two-syllable words
- helps children move to silent reading—oral reading reappears in difficult text

YOUR TURN . . .

1. Collect samples of focused and unfocused writing from several children in the developing stage and make some general determinations about what they know about words. Based on the writing samples, what types of word knowledge activities might be planned that would be developmentally appropriate?
2. Select a set of words for a focused assessment of word knowledge for the developing stage. Explain how each word reflects knowledge that is developed in this stage.
3. Survey the word knowledge activities from a first- or second-grade basal reading text. Make a list of the basal skills in the suggested sequence. How do the expectations of the basal compare with the expectations of word knowledge for developing readers and writers discussed in this chapter? Are the sequences of instruction similar? Explain your thinking.
4. Survey the word lists of one grade level of a basal spelling series. Make a list of the phonics and structural patterns in the suggested order of instruction. How do the expectations of the spelling series compare with the expectations of word knowledge stages? How might you explain any differences that exist?
5. Begin a file of other suggested activities to develop word knowledge in phonics. Organize the activities according to the phonetic elements that are being emphasized.

Aa Bb Cc Dd Ee Ff Gg Hh Ii Jj Kk Ll Mm

CHAPTER

10

Word Study III: Integrating Phonics and Structure

Adding to our literacy framework . . .

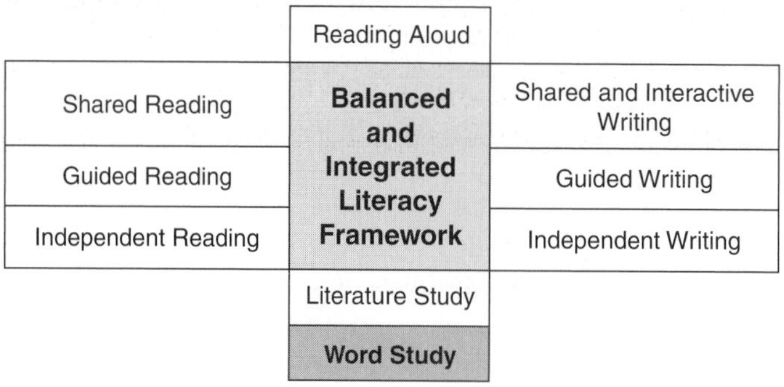

	Reading Aloud	
Shared Reading	**Balanced and Integrated Literacy Framework**	Shared and Interactive Writing
Guided Reading		Guided Writing
Independent Reading		Independent Writing
	Literature Study	
	Word Study	

In this chapter, we . . .

- Examine the ways that many English words are composed of structural units.
- Consider the development of readers and writers during the transitional stage, beginning at third-grade reading level.
- Explore elements of instruction to help children link their knowledge of phonics with the structural makeup of words, including whole-class and small-group word building and word sorting.

Looking into Classrooms . . .

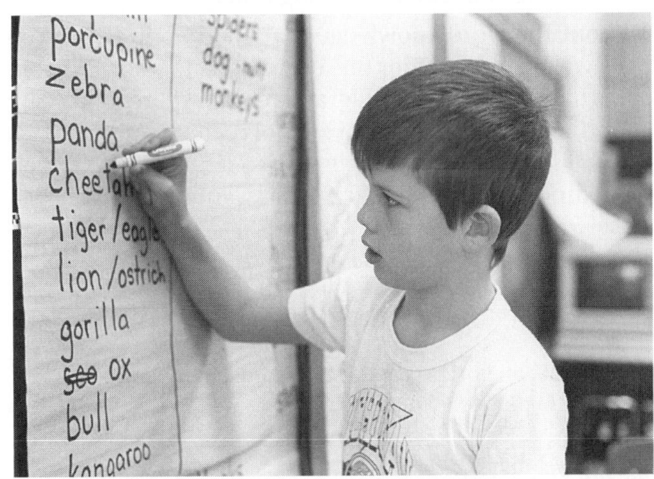

It is time for daily word study in Lori's third-grade classroom. The children move to the section of the room where their word study group meets. For the twenty children in Lori's classroom, there are four levels of developmental word study: early developing stage (single long vowels), later developing stage (double vowels), inflected endings with no change to the base word (early transitional), and syllabication patterns (middle transitional). The children settle into their word study groups. It is Tuesday, so they know that this day is for closed word sorts and to examine patterns within their words for the week. Lori sits with the syllabication group because they are struggling to understand how their phonics knowledge can help them with words that are more than one syllable. Lori understands that children frequently experience some confusion over using their phonics knowledge for one-syllable words with the longer, more complex words they find in their third-grade reading materials. As she talks with the children, Lori discovers that the children are not aware of how to look at words to see the phonics patterns they already know. Lori decides to restructure the next several weeks of word study lessons to help children first consider patterns that focus on familiar words that have only one consonant between two vowels. Lori chose this pattern because she knows that the first syllable in these words can decode as either a long-vowel or a short-vowel syllable. Children in this group know both long-vowel and short-vowel patterns in one-syllable words.

Building a Theory Base . . .

With utmost certainty, all readers will encounter words that are unfamiliar. "The vocabulary of written English consists of a relatively small number of words that occur frequently and an extremely large number of words that occur only infrequently" (Winsor, Nagy, Osborn & O'Flahavan, 1993, p. 5). Thus, in almost any text we read, many words will appear only once and some of those words may either be unfamiliar or ones we have not seen for a long time.

To help us begin to think about the word knowledge that children in the developing and transitional stages will need, consider this example. Anderson, Wilson, and Fielding (1992) estimate that the average fifth-grade reader will read about 1 million words in a year, counting both in and out of school reading. At least 10% or 10,000 of those words will be seen only once during that year. Winsor, Nagy et. al. (1992) estimate that the composition of the 10,000 words would be as follows:

- 40% or 4,000 derivatives of more frequent words (*indebtedness* from *debt*)
- 13% or 1,300 inflections of more frequent words (*merges* from *merge, merited* from *merit*)
- 15% or 1,500 proper nouns
- 22% or 2,200 words in several categories (capitalized words, numbers, deliberate misspellings, mathematical expressions)
- 10% or 1,000 truly new words

According to these figures, we can see that many of these infrequent words will be partially known. Readers who cannot discern the relationships among words will face real difficulties in reading (Winsor, Nagy et al., 1992).

While phonics patterns enable children to understand more about letter–sound relationships within syllables, it is structural patterns that enable children to find meaningful units within multisyllabic words. Linking meaningful units within words helps children enlarge their vocabulary by seeing how words are related to one another through word parts or chunks (Beck, Perfetti, & McKeown, 1982).

Our figures suggest that slightly over half of the words children will encounter in text will be longer words that include meaningful units. Knowledge of structural units should increase children's opportunity to relate unfamiliar words to known words that contain some of the same meaningful units. When the combination of units is immediately unfamiliar, phonics knowledge will assist children as they begin to decode chunks of words.

Approximately 10% of the words will be truly new words, as mentioned, and are likely to contain multiple syllables. A combination of phonics and structural knowledge will equip children with the tools to predict pronunciations that can be cross-checked by the knowledge of language and contextual meaning.

CHILDREN'S KNOWLEDGE OF WORDS IN THE TRANSITIONAL STAGE

What do developing readers add to their knowledge of words as they move to the transitional stage? They come to the transitional stage with a strong concept of words in print and a foundation in letter–sound patterns. We build on this knowledge to help children acquire increased proficiency in reading and writing multisyllable words. With multisyllable words, children must be flexible in applying both phonetic and structural knowledge about words.

Transitional readers, children who are functioning between early third-grade and sixth-grade reading levels, have the ability to be quite fluent and are ready to be challenged as they think about written language. They have made the transition from picture books to chapter books, or novels, and are able to sink into periods of silent reading for 30 minutes or more. They will soon make the transition to mature reading, a stage in which they will have enough knowledge and skill to make connections to known words and teach themselves about new words.

The texts that children read at this level are becoming quite challenging. Not only do they find sentence structures becoming more complex, but they also encounter many multisyllabic words. An increasing number of these words include base words or roots with a prefix, a suffix, or both attached. Children must not only draw upon their knowledge of phonics patterns, but they must also expand their understanding of the structural units from which words can be composed.

Transitional writers wrestle with decoding multisyllable words and how to best use phonics generalizations derived from work with syllables. Transitional children typically know much more about word patterns than they are able to show in their writing. Continued attention to patterns in words during daily literacy activity enables them to further close the gap between what they read and write conventionally.

INTRODUCING STRUCTURAL UNITS

During the developing stage children will begin to encounter words in reading materials that are composed of familiar words plus "something more" added on. That "something more" is an affix—a prefix or suffix—added to the base word to alter or clarify in a particular context. This is the beginning of the study of multisyllable words, the words that dominate the English language. An overview of basic elements of multisyllable words is shown in Figure 10.1. This section discusses the characteristics of the structural elements that compose multisyllabic words.

The basic structural unit is the *morpheme.* Morphemes include roots or base words, and affixes. Morphemes can be either free from or bound to other morphemes.

- *Free morphemes* function as words without needing to be attached to other morphemes.
- *Bound morphemes* must be attached to at least one other morpheme to make a recognizable word. Most multisyllable words are created from combinations of free and bound morphemes.

Example:	crosswalk	=	cross(free) + walk(free)
	repaint	=	re(bound) + paint(free)
	richest	=	rich(free) + est(bound)
	inspection	=	in(bound) + spec(bound) + tion(bound)

As children study longer words they should learn to distinguish morphemes that are free from those that must be bound together. It is often easier to determine the

Overview of Structural Patterns			
Base Word + Base Word		**Base Word + Affix**	
Compound Words • literal (dog+house)* • implied (over+drawn) • two word (ice cream) • hyphenated (son-in-law)	**Contractions** • not family (can't) • are family (we're) • will family (I'll) • is family (he's) • have family (we've) • would family (I'd)	**Prefix + Base Word/Root** • independent (un+tie) • dependent (con+cern)	**Base Word/Root + Suffix** • inflected suffix *(jump+ing, hop+p+ing) • derivational suffix (care+ful)
		Prefix + Base Word/Root + Suffix (in+habit+ed, dis+organ+iz+ed)	

***Bold = introduced in the developing stage**

FIGURE 10.1
Overview of Structural Patterns

meaning of longer words that are made from free morphemes than those that are made from bound morphemes.

Base Words or Roots

Multisyllable words contain at least one base word or root. The essential meaning of longer words can be found by identifying the meaning of either the base word or the root.

Base words:
Base words are free morphemes and can function as words by themselves or have affixes added to create related words. We often know a meaning of a base word from our early language experiences, which is useful in determining the meaning of longer words that contain the same base.

Example: joy
joy + ful
en + joy + ment

Joy can stand by itself as a word. We have a meaning for the word. When we find it within a longer word, we use our meaning for the base word to help us determine the related meaning.

Roots:
Roots can also serve as the core of a word, but roots are typically morphemes that must be bound to an affix to be recognized as a meaningful word. Typically, the meaning of a root is not as familiar to children as the meaning of a base word.

Example:	*graph*	(to write or record)
	auto*graph*	(auto = self or same)
	photo*graph*y	(photo = light)

Through experiences in school, children may only think of *graph* as a chart for recording data in mathematics. They may not relate its broader meaning, "to write or record," to other words that contain the root, *graph*.

Children can dramatically expand their knowledge of words if they use meanings of word parts in known words to figure out meanings of unfamiliar words. Flexibility with language is an important part of expanding reading and writing vocabulary beyond one-syllable words. Children must understand that meaningful units can be included in more than one word and that the unit carries its meaning with it in some way. Roots are typically studied late in the transitional stage, well beyond the development of most primary-grade children.

Affixes

Affixes are bound morphemes that can modify or change the meaning of a base word or root. There are two types of affixes, prefixes and suffixes. Prefixes are morphemes that are added before a base word or root, and suffixes are morphemes that follow a base word or root. Neither prefixes nor suffixes can stand alone as words. They must be combined with at least one base or root word.

Prefixes:
A prefix modifies the meaning of the base word or root to which it is added. The modified meaning is easier to determine if the prefix is attached to a base word, a free morpheme, rather than a root.

Example: rejoin (re = again, join = bring together)
revive (re = again, vive = from *vivere,* live)

The unit *join* is a base word, whereas *vive* is a root. Using the meaning of the word parts, the overall meaning of *rejoin* is easier to determine than the meaning of *revive.*

A prefix is considered to be *independent* if it is attached to a base word that can function without the prefix. A prefix is *dependent* if it must be attached to a root to create a meaningful word.

Example: rejoin = re (independent prefix) + join (base)
revive = re (dependent prefix) + vive (root)

This is an important distinction for children who are trying to use their knowledge of structural patterns to determine the pronunciation and meaning of new words. The meaning of the base word *join* is modified by the meaning of the prefix *re.* In contrast, children typically do not have a separate meaning for the root *vive.* They know the meaning of *revive* as a word found in meaningful contexts, and not by relating the meanings of parts *re* + *vive.*

Suffixes:
There are two types of suffixes that can be attached to the end of a base word or root: inflectional suffixes and derivational suffixes.

Inflectional suffixes are added to a base word and include the endings s, 's, es, ed, ing, er, and est. These suffixes affect the number or possession of nouns, the tense of verbs, or the comparison or degree of adjectives.

Example: dog + s—singular to plural noun
jump + ed—present to past verb tense
small + er—comparative adjective

Adding an inflectional suffix typically does not change the part of speech or usage of the base word, except in the cases of +ing (*build* to *building*). Determining the meaning of the new word with an inflected suffix is relatively easy.

In comparison, *derivational suffixes* do affect the meaning and usage of base and root words, and add greatly to the richness of language. Adding a derivational suffix usually changes the part of speech of a base word, thereby changing the way that the word may be used.

Example:	pain (noun) + less	=	painless (adjective)
	assign (verb) + ment	=	assignment (noun)
	week (noun) + ly	=	weekly (adverb)

Focusing on the structure of words provides the opportunity to help children combine their knowledge about phonics patterns within syllables with a growing knowledge of the meaningful units in more complex words. This knowledge will become the foundation for mature reading.

REFINING CONCEPTS ABOUT WORDS IN PRINT

As children encounter greater numbers of multisyllable words in the developing and transitional stages, they must enlarge their understanding of what constitutes a "word" to include both meaning units (morphemes) and sound units (phonemes). They must learn to integrate their knowledge of phonics generalizations in one-syllable words with the meaningful syllables found in longer words. During the developing and transitional stage, children learn the following:

- The syllables in multisyllable words contain some of the same patterns that are known from smaller, one syllable, words.

  Example: Compound words, like *upstairs,* often contain two one-syllable base words that are already known.

  Example: In the two-syllable word *after,* the first syllable, *af,* is like the word *at* and the second syllable, *ter,* is like the word *her.*

- Multisyllable words can be composed of parts, or chunks, that contribute to the overall meaning of the word.

  Example: untie = un (not) + tie (to fasten or join) means to loosen or undo.

  Example: childish = child + ish (like, adjective forming) means like a child.

- Joining syllables to make multisyllable words can cause changes in the sounds or spelling of individual syllables.

  Example: The *o* in *sec-ond* does not receive vocal emphasis or stress and is pronounced like the *u* in *up.*

  Example: Joining *run* + *ing* to make *running* requires the addition of another *n* to preserve the short *u* sound.

- Multisyllable words can be made of sound chunks, meaning chunks, or both.

Example: sound chunks (*dam-age, fiz-zle*) meaning chunks (club-house, treatment), both meaning chunks and sound chunks (market-able).

To support children's concepts about multisyllable words, we must consider basic principles that will guide our instructional planning.

GUIDING PRINCIPLES FOR INSTRUCTION IN STRUCTURAL PATTERNS

Principles of instruction consider the nature of the learner and what is to be learned. Consequently, we must consider the vocabulary knowledge of young children, their experiences with words, and our knowledge of the ways that structural units can be joined to create words.

The principles for planning learning experiences with structural words, composed of two or more meaning units, that will guide us in this chapter are:

- base word patterns before root word patterns,
- suffix patterns before prefix patterns,
- consistent patterns before variable patterns, and
- frequency/utility.

Base words are not only introduced in children's reading materials before words with roots, but are also known to children through oral language. Children will use their knowledge of base words in personal reading and writing during first grade.

The meaning of a base word with a suffix attached is easier for children to determine, in a left-to-right manner, than when a prefix is attached. Children will encounter base words with an inflected suffix in their reading materials before any prefix pattern. Patterns in which the base is represented completely are more recognizable than when base words have been altered by a suffix. It is always easier for children to see the whole before they see parts. Children will recognize a whole base word, within a larger word, before they will recognize a partial base word.

As always, we let utility be our guide. Children must be able to apply what they are learning if they are to refine their understandings of how words can be made from smaller units. Exposure to multisyllable words in their reading provides the opportunity for closer examination of meaningful parts.

Take a moment to reflect on your theory base for the integration of phonics and structural patterns . . .

Words in the English language are composed of structural units that combine to create new words:

- familiar base words to which an affix is added.
- affixes (prefixes and suffixes) which can be added to base words to alter meaning or expand the ways in which a word may be used.

- prefixes may be either independent of or dependent on a base word or root.
- suffixes may be inflections of speech or change the part of speech, deriving a new word from an old.

During the transitional stage, children should learn:

- that words can be composed of meaningful units as well as sound units, with which they are already familiar.
- to integrate their knowledge about phonics with newly acquired knowledge about the structure of words.

Children must understand the possibilities for the composition of multisyllable words:

- can be composed of familiar words and other meaningful units that have appeared in other known words.
- can be composed of syllables that are either meaning chunks or sound chunks, or both.
- knowledge of phonics instruction with smaller words can be helpful in figuring out multisyllable words.
- the joining of syllables can alter the expected sounds of some letters.

Certain principles should guide us as we plan learning experiences for developing and transitional readers. In general, we should emphasize:

- Base word patterns before root word patterns,
- Suffix patterns before prefix patterns,
- Consistent patterns before variable patterns, and
- Frequency/utility.

Putting Theory into Practice . . .

In this portion of the chapter we focus on issues of instruction in structural patterns within words, as well as how we can support children's work with multisyllable words that require both phonics and structural knowledge to decode. We begin with an overview of the transitional stage, which focuses primarily on patterns in multisyllable words.

OVERVIEW OF INSTRUCTION IN THE TRANSITIONAL STAGE

A major focus of instruction during the transitional stage is the integration of knowledge about phonics with knowledge of structural units within the English language. The reading materials that we find for third- to sixth-grade level contain an ever-increasing number of multisyllable words. Transitional readers and

FIGURE 10.2
Overview of Instruction in the Transitional Stage

Transitional Readers and Writers	In this stage, students learn . . .
Function between third- to sixth-grade reading level **read–** multisyllable words, structural and phonetic solidifying silent reading becoming flexible readers **write–** multisyllable words, structural and phonetic spelling still lags behind decoding	• base + base (compound words, contractions) • independent prefix + base (untie) • base + inflected suffix, no change to base (s, es, ed, ing) • base + inflected suffix, change to base (consonant double, e drop, y to i) • phonic syllable patterns v/cv—ci/der vc/cv—mar/ket vc/v—ri/ver /c+le—wig/gle, tri/ple

writers who are able to see familiar units within unfamiliar words will be able to decode many new words to make meaning in increasingly complex text. Instruction about multisyllable words will span compound words to complex combinations of affixes and base words/roots, all of which require the efficient use of phonics to determine pronunciation. Figure 10.2 provides an overview of instruction during the transitional stage.

Given what we know about developing and transitional readers and writers, how will we plan effectively for whole-class and small-group word study that focuses on the integration of structural and phonetic patterns? We will draw upon our plans for instruction in phonics in the previous chapter. As always, the sequence we follow and the example words we select are determined by utility in reading and writing experiences.

WHOLE-CLASS WORD STUDY: BUILDING STRUCTURAL WORDS

To challenge children's understanding of words and their meanings, we might alter the word building lessons introduced in Chapter 9 to include the construction of structural words from meaningful units. Word building activities that focus on structural units provide opportunities for transitional readers and writers to refine their understanding of ways in which units can be combined.

Selecting Words

We can structure our study in two ways:

- Select a common base word and a variety of affixes that can enhance or alter the meaning of the base. We focus on the ways in which affixes can alter the meaning of a base word.

Example: *cares, cared, careful, carefully, caring, uncaring, careless*

To build structural words children need a variety of word chunk cards. To build words related to *care,* children will need: *care, -s, -ed, -ing, -ful, -ly, -less, un-.*

- Select a common prefix or suffix to use with a variety of base words. We focus on the meaning of an individual prefix or suffix and the pattern of how it impacts a base word.

Example: +*ing*
barking, jumping, sleeping, playing, thinking, flying
raking, hitting, running, using, making, hopping, hoping

To build structural words we select a variety of base words to which +*ing* can be added. Notice that +*ing* changes the spelling of some base words.

To build these words children will need each base word, +*ing,* and single consonants *t-, n-,* and *p-.*

Procedure

The procedure of building with word chunks is similar to the procedure for building with the letters of one word (see Chapter 9 for other examples).

- The teacher holds up each chunk, one at a time, and names the chunk. Children do the same.
- The teacher states the number of chunks and the word to be made, such as "Let's make the two-chunk word *careful.*" The teacher then observes to see that children understand the direction.
- One child who makes the word correctly then comes to the front of the room and places the large cards with the word chunks in the pocket chart for everyone to see.
- The teacher helps children check their building of the word against the model in the pocket chart. The teacher calls attention to ways that readers integrate structural and phonetic knowledge in reading words.
- The children continue building all of the words possible, until they have used every chunk at least once.
- After children build the words for the day, the teacher uses large word cards for each word to help children sort words in the pocket chart that have similar patterns and to consider the meaning of particular words.
- To end the lesson, the teacher asks children to speculate on how a word might be spelled that contains a chunk of a word made that day.

To provide ample opportunity for all children to participate, ask questions, spell, sort, and write words, it may take several days to complete the activities for word building with a particular set of words.

Sample Lesson—Words with the Base Word Care

Imagine that during our discussions about fire safety we have been using the words *careful* and *carefully* quite often. The children notice that both words contain the word *care.* It seems appropriate to discuss how affixes enable us to create many related words in English, so we develop a word building lesson. The following words contain suffixes that children have seen attached to other base words.

cares, careful, carefully, carefulness, careless,
carelessness, cared , caring, uncaring

Let us build these words. Children will need a word card containing the base word *care.* They will also need prefix cards that contain *un-.* They will need suffix cards for *-s, -ed, -ing, -ful, -ly, -less,* and *-ness* as shown in Figure 10.3. Consider making base word, prefix, and suffix cards each a different color to call attention to the placement within words (for example, base word = black, prefix = red, suffix = green).

Call attention to the *-are* vowel pattern in *care.* Also note that in the previous list of words, three words have a change to the base word when the suffix is added: *care+ed, care+ing, un+care+ing.* As children build these words, we want to observe how they deal with the silent *e* at the end of *care.*

When we build words with letters, we begin with the smallest words and work our way up to the longest word. What order should we consider for building structural words? Should we begin with the least complex? Which words are the least complex? We might say that words with one affix (*care+less*) are less complex than words with more than one affix (*care+less+ness*). We also might say that words in which the base word changes (*car+ing*) are more complex than base words that do not change (*care+ful*). The order we choose depends upon our children's experience with base words that change. If children have had some experience, we may want to use this time to observe who understands such changes.

The day of the lesson, children pass out the needed cards. We build words one at a time and check their understanding of each word. We discuss not only spelling changes that can occur but also how the meaning of the base word is affected by the addition of prefixes and suffixes.

To build the word *cares* from *care+ing,* children must lay the suffix *–ing* over the end of the base word *care* to cover the final *e.* This demonstrates understanding that when a base word ends with a silent vowel and has a suffix added that begins with a vowel, there will most likely be a change to the base word.

After all words have been built, we use word cards and a pocket chart for children to sort words by the patterns they have observed. What patterns might they notice? They might notice that some words share the same suffixes, and also similar meanings:

Meaning pattern:

careful	careless	caring
carefully	carelessness	uncaring
carefulness		

Because of the attention to we gave to the change to the base word *care,* children might sort words with a change to the base words, and those with no change.

Visual pattern:

base changes	**no change to base**	
cared	cares	careful
caring	careless	carefully
uncaring	carelessness	carefulness

FIGURE 10.3
Building Words with the Base Word *Care*

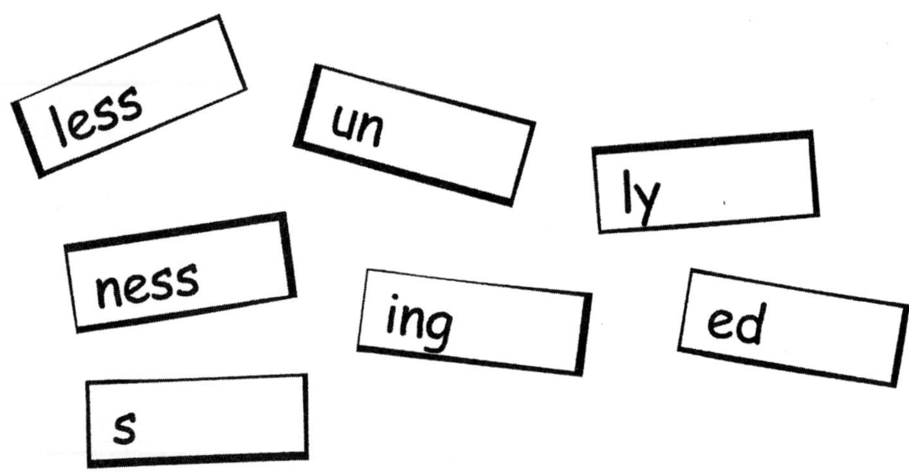

To help children consolidate their understanding of meaning changes, consider having them use words in sentences and identify their parts of speech as one way to consider changes in meaning.

care (verb)	I don't *care* if it rains.
careless (adjective)	Please don't be *careless* with my car.
carefully (adverb)	She cut the vegetables *carefully.*
carelessness (noun)	This accident is because of your *carelessness.*

Changing part of speech changes the ways in which we can use words to express ideas. Derivational suffixes change the part of speech and, thus, the meaning of base words.

Sample Lesson—Words with +ing

To focus children's attention on the power of a prefix or suffix, we can build words using only that particular affix.

Example: +*ing*
barking, painting, sleeping, thinking, flying, building, raking, hitting, running, using, making, hopping

To build these structural words we select a variety of base words to which +*ing* can be added. When we add +*ing* to *bark,* we change the verb *bark* from present tense to a participle that can be used to describe past (was barking), present (is barking), or future (will be barking) action. Consider *paint* and *painting. Paint* can be both a noun and a verb; adding +*ing* maintains both the noun (object) and the verb form (action).

Notice also that +*ing* changes the spelling of some base words. Do you notice the pattern? Words that end in silent *e*, lose that *e*. Words that end in a single consonant have the consonant doubled before adding +*ing*. This relates to preserving the vowel sound in the base word.

To build these words children will need a card for each base word, +*ing*, and single consonants cards for *t*-, *n*-, and *p*-.

As with *care* words, we will build each word, discuss potential changes in meaning or word usage, and notice spelling changes when they occur. After word building, children will sort for patterns. What patterns might they notice?

Visual pattern:

Drop *e*	**Double Consonant**	**No Change to Base**	
raking	hitting	sleeping	painting
using	hopping	flying	thinking
making	running	building	

Meaning pattern:

Verb	**Verb or Adjective**	**Verb or Noun**
raking	sleeping	building
hopping	flying	painting
using		
running		
making		
hitting		

Sample word building and word sorting are shown in Figures 10.4 and 10.5. We will try building sentences with words to notice potential changes in meaning when +*ing* is added. With a number of words, we must consider possible contexts in which words can be found.

> The new apartment **building** had three floors. (noun)
> The workers are **building** some new apartments. (verb)
> The geese are **flying** in a V-shaped formation. (verb)
> A **flying** fish can glide in the air for a short distance. (adjective)

Again, we challenge the children to hunt for similar words in their reading materials to help them solidify their understandings about structural units.

Selecting structural words for study can be guided by the words that are showing up in children's reading materials or words that children are trying to use in their writing. We know that utility is important. Children must be able to apply their new knowledge to print in some manner fairly soon after word building lessons.

When children are sorting structural patterns, the words are typically categorized according to meaning or visual patterns as we found in the previous example. Since structural units are also meaning units, we must be sure to emphasize meaning at some point in the sorting of structural words.

FIGURE 10.4
Building Words with the Suffix-*ing*

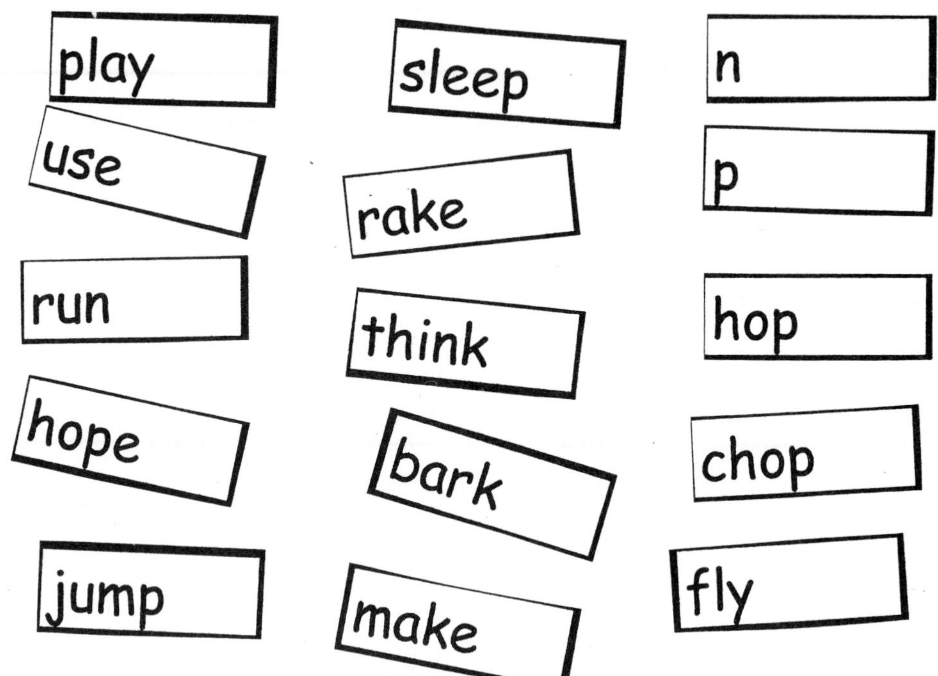

SMALL-GROUP WORD STUDY: SORTING, BUILDING, AND HUNTING FOR WORDS

In Chapter 9, we discussed the organization of small-group word study and possible weekly routines. We know how to form small groups for word study by evaluating each child's knowledge of words (see discussion in Chapter 9). Words are selected that are at an appropriate level of challenge. Typically, small-group study takes the place of traditional spelling instruction. The small groups meet for approximately twenty minutes per day for focused word study. This time is in addition to whole-class word building and/or word study that is integrated into other daily literacy components.

For the most efficient use of time, children in the same group should move to a central place in the classroom for activities and discussion. We are able to

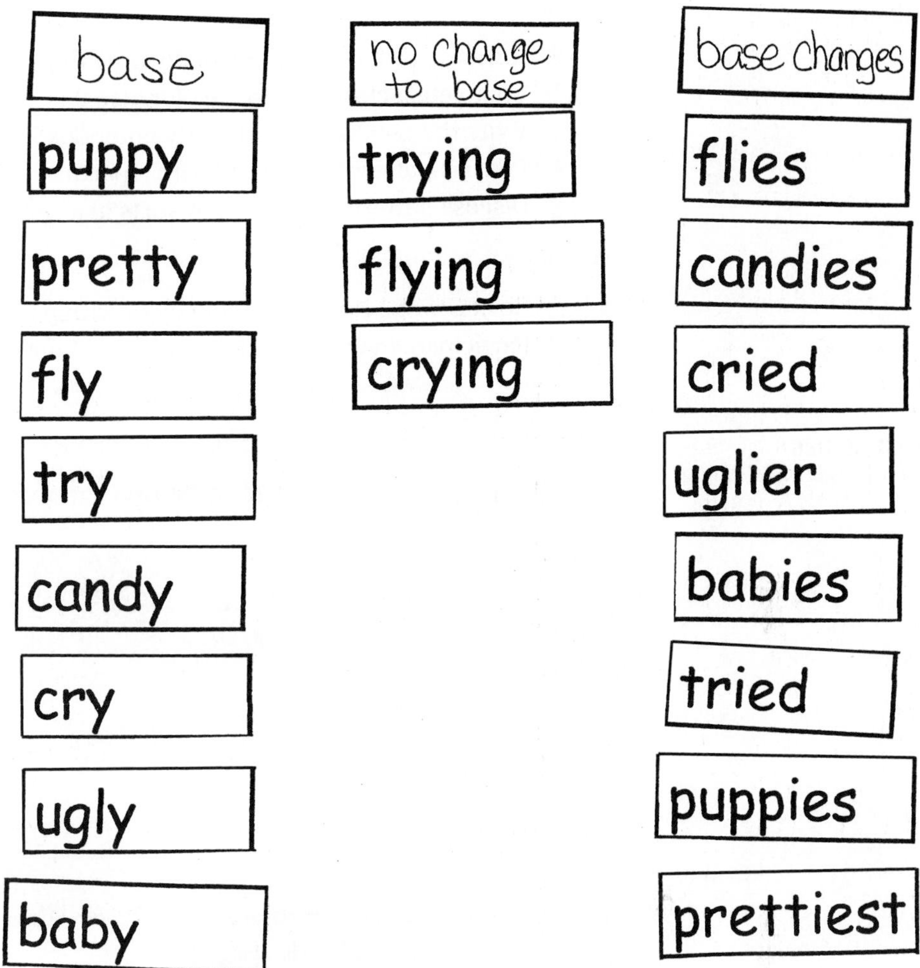

FIGURE 10.5
Structural Word Sort

monitor group activity as we move about the classroom. We can listen in informally or plan to sit with a group for part of the word study period. We can focus children's attention on patterns and help them integrate understandings. We ask children to record their observations about words (see Figure 10.6). When small groups work with multisyllable words, the weekly routine described in Chapter 9 remains useful.

Small-group routine:
Monday

- Get new list of appropriate words.
- Children check to be sure they can read each word.
- Write list of words in word study notebook.
- Make word cards (about 1" × 3") for sorting activities.
- Take a spelling pretest with a partner.

Tuesday

- Review word cards, individually or with partner.
- Complete a closed word sort for visual or meaning pattern.
- Write the results in word study notebook.
- Discuss patterns observed with a partner.
- Discuss patterns observed in sorts in a word study group.

Wednesday and Thursday

- Review word cards, individually or with partner.
- Participate in word building and word hunting activities.

FIGURE 10.6
Word Study Notebook—V/CV and VC/V Patterns

Word Study Notebook

4/1 Word List

cider	radish	open
linen	rocket	lizard
later	diner	ticket
travel	music	pilot

4/3 Word Building—Syllables

V/CV	VC/V
ci-der	rad-ish
o-pen	rock-et
pi-lot	trav-el
di-ner	tick-et
la-ter	liz-ard
mu-sic	lin-en

4/2 Closed word sort—listen for the first vowel sound to be long or short.

secret	river
cider	radish
open	linen
later	rocket
diner	lizard
music	ticket
pilot	travel

Words like secret have a long vowel first.

Words like river have a short vowel first.

4/4 Word Hunting in *Chocolate Fever*

V/CV	VC/V
be-lieve	com-ical
be-cause	choc-olate
u-sual	prob-ably
u-sually	im-agine
co-coa	ev-ery
	sep-arate
	ex-act

Our group looked for words that have a VCV pattern at the beginning. Then we tried long- and short-vowel sounds to see what made sense.

- Write results in word study notebook.
- Compare new words and word list, note similarities and differences in notebook.
- Discuss results with partner.
- Discuss patterns with word study group.

Friday

- Take posttest including two to three new words that fit the pattern to test ability to generalize pattern.
- Correct posttest.
- Discuss comfort/confidence with patterns following test.
- Plan for next week of word study, including words to be carried over.

Our small-group word study with multisyllable words utilizes the same types of sorting, word building, word hunts, discussion, recording activities, and teacher guidance that we discussed in Chapter 9. The pretest and posttest, however, take on greater importance as children focus on more complex words.

The purpose of a weekly pretest is to help children identify understanding and misconceptions related to the focus words. Partners within each group can learn to administer the pretest to each other. Through whole-class modeling and guided self-correction, children can learn how to check their spellings, letter by letter. The outcome of the pretest should guide teacher–student and student–student interactions during the week of study. Children want to improve their spelling, but they need to know how to correct their thinking when it interferes with spelling patterns.

The posttest can be administered in the same manner. If the purpose of word study is personal improvement, then it is best for children to learn to correct their own work. Focusing on personal growth, rather than class competition, may reduce the anxiety some children have about being "right." Learning must become its own reward.

With a basic framework for whole-class and small-group word study in mind, we consider possible sequences of instruction, beginning with the developing stage.

POSSIBLE SEQUENCE FOR STRUCTURAL PATTERNS FOR DEVELOPING READERS AND WRITERS

In the developing stage, children begin to consider morphology, or meaningful units of language. These patterns are introduced for recognition and should not be required for spelling. Practice in recognition is setting the stage for spelling multisyllable words during the transitional stage. Figure 10.7 provides a detailed listing of the structural elements we will teach during the developing and transitional stages. In this section we explore the structural elements that are appropriate for developing and transitional readers and writers.

Base + Base		Base + Affix(es)	
Compound Words	**Contractions**	**Prefixes**	**Suffixes**
literal meaning dog+house bed+room gold+fish play+ground after+noon play+time eye+sight wild+life **implied/accepted meaning** every+one out+side run+away over+drawn fall+out soft+ware butter+fly **two words** fly paper ironing board steam engine wagon wheel **hyphenated** cut-off part-time play-offs tongue-tied	**not family** are+not = aren't can+not = can't have+not = haven't do+not = don't will+not = won't would+not = wouldn't could+not = couldn't should+not = shouldn't **Pronouns** **are family** you+are = you're they+are = they're we+are = we're **will family** I+will = I'll you+will = you'll we+will = we'll they+will = they'll **is family** he+is = he's she+is = she's it+is = it's I+am = I'm **have family** I+have = I've you+have = you've	we+have = we've they+have = they've **independent - not bound to base** dis disobey en enjoy for forgive fore foretold im impure in inactive inter interview mis mislead non nonstop pre preview re repay un undo **dependent - bound to base/root** com combine con concern de decide dis disturb ex excuse	pre prefer pro process **inflectional nouns** s dog+s es dish+es horse+es 's one boy's two boys' **verbs** s jump+s ed jump+ed bat+t+ed bake+ed ing jump+ing hit+t+ing bake+ing **adjective** er tall+er big+g+er pretty+er nice+er est tall+est big+g+est pretty+est nice+est **derivational** able comfortable ance allowance ess princess ful careful ify classify ion addition division ish foolish ism criticism ist finalist ity ability ive productive ize organize less painless ly friendly ment payment ness kindness

FIGURE 10.7
Structural Patterns

Base + Inflectional Suffix

The inflectional suffixes include *-s, -'s -es, -ed, -ing, -er,* and *-est.* As early as first and second grade, we use instructional reading materials to introduce children to familiar base words that have inflectional suffixes added.

First Grade Example:	asked	boats	cookies
	goes	grapes	its
	things	wheels	cried

Notice that in the group of first-grade words the base remains the same when the inflectional suffix is added, with the exception of *cried.* Children must learn to see that a recognizable base word is included in the new word. For some children, a suffixed word appears to be a completely new word, not one that includes a familiar word.

First-Grade Example:	ask+ed	boat+s	cookie+s
	go+es	grape+s	it+s (possessive)
	thing+s	wheel+s	cried (cry-ied)

In second-grade reading materials children add to their knowledge of the possibilities of inflectional suffixes. The base words become more challenging. In addition, they are introduced to base words that change when an inflectional suffix is added.

Second-Grade Example:	blinking	branches	building
	crossed	dribbling	hugging
	pulled	stories	tracing

Notice the change to the base words in *hugging, stories, dribbling,* and *tracing.*

Example:	hug	hugging (*g* is doubled)
	story	stories (*y* changes to *i*)
	dribble	dribbling (*e* is dropped)
	trace	tracing (*e* is dropped)

We delay introducing children to such changes in base words until they are able to consistently use a base and a suffix, with no change, to pronounce a new word.

Inflectional suffixes appear in children's oral language quite early. It makes sense that early reading materials begin to introduce inflectional words. Children are able to use their oral language to self-monitor for meaning as they read and write.

- Work with base words that do not change when the inflected suffix is added.
- Select words in familiar text that have inflected endings and known base words.
- Select sight words, add inflected suffixes, and have children read and write the new words.

We want to encourage children to see a familiar base word + something extra. For example, think of the pattern in the book *Brown Bear, Brown Bear, What Do You See?*

Brown Bear, Brown Bear, What do you see?

I see a red bird *looking* at me.

The repeated pattern includes an inflectional word, *looking*. The base word *look* is a high-frequency word. Throughout this predictable text children read, "looking," over and over again with each new animal. If the word *look* is known to children, *looking* can be studied to help children become familiar with the function of inflectional suffixes. Other simple texts offer words for study, focusing on plural nouns (-s, -es), as well as the change in tense for verbs.

- Sort inflectional suffixes to notice visual differences in words.

Two-level sort	*-ing*	not *-ing*	
	plural	not plural	
Three-level sort	*-s*	*-ing*	neither

Compound Words (Base + Base)

New words can be brought into our language by compounding, or joining, existing words to represent a new meaning. Typically two base words are combined to make the compound. Compounds can be written as one word or two words, with or without a hyphen. If the compound has been in the language for a while or is commonly used, it tends to be written as one word.

While the majority of compound words in the English language are nouns, we also find pronouns, verbs, and adjectives with compound structures.

Example: raincoat (noun) anyone (pronoun)
withdraw (verb) breathtaking (adjective)

Compounds drawn from different parts of speech provide diversity for expressing ideas.

During the developing stage, children learn compound words that have fairly literal meanings, determined by knowing the two base words from which the compound is made. The meaning of some compound words may be implied or accepted through their use. More challenging compounds are studied during the transitional stage.

To understand the meaning of literal compounds, we think about the relationship between the two words.

Example: earache—an *ache* in the *ear*
dressmaker—a *maker* of *dresses*
fingerprint—a *print* made with the *finger*

The ability to make such direct connections between words makes literal compounds easy to learn.

- Children know compound words in oral language and they will also encounter them early on in written language. The compound words children study should be composed of two known sight words. The thinking strategy requires children to see compound words as two known words that have been put together. The "putting together" should signal the children to puzzle over how the words are related to each other.
- Focus first on words that are concrete. Clustering words around the topics such as people, places, things, animal life, and time is suggested

by Rinsky (1993) and seems to be a beneficial way to study compounds. Word sorts can center on these categories to help children get started. Children can also hunt for compounds in their reading materials and add compounds to a word wall.

People	Places	Things	Animal Life	Time
fireman	bedroom	doghouse	starfish	bedtime
nobody	playground	snowball	goldfish	birthday

As with inflections, begin by selecting only compound words that are showing up in children's reading materials or are known sight words.

Sorting compound words

Two-level sort	compound not compound
Three-level and four-level sorts	(sort by meaning) people, places, things, etc.

Contractions (Base + Base)

Contractions are actually contracted forms of two base words. These expressions are common in conversational speech. When represented in print, an apostrophe is used to show the place in the word where sounds and letters are omitted in pronunciation.

Example: I will—I'll
cannot—can't

Contractions with *not* are actually two base words that began as a compound word, then become contracted.

Example: cannot can't
shouldnot shouldn't

Knowledge of compound words should help children understand these contracted words. In most contractions, the first word can still be seen, while the second word has been contracted. However, a few contractions will result in a change to both words.

Example: willnot wo+n't
cannot ca + n't

In addition, one contraction results in a change in pronunciation of the first vowel, changing from long /oo/ to long /o/.

Example: donot don't

The variation of these contractions provides some challenge for readers and writers.

Many contractions include a pronoun combined with a verb such as *are, will, is,* or *have.* Pronoun contractions are used like pronoun referents, referring back to a person(s) who has already been identified.

Example: we are we're
she will she'll
he is he's
they have they've

The study of compound words and contractions enables children to think about longer words using meaningful word parts that are already known from earlier reading and writing experiences.

- It is best to begin with contractions that are more predictable, in which a base word is intact. Children look for what is familiar. Also consider the pronunciation—it will help if the contraction matches the pronunciation of the base word.

Example:		
	more predictable:	we are = we're (original base is seen)
	less predictable:	will not = won't (original base is not seen)

- Children usually know how to read contractions as a unit before they are able to write them. In writing, they may substitute the two words that stand for the contraction, especially if they are writing "book talk" and not dialogue. Working with a contraction family can be quite successful. We may want to begin with contractions that are already in the children's speaking vocabularies.
- For some children, it may be helpful to develop the concept of contractions using individual letter cards or magnetic letters to write both words of the contraction, then remove letters and add the apostrophe to hold the place of those letters.

  can not
  ca_ n_t
  ca_ n't
  can't

- Matching activities can also be used to reinforce contractions. Using three word cards for each contraction—*can, not, can't*—children make matches to show the meaning of contractions. Matching can also be played as a card game like "Go Fish."
- Sorting activities for contractions might include:

Two-level sorts		
	can't (contraction)	can (not a contraction)
	we're (are family)	can't (not in the are family)
	won't (first base word changes)	aren't (base does not change)

Independent Prefix + Base

When children meet a word that is composed of an independent prefix and a base word, they often know the meaning of the base word from prior experience.

- Children must learn that a prefix also has a meaning that, when joined with the base word, creates a new word with a meaning that is related to the base word.

Example:		
	open	re (again) + open
	safe	un (not) + safe
	like	dis (not) + like

- The challenge for children is to realize that the meaning is determined by first identifying the base word, thinking of its meaning, then modifying that meaning by adding on the meaning of the prefix.

  Example: reopen
  -see re + open
  -think of the meaning of open
  -add the meaning of the prefix, re

  The prefixes *un* (meaning "not or back") and *mis* (meaning "bad, not, or amiss) are consistently combined with base words to make new words whose meaning can be decoded through the strategy described above. The prefix *mis*, however, is often joined to base words that appear in higher-level reading materials.

  Example: uncooked uncurl uneaten
  unhurt unkind unopened
  unsafe untie unused

  Example: misadvise misfortune misinform
  mislead misprint mistrust

- The prefixes *re* (meaning "again or back") and *dis* (meaning "not, apart, or reversed") are frequently combined with base words to create new words, but can also be combined with root words (see dependent prefix + root).

  Example: rebuild recall recopy
  refill relive rename
  reopen repaid reread

  Example: disagree disarm dishonest
  dislike disown distrust

  Other prefixes may also be combined with base words, but are more likely to be combined with roots that are more challenging for determining word meaning.

- To help children study independent prefixes, focus on joining and separating prefixes and bases, with discussion of changes in meaning. Separate word cards are best for word building.
- Sorting focuses on visual discrimination of bases with different prefixes. Multilevel sorts can be used depending upon the number of different prefixes being studied at one time.

Sorting by prefix:

untie	review	preview
undo	retake	prepay
unfair	recall	

Sorting by base:

untie	preview
retie	review

Base + Derivational Suffix

- Using base words that are well known, help children consider the subtle changes in meaning that occur when derivational suffixes are added. The suffixes that are in children's reading are best for this instruction and will probably include *-ly, -ful, -en, -less,* and *-self.* Remember to begin with words in which neither the base nor the prefix is changed in the joining of syllables.
- Word study can proceed in two directions, clustering words that share the same base or clustering words that share the same suffix.

Base Cluster	Suffix Cluster
careful	helpful
carefully	careful
careless	playful

For adding to children's meaningful vocabulary clustering by the base is preferable because words share related meaning and are easier to learn (Beck, Perfetti, & McKeown, 1982).

When developing readers and writers focus on phonics, they focus on the internal structure of syllables to make sense out of consonants and vowels. When they focus on structural patterns, they are able to use known words and word parts to enhance their understanding of words.

Attention to base words and affixes in this stage should not require new decoding skills, but rather address thinking strategies. Spelling instruction still focuses on one-syllable words. Recognition and understanding of two-syllable structural patterns continues to develop.

STRUCTURAL PATTERNS FOR TRANSITIONAL READERS AND WRITERS

Compound Words

- *Implied compounds.* In contrast, the meaning of some compounds is implied and must be determined by the context in which the new word is used. The meaning of many such compounds has, over time, come to be accepted in our language. Building a relationship between the two words in this type of compound is not helpful in determining an appropriate meaning.

Example: dragonfly—Is it a drago n that flies?
starboard—Is it a board made of stars?
carpool—Is it a pool for cars?

Children must be aware that as words have been compounded and used in our language some meanings have been modified. Through the use of words in the context of our language, we begin to realize those compounds that have implied meanings.

- *Two-word compounds.* If a base word is more than two syllables, the compound may be written as two words that carry one meaning.

  Example: bulletin board (bul-le-tin + board)
  mail carrier (mail + car-ri-er)

  A space between the two words makes it easier for the reader to decode each word, instead of reading *bulletinboard.*

- *Hyphenated compounds.* Compounds may also be written with a hyphen (-). This form tends to be used when the compound describes a noun.

  Example: able-bodied person
  white-tailed deer

  Notice how the hyphen emphasizes each of the words used to create the compound. Hyphenated compounds may either be new to our language and, thus, an experiment in adding new words, or they may serve a specific purpose.

- *Sorting compounds.* Begin by sorting against literal compounds that are the easiest for children to understand. Then compare compounds.

Three-level sort	literal compound	implied compound	neither
	one-word compound	two-word compound	neither

Compounding words that are already in the English language enables us to experiment with known words to express current ideas. Appendix B provides a list of useful compound words for study. Children should be aware that compounds are more than just "two words that have been put together into one word."

Base + Inflected Suffix (Base Changes)

Inflectional suffixes enable nouns to show number and possession, verbs to show tense, and adjectives to show comparison. In the case of +*ing,* however, some words do change a part of speech. In the developing stage we gave attention only to inflections in which the base word remained unchanged. However, there are conditions under which the base will be altered when joined with an inflected suffix.

In the transitional stage, there are several generalizations that are beneficial for children to study:

- When adding *-es, -ed,* or *-ing* to a base word that ends with an *e,* the *e* in the base word is usually dropped. This is often done to avoid changing the vowel sound in the suffix.

  horse + es = horses, not horsees
  rake + ed = raked, not rakeed
  hide + ing = hiding, not hideing

- When adding *-ed* or *-ing* to a base word that ends with a single consonant, the consonant is usually doubled to preserve the short vowel sound in the base.

grab +bed = grabbed, not grabed
hop + ing = hopping, not hoping

- Sorting inflected suffixes that cause change should focus on the following:

Two-level sort	base changes, no change to base
Three-level sort	letter doubled, letter dropped, no change

- In addition to sorting, it may be helpful for children to manipulate letters that form these words to demonstrate their understanding of the generalization. Word cards or letter cards can be used to form a base word, form the suffix, join the two syllables, then show and explain what must be done to preserve the pronunciation of the vowel in the new word.

More Independent Prefixes + Base Words

- Independent prefixes were introduced in the developing stage for recognition.
- Give attention to multisyllable words that are made from other independent prefixes and are now a part of children's reading vocabulary. Encourage a thinking strategy that combines the meaning of the base with the meaning of the prefix, when the syllables are joined. A list of independent prefixes is provided in Figure 10.7.
- Sorting activities are similar to those described for developing readers and writers; compare words with the same prefix or the same base.

More Base Words + Derivational Suffixes

- In the transitional stage, children continue to add derivational suffixes to their storehouse of words. Instruction should continue to focus on words in which the base remains identifiable.
- Sorting activities should continue to focus children's attention on adding on to base words to examine change in meaning and part of speech. Frequency of usage should guide the selection of words for study.

Introduction to Dependent Prefixes + Roots

During the transitional stage the vocabulary in children's reading materials will begin to contain words that are composed of dependent prefixes.

- In contrast to an independent prefix, which can be separated from a base word, a dependent prefix must be attached to its root to form a meaningful word. The root cannot stand alone as a meaningful word.

  Example: reduce = re + duce
  distinct = dis + tinct

  Identifying the root of each word above, *duce* and *tinct,* does not help to find the meaning of *reduce* or *distinct* without knowledge of Latin, from which the words came. The thinking strategy we use to make meaning with an independent prefix + base word is not helpful.

- To determine the meaning for words that are composed of a dependent prefix and a root, readers must either use context and prior language experience, or be introduced to the meaning of Latin roots. In elementary grades the most feasible thinking strategy is the use of context and language knowledge to determine meaning.

  When meeting such a prefixed word, children must be able to:

  1. see the units within words,
  2. use phonics knowledge to determine the probable sounds for each unit, then
  3. move to context and language as a check for word meaning.

- As early as third grade, children are guided to think about words that have dependent prefixes. In a current basal reading/language arts series for third grade we find dependent prefixes identified for study in the vocabulary words that are considered essential to the comprehension of the story.

Examples:			
	insisted	recognize	inspired
	infection	proposal	adoration
	assured	disturb	embarrassed
	relieved	reluctantly	

Because these words do not contain base words, children are not able to use their base word + prefix thinking strategy to determine a new word meaning. Instead, children will need to use phonics to decode the words above, then use context and language knowledge to determine word meaning.

Example: in/sis/ted

Decode *in*—short-vowel pattern
sis—short-vowel pattern
ted—short-vowel pattern with *-ed* suffix

Context "But I *love* snow," Irene *insisted.*
(*Brave Irene,* William Steig)

The clues provided by the author, combined with children's language knowledge, should help students determine a general meaning for the word. Using the meaning of the prefix and root requires knowledge that most third-grade children have not yet developed.

Example: insisted
in—from Latin, meaning "on"
sist—from Latin, *sistere,* meaning "stand"
ed—past tense form of the verb

In the later elementary grades and middle school, students will be exposed to the meanings of frequently used roots to add to their decode + context/language strategy for dependent prefixed words. Knowledge of roots will expand the vocabulary of mature readers and writers.

SYLLABICATION—INTEGRATING STRUCTURE AND PHONICS ACROSS SYLLABLES

Children who are able to see meaning units and sound units in words are likely to be more successful readers. There are useful generalizations that can help children work with multisyllable words. To find the generalizations useful, children must first have a good sense of the types of structural units (meaning) and phonic units (sound).

Children must learn to recognize when there are familiar meaning units in unfamiliar words. To find meaning, children must be able to identify the base word or root in an unfamiliar word as an anchor for pronunciation and meaning.

Children must also be able to recognize when a longer word is not composed of meaning units. In such cases their knowledge of phonics in one-syllable words becomes very useful. As early as first grade, instructional reading materials introduce children to words that have more than one syllable. Some words are composed of a familiar one-syllable word plus something more, such as *lead+er.* Other words are composed of letter–sound units, such as *cac+tus* and *muf+fin,* which are similar to other known syllables. Learning to see longer words as parts that have familiar patterns is an aid to unlocking words that are unfamiliar.

Children should look for meaning units first in words, then apply their phonics knowledge. Structural words are primarily base words or roots and affixes. Teach children to look for the base words and affixes, then to apply phonics to read any units that they do not immediately recognize. Can you recognize the structural units and phonics units in words? Think about the words we looked at earlier—

market	uncaring	dangerous

How do we divide these words into chunks, or syllables?

mar + ket	un + car + ing	dan + ger + ous

When words are divided into syllables, the divisions can create different types of syllables. Those syllables can be:

Long-vowel syllables—have a vowel sound that is consistently long. They may end with a vowel or contain a consistent double vowel. These are also called open syllables.

Short-vowel syllables—have one vowel and end with one or more consonants. These are also called closed syllables.

R-controlled syllables—have a vowel followed by *r,* which produces a special r-controlled vowel sound.

Variable syllables—have vowel and/or consonant patterns that can have variable sounds, so several possibilities must be tried to find an appropriate pronunciation.

What types of syllable patterns do we have in the words above?

mar + ket = mar (r-controlled) + ket (short vowel)

un + car + ing = un (short vowel) + car (from *care,* r-controlled) + ing (short vowel) dan + ger + ous = dan (short vowel) + ger (r-controlled) + ous (variable because of *ou*)

To use phonics effectively, children must learn to see these same basic one-syllable patterns in longer words. These patterns provide a place to begin to decode or encode unfamiliar words.

The following structural generalizations are worth teaching for syllabication.

1. base + base (compound, contraction)
2. prefix + base or base + suffix (This pattern could also include words with more than one affix, such as *un+break+able.*)

These phonics generalizations are worth teaching for syllabication.

3. V/CV—single consonant between vowels, first vowel can be open (long vowel) (*fa+vor, mu+sic*) or
   VC/V—closed syllable (short vowel) (*riv+ er, hab+it*)
4. VC/CV—two consonants between vowels, not a blend or digraph (*dol+lar, mar+ket*) (closed or variable syllables)
5. C+le—preceding consonant stays with *le,* except for *ck* (*ta+ble, pick+le*) (most likely an open syllable, except for *ck*)

For word study, children should be encouraged to talk about the generalizations they use for familiar multisyllable words. Then introduce unfamiliar words that use the generalizations above for children to apply new knowledge.

Sorting activities should cause children to discriminate words according to the makeup of words and the syllabication generalizations that would be most helpful in decoding a word.

Two-level word sort examples	structural word, not a structural word
	base + base, not base + base
	begin with structure, begin with phonics
	V/CV, VC/V
Three-level word sort examples	prefix + base, base + suffix, neither
	VC/V, VC/CV, neither
	V/CV, VC/V, neither
Four-level word sort examples	base + base, prefix + base, base + suffix, none V/CV, VC/V, VC/CV, none

For an example of two-level sorting in syllabication patterns, refer back to Figure 10.6, in which children examine words with the V/CV and VC/V patterns.

Unaccented or Unstressed Syllables

When we pronounce words in English, all syllables do not receive equal emphasis. When we do not stress all syllables equally, we may change the pronunciation of a vowel in an unaccented, or unstressed, syllable. The vowel sound often changes to the sound of a short *u*. Pronounce the following words and listen for the schwa. Can you identify the unstressed syllable? Does the vowel in that syllable sound like short *u?*

about = a + bout   pencil = pen + cil
second = sec + ond   signal = sig + nal

There is a schwa in each word above. In *about,* the unstressed syllable is the first syllable, the *a* sounds like short *u*. In each of the other words the unstressed syllable is in the second syllable and sounds like short *u*.

A schwa sound does not typically occur in base words + affixes, because each morpheme unit is stressed. Consider these words. Is there a schwa? Is there an unstressed syllable?

foolish = fool + ish   repaid = re + paid
enrage = en + rage   raincoat = rain + coat

Notice how each structural part, or meaning unit, is stressed? In syllables that are stressed, the vowel sound is not likely to have a schwa sound. Children will need help to notice that words without affixes are more likely to have a vowel that has a schwa sound, rather than affix + base or base + base combinations. A schwa sound is most likely to occur in words that are made of sound units rather than meaning units.

Sorting activities should cause children to discriminate the presence or absence of a schwa as shown in Figure 10.8:

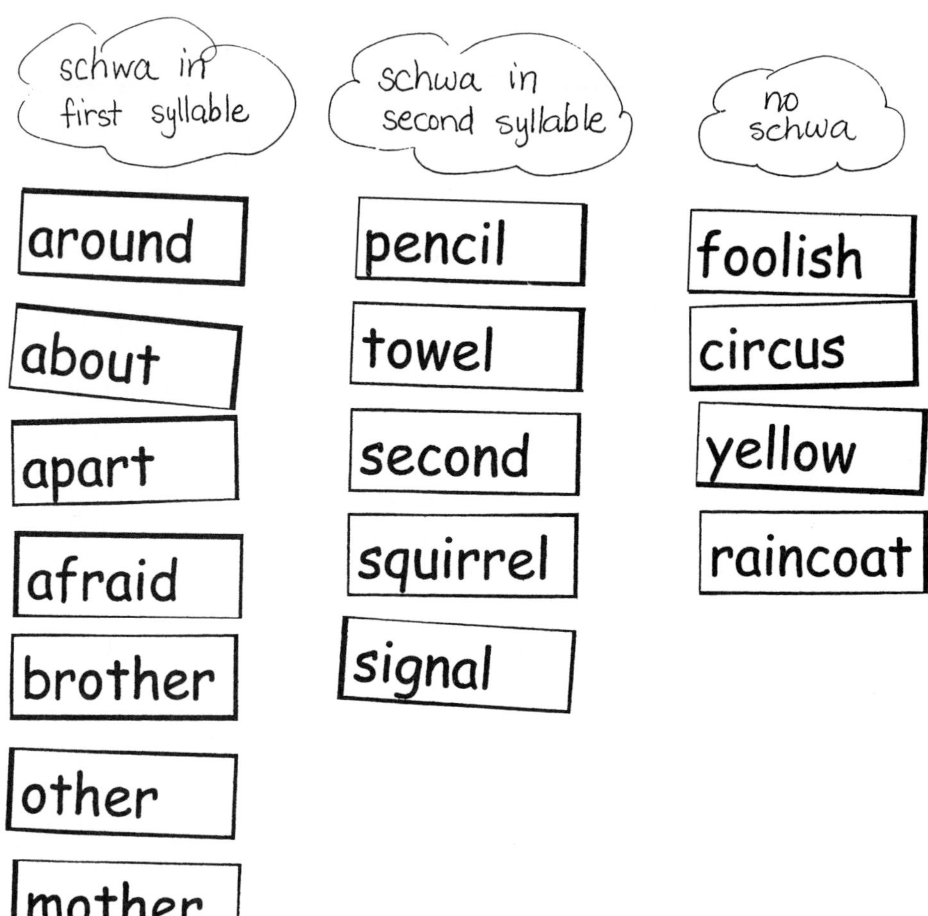

FIGURE 10.8
Sorting Words with a Schwa Vowel Sound

Two-level sorts	has a schwa	does not have a schwa	
Three-level sorts	schwa in first syllable	schwa in second syllable	neither

SELF-MONITORING STRATEGIES IN THE TRANSITIONAL STAGE

In this stage children focus on patterns that occur as syllables are joined. With this focus on units within words, not just letter–sound patterns, children should be encouraged to expand their "context +___" strategy to include syllables. As they meet an unfamiliar word, children should examine the word enough to know if there are structural patterns that should be chunked or if use of their phonics knowledge will be sufficient.

Once this decision is made the steps become:

Primarily Structural: context + base word,
checked by sense and remaining syllables

Primarily Phonetic: context + first syllable,
checked by sense and remaining syllables.

Deciding whether to apply structural patterns first or phonics patterns will cause the child to rely on different syllabication generalizations. Such decisions will increase children's efficiency in word identification.

SOLIDIFYING SILENT READING TO CONNECT WITH TEXT

During the transitional stage children begin to solidify their ability to read silently. The skills that are acquired during this stage make most words available to readers. Material for instruction can be more challenging for children if we are there to assist their attempts to use new skills. However, extensive practice in low-challenge materials must still take place to allow children to consolidate all of the word knowledge they have gained, moving it predominately to sight vocabulary. To break through into more mature reading, skills must become automatic so that attention can be given almost exclusively to ideas in text.

ASSESSMENT: MONITORING WORD KNOWLEDGE DEVELOPMENT WITH MULTISYLLABLE WORDS

As children progress to the transitional stage of development, we want to be sure that their basic knowledge of words in print is solid. We do not want their lack of knowledge about words in print to hold them back from breaking into mature reading. Therefore, we ask ourselves the following questions:

Transitional Stage

- Does the child have a large enough sight vocabulary to read fluently in appropriate text?
- Is the child able to use structural knowledge with words in which the base has been changed by the joining of syllables? What behaviors have been observed?
- Is the child beginning to integrate phonics and structural patterns to decode unfamiliar multisyllable words? How consistently is the child able to use the context + syllables strategy to decode?
- What behaviors suggest that the child is about ready to break into mature reading?

Gathering data to address these questions guides the learning experiences we plan for reading and writing. Conferring with children about their reading and writing and collecting samples of reading and writing over time is essential for planning effective instruction.

From our discussions in Chapter 9, we know that samples of children's reading and writing can be used to inform us about their knowledge of letter–sound patterns in words. The same holds true for children's knowledge of structural patterns in words. As we make reading records, we pay careful attention to the types of miscues children make and which miscues they are able to self-correct. In their writing, we look for patterns in the way they use base words and affixes to make multisyllable words. Our observations of children's reading and writing direct us to the types of words they may need to study more closely in order to generalize patterns to other English words.

Keeping Records of Word Knowledge Development

Each time that you evaluate children's reading or a piece of focused or unfocused writing for evidence of word knowledge, it will be helpful for you to record your observations. Record-keeping forms, such as provided in Figure 10.9, can be made to reflect the knowledge and strategies for which you provide instruction and expect to see develop at each stage. Such forms are combined with your anecdotal notes to form a more complete picture of student development.

Take a moment to reflect on putting theory into practice with multisyllable words . . .

During the transitional stage, children:

- focus on how inflected suffixes can change base words,
- add to their knowledge of words with independent prefixes,
- add to their knowledge of words with derivational suffixes,
- learn to combine their knowledge of structure and phonics to identify multisyllable words more proficiently,
- learn generalizations for identifying syllables in multisyllabic words,
- become aware of the impact the relationships between stressed/unstressed syllables and vowels (schwa),

Context:	Usually	Sometimes	Rarely
Uses written context to determine unfamiliar words and word meanings.			
Sight Vocabulary:			
Adds meaningful words to sight vocabulary.			
Reads widely.			
Frequently reads low-challenge text.			
Increases amount of independent reading time.			
Phonics Patterns:			
Continues to refine ability to use sound chunks to decode unfamiliar multisyllable words.			
Recognizes/uses syllabication generalizations in reading. V/CV or VC/V VC/CV C+le			
Recognizes/uses syllabication generalizations in writing. V/CV or VC/V VC/CV C+le			
Structural Patterns:			
Recognizes/uses base words with inflectional suffixes that change the base word. drop silent *e* double final single consonant change *y* to *i*, add suffix			
Reads/writes independent prefix + base word.			
Reads/writes base + derivational suffix.			
Begins to read/write dependent prefix + root.			
Integrates use of structure + phonics as needed in multisyllable words.			
Self-Monitoring Strategy:			
Uses context + beginning syllable strategy, checked by sense and other syllables.			
Oral reading is fluent in low-challenge materials.			
Silent reading is rapid in low-challenge text.			
Decoding is becoming fairly automatic.			

FIGURE 10.9
Development of Word Knowledge: Transitional Stage

- integrate their knowledge of syllables into their "context +" strategy, and
- solidify their ability to read silently.

Word study in the transitional stage:

- emphasizes changes to words with the joining of syllables
  - -inflectional and derivational suffixes
  - -adding and dropping consonants to preserve vowel sounds in base words
  - -more independent prefixes
  - -introduction to dependent prefixes
- syllabication
  - -noticing differences in multisyllable words
  - -integrating the use of phonics and structural patterns
- generalizations
  - -base + base
  - -base + affix
  - -V/CV, VC/V, or VC/CV
  - -C+le
  - -schwa—vowels in unaccented syllables
- self-monitoring
  - -context + first syllable, checked by context and remaining syllables
- solidify silent reading

YOUR TURN . . .

1. Develop sets of words for focused assessment that represent the structural units and syllabication generalizations that are the focus of the transitional stage. For example, which words would you select to assess children's understanding of base + suffix words? You should be able to explain how each word in the set reflects knowledge that is developed in this stage.
2. Survey the activities in one level of a basal reading series that focus on helping children understand structural patterns. Make a list of the skills, in the sequence in which they are suggested in the basal reader. How do the expectations of the basal compare with the expectations of the transitional stage? Are the sequences of instruction similar? Explain your thinking.
3. Survey the multisyllable words suggested in second-grade and third-grade levels of a basal spelling series. How does the spelling series help children use their knowledge of phonics and structure to spell multisyllable words? How does the approach of the spelling series compare/contrast to the word study programs discussed in this chapter?
4. Begin to collect words that will be appropriate for structural word sorts and word building. Challenge yourself to categorize the words according to sequences suggested in this chapter. Compare your lists with those suggested in Appendix B.
5. Begin a file of other suggested activities to develop word knowledge for multisyllables. Organize the ideas according to the structural element that is emphasized or most appropriate.

Part II

Making Connections: Linking Children's Learning Experiences within a Balanced Literacy Program

An Integrated Unit Study:

Learning about Amphibians in Two Second-Grade Classrooms

Linking the components in our literacy framework . . .

	Reading Aloud	
Shared Reading	Balanced and Integrated Literacy Framework	Shared and Interactive Writing
Guided Reading		Guided Writing
Independent Reading		Independent Writing
	Literature Study	
	Word Study	

In this unit study, we . . .

- Explore a unit of study prepared for second-grade students, organized around the components of a balanced literacy program.
- Consider how to link children's learning experiences to enhance literacy development.

Putting Theory into Practice in Second-Grade Classrooms . . .

We began this text by considering the components of balanced literacy, how to create meaningful learning environments for young children, and the importance of our role as teachers. In each chapter that followed, we considered the purpose of particular literacy components and the possibilities for each component as it is implemented in the classroom. In this chapter, we take a final opportunity to visit two second-grade team-teaching classrooms, where the teachers have been working for the past two years to develop and implement a balanced and integrated approach to literacy learning.

SETTING THE STAGE

Before we visit the classrooms, consider the following ideas. We know that the most meaningful learning experiences are integrated in natural ways, like the learning experiences we have outside of school. We also know that effective literacy learning is the central focus of instruction in the primary grades. Learning to integrate literacy components to enhance children's learning, however, is not an easy task and requires a great deal of study and reflection on the effectiveness of the instructional decisions we make in the classroom. Effective teachers strive to teach themselves how to integrate literacy components around a central topic or concept. They know that focusing instruction in this way provides more in-depth learning experiences for children.

The emphasis in such classrooms is on engaging children in inquiry experiences that are integrated through the literacy components teachers select to enhance children's learning. Integrating instruction demonstrates to children that literacy is a tool for learning about the world, as well as themselves. In an integrated curriculum, the tools for exploration and inquiry are oral and written language. Integrated learning experiences teach children that listening, speaking, reading, and writing are vehicles for exploring ones' own thinking and inquiring into the thinking of others.

To make effective instructional decisions, we must realize that learning how to link literacy components for integration hinges on our ability to select the component(s) that provide the most appropriate levels of assistance to support and extend children's learning, moving them toward independence. To remind us about the levels of assistance that each component provides, the components of our literacy framework are listed below from most to least assistance.

Most assistance:	Read Aloud/ Whole-Class Literature Study	
	Shared Reading	Shared and Interactive Writing
		Whole-Class Word Study— Word Building
	Guided Reading	Guided Writing
	Small-Group Literature Study	Small-Group Word Study— Word Sorting and Building
Least assistance:	Independent/ Reading/Literature Study	Independent Writing

To link components, teachers begin by selecting those that provide high teacher support. Then as children acquire background, skills, and strategy, teachers select components that enable children to be more independent, thus gaining control over their own learning.

MEETING THE TEACHERS

To observe the linking of components in our literacy framework, we visit two team-teaching second-grade classrooms where the teachers deliberately select components to provide the appropriate support to children as they learn about the world of amphibians. Each team of teachers (Jeana and Marcie) (Nicki and Mary) shares a group of thirty to thirty-two children, who are predominantly speakers of languages other than English. The school in which they teach has a high percentage of children who receive free or reduced-cost breakfast and lunch. Three years ago the faculty began investigating balanced literacy as a framework for a schoolwide literacy program. For the past two years, Jeana, Marcie, Nicki, and Mary have been working to implement the components in ways that work best for their children. They believe that linking instructional experiences through the components maximizes language development and conceptual learning for all of their children.

GETTING STARTED

The units of study that these teachers create are driven by two factors: the school district's academic standards and the importance of leading children's development in literacy.

> **Science standards** for second-grade children in this school district identify concepts about ecosystems and the diversity of living things. Experience has taught Jeana, Marcie, Nicki, and Mary that their children are fascinated with animals and very motivated to learn about the environments in which various animals live. They decide upon a unit that focuses on amphibians—primarily frogs, toads, and salamanders—as an example of diversity within a classification of animals, how all living things move through life cycles, and how living things interact with their environment.
>
> **Language arts standards** for second-grade children focus on acquiring language skills that encourage and support fluent reading and writing. Knowing that a majority of children in their classrooms speak Spanish at home, these teachers focus intensely on the development of English through a unit of study such as amphibians. Learning about the world becomes an anchor for learning language. These experiences also provide motivation for extending skills and strategies in reading and writing. This unit will focus on gathering accurate information while reading and comparing/contrasting sources of information. In writing, children will focus on organizing ideas around a topic and comparing/contrasting two animals.

Several weeks before a unit of study begins, the teachers brainstorm ideas together, share the materials they already have, and search for additional songs, poems, chants, and books to support the study. Their experience with second-grade children has taught them that a unit of approximately three to four weeks provides an appropriate amount of time to develop the language and concepts of a topic. While the teachers want variety in their teaching materials, they also want to limit the number of different materials they use in order to provide ample time for revisiting. They have learned that repeated exposure in meaningful contexts is a key to helping their children acquire language to support reading and writing skills/strategies.

Daily routine:
During the unit, the classes will follow this general routine:

Morning

- Shared reading—poem of the week
- Read-aloud—fiction and information

Shared/interactive writing—a response to read-aloud

Guided/independent writing

Whole-class literature study

Whole-class word study (word building, also integrated into shared and guided reading)

Afternoon

Guided reading/independent reading/activity centers

Math

Instruction in science and social studies always occurs through the literacy components. Working in a school in which children are considered to be at risk for academic success causes these teachers to make each learning experience a literacy experience.

MAKING INSTRUCTIONAL DECISIONS

As the teachers plan together, they consider how to best use each component to build children's background knowledge and teach literacy skills and strategies. Let us consider ideas they have for each component:

Shared Reading—Poem of the Week

Each week, the children are introduced to a new poem that emphasizes oral language and vocabulary. The children practice all week and individually recite the poem on Friday.

Monday:

The children listen to the teacher read the poem aloud, pointing to the words.

The teacher rereads the poem and encourages children to join in.

They discuss the meaning of the poem and any vocabulary they are not sure about.

Teacher shows pictures and links back to children's experiences.

The class creates movements and gestures to fit the poem, connecting language to action.

Children receive a personal copy for practicing at home.

Tuesday–Friday:

Teacher illustrates favorite or important parts of the poem on class chart and individual copies.

Poem is reread in whole group, in guided reading, buddy read during independent reading and center time.

Practice handwriting by writing the poem.

Individually recite poem on Friday.

Teaching points:

Draw teaching points from what each text offers that might be new knowledge for the children. The teachers also consider which teaching points are most emphasized by the language arts standards. Possible teaching points from the poems of the week will be emphasized during shared reading, then in shared/interactive writing.

Mediated Read-Aloud

Each day the teachers read aloud both fiction and information texts to extend children's background knowledge and their engagement with the topic. Children are encouraged to be very interactive, as in the sample mediated read-aloud presented in Chapter 2. The discussion that grows out of the mediated read-aloud becomes the base for whole-class shared writings. A fiction text is read first each day during the read-aloud time to set the stage for the information text. Reading both types of text provides an additional opportunity to compare the depiction of reality and fantasy in literature, another language arts standard for second grade.

Shared/Interactive Writing

Following the read-aloud, the teachers engage the children in a variety of compositions that utilize children's growing knowledge base, and model various composition styles identified in the second-grade language arts standards (compare/contrast, sequence, description, explanation). The teachers decide whether the writing will be shared or interactive, or both depending upon the nature of the composition.

In general, it takes these second-grade children twenty to thirty minutes to interactively compose and write one to two sentences, depending upon length. Such texts are typically a cumulative composition written over several days. Sequential compositions, such as retelling the life cycle of a frog, make excellent interactive writings. Interactive compositions provide opportunities for children to learn how to self-monitor writing, as well as how to self-help when "stuck" while writing. For example, the teachers encourage children to make analogies to familiar words to figure out new words, such as asking, "If I know *long,* how can I figure out *song?*

The teachers choose shared writing to label drawings of amphibians and engage children in discussion as a way of developing vocabulary (a narrative drawing), model how to compare two things using a Venn diagram, create charts to compare attributes of amphibians, and compose paragraphs with a topic sentence and supporting details that explain or describe.

Guided Writing

Following read-aloud and shared/interactive writing, children are invited to work on their own compositions, while the teachers are available to assist. While the children are gathered on the carpet at the end of shared writing, the children are encouraged to verbalize ideas for their compositions, to say the sentences as they might write them. The teachers find that having ideas in mind for the composition increases children's fluency. During guided writing, children have the opportunity to carry their writing over several days, to develop their ideas, and practice monitoring their own writing so that it communicates what the child has in mind. If children encounter some difficulty in composing, whether it is ideas/content, organization, or the use of conventions, they are encouraged to search for ways to help themselves. They might find what they need on the word wall, in a past composition, somewhere else in the room, from a friend, and so forth. These teachers encourage children to believe they can solve their own writing problems, but the teachers always keep a watchful eye for how well the children are making decisions.

Literature Study

During this unit, the teachers have chosen two types of literature study. During the second week they study a class set of *Frog and Toad Are Friends* by Arnold Lobel. In contrast to guided reading of texts for fluency, the focus of this literature study is children's response to the literature, to the characters, and to their actions. There is also discussion of reality versus fantasy, discussing what frogs and toads are like in the real world versus the characters they portray in the book. Near the end of the unit, the children will study versions of the story about *The Frog Prince* and make comparisons between versions.

Word Study

Whole-class word building occurs several times each week to support children's exploration with letter–sound patterns with their teachers' support. To catch children's interest, the teachers often choose a word related to the unit. Selecting a variety of words enables the children to maintain familiar letter–sound patterns and, over time, practice new patterns in a supportive environment. In addition to word building, the teachers lead the children to think about words during read-aloud, and to examine words during shared reading and writing and guided reading.

Guided Reading Groups

Each afternoon the teachers provide time for children to meet in guided reading groups, practice reading with familiar texts from their book boxes, and to work in one activity center. Each guided reading group usually lasts about twenty to twenty-five minutes. In a team-teaching classroom, with approximately thirty children, there are typically five to six guided reading groups. Children who read at first-grade level meet for guided reading every day. Children who read at grade level or above meet every other day. Grade-level readers are able to have an instructional text introduced and read in the group one day, then buddy read that text the next day. After a text is introduced and read in the group, it is moved to the independent book boxes.

While one team-teacher is with a guided reading group, the other team-teacher listens in on several focus children's independent reading. The activity centers are set up to be independent activities in which children explore or practice ideas/concepts from the unit or other current interests.

The teachers try to find multiple copies of texts at children's instructional level that compliment the unit. Sometimes it is difficult, however, to find enough instructional-level texts for guided reading throughout a unit. These teachers know that it is more important for children to be in appropriate-level materials than to have all guided reading texts tied into the unit. When there is a shortage of appropriate texts, personal copies of shared/interactive writings can be used for some guided readings, as well as other instructional texts that are not related to the unit.

The teachers use resources such as *Matching Books to Readers* (Fountas & Pinnell, 1999) and *Guided Reading* (Fountas & Pinnell, 1996), published by Heinemann Books, to identify appropriate texts. Their school has purchased many of these texts in sets specifically for guided reading. The following materials are available for instructional-level reading that relates to the unit:

Early first grade:

Farley Frog (Pair-it Books, Steck-Vaughn)
Frogs (Joy Readers, Dominie)
Frogs Can Jump (Book Bank, Wright Group)
Frogs (Twig Books, Wright Group)
Happy Birthday, Frog (Story Box, Wright Group)
Jump, Frog: (Steward & Salem, Seedling)

Mid-first grade:

Frog's Lunch (Lillgard & Zimmerman, Scholastic)
Frogs on a Log (Teacher's Choice Series, Dominie)
Frogs (Pebble Books, Grolier)
Freddie the Frog (First Start, Troll)
The Frog and the Fly (Cat on the Mat Books, Oxford University Press)
Jog, Frog, Jog (Barbara Gregorich, School Zone)
Little Frog's Monster Story (Ready Readers, Modern Curriculum)

Late first grade:

Frog Prince (Sunshine Books, Wright Group)
Frog Prince (Traditional tales, Dominie)
Frogs (Storyteller-First Snow, Shortland Publications)
Freddy Frog's Note (Ready Readers, Modern Curriculum)
How Do Frogs Grow? (Discovery Links, Newbridge)

Early second grade:

Days with Frog and Toad (Arnold Lobel, HarperTrophy)
Froggy Learns to Swim (Jonathan London, Scholastic)
(This level must be supplemented with other materials.)

Mid-second grade:

Frog and Toad All Year (Arnold Lobel, Houghton Mifflin)
Frog and Toad Are Friends (Arnold Lobel, Harper & Row)
Frog and Toad Together (Arnold Lobel, HarperCollins)
Frog or Toad? (Ready Readers, Modern Curriculum Press)
Frog Prince (Literacy 2000, Ribgy)
Commander Toad series (Jane Yolen, Putnam & Grosset)

Late second grade:

The Frog Who Thought He Was a Horse (Literacy 2000, Rigby)
(This level must be supplemented with other materials.)

Independent Reading

Each day the children spend twenty to thirty minutes reading texts from their designated book boxes. Each text in their book boxes has been read during guided reading. The children practice fluent reading with these familiar texts. Children usually sit with another child from the guided reading group to participate in buddy reading and to provide assistance as needed for each other. While one team-teacher is with a guided reading group, the other is listening to a few focus children read from their book boxes. These teachers know that focusing on children during independent reading is an excellent way to gauge how well children are independently using what they have been learning through other literacy components. This is an excellent time to make an unscripted reading record (see assessment section in Chapter 5) to document the strategies children use independently. These teachers believe that children will get to be better readers by practicing fluent, skilled reading every day.

Independent Writing

The teachers include independent writing in the afternoon activity centers. Children are invited to respond to unit experiences, write facts about amphibians, or continue a piece they started in their journal. Children can also make their own amphibian books, record observations of the amphibians in the science center (frog, salamander, and newt), label illustrations of amphibians with appropriate vocabulary as modeled by a teacher, or create their own Venn diagram comparing two amphibians as modeled by a teacher. Another activity is "write the room," during which time children look for ideas in the room to write about such as on the word wall, shared writing charts, or the poem of the week.

PUTTING THE PIECES TOGETHER

We now examine how each week comes together. What types of things did the teachers select to do each week? With four teachers sharing ideas, they find that they begin to adjust activities throughout the unit as they discuss their observations of children's engagement and response. Sometimes they find that what they thought was a good idea does not work well with this particular group of children at this time. Through trial and error they have learned that integrating the components well requires them to remain flexible and to take their direction from the children's responses.

Week 1—Introduction to Amphibians, Frogs, and Toads

***Poem of the week*—Frogs and Toads:**

- Composed by the teachers, in the pattern of "The Farmer in the Dell" (see Figure 1)
- Teaching point: Identify describing words (*strong, webbed, bulging, sticky*), discuss how these words make the poem more interesting, to help make mental pictures.

FIGURE 1

Week 1– Poem of the Week

Frogs and Toads

Frogs and toads here,
Frogs and toads there,
Frogs and toads, frogs and toads, everywhere.

Strong legs jumping
Webbed feet swimming
Bulging eyes looking
And sticky tongues flicking

Frogs near a bog
Toads under ground
Frogs on a lily pad
Toads on land

Frogs and toads here,
Frogs and toads there,
Frogs and toads, frogs and toads, everywhere.

Frogs and toads!
Frogs and toads!

(to the tune of "Farmer in the Dell")

- Teaching point: Identify words that are base words + inflected suffix (*jumping, swimming, looking, flicking*), how we can figure out the word by finding the base word inside, then adding the ending.
- Teaching point: Learn to decode words using a familiar rime, such as *-og* (build the words *frog, bog, log* from poem, make analogy to new word, *hog*).

Texts for mediated read-aloud:
Begin to build background and extend personal knowledge through read-aloud. To provide time to build background, the first few days of the unit emphasize read-aloud and shared/interactive writing over guided writing time.

Fiction

Jump, Frog, Jump, by Robert Kalan (predictable, cumulative tale)

Fish is Fish, by Leo Leonni

Days with Frog and Toad, by Arnold Lobel

Frog and Toad All Year

A Boy, a Dog, a Frog, and a Friend, by Mercer Mayer (a wordless book to encourage story telling; other books in series)

Information Texts

Very first things to know about frogs, by Patricia Grossman

Hiding Toads, by Suzanne Paul Dell'Oro

Jumpy, Green, and Croaky. What am I? by Moira Butterfield & Wayne Ford

Toad Overload, by Patricia Seibert

Why Frogs Are Wet, by Judy Hawes

***Interactive writing*—Frog and Toad Differences:**

- This piece is composed over the course of the week, as the children gather information about frogs and toads. (see Figure 2)
- As each attribute is identified, the children are led to compare and contrast frog and toads, verbalize the statement that the class wants to write, then individual children are selected to come to the chart to write whole words or parts of words they know.
- Because these are team-teachers, one teacher supports the child who is writing on the chart, the other uses a small white board and marker to engage the class in thinking about particular features of the words in the composition.

***Shared writing*—Narrated Drawing of a Frog:**

- On a large chart, a teacher lightly sketches a frog and places penciled notes around the edge as reminders of attributes to be labeled on the drawing. (see Figure 3)

FIGURE 2

Week 1—Interactive Writing
Frog and Toad Differences
Frogs have bright colors and toads have dull colors. Toads have dry, bumpy skim. Frogs have smooth, moist skin. Toads are plump and frogs are thin. Long leaps are for frogs, short hops are for toads. Frogs like the water and toads like the land.

- Following the daily read-aloud, the teacher engages the children in discussion about frogs, and as the discussion develops, the teacher narrates the drawing and labeling of the frog.
- The teacher uses a marking pen to "draw" the frog, label its parts, and make notes about its behavior.
- To the children this appears to be a creation of the moment, not tracing by the teacher.
- The drawing serves as a review of facts about frogs and supports children's development of technical vocabulary.
- A version of this activity is placed in the activity centers during week 2.

***Shared writing*—Venn Diagram Comparing Frogs and Toads:**

- At the end of the first week, the teachers engage the children in comparing and contrasting what they know about frogs and toads.
- A Venn diagram, overlapping circles, is used to show what is similar and what is different (see Figure 4).
- The teacher does the recording to maximize time.
- A version of this activity is placed in the activity centers during week 2.

FIGURE 3

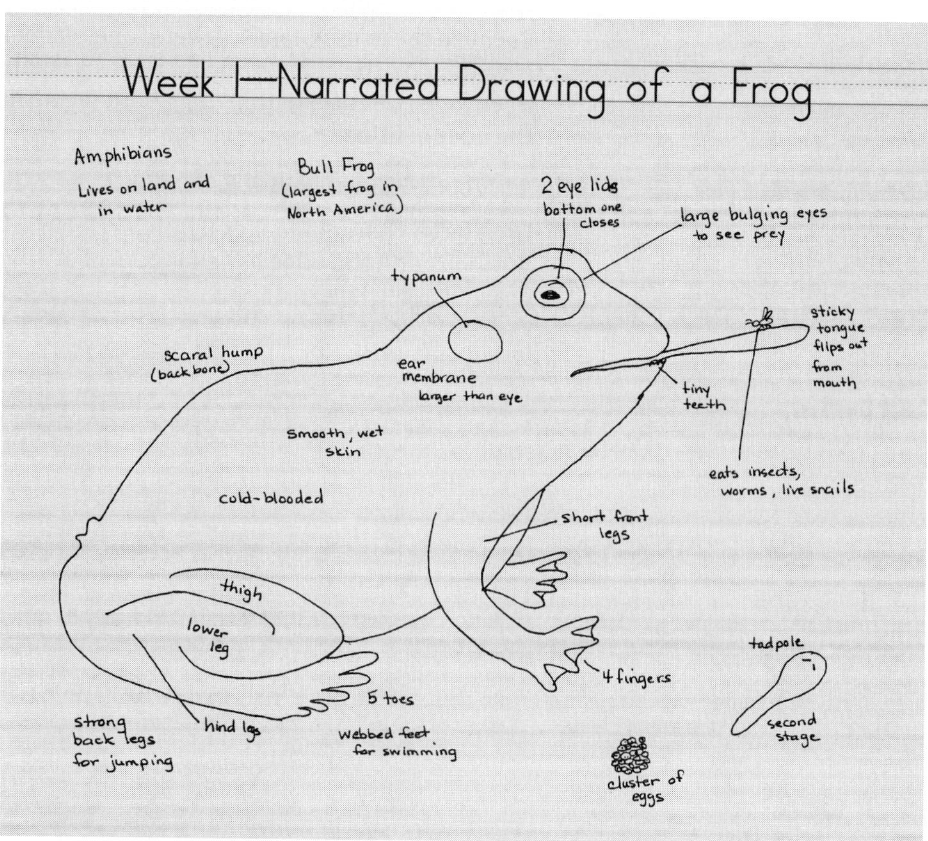

FIGURE 4

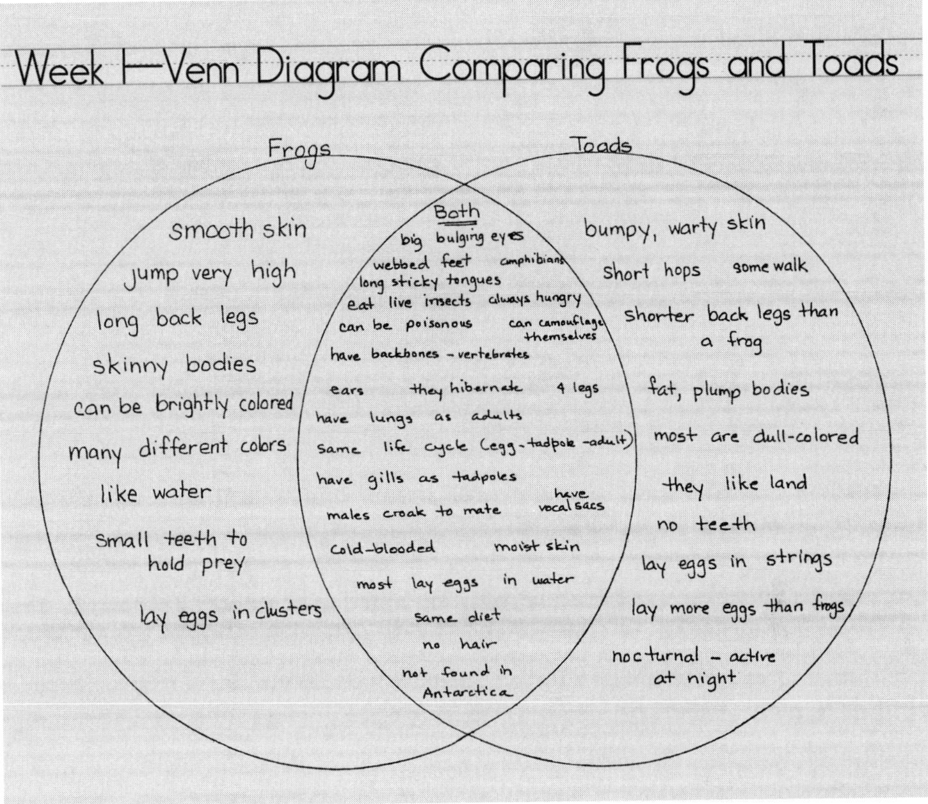

Guided writing—journals:

- Guided writing begins on day 3 of the first week. The first two days are given to read-aloud and shared/interactive writing to build background and model writing.
- Children are encouraged to begin to record things they are learning about frogs and toads. (see excerpts from Ricardo's Journal in Figure 5)

Whole-class word building:

- Use the letters in the word *jumping* to build *in, up, pin/nip, pig, jug, mug/gum, gun, jump, jumping.*
- Use the letters in the word *splash* to build *pal/lap, has, pass, pals, laps, slap, slaps, slash, splash.*
- Because this is early in the school year, the selection of words provides practice with short vowels for first-grade-level readers and review for grade-level readers.
- Two days are spent on each word to provide ample review and practice with building and sorting the words, noticing patterns.

FIGURE 5
Excerpts from Ricardo's Journal

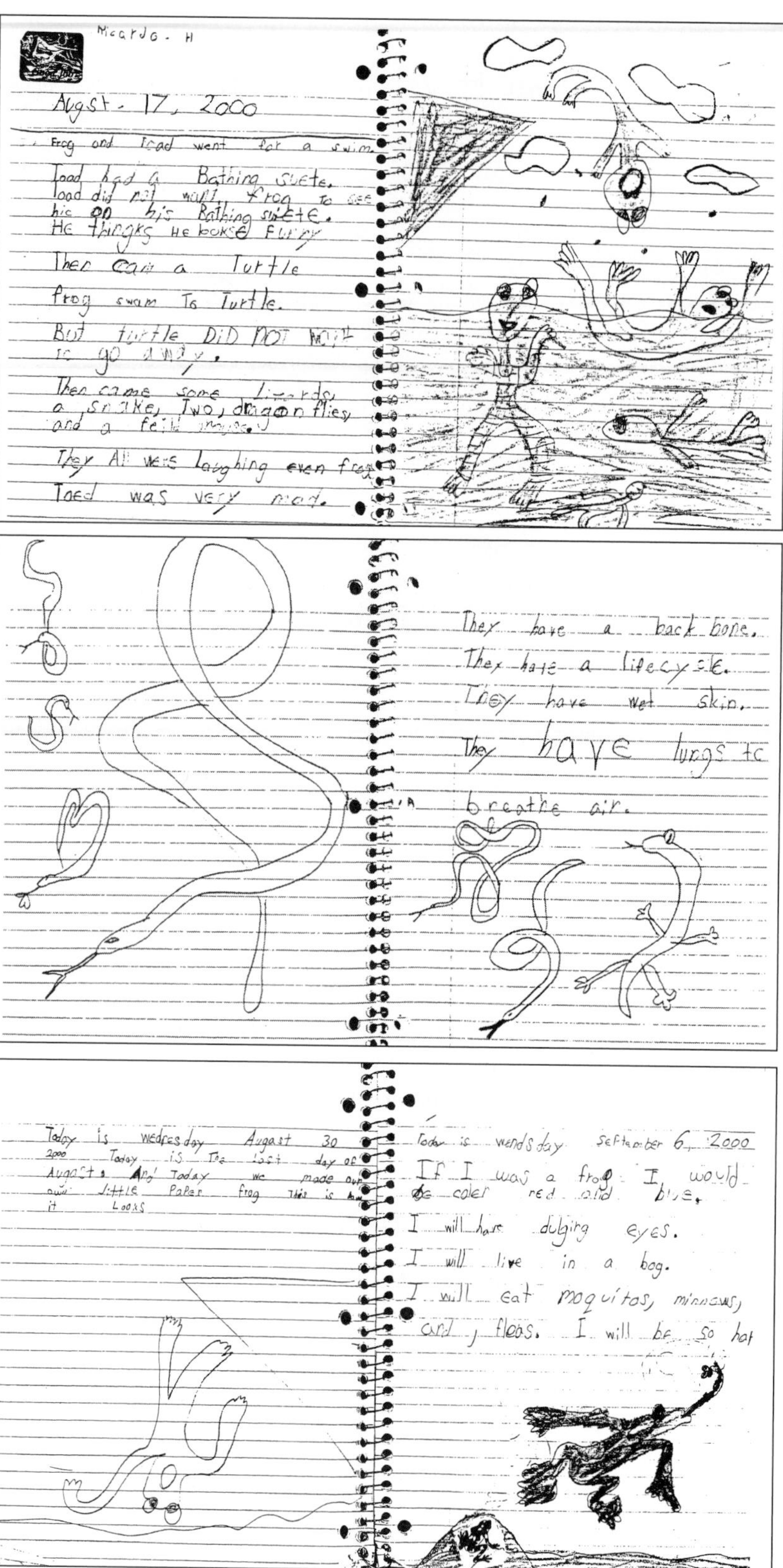

Ricardo. H
Augst. 17, 2000
Frog and Toad went for a swim.
Toad had a Bathing suete.
Toad did not want Frog to see him on his Bathing suete.
He thingks He lookse funny
Then cam a Turtle
frog swam To Turtle.
But turtle DiD NOT want to go away.
Then came some lizards, a snake, Two, dragon flies and a feild mouse.
They All were laughing even frog
Toed was very mad.
They have a back bone.
They have a lifecycle.
They have wet skin.
They have lungs to breathe air.
Today is wednesday August 30 2000 Today is The last day of August. And Today we made our own little Paper frog This is how it Looks
Today is wendsday September 6, 2000
If I was a frog I would be coler red and blue.
I will have bulging eyes.
I will live in a bog.
I will eat moquitos, minnows, and fleas. I will be so hap

FIGURE 5 (continued)
Excerpts from Ricardo's Journal

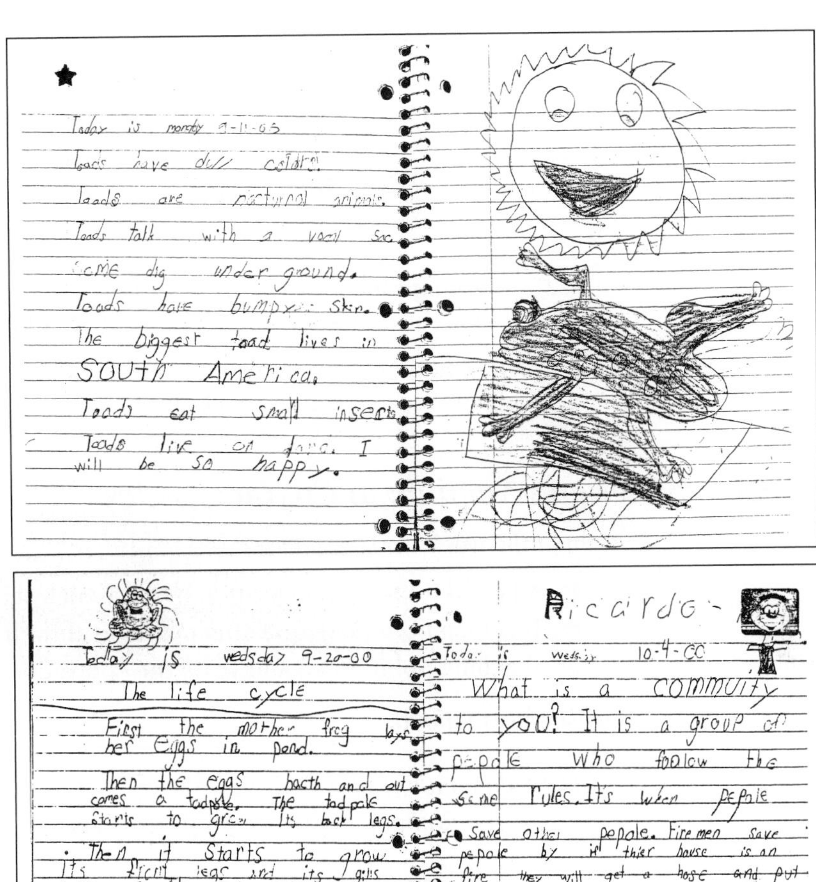

Today is monday 9-11-00
Toads have dull colors.
Toads are nocturnal animals.
Toads talk with a vocal sac.
Some dig under ground.
Toads have bumpy skin.
The biggest toad lives in South America.
Toads eat small insects.
Toads live on land. I will be so happy.

Today is wedsday 9-20-00
The life cycle
First the mother frog lays her eggs in pond.
Then the eggs hacth and out comes a tadpole. The tadpole starts to grow its back legs.
Then it starts to grow its front legs and its gills dissappear. Its tail gets shorter and the lungs develop. Now the tadpole can live on land and water because its an Adult now!

Ricardo
Today is Wedsday 10-4-00
What is a commuity to you? It is a group of pepole who foolow the same rules. It's when pepole save other pepole. Fire men save pepole by if their house is on fire they will get a hose and put the fire out.

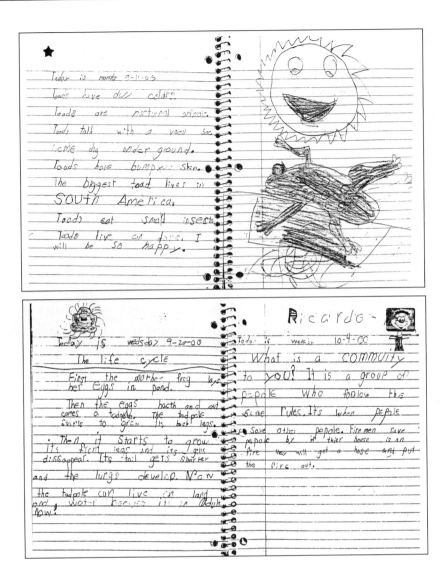

Guided reading, independent reading, activity centers:

- Teachers select appropriate text for each group of children.
- Each day the teachers meet with four groups.
- First-grade-level groups meet every day, grade-level groups meet every other day.
- Teaching points are determined by each individual text and teacher's observations of children's reading. In general, teachers strive for oral fluency and comprehension of text during discussion.
- During the first week of the unit, independent reading texts used are from the previous weeks of guided reading and do not relate to the unit.

- During the first week of the unit, activity centers include:

  Library corner, which also displays a collection of unit books, including wordless books by Mercer Mayer,

  Science center, which houses an aquarium set up as a habitat for several small frogs,

  Listening station, with a tape recorded book about frogs and toads, and a

  Writing center, with a variety of papers, writing implements, and an interesting display of pictures of amphibians.

As new activities are introduced during the week, the teachers place that activity in a center to let children explore further.

Week 2—Salamander and Amphibian Characteristics

Poem of the week—salamanders:

- Adapted from a poem written by a parent volunteer (see Figure 6)
- Teaching point: Use question marks to show a question.
- Teaching point: Read and write the contraction *you're.*

Mediated read-aloud:

Fiction

The Salamander Room, by Anne Mazer

Would You Rather be a Bullfrog? by Dr. Seuss

FIGURE 6

Week 2—Poem of the Week

Salamander, Salamander

Salamander, salamander,
Where do you hide?
Under rocks in the woods,
Wiggling side to side.

You look like a lizard,
But like frogs, toads, and caecilians,
You're in a family
Called amphibians.

(adapted from a poem by Mrs. Cassas)

Tuesday, by David Wiesner (almost wordless, great for encouraging predictions)

Frog and Toad Together, by Arnold Lobel

Frog Goes to Dinner, by Mercer Mayer (wordless)

Information

A Salamander's Life, by John Himmelman

Sneaky Salamanders, by Suzanne Paul Dell'Oro with Andres Varela-Paul

Salamanders Secret, Silent Lives, by Sara Swan Miller

Extremely Weird Frogs, by Sarah Lovett

Frogs, by Kevin Holmes

Interactive writing—amphibian characteristics:

- Same procedure as week 1
- Verbal composition by children, children take turns writing a word or partial word, while others discuss spelling patterns and word knowledge needed to compose. (see Figure 7)
- Self-monitoring strategies are encouraged.

Guided writing—journals:

- As children have had some opportunity to build vocabulary, the teachers provide a "word splash" for guided writing. A word splash is a half-page of words "splashed on to the paper." Children compose sentences using the vocabulary. They are encouraged to relate the sentences to the content of the unit. (see Figure 8)
- Teachers continue to encourage children to use their knowledge to write facts about amphibians, to imagine themselves as one of the amphibians being studied. (see Figure 9)

FIGURE 7

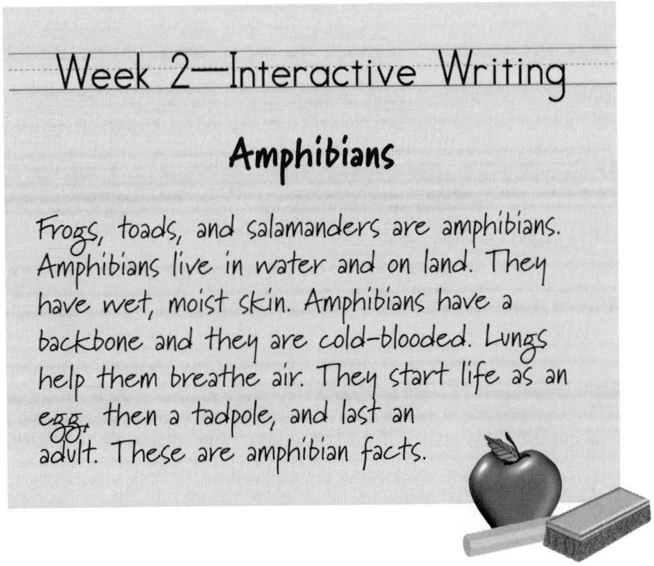

Week 2—Interactive Writing

Amphibians

Frogs, toads, and salamanders are amphibians. Amphibians live in water and on land. They have wet, moist skin. Amphibians have a backbone and they are cold-blooded. Lungs help them breathe air. They start life as an egg, then a tadpole, and last an adult. These are amphibian facts.

FIGURE 8

Karen's Word Splash

insects
egg
toad
smooth
tadpole
frog
amphibian
sticky
bulging
webbed
bumpy

Karen's word splash

Tadpoles are baby frogs or toads.
Toads and frogs have sticky toungs.
Toads have bumpy skin.
Mother frog/toad lays her eggs in the pond. Frogs have smooth skin.

Frogs and toads have webbed feet.
Toads and frogs have bulging eyes.
Frogs, toads and salamanders are amphibians

Ricardo's Word Splash

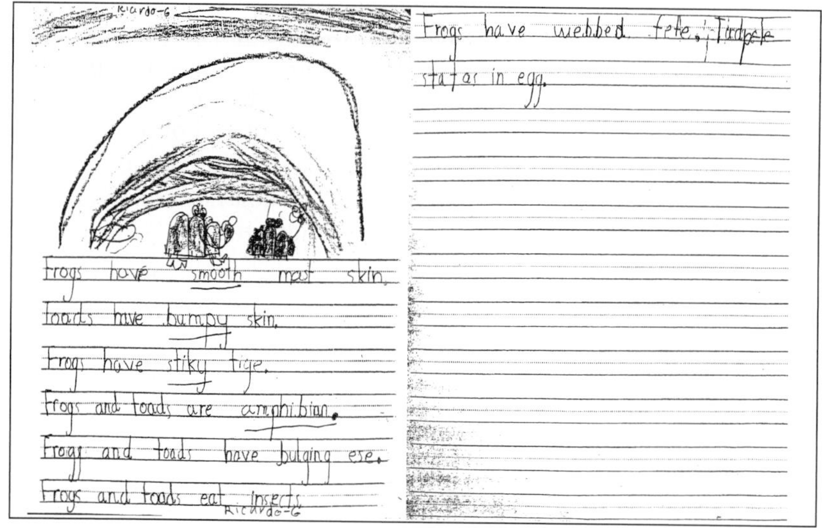

Frogs have smooth skin.
toads have bumpy skin.
Frogs have stiky tiqe.
Frogs and toads are amphibian.
Frogs and toads have bulging ese.
Frogs and toads eat insects
Frogs have webbed fete.
stat as in egg.

***Literature study*—Frog and Toad Are Friends:**

- Whole-class read-along is one chapter per day.
- Discussion/response begins with a focus on friendship.
- As children gather background about frogs and toads, discussion focuses on comparing/contrasting real frogs and toad with make-believe.
- Buddy rereading is encouraged during afternoon activity center time.

FIGURE 9
Excerpts from Karen's Journal

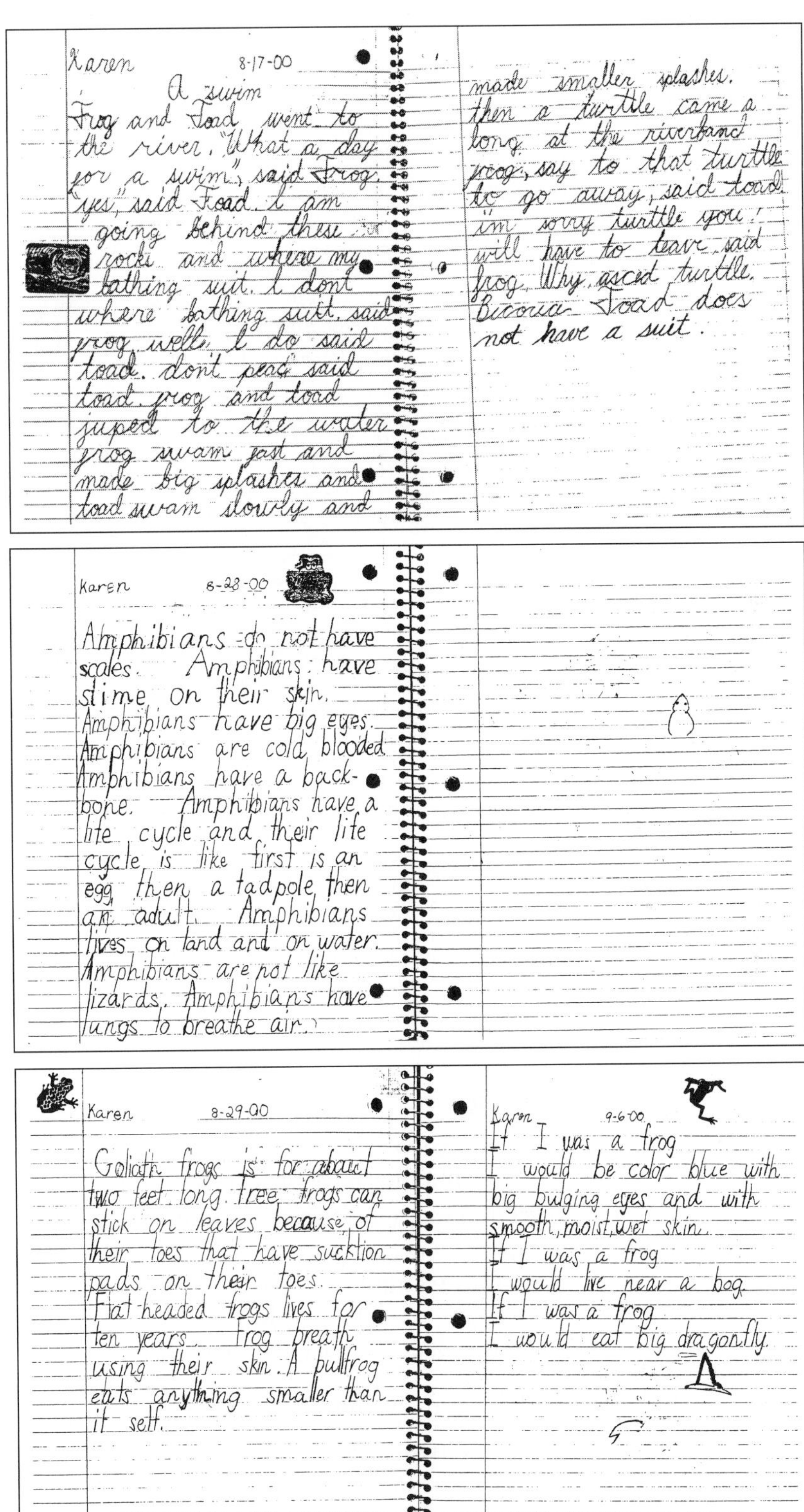

Karen 8-17-00

A swim

Frog and Toad went to the river. "What a day for a swim", said Frog. "yes", said Toad. I am going behind these rocks and where my bathing suit. I dont where bathing suit, said frog. well. I do said toad. dont peak said toad. frog and toad juped to the water frog swam fast and made big splashes and toad swam slowly and made smaller splashes. then a turtle came a long at the riverband frog, say to that turtle to go away, said toad i'm sorry turtle you will have to leave, said frog. Why asced turtle. Bicozia Toad does not have a suit.

Karen 8-28-00

Amphibians do not have scales. Amphibians have slime on their skin. Amphibians have big eyes. Amphibians are cold blooded Amphibians have a back-bone. Amphibians have a life cycle and their life cycle is like first is an egg then a tadpole then an adult. Amphibians lives on land and on water. Amphibians are not like lizards. Amphibian's have lungs to breathe air.

Karen 8-29-00

Goliath frogs is for about two feet long. tree frogs can stick on leaves because of their toes that have sucktion pads on their toes. Flat headed frogs lives for ten years. Frog breath using their skin. A bullfrog eats anything smaller than it self.

Karen 9-6-00

If I was a frog
I would be color blue with big bulging eyes and with smooth, moist, wet skin.
If I was a frog
I would live near a bog.
If I was a frog
I would eat big dragonfly.

FIGURE 9 (continued)
Excerpts from Karen's Journal

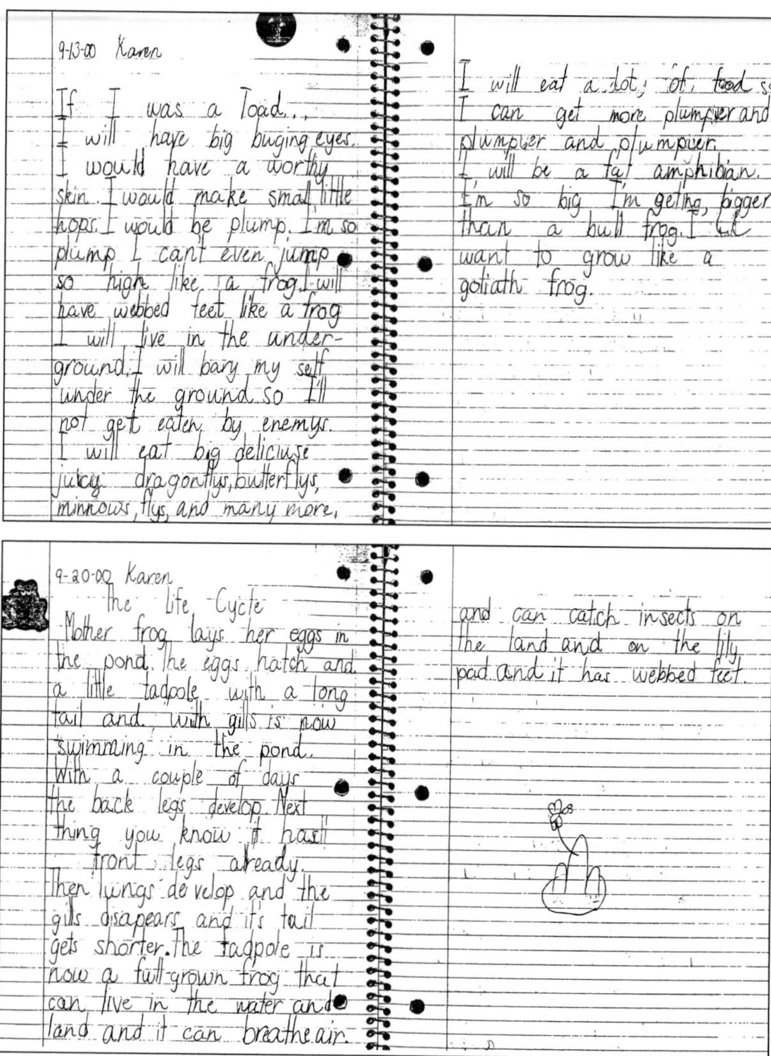

9-13-00 Karen

If I was a Toad...
I will have big buging eyes. I would have a worthy skin. I would make small little hops. I would be plump. I'm so plump I can't even jump so high like a frog. I will have webbed feet like a frog. I will live in the under-ground. I will bary my self under the ground so I'll not get eaten by enemys. I will eat big deliciuse juicy dragonflys, butterflys, minnows, flys, and many more, I will eat a lot of food so I can get more plumper and plumpuer and plumpuer. I will be a fat amphibian. I'm so big I'm geting bigger than a bull frog. I want to grow like a goliath frog.

9-20-00 Karen

The Life Cycle
Mother frog lays her eggs in the pond. The eggs hatch and a little tadpole with a long tail and with gills is now swimming in the pond. With a couple of days the back legs develop. Next thing you know it has front legs already. Then lungs develop and the gils disapears and it's tail gets shorter. The tadpole is now a full-grown frog that can live in the water and land and it can breathe air and can catch insects on the land and on the lily pad and it has webbed feet.

Shared writing—response to Frog and Toad's friendship:

- Near the end of the week, children compose their response to the friendship they have observed between Frog and Toad. (see Figure 10)
- Shared writing is used to maximize instructional time.
- Ideas in the composition have been discussed over the week of literature study.
- Teachers model composing a well-organized paragraph, with topic sentence, supporting details, and a concluding statement.

Whole-class word building:

- Use the letters in the word *lizards* to build *is, as, ad, ads, sad, lad, lid, lids, lads, rail, sail, sails, lizard, lizards.*
- Use the letters in the word *salamander* to build *as, man, land, sand, lean, leans, mean, dream, dreams, near, dear, salamander.*

FIGURE 10

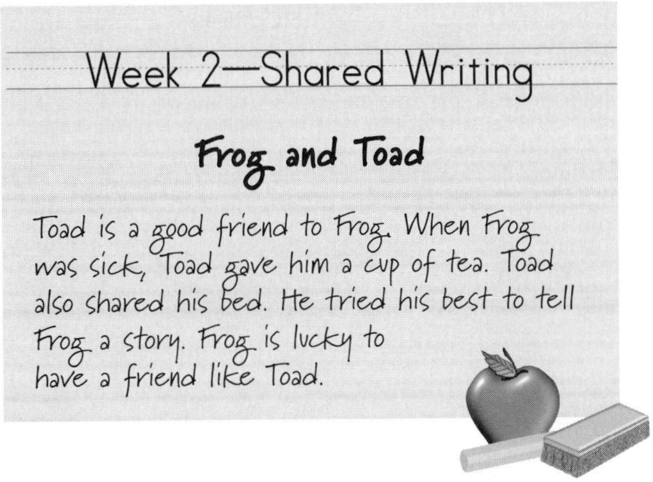

Week 2—Shared Writing

Frog and Toad

Toad is a good friend to Frog. When Frog was sick, Toad gave him a cup of tea. Toad also shared his bed. He tried his best to tell Frog a story. Frog is lucky to have a friend like Toad.

Guided reading, independent writing, activity centers:

- Same basic procedure as week 1.
- During week 2 of the unit, independent reading texts are a combination of previous weeks of guided reading texts, including texts from week 1.
- During week 2 the activity centers include:

  Library corner, which also displays a collection of unit books, with the addition of books from the Frog and Toad series by Arnold Lobel,

  Science center, which now houses two aquariums for observation. One set up as a habitat for several small frogs and one for a salamander. Children are encouraged to record observations in a science center log,

  Listening station, with a tape recorded book about salamanders,

  Writing center, with a variety of papers, writing implements, and an interesting display of pictures of amphibians, and

  Narrated drawing of the frog from week 1 with individual copies of a frog drawing and a toad drawing for children to narrate/label.

Week 3—Life Cycles

***Poem of the week—tadpoles,* Tadpoles:**

- Teaching point: Use a pronoun to stand for a noun. (see Figure 11)
- Teaching point: Use words that signal sequence (first, then, finally).
- Longer words have more chunks (clap syllables, count chunks, compare long and short words).

Mediated read-aloud:

Fiction

Toad on the Road, by Jon Buller

Can You Jump Like a Frog? by Marc Brown

Frog and Toad are Friends

FIGURE 11

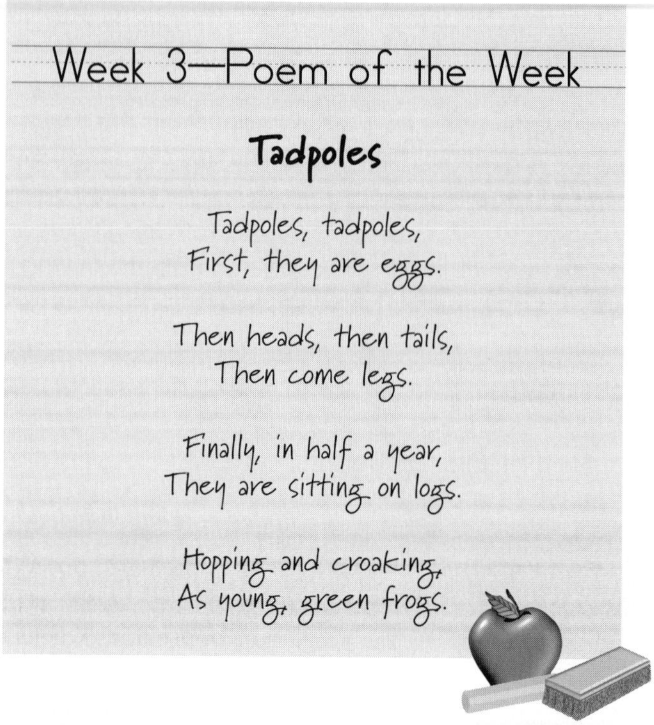

Week 3—Poem of the Week

Tadpoles

Tadpoles, tadpoles,
First, they are eggs.

Then heads, then tails,
Then come legs.

Finally, in half a year,
They are sitting on logs.

Hopping and croaking,
As young, green frogs.

The Frog and Toad Pop-up Book
Frog, Where Are You? by Mercer Mayer (wordless)

Information

From Tadpole to Frog, by Wendy Pfeffer
From Tadpole to Frog, by David Stewart
The Life Cycle of a Frog, by John Williams
How to Hide a Gray Tree Frog and Other Amphibians, by Ruth Heller (very descriptive)
Climbing Tree Frogs, by Ruth Berman
A Wood Frog's Life, by John Himmelman

Interactive writing—life cycle:

- Same procedure as weeks 1 and 2 (see Figure 12)
- Verbal composition by children; children take turns writing a word or partial word, while others discuss spelling patterns and word knowledge needed to compose.
- Self-monitoring strategies are encouraged.

Guided writing—journals:
In addition to all of the possibilities proposed thus far:

- Children are asked to explain amphibian life cycles.
- Children are encouraged to write about the versions of *The Frog Prince* that have been studied. (see Kaylo's journal in Figure 13)

FIGURE 12

Week 3—Interactive Writing

The Life Cycle

The mother frog lays her eggs in the pond.
When the eggs hatch, tadpoles swim around.
The tadpoles grow their back legs. The
tadpoles grow their front legs. The lungs
develop and the gills disappear.
The tail is gone. It's a frog!

FIGURE 13
Excerpts from Kaylo's Journal—Responses to *The Frog Prince*

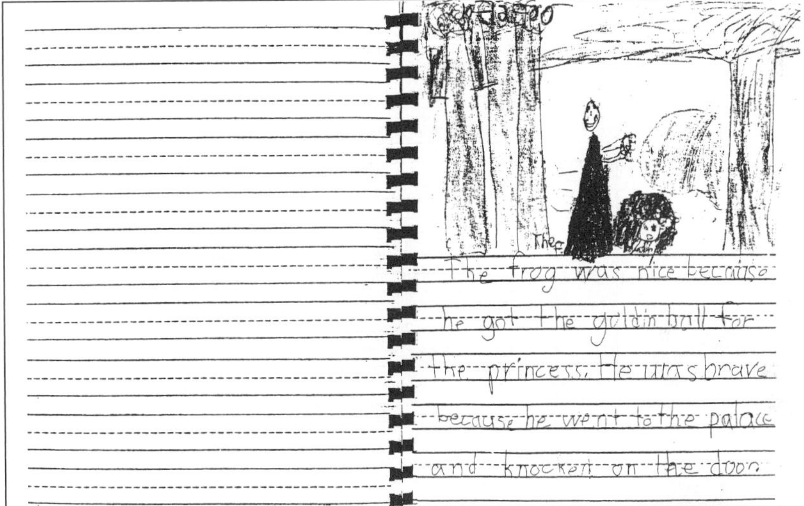

The frog was nice becaus
he got the guldin ball for
the princess. He was brave
because he went to the palace
and knocken on the door.

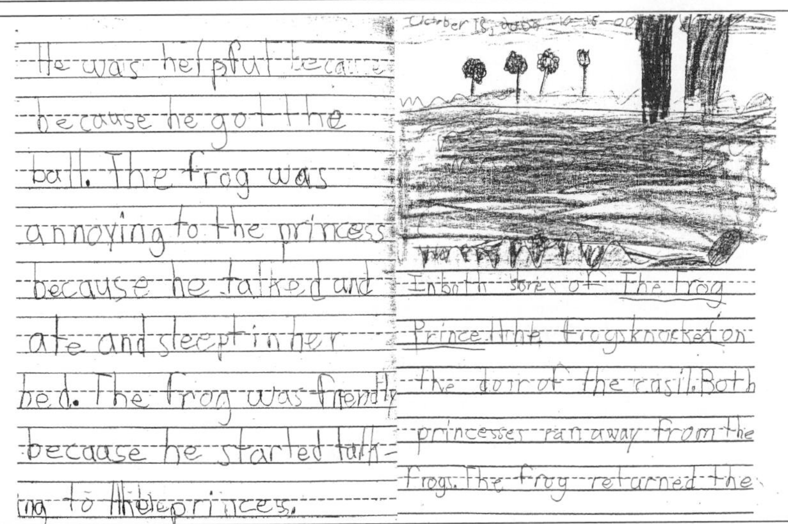

He was helpful because
because he got the
ball. The frog was
annoying to the princess
because he talked and
ate and sleept in her
bed. The frog was frendly
because he started talk-
ing to the princes.
October 18,
In both stories of The Frog
Prince the frogs knocked on
the dorr of the casil. Both
princesses ran away from the
frogs. The frog returned the

FIGURE 13 (continued)
Excerpts from Kaylo's Journal—Responses to *The Frog Prince*

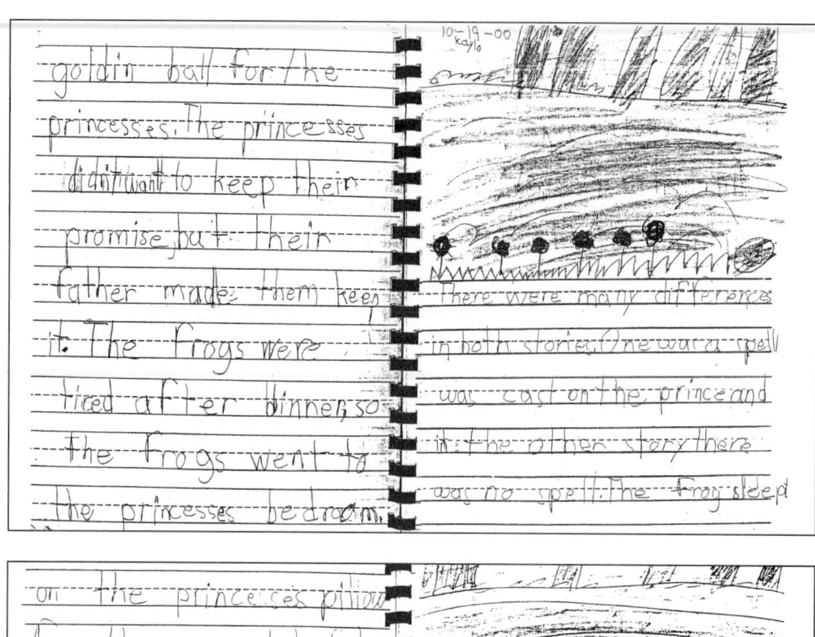

goldin ball for the princesses. The princesses didn't want to keep their promise but their father made them keep it. The frogs were tired after dinner, so the frogs went to the princesses bedroom.

10-19-00
Kaylo

There were many differences in both stories. One was a spell was cast on the prince and in the other story there was no spell. The frog sleep

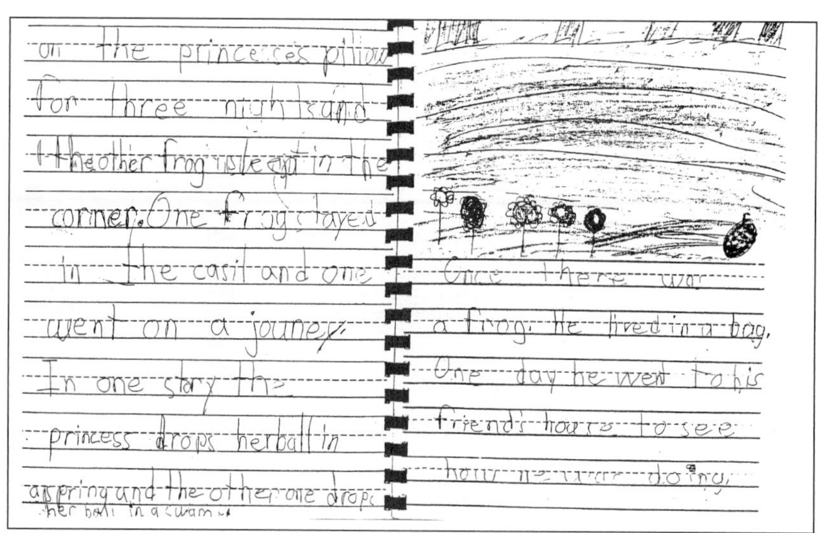

on the princeses pillow for three nights and the other frog slept in the corner. One frog stayed in the casil and one went on a jouney. In one story the princess drops her ball in a spring and the other one drops her ball in a swamp.

Once there was a frog. He lived in a bog. One day he went to his friend's house to see how he was doing.

When he got there, he knocked on the door. "Come in" said his friend. He went in. He saw his friend. He knew he was sick. He said "you will get better soon"

Whole-class literature study:

- Begin to study several versions of *The Frog Prince.*
- Whole-class read-aloud due to lack of multiple copies.
- Discussion of story elements—characters, setting, problem, solution.

Shared writing:

- Begin a story element chart (also called literary elements for older students) to help children remember the characters, setting, problem, and solution for each of the four books read aloud. (see Figure 14)
- The chart sets the stage for a Venn diagram during week 4 to carefully compare the two versions that emerge as the children's favorites.
- Shared writing is chosen to maximize use of time.

Whole-class word building:

- Use the letters in the word *tadpoles* to build *ad, tad, pad, pads, lads, let, pet, pets, pole, poles, tale, tales, told, late, plate, plates, pedal, pedals, tadpole, tadpoles.*
- Use letters in the word *prince* to build *in, pin, rip, pen, ice, rice, nice, ripe, pine, cried, price, prince.*

Week 3—Charting Story Elements for Versions of The Frog Prince

Book	Characters	Setting	Problem	Solution
The Frog Prince, Continued by Jon Scieszka				
The Princess and the Frog retold by Rachel Isadora				
A Frog Prince by Alex Berenzy				
The Frog Princess by Elizabeth Isele				

FIGURE 14

Guided reading, independent writing, activity centers:

- Same basic procedure as weeks 1 and 2.
- During week 3 of the unit, independent reading texts are a combination of previous weeks of guided reading texts, including texts from weeks 1 and 2. Now children have many related texts to reread.
- During week 3 the activity centers include:

  Library corner, which also displays a collection of unit books, with the addition of *The Frog Prince* versions,

  Science center, which now houses two aquariums for observation. One set up as a habitat for several small frogs and one for a salamander. Children are encouraged to record observations in a science center log,

  Listening station, with a tape recorded book of *The Frog Prince.*

  Writing center, with a variety of papers, writing implements, and an interesting display of pictures of amphibians, and

  Blank copies of a Venn diagram, for children to compare two amphibians. The Venn diagram that was prepared by the class in shared writing is also displayed.

Week 4—Writing Group Reports

Note: Due to the time needed for composing and editing the group reports, word study and literature study are deleted during week 4. Read-aloud includes only fiction, due to the guided and independent reading in information texts that children will do to gather information for their reports.

***Poem of the week*—Five Little Bumpy Toads:**

- Teaching point: What happens when we add *y* to words like *bump* to make *bumpy?* (see Figure 15)
- Teaching point: Use context to figure out the meaning of words like *burrowed.*

***Read-aloud/literature study—versions of* The Frog Prince:**
Fiction

The Princess and the Frog, retold by Rachel Isadora

The Frog Prince, continued by Jon Scieszka

A Frog Prince, by Alex Berenzy

The Frog Princess, by Elizabeth Isele

Shared writing—Venn diagram:

- To prepare for writing a paragraph about comparing two texts, the children participate in a shared writing to create a Venn diagram comparing the two versions. (see Figure 16)

Shared writing—a comparison:

- At the end of the week the children use ideas from the Venn diagram to explain the comparison between their two favorite versions of *The Frog Prince.* (see Figure 17)

FIGURE 15

Week 4—Poem of the Week

Five Little Bumpy Toads

Five little bumpy toads
Hopped across a bumpy road
To find some most delicious bugs.
Yum! Yum!

One burrowed under ground
Where it could not be found
Now there are four little bumpy toads.
Croak! Croak!

Continue to count down to zero toads.
(adapted from the song, "Five Little Speckled Frogs")

FIGURE 16

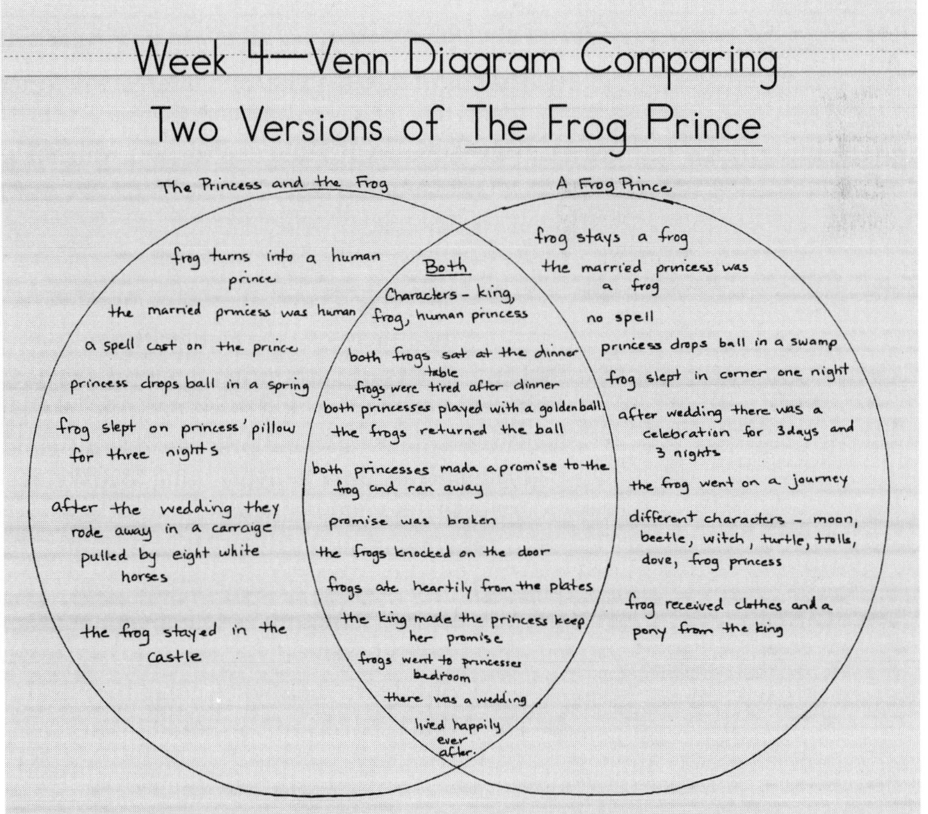

FIGURE 17

Week 4—Shared Writing

A Comparison

We compared two stories based on a book called The Frog Prince. In both stories some parts were different and some parts were the same. One difference was in one story the frog remains a frog, and in the other story the frog becomes a prince. One similarity was the king makes the princess keep her promise to the frog.

Guided writing—reports:

- Groups of mixed ability and interest are formed for amphibians, frogs, toads, salamanders, and caecilians.
- The class decides that each report will include a section about
    - characteristics,
    - habitat,
    - diet,
    - life cycle, and
    - identification (see Figure 18)
- Large blocks of time during the week are devoted to rereading, discussion, and writing to prepare the group reports.
- The teachers guide the process, helping children use their participation in shared and interactive writing to make decisions about the writing traits that should be included:
    - What ideas and content to include
    - How to organize their ideas
    - How to monitor use of conventional language to communicate their ideas
    - How to let their voice come through in the writing
- The group reports are presented to the class on Friday.

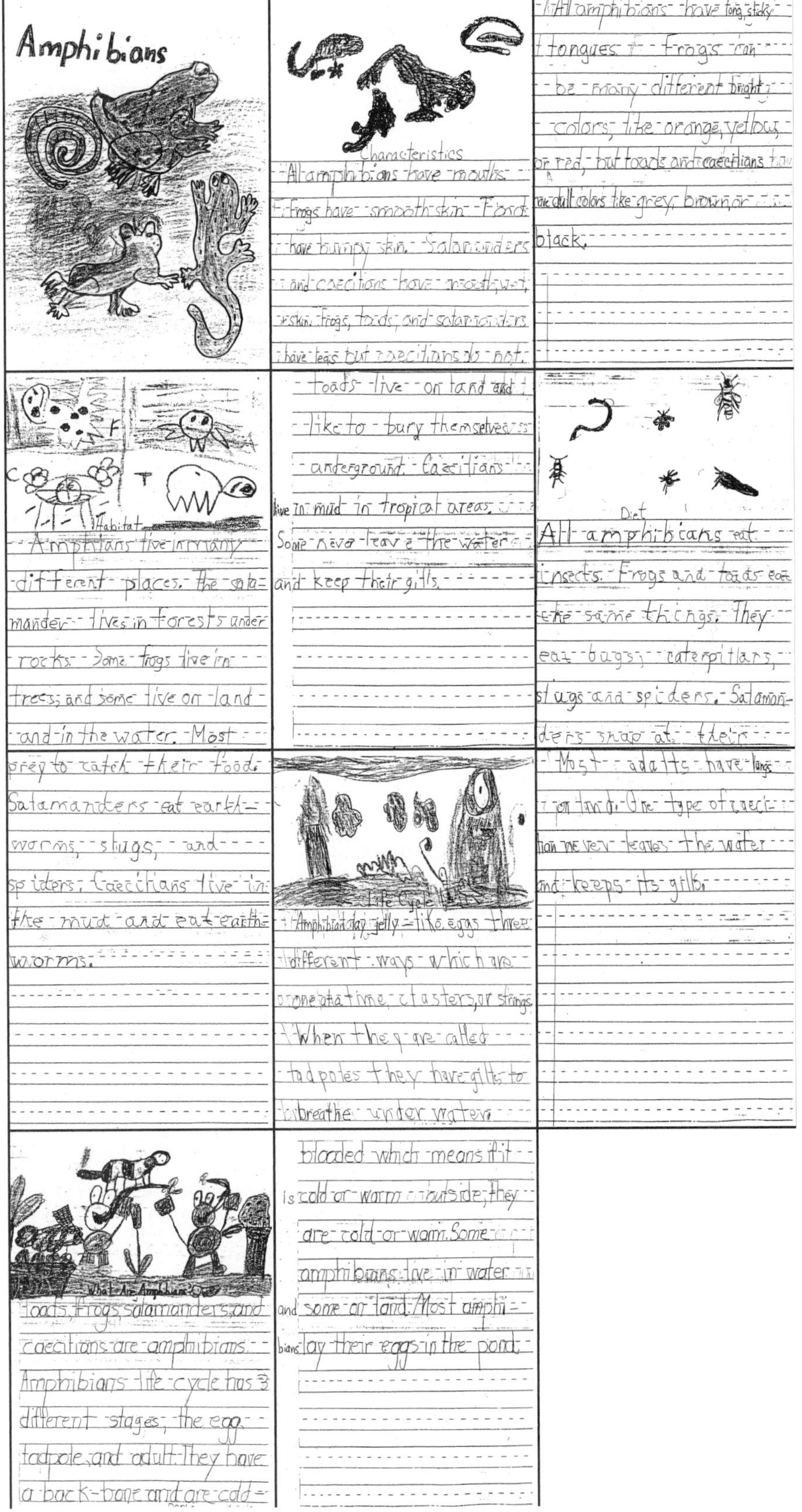

Amphibians
Characteristics
All amphibians have mouths. Frogs have smooth skin. Toads have bumpy skin. Salamanders and caecitions have smooth, wet skin. Frogs, toads, and salamanders have legs but caecitians do not.
All amphibians have long, sticky tongues. Frogs can be many different bright colors, like orange, yellow, or red, but toads and caecitians have dull colors like grey, brown, or black.
Habitat
Amphibians live in many different places. The salamander lives in forests under rocks. Some frogs live in trees, and some live on land and in the water. Most
toads live on land and like to bury themselves underground. Caecitians live in mud in tropical areas. Some never leave the water and keep their gills.
Diet
All amphibians eat insects. Frogs and toads eat the same things. They eat bugs, caterpitlars, slugs and spiders. Salamanders snap at their
prey to catch their food. Salamanders eat earthworms, slugs, and spiders. Caecitians live in the mud and eat earthworms.
Life Cycle
Amphibians lay jelly-like eggs three different ways which are one at a time, clusters, or strings. When they are called tadpoles they have gills to breathe under water.
Most adults have lungs on land. One type of caecitian never leaves the water and keeps its gills.
What Are Amphibians
Toads, frogs, salamanders, and caecitians are amphibians. Amphibians life cycle has 3 different stages, the egg, tadpole, and adult. They have a back-bone and are cold-
blooded which means if it is cold or warm outside, they are cold or warm. Some amphibians live in water and some on land. Most amphibians lay their eggs in the pond.

FIGURE 18
Group Book—Amphibians

Guided reading, independent writing, activity centers:

- Same basic procedure as previous weeks.
- During this final week of the unit, independent reading texts are a combination of previous weeks of guided reading texts. Children have at least six related texts in the book box to reread.
- During week 4 the activity centers include:
    - *Library corner,* which also displays a collection of unit books, including the versions of *The Frog Prince,*
    - *Science center,* with two aquariums for observation. One set up as a habitat for several small frogs and one for a salamander. Children are encouraged to record observations in a science center log,
    - *Listening station,* with tape recorded copies of the favorite books of the unit,
    - *Writing center,* with a variety of papers, writing implements, and an interesting display of pictures of amphibians, and
    - *Pocket chart,* for putting sentence strips with the stages of the life cycle in order. Individual copies of a cut-and-paste activity to put the stages of the life cycle in order and illustrate.

CONCLUDING THOUGHTS

Throughout Making Connections we observe how four second-grade teachers weave together the components of a balanced literacy program to provide their students with rich and meaningful learning experiences. To learn more about each individual component we can revisit Chapters 2 through 10, then compare our understandings with the ways in which these teachers utilize each component. We must remember that orchestrating literacy components in a balanced and effective manner develops slowly over time as we continue to gain a greater understanding of children's literacy development.

Appendix A

Handbook of Children's Literature

I. Genres of Children's Literature

Lukens (1998) defines genre as a "kind or type of literature in which the members share a common set of characteristics" (p. 13). There are different genres in literature because writing is used for different purposes or intentions. You will encounter the following genres in children's literature:

- contemporary realistic fiction
- historical fiction
- fantasy
- folk literature
- biography and autobiography
- information
- poetry

An author's intention or purpose influences the organization of ideas in particular ways and the selection of words to serve particular purposes. With each genre, you may find similarities and differences in the ways that authors share their ideas, but you will also find that each genre is unique in some way.

Contemporary Realistic Fiction

It is necessary for each of us to learn about our own world. Realistic fiction enables children to explore the reality of their lives and the lives of others. In quality realistic fiction, authors create the following:

- Believable characters who think and act like people who are or could be known to us
- Contemporary settings that could exist and support the telling of a believable story
- Plots and themes that reflect contemporary issues, problems, and values
- Stories that are appropriate for the audience for whom they are intended

Realistic fiction is found in both picture book and chapter book forms and should be an essential part of your literature program. Picture storybooks such as *The Wednesday Surprise* (Bunting, 1989) let children explore the role they can have in helping a relative learn to read. As children follow the actions of the characters, they can think about people who care about and help others, do everyday things that we all do to live our lives, and work to solve problems to make their lives more satisfying. All of this is wrapped in a story of usually no more than thirty-two pages of print and illustrations.

In chapter books, children encounter more complex plot and character development, and continue to explore life situations. The Ramona series, including *Ramona Quimby, Age 8* (1981), by Beverly Cleary, has been a favorite of many schoolchildren. Primary-grade children watch Ramona grow and change through her own primary-grade years. Ramona's feelings and predicaments are often familiar and humorous. Similarly, the story of *Felita* (Mohr, 1989) lets children explore the dilemmas of a young Puerto Rican girl when her family decides to leave their old neighborhood. Both books are chapter books, and children are able to follow Ramona and Felita through 100+ pages of people and events that affect their lives. Chapter books bring contemporary realistic fiction to life for a reader.

Historical Fiction

Historical fiction bears a strong resemblance to contemporary fiction. Both are realistic, differing mainly in the impact of the setting on the telling of the story. When authors move to a time period other than their own, they are obligated to help readers understand how the time of the story affects the characters and the events of the plot. Writers of historical fiction must be true to the period in which they set the story. The characters do not have to be people that actually lived, but they must be realistic.

Historical picture books are available in limited number. One excellent example is *Nettie's Trip South* (Turner, 1987). The setting is the South, during pre–Civil War days. Although Nettie is a fictional character, the life that she lived is in keeping with lives of white children during that time. Through Nettie's letter to her friend Addie, children can explore what it might have been like to be confronted with the realities of slavery. Turner creates a fictional character in Nettie to share actual events from the life of Turner's great-grandmother as told in diary entries from 1859.

Many wonderful pieces of historical fiction are available in chapter book form. However, many will be challenging for the majority of primary-grade readers. One example of historical fiction that is appropriate for the primary grades is *Sarah, Plain and Tall* (MacLachlan, 1985), which tells the story of a mail-order bride from Maine who comes to be mother and wife for a pioneer family living on the plains. Through this family, children cannot only experience life in a time when modern conveniences were not available, but may also see that family relationships have always been important.

Fantasy

Fiction that contains elements not found in the natural world is called *fantasy*. Early fantasy comes in the form of picture books, with illustrations that help children develop images of fantastic people and places. Fantasy helps young children begin to distinguish what is real from what may be imaginary. Fantasy also helps young children think of possibilities beyond their everyday lives. In the picture storybook fantasy *Sylvester and the Magic Pebble* (Steig, 1969), a donkey family and a magic pebble help children explore the theme that love conquers all.

As children advance as readers, fantasy becomes more of an issue of other worlds and times, as in *James and the Giant Peach* (Dahl, 1961). Living in the imaginary world becomes a delight in itself, letting children explore the possibilities of what could be, without needing to distinguish what is "real." Children (and adults) may enjoy the fantasy for its own sake. Description takes the place of illustration, freeing children to create their own images of imaginary characters and worlds.

Quality fantasy rests on the author's ability to create a willing suspension of disbelief—imaginary worlds and characters must seem possible to the reader. In *Charlotte's Web* (1952), E. B. White roots his fantasy in the reality of farm life. He creates characters that seem so believable that the reader accepts animals talking and thinking as if they were human. While the reader knows that animals cannot actually behave in this way, the behavior is so integral to the story that the fantasy is not questioned.

Folk Literature

For as long as people have lived their lives with others, telling stories has been part of sharing the lessons of life. Folk literature has its roots in oral storytelling tradition. You are probably quite familiar with this genre of literature from your own background of reading in school. This category includes folktales, fairytales, fables, tall tales, myths, and legends. Myths and legends, however, are not widely used in primary-grade classrooms because of the frequent maturity of their content.

When storytellers share a story, they often concentrate on the development of the plot, using recognizable characters and settings. Because folk literature comes out of an oral tradition, it often has simple plots, rather stock characters with easily identifiable characteristics, and settings in "long ago" or "far away" times. Such stories usually have strong, clear, and often explicit themes that clearly teach a lesson or moral. Such explicit themes are helpful to young children, who are usually not yet able to judge behavior according to situational conditions.

One of the greatest values of folk literature is the possibility of sharing stories across cultures. For example, Cinderella stories, coming to us from different countries, let us see commonalities, as well as differences, across cultures. We can see similarities to the Cinderella tale that is familiar to most of us (Perrault, 1981) in such stories as the following:

- *Tattercoats* from England (Steele, 1976)
- *Mufaro's Beautiful Daughters* from Africa (Steptoe, 1987)
- *Moss Gown* from eastern North Carolina (Hooks, 1987)
- *Yen-Shen* from China (Louie, 1982)

Through folk literature, we are able to see that, across other time periods and cultures, life has taught many others the same lessons that we, too, have learned.

Biography and Autobiography

Biography, in which an author tells the story of another person's life, often mixes the accuracy of information texts with the literary elements of fiction. The writer of biography is obliged to accurately present the facts of a person's life while using an interesting writing style to bring that person to life for the reader. *Autobiography* is a firsthand account of a person's own life, and should be an accurate retelling.

The difficulty for the writer of biography for young children lies in telling stories out of a time period that is unknown to the young reader. To be appropriate and appealing to primary-grade children, authors often present biographies in picture book format with illustrations to support the text. Illustration can fill in information the reader needs to relate to unfamiliar settings and circumstances. David Adler has created a fine series of picture book biographies of famous Americans, such as Martin Luther King, Jr. and John F. Kennedy.

Authors of biographies for developing readers in third and fourth grade must also consider the match between the reader's life and the time period addressed in the biography. Through careful development of setting, character, and plot, biographers should help readers connect to time periods and living conditions that may be dramatically different from what they personally know. A good example is *Sadako and the Thousand Paper Cranes* (Coerr, 1977), the story of a young Japanese girl who survived the bombing of Hiroshima in 1945, but later died as a result of radiation from the bomb.

Autobiographies are more difficult to find for primary-grade children. A new series, called Meet the Author (published by Richard C. Owens), offers autobiographies of children's authors with particular emphasis on aspects of their lives that have influenced their writing. One example is *A Letter from Phoenix Farm* by Jane Yolen (1992).

Information Books

Children are curious about the world. Information books offer children opportunities to explore the world through both images and ideas. Quality information books should have photographs and/or illustrations that accurately depict a topic, such as Aliki's *How a Book Is Made* (1986). Young children should be able to gain content background through close inspection of the illustrations. The text of information books should be well organized, allowing developing readers to successfully think their way through text as you share it aloud.

Children's first information books often focus on familiar people, objects, or events. As children become acquainted with books, we want them to see that familiar things can be represented, first through photographs and illustrations and eventually through words. Alphabet, counting, and concept books for young children typically have limited amounts of text. Photographs or illustrations carry a great deal of the "message" of the book. The absence of text encourages interaction between the reader and the illustrations, particularly in early read-aloud experiences. For a good example, examine books by Tana Hoban or Bruce McMillan. These two authors use photography to help children relate to information available in the environment, such as shapes and pairs of things. For excellent information books with simple, clear drawings, consider books by Gail Gibbons, Richard Scarry, and Sandra Boynton.

Young children need extensive experiences with quality information books before you can expect them to read such books independently. Children must learn that the writing in information books is different than that in other genres. An author's intention for writing an information book about spiders and how they live is different than an author's intention when retelling a folktale about a spider, such as *Anansi and the Moss-Covered Rock* (Kimmel, 1988), in which Anansi uses his cleverness to outwit much larger animals. Different intentions lead to different styles of writing. Because the writing in information books is different, children should approach information books with different expectations than they have for stories. Later in this chapter you will have the opportunity to consider how different genres give us different types of writing.

Poetry

Children and poetry are a natural match. The sensations created by the ways that poets use language appeal to the sensory nature in young children. Watching young children at work and play has probably taught you that children love the sounds and the feel of language. Young children pick up a new word or jingle and repeat it many times to experience the sounds and sensations it produces. Poetic elements such as rhythm, rhyme, and repetition help to make language seem more concrete to young children because they can *feel* it.

Poetry that is appropriate for young children should invite them to become involved in "trying on" language. For young children, poetry should contain familiar objects and experiences, tell stories of the familiar, express familiar feelings, and contain rhythm, rhyme, and repetition. Poetic language for young children should be concrete, using words from children's background experience. Abstract poetry forms such as haiku or cinquain are best saved until children have developed their ability to deal with abstraction.

Children's favorite poets are often humorous ones, such as Jack Prelutsky and Shel Silverstein. Illustrated picture books of poetry such as *Tyrannosaurus Was a Beast* by Jack Prelutsky (1988) not only provide images through language but also through colorful illustrations. Collections of poetry can offer an in-depth exploration of one topic or a wide variety of topics and styles. Silverstein's collection *Where the Sidewalk Ends* (1974) is "credited with bringing more converts to poetry than any other volume" (Cullinan, 1989, p. 347).

Poetry has made its way into emergent reading instruction through predictable patterned texts, such as *Brown Bear, Brown Bear, What Do You See?* (Martin, 1983) and *The Napping House* (Wood & Wood, 1984). Developing readers meet poetry in book form through examples such as *Dancing with the Indians* (Medearis, 1991). You will find that the rhythm and rhyme of poetry provide support as children are learning the ins and outs of written language.

II. Narrative Writing: Becoming Aware of Literary Elements

You will often find narrative writing in the picture books and chapter books that primary-grade children will read. This writing is characterized by the use of the following literary elements:

- setting
- characters
- plot
- point of view
- theme
- style

In this section, we examine the literary elements used in children's literature and consider the importance of each. We will consider both picture and chapter books from the perspective of both literature and reading instruction. We will draw our examples most often from picture storybooks, because they provide excellent samples in a short text.

Setting

One of the first elements that a reader might notice in any text is the author's use of setting. Simply speaking, *setting* helps you develop a sense of time and place, but it is in reality much more. If you consider an author's intention for writing, you will understand setting's potential.

Types of Settings. In some stories, the author focuses on the development of characters, and where the story is taking place seems somewhat unimportant. In such cases, the setting is merely a *backdrop* and you may not pay much attention to it. The author probably intends for you to devote your attention to other elements in the story. The author creates a setting that does not exert much influence on the characters or plot. *The Terrible Thing That Happened at Our House* (Blaine, 1975) provides an example of a backdrop setting. As a reader, you realize where and when the story is taking place, but you also realize that the setting does not influence your attention to the conflict the main character is experiencing.

Functions of Setting. In contrast, the author may choose to use the setting in a more integral way. When settings are integral to the telling of the story, the setting actually plays a part in the story and can serve several different functions. Lukens (1998) writes that authors might use integral settings to (1) affect the mood of the story, (2) show a particular side of a character, (3) act as an antagonist, or (4) symbolize a figurative meaning. To explore these functions of integral settings, we focus on one picture storybook, *The Ghost-Eye Tree* (Martin & Archambault, 1985). In it, we may observe all of the functions of setting.

How setting affects the mood of the story is easy to see in *The Ghost-Eye Tree* because of the power of Ted Rand's illustrations. The placement of the illustrations on the page and the predominance of black and grays give an eerie feel to the story as you begin to read: "One dark and windy autumn night when the sun had long gone down. . . ." The teller of the story, a young boy, continues as we hear, "Oooo . . . . I dreaded to go. . . . I dreaded the tree. . . ." The mood is set. The setting already affects you as reader. You have expectations that the setting will be important to the upcoming events.

Sometimes an author uses a setting to illuminate a character, or show you a side of a character that might not be evident in any other way. You often see this when there is a person-against-nature conflict in a story. As you are introduced to the older sister in *The Ghost-Eye Tree,* you hear her call her younger brother a "'fraidy cat," the beginning of a conversation that shows the older sister's impatience with her brother's fear. As they return from fetching a bucket of milk and must pass by the dreaded tree, both children are scared by noises from the tree and run the rest of the way home. The boy discovers that he has lost his hat. The sister, realizing how important the hat is to her brother, returns to the tree to find it. Without the influence of this setting you might not have seen the softer, sympathetic side of the sister.

Settings can also act as an antagonist. Lukens (1998) defines *antagonist* as an opposing force to the *protagonist,* or main character. It is the conflict between the protagonist and antagonist that creates plot in most stories. In *The Ghost-Eye Tree,* the tension in the plot is based on the conflict between the setting and the characters. Without a setting that scared the children, they would likely not have behaved as they did.

While the setting creates a mood and brings out certain behaviors in the characters, you also realize that it represents more, that it symbolizes a figurative meaning. In *The Ghost-Eye Tree,* the darkness, the wind, and the cloudy sky suggest fear of the unknown. The ghost-eye tree itself, looking like the eye of a terrible monster, symbolizes evil. The reader senses the evil as the illustrations and the text reinforce the young boy's fear.

Characters

Many writers would say that characters are at the heart of their writing. Through the characters' actions and reactions the plot is created. Authors reveal their characters through description and dialogue. Characters come in a variety of types and serve different functions.

Learning about Characters. Readers learn about characters through description and dialogue. As you read an author's description of a character, you learn about the character's physical appearance, actions, possibly the character's thoughts, and, if the author is narrating the story, you will know what the author thinks about the character. Through dialogue, you "listen" to the character's words and also to what others say about the character. It is then your job as the reader to put these pieces of information together to form your own understanding of the character. As you begin to read *The Ghost-Eye Tree,* for example, you immediately meet the main character, a young boy, who will be narrating the story. To learn about the character of this young boy you will need to attend carefully to his words as he tells you about the dark autumn night, his older sister, and the task of getting a bucket of milk for his mother, which will take him by the dreaded ghost-eye tree.

Types of Characters. Characters are described in part by how much the reader knows about them. When an author focuses a story around one or two characters, you often know much about them. Characters about which readers come to know many different aspects are referred to as *round* characters. Main characters are often round, because readers need information about them to buy into the plot. In picture storybooks that focus mainly on developing the plot or that are drawn from a genre such as folk literature that uses stock characters, you may learn very little about some characters. Such characters are called *flat* characters. Both the sister and brother in *The Ghost-Eye Tree* are round characters; you learn a great deal about them through dialogue and the brother's telling of the story. In contrast, the mother is a flat character; you really don't need to know much about her to understand her role in the story.

Characters can also be described by how much they change during the development of the plot. The events of the plot affect some characters, and you can see how they grow and change as a result of their experiences. Characters that change are referred to as *dynamic* characters. In contrast, some characters show consistent traits throughout a story. These *static* characters can be like the people in your life that you depend on to always be a certain way, or like the type of people who remain unchanged by life's events. Depending on the duration of the plot, the author may need both types of characters to tell a believable story. As you follow the brother and sister in *The Ghost-Eye Tree* as they get a bucket of milk, you see two consistent characters: The young boy tries to overcome his fears while the older sister keeps trying to show him that his fear is in his mind. Throughout the episode you see glimpses of softness and caring in the older sister, especially when she goes back to get her brother's hat. You do not see a (dynamic) character change because the duration of the plot, one night, is too short to realistically expect to see change in a person.

Two other types of characters that you are likely to meet in various genres are the stereotyped and the anthropomorphic characters. When authors describe characters as if they represent generalized characteristics of a group rather than as developed individuals, we say the character is *stereotyped.* In folk literature, stereotyped characters such as evil witches are common because one intent of the genre is to teach lessons about life and readers must easily identify character traits. In contrast, you would not want stereotyped characters in realistic fiction because the author should be developing individuals who are unique and believable. Any characters, whether round, flat, or stereotyped, that are animals that act like humans, are called *anthropomorphic* characters. This type of character is often found in fantasies when the author wants the reader to suspend disbelief and respond to a world created by the author.

Functions of Characters. As part of using characters to create an interesting story, an author can consciously use characters to serve specific purposes. The author will usually develop a main character, referred to as the *protagonist,* who leads or propels the action. To keep the plot moving along, the author will also create an *antagonist,* an opposing force(s) that pushes or challenges the main character. Sometimes (as noted previously) the opposing force is the setting, but most often it is another character.

Characters also serve a third function, that of a *foil.* When the author needs to push the protagonist in a particular direction or cause characters to show a particular side of themselves, but the antagonist cannot serve that purpose, the author will create a character with a limited and short-lived role. This character, a foil, has a specific purpose and will usually disappear after serving that purpose.

Unity between Characters and Actions. As you read, you look for consistency between characters and their actions. A well-developed character's actions should fit with what you have learned about that person. How you view the character should suggest possible behaviors that you would expect. This unity of character and action is part of what makes a story believable. If an author wants the reader to invest belief in a character, unity is vitally important, especially in the genres of realistic and historical fiction, fantasy, and biography.

Plot

Plot gives structure to a story. Plot organizes the telling of the story in a chronological fashion. The actions and reactions of the characters create problems and tensions that build toward a resolution.

Types of Plots. As authors move characters through a series of actions and reactions, two basic types of plots emerge: progressive and episodic. In a *progressive* plot you sense when the author builds the tension between characters and events as the plot develops. *Where the Wild Things Are* (Sendak, 1963) is a good example of a progressive plot in a picture book. You follow Max from his bedroom to the island where he finds the wild things, then back to his bedroom. In a chapter book, a progressive plot usually keeps you involved from chapter to chapter, anticipating what will happen next. *Charlotte's Web* (White, 1952) is an example of a progressive plot in which the author involves you in the trials and tribulations of life, friendship, and death.

In contrast, an *episodic* plot focuses on one life event in a picture book, and seems to begin anew with each new chapter in a chapter book. As a reader, you probably do not feel the same type of tension in the development of an episode. While you follow a main character or two, each chapter is usually a new episode in the character's life and is not necessarily linked directly to the previous chapter. *The Ghost-Eye Tree* is a good example of one episode that is developed into a picture storybook. The Little House books by Laura Ingalls Wilder are examples of episodic plots in chapter books, with each chapter beginning a new episode that may or may not be connected to the previous episode/chapter.

Order in Plots. Probably one of the most noticeable aspects of plot is order. For most stories, it makes sense for an author to tell the story in a *chronological* order. *The Ghost-Eye Tree* is an example of a chronological plot. You have a stronger interest in the feelings of the brother and sister after following their milk-getting adventure that takes them past the dreaded tree. A chronological plot allows you to have time to build a relationship with the author and characters. Sometimes it is easier for an author to "hook" you by beginning the telling of a story after the event has taken place, then reconstructing a portion or all past events for you. Such a *flashback* plot can be seen in *The Day Jimmie's Boa Ate the Wash* (Noble, 1980), where the story opens at home after a school field trip is over, then reconstructs the story a young girl tells her mother about the exciting day. The illustrator, Steven Kellogg, helps to make the flashback understandable to young children by showing the beginning of the retelling in thought bubbles above the heads of the characters. The thought bubbles gradually enlarge to become a full-page display of the flashback.

Action in Plots. Good stories keep readers or listeners engaged, waiting to find out what happens. The "what happens" is usually tied to the solving of a problem or dilemma that faces a significant character. As you follow the character through the plot, a skillful author builds in just enough action or tension to keep you wanting to see how the character resolves the problem. The author may structure the story using several literacy devices. Tension may build to a breaking point, called the *climax,* as you follow the characters. Some authors may choose to leave you at that exciting point, letting you decide how the problem resolved itself. Such a story is called a *cliffhanger.* Adults often enjoy this type of participation in a plot, but children can find the lack of closure unsettling. Consequently, you will not find many books for young children written in a cliffhanger style.

Realistically, most of the events of our lives do not climax, yet are interesting and can help us learn about life. Stories written in this manner have *tension,* but no climax. Exposure to such stories can help children appreciate the drama of their own lives as they watch others live. Realistic fiction is a genre that contains many such stories. *Nettie's Trip South* (Turner, 1987) is an example of a historical story with tension, but no climax. The author's intention was perhaps to help children consider the seriousness of slavery, and perhaps felt this was best accomplished without the added emotion of climactic events. Beverly Cleary's series of chapter books about Ramona also let children consider the realism and humor of life without dramatic conclusions. There is a building of tensions, however, that are a part of everyday life.

Some readers like the exhilaration of a climax, but prefer for the author to show how the characters reacted to the climax. This reaction, usually the conclusion of the story, is called the *resolution.* Authors can resolve a story in two ways: closed and open. A *closed resolution* leaves little doubt in your mind about what followed the climax. Bringing closure can be very comforting for young children who still see life as definitive and want to know "the answer." As a genre, folk literature, which developed out of telling stories about life, provides many good examples of closed resolutions. In *The Paper Crane* (Bang, 1985) for example, the author provides closure with the words, "But neither the stranger nor the dancing crane has ever been seen again." Realistic fiction also provides many good examples of closed resolutions in contemporary settings. *The Ghost-Eye Tree* lets you know how the young boy resolved his fear of having to go by the dreaded tree to get milk for his mother. In *The Terrible Thing That Happened at Our House,* you find out how the family coped with working parents.

In contrast, some authors end with an *open* resolution, leaving some doubt about the outcomes and letting you contribute to the ending. *The Day Jimmie's Boa Ate the Wash* and *Jumanji* (Van Allsburg, 1981) are examples of an open resolution following a climax. In both of these books you are aware of possibilities for future events, but the authors allow you to complete the story. Open resolutions are very effective with older children who are able to use their knowledge of life and story characters to carry on the story.

Conflict in Plots. Conflicts in our everyday lives influence many of our actions and reactions. You are probably aware of things that you do that are motivated by struggles and desires within yourself, with other people, with your environment, or with the conventions of society. Your life is influenced by the ways that you act and react with the conflicts you encounter. Because narrative tells the stories of people's lives, it naturally centers around the conflicts in which people find themselves. There are at least four types of conflict found in narrative:

conflict *with self, with people, with nature,* and *with society.* Without these conflicts, there can be no tension in a plot, because tension could not build to a point that requires a climax to resolve it. Without conflict, what would keep you interested in reading to find out what happens next?

As you read *The Ghost-Eye Tree,* did you sense the conflicts that helped the plot develop? You may see the conflict the boy had with himself, coping with his fear of the tree, and the conflicts he had with his older sister, not wanting her to think he was afraid. You also may see conflicts the children had with the dreaded tree and the spooky effects of wind and darkness. When you recognize these conflicts, you can better understand the actions of the boy and identify with him from times in your life when you experienced similar conflicts. By recognizing the conflicts and associating them with conflicts from your own life, you anticipate what he would do and can better understand his reasons for acting as he did.

The Ghost-Eye Tree shows you conflicts characters have with self, other people, and nature. *Nettie's Trip South* clearly shows you conflict with society. Nettie could not understand how the people of the South could treat slaves as they did. In her letter to her friend, Addie, Nettie expresses her conflict with Southern society's views of slaves.

Point of View

Types of Point of View. Considering who is telling the story becomes increasingly important as children are able to see things from the perspective of another. Young children see the world through their own eyes and often do not realize that others may see that same world differently. At this stage of development, it may be best to engage children with literature written from an objective perspective, allowing them to see all sides of an issue and not be influenced by the view of a particular individual who may be telling a personal version of the story. Sendak tells *Where The Wild Things Are* (1963) through an *objective narrator,* who seems to be suspended over the characters and setting, with the ability to see and hear all that goes on. The narrator introduces the characters and the setting, then proceeds to retell the dialogue and events as they happen. It is then up to you, the reader, to judge the value or meaning of the characters' actions.

If the narrator had allowed you to know the thoughts of one or more of the characters, in addition to knowing and hearing all that was done and said, the point of view would have been that of a *limited omniscient* narrator. In some plots it is important for you to know what a character, often the main character, is thinking to become more involved with the characters or to better understand a character's motivations.

As a contrast to the narrator's point of view, *The Ghost-Eye Tree* is told from the point of view of the young boy, a *first-person* point of view. You see all of the events of plot through his eyes. He interprets his sister's actions, the mood of the night, the fear of the tree, and his own feelings and actions. Is it possible that his view influences your reactions to the story? When you read a story written from a first-person point of view, it is important to realize that you are seeing one view of the events and that that view is influenced by the teller's feelings. Very young children may not understand the difference between a narrator's view and a single person's view of story events.

Point of view can influence the interpretations that your children make about characters and story events. When you share literature with children, you must consider who is telling the story and whether your children will be able to detect the influence of point of view on their personal interpretation of character actions and reactions.

Theme

Types of Themes. The themes of stories help us think about important aspects of life: friendships, loyalty, death, courage, cleverness, and so on. In some genres and among certain writers, the theme is rather *explicit*—its point is easy to detect. Folk literature often has explicit themes, especially in fables, which usually state a moral at the end. *Miss Rumphius* (Cooney, 1982) is an example of realistic fiction that provides an explicit theme: Do something to leave the world more beautiful. While very young, Alice Rumphius is told by her grandfather that during her life she must do something to make the world more beautiful. Through all of her travels Miss Rumphius remembers her grandfather's words, and finally discovers something she can do. You hear the theme again at the end of the story when Miss Rumphius tells her niece, "You must do something to make the world more beautiful."

The theme of *The Ghost-Eye Tree* is more of an *implicit* theme—one that you must infer from the characters' actions. As a reader, you make inferences based upon what you think is important about a story, influenced by your experience as a reader and in life. Because inference is involved in interpreting implicit themes, it is possible for different readers to "see" these themes differently.

As you select literature to share with children, you will want to consider the clarity of the theme or themes in a story and the possible interpretations that your students may make based on their experiences as readers and in life. Your expectations for what students will take from a story may be based on their ability to infer about life themes. Explicit themes are most appropriate for very young children, who see the world as either right or wrong. Implicit themes become more appropriate as children are able to understand and see the world from more than one perspective.

Style

For many of us, a writer's style can have a tremendous impact on our response to a story. Writers use language in distinctive ways, ways that can draw us in as readers or push us away. Style is an important element to consider when selecting literature for young children. Reading involves meaning making, which will be difficult for young children who cannot relate to the way that an author is using language.

Sentence Structure and Patterns. One of the first things you may notice about writing is the sentence *structure*. Are sentences complicated and confusing or fairly easy to follow? This is an important consideration when you are selecting literature to share with young children. Book language is more formal than spoken language, and books often introduce young children to sentence structures that they do not hear frequently in the language spoken in familiar surroundings. As you select literature you must consider how familiar your children will be with the sentence structures that a particular author uses.

Consider the sentence structure used by Eric Kimmel to introduce the folktale of *Anansi and the Moss-Covered Rock* (1988): "Once upon a time Anansi the Spider was walking, walking, walking through the forest when something caught his eye. It was a strange moss-covered rock." If you have read much folk literature this is probably a familiar opening to you. The nature of folk literature, drawn from storytelling, brings with it certain uses of language that can affect the structure and pattern of sentences. You would select this folktale to share with children in part on the basis of your children's experience with the language of folk literature.

Authors use words and sentence structures purposefully. For example, in *The Wednesday Surprise* (1989), Eve Bunting lets you know how Anna feels about her Grandmother when she says, "I show Grandma my breath picture, if it's still there. Mostly she knows what it is. Mostly she's the only one who does." In *The Snowy Day* (1962), Ezra Jack Keats arranges his sentences to show the reader something about the meaning of the words. For example, describing what Peter does in the snow, Keats says, "Then he dragged his feet s-l-o-w-l-y to make tracks."

Sentence *patterns,* found more and more frequently in books intended for very young children, provide children with repeated exposure to particular sentence structures. For example, you find the following pattern in *Brown Bear, Brown Bear, What Do You See?* (Martin, 1983):

> Brown Bear, Brown Bear,
> What do you see?
> I see a redbird
> Looking at me.

The same pattern continues as each new animal is introduced. Continuing the pattern allows young children time to develop comfort with understanding the structure of the sentences. While this is a simplistic example of pattern, you can see how predictability in sentence structure could aid a child's understanding.

Uses of Language. As you consider the maturity and experience that your children have with language, particularly book language, you will also consider the ways in which authors use words. Some authors will use words to help readers make mental images, or comparisons that are more concrete. Some authors will play with language in new and creative ways. Some authors will appeal to your senses through the use of language.

Imagery is the term most frequently used to describe an author's use of words to appeal to your senses. Imagery that reminds you of pleasant memories is likely to draw you in to listen to an author's ideas. You are reminded of childhood treasures when you read about Sylvester finding a pebble that "was flaming red, shiny, and perfectly round, like a marble" (*Sylvester and the Magic Pebble* [Steig, 1969]). Imagery can also be instrumental when an author is trying to help you understand situations in which you may lack firsthand experience. In *Nettie's Trip South,* Nettie struggles to explain in her letter to Addie her reaction to seeing slaves sold at auction: "Someone called out a price and she was gone.

Gone, Addie, like a sack of flour pushed across a store counter." In each example, imagery helps the author reach out to you, encouraging you to respond to the sensations that words can evoke.

You may wonder why imagery would be important for young children. You might ask, "Aren't primary-grade children too young to think about imagery?" The children with whom you will share literature are still very sensory in their responses to the world around them. They are curious about their world. If you are aware of an author's use of imagery to appeal to a reader's senses, you will be able to help children use their sensory responses with literature. You will call attention to interesting images as you read aloud. You will emphasize language that appeals to the senses. You will help children use images to build new understandings of the world they know and the world they are learning about each day. Imagery is especially important for primary-grade children.

Figurative language can be thought of as, "using words in a nonliteral way, giving them meaning beyond their usual, everyday definitions" (Lukens, 1990, p. 143). For young children, figurative language will also include personification and simile. Other figurative devices, such as metaphor, hyperbole, understatement, allusion, symbol, and puns, will require further maturation and are more appropriate for intermediate and middle school–age students.

Our language is full of multiple meanings and phrases that cannot be interpreted literally. Young children will need experience with language to appreciate an author's use of figurative language. In *The Wednesday Surprise,* Grandma surprises everyone by showing that she has learned how to read. To describe this situation Bunting writes, "Grandma *has the floor.* She . . . gives back the book and *beams all over her face* (emphasis added)." Bunting has used contemporary, yet figurative, language that cannot be interpreted literally. Young children will need experience with figurative language to fully appreciate many stories. Figurative language can also create humorous situations. When Amelia Bedelia, the maid, is asked to draw the drapes, she sits down with crayons and makes a picture of curtains at the window.

Young children who have been read to already have experience with *personification.* Many books for young children use anthropomorphic animal characters, which take on human qualities. Think of the classic tales of childhood—"Goldilocks and the Three Bears," "The Three Little Pigs," and "Little Red Riding Hood." The animals in these classic tales speak as humans, show human feelings, and live human lives. As young children interact with these anthromorphic, personified characters, it is possible that they will consider the realities of human behavior. Personification accentuates human behavior, calling attention to what might otherwise go unnoticed.

To accentuate the qualities of an object or person, an author may use a comparative relationship between unlike things. This comparison, called a *simile,* usually includes the words *as, like,* or *than* to show the relationship in a directly stated comparison. To accentuate the atmosphere on a plantation in *Netties's Trip South,* Turner says, "Trees were like old men with tattered gray coats." Trees and old men are certainly unlike things, yet Turner uses this comparison to help you sense what Nettie might have been feeling about the plantation. To emphasize the color of snow in *Owl Moon,* Yolen states that it "was whiter than the milk in a cereal bowl." Similes, which are rather explicit comparisons, are excellent stylistic devices to introduce to young children.

Devices of *sound* appeal to what readers find pleasing, such as onomatopoeia, alliteration, and rhythm. Children's interest in sound is evident in their play, as they chant jingles from television commercials and the like.

You will want to use books that feature *onomatopoeia,* descriptive words that mimic the sounds that people and objects make. *In The Snowy Day,* Peter hears his feet make *crunch, crunch, crunch* sounds as he walks in the snow. The wind *swishes* and *swoooshes* around the housetops in *Mirandy and Brother Wind.* Onomatopoeia can make descriptions more concrete for young children.

Alliteration is the repetition of initial consonant sounds to accentuate particular words and phrases. In *Owl Moon,* to set the mood for going owling on a cold winter night, Yolen writes, "Somewhere behind us a train whistle blew, long and low, like a sad, sad song." Do you notice how her repetition of words that begin with *l* and *s* adds to the mood she is trying to create? Alliteration is most effective when read aloud to children so they can appreciate the beauty of the language.

Using words to create *rhythm,* repeating cadences of sounds and syllables, in the phrases and sentences of a story can also appeal to the senses of young children and add to their appreciation of literature. Some rhythms are so obvious that children join the author and chant a particular part of a story. Children cannot resist the rhythm of, "they roared their terrible roars and gnashed their terrible teeth and . . ." in *Where the Wild Things Are.* This portion of the story soon becomes a chant that is often repeated long after the reading is over. A more subtle, yet equally effective, use of rhythm is found in *The Ghost-Eye Tree.* The young narrator asks,

> Why does Mama always choose me
> when the night is so dark
> and the mind runs free?

Rhythm combined with predictable sentence patterns makes excellent literature for emerging readers. The rhythm of language makes language patterns easier to remember for young children as they are learning to read.

As you select literature to share with children, you will want to consider the author's style of using words and anticipate how your students will respond to that particular style. Selecting appropriate literature for young children means more than finding content or plots that will be interesting or that focus on a particular topic. If children cannot relate to an author's style, they may miss much of what a book has to offer.

We have been discussing literary elements that authors use to develop narrative texts. Although this may be the dominant type of writing that children read before school, you will want to provide more balance in your class between narrative and information writing, because information writing is the writing most used for life purposes.

III. Information Writing: Becoming Aware of Text Structures

Information is available in many genres. *Bread Bread Bread* (Morris, 1989) and *What Will the Weather Be Like Today?* (Rogers, 1989) offer information embedded in poetic writing. The *Magic School Bus Inside the Human Body* (Cole, 1989) teaches science information through fantasy. Children learn about the act of writing through fiction in *If You Were a Writer* (Nixon, 1988). When compared with other genres, however, information writing offers contrasting structures for sharing an author's ideas. As information writers organize their ideas to describe, inform, persuade, respond, or compare, their writing takes on structures that are different from narrative writing.

Common Text Structures

Authors use several common structures or organization patterns repeatedly in information writing (Meyer & Freedle, 1984; Niles, 1974):

- comparison
- cause and effect
- description
- problem and solution or question and answer
- ordered list or sequence

Narrative writers describe life situations and problems by skillfully using literary elements to develop believable settings, plots, and characters that will touch your emotions and draw you into the story. Information writers also arrange ideas to serve their purpose(s) for writing. For example, to inform you about the dangers of pollution, an information writer may identify causes of pollution and inform you about the harmful effects or potential harm for humans and for nature. In contrast, an information writer whose purpose is to teach you how to determine if water is polluted will need to organize ideas differently, to list the procedures for testing samples of water.

Description. Paragraph [A] is an example of descriptive writing.

> [A] Life in a high desert town is quite nice. The sky is almost always blue and the sun shines more than 300 days of the year. The air is dry, so that even on hot days your skin does not perspire. The nights are cool, making summer evenings especially pleasant. Winters are mild, with limited snowfall. Snow melts quickly in the valley, but stays on the mountains that surround us to make a very pleasing sight.

In paragraph A, we find out about the characteristics of a desert town. The description does not have to be presented in a particular order for us to have an image of the town. In descriptive writing, there typically are very few clues to tell us how to arrange the ideas in a way that makes sense to us. All of the ideas together relate to the topic, but in no particular order. Descriptive writing requires us, the readers, to link the ideas. We know the topic and the details from the author. We must decide how the ideas are related.

Description can be difficult writing for children because they must establish the relationships among the details and the main idea. If the topic of the writing is unfamiliar, the task of linking ideas is more difficult. Unfortunately, much information writing in school is descriptive writing, in which children must learn to link the ideas.

Ordered List or Sequence. Paragraph [B] provide an ordered list of directions to follow.

> [B] The best way to see Lake Tahoe for the first time is to go west from Reno on Hwy 431. As you twist and turn your way up the Mount Rose Highway, you will

pass two downhill ski areas and several rustic restaurants. Soon you will pass the mountain summit and begin your descent into the Tahoe Basin. Next you will pass a large open meadow that is excellent for cross-country skiing. Just after you get your first glimpse of Lake Tahoe there will be a scenic overlook on the left side of the road. Stop there for a breathtaking view of the lake.

In paragraph [B], we can follow the order of the directions for the best way to get to Lake Tahoe. The author uses language suggesting that there is an order to follow. The directional words help us sense that order, such as "As you twist and turn . . ., Soon you . . . ., Next . . . ., and Just after . . . ." Directions are usually sequences of steps. Ordered lists or sequences are most understandable when they include language related to sequence or time. Without such language, we would need firsthand experience to understand the order.

Comparison. Paragraph [C] is an example of comparison text.

[C] When I am driving in my town, I can always tell what direction I am going by looking at the mountains. On the west side of town the mountains are higher and more rugged looking, and have more trees than the mountains to the east. Two of the mountains on the west stay snow covered most of the year and trees have been cut to make ski runs. The mountains on the east are very dry, brown, and rounded compared to the mountains on the west.

Paragraph [C] compares and contrasts the mountains on the east and west sides of a city to show how they are used to tell direction. Comparative words help us understand: *higher, more rugged, more trees.* Distinctive features that set each mountain apart are described. Do you see those contrasts? In comparison writing, the author establishes relationships between the objects or ideas being compared.

Cause and Effect. Paragraph [D] is an example of text that sets up a cause/effect relationship.

[D] A desert is considered to be a dry climate, with limited precipitation and low humidity. The result of limited precipitation is often a shortage of water in the hot, dry summer months when trees and grass most need moisture. The low humidity causes moisture to evaporate quickly from skin. The effect of this evaporation is dry, flaky, and sometimes cracking skin.

In paragraph D, the cause-and-effect relationship is evident as the author explains the effects of a dry desert climate. We can infer that the cause is the dry climate, because the effects of that climate are described. The order of the cause and the effects could have been reversed without altering the meaning of the paragraph. The emphasis, however, in this paragraph is on the effects. Sometimes in cause-and-effect writing, the author gives clues by using words such as *cause, effect, result,* or *because.* These clue words help us know which ideas to link together.

Problem and Solution. In paragraph [E] a problem and its solution are presented in the same text.

[E] During the winter months our town has "red" days when the air quality is hazardous to living things. To alleviate this problem, the city council requires that from November to March gas stations must sell a special gasoline that helps to reduce the particles that car exhaust puts into the air. People are also encouraged to car pool. In addition, no burning is allowed on "red" days because the particles in the smoke further contaminate the air.

In paragraph [E], by the time that we read the second sentence we are aware of being asked to think about a particular problem and some possible solutions. When we read the phrase, "to alleviate this problem," we might question whether we understand what the problem is and if more than one solution is possible. The author does not explicitly state what the problem is, although we do know the effect of the problem. In addition, we do know about solutions for the problem. Problem/solution and question/answer structures suggest that at least two parts must be understood. As the reader, we need to be sure that we understand what the parts are.

Text Structures in Children's Literature

Let us shift our focus to the actual use of different text structures in information books used by primary-grade children. In this section, you will consider two information texts, *Fire Fighters* (Maass, 1989) and *Rain Forest Secrets* (Dorros, 1990), as examples of how authors use text structures in book-length writings.

Fire Fighters begins with a question-and-answer paragraph about what firefighters do. What follows in just the first ten pages is a mixture of structures:

- A descriptive section about what firefighters must learn about hoses
- An ordered list to help the reader understand the procedure firefighters use to get water from hydrants to the fire
- A descriptive section about the tools that firefighters use
- An ordered list of a firefighter's training

Each time Maass changes the structure of the writing, you must adjust your thinking as a reader to follow his ideas. This means that in the first ten pages of *Fire Fighters* you had to change your thinking at least four times. These changes are part of what makes information writing so challenging for children.

As in *Fire Fighters,* in *Rain Forest Secrets,* Dorros tries to capture your interest in rain forests by first asking a question: "Have you ever been to a rain forest?" He then gives the following descriptions:

- a general rain forest environment
- rain forest location
- rainfall
- the Amazon River
- the ecology of the forest floor
- the canopy
- the understory
- uses of rain forest plants

The first twenty-three pages of text consist of detailed description, details about which the reader may lack experience and knowledge.

You will remember that in descriptive writing, the reader generally must link the ideas together. This means that the reader must be able to tell which ideas go together and which do not. Being aware that the structure of this book is predominantly description might lead you to help children learn how to organize the information in the descriptions so they may then use it. *Rain Forest Secrets* contains information that is important for children to have, but the structure of the writing may make the text inaccessible for many primary-grade children.

In thinking about these two examples, you can see that information writing will present challenges to you in your teaching of reading and writing. You must consider the structure of the writing and what readers must know to make sense of the author's ideas. Look carefully at how well the author helps readers to do this. Children deserve information writing that is considerate of their background as readers and that supports them as they try to learn from information text.

Description, ordered lists or sequences, cause and effect, problem/solution or question/answer, and comparison are the major text structures that you will encounter in information books for young children. Spend some time with your favorite information books to identify their structures. Try to become aware of how you detect and use the different information writing structures in learning.

Children's Literature

Adler, D. (1989). *A picture book of Martin Luther King, Jr.* New York: Holiday House.

Aliki. (1982). *We are best friends.* New York: Greenwillow Books.

Aliki (1986). *How a book is made.* New York: Cromwell.

Bang, M. (1983). *Ten, nine, eight.* New York: Crowell.

Bang, M. (1985). *The paper crane*. New York: Greenwillow Books.

Bayer, J. (1984). *A my name is Alice.* New York: Dial.

Blaine, M. (1975). *The terrible thing that happened at our house.* New York: Scholastic.

Blume, J. (1974). *The pain and the great one.* New York: Dell.

Blume, J. (1981). *The one in the middle is a green kangaroo.* New York: Dell.

Brett, J. (1989). *The mitten.* New York: Scholastic.

Bulla, C. R. (1955). *The poppy seeds.* New York: Penguin.

Bunting, E. (1989). *The Wednesday surprise.* New York: Clarion.

Byars, B. (1988). *Beans on the roof.* New York: Bantam Doubleday.

Carle, E. (1969). *The very hungry caterpillar.* New York: Scholastic.

Carle, E. (1971). *Do you want to be my friend?* New York: Crowell-Collier.

Charles, O. (1988). *How is a crayon made?* New York: Simon Schuster.

Cleary, B. (1981). *Ramona Quimby, age 8.* New York: Dell.

Coerr, E. (1977). *Sadako and the thousand paper cranes.* New York: Putnam.

Cole, J. (1989). *The magic school bus inside the human body.* New York: Scholastic.

Conrad, P. (1988). *Staying nine.* New York: HarperCollins.

Cooney, B. (1982). *Miss Rumphius.* New York: Scholastic.

Crews, D. (1978). *Fright train.* New York: William Morrow & Company.

Dahl, R. (1961). *James and the giant peach.* New York: Knopf.

dePaola, T. (1979). *Oliver Button is a sissy.* New York: Harcourt Brace Jovanovich.

dePaola, T. (1981). *Now one foot, now the other.* New York: Putnam.

Dorros, A. (1990). *Rain forest secrets.* New York: Scholastic.

Fox, M. (1986). *Hattie and the fox.* New York: Bradbury Press.

Galdone, P. (1973). *The little red hen.* New York: Clarion.

Gardiner, J. R. (1980). *Stone fox.* New York: Harper & Row.

Gibbons, G. (1987). *Trains.* New York: Holiday House.

Gibbons, G. (1990). *Weather words and what they mean.* New York: Holiday House.

Ginsburg, M. (1972). *The chick and the duckling.* New York: Macmillan.

Hoffman, M & Binch, C. (1991). *Amazing Grace.* New York: Dial Books.

Hooks, W. (1987). *Moss gown.* New York: Clarion.

Hutchins, P. (1968). *Rosie's walk.* New York: Simon & Schuster.

Keats, E. J. (1962). *The snowy day.* New York: Viking Press.

Kimmel, E. (1988). *Anansi and the moss-covered rock.* New York: Scholastic.

Lear, E. (1983). *An Edward Lear alphabet.* New York: Mulberry Books.

Lobel, A. (1981). *On Market Street.* New York: Greenwillow.

Louie, A. (1982). *Yen-Shen: A Cinderella story from China.* New York: Philomel.

Maass, R. (1989). *Fire fighters.* New York: Scholastic.

MacLachlan, P. (1985). *Sarah, plain and tall.* New York: Harper & Row.

Martin, B. & Archambault, J. (1989). *Chicka chicka boom boom.* New York: Holt, Rinehart & Winston.

Martin, B. & Archambault, J. (1985). *The ghost-eye tree.* New York: Scholastic.

Martin, B. (1983). *Brown bear, brown bear, what do you see?* New York: Henry Holt and Company.

McKissack, P. (1988). *Mirandy and brother wind.* New York: Alfred A. Knopf.

Medearis, A. S. (1991). *Dancing with the Indians.* New York: Scholastic.

Mohr, N. (1989). *Felita.* New York: Bantam Skylark.
Morris, A. (1989). *Bread, bread, bread.* New York: Lathrop, Lee, & Shepard.
Nixon, J. L. (1988). *If you were a writer.* New York: Simon & Schuster.
Noble, T. H. (1980). *The day Jimmie's boa ate the wash.* New York: Dial.
Pallotta, J. (1986). *The icky bug alphabet book.* New York: Trumpet.
Perrault, C. (1981). *Cinderella.* Illustratd by Marcia Brown. New York: Simon & Schuster.
Prelutsky, J. (1988). *Tyrannosaurus was a beast.* New York: Greenwillow.
Rees, M. (1988). *Ten in a bed.* Boston, MA: Little Brown.
Rogers, P. (1989). *What will the weather be like today?* New York: Scholastic.
Scott, A. H. (1990). *One good cow: A cowpuncher's counting book.* New York: Greenwillow.
Sendak, M. (1963). *Where the wild things are.* New York: Harper & Row.
Shaw, C. G. (1947). *It looked like spilt milk.* New York: Harper & Row.
Silverstein, S. (1974). *Where the sidewalk ends.* New York: Harper & Row.
Slepian, J. & Seidler, A. (1967). *The hungry thing.* New York: Scholastic.
Slepian, J. & Seidler, A. (1990). *The hungry thing returns.* New York: Scholastic.
Smith, R. K. (1972). *Chocolate fever.* New York: Dell Publishing.
Steele, F. A. (1976). *Tattercoats: An old English tale.* New York: Bradbury.
Steig, W. (1969). *Sylvester and the magic pebble.* New York: Simon and Schuster, Inc.
Steptoe, J. (1987). *Mufaro's beautiful daughters.* New York: Scholastic.
Talanda, S. (1983). *Dad told me not to.* Milwaukee, WI: Raintree.
Turner, A. (1987). *Nettie's trip south.* New York: Scholastic.
Van Allsburg, C. (1981). *Jumanji.* New York: Scholastic.
White, E. B. (1952). *Charlotte's web.* New York: Harper & Row.
Wells, R. (1985). *Hazel's amazing mother.* New York: Trumpet.
Williams, V. B. (1982). *A chair for my mother.* New York: Greenwillow.
Wood, A. & Wood, D. (1984). *The napping house.* San Diego, CA: Harcourt Brace Jovanovich.
Yolen, J. (1972). *The girl who loved the wind.* New York: Crowell.
Yolen, J. (1987a). *Owl moon.* New York: Scholastic.
Yolen, J. (1987b). *The Three Bears rhyme book.* San Diego: Hardcourt Brace Jovanovich.
Yolen, J. (1992). *A letter from Phoenix Farm.* Katonah, NY: Richard C. Owens.

References

Cullinan, B. (1989). *Literature and the child.* San Diego, CA: Hardcourt Brace Jovanovich.
Gonzalez, R. D. (1990). When minority becomes majority: The changing face of English classrooms. *English Journal,* 79, 16–23.
Lukens, R. (1990). *A critical handbook of children's literature.* Glenview, IL: Scott, Foresman.
Martinez, M., & Nash, M. F. (1990). Bookalogues: Talking about children's liturature. *Lanuage Arts, 67,* 599-606.
Meyer, B. J., & Freedle, R. O. (1984). Effects of discourse type on recall. *American Educational Research Journal, 21,* 121–143.
Morrow, L. (1989). *Literacy developement in the early years.* Englewood Cliffs, NJ: Prentice Hall.
Niles, O. S. (1974). Organization perceived. In H. L. Herber (Ed.), *Perspectives in reading: Developing study skills in secondary schools* (pp. 57–76). Newark, DE: International Reading Association.
Rasinski, T., & Padak, N. D. (1990). Multicultural learning through children's literature. *Lanuage Arts, 67,* 576–580.
Reimer, K. M. (1992). Multiethnic literature: Holding fast to dreams. *Lanuage Arts, 69,* 14–21.
Sims, R. (1983). What has happened to the "all white" world of children's books? *Phi Delta Kappa, 64,* 650–653.
Sulzby, E. (1995). Children's emergent reading of favorite storybooks. *Reading Research Quarterly, 20,* 458–481.

Appendix B

Sample Word Lists and Word Sorts

The word lists and sorts that follow are appropriate examples for developing and transitional readers and writers. The words are drawn from high-frequency word lists and current basal reading series. Before sorting words, children should be able to segment a specific phonetic element through picture sorts. Word sorts should contain words that are sight words and that appear frequently in independent and instructional reading materials.

Word Lists and Sorting for Phonic Patterns

Children in the developing stage refine their knowledge of single consonants, developed in the emergent stage through picture sorting, as they add new knowledge about short vowels and consonant teams. Transitional readers and writers continue to develop their phonics knowledge, but typically in multisyllable words.

Notice that in the suggested sequence for word sorts, short vowels, consonant blends/clusters, and consonant digraphs are mixed to provide a constant review of basic phonic elements.

1. Suggested sequence for word study: short vowels, consonant blends, and digraphs

short *a*	not short *a*					
short *i*	not short *i*					
short *a*	short *i*	neither				
l blend	not *l* blend					
bl	*cl*	*fl*	*gl*	*pl*	*sl*	
sh (initial)	*sh* (final)	neither				
short *o*	not short *o*					
short *a*	short *i*	short *o*	none			
r blends	not *r* blends					
br	*cr*	*dr*	*fr*	*gr*	*pr*	*tr*
ch	*sh*	neither				
short *u*	not short *u*					
short *o*	short *u*	neither				
s blends	not *s* blends					
sk	*sn*	*sp*	*st*	*sw*	*scr*	*spl*
th (voiced)	*th* (voiceless)	neither				

Note: Words are selected so that the focus of the sort is the only new phonetic element in the word. Words chosen for the crazy (discard) pile are always sight words or known words from previous sorts.

Sample Word Sorts (in suggested sequence)

short a (only single consonants)			**not short a (sight words)**	
had	ham	at	the	is
bad	jam	cat	to	me
mad	am	sat	I	be
sad	map	hat	go	in
rag	nap	an	my	you
bag	cap	can		
tag	man	ran		

short i (only single consonants)			**not short i (sight words/short a)**	
did	dip	hit	I	tan
pin	tip	kit	go	zap
in	zip	fit	the	pad
sit	big	if	me	bag
it	dig	six	to	ax

short o (only single consonants)			**not short o (sight words/short a/i)**	
not	on	pop	hip	was
got	box	hop	lap	am
pot	fox	top	sip	did
hot	job	log	six	rag
lot	dog	mom		

l blend (only short a and i)		**not l blend**	
clap	glad	lap	fat
clip	plan	lip	pan
flip	slap	can	sip
flag	slam	tag	pig
flat	slip		

same l blend

bl	**cl**	**fl**	**gl**	**pl**	**sl**
black	clap	flag	glad	plan	slam
	clip	flat			slap
		flip			slip

initial sh	**final sh**	**neither**
ship	wish	and
shin	fish	of
she	dish	flip
shot	dash	
shop	flash	

r blends		not r blend
brag	drop	bag
brat	drag	plan
crab	frog	shop
crop	grin	have
drip	trip	was
trap	prop	pop

same r blend

br	cr	dr	fr	gr	pr	tr
brag	crab	drag	frog	grin	prop	trip
brat	crop	drip	trap			trap
		drop				

ch		sh		neither
chop	rich	shin	fish	crab
chat	much	she	flash	grin
chip	such	ship		glad
chin				slip

short u			not short u	
but	fun	rug	chop	hat
cut	run	bug	frog	cab
up	sun	us	stop	drag
cup	bun	bus		
rub	tub	mud		

short e			not short e	
get	bed	jet	fun	glad
let	red	met	she	big
yet	hen	leg	mud	ship
pet	men	beg		
set	ten	yes		

s blend		not s blend	
scrub	spot	bus	yes
skin	spit	sun	chat
skip	splash	men	frog
snap	stop		
spin	step		
split	swim		

same s blend

sk	*sn*	*sp*	*st*	*sw*	*scr*	*spl*
skin	snap	spin	stop	swim	scrub	splash
skip		spot	step			split
						spit

th (voiced)		th (voiceless)	neither
then	the	thin	chin
them	that	bath	chat
this	three	both	shin
than		with	are

2. Suggested sequence for word study: adding single long vowels

long *a*_e	short *a*		
long *i*_e	short *i*		
long *a*_e	long *i*_e	neither	
long *o*_e	short *o*		
long *o*_e	long *a*_e	long *i*_e	none
long *u*_e	short *u*		
long *e*	short *e*		
long *u*_e	long *e*	neither	

Sample Word Sorts (in suggested sequence)

long a_e			**short a**	
name	tape	plate	mad	bath
same	shape	plane	at	snap
game	make	grade	plan	that
gave	lake	brave	jam	tap
late	case	made		
gate	chase	skate		

long i_e		**short i**	
I	bike	big	if
time	slide	six	slid
wife	smile	drip	rid
five	nine		
like	ride		

long a_e	**long i_e**	**neither**
game	nine	had
skate	smile	lip
plane	time	six
lake	five	bag
chase	bike	

long o_e		**short o**
so	pole	not
no	bone	stop
go	stone	mom
rope	joke	hop
home	broke	dot
note	stove	frog

long o_e	**long a_e**	**long i_e**	**none**
no	gate	wife	do
joke	shape	ride	him
stove	made	hike	ham
home	name		
bone			

long u__e		**short u**
cute	tube	plug
cube	June	cup
mule	rude	bus
rule	flute	drum
tune		sun

long e		**short e**
he	tree	them
we	sweet	then
me	free	yes
be	see	red
she	feet	step

long u	**long e**	**neither**
cube	tree	but
flute	she	sun
rule	feet	red
June	green	
me		

3. Suggested sequence for word study: adding variant consonants, variant vowels, and silent letters:

final double consonant		not double consonant		
single and double consonants (same sound)				
hard *c/g*	soft *c/g*			
final *s* as *z*	*s* as *s*			
ar	short *a*	neither		
or/ore	short *o*	neither		
er/ir/ur	short *e*	short *i*	short *u*	
ai/ay	*a__e*	short *a*		
oa	*o__e*	short *o*		
igh/ight	*i__e*	short *i*		
ea (long *e*)	*ea* (short *e*)	*ea* (long *a*)	short *e*	
silent consonant digraph		no silent consonant digraph		
final consonant blend		no final blend		
oo (long)	*oo* (short)	long *o*	short *o*	
ow (*ow*)	*ow* (long *o*)	short *o*		
au/aw	long *a*	short *a*		
oi/oy	long *o*	short *o*		
ou (*ow*) -	(long *oo*)	(short *oo*)	(long *o*)	(short *u*) (*au*)
ui/ue/ew/u__e		short *u*		
are/air	*ar*	neither		
ear/eer/ere (*eer*)	*ear* (*er*)	*ear* (*air*)	*ear* (*ar*)	
ire	*ir*	neither		
ure	*ur*	neither		

long *a* (*a__e, ai, ay, ea, ei, ey*)	short *a*
long *e* (*e, ee, ea, ie, ey*)	short *e*
long *i* (*i__e, y, ie, igh*)	short *i*

Sample Word Sorts (in suggested sequence):

double consonant			**not double consonant**	
will	dress	mess	sled	if
all	off	class	leg	pal
small	sniff	add	bus	is
well	egg	buzz		

final l/ll	**final s/ss**	**final f/ff**	**final g/ggfinal**	**d/dd**
will	bus	off	leg	mad
pal	dress	if	egg	slid
small	class	sniff	bag	add
well	yes			odd
pill				
doll				

soft c/g		**hard c/g**
face	mice	cat
place	cage	cape
race	age	bag
nice	stage	frog
ice	huge	game

initial s /s/	**final s /s/**		**final s /z/**	
said	dress	yes	his	has
sing	glass	us	as	nose
six	kiss	bus	wise	use
sun			these	was

ar		**short a**	**neither**
car	barn	ran	run
star	arm	jam	frog
jar	far	fan	game
farm	mark	flag	
sharp		bath	

or/ore	**short o**	**neither**
for	on	rob
more	pot	rope
store	stop	crab
or	frog	
chore		
fork		

er/ir/ur		**short e**	**short i**	**short u**
her	first	hen	did	fun
bird	dirt	bed	slip	bud
girl	stir	step		gun
fur	burn			

ai/ay		a_e	short a
train	tray	gate	pat
rain	may	game	ran
stain	play	made	clap
mail	say	shake	plan
pail	day	shave	
wait	way		

oa		o_e	short o
boat	road	joke	drop
coat	toad	rope	spot
float	loaf	stove	dog
goat	goal	home	
soap	toast		

igh/ight		i_e	short i
sigh	tight	five	big
high	might	smile	him
right	sight	nine	sit
light	flight	kite	grin
fight	night		clip

ea (long a)	ea (short e)	ea (long a)	short e
clean	spread	great	step
team	dead	break	red
beat	head	steak	then
sea	deaf		
teach	bread		
please			
each			
meat			

silent consonant digraph			no silent digraphs
write	white	lamb	ride
wrote	witch	comb	way
know	catch	fudge	no
knife	wheel	bridge	grin
knit	match	sign	make
ghost	whale	half	with
who	black	calf	
when	trick	duck	

same silent digraphs (initial)

wr(w)	kn(k)	gh(g)	wh(w)	wh(h)
write	know	ghost	when	who
wrote	knife	ghost	white	
	knit		whale	
			wheel	

same silent digraphs (final)

ck(k)	*mb*(m)	*gn*(n)	*lf*(f)	*tch*(ch)	*dge*(j)
duck	comb	sign	calf	match	fudge
trick	lamb	reign	half	witch	bridge
black				catch	

final blend (short vowel)			**not final blend**	
belt	next	fast	mat	hike
milk	left	must	hid	had
help	pink	ask	cap	let
and	think	plant		
hand	bank	thank		

final blend (long vowel)		**not final blend**	
old	kind	odd	that
cold	wild	fin	thin
told	child	kid	pin
find			

oo (long)		**oo (short)**		**long o**	**short o**
boot	tool	foot	good	stone	hop
soon	cool	look	wood	robe	not
boom	shoot	book	hook	road	got
moon	tooth	took		goat	
hoop	broom				

ow (ow)		**ow (long o)**		**short o**
cow	down	row	throw	hot
now	crown	bow	slow	box
bow	brown	know	show	sock
how	plow	grow	flow	

au/aw		**long a**	**short a**
haul	jaw	lake	snap
law	crawl	day	chat
draw	dawn	clay	match
paw	saw	rain	
saw		snail	

oi/oy		**long o**	**short o**
oil	toy	bone	on
coin	boy	road	not
boil	joy	rope	box
noise		stove	job
join		boat	stop

ou(ow)	(long oo)	(short oo)	(long o)	(short u)	(au)
out	you	would	though	tough	ought
cloud	through	could	soul	rough	fought
mouse	soup	should		young	bought
sound	group				
shout					
bounce					
round					
couch					
mouth					

ue/ui	ew/u_e	short u
blue	flute	bug
true	tube	sun
suit	use	club
fruit	stew	crush
juice	blew	

are/air		ar		neither
care	stairs	far	mark	game
rare	chair	car	cart	can
share	pair	barn	dark	glad
scare	fair	start		flake

ear/eer/ere (eer)		ear (er)	ear (air)	ear (ar)
ear	here	earth	bear	heart
dear	deer	learn	pear	
fear	clear	earn	wear	
near	year			

ire	ir	neither
fire	dirt	bike
wire	girl	hide
tire	first	fit
hire	third	clip

ure	ur	neither
pure	fur	cute
sure	burn	suit
cure	turn	fun
	nurse	

a_e, ai, ay, ea, ei, ey (long a)		short a
cape	they	sand
shake	eight	rag
mail	rein	clap
rain	great	that
stay	break	chat
play	steak	

e, ee, ea, ie, ey (long e)		short e
she	key	step
need	field	net
sheep	chief	egg
sweet	dream	when
each	treat	left

i_e, y, ie, igh (long i)		**short i**
five	light	will
smile	high	stick
pipe	knight	fish
drive	tie	which
fly	lie	hip
try	pie	with
sky		

o_e, oa, ou, ow (long o)		**short o**
bone	home	rock
boat	float	plop
soap	toast	box
joke	know	spot
stove	show	frog
though	grow	

Word Lists and Sorts for Structural Patterns

1. Suggested sequence of word sorts: structural units

compound word	not a compound	
compound-literal	compound-implied	
contraction	not a contraction	
contractions by families		
inflected ending	no inflected ending	
e drop	no *e* drop	
consonant double	no consonant double	
ends with *y*	*y* changes to *i*	*y* does not change
independent prefix	no independent prefix	
same prefix		
derivational suffix	no derivational suffix	
dependent prefix	no dependent prefix	

Sample Word Sorts (in Sequence)

compound word		***not a compound word***
bedroom	snowman	room
goldfish	baseball	dog
houseboat	daydream	house
doghouse	playground	ground
armchair	wheelchair	chair

compound—literal meaning		***compound—implied meaning***	
bedroom	cheerleader	starfish	runaway
doghouse	salesperson	butterfly	breakfast
wheelchair	shipyard	homesick	fallout
daytime	eyesight	software	everywhere
weekend	newscast	overdrawn	

contraction		***not a contraction***	
can't	you'll	can	have
didn't	haven't	did	her
you're	we've	you	I
we'll	he's	not	will
I'm			

contractions by families

not		**are**	**will**	**is**	**have**
aren't	shouldn't	you're	I'll	he's	I've
can't	couldn't	we're	you'll	she's	you've
didn't	wouldn't	they're	we'll	it's	we've
don't	hadn't	they'll	I'm		they've
won't	haven't				

inflected suffix		***no inflected suffix***	
dogs	smartest	dog	smart
horses	taller	horse	tall
dishes	barking	dish	bark
hits	washed	hit	wash
writes	jumped	write	jump

e drop		***no e drop***
raked	making	jumped
baking	liking	washed
nicer	smiling	thinking
hoping	using	sleeping
		playing

consonant double		***no consonant double***
hitting	rubbed	thinking
runner	chopped	watching
hottest	hopping	shorter
stopping	bigger	tallest
		smartest

ends with y		***y changes to i***		***y does not change***
baby	ugly	babies	tried	flying
fly	puppy	candies	flies	trying
pretty	cry	prettiest	uglier	crying
try	candy	cried	puppies	

independent prefix		***no independent prefix***	
untie	forget	tie	get
preview	forgive	view	load
reuse	unload	use	give
prepay	unkind	pay	kind
repay	undo	call	do
recall			

same prefix (meaning)			
un	re	pre	for
untie	reuse	preview	forgive
unkind	review	prepay	forget
unload	repay		
undo	recall		

derivational suffix		***no derivational suffix***	
careful	helpful	care	help
slowly	wisely	slow	wise
sleepy	waiter	sleep	kind
cloudy	really	cloud	real
painless	kindness	pain	wait
friendly		friend	

dependent prefix		***no dependent prefix***	
insist	recognize	unload	disagree
inspire	proposal	repay	recall
infection	reluctant	unkind	reappear
assure	disturb	preview	incorrect
embarrass	relieve		

Word Lists and Sorts for Syllabication Generalizations

Suggested Sequence for Word Study: Integrating Phonics and Structure

structural word	phonetic word	
base + base	prefix + base	base + suffix
VC/CV (same letters)	VC/CV (different letters)	
V/CV	VC/V	
VC/CV	V/CV VC/V	C+le

Sample Word Sorts (in sequence)

structural word		***phonetic word***	
floating	starlight	towel	family
thirsty	friendly	river	butter
winner	dresses	bubble	early
carefully	repay	giant	squirrel
we're	driver	dollar	buffalo
untie			

base + base	***prefix + base***	***base + suffix***
starfish	untie	swimming
didn't	prepay	horses
I'll	recall	washed
daydream	forgive	careful
you're	unkind	slowly
houseboat		kindness
weekend		

VC/CV **(same letters)**		***VC/CV*** **(different letters)**	
kitten	dollar	picnic	signal
summer	hammer	pencil	person
rabbit	lesson	garden	monkey
pillow	yellow	circus	winter
little	pretty	doctor	

V/CV		***VC/V***	
cider	open	river	rocket
pilot	secret	second	linen
later	student	clever	lizard
water	apart	sugar	pocket
music	father	ticket	radish

VC/CV	***V/CV***	***VC/V***	***C+le***
after	recess	brother	purple
balloon	cement	cousin	eagle
basket	diner	never	fable
carrot	equal	travel	fiddle
chimney	hotel	visit	pebble
dinner	music	lizard	turtle
harvest	open	pocket	candle
hungry		river	cycle

Appendix C

Pictures for Sorting Activities

Suggested Sequence for Word Study and Picture Sorting: Initial Consonants

b	not b			
f	not f			
b	f	neither		
m	not m			
b	f	m	none	
s	not s			
t	not t			
s	t	neither		
d	not d			
s	t	d	none	
l	not l			
s	t	d	l	none
n	not n			
l	n	neither		
r	not r			
l	n	r	none	
p	not p			
n	l	r	p	none
j	not j			
k	not k			
j	k	neither		
v	not v			
j	k	v	none	
z	not z			
j	k	v	z	none
h	not h			
w	not w			
h	w	neither		
y	not y			
h	w	y	none	

Suggested Sequence for Word Study and Picture Sorts: Final Consonants

final d	not final d	
initial d	final d	neither
final g	not final g	
initial g	final g	neither
final d	final g	neither
final b	not final b	
initial b	final b	neither
final t	not final t	
initial t	final t	neither
final b	final t	neither
final n	not final n	
initial n	final n	neither
final p	not final p	
initial p	final p	neither
final n	final p	neither
final m	not final m	
initial m	final m	neither
final r	not final r	
initial r	final r	neither
final m	final r	neither

initial b		initial c (hard)	

bell	bird	cat	cake
box	barn	car	comb
bus	bat	cup	camel
ball	book	can	coat
bed	boat	candle	cap

door	duck	four	fire
dinosaur	desk	fence	finger
doll	dishes	fork	feet
dog	dime	fish	feather
deer	domino	fan	five

ghost	gum	hamburger	hanger
goat	gorilla	heart	hair
girl	gate	hammer	hat
garden	gun	hook	horse
game	goose	hand	hose

initial j		initial k	

jar	jack-o-lantern	ketchup	kitten
jet	jacket	kangaroo	kettle
jacks	jack-in-the-box	king	kitchen
jeep	jug	key	kite
jam	jumprope	kick	kiss

lion	ladder	money	mop
lock	lemon	mail	mouse
lightbulb	legs	monkey	mailbox
leaf	lamp	map	man
lizard	lawn mower	mitten	matches

newspaper
nail
nest
nickel
nine

nose
nuts
net
needle
night

pin
pencil
pig
pear
pillow

pan
pie
purse
pitcher
paper

question mark
quarter
quack

queen
quilt

rug
rabbit
rain
rat
rocket

ring
rake
radio
rooster
road

sandbox
suit
sandwich
six
soap

saw
sun
seven
sink
sock

two
turtle
telephone
tire
top

tent
table
television
toaster
ten

whale
web
well
windmill
wagon

watch
window
watermelon
witch
worm

vacuum
vine
violin
vegetables
volcano

vase
valentine
veterinarian (vet)
vest
van

yolk yoyo yard yellow	yawn yarn yell	zero zipper zigzag	zebra zoo

final b		final d	

color

tub	bulb	bread	bird
crib	cab	bed	sled
scrub	web	red	lid
bib	tube	hand	lizard
globe		road	record

final f		final g	

leaf
scarf
giraffe
cuff

wolf
knife
roof
chef

bug
egg
pig
bag
rug

leg
frog
tag
dog
log

final k		final l	

duck	fork	well	kettle
rake	rock	mail	camel
sink	lake	ball	turtle
hook	book	shell	hill
cake	lock	bell	doll

final m		final n	

jam	arm	ten	pan
broom	steam	lion	fan
gum	thumb	wagon	pin
drum	swim	seven	man
ham		sun	mitten

final p		final r	

mop
cap
sleep
clap
cup

top
map
jeep
stamp
rope

door
bear
pear
jar
hair

hammer
four
deer
car

final s		final t	
horse	vase	boat	bat
goose	house	goat	cat
glass	dress	suit	heart
lips	mouse	foot	mat
bus		net	hat

final v		final x	
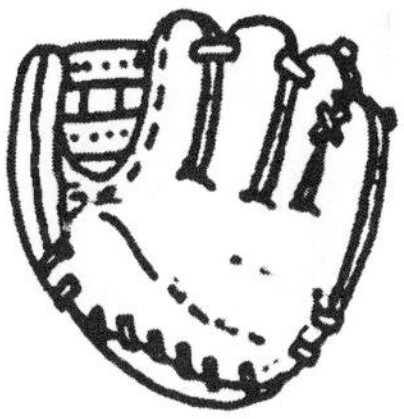	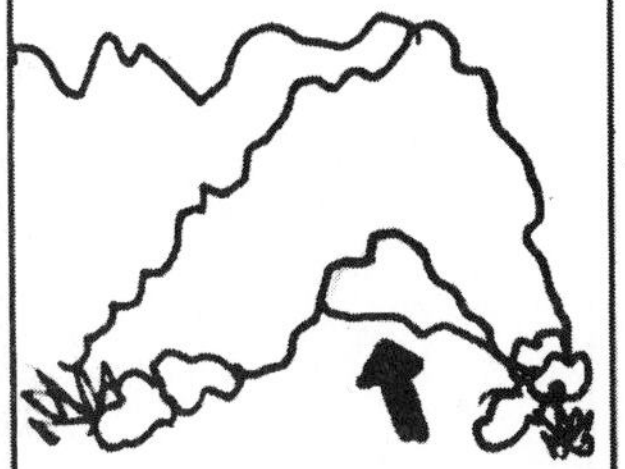	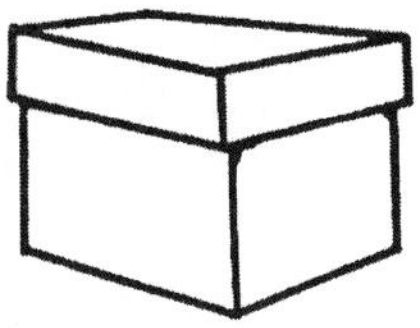	

glove
five
shave
dive

cave
wave
twelve

box
fox
ax
mix

six
wax
ox

block
blind
blanket
blouse
blade

clown
cloud
club
clock
clam

fly
flowers
flashlight
flag
flute

glasses
glove
globe
glue
glass

pl	sl	br	cr
			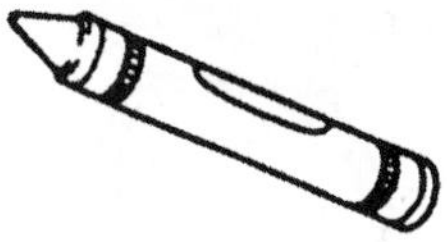
	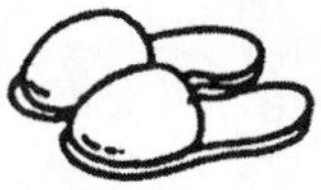		

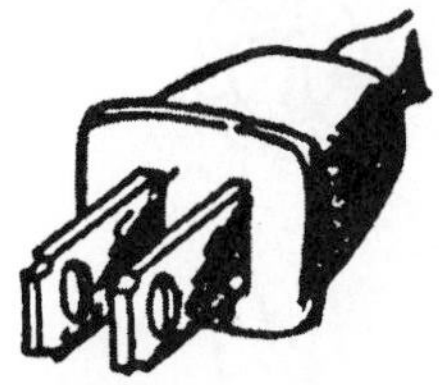			

plate	slide	broom	crayon
pliers	slippers	bread	crack
plane	sled	brush	cry
plug	slingshot	bride	crab
plant	sling	bridge	crib

dress
drawer
dragon
drum
drive

frame
frog
fruit
freckles
fry

grasshopper
grin
groceries
grapes
green

present
pretzel
prince
prize
press

tr	sc/sk	sm	sn

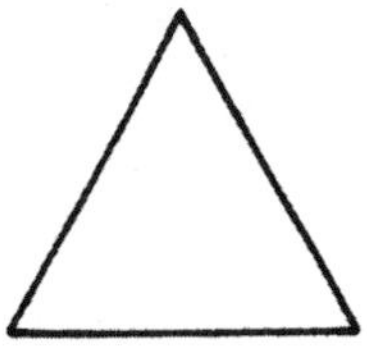			

track
truck
tree
train
triangle

skis
scout
skull
skate
skunk

smile
smoke
smell

snake
snail
snowman

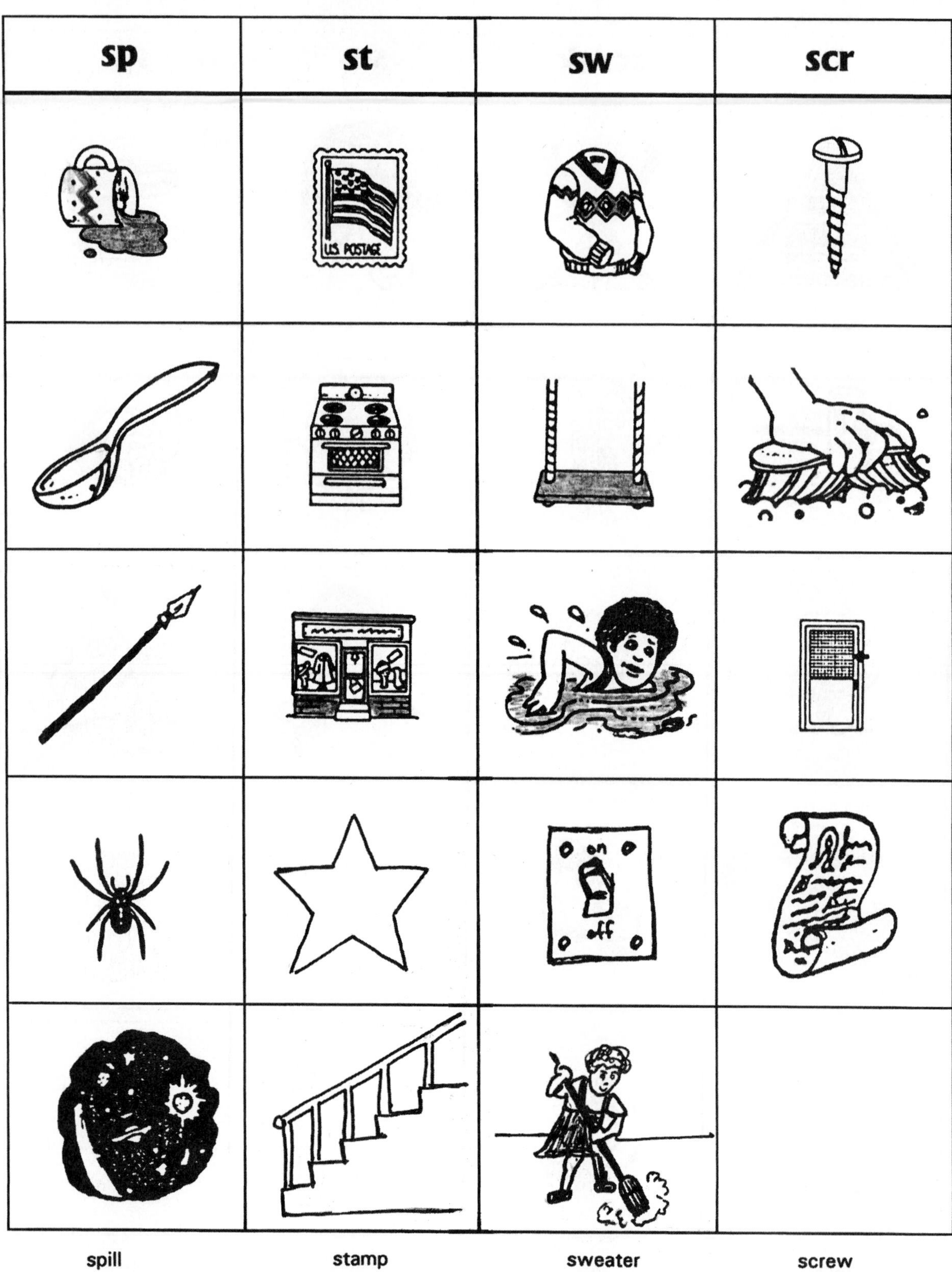

spill	stamp	sweater	screw
spoon	stove	swing	scrub
spear	store	swim	screen
spider	star	switch	scroll
space	stairs	sweep	

spr	str	initial sh	final sh
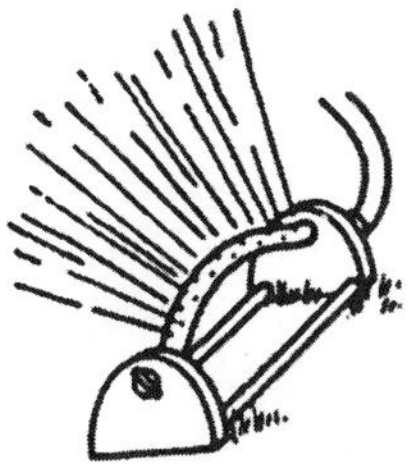		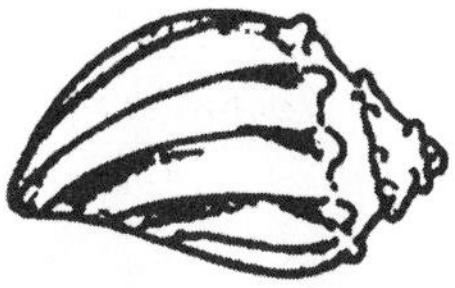	
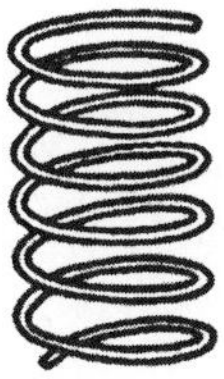			
	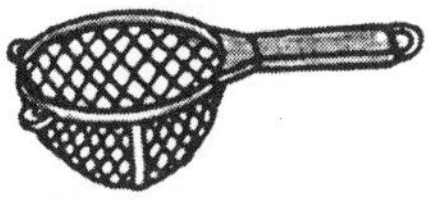		

sprinkler
spring
spray

straw
street
strainer
strawberry

shell
ship
shoe
shovel
sheep

dish
brush
bush
trash
fish

(voiceless)

initial th	final th	initial ch	final ch
three	wreath	chin	match
thumb	tooth	chick	sandwich
thimble	teeth	chair	watch
throne	moth	check	peach
thermometer		cheese	catch

short a		long a	
	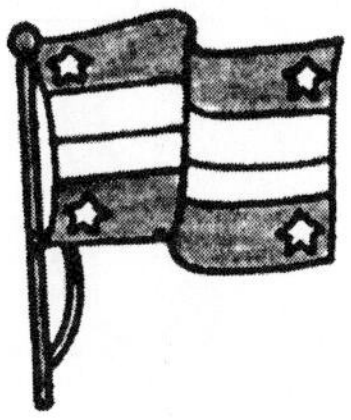		

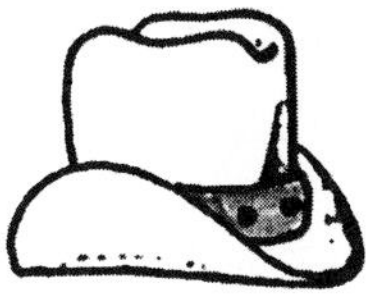			

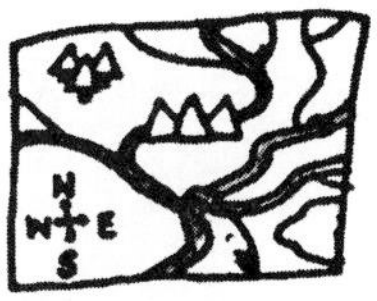			

crab	flag	cane	rain
glass	fan	whale	skate
hat	man	train	snake
bat	hand	cape	chain
map	apple	frame	tape

desk
dress
well
net
belt

ten
web
bed
shell
bell

three
teeth
street
queen
leaf

sheep
cheese
key
jeep
tree

short i		long i	
chick	whip	kite	five
ship	milk	cube	spider
brick	swim	prize	tire
spill	chin	nine	bride
hill	crib	bike	slide

short o		long o	

frog	stop	nose	rope
clock	box	hose	globe
block	top	bow	road
dog	fox	hoe	coat
lock	cross	cone	smoke

short u		long u	

scrub
plug
skunk
bus
rug

cup
drum
duck
truck
brush

tube
fruit
music
ruler

suit
cube
mule
tulip

References

Adams, J. & Collins, A. (1985). A schematic-theoretic view of reading. In H. Singer & R. B. Ruddell (Eds.), *Theoretical models and processes of reading* (3rd ed.) (pp. 404–425). Newark: DE: International Reading Association.

Adams, M. J. (1990). *Beginning to read: Thinking and learning about print.* Cambridge, MA: MIT press.

Adams, M. J. & Bruck, M. (1995). Resolving the "Great Debate." *American Educator,* 8, 7–20.

Adams, M. J. & Osborn, J. (1990). *Beginning reading instruction in the United States.* Paper presented at the Meeting of the Educational Policy Group, Washington, D.C. ERIC Document No. ED 320 128.

Allington, R. (1977). If they don't read much, how they ever gonna get good? *Journal of Reading,* 21(2), 57–61.

Allington, R. & McGill-Franzen, A. (1989). Different programs, indifferent instruction. In D. K. Lipsky & A. Gartner (Eds.), *Beyond separate education: Quality education for all.* Baltimore, MD: Paul H. Brooks.

Allington, R. L. (1994). The schools we have. The schools we need. *The Reading Teacher,* 48(1), 14–29.

Anderson, R. A. & Pearson, P. D. (1984). A schematic-theoretic view of reading comprehension. In P. D. Pearson (Ed.), *Handbook of reading research.* New York: Longman.

Anderson, R. C., Hiebert, E. H., Scott, J., & Wilkinson, I. A. G. (1985). *Becoming a nation of readers.* Champaign-Urbana, IL: Center for the Study of Reading.

Anderson, R. C., Wilson, P. T., & Fielding, L. G. (1992). Growth in reading and how children spend their time outside of school. *Reading Research Quarterly,* 23, 285–303.

Ashton-Warner, S. (1963). *Teacher.* New York: Simon & Schuster.

Atwell, N. (1998). *In the middle: Writing, reading and learning with adolescents* (2nd ed.). Portsmouth, NH: Heinemann.

Barbe, W. B, Wasylyk, T. M., Hackney, C. S., & Braun, L. A. (1984). *Zaner-Bloser creative growth in handwriting (Grades K–8).* Columbus, OH: Zaner-Bloser.

Barnitz, J. (1986). *Reading development of nonnative speakers of English.* Orlando, FL: Harcourt, Brace Jovanovich and the Center for Applied Linguistics.

Barone, D. (1990). The written responses of young children: Beyond comprehension to story understanding. *The New Advocate,* 3, 49–56.

Barrett, F. L. (1982). *A teacher's guide to shared reading.* Ontario, Canada: Scholastic-TAB.

Beach, S. A. (1990). *The interrelationship of phonemic segmentation, auditory abstraction and word recognition.* A paper presented at the annual meeting of the International Reading Association, Atlanta, GA, May 1990.

Bear, D. R. & Barone, D. (1989). Using children's spellings to group for word study and directed reading in the primary classroom. *Reading Psychology,* 10, 275–292.

Beaver, J. M. (1982). Say it! Over and over. *Language Arts,* 59(2), 143–148.

Beck, I. & Juel, C. (1995). The role of decoding in learning to read. *American Educator,* 8, 21–25, 39–42.

Beck, I. L., Perfetti, C. A., & McKeown, M. G. (1982). The effects of long-term vocabulary instruction on lexical access and reading comprehension. *Journal of Educational Psychology,* 74, 506–521.

Bedrova, E. & Leong, D. J. (1996). *Tools of the mind: The Vygotskian approach to early childhood education.* Englewood Cliffs, NJ: Merrill/Prentice-Hall.

Beldin, H. L. (1970). Informal reading tests: Historical review and review of the research. In W. D. Durr (Ed.), *Reading difficulties: Diagnosis, correction and remediation.* Newark, DE: International Reading Association.

Betts, E. A. (1946). *Foundations of reading instruction.* New York: American Book Company.

Biemiller, A. (1970). The development and use of graphic and contextual information as children learn to read. *Reading Research Quarterly,* 6, 75–96.

Biemiller, A. (1977/78). Relationships between oral reading rates for letters, words, and simple text in the development of reading achievement. *Reading Research Quarterly,* 13, 223–253.

Bissex, G. L. (1980). *Gnys at wrk: A child learns to read and write.* Cambridge, MA: Harvard University Press.

Blachman, B. (1991). Getting ready to read: Learning how print maps to speech. In J. Kavanagh (Ed.), *The language continuum: From infancy to literacy.* Parkton, MD: York Press.

Blackburn, E. (1985). Stories never end. In J. Hansen, T. Newkirk, & D. Graves (Eds.), *Breaking ground: Teachers relate reading and writing in the elementary school.* Portsmouth, NH: Heinemann.

Bode, B. A. (1989). Dialogue journal writing. *The Reading Teacher,* 42, 568–571.

Bond, G. L. & Dykstra, R. (1967). The cooperative program in first grade reading instruction. *Reading Research Quarterly,* 2, 5–142.

Bowyer, T. (1988). *Implementing the language experience approach in an E.M.H. classroom.* Creative component completed in partial fulfillment of master's degree. Oklahoma State University.

Bridge, C. A., Winograd, P. N., & Haley, D. (1983). Using predictable materials vs. preprimers to teach beginning sight words. *The Reading Teacher,* 36, 884–891.

Britton, J. (1970). *Language and learning.* New York: Penguin.

Brown, K. J. (1999/2000). What kind of text—For whom and when? Textual scaffolding for beginning readers. *The Reading Teacher,* 53, 292–307.

Bus, A. G., van Ijzendoorn, M., & Pellegrini, A. (1995). Joint book reading makes for success in learning to read: A meta analysis on intergenerational transmission of literacy. *Review of Educational Research,* 65, 1–21.

Butler, A. (1987). *Shared book experience.* Crystal Lake, IL: Rigby.

Byrne, B., Freebody, P., & Gates, A. (1992). Longitudinal data on the relations of word-reading strategies to comprehension, reading time, and phonemic awareness. *Reading Research Quarterly,* 27, 141–151.

Calkins, L. M. (1986). *The art of teaching writing.* Portsmouth, NH: Heinemann.

Calkins, L. M. (1994). *The Art of Teaching Writing* (new edition). Portsmouth, NH: Heinemann.

Center for the Study of Reading. (1990). *Teachers and independent reading: Suggestions for the classroom.* Urbana, IL: Author.

Chall, J. S. (1967). *Learning to read: The great debate.* New York: McGraw-Hill.

Chall, J. S. (1979). The great debate: Ten years later, with a modest proposal for reading stages. In L. B. Resnick & P. A. Weaver (Eds.), *Theory and practice of early reading* (Vol. 1, pp. 29–54). Hillsdale, NJ: Erlbaum.

Chall, J. S. (1983). *Stages of reading development.* New York: McGraw-Hill.

Clay, M. M. (1966). *Emergent reading behavior.* Unpublished doctoral dissertation. University of Aukland, NZ.

Clay, M. M. (1967). The reading behavior of five-year-old children: A research report. *New Zealand Journal of Educational Studies,* 2, 11–31.

Clay, M. M. (1975). *What did I write? Beginning writing behaviour.* Portsmouth, NH: Heinemann.

Clay, M. M. (1979). *Reading: The patterning of complex behavior.* Portsmouth, NH: Heinemann.

Clay, M. M. (1985). *Early detection of reading difficulties* (3rd ed.). Portsmouth, NH: Heinemann.

Clay, M. M. (1991). *Becoming literate: The construction of inner control.* Portsmouth, NH: Heinemann.

Clay, M. M. (1993). *An observation survey of early literacy achievement.* Portsmouth, NH: Heinemann.

Clay, M. M. (1998). *By different paths to common outcomes.* York, ME: Stenhouse Publishers

Combs, M. (1993). Thinking and informal writing in science. *Think,* 2(3), 39–43.

Cooper, J. D. (1993). *Literacy: Helping children construct meaning.* Boston, MA: Houghton Mifflin.

Cullinan, B. E. (1989). *Literature and the child.* San Diego, CA: Harcourt Brace Jovanovich.

Cullinan, B. E. (1992). Leading with literature. In B. E. Cullinan (Ed.), *Invitation to read: More children's literature in the reading program.* Newark, DE: International Reading Association.

Cunningham, P. M. (1995). *Phonics they use: Words for reading and writing* (2nd ed.). New York: HarperCollins.

Cunningham, P. M. & Cunningham, J. W. (1992). Making words: Enhancing the spelling-decoding connection. *The Reading Teacher,* 46(2), 106–115.

Cunningham, P. M. & Hall, D. P. (1994). *Making words: Multilevel, hands-on, developmentally appropriate spelling and phonics activities.* Torrance, CA: Good Apple.

Cunningham, P. M., Moore, S. A., Cunningham, J. W., & Moore, D. W. (1989). *Reading in elementary classrooms: Strategies and observations.* New York: Longman.

Daniel, T. B., Fehrenbach, C. R., & Greer, F. S. (1986). Supporting concept development with LEA. *Science and Children,* (3), 15–17.

Daniels, H. (1994). *Literature circles: Voice and choice in the student-centered classroom.* York, ME: Stenhouse.

D'Arcy, P. (1989). *Making sense, shaping meaning: Writing in the context of a capacity-based approach to learning.* Portsmouth, NH: Heinemann.

Davey, B. (1983). Think-aloud—modeling the cognitive processes of reading comprehension. *Journal of Reading,* 27, 44–47.

DeFord, D. (1981). Literacy: Reading, writing and other essentials. *Language Arts,* 58(6), 652–658.

Depree, H. & Iversen, S. (1994). *Early literacy in the classroom: A new standard for young readers.* Bothell, WA: The Wright Group.

Dixon-Krauss, L. (1994, September). *A mediation model for dynamic literacy instruction.* Paper presented at the International Conference on L. S. Vygotsky and the Contemporary Human Sciences in Moscow, Russia.

Dixon-Krauss, L. A. & Powell, W. R. (1995). Lev Semyonovich Vygotsky: The scholar/teacher. In Dixon-Krauss, L. (Ed.), *Vygotsky in the classroom: Mediated literacy instruction and assessment.* New York: Longman.

Douglas, D. J. (1988). *Factors related to choice of topic in a first grade process writing classroom.* Unpublished doctoral dissertation. Oklahoma State University.

Dowhower, S. (1987). Effects of repeated reading on second-grade transitional readers' fluency and comprehension. *Reading Research Quarterly,* 22, 389–406.

Durkin, D. (1966). *Children who read early.* New York: Teachers College Press.

Durrell, D. D. (1937). *Durrell analysis of reading difficulties.* New York: Harcourt Brace Jovanovich.

Dykstra, R. (1968). Summary of the second grade phase of the cooperative research program in primary reading instruction. *Reading Research Quarterly,* 4, 49–70.

Eeds, M. & Wells, D. (1989). Grand conversations: An exploration of meaning construction in literature study groups. *Research in the Teaching of English,* 23, 4–29.

Ehri, L. C. (1991). Development of the ability to read words. In R. Barr, M. L. Kamii, P. Mosenthal, & P. D. Pearson (Eds.), *Handbook of reading research* (Vol. 2, pp. 383–417). Mahway, NJ: Lawrence Erlbaum.

Ehri, L. C. (1998). Grapheme-phoneme knowledge is essential for learning to read words in English. In J. L. Metsala & L. C. Ehri (Eds.), *Word recognition in beginning literacy* (pp. 3–40). Mahwah, NJ: Erlbaum.

Ehri, L. C., Duffner, N. D., & Wilce, L. S. (1984). Pictorial mnemonics for phonics. *Journal of Educational Psychology,* 76, 880–893.

Elster, C. A. (1995). Importations in preschoolers' emergent readings. *Journal of Reading Behavior,* 27, 65–84.

Elster, C. A. (1998). Influences of text and pictures on shared and emergent readings. *Research in the Teaching of English,* 32, 43–78.

Ewoldt, C. & Hammermeister, F. (1986). The language-experience approach to facilitating reading and writing for hearing-impaired students. *American Annal of the Deaf,* 131, 271–274.

Farris, P. J. (1991). Handwriting instruction should not be extinct. *Language Arts,* 68, 312–314.

Ferguson, A. M. & Fairburn, J. (1985). Language experience for problem solving in mathematics. *The Reading Teacher,* 38, 504–506.

Fielding, L. G., Wilson, P. T., & Anderson, R. (1984). A new focus on free reading: The role of trade books in reading instruction. In T. E. Raphael, (Ed.), *The contexts of school-based literacy.* New York: Random House.

Filby, N., Barnett, B., & Bossart, S. (1982). *Grouping practices and their consequences.* San Francisco, CA: Far West Laboratory for Educational Research and Development.

Fischer, K. W. & Bulloch, D. (1984). Cognitive development in school-aged children: Conclusions and new directions. In W. A. Collins (Ed.), *Development during middle childhood: The years from six to twelve* (pp. 70–146). Washington, DC: National Academy Press.

Five, C. L. (1988). From workbooks to workshop: Increasing children's involvement in the reading process. *The New Advocate,* 1(Spring), 103–113.

Fountas, I. C. & Pinnell, G. S. (1996). *Guided reading: Good first teaching for all children.* Portsmouth, NH: Heinemann.

Fountas, I. C. & Pinnell, G. S. (1999). *Matching books to readers.* Portsmouth, NH: Heinemann.

Fox, B. & Routh, D. (1984). Phonemic analysis and synthesis as word attack skills: Revisited. *Journal of Educational Psychology,* 76, 1059–1064.

Freeman, J. (1992). Reading aloud: A few tricks of the trade. *School Library Journal,* 38(7), 26–29.

Freppon, P. A. & Dahl, K. L. (1991). Learning about phonics in a whole-language classroom. *Language Arts,* 68, 190–197.

Fulwiler, T. (1985). Writing and learning, grade 3. *Language Arts,* 62, 55–59.

Gambrell, L. B. (1985). Dialogue journals: Reading-writing interaction. *The Reading Teacher,* 38, 512–515.

Gates, A. I. (1935). *The improvement of reading.* New York: Macmillan.

Gilmore, J. V. & Gilmore, E. C. (1951). *Gilmore oral reading tests.* New York: Harcourt, Brace Jovanovich.

Goodman, Y. M. & Burke, C. L. (1970). *Reading miscues inventory.* New York: Macmillan.

Gough, P. B. & Tunmer, W. E. (1986). Decoding, reading, and reading disability. *Remedial and Special Education,* 7, 6–10.

Graves, D. H. (1973). *Children's writing: Research directions and hypotheses based upon an examination of the writing processes of seven-year-old children.* Unpublished doctoral dissertation. State University of New York at Buffalo.

Graves, D. H. (1983). *Teaching writing.* Portsmouth, NH: Heinemann.

Graves, D. H. (1994). *A fresh look at writing.* Portsmouth, NH: Heinemann.

Gray, W. S. (1915). *Standardized oral reading paragraphs.* Bloomington, IL: Public School Publishing Company.

Griffith, P. L. (1991). Phonemic awareness helps first graders invent spellings and third graders remember correct spellings. *Journal of Reading Behavior,* 23, 215–233.

Griffith, P. L. & Klesius, J. P. (1990). *The effect of phonemic awareness ability and reading instructional approach on first grade children's acquisition of spelling and decoding skills.* A paper presented at the National Reading Conference, November 1990.

Griffith, P. L. & Olson, M. W. (1992). Phonemic awareness helps beginning readers break the code. *The Reading Teacher,* 45, 516–523.

Hagerty, P. (1992). *Reader's workshop: Real reading.* Ontario, Canada: Scholastic Canada Ltd.

Hall, M. (1978). *The language experience approach for teaching reading, a research perspective.* Newark, DE: International Reading Association.

Hall, M. (1981). *Teaching reading as a language experience* (3rd ed.), Columbus, OH: Merrill.

Halliday, M. A. K. (1975). *Learning how to mean: Exploration in the development of language.* London: Edward Arnold.

Hansen, J. (1987). *When writers read.* Portsmouth, NH: Heinemann.

Harris, V. J. (1994). Multiculturalism and children's literature. In F. Lehr & J. Osborn (Eds.), *Reading, language and literacy* (pp. 201–214). Hillsdale, NJ: Lawrence Erlbaum Associates.

Hart, B. & Risley, T. R. (1995). *Meaningful differences in the everyday experience of young American children.* Baltimore: Brookes.

Heald-Taylor, G. (1987). How to use predictable books for K–2 language arts instruction. *The Reading Teacher,* 40, 656–661.

Heibert, E. H. & Colt, J. (1989). Patterns of literature-based reading instruction. *The Reading Teacher,* 43, 14–20.

Henderson, E. (1985). *Teaching spelling.* Boston, MA: Houghton Mifflin.

Henderson, E. H. & Beers, J. W. (1980). *Developmental and cognitive aspects of learning to spell: A reflection of word knowledge.* Newark, DE: International Reading Association.

Herman, P. A. (1985). The effect of repeated readings on reading rate, speech pauses, and word recognition accuracy. *Reading Research Quarterly,* 20, 553–564.

Hill, B. C., Johnson, N. J., & Schlick Noe, K. L. (Eds.) (1995). *Literature circles and response.* Norwood, MA: Christopher-Gordon Publishers.

Hilliard, A. (1994). Foreword. In E. W. King, M. Chipman, & M. Cruz-Janzen (Eds.), *Educating young children in a diverse society* (p. x). Boston, MA: Allyn & Bacon.

Holdaway, D. (1979). *Foundations of literacy.* Sydney, Australia: Ashton Scholastic.

Holdaway, D. (1980). *Independence in reading.* Portsmouth, NH: Heinemann.

Holdaway, D. (1984). *Stability and change in literacy learning.* Portsmouth, NH: Heinemann.

Johnson, D. M. (1981). The effects of cooperative, competitive and individualistic goal structures on achievement: A meta-analysis. *Psychological Bulletin,* 89, 47–62.

Juel, C. (1991). Beginning reading. In R. Barr, M. Kamil, P. Mosenthal, & P. D. Pearson (Eds.), *Handbook of reading research* (Vol. 2, pp. 759–788). New York: Longman.

Juel, C., Griffith, P. L., & Gough, P. B. (1986). Acquisition of literacy: A longitudinal study of children in first and second grade. *Journal of Educational Psychology,* 78, 243–255.

Kawamaki, A. J. (1985). *A study of the effects of repeated story reading on kindergarten children's story comprehension.* Paper presented at the annual meeting of the National Reading Conference, San Diego.

Kinney, M. (1985). A language experience approach to teaching expository text structure. *The Reading Teacher,* 39, 854–856.

Kreeft, J. (1984). Dialogue writing—Bridge from talk to essay writing. *Language Arts,* 651, 141–150.

Lindfors, J. W. (1987). *Children's language and learning* (2nd ed.). Englewood Cliffs, NJ: Prentice-Hall.

Lukens, R. (1998). *A critical handbook of children's literature.* Glenview, IL: Scott Foresman.

Lynch, P. (1986). *Using big books and predictable books.* New York: Scholastic.

Maclean, M., Bryant, P., & Bradley, L. (1987). Rhymes, nursery rhymes, and reading in early childhood. *Merrill-Palmer Quarterly,* 33, 255–282.

Madura, S. (1995). The line and texture of aesthetic response: Primary children study authors and illustrators. *The Reading Teacher,* 49, 110–118.

Mason, J. (1984). Early reading: A developmental perspective. In P. D. Pearson (Ed.), *Handbook of reading research* (pp. 505–544). New York: Longman.

McCarrier, A., Pinnell, G. S., & Fountas, I. C. (2000). *Interactive writing: How language and literacy come together,* K–2. Portsmouth, NH: Heinemann.

McGee, L. M. (1992). Focus on research: Exploring the literature-based reading revolution. *Language Arts,* 69, 529–537.

McKenzie, M. G. (1985). *Shared writing: Apprenticeship in written language matters.* London: Centre for Language in Primary Education.

McMahon, S. I. (1991). *Book club: How written and oral discourse influence the development of ideas as children respond to literature.* Paper presented at the annual meeting of the American Educational Research Association.

Meyer, B. J. & Freedle, R. O. (1984). Effects of discourse type on recall. *American Educational Research Journal,* 21, 121–143.

Morris, D. (1981). Concepts of words: A developmental phenomenon in the beginning reading and writing processes. *Language Arts,* 58, 659–668.

Morrison, B. B. (1983). Language experience reading with the microcomputer. *The Reading Teacher,* 36, 448–449.

Morrow, L. M. (1985). Retelling stories: A strategy for improving young children's comprehension of story structures and oral language complexity. *Elementary School Journal,* 85, 647–661.

Morrow, L. M. (2001). *Literacy development in the early years: Helping children read and write* (4th ed.). Boston: Allyn and Bacon.

Mullis, I. V. S., Campbell, J. R., & Farstrup, A. E. (1993). *NAEP 1992 reading report card for the nation and states.* Washington, DC: Office of Education Research and Improvement.

Murray, D. (1985). *A writer teaches writing* (2nd ed). Boston: Houghton Mifflin.

National Assessment of Educational Progress 2000 (NAEP). (2000). Washington, DC: Office of Education Research and Improvement.

National Literacy Standards for Language Arts (1996). National Council for Teachers of English and International Reading Association: Urbana-Champaign, IL.

Nessel, D. D. & Jones, M. B. (1981). *The language-experience approach to reading.* New York: Teachers College Press.

Niles, O. S. (1974). Organization perceived. In H. L. Herber (Ed.), *Perspectives in reading: Developing study skills in secondary schools* (pp. 57–76). Newark, DE: International Reading Association.

Ogle, D. (1986). The K-W-L: A teaching model that develops active reading of expository text. *The Reading Teacher,* 39, 364–370.

Pappas, C. C., Kiefer, B. Z., & Levstik, L. S. (1999). *An integrated language perspective in the elementary school,* (2nd ed.). New York: Longman.

Paris, S. G., Wasik, B. A., & Turner, J. C. (1991). The development of strategic readers. In R. Barr, M. L. Kamil, P. Mosenthal, & P. D. Pearson (Eds.), *Handbook of reading research* (Vol. 2). New York: Longman.

Pennington, B. F., Grossier, D., & Welsh, M. C. (1993). Contrasting cognitive deficits in attention deficit hyperactivity disorder versus reading disability. *Developmental Psychology,* 29, 511–523.

Perfetti, C. A. (1985). *Reading ability.* New York: Oxford University Press.

Peterson, R. & Eeds, M. (1990). *Grand conversations: Literature groups in action.* Ontario, Canada: Scholastic-TAB.

Piaget, J. & Inhelder, B. (1969). *The psychology of the child.* New York: Basic Books.

Powell, W. R. (1993). *Classroom literacy instruction and assessment from the Vygotskian perspective.* Paper presented at the Thirty-Eighth Annual Convention of the International Reading Association, San Antonio, TX.

Pressley, M. (1997). The cognitive science of reading. *Contemporary Educational Psychology,* 22, 247–259.

Pressley, M. (1998). *Reading instruction that works: A case for balanced teaching.* New York: The Guilford Press.

Rack, J., Snowling, M., & Olsen, R. (1992). The nonword reading deficits in developmental dyslexia: A review. *Reading Research Quarterly,* 27, 28–53.

Ramirez, G. & Ramirez, J. L. (1994). *Multiethnic children's literature.* Albany, NY: Delmar.

Raphael, T. E. & McMahon, S. I. (1994). "Book Clubs": An alternative framework for reading instruction. *The Reading Teacher,* 48, 102–116.

Rasinski, T. V. (1990). Effects of repeated reading and listening-while-reading on reading fluency. *Journal of Educational Research,* 83, 147–150.

Read, C. (1975). *Children's categorizations of speech sounds in English* (NCTE Res. Rep. No. 17). Urbana, IL: National Council of Teachers of English.

Rhodes, L. K. (1981). I can read! Predictable books as resources for reading and writing instruction. *The Reading Teacher,* 34, 511–518.

Rigg, P. (1986). Reading in ESL: Learning from kids. In P. Rigg & D. S. Enright (Eds.), *Children and ESL: Integrating perspectives.* Washington, DC: Teachers of English to Speakers of Other Languages.

Rigg, P. (1989). Language experience approach: Reading naturally. In P. Rigg & R. Van Allen (Eds.), *When they don't all speak English: Integrating the ESL student into the regular classroom.* Urbana, IL: National Council of Teachers of English.

Rinsky, L. A. (1993). *Teaching word recognition skills* (5th ed.). Scottsdale, AZ: Gorsuch Scarisbrick.

Rosen, H. & Rosen, C. (1973). *The language of primary school children.* London: Penguin/Education for the Schools Council.

Rosenblatt, L. M. (1978). *The reader, the text, the poem: The transactional theory of the literary work.* Carbondale, IL: Southern Illinois University Press.

Samuels, S. J. (1979). The method of repeated reading. *The Reading Teacher,* 32, 403–408.

Schank, R. & Abelson, R. (1975). *Knowledge structures.* Hillsdale, NJ: Erlbaum.

Senick, G. J. (Ed.). (1976–1995). *Children's literature review* (Vol. 1–34). New York: Gale Research.

Shanklin, N. K. (1982). *Relating reading and writing: Developing a transitional model of the writing process.* Bloomington, IN: Monographs in Teaching and Learning, School of Education, Indiana University.

Shannon, P. (Ed.). (1992). *Becoming political: Reading and writing in the politics of literacy education.* Portsmouth, NH: Heinemann.

Siera, M. & Combs, M. (1990). Transitions in reading instruction: Handling contradictions in beliefs and practice. *Reading Horizons,* 31, 113–126.

Slavin, R. E., Madden, N. A., Karweit, N. L., Dolan, L. J., & Wasik, B. A. (1991). Success for all: Ending reading failure from the beginning. *Language Arts,* 68, 404–409.

Slocum, T. A., O'Connor, R. E., & Jenkins, J. R. (1993). Transfer among phonological manipulation skills. *Journal of Educational Psychology,* 85, 618–630.

Smith, F. (1982). *Writing and the writer.* New York: Holt, Rinehart & Winston.

Snow, C. E., Burns, M. S., & Griffin, P. (Eds.). (1998). *Preventing reading difficulties in young children.* Washington, DC: National Academy Press.

Soderman, A. K., Gregory, K. M., & O'Neill, L. T. (1999). *Scaffolding emergent literacy: A child-centered approach for preschool through grade 5.* Boston, MA: Allyn & Bacon.

Spache, G. D. (1963). *Diagnostic reading scales.* Monterey, CA: CTB/McGraw-Hill.

Speigel, D. L. (1985). Developing independence in decoding. *Reading World,* 75–80.

Stahl, S. (1992). Saying the "p" word: Guidelines for exemplary phonics instruction. *The Reading Teacher,* 45, 618–625.

Stahl, S. & Miller, P. (1989). Whole language and language experience approaches for beginning reading: A quantative research synthesis. *Review of Educational Research,* 59, 87–116.

Stahl, S. A. & Murray, B. A. (1994). Defining phonological awareness and its relationship to early reading. *Journal of Educational Psychology,* 86, 221–234.

Standards for the English Language Arts. (1996). Newark, DE & Urbana, IL: International Reading Association and the National Council of Teachers of English.

Stanovich, K. (1986). Matthew effects in reading: Some consequences of individual differences in the acquisition of literacy. *Reading Research Quarterly,* 21, 360–407.

Stanovich, K. E. (1982). Individual differences in the cognitive processes of reading: I. Word decoding. *Journal of Learning Disabilities,* 15, 485–493.

Stanovich, K. E., Cunningham, A. E., & West, R. F. (1981). A longitudinal study of the development of automatic recognition skills in first graders. *Journal of Reading Behavior,* 13, 57–74.

Staton, J. (1980). Writing and counseling: Using a dialogue journal. *Language Arts,* 57, 514–518.

Staton, J. (1987). The power of responding in dialogue journals. In T. Fulwiler (Ed.), *The journal book* (pp. 47–63). Portsmouth, NH: Heinemann.

Stauffer, R. G. (1975). *Directing the reading-thinking process.* New York: Harper & Row.

Stauffer, R. G. (1980). *The language experience approach to the teaching of reading.* New York: Harper & Row.

Stauffer, R. G. & Hammond, W. D. (1967). The effectiveness of language arts and basal reader approaches to first grade reading instruction. *The Reading Teacher,* 20, 740–746.

Stauffer, R. S. (1959). A directed reading-thinking plan. *Education,* 79, 527–532.

Sulzby, E. (1985). Children's emergent reading of favorite storybooks. *Reading Research Quarterly,* 20, 458–481.

Sulzby, E. & Teale, W. H. (1991a). Emergent literacy. In R. Barr, M. L. Kamil, P. Mosenthal, & P. D. Pearson (Eds.), *Handbook of reading research* (Vol. 2, pp. 727–757) New York: Longman.

Sulzby, E. & Teale, W. H. (1991b). Emergent reading. In R. Barr, M. Kamil, P. Mosenthal, & P. D. Pearson (Eds.), *Handbook of reading research* (Vol. 2, pp. 861–883). New York: Longman.

Taylor, D. (1983). *Family literacy: Young children learning to read and write.* Exeter, NH: Heinemann.

Teale, W. H. (1986). Home background and children's literacy development. In W. H. Teale & E. Sulzby (Eds.), *Emergent literacy: Writing and reading* (pp. 173–206). Norwood, NJ: Ablex.

Telgen, D. (Ed.). (1971–1994). *Something about the author* (Vol. 1–76). Detroit, MI: Gale Research.

Temple, C., Nathan, R., Temple, F., & Burris, N. (1993). *The beginnings of writing* (2nd ed.). Boston, MA: Allyn & Bacon.

Tharp, R. G. & Gallimore, R. (1988). *Rousing minds to life: Teaching, learning, and schooling in social context.* Cambridge, UK: Cambridge University Press.

Tompkins, G. E. (1993). *Teaching writing: Balancing process and product.* New York: Macmillan.

Trachtenburg, P. & Ferruggia, A. (1989). Big books from little voices: Reaching high risk readers. *The Reading Teacher,* 43, 284–289.

Treadway, J. (1993). *Language experience and whole language for the second language student.* Unpublished course materials, San Diego State University.

Trelease, J. (1989). *The new read-aloud handbook.* New York: Viking Penguin.

Tunnel, M. O. & Jacobs, J. S. (1989). Using "real" books: Research findings on literature based reading instruction. *The Reading Teacher,* 42, 470–477.

U.S. Department of Education (1997, July). *The seven priorities of the U.S. Department of Education.* Working Document. Washington, DC: Author.

Vygotsky, L. S. (1962). *Thought and language* (E. Hanfmann & G. Vakar, Eds. & Trans.). Cambridge, MA: MIT Press.

Vygotsky, L. S. (1978). *Mind in society* (M. Cole, V. John-Steiner, S. Scribner, & E. Sounerman, Eds. & Trans.). Cambridge, MA: Harvard University Press.

Wagner, R. K., Torgenson, J. K., Laughon, P., Simmons, K., & Rashotti, C. A. (1993). Development of young readers' phonological processing abilities. *Journal of Educational Psychology,* 85, 83–103.

Wells, G. (1986). *The meaning makers: Children learning language and using language to learn.* Portsmouth, NH: Heinemann.

Winsor, P., Nagy, W. E., Osborn, J., & O'Flahavan, J. (1993). *Structural analysis: Toward an evaluation of instruction.* Center for the Study of Reading, Technical Report No. 581. (ERIC Document Reproduction Service, No. ED 360 625).

Wood, S. S., Bruner, J. S., & Ross, G. (1976). The role of tutoring in problem solving. *Journal of Child Psychology,* 17, 89–100.

Yaden, D. (1988). Understanding stories through repeated read-alouds: How many does it take? *The Reading Teacher,* 41, 556–560.

Yolen, J. (1992). *A Letter from Phoenix Farm.* Katonah, NT: Richard C. Owens.

Yopp, H. (1988). The validity and reliability of phonemic awareness tests. *Reading Research Quarterly,* 23, 159–177.

Yopp, H. K. (1992). Developing phonemic awareness in young children. *The Reading Teacher,* 45, 696–703.

Yopp, H. K. & Yopp, R. H. (2000). Supporting phonemic awareness development in the classroom. *The Reading Teacher,* 54, 130–143.

Zarrillo, J. (1989). Teachers' interpretations of literature-based reading. *The Reading Teacher,* 43, 22–28.

Name Index

Subject Index